The Global Agenda

Issues and Perspectives

The Global Agenda

Issues and Perspectives

Charles W. Kegley, Jr.
University of South Carolina

Eugene R. Wittkopf
University of Florida

Random House
New York

For Pamela and Barbara,
Suzanne, Debra, and Jonathan

First Edition

987654321

Copyright © 1984 by Random House, Inc.

LIBRARY OF CONGRESS CATALOGING IN PUBLICATION DATA

Main entry under title:

The Global agenda.

   1. International relations—Addresses, essays,
lectures. I. Kegley, Charles W.   II. Wittkopf,
Eugene R., 1943-   .
JX1395.G575   1984   327   83-22025
ISBN 0-394-33414-0

Cover design by Chris Welch.

Manufactured in the United States of America

Preface

There is no scientific antidote [to the atomic bomb], only education. You've got to change the way people think. I am not interested in disarmament talks between nations. . . . What I want to do is to disarm the mind. After that, everything else will automatically follow. The ultimate weapon for such mental disarmament is international education.

—Albert Einstein

Constancy and change seem to describe most accurately the nature of contemporary international politics. Global transformations and emergent trends have produced new issues and cleavages in international politics. Simultaneously, traditional controversies continue to color relations among nations. Hence the study of contemporary international politics must give attention to the factors that produce change and also to those that promote changelessness in relations among world political actors. Our purpose in gathering together this collection is to make available between the covers of a single volume, for students of international relations, what we believe to be the best introduction to the contemporary issues that animate contemporary world politics *and,* also, an introduction to the major analytical perspectives scholars have fashioned to make these issues comprehensible. It seems to us, that to a greater or lesser degree, coverage of both these elements is missing in standard texts (by design and necessity), and that a supplementary anthology is the logical place for them.

The Global Agenda: Issues and Perspectives categorizes readings into four "baskets" that build on the distinction between "high politics" (peace and security issues) and "low politics" (non-security issues). The criteria that guided the selection of particular articles within each part and the rationale that underlies the organization of the book are made explicit in our introductions to each part, which are designed to help students connect individual readings to common themes.

The innovative organization of the book is intended to capture the diversity of global issues and patterns of interaction that presently dominate the attention of world political actors and that precipitate policy responses. The thematic organization of the book allows treatment of the breadth of global issues and of the analytical perspectives that give them meaning, ranging from classic theoretical formulations to the newer conceptual foci that have arisen to account for recent developments in world affairs. In preparing the volume in this manner we have proceeded from the assumption that there is need for educational materials that balance concern for substance with process and for description with theoretical exposition, and that expose a variety of normative interpretations without advocating any particular one.

Several people contributed to the development of this book. We wish especially to acknowledge the contributions of Lawrence M. Jackson, John W. Outland, Lucia Wren Rawls, Joseph Sausnock, and Thomas J. Volgy. The helpful suggestions of a number of anonymous reviewers is also gratefully acknowledged. At Random House we are indebted to Bertrand W. Lummus and Fred H. Burns for their support and professional assistance.

Charles W. Kegley, Jr.
Eugene R. Wittkopf

Contents

The Global Agenda

Issues and Perspectives

Part ONE

Arms and Influence

The contemporary international political system began to acquire its present shape and definition over three centuries ago with the emergence of a state system in Europe following the Thirty Years War. As political, economic, and social intercourse grew among the states of Europe, legal norms were devised to regulate inter-state behavior. The doctrine of state sovereignty, according to which no legal authority is higher than the state, emerged supreme. Thus the emergent international system was based on the right of states to control, without interference from others, their internal affairs and to manage their relations with other states, with which they collaborated or competed as they saw fit. Foremost in this system was the belief, reinforced by law, that the state possessed the right, indeed, the obligation, to take whatever measures it deemed necessary to insure its preservation.

Although the international system and the patterns of interaction among its political actors have changed profoundly since the 1648 Peace of Westphalia gave birth to the state system, contemporary world politics remain significantly colored by the legacy of the past. World politics continue to be conducted in an atmosphere of anarchy. As in the past, the system remains fragmented and decentralized, with no higher authority above nation-states, which, as the principal actors in world politics, remain free to behave toward one another largely as they choose.

This is not meant to imply that states exercise their freedoms with abandon, or that they are unconstrained in the choices they make. The political, legal, moral, and structural constraints on states' freedom of choice are formidable. Moreover, states' national interests are served best when they act in a manner that does not threaten the stability of their relations with

1

others or of the global system that protects their autonomy. Hence, the international system, as the British political scientist Hedley Bull reminds us, may be an anarchical society, but it is one of "ordered anarchy" nonetheless.

The world has grown increasingly complex and interdependent as contact, communication, and exchange have increased among the actors in the state system and as the number of nation-states and other non-state international actors has grown during the past four decades. Expanded interaction among increased numbers of actors reflects the increased range of possible mutually beneficial exchanges between states. But just as opportunities for cooperation have expanded, so have the number of possible sources of disagreement. That we live in an age of conflict is a cliché that contains elements of truth, for differences of opinion and efforts to resolve disputes to one's advantage, often at the expense of others, are part of any long-term relationship. Thus, as the world has grown smaller, the mutual dependence of world political actors on one another has grown, and the number of potential rivalries, antagonisms, and disagreements has increased correspondingly. Friction and tension thus appear to be a characteristic of relations between nations; the image of world politics conveyed in newspaper headlines does not suggest that a shrinking world has become a more peaceful one. Instead, competition and conflict appear endemic.

Given the characteristics of contemporary world politics, the number of *issues* that at any one time are in dispute among global political actors appears to have increased greatly. The multitude of contentions render the *global agenda*—the list of issues that force their way into consideration and command that they be addressed, peacefully or not—more crowded and complex. Because the responses that are made to the issues on the global agenda shape our lives both today and into the future, it is appropriate that we direct attention to those matters that animate world politics and stimulate the attention and activities of national decision makers. At the same time, as different state and non-state actors view global political issues from often widely varying vantage points, it is appropriate that we remain sensitive to the various perceptual lenses through which the items on the global agenda are viewed. Accordingly, *The Global Agenda: Issues and Perspectives* seeks to focus on the range of issues that dominate world politics and also on the multitude of analytical and interpretive perspectives from which those issues are viewed.

The issues and perspectives discussed in *The Global Agenda* are grouped into four broad, somewhat overlapping, but analytically distinct issue-areas: (1) arms and influence, (2) discord and collaboration, (3) politics and markets, and (4) ecology and politics. Broadly speaking, the first two issue-areas deal with states' security interests, often referred to as matters of *high politics*. The latter two, again broadly speaking, deal with the non-security issues, often referred to as matters of *low politics,* that increasingly have come to share, if not dominate, the attention of world political actors. In all four issue-areas, we seek to convey not only the range of issues now facing those responsible for political choices, but also the many vantage points from which they are typically viewed.

We begin in Part I with consideration of a series of issues appropriately subsumed under the collective rubric *Arms and Influence.* As the term *high politics* suggests, the issues and perspectives treated here focus on the prospects for peace and security in a world of competitive nation-states armed with increasingly lethal weapons of violence and destruction.

ARMS AND INFLUENCE

It is often argued that states strive for power, security, and domination in a global environment punctuated by the threat of violence and, increasingly, the fear of extinction. This perspective flows naturally from the characteristics of the international political system, which continues to be marked by the absence of central institutions capable of conflict management and resolution. Hence, preoccupation with preparations for defense to promote national security becomes understandable, for the fear persists that one adversary might use force against another to realize its goals or to vent its frustrations. In such an environment, arms not only enhance security, but also become the means to realize and extend one's influence. Hence, nations frequently see their interests best served by a search for power, by whatever means. Understandably, therefore, *power* and *influence* remain perhaps *the* principal concepts in the study of world politics.

Appropriately, our first essay, "Power, Capability, and Influence" by K. J. Holsti, provides a thoughtful discussion of the meaning of power, capability, and influence as these concepts relate to the foreign policy behavior of states in contemporary world politics. The essay provides insights important not only for evaluating the subsequent essays in this book, but also for evaluating the use to which these necessary but ambiguous terms are often put in other interpretations of global issues. For almost invariably such discussions make reference, implicitly or explicitly, to the interrelationships among power, capability, and influence.

Robert L. Paarlberg's essay on "Coercive Resource Power" extends Holsti's discussion by examining the possibilities and problems of exercising influence through means other than military instruments. His discussion of oil and food as tools of coercion alerts us to the complexities involved in influencing others. It also cautions us not to assume that barrels of oil and bushels of grain can be used in the same way for similar ends. Paarlberg thus offers sobering thoughts for those who assume that resource power can be translated automatically into political leverage.

Our third selection, "Arms Sales: The New Diplomacy" by Andrew J. Pierre, also addresses the matter of influence. In this case, arms are the focus. Arms transfers, as Pierre notes, have become a pervasively used device whereby states seek to expand their influence with allies and to extend it even to other not-so-friendly but eager consumers of the weapons of destruction. Arms aid and arms sales have become so commonplace that Pierre aptly characterizes arms transfers as a growing substitute for more traditional means of pursuing foreign policy objectives, indeed, "as foreign policy writ large." The consequences of such policies will no doubt dominate the future global agenda, as present trends promise to create future dangers (and, perhaps for some, opportunities) that will necessarily have to be confronted.

A dramatic increase in the capacity to destroy is among the inevitable consequences of nations' efforts to enhance their influence through the purchase or production of increasingly sophisticated armaments. Many political analysts see the prospects for peace dramatically reduced by this development. Others, including many policy makers, see a greater capacity for self-protection. Because arms both threaten and protect, we can rightly ask, What are the causes of violent conflict—of war? Quincy Wright, in "The Causes of War," argues the answer depends on a varied combination of tangible and intangible factors. Arms, therefore, may be necessary instruments of modern warfare, but the call to arms—and the means to its control—must be located elsewhere, for the reasons for arming and engaging in violence typically derive from deep-seated underlying factors.

This background on the roots of war forces us to consider the road to peace. The "balance of power" is perhaps the most common prescription for regulating power and the resort to force in a decentralized, anarchical system. However, as Inis L. Claude demonstrates in his essay on "The Management of Power in International Relations," despite the ubiquity of the balance-of-power concept, its meaning remains ambiguous and its guidelines for the future uncertain. In making this argument, Claude usefully incorporates a critical analysis of two popular perspectives on world politics. The first, known as *political realism,* or *realpolitik,* sees the pursuit of power as the dominant foreign policy objective of nation-states. Claude evaluates this perspective by critically analyzing the ideas of the late Hans J. Morgenthau, perhaps the most famous proponent of the realist perspective and prescription. Additionally, Claude briefly examines the so-called *idealist* perspective that is often juxtaposed to realism. Because both realism and idealism continue to influence the way national security issues are debated and evaluated, both deserve careful scrutiny.

Nuclear weapons are doubtless the most destructive form of lethal power and hence the most threatening instruments of influence that must be managed successfully. For these reasons, the prevention of a nuclear World War III is an issue of explosive global interest. *The Fate of the Earth,* as Jonathan Schell's popular book on the subject is titled, is at stake. Designed to raise consciousness about the devastating effects of nuclear weapons and war, Schell's book is regarded by some as having contributed significantly to the nuclear freeze movement of the early 1980s. In "Nuclear Weapons and the Institution of War," taken from that book, Schell focuses attention on the relationship of nuclear weapons to the contemporary functions of warfare. His conclusion that civilization will be destroyed if nuclear weapons are not, and his prediction that warfare itself has been rendered obsolete by weapons that make it suicidal, underscore the urgency of grappling with the multiple issues that nuclear weapons pose.

In our seventh selection, "On the International Uses of Military Force in the Contemporary World" by Klaus Knorr, the author takes exception to the thesis that force no longer makes sense or plays a role in world politics. Contrary to Schell's argument, Knorr maintains that the usability and usefulness of military force have not diminished, and that, even in the era of thermonuclear weapons, the threat and actual use of military force retain many of their traditional functions. Although recognizing the issues of cost and destructiveness that the application of military force poses, Knorr concludes that war has not decreased in frequency. Particularly in the Third World, the developing nations of Asia, Africa, and Latin America, war remains a recurrent, even institutionalized, mode of inter-state behavior. Hence, Knorr concludes, the relationship between military power and political influence has not eroded. The issue of conventional war thus continues to join the threat of nuclear extinction as a salient issue on the global agenda. And Knorr's thesis serves as a counter to the perspective of those who agree with the views of Schell.

The problem of international security is compounded further by another harsh reality—the possibility, perhaps likelihood, that the number of states possessing nuclear weapons will increase beyond the small club that presently possess them. Controlling nuclear proliferation is a major arms control issue. But, as Hedley Bull astutely warns in "Rethinking Non-Proliferation," the proliferation issue is complex and many states have powerful, and often legitimate, incentives to join the nuclear club. Offering a perspective on proliferation unusually sensitive to the needs, claims, and aspirations of states presently outside the charmed circle of nuclear powers, Bull inventories the problems and prospects confronting the world community on this global issue. The absence of compelling solutions acceptable to all frames the issue and underscores the risks entailed, all of which explain why easy solutions are unlikely and why the proliferation debate is destined to remain intense.

If disagreement characterizes answers to the question "How many countries should have the bomb?" near consensus exists on avoiding its use. Since the atomic age began in 1945, considerable effort has been devoted to devising strategies to avoid resort to nuclear weapons. *Deterrence*— preventing a potential adversary from doing something he might otherwise do—has dominated strategic thinking about nuclear weapons during most of the post–World War II era. The failure of deterrence, particularly between the superpowers, the United States and the Soviet Union, could, of course, ignite a global conflagration, which means that the entire world has a stake in the successful operation of a deterrent strategy.

Spurgeon M. Keeny, Jr., and Wolfgang K. H. Panofsky argue, in their essay "MAD Versus NUTS," that the policies of the superpowers have ironically put them into a "mutual hostage relationship." They are destined to continue in that precarious state, the authors argue, because they cannot escape the circumstances to which they have both contributed. Reviewing the mutual assured destruction (MAD) doctrine and recent challenges to it mounted by nuclear utilization theorists (NUTs) in the United States, Keeny and Panofsky conclude that the former doctrine is inadequate, but that the latter is unacceptably dangerous. In the absence of real disarmament, the most that can be hoped for is a continuation of the tenuous stability that results from the assurance of mutual destruction. The superpowers cannot escape the grim realities of a MAD world.

Fortunately, the superpowers have managed to avoid the nuclear precipice. Doing so has required that they successfully manage the many crises that have punctuated their relationship during the past several decades. Many

of these crises have involved countries in the Third World that have themselves frequently faced crises. Indeed, crises have become so prevalent a
feature of world politics that some have argued they are a substitute for
war.

What constitutes a crisis, however, is not entirely clear. Glenn H. Snyder
and Paul Diesing, in their essay "The Anatomy of International Crises,"
examine the nature of these recurrent phenomena. Tying their definition of
a crisis to the incipience of war, they provide an insightful discussion of
the causes, evolution, and outcomes of crises.

Finally, Part I concludes with a treatment of yet another dimension of the
link between arms and the search for influence: the threats posed by international terrorism. In "The Politics of International Terrorism," Andrew
J. Pierre offers a timely and illuminating discussion of the nature of international terrorism and the prospects for its control. Because, as with the
other salient items on the global agenda, different states view the issue of
international terrorism differently, Pierre is pessimistic about the possibility of bringing this terrifying force under control.

The issues discussed in the eleven essays in Part I—capabilities and influence, resource power, arms sales, war, the balance of power, nuclear destruction, the use of force, nuclear proliferation, deterrence, crises, and
terrorism—do not exhaust the range of security problems that populate the
global agenda. However, in focusing attention on some of the many issues
relating to the role of arms and influence in a world of interdependent and
often competitive states, they offer insight into the complexities of the
issues of high politics with which national decision makers must grapple.
Part II will add further insight into the politics of peace and security when
we shift attention to the nature of discord and collaboration in world politics.

1

Power, Capability, and Influence

K. J. HOLSTI

In this essay, K. J. Holsti clarifies the meaning of three concepts crucial to the conduct of international politics—power, capability, and influence—and examines the complexities of each as it relates to states' efforts to realize their foreign policy objectives. Holsti is professor of political science at the University of British Columbia. He is a frequent contributor to the professional literature on international politics, and his publications include *Why Nations Realign* (1982).

[A foreign policy] act is basically a form of communication intended to change or sustain the behavior of those upon whom the acting government is dependent for achieving its own goals. It can also be viewed as a "signal" sent by one actor to influence the receiver's image of the sender.[1] In international politics, acts and signals take many different forms. The promise of granting foreign aid is an act, as are propaganda appeals, displays of military strength, wielding a veto in the Security Council, walking out of a conference, organizing a conference, issuing a warning in a diplomatic note, sending arms and money to a liberation movement, instituting a boycott on the goods of another state, or declaring war. These types of acts and signals, and the circumstances in which they are likely to succeed, will be discussed. . . . Our organizing principle will be the amount of threat involved in the various techniques of influence. Diplomatic persuasion seemingly involves the least amount of threat; economic pressures, subversion, intervention, and various forms of warfare involve increasingly great amounts of threat and punishment. To help understand what all these types of action or techniques of influence have in common, however, we will discuss in a more abstract manner the behavior governments show when they turn toward each other to establish orientations, fulfill roles, or achieve and defend objectives.

The international political process commences when any state—let us say state A—seeks through various acts or signals to change or sustain the behavior (for instance, the acts, images, and policies) of other states. Power can thus be defined

Reprinted from K. J. Holsti, *International Politics: A Framework for Analysis,* 4th ed. (Englewood Cliffs, N.J.: Prentice-Hall, 1983), pp. 144–159. © 1983. Adapted by permission of Prentice-Hall, Inc. Some footnotes have been deleted.

[1] A comprehensive treatment of how governments "signal" each other is in Robert Jervis, *The Logic of Images in International Relations* (Princeton, N.J.: Princeton University Press, 1970).

as the general capacity of a state to control the behavior of others. This definition can be illustrated as follows, where the solid line represents various acts:

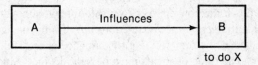

A seeks to influence B because it has established certain objectives that cannot be achieved (it is perceived) unless B (and perhaps many other states as well) does X. If this is the basis of all international political processes, the capacity to control behavior can be viewed in several different ways:

1. Influence (an aspect of power) is essentially a *means* to an end. Some governments or statesmen may seek influence for its own sake, but for most it is instrumental, just like money. They use it primarily for achieving or defending other goals, which may include prestige, territory, souls, raw materials, security, or alliances.

2. State A, in its acts toward state B, uses or mobilizes certain *resources*. A resource is any physical or mental object or quality available as an instrument of inducement to persuade, reward, threaten, or punish. The concept of resource may be illustrated in the following example. Suppose an unarmed robber walks into a bank and asks the clerk to give up money. The clerk observes clearly that the robber has no weapon and refuses to comply with the order. The robber has sought to influence the behavior of the clerk, but has failed. The next time, however, the robber walks in armed with a pistol and threatens to shoot if the clerk does not give up the money. This time, the clerk complies. In this instance, the robber has mobilized certain resources or capabilities (the gun) and succeeds in influencing the clerk to comply. But other less tangible resources may be involved as well. The appearance of the person, particularly facial expression, may convey determination, threat, or weakness, all of which may subtly influence the behavior of the clerk. In international politics, the diplomatic gestures and words accompanying actions may be as important as the acts themselves. A government that places troops on alert but insists that it is doing so for domestic reasons will have an impact abroad quite different from the government that organizes a similar alert but accompanies it with threats to go to war. "Signals" or diplomatic "body language" may be as important as dramatic actions such as alerts and mobilizations.

3. The act of influencing B obviously involves a *relationship* between A and B, although, as will be seen later, the relationship may not even involve overt communication. If the relationship covers any period of time, we can also say that it is a *process*.

4. If A can get B to do something, but B cannot get A to do a similar thing, then we can say that A has more power than B regarding that particular issue. Power, therefore, can also be viewed as a *quantity,* but as a quantity it is only meaningful when compared to the power of others. Power is therefore relative.

To summarize, power may be viewed from several aspects: It is a means; it is based on resources; it is a relationship and a process; and it can be measured, at least crudely.

We can break down the concept of power into three distinct analytic elements: power comprises (1) the *acts* (process, relationship) of influencing other states; (2) the *resources* used to make the wielding of influence successful; and (3) the *responses* to the acts. The three elements must be kept distinct. Since this definition may seem too abstract, we can define the concept in the more operational terms of policy makers. In formulating policy and the strategy to achieve certain goals, they would explicitly or implicitly ask the five following questions:

1. Given our goals, what do we wish B to do or not to do? (X)
2. How shall we get B to do or not to do X? (implies a relationship and process)
3. What resources are at our disposal so that we can induce B to do or not to do X?
4. What is B's probable response to our attempts to influence its behavior?
5. What are the *costs* of taking actions 1, 2, or 3—as opposed to other alternatives?

Before discussing the problem of resources and responses, we have to fill out our model of the influence act to account for the many patterns of behavior that may be involved in an international relationship. First, the exercise of influence implies more than merely A's ability to *change* the behavior of B. Influence may also be seen when A attempts to get B to *continue* a course of action or policy that is useful to, or in the interests of, A.[2] The exercise of influence does not always cease, therefore, after B does X. It is often a continuing process of reinforcing B's behavior.

Second, it is almost impossible to find a situation where B does not also have some influence over A. Our model has suggested that influence is exercised only in one direction, by A over B. In reality, influence is multilateral. State A, for example, would seldom seek a particular goal unless it has been influenced in a particular direction by the actions of other states in the system. At a minimum, there is the problem of feedback in any relationship: If B complies with A's wishes and does X, that behavior may subsequently prompt A to change its own behavior, perhaps in the interest of B. The phenomenon of feedback may be illustrated as follows:

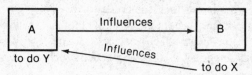

Third, there is the type of relationship that includes "anticipated reaction."[3] This is the situation where B, anticipating rewards or punishments from A,

---

[2] J. David Singer, "Inter-Nation Influence: A Formal Model," *American Political Science Review*, 57 (1963), 420–30. State A might also wish state B to do W, Y, and Z, which may be incompatible with the achievement of X.

[3] Herbert A. Simon, "Notes on the Observation and Measurement of Political Power," *Journal of Politics*, 15 (1953), 500–16. For further analysis, see David A. Baldwin, "Inter-Nation Influence Revisited," *Journal of Conflict Resolution*, 15 (December 1971), 478–79.

changes his behavior, perhaps even before A makes any "signals" about possible action. Deterrence theory clearly assumes that B—the potential aggressor against A—will not attack (where it might, were there no deterrent), knowing that an unacceptable level of punishment would surely result. A similar situation, but in reverse, is also common in international politics. This is where A might wish B to do X, but does not try to influence B for fear that B will do Y instead, which is an unfavorable response from A's point of view. In a hypothetical situation, the government of India might wish to obtain arms from the United States to build up its own defenses, but does not request such arms because it fears that the United States would insist on certain conditions for the sale of arms that might compromise India's nonalignment. This anticipated reaction may also be multilateral, where A wishes B to do X, but will not try to get B to do it because it fears that C, a third state, will do Y, which is unfavorable to A's interests. India wants to purchase American arms, but does not seek to influence the United States to sell them for fear that Pakistan (C) will then build up its own armaments and thus accelerate the arms race between the two countries. In this situation, Pakistan (C) has influence over the actions of the Indian government even though it has not deliberately sought to influence India on this particular matter or even communicated its position in any way. The Indian government has simply perceived that there is a relatively high probability that if it seeks to influence the United States, Pakistan will react in a manner contrary to India's interests.

Fourth, power and influence may be measured by scholars, but what is important in international politics is the *perceptions* of influence and capabilities held by policy makers and the way they interpret another government's signals. The reason that governments invest millions of dollars for gathering intelligence is to develop a reasonably accurate picture of other states' capabilities and intentions. Where there is a great discrepancy between perceptions and reality, the results to a country's foreign policy may be disastrous. To take our example of the bank robber again, suppose that the person held a harmless toy pistol and threatened the clerk. The clerk perceived the gun to be real and deduced the robber's intention to use it. As a result, the clerk complied with the demand. In this case, the robber's influence was far greater than the "objective" character of the robber's capabilities and intentions; and distorted perception by the clerk led to an act which was unfavorable to the bank.

Finally, as our original model suggests, A may try to influence B *not to do* X. Sometimes this is called negative power, or deterrence, where A acts in a manner to *prevent* a certain action it deems undesirable to its interests. This is a typical relationship in international politics. By signing the Munich treaty, the British and French governments hoped to prevent Germany from invading Czechoslovakia; Israeli attacks on PLO facilities in Lebanon are designed to demonstrate that PLO guerrilla operations against Israel will be met by vast punishments, the costs of which to the PLO would far outweigh the gains of the terrorist acts. Such a cost-benefit analysis, the Israelis hope, would deter the PLO from undertaking further operations. The reader should keep in mind the distinction between compellance and deterrence.

RESOURCES

The second element of the concept of power consists of those resources that are mobilized in support of the acts taken to influence state B's behavior. It is difficult to assess the general capacity of a state to control the actions and policies of others unless we also have some knowledge of the capabilities involved.[4] Nevertheless, it should be acknowledged that social scientists do not understand all the reasons why some actors—whether people, groups, governments, or states—wield influence successfully, while others do not.

It is clear that, in political relationships, not everyone possesses equal influence. In domestic politics, it is possible to construct a lengthy list of capabilities and attributes that seemingly permit some to wield influence over large numbers of people and important public decisions. Robert Dahl lists such tangibles as money, wealth, information, time, political allies, official position, and control over jobs, and such intangibles as personality and leadership qualities.[5] But not everyone who possesses these capabilities can command the obedience of other people. What is crucial in relating resources to influence, according to Dahl, is that one *mobilize them for one's political purposes* and possess the skill to mobilize them. One who uses wealth, time, information, friends, and personality for political purposes will probably be able to influence others on public issues. A person, on the other hand, who possesses the same capabilities but uses them to invent a new mousetrap is not apt to be important in politics. The same propositions also hold true in international politics. The amount of influence a state wields over others can be related to the capabilities *mobilized* in support of *specific* foreign-policy objectives. To put this proposition in another way, we can argue that resources do not determine the uses to which they will be put. Nuclear power can be used to provide electricity or to deter and perhaps destroy other nations. The use of resources depends less on their quality and quantity than on the external objectives a government formulates for itself.

The *variety* of foreign-policy instruments available to a nation for influencing others is partly a function of the quantity and quality of capabilities. What a government seeks to do—the type of objectives it formulates—and how it attempts to do it will depend at least partially on the resources it finds available. A country such as Thailand, which possesses relatively few resources, cannot, even if it would desire, construct intercontinental ballistic missiles with which to intimidate others, establish a worldwide propaganda network, or dispense several billion dollars annually of foreign aid to try to influence other countries. We can conclude, therefore, that how states *use* their resources depends on their external objectives, but the choice of objectives and the instruments to achieve those objectives are limited or influenced by the quality and quantity of available resources.

---

[4] We might assess influence for historical situations solely on the basis of whether A got B to do X, without our having knowledge of either A's or B's capabilities.

[5] Robert A. Dahl, *Who Governs?* (New Haven, Conn.: Yale University Press, 1961).

THE MEASUREMENT OF RESOURCES

For many years, students of international politics have made meticulous comparisons of the potential capabilities of various nations, assuming that a nation was powerful, or capable of achieving its objectives, to the extent that it possessed certain "elements of power." Comparative data relating to production of iron ore, coal, and hydroelectricity, economic growth rates, educational levels, population growth rates, military resources, transportation systems, and sources of raw materials are presented as indicators of a nation's power. Few have acknowledged that these comparisons do not measure a state's power or influence but only its potential capacity to wage war. Other resources, such as diplomatic or propaganda skills, are seldom measured; but surely they are as important as war-making potential. Measurements and assessments are not particularly useful anyway unless they are related to specific foreign-policy issues. Capability is always the capability to do something; its assessment is most meaningful when carried on within a framework of certain foreign-policy objectives.

The deduction of actual influence from the quantity and quality of potential and mobilized capabilities may, in some cases, give an approximation of reality, but historically there have been too many discrepancies between the basis of power and the amount of influence to warrant adopting this practice as a useful approach to international relations. One could have assumed, for example, on the basis of a comparative study of technological and educational levels and general standards of living in the 1920s and 1930s that the United States would have been one of the most influential states in international politics. A careful comparison of certain resources, called the "great essentials,"[6] revealed the United States to be in an enviable position. In the period 1925 to 1930, it was the only major country in the world that produced from its own resources adequate supplies of food, power, iron, machinery, chemicals, coal, iron ore, and petroleum. If actual diplomatic influence had been deduced from the quantities of "great essentials" possessed by the major nations, the following ranking of states would have resulted: (1) United States, (2) Germany, (3) Great Britain, (4) France, (5) Russia, (6) Italy, (7) Japan. However, the diplomatic history of the world from 1925 to 1930 would suggest that there was little correlation between the resources of these countries and their *actual influence*. If we measure influence by the impact these states made on the system and by the responses they could invoke when they sought to change the behavior of other states, we would find for this period quite a different ranking, such as the following: (1) France, (2) Great Britain, (3) Italy, (4) Germany, (5) Russia, (6) Japan, (7) United States.

Indeed, many contemporary international relationships reveal how often the "strong" states do not achieve their objectives—or at least have to settle for poor substitutes—even when attempting to influence the behavior of "weak" states. How, for instance, did Marshal Tito's Yugoslavia effectively resist all sorts of

---

[6] Frank H. Simonds and Brooks Emeny, *The Great Powers in World Politics* (New York: American Book, 1939).

pressures and threats by the powerful Soviet Union after it was expelled from the Communist bloc? Why, despite its overwhelming superiority in capabilities, was the United States unable in the 1960s to achieve its major objectives against a weak Cuba and North Vietnam? How have "small" states gained trading privileges and all sorts of diplomatic concessions from those nations with great economic wealth and military power? The ability of state A to change the behavior of state B is, we would assume, enhanced if it possesses physical resources to use in the influence act; but B is by no means defenseless or vulnerable to diplomatic, economic, or military pressures because it fails to own a large modern army, raw materials, and money for foreign aid. The successful exercise of influence is also dependent upon such factors as personality, perceptions, friendships, and traditions, and, not being easy to measure, these factors have a way of rendering power calculations and equations difficult. . . .

VARIABLES AFFECTING THE EXERCISE OF INFLUENCE

One reason that gross quantities of resources cannot be equated with effective influence relates to the distinction between a state's overall capabilities and the *relevance* of resources to a particular diplomatic situation. A nuclear force, for example, is often thought to increase the diplomatic influence of those who possess it. No doubt nuclear weaponry is an important element in a state's general prestige abroad and may be an effective deterrent against a strategic attack on its homeland or "core" interests. Yet the most important aspect of a nuclear capability—or any military capability—is not its possession, but its relevance and the ability to signal one's determination to use it. Other governments must know that the capability is not of mere symbolic significance. The government of North Vietnam possessed a particular advantage over the United States (hence, influence) because it knew that in almost no circumstances would the American government use strategic nuclear weapons againsts its country. It therefore effectively broke through the significance of the American nuclear capability as far as the Vietnam War was concerned. A resource is useless unless it is both mobilized in support of foreign-policy objectives and made credible. Likewise, nuclear weapons would be irrelevant in negotiations on cultural exchanges, just as the Arab countries' vast oil resources could not be effectively mobilized to influence the outcome of international negotiations on satellite communications. Influence is always specific to a particular issue, and resources must be relevant to that issue.

A second variable that determines the success or failure of acts of influence is the extent to which there are *needs* between the two countries in any influence relationship. In general, a country that needs something from another is vulnerable to its acts of influence. This is the primary reason that states that are "weak" in many capabilities can nevertheless obtain concessions from "strong" countries. Consider the case of France and Germany and some of the "weak" states in the Middle East. Both European countries are highly dependent upon Arab lands for oil supplies. They have an important need, which only the Arab countries can satisfy at a reasonable cost. On the other hand, the Middle Eastern countries that control these oil resources may not be so dependent upon Germany and France, particularly if they can sell their oil easily elsewhere. Because, in this situation, needs are not equal on both sides, the independent states (in terms of needs) can make demands (or resist demands made against them) on the dependent great powers and obtain important concessions. The German and French governments know that if they do not make these concessions or if they press their own demands too hard, the Arab states can threaten to cut off oil supplies. Their dependence thus makes them vulnerable to the demands and influence acts of what would otherwise be considered "weak" states. To the Arab states, oil is much more important as a capability than military forces—at least in their relations with major powers. In the form of a general hypothesis, we can suggest that, regardless of the quantity, quality, and credibility of a state's capabilities, the more state B needs, or is dependent upon, state A, the more likely that state A's acts—threats, promises, rewards, or punishments—will succeed in changing or sustaining B's behavior.

A third variable that has assumed increasing importance in the past several decades, and one that can be considered an important resource, is level of technical expertise. An increasing number of issues on the international and foreign-policy agendas are highly technical in nature: law of the sea, satellite broadcasting, international monetary matters, and the like. Many of these issues are discussed in international fora, where leadership often depends more on knowledge of the technical issues than on other types of resources. Those governments which come armed with technical studies, have a full command of the nature of the problem, and are prepared to put forth realistic solutions are more likely to wield influence than are governments which have only rudimentary knowledge of the problem and no scientific studies to back their national positions. A number of recent case studies have demonstrated conclusively that the outcomes of negotiations on technical questions cannot be predicted from the gross power of the participants and that knowledge, among other factors, accounts for more than raw capabilities.[7]

Understanding the dynamics of power relationships at the international level would be relatively easy if resource relevance, credibility, need, and knowledge were the only variables involved. Unfortunately, political actions do not always conform to simple hypotheses, because human characteristics of pride, stubbornness, prestige, and friendship enter into all acts of influence as well. A government may be highly dependent upon some other state and still resist its demands; it may be willing to suffer all sorts of privations, and even physical destruction and loss of independence, simply for the sake of pride. The government of North Vietnam was willing to accept a very high level of destruction of lives and productive facilities by American bombers rather than make diplomatic or military concessions to the United States.

---

[7] See, for example, the case studies in Robert O. Keohane and Joseph S. Nye, *Power and Interdependence: World Politics in Transition* (Boston: Little, Brown and Company, 1977). See also David Baldwin's strong emphasis on the relevance of resources to particular situations in "Power Analysis and World Politics," *World Politics*, 31 (January 1979), 161–94.

· Additional variables affecting the exercise of influence can be observed in the situation where two small states of approximately equal capabilities make similar demands upon a "major" power and neither of the small states is dependent upon the large—or vice versa. Which will achieve its objectives? Will both exercise influence equally? Hypothetically, suppose that the ambassadors of Norway and Albania go to the British Foreign Office on the same day and ask the British government to lower tariffs on bicyles, a product that the two countries would like to export to England. Assume that the quality and price of the bicycles are approximately the same and that the British government does not wish to allow too many imports for fear of damaging the domestic bicycle industry. Assume further that both the Norwegian and Albanian ambassadors offer roughly equal concessions if the British will lower their tariffs on bicycles. Both claim they will lower their own tariffs on English automobiles. Which ambassador is most likely to succeed—that is, to achieve his government's objectives? Chances are that the British government would favor the request of the Norwegian ambassador and turn down the representation by the diplomat from Tirana. The explanation of this decision can probably not be found in the resources of either of the small countries (both offered approximately equal rewards) or in need, since in this hypothetical situation Britain needs neither of the small countries' automobile markets. Norway would get the favorable decision because British policy makers are more *responsive* to Norwegian interests than to those of Albania. Albania represents a Communist state whose government normally displays through its diplomacy and propaganda strong hostility toward England.

After relevant resources, need, and knowledge, the fourth variable that determines the effectiveness of acts of influence is thus the ephemeral quality of responsiveness.[8] Responsiveness can be seen as a disposition to receive another's requests with sympathy, even to the point where a government is willing to sacrifice some of its own values and interests in order to fulfill those requests; responsiveness is the willingness to be influenced. In one study, it was shown that members of the State Department in the United States may take considerable pains to promote the requests and interests of other governments among their superiors and in other government agencies, provided that the requesting government feels that the issue is important or that the need must be fulfilled.[9] In our hypothetical case, if the quality of responsiveness is present in the case of the Norwegian request, members of the British Foreign Office would probably work for the Norwegians and try to persuade other government agencies concerned with trade and commerce to agree to a lowering of the tariff on bicycles. In the British reaction to the Albanian request, it is not likely that the government would display much responsiveness. Suspicion, traditional animosities, lack of trust, and years of un-

---

[8] The concept of responsiveness is introduced by Karl W. Deutsch et al., *Political Community and the North Atlantic Area* (Princeton, N.J.: Princeton University Press, 1957); developed by Dean G. Pruitt, "National Power and International Responsiveness" *Background,* 7 (1964), 165–78. See also Dean G. Pruitt, "Definition of the Situation as a Determinant of International Action," in *International Behavior: A Social-Psychological Analysis,* ed. Herbert C. Kelman (New York: Holt, Rinehart & Winston, 1965), pp. 393–432.

[9] Pruitt, "National Power," 175–76.

favorable diplomatic experience would probably prevent the development of much British sympathy for Albania's needs or interests. . . . When the other variables, such as resources or need, are held constant or made equal, the degree of responsiveness will determine the success or failure of acts taken to influence other states' behavior.

If effective influence cannot be deduced solely from the quantity and quality of physical capabilities, how do we proceed to measure influence? If we want to assess a situation that has already occurred, the easiest way to measure influence is to study the *responses* of those in the influence relationship.[10] If A can get B to do X, but C cannot get B to do the same thing, then in that particular issue, A has more influence. If B does X despite the protestations of A, then we can assume that A, in this circumstance, did not enjoy much influence over B. It is meaningless to argue that the Soviet Union is more powerful than the United States unless we cite how, for what purposes, and in relation to whom the Soviet Union and the United States are exerting influence. . . .

HOW INFLUENCE IS EXERCISED

Social scientists have noted several fundamental techniques that individuals and groups use to influence each other. In a political system that contains no one legitimate center of authority that can command the members of the group or society, bargaining has to be used among the sovereign entities to achieve or defend their objectives. Recalling that A seeks one of three courses of conduct from B (B to do X in the future, B not to do X in the future, or B to continue doing X), it may use six different tactics, involving acts of:

   1. PERSUASION. By persuasion we mean simply initiating or discussing a proposal with another and eliciting a favorable response without explicitly holding out the possibility of rewards or punishments. We cannot assume that the exercise of influence is always *against* the wishes of others and that there are only two possible outcomes of the act, one favoring A, the other favoring B. For example, state A asks B to support it at a coming international conference on the control of narcotics. State B might not originally have any particular interest in the conference or its outcome; but it decides, on the basis of A's initiative, that something positive might be gained, not only by supporting A's proposals, but also by attending the conference. In this case, B might also expect to gain some type of reward in the future, although not necessarily from A. Persuasion would also include protests and denials that do not involve obvious threats.
   2. THE OFFER OF REWARDS. This is the situation where A promises to do something favorable to B if B complies with the wishes of A. Rewards may be of almost any type in international relations. To gain the diplomatic support of B at the narcotics conference, A may offer to increase foreign-aid payments, lower tariffs on goods imported from B, support B at a later conference on communi-

[10] Robert A. Dahl, "The Concept of Power," *Behavioral Science,* 2 (1957), 201–15.

cations facilities, or promise to remove a previous punishment. The last tactic is used often by negotiators. After having created an unfavorable situation, they promise to remove it in return for some concessions by their opponents.

3. THE GRANTING OF REWARDS.   In some instances, the credibility of a government is not very high, and state B, before complying with A's wishes, may insist that A actually give the reward in advance. Frequently, in armistice negotiations neither side will unilaterally take steps to demilitarize an area or demobilize troops until the other shows evidence of complying with the agreements. One of the clichés of cold-war diplomacy holds that deeds, not words, are required for the granting of rewards and concessions.

4. THE THREAT OF PUNISHMENT.   Threats of punishment may be further subdivided into two types: (a) positive threats, where, for example, state A threatens to increase tariffs, institute a boycott or embargo against trade with B, or use force; and (b) threats of deprivation, where A threatens to withdraw foreign aid or in other ways withhold rewards or other advantages that it already grants to B.

5. THE INFLICTION OF NONVIOLENT PUNISHMENT.   In this situation, threats are carried out in the hope of altering B's behavior, which, in most cases, could not be altered by other means. The problem with this tactic is that it often results in reciprocal measures by the other side, thus inflicting damage on both, and not necessarily bringing about a desired state of affairs. If, for example, A threatens to increase its military capabilities if B does X and then proceeds to implement the threat, it is not often that B will comply with A's wishes, because it, too, can increase its military capabilities. In this type of situation, both sides indulge in the application of punishments that may escalate into more serious forms unless the conflict is resolved. Typical acts of nonviolent punishment include breaking diplomatic relations, raising tariffs, instituting boycotts and embargoes, holding hostages, organizing blockades, closing frontiers, or walking out of a diplomatic conference.

6. FORCE.   In previous eras, when governments did not possess the variety of foreign-policy instruments available today, they frequently had to rely upon the use of force in the bargaining process. Force and violence were not only the most efficient tactics, but in many cases the only means possible for influencing. Today, the situation is different. As technological levels rise and dependencies develop, other means of inducement become available and can serve as substitutes for force.

PATTERNS OF INFLUENCE
IN THE INTERNATIONAL SYSTEM

Most governments at some time use all their techniques for influencing others, but probably over 90 percent of all relations between states are based on simple persuasion and deal with relatively unimportant technical matters. Since such interactions seldom make the headlines, we often assume that most relations between states involve the making or carrying out of threats. But whether a government is communicating with another over an unimportant technical matter or over a subject of great consequence, it is likely to use a particular type of tactic in its attempts to influence, depending on the past tradition of friendship or hostility between those two governments and the amount of compatibility between their objectives and interests. Allies, for example, seldom threaten each other with force or even make blatant threats of punishment, but governments that disagree over a wide range of policy objectives and hold attitudes of suspicion and hostility toward each other are more likely to resort to threats and imposition of punishments. The methods of exerting influence between Great Britain and the United States are, typically, persuasion and rewards, whereas the methods of exerting influence between the Soviet Union and the United States in the early post–World War II era were typically threatening and inflicting punishments of various types. . . .

To summarize this analysis of power, we can suggest that power is an integral part of all political relationships; but in international politics we are interested primarily in one process: how one state influences the behavior of another in its own interests. The act of influencing becomes a central focus for the study of international politics, and it is from this act that we can best deduce a definition of power. If we observe the act of influencing, we can see that power is a process, a relationship, a means to an end, and even a quantity. Moreover, we can make an analytical distinction among the act of influencing, the basis, or resources, upon which the act relies, and the response to the act. Resources are an important determinant of how successful the wielding of influence will be, but they are by no means the only determinant. The nature of a country's foreign-policy objectives, the skill with which a state mobilizes its capabilities for foreign-policy purposes, its needs, responsiveness, costs, and commitments are equally important. Acts of influencing may take many forms, the most important of which are the offer and granting of rewards, the threat and imposition of punishments, and the application of force. The choice of means used to induce will depend, in turn, upon the general nature of relations between any two given governments, the degree of involvement between them, and the extent of their mutual responsiveness. . . .

2

Coercive Resource Power

ROBERT L. PAARLBERG

In the following article, Robert L. Paarlberg critically evaluates the comparative strengths of oil and food as instruments of influence in international politics. He concludes that the nature of domestic politics in countries seeking to exercise resource power and in those designated as target nations, and the nature of the international resource markets, render agripower "a much less promising source of diplomatic leverage than petropower." Paarlberg is assistant professor of political science at Wellesley College and has been a research associate, Harvard University Center for International Studies. He is editor of *Diplomatic Dispute: U.S. Relations with Iran, Japan, and Mexico* (1978).

It was fashionable several years ago to argue that both food and oil could be used as tools for coercion. International security, once defined and preserved by military might, had suddenly been threatened by the uncertain availability of critical economic resources. Nations seemed in a position to struggle for dominance over one another by offering or refusing access to increasingly scarce primary commodities and raw materials. In one view, the most dramatic aspect of this struggle was to occur between producers of food and oil. Food power was to be arrayed against oil power. The oil-starved industrial countries, some of which exported food, would confront food starved non-industrial countries, some of which exported oil.[1]

This looming contest between "agripower" and "petropower" was not unwelcome to some in the United States who foresaw their own ultimate triumph, with what had come to be called the "food weapon." Having earlier identified food as "one of the principal tools in our negotiating kit," Secretary of Agriculture Earl L. Butz predicted in 1975 that, "In the long run, agripower has to be more important than petropower." Assistant Secretary of State Thomas O. Enders warned in November 1974, at the time of the World Food Conference, that U.S. food power was a natural counter to Middle East oil power. He claimed that "The food producers' monopoly exceeds the oil producers' monopoly." Other State Department officials asserted in 1975 that "we could make OPEC look sick if we were just to use what our agriculture gives us." The Central Intelligence Agency

Reprinted from Robert L. Paarlberg, "Food, Oil, and Coercive Resource Power," *International Security* 3 (Fall 1978), pp. 3–19 by permission of the M.I.T. Press, Cambridge, Massachusetts. Copyright © by the President and Fellows of Harvard College. Some footnotes have been deleted; others have been renumbered to appear in consecutive order.

[1] For an elaboration of this viewpoint, see Barraclough, "Wealth and Power: The Politics of Food and Oil," *The New York Review of Books* XXII, no. 13 (August 7, 1975), p. 23.

published its speculation that food abundance might allow the United States to regain the primacy in world affairs which it had enjoyed at the close of the Second World War, when it was the only nation to possess nuclear weapons. Lester R. Brown concurred with these official assessments, observing that, "The issue is no longer whether food represents power, but how that power will be used."[2]

Yesterday's prophets of food power have today fallen silent. Exportable oil has indeed become a prime ingredient of national power in the contemporary international system, but food has not. Since the effective wielding of their "oil weapon" in 1973–74, the Arab oil exporting nations have gained discernable leverage over the diplomatic behavior of oil importing countries in the industrial world. Even as the real price of oil now declines, amid predictions of an interlude of abundant world supplies, the threat of another Arab oil embargo remains sufficient to inspire, among oil importing countries, far more generous policies toward the Arab world than would otherwise be the case. Non-Arab oil exporting countries enjoy enhanced diplomatic leverage as well, merely by posing as "dependable" sources of supply. No parallel growth of food power has yet occurred. This is due in part to recent conditions of relative abundance in the world food market. Yet the failure of food power to emerge as a counterweight to oil power goes far beyond current market conditions. Whatever the changing condition of the market, food can never provide as much diplomatic leverage to an exporting nation as does oil.

BARRIERS TO THE EXERCISE OF RESOURCE POWER

We define resource power as the ability of one nation to influence the behavior of another nation through the manipulation of international resource transfers. This definition excludes from consideration the export of resources such as food and oil for the sole purpose of earning foreign exchange, however beneficial such earnings may be in a commercial sense. To be worthy of its name, resource power must make possible more than the accumulation of wealth. It must enable the user to influence the behavior of other nation-states. Working from this definition, there will be at least three separate points at which any effort to wield resource power can meet frustration:

1. Within the domestic system of the subject nation (i.e., the nation seeking to exercise resource power). Here, for either practical or political reasons, foreign policy leaders may be unable to control the volume and the direction of their own external resource transfers.

2. Within the domestic system of the target nation. Here the threat or even the

---

[2] These predictions of food power are found in Earl L. Butz, "Food Power—A Major Weapon" (speech), Washington, D.C., 24 June 1974; "Food Power: The Ultimate Weapon in World Politics?" *Business Week*, 15 December 1975, pp. 54–60; Central Intelligence Agency, Office of Political Research, *Potential Trends in World Population, Food Production, and Climate* (OPR 401), August 1974; and Lester R. Brown, "The Politics and Responsibility of the North American Breadbasket," World Watch Paper No. 2, Worldwatch Institute, Washington, D.C., October 1975.

reality of resource trade manipulation may be inadequate or inappropriate to produce the desired modification of behavior.

3. Between the subject and the target nation, within the international resource market itself. Here options for control over supply may not exist, while low cost options to reduce dependence upon any one source of supply may abound.

If an attempt to exercise resource power fails at any one of these three points, it will fail altogether. For the Arab nations to enjoy oil power, their leaders must be able to manipulate oil exports at will, political authorities within target nations must be sufficiently affected by these manipulations to react in the desired fashion, and the international oil market must allow no low cost escape from oil trade dependence upon Arab sources of supply. All three of these rather strict conditions are simultaneously met under present conditions, and as a consequence oil has emerged as an exceptional source of resource power.

Not one of these three critical conditions can be met in the case of food. Political leaders in food exporting countries, such as the United States, are *not* capable of manipulating food exports at will. Even if they could, political authorities in target nations would *not* be sufficiently affected by food trade interruptions, or they would *not* be inclined to react in the direction of U.S. diplomatic preferences. And in any case, the world food trading system does *not* force target nations to accept food trade dependence upon any one source of supply, such as the United States. Let us consider each of these three points of probable food power failure in turn.

Difficulty Manipulating Food Exports

Food exports are far more difficult for national leaders to manipulate than oil exports. In the first instance, this is because the production of food is more difficult to adjust than the production of oil. Oil is a natural resource, available in uncertain quantities below the ground but in easily controlled quantities at the wellhead. National political leaders seeking to exercise oil power abroad can strengthen their hand by manipulating rates of production at home. As an accompaniment to their 1973 embargo, the Arab oil exporting countries were able to agree upon a finely tuned schedule of punitive production cutbacks: in October a minimum 5 percent cutback from September production levels, to be followed by an additional 5 percent cutback each month thereafter. Political leaders seldom enjoy such power over food production. Food is not a natural resource. Its annual availability depends largely upon matters which defy political control. In the United States, for example, each year's food production depends primarily upon the weather, and secondarily upon many separate decisions made throughout the growing season by thousands of private business firms and millions of individual farmers. Political leaders may sometimes be able to influence a few of these decisions at the cost of multi-billion dollar price support and acreage control policies. They can do little or nothing about the weather.

Even when blessed with a desired level of domestic food production, political leaders seeking to exercise international food power still must gain control over the volume and the direction of food exports. Both practical and political concerns complicate this task. By its very nature, food is far more difficult to withhold from the world market than oil. Oil withheld from the market, either in storage above ground or left untouched below ground, can increase in value. Food left too long in the ground, or held too long in expensive storage, loses whatever value it may have had. Hence the laughability of a sometimes imagined Central American "banana embargo." Political constraints are also important, particularly since the major food surplus nations, unlike the major oil surplus nations, adhere to procedures of representative democracy. Few political leaders in these food surplus democracies will wish to invite the hostile reaction of farm constituents to a termination or redirection of overseas food sales. . . .

Political questions aside, a food embargo strategy may simply exceed the legal capabilities of the U.S. Government. The United States (unlike most of its export competitors) is not a state trading nation. Approximately 95 percent of U.S. food exports are not handled by the government at all, but rather by private food trading companies, several of which are based in other countries as well as in the U.S. Before the embarrassment of the 1972 Soviet grain purchase, the so-called "great grain robbery," national political leaders were not even notified in a timely fashion of when, or to whom, these sparsely regulated private firms were selling American food. The exporting companies must now report large sales promptly, but they are not constrained to seek prior government approval. In 1975 the House Committee on Agriculture conclusively rejected a proposal to place private grain sales under the control of an official export marketing board. This lack of national political control over food exports has been judged appropriate to the larger task of maintaining commercial incentives for abundant food production. If national political leaders in the United States were to opt for complete control over U.S. food exports, they might find themselves in a better position to exercise food power—but with less food. Oil exporting countries need not face this dilemma, since political control of oil exports does not affect the quantity of oil available for export.

Despite political and legal restrictions, the United States has, at times, blocked commercial food exports. In June 1973, for example, the government placed a brief but general embargo on soybean exports. Also, during the depths of the cold war commercial food sales were effectively blocked to the Soviet Union. Yet it would be inappropriate to cite either case as a successful exercise of food power. The 1973 soybean embargo (made possible by authority in the 1969 Export Administration Act to limit exports in the face of an excessive drain on domestic supplies) was undertaken not for the purpose of gaining diplomatic leverage over foreign food customers, but to control food price inflation for consumers at home. The State Department was not even invited to participate in the domestic policy debate which led up to the soybean embargo decision. If given a chance, those with foreign policy interests in mind would have strongly warned against suddenly interrupting soybean exports to trusting allies in Western Europe and Japan. Far from constituting a successful exercise of food power, the 1973 soybean embargo weakened the hand of U.S. foreign policy.

Nor did cold war restrictions on food sales to the Soviet Union constitute an effective exercise of food power. Quite the opposite. The 1949 Export Control Act had not prohibited commercial sale of foodstuffs to any country, but an amendment to the Agricultural Act of 1961 did express Congressional objection to the subsidized sale of agricultural commodities to the Russians. This restriction carried very little meaning at the time, since the Soviet Union was still a net exporter of food. But in 1963, following a serious crop failure, the Russians turned to the world market to purchase wheat, and Congressional objections to U.S. sales suddenly began to have an effect—a painful, unwelcome effect. President Kennedy, eager to sell wheat to the Russians to advance the progress of détente, found himself unable to do so. In his effort to escape domestic objections to a Russian wheat deal, Kennedy was forced to yield to labor demands that half the grain be shipped in U.S. vessels, an expensive proposition which dampened Soviet interest in the sale. The International Longshoreman's Association signalled its determination to police this restriction by refusing at one point to load any grain at all on ships bound for the Soviet Union. All the while the grain sale scheme met effective resistance from those Republican partisans who opposed "trading with the enemy." One notable opponent of the sale was former Vice President Richard M. Nixon, who joined critics in Congress by arguing that a wheat sale to the Soviet Union might turn out to be "the major foreign policy mistake of this Administration, even more serious than fouling up the Bay of Pigs." In the end, internal opposition of one form or another held the final sale to less than half of its originally intended size.[3]

These restrictions on grain sales to Russia remained effective for another eight years, until 1971, when the Nixon White House, in its own early pursuit of détente, finally struck a bargain with the still reluctant maritime unions to permit larger food sales to the Soviet Union. Even then, however, food was destined to remain an elusive diplomatic tool. Nixon's 1972 grain sale so outraged American consumers that they demanded re-imposition of export controls. These controls brought forth, in turn, howls of indignation from American farmers who had grown accustomed to the Soviet market. On balance, efforts to manipulate U.S. food sales to the Soviet Union seem to have caused much more political discomfort in Washington than in Moscow. . . .

At this first point of comparison, within the domestic system of the nation seeking to exercise resource power, food exports prove far more resistant to willful political manipulation than oil exports.

Ineffective Impact Within Target Nations

Food and oil further differ at a second point in the process of exercising resource power—at the point of impact within "target" nations. In the eyes of target nation leaders, food trade interruptions are usually far less threatening than oil trade interruptions.

First, imports of food usually satisfy a much smaller share of total domestic consumption than imports of oil. Oil importing countries typically rely upon the world market for almost all of the oil they consume, while food importing coun-

---

[3] See James Trager, *The Great Grain Robbery* (New York: Ballantine Books, 1975), pp. 14–16.

tries seldom import to satisfy more than 5 to 10 percent of their total food consumption. For example, during the . . . 1973–76 period of unusually high world-wide food import demand, the major food importing nations of Western Europe relied upon the world market to satisfy only 9 percent of their total food calorie consumption. During the same period, these same nations relied upon imports to satisfy approximately 90 percent of their total oil consumption. . . .

Among one very important group of food importing countries, those which also export oil, few have developed more than a modest dependence upon the world food market. The OPEC countries of North Africa and the Middle East have dramatically increased their food imports in recent years, but still produce enough at home to satisfy two thirds of their own total cereal consumption. Both Indonesia and Nigeria are more than 94 percent self-sufficient in cereal supplies. Mexico, a non-OPEC oil exporting country with substantial food import needs, nonetheless provides for more than three quarters of its own grain consumption. The Soviet Union, sometimes depicted as an oil surplus nation which is highly vulnerable to food trade interruptions, is still only modestly dependent upon the world food market. Over the period 1973–76, despite an unprecedented volume of food imports, the Soviets remained 97 percent self-sufficient in total kilocalorie supplies, and 94 percent self-sufficient in grain consumption.[4] When food imports satisfy such a small share of total internal consumption, the impact of a food trade interruption can hardly be expected to match that of an oil trade interruption.

Second, food and oil shortages tend to produce pain at different points within target nations. Faced with an oil trade interruption, leaders in most industrial democracies may anticipate a simultaneous increase in both inflation and unemployment, followed by a chorus of competing demands from their most vocal and visible political constituents—business leaders deprived of production and sales, workers deprived of jobs, and citizens deprived of economical fuels for home and for transportation. By contrast, food shortages may present political leaders with a somewhat more manageable problem. In most poor countries, to begin with, food shortages can usually be allocated to politically powerless citizens living in the countryside. Food distribution systems in poor countries are frequently biased to provide first for the needs of small but politically active urban elites. Even under conditions of desperate overall scarcity, these politically powerful groups may not suffer, and pressures to comply with food power demands may not develop. Those who will suffer most from a food trade interruption will be the least visible, the least vocal, and the least powerful segment of the national population, the rural poor.[5]

---

[4] See "Meeting Food Needs in the Developing World," Research Report No. 1, International Food Policy Research Institute, Washington, D.C., February 1976. Also, USDA, Foreign Agriculture Circular, Grains, FG 1–76, 21 January 1976.

[5] Consider, for example, the experience of Bangladesh, as described by Donald F. McHenry and Kai Bird, "Food Bungle in Bangladesh," *Foreign Policy*, no. 27 (Summer 1977), 72–88. Food shortages are not so easily allocated to politically invisible segments of the population in all third world countries. Where a very large and politically active middle class may exist, as in Chile, food shortages will create a difficult dilemma for political leaders, as during the Allende period when food aid from the U.S. was discontinued. See data and discussion by Cheryl Christensen, "Food and National Security," in Klaus Knorr and Frank N. Trager, eds., *Economic Issues and National Security* (Lawrence, Kansas: Regents Press of Kansas, 1977), p. 300.

Among industrial food importing nations, adjustment to a food trade interruption may prove politically manageable for quite a different reason. Industrial countries do not usually import large quantities of food to satisfy human needs directly. Western Europe, Japan, and the Soviet Union, for example, together import nearly 85 percent of their grain in the form of coarse animal feed for livestock. When faced with a food trade interruption, these nations have the option of falling back to a more efficient means of feeding their people, relying upon abundant non-meat food supplies while reducing livestock herds. . . .

Because food trade interruptions tend to disrupt much smaller shares of internal consumption, and because that disruption tends to be allocated to the least visible extremities of the political system, efforts to exercise "food power" are unlikely to produce a sufficient impact within target nations to evoke the intended reaction. It is more likely that those efforts will produce either no effect or an entirely unintended effect within target nations. . . .

Escape from Dependence Within the International Food Market

The final point at which food power proves inferior to oil power is within the international market, where large food exporting nations such as the United States enjoy fewer options to exercise monopoly or oligopoly power, and fewer opportunities to use that market power for political purposes.

At first glance, the world food market appears to be no less dominated by a few large sellers than the world oil market. The United States and Canada, together, have been in some years the source of up to 65 percent of the world's grain exports. The total OPEC share of world oil exports is higher at 85 percent, but within the thirteen nation OPEC group the share of the two largest exporting nations alone (Saudi Arabia and Iran) stands at only 38 percent, and the total Arab share of world oil exports stands at just 54 percent, less than the North American share of world grain exports.[6] Some observers have argued from this evidence that the U.S. and Canada, together, enjoy a power position in the world food market which more than matches the position of any two nations or of all Arab nations together within the world oil market. This popular comparison is flawed in several important respects.

First, the United States and Canada do not coordinate their food export policies in pursuit of any common purpose. They are, in fact, direct competitors. Canada irritates the United States when it produces for export at full capacity even during times of abundant supply, when the United States often seeks to support prices by restricting its own production. Tellingly, Canadian food sales to the Soviet Union continued during the brief U.S. effort in 1975 to enforce a "food power" embargo. The U.S., in turn, irritates Canada whenever it uses export subsidies, government credits, and "food aid" shipments to further enlarge its much greater share of the export market at Canada's expense. To speak of a

[6] James W. Howe and the Staff of the Overseas Development Council, *The U.S. and World Development: Agenda for Action 1975* (New York: Praeger, 1975), p. 236.

"North American" monopoly on exportable grain supplies is to conclude too much from simple continental geography.

Second, dominance in the world food market counts for much less than dominance in the world oil market. The United States and Canada may account for two thirds of the world's wheat exports, but they account for less than one fifth of world wheat production. Most of the world's food production never enters the international market. More than 80 percent of the people in the world live in countries which are at least 95 percent self-sufficient in their total food calorie supply.[7] The world's food system does not, in fact, consist of a single "interdependent" world market. It would be more accurate to describe that system as a collection of many separate national food markets, frequently protected from one another by government policies specifically designed to prevent too much food trade interdependence. Most of the international food trade which does occur performs only a residual function. Nations typically turn to the international market to fill marginal needs not met by their own substantial domestic food production, or to find an outlet for an unwanted domestic surplus. To "control" even a large portion of this residual market is not to determine who gets food and who does not.

By contrast, the international oil market is the principal market from which most consumption must be satisfied. More than half of the world's oil consumption is satisfied through imports, compared to only one eighth of all consumption of the world's most traded food source, grain. A large export share in the world oil market is more likely, as a result, to translate into real political power.

Third, as well as performing its lesser role, the international food market remains far more competitive than the world oil market. This is true despite the fact that five large multinational grain trading firms handle 85 percent of all U.S. grain entering international trade. These five firms may appear to "control" U.S. exports, but (unlike the seven major international oil companies) they have never performed more than the restricted intermediate function of transporting and handling grain. They do not own farms, grain on farms, or the means of producing grain on farms. They do not determine the price, the volume, or the direction of exports.[8] Most export prices continue to be set in an open market, through competitive bid, where foreign customers enjoy potential access to virtually the entire U.S. domestic grain supply. More than fifty private firms actually engage in the U.S. grain export business, assuring the competitive character of most contracts. While the world food system as a whole consists largely of politically regulated and non-competitive national markets, the smaller residual international market takes its character from the more open and competitive nature of the United States, the principal exporting nation in that market. The world oil market, by contrast, is less competitive, taking its character from the near-total regulation

[7] J. P. O'Hagan, "National Self-Sufficiency in Food," *Food Policy*, vol. 1, no. 5 (November 1976), p. 355.

[8] See Gary L. Seevers, "Food Markets and Their Regulation." In the face of OPEC member nation demands for "participation" in ownership, and for control over pricing and production, the role of the major international oil companies now begins to resemble more nearly the rather modest middleman function of the international grain companies.

practiced within and among the principal oil exporting nations of the Middle East.

The world food market is also highly competitive in the sense that most food importing nations have ample means to escape dependence upon any one source of supply. Of the 120 or so food importing nations which make regular purchases in the market, few purchase in large enough quantities to make them truly dependent upon a single large supplier, such as the United States. . . .

Even when a nation's import requirements may be very large, and even when supplies are very tight, the competitive character of the world food market tends to frustrate those seeking to exercise food power. . . .

Also, it must be remembered that the high prices which accompany tight food supplies will quickly bring new producers into the world food market. New oil producers can also appear as prices increase, but not so quickly and not in so many varied locations. . . .

Finally, the condition of the world food market, more often than not, is one of abundance rather than scarcity. Food may be scarce today in relation to nutritional needs, but it is once again abundant in relation to effective commercial and political demand. . . .

QUALIFICATIONS AND CONCLUSION

Food power is inferior to oil power at each critical point in the process of exercising coercive resource diplomacy: within the domestic system of the nation seeking to exercise resource power, within the domestic system of the target nation, and also within the larger realm of the international resource market. Formidable barriers to the successful exercise of food power exist at each of these three points, while comparable barriers to the exercise of oil power are presently absent. In combination, such barriers to the exercise of food power greatly diminish its value to the user.

Exceptions may be found to this general rule of food power failure. Recall, for example, the U.S. suspension of food aid to the Marxist government of Salvador Allende in Chile. That government was subsequently weakened by middle class discontent over food shortages, among other things, and fell to a military coup in 1973. Within five days the new government received food aid credits to buy U.S. wheat. The appearance of food power in this case is deceptive. At best, food was only one of many instruments of power wielded against the Allende government, and alongside these other instruments of economic coercion, probably the least important.[9] What is more, food power appears in this instance as a rather blunt instrument of diplomatic influence. It did not influence the Chilean government to alter its policies; instead, its contribution was to the downfall of that government, and to the emergence of a military regime which has become, in its own way, no less troublesome to United States foreign policy. Also, it was precisely this cynical use of food aid in Chile which inspired many of the detailed

---

[9] The Allende government was exceptionally unstable in any case; indigenous middle class resistance to Allende's brand of socialism might have been sufficient to bring about a collapse even in the absence of destabilizing foreign policy actions by the U.S.

restrictions on food aid which now help to insure against any repetition of this episode. In this respect, the success of food power in Chile was not only dubious but self-terminating.

A second exception to the rule of food power failure might also be acknowledged. This was the successful use of promised food sales by President Nixon, in 1972, as one means to entice the Soviet Union into a more forthcoming diplomatic posture at the time of the first Moscow summit, amid a troublesome North Vietnamese Easter offensive, and during the final stages of the SALT I negotiations. In the end, however, this exercise of food power proved to be politically and commercially costly at home, and scarcely worth the increment of leverage gained abroad. As in the case of Chile, it was also a self-terminating use of food power. Once the initial 1972 grain sale to the Soviet Union had been made, leverage over the Soviet Union was immediately lost. . . .

Remember that this high probability of food power failure applies only to the realm of behavioral control. There is no doubt that exportable food supplies are a useful source of foreign exchange, and perhaps by that avenue they do constitute a derivative source of national strength or power. . . .

One last food power claim remains to be considered. This is a claim that food abundance confers an even more derivative form of "structural power" upon U.S. policymakers. Even if the United States cannot use food to control discrete actions, it may be able to set the bounds within which some of those actions are taken, by virtue of its very large influence over the structure of the world food market. For example, by offering unrestricted commercial access to its own very large food supply, the United States can unilaterally maintain the semblance of an open world food trading system, regardless of restrictions which smaller nations place upon their exports in times of scarcity. Similarly, by holding large surplus food stocks in times of abundance, as in the years before 1972, the United States can unilaterally stabilize world food prices, protecting consumers and producers alike from disruptive price fluctuations. No other nation holds this sort of unilateral structuring power over the character of the world food market.

But in what sense is this structuring power a diplomatic asset? If anything, it may be a diplomatic liability. Since the United States can perform certain tasks alone, it is expected to do so—alone. The United States, which now ships up to one third of its annual harvest abroad, has grown heavily dependent upon an open and stable international food trading system. If system maintenance tasks are not performed, it has the most to lose. By shouldering the leadership burden alone, it may indeed exercise some "structural power" over the world food system, but this kind of power may actually be accompanied by commercial sacrifice and diplomatic constraint.

In conclusion, the power which food confers is much less than meets the eye. Agripower, in the long run as well as in the short run, is a much less promising source of diplomatic leverage than petropower. This lesson may disappoint those searching for a response in kind to the power now being wielded by those with exportable supplies of oil. To counter that power requires not a response in kind, not an exercise of food power, but a disciplined and deliberate response to oil power on its own terms, through reduced national vulnerability to a future oil trade interruption.

3

Arms Sales: The New Diplomacy

ANDREW J. PIERRE

Arguing that arms transfers are inherently neither "bad" nor "good," Andrew J. Pierre concludes from his survey of trends in conventional arms transfers that recent developments regarding this issue mirror the transformation of world politics shown in the global diffusion of power from industrialized to Third World countries. Pierre is a senior fellow at the Council on Foreign Relations and author of *The Global Politics of Arms Sales* (1982).

. . . Arms sales have become, more than ever before, a crucial dimension of world politics. They are now major strands in the warp and woof of international affairs. Arms sales are far more than an economic occurrence, a military relationship, or an arms control challenge—*arms sales are foreign policy writ large.*

II

A number of trends combine to give arms sales greater saliency. The first is the sheer increase in the quantity of weapons being supplied. Arms transfers worldwide have more than doubled in the past decade, from $9.4 billion in 1969 to over $20 billion in 1980 (in constant 1977 dollars). The United States has been the largest supplier during this period and has seen its foreign military *sales* (as distinct from arms *delivered,* and measured so as to include items such as training and logistical assistance) rise from $1.1 billion in 1970 to approximately $16 billion [in 1981] (in current dollars).[1] The Soviet Union has also sharply increased its arms transfers and by some measurements has begun to overtake the United States. The level of French and British arms sales has quadrupled since 1970 and a number of smaller suppliers have significantly increased their sales.

Reprinted from Andrew J. Pierre, "Arms Sales: The New Diplomacy," *Foreign Affairs* 60 (Winter 1981/82), 266–286. Abridged by permission of Foreign Affairs. Copyright 1982 by the Council on Foreign Relations, Inc. Some footnotes have been deleted.

[1] This does not include the recent $8.5 billion sale to Saudi Arabia. Most of the arms sales data in this article are drawn from U.S. Arms Control and Disarmament Agency, *World Military Expenditures and Arms Transfers;* U.S. Department of Defense, *Foreign Military Sales and Military Assistance Facts;* Central Intelligence Agency, *Communist Aid to Less Developed Countries of the Free World;* International Institute for Strategic Studies, *The Military Balance;* and Stockholm International Peace Research Institute, *Yearbook of World Armaments and Disarmament.* Each of these is published annually. Due to variations in methodology, however, comparisons among these are difficult and may be misleading.

A second trend is the qualitative upgrading of arms sales. Prior to the 1970s, most arms supplied (especially to the developing countries) were the surplus and obsolete weapons of the major powers, which they wanted to eliminate from their inventories (often as military assistance grants) so as to make room for new, more advanced equipment. Even in the early 1960s the aircraft transferred to the developing world more often than not were ten-year-old American F-86 and Soviet MiG-17 fighters rather than the first-line planes of the period such as F-4s and MiG-21s. In contrast, today some of the arms being transferred, such as F-15s, MiG-23s and AWACS, are among the most sophisticated in the inventories of the supplier states.

A noteworthy aspect of the qualitative improvement has been the spread of sophisticated weaponry through co-production agreements. These enable countries to acquire through licensing arrangements the knowledge to manufacture or to assemble a weapons system. More than two dozen developing countries now participate in such arrangements with outside suppliers.

A third trend is in the changed direction of the arms flows. Until the mid-1960s most weapons went to developed countries, usually the NATO allies of the United States or the Warsaw Pact allies of the Soviet Union. It was not until the war in Southeast Asia in the second half of the decade that the dominant portion went to the developing world. Nor was the trend reversed at the end of the Vietnam War. During the late 1970s the Persian Gulf and Middle East countries received by far the largest portion of arms, with a fourfold rise in the value of arms imports (in constant dollars) during the decade. Iran, Saudi Arabia and Israel were the major recipients of Western arms, while most Soviet weapons were shipped to Syria, Iraq, Libya, and, a little earlier, Egypt. Indeed, by 1980 this region was receiving 50 percent of all weapons shipped to the Third World. This has led some observers to conclude that the arms sales "problem" is solely a Middle East problem—but this is far too simplistic an analysis. Arms sales to Africa increased 20-fold from 1969 to 1978 and to Latin America tripled (again, in constant dollars). Although the totality of these sales was small compared to the Middle East figure, these increases were important in the context of the respective regions. Over three-quarters of the global arms trade now goes to the Third World.

A fourth trend is the establishment of indigenous armament industries within the Third World. Twenty-four developing countries now produce weapons of some type. This, too, is a recent change; two decades ago hardly any of these nations manufactured arms locally. The prime incentives for the creation of these national industries have been political or security concerns rather than commercial ones, as sometimes averred. Nations have been motivated by the desire to reduce their dependence upon outside suppliers in order to bolster their national security. But once the industry is created, exports are seen as a way of reducing unit costs, offsetting research and development expenses, and providing trade benefits. Among the states which have sought to augment their self-sufficiency because of the perceived unreliability of outside suppliers have been Israel, South Africa, Taiwan, South Korea and India. Others have been motivated less by perceptions of a threat to their security than by broad political considerations relating to their status within their region: Argentina, Brazil, Venezuela and Indonesia.

While arms production in the Third World is certain to continue expanding at a steady rate, its impact upon the global arms trade is likely to remain marginal. Four states accounted for 87.5 percent of the value of major weapons transferred to the developing world during the decade of the 1970s: the United States (45 percent), the Soviet Union (27.5 percent), France (10 percent) and Britain (5 percent). When West Germany, Canada, Italy, the Netherlands, and Czechoslovakia are added in, the figure goes up to 94.3 percent. The new Third World suppliers are mainly producing second-echelon weapons and do not have the technological base to compete with the principal suppliers. No Third World country has yet become the principal supplier of a developing country.

III

These trends in the transfer of arms must be viewed as an integral part of the broader transformations in the international system. As is well recognized, the world is undergoing a diffusion of power, political and economic, from the industrialized states to the developing nations. There is an important military component to that diffusion as well. The acquisition of conventional arms, often sophisticated and in far larger quantities than the recipient states have previously possessed, is a critical element of that diffusion. Arms are a major contributing factor to the emergence of regional powers such as Israel, Brazil and South Africa; their purchase can make a deep impact upon regional balances and local stability.

Arms sales, moreover, have become a key instrument of diplomacy for the weapons suppliers, in some cases the best one available to them. There has been a decline in the traditional instruments of reassurance and diplomacy, such as formal alliances, the stationing of forces abroad, and the threat of direct intervention. At a time when the major powers are less likely to intervene with their own armed forces, they are more prone to shore up friendly states through the provision of arms or to play out their own competition through the arming of their proxies. A contributing factor has been the reduction of other instruments of diplomacy, such as developmental aid. Both the United States and the Soviet Union now give less in economic than in military assistance. Even ideology ("Free World" versus Communism) no longer has the cementing influence that it once had.

Arms sales must also be seen in the context of North-South issues. They constitute a redistribution of power whose significance in certain cases may be equal to or greater than that of some of the better-recognized economic forms. Certainly the withholding or granting of arms can have a great political and psychological impact upon Third World leaders. Then, too, arms sales can be a method of technology transfer; an increasing number of states do not want the weapons fresh out of the crates but rather the technology that will enable them to build, or coproduce, at home.

Finally, arms sales have become, and surely will remain, a crucial aspect of the continuing East-West competition in the Third World. Indeed, they are now the prime instrument used by the Soviet Union, and an important one for the United States, in the rivalry for the allegiance of much of the world. The capability of the Soviet Union to project its military presence to distant places expanded greatly during the 1970s, and Moscow shows no reluctance to use arms transfers to support its political aims. The energy vulnerability of the West has made the security of the Persian Gulf and the stability of the Middle East matters of the highest importance; arms sales have become an important means used by the West to safeguard these interests, quite apart from the economic benefits to be gained from sales to the oil-rich countries.

IV

The greater prominence of arms sales today has not been matched by new insights as to their utility. Judgments about arms sales are often extremely difficult to reach. . . . This is due, in part, to the lack of norms about the requirements of international security. In dealing with the spread of nuclear weapons, most observers agree about the goal of preventing nuclear proliferation, and the disagreements, important as they are, are about tactics for achieving this. No similar principle is applicable to the spread of conventional arms.

A particular sale may be destabilizing or it may restore a balance. It may promote an arms race in a region, or it may help deter a potential conflict. Moreover, what is true in the short run may not be valid for the longer term. Who is to say how a weapon transferred now could be employed in ten years' time (e.g., U.S. weapons given to South Vietnam)? And who can vouchsafe that the future political leadership of a country will be as "responsible" about the use of weapons in the future as it is at present (e.g., the Shah [of Iran])? Or that the alliances and foreign policy alignments of today—upon which the prospective supplier must base his decision—will be the same tomorrow (e.g., Somalia and Ethiopia)?

Arms sales decisions are thus fraught with policy dilemmas. Even when a supplier country has adopted general policy guidelines, each weapons transfer decision must be made individually, and often it will involve complex judgments and trade-offs. Short-term benefits should be weighed against longer term risks. Economic advantages may have to be balanced against potential political disadvantages. One important foreign policy goal, such as strengthening an alliance relationship or a nation's capacity for self-defense, may run counter to another goal, such as promoting human rights (e.g., South Korea). Assisting one nation (e.g., China) could cause a deterioration of relations with another (e.g., the Soviet Union). Or, yet again, such indirect pressure may moderate the other's behavior. Providing substantial amounts of conventional arms may or may not reduce incentives for the acquisition of nuclear weapons (e.g., Pakistan). As the debates in recent years on a large number of arms sales show, one can almost take for granted that every decision will involve competing objectives. . . . [The author next provides a survey of recent arms sales politics and practices of the major suppliers, notably the Soviet Union, France, and the United States—*eds.*]

V

Clearly, the need for some international restraints on the transfer of arms is greater than ever. Unfortunately, this is not an auspicious time for new initiatives in this regard, given the marked deterioration in Soviet-American relations and the current European-American difficulties. Any specific proposals for early action would have a distinct air of unreality.

Nonetheless, it is not too early to think constructively about the problem. That the Third World is likely to be an increasingly unstable environment in the coming decades, with a propensity for conflict, is by now a widely accepted judgment. Yet we have not even begun to sort out "rules of the game" to maintain a lid on the competition between the Soviet Union and the West in the Third World. Restraints on the competitive transfer of arms should be an important component of such an undertaking. Nor is there a system for regular consultations between the United States and its European allies on arms sales to the developing world. This global problem is not discussed in NATO because it is thought to be outside of its charter. Yet uncoordinated Western arms sales, without an accepted "code of conduct," can undermine regional balances and may also conflict with the diplomacy of other Western nations in such a way as to prevent a political evolution desired by all of them. . . . [Here Pierre briefly summarizes the failed attempt of the United States and the Soviet Union between 1977 and 1978 to achieve an agreement to limit conventional arms transfers—*eds.*]

Any future attempt to develop cooperative, multilateral regulation of arms sales should be undertaken in the following manner:

First, priority should be placed upon arrangements between the West European suppliers and the United States rather than the negotiation of Soviet-American accords. The latter is a long-term aim, which will remain difficult to achieve because of the basic East-West political and ideological competition in the Third World. On the other hand, there already is a pressing need for greater cooperation within the West on policies in dealing with Third World instabilities. In the Middle East and Persian Gulf, for example, a coordinated approach on arms sales could become an important component of an overall, more unified foreign policy toward the area. The present pattern of competitive, uncoordinated sales to a country or region can be contrary to Western political interests. There is too much truth to the statement: "If we don't sell, someone else will.". . .

Second, at the point when the international atmosphere has become considerably more propitious than today, and after consultations have been held within the West, a new attempt should be made to discuss arms sales with the Soviet Union. This time, however, the Europeans should be full partners from the outset. Initially the discussions should involve a frank exchange of views on regional security and local political developments in sensitive areas. There may be common incentives to seek to insulate some local conflicts from East-West tensions. When interests sharply conflict, as they inevitably will at times, such discussions may provide a venue for crisis management. Maintaining contact can reduce some misunderstandings of each other's purposes and foster much needed predictability in a period of tension or crisis.

It would be unrealistic, of course, to expect the Soviets to call a halt to their use of arms transfers as an instrument of policy, and even in the West there would be resistance to following such a course of self-denial. But we should seek some "rules of the game" that introduce a pattern of restraint. The understanding worked out after the 1962 Cuban missile crisis regarding the nontransfer of "offensive" weapons to the island may provide one type of precedent. . . .

Third, the suppliers should seek to involve the recipients in planning for restraints. The political and psychological dimensions are important. Proposals for restraint should not be seen as inherently discriminatory. For some time such proposals were characterized as arrogant manifestations of paternalistic attitudes. But in the past several years Third World attitudes have been gradually changing, as evidenced in U.N. debates. Now there is an emerging tendency to see arms sales as a mechanism by which the industrialized world manipulates the developing nations, creating new forms of dependence and drawing them into the superpower confrontation.

Both of these points of view are extreme. The best plans for restraint would be regionally based, involve intensive discussions between the producers and the purchasers regarding real security needs, and should lead to a kind of symbiotic relationship beneficial to all.

In undertaking the above steps it should be borne in mind that the challenge is to *manage* the process of arms sales so as to enhance international security. Of themselves arms sales are neither "bad" nor "good"—it all depends upon how they are used—so that there is no a priori case for either reducing or increasing them. An arms control approach is desirable, but to be successful, care must be taken that it is not artificially separated from the realities of foreign policy. Arms sales, whether we like them or not, have become a common coin of today's world politics. Because they are instruments of diplomacy as well as of security, they will gain in currency in the years to come.

4

The Causes of War

QUINCY WRIGHT

Recognizing the multiple causes of war, Quincy Wright argues that these causes are rooted in the relations of political groups to one another, and that its explanation must be found in sociological, psychological, technological, and legal factors. Wright was professor emeritus of international law at the University of Chicago and is especially well-known for his encyclopedic *A Study of War,* a portion of which is excerpted here.

Wars arise because of the changing relations of numerous variables—technological, psychic, social, and intellectual. There is no single cause of war. Peace is an equilibrium among many forces. Change in any particular force, trend, movement, or policy may at one time make for war, but under other conditions a similar change may make for peace. A state may at one time promote peace by armament, at another time by disarmament; at one time by insistence on its rights, at another time by a spirit of conciliation. To estimate the probability of war at any time involves, therefore, an appraisal of the effect of current changes upon the complex of intergroup relationships throughout the world. Certain relationships, however, have been of outstanding importance. Political lag deserves attention as an outstanding cause of war in contemporary civilization.

POLITICAL LAG

There appears to be a general tendency for change in procedures of political and legal adjustment to lag behind economic and cultural changes arising from intergroup contacts. The violent consequences of this lag can be observed in primitive and historic societies, but its importance has increased in modern times. The expansion of contacts and the acceleration of change resulting from modern technology has disturbed existing power localizations and has accentuated the cultural oppositions inherent in social organization. World-government has not developed sufficiently to adjust by peaceful procedures the conflict situations which have arisen. Certain influences of this political lag upon the severity and frequency of wars will be considered in the following paragraphs.

War tends to increase in severity and to decrease in frequency as the area of political and legal adjustment (the state) expands geographically unless that area

Reprinted from Quincy Wright, *A Study of War,* Vol. 2 (Chicago: University of Chicago Press, 1942), pp. 1284–1295. Reprinted by permission of the University of Chicago Press. Copyright 1942 by the University of Chicago. Footnotes have been deleted.

becomes as broad as the area of continuous economic, social, and cultural contact (the civilization). In the modern period peoples in all sections of the world have come into continuous contact with one another. While states have tended to grow during this period, thus extending the areas of adjustment, none of them has acquired world-wide jurisdiction. Their growth in size has increased the likelihood that conflicts will be adjusted, but it has also increased the severity of the consequences of unadjusted conflicts. Fallible human government is certain to make occasional mistakes in policy, especially when, because of lack of universality, it must deal with conflicts regulated not by law but by negotiation functioning within an unstable balance of power among a few large units. Such errors have led to war.

War tends to increase both in frequency and in severity in times of rapid technological and cultural change because adjustment, which always involves habituation, is a function of time. The shorter the time within which such adjustments have to be made, the greater the probability that they will prove inadequate and that violence will result. War can, therefore, be attributed either to the intelligence of man manifested in his inventions which increase the number of contacts and the speed of change or to the unintelligence of man which retards his perception of the instruments of regulation and adjustment necessary to prevent these contacts and changes from generating serious conflicts. Peace might be kept by retarding progress so that there will be time for gradual adjustment by natural processes of accommodation and assimilation, or peace might be kept by accelerating progress through planned adjustments and new controls. Actually both methods have been tried, the latter especially within the state and the former especially in international relations.

Sovereignty in the political sense is the effort of a society to free itself from external controls in order to facilitate changes in its law and government which it considers necessary to meet changing economic and social conditions. The very efficiency of sovereignty within the state, however, decreases the efficiency of regulation in international relations. By eliminating tensions within the state, external tensions are augmented. International relations become a "state of nature." War therefore among states claiming sovereignty tends to be related primarily to the balance of power among them.

Behind this equilibrium are others, disturbances in any one of which may cause war. These include such fundamental oppositions as the ambivalent tendency of human nature to love and to hate the same object and the ambivalent tendency of social organization to integrate and to differentiate at the same time. They also include less fundamental oppositions such as the tendency within international law to develop a world-order and to support national sovereignty and the tendency of international politics to generate foreign policies of both intervention and isolation. Elimination of such oppositions is not to be anticipated, and their continuance in some form is probably an essential condition of human progress. Peace, consequently, has to do not with the elimination of oppositions but with the modification of the method of adjusting them.

With an appreciation of the complexity of the factors involved in the causation of war and of the significance of historic contingency in estimating their influence, caution is justified in anticipating results from analytical formulations of the problem. . . .

Warfare cannot exist unless similar but distinct groups come into contact. Its frequency and its intensity are dependent upon the characteristics of the groups and are roughly proportionate to the rapidity with which these contacts develop so long as the groups remain distinct and self-determining. However, when these contacts have passed a critical point of intensity, sympathetic feelings and symbolic identifications tend to develop among individuals of different groups sufficiently to permit the functioning of intergroup social, political, and legal institutions, adjusting conflicts and broadening the area of peace. The smoothness of this process is greatly influenced by the policies pursued by groups and the degree of the consistency of these policies with one another.

It is in the relation of political groups to one another and to their members and in the relation of group policies to one another and to the world-order that the explanation of war is to be found. War may be explained sociologically by its function in identifying and preserving political groups, psychologically by the conflict of human drives with one another and with social requirements, technologically by its utility as a means to group ends, and legally by inadequacies and inconsistencies in the law and procedure of the whole within which it occurs.

SOCIOLOGICAL FUNCTIONS OF WAR

Animal warfare is explained by the theory of natural selection. The behavior pattern of hostility has contributed to the survival of certain biological species, and consequently that behavior has survived. In the survival of other species other factors have played a more important role. The peaceful herbivores have on the whole been more successful in the struggle for existence than have the predators and parasites.

Among primitive peoples before contact with civilization warfare contributed to the solidarity of the group and to the survival of certain forms of culture. When population increased, migrations or new means of communication accelerated external contacts. The war-like tribes tended to survive and expand; furthermore, the personality traits of courage and obedience which developed among the members of these tribes equipped them for civilization.

Among peoples of the historic civilizations war tended both to the survival and to the destruction of states and civilizations. Its influence depended upon the stage of the civilization and the type of military technique developed. Civilized states tended to fight for economic and political ends in the early stages of the civilization, with the effect of expanding and integrating the civilization. As the size and interdependence of political units increased, political and economic ends became less tangible, and cultural patterns and ideal objectives assumed greater importance. Aggressive war tended to become a less suitable instrument for conserving these elements of the civilization. Consequently, defensive strategies and peaceful sentiments developed, but in none of the historic civilizations were they universally accepted. War tended toward a destructive stalemate, disintegrating the civilization and rendering it vulnerable to the attack of external barbarians of younger civilizations which had acquired advanced military arts from the older civilization but not its cultural and intellectual inhibitions.

In the modern period the war pattern has been an important element in the creation, integration, expansion, and survival of states. World-civilization has, however, distributed a singularly destructive war technique to all nations, with the consequence that the utility of war as an instrument of integration and expansion has declined. The balance of power has tended to a condition such that efforts to break it by violence have increasingly menaced the whole civilization, and yet this balance has become so complex and incalculable that such efforts have continued to be made.

PSYCHOLOGICAL DRIVES TO WAR

Human warfare is a pattern giving social sanction to activities which involve the killing of other human beings and extreme danger of being killed. At no period of human development has this pattern been essential to the survival of the individual. The pattern is a cultural acquisition, not an original trait of human nature, though many hereditary drives have contributed to the pattern. Of these, the dominance drive has been of especial importance. The survival of war has been due to its function in promoting the survival of the group with which the individual identifies himself and in remedying the individual problem arising from the necessary repression of many human impulses in group life. The pattern has involved individual attitudes and group opinion. As the self-consciousness of personality and the complexity of culture have increased with modern civilization, the drive to war has depended increasingly upon ambivalences in the personality and inconsistencies in the culture.

A modern community is at the same time a system of government, a self-contained body of law, an organization of cultural symbols, and the economy of a population. It is a government, a state, a nation, and a people.

Every individual is at the same time subject to the power and authority of a government and police, to the logic and conventions of a law and language, to the sentiments and customs of a nation and culture, and to the caprices and necessities of a population and economy. If he fights in war, he does so because one of these aspects of the community is threatened or is believed by most of those who identify themselves with it to be threatened. It may be that the government, the state, the nation, and the people are sufficiently integrated so that there is no conflict in reconciling duty to all of these aspects of the community. But this is not likely because of the analytical character of modern civilization which separates military and civil government, the administration and the judiciary, church and state, government and business, politics and the schools, religion and education. Furthermore, it may be that the threat is sufficiently obvious so that no one can doubt its reality, but this is also seldom the case. The entities for whose defense the individual is asked to enlist are abstractions. Their relations to one another and the conditions of their survival are a matter of theory rather than of facts. People are influenced to support war by language and symbols rather than by events and conditions.

It may therefore be said that modern war tends to be about words more than about things, about potentialities, hopes, and aspirations more than about facts, grievances, and conditions. When the war seems to be about a particular territory, treaty, policy, or incident, it will usually be found that this issue is important only because, under the circumstances, each of the belligerents believed renunciation of its demand would eventually threaten the survival of its power, sovereignty, nationality, or livelihood. . . .

. . . War, therefore, rests, in modern civilization, upon an elaborate ideological construction maintained through education in a system of language, law, symbols, and ideals. The explanation and interpretation of these systems are often as remote from the actual sequence of events as are the primitive explanations of war in terms of the requirements of magic, ritual, or revenge. War in the modern period does not grow out of a situation but out of a highly artificial interpretation of a situation. Since war is more about words than about things, other manipulations of words and symbols might better serve to meet the cultural and personality problems for which it offers an increasingly inadequate and expensive solution. . . .

It may be questioned whether a rational consideration of the symbols, for the preservation of which wars have been fought, demonstrate that they have always been worth fighting for or that fighting has always contributed to their preservation. The actual values of these entities as disclosed by philosophy and the actual means for preserving them as disclosed by science are, however, less important in the causation of war than popular beliefs engendered by the unreflecting acceptance of the implications of language, custom, symbols, rituals, and traditions. It is in the modification of these elements of national cultures so that they will conform more precisely to the ends accepted by modern civilization and to the means likely to secure those ends that a more peaceful world-order can gradually be developed. Such a work of education and propaganda cannot be effective unless it proceeds simultaneously in all important national cultures. A minimum acceptance by all of certain world-standards is the price of peace. The definition and maintenance of such standards require the co-operation of international education, international jurisprudence, international administration, and international politics.

5

The Management of Power in International Relations: The Balance of Power

INIS L. CLAUDE, JR.

Although the balance-of-power concept is central to the theory and practice of international politics, Inis L. Claude, Jr., demonstrates in this essay that it is often ambiguously used to refer to vastly different phenomena. His essay focuses particular attention on the work of the late Hans J. Morgenthau, whose perceptive writing over many decades on the elements of "political realism" uses "balance of power" as a core idea. Claude is Edward R. Stettinius, Jr., Professor at the University of Virginia. Among his well-known works is *Swords Into Plowshares* (1971).

The crucial fact about the human situation . . . may be simply and starkly expressed: Mankind stands in grave danger of irreparable self-mutilation or substantial self-destruction. The circumstances which underlie this perilous condition may be succinctly described: Humanity is divided into basic units called states; some of these units possess the awesome capacity to destroy others. Once this power is unleashed, there is the high probability of a competitive struggle which may draw the whole world into its devastating vortex. It is not certain that the technology of destruction has yet advanced to the point of making it possible for a global war to render the planet uninhabitable in the absolute sense. In any case, such definitive devastation has not yet become the inevitable result of a general war. Yet, the march of military technology is so rapid that it is no longer premature to contemplate the danger of the annihilation of the human race. . . .

This catastrophe may not occur. In principle, it is doubtless avoidable. But the hard fact is that humanity has developed no means for providing reasonable assurance, let alone confident certainty, that it *will* be avoided. The conclusion is inescapable that a high priority on the human agenda must be assigned to the task of achieving maximum safeguards against both the penultimate tragedy of the smashing of human civilization and the ultimate tragedy of human extinction. We may hope that it is not too late to face the issue of the survival of human values; we may assume that it is not too early to confront the issue of the survival of the human species. . . .

However one may resolve the question of the priority to be assigned to the maintenance of peace, it is clear that the problem of the management of power in international relations looms as the central issue of our time. Power exists in states. It may be used in competitive struggle, producing intolerable destruction. It may be used unilaterally, producing enslavement and degradation of its victims. In short, both survival and freedom, both existence itself and the higher values that enrich existence, are implicated in the problem of power. We may assert nobility of character as well as tactical wisdom in rejecting the doctrine of peace at any price, but the price of war, in the sense of the total unleashing of the destructive resources available to states, may well be insupportable.

This . . . is a study of the problem of the management of power in international relations. Except where clearly indicated otherwise . . . I use the term *power* to denote what is essentially military capability—the elements which contribute directly or indirectly to the capacity to coerce, kill, and destroy. I am aware that power may be defined much more broadly, to include the variety of means by which states may pursue their purposes and affect the behavior of other units. My adoption of a more restricted usage is not to be construed as a denial of the complexity of the process whereby human individuals and groups achieve desired results in their relations with each other, or as an assertion that in international relations brute force is all that counts. Nevertheless, the capacity to do physical violence is the central factor in this study. It is the variety of power which most urgently requires effective management, and I have found it convenient to refer to the task of keeping war-making potential under control as the problem of the management of power. . . .

The theory of international relations contains three basic concepts which may be regarded as relevant to the problem of the management of power: balance of power, collective security, and world government. . . . [The remainder of this essay will focus exclusively on the first, and perhaps most prominent concept, since it continues to receive primary emphasis in debates about international relations—*eds.*]

The concept of the balance of power is, by any standard, an ancient notion in the field of international relations. Whether it is also an honorable one is a question to which the history of thought provides no uniform and consistent answer. The concept has sometimes been highly regarded and sometimes not, and differing opinions have flourished at all times. With generous allowance for such differences, one may say that the doctrine of balance of power had its heyday in the eighteenth and nineteenth centuries, that it suffered disrepute during the greater part of the first half of the twentieth century, and that it has recently made a most impressive comeback. . . .

Although the validity of the balance of power concept is generally acknowledged to be an arguable issue, it is frequently assumed that the meaning of the concept is self-evident, or clearly established and generally understood. Thus, the term is used as common coin, often without any attempt at definition or explanation. Indeed, the phrase *balance of power* might be regarded as a cliché in the literature of international relations—a standard expression, a phrase which literally rolls off the tongue or the pen. "Balance of power" is to writers on international relations as "a pinch of salt" is to cooks, "stellar southpaw" to baseball writers, and "dialectical materialism" to Marxist theoreticians.

Unfortunately for the scholar who wants to understand and evaluate, the meaning of the balance of power is not so definitively established as those who glibly use the phrase seem to imply. If its meaning is not shrouded in mystery, it is at least cloaked in ambiguity. . . .

. . . The trouble with the balance of power is not that it has no meaning, but that it has too many meanings.

THE MULTIPLE MEANINGS OF THE BALANCE OF POWER

Balance of Power as a Situation

The balance of power sometimes means equilibrium—*l'équilibre, das Gleichgewicht*. In this sense, it is a purely descriptive term, designed to indicate the character of a situation in which the power relationship between states or groups of states is one of rough or precise equality. The image is that of two scales suspended upon a fulcrum, balancing only when equal weights are placed upon the two sides. Alternatively, the image of the chandelier is invoked when a more complex situation is envisaged, but in either case the basic idea is the same: Balance of power refers to a situation in which power is literally "balanced" by equivalent power. . . .

A second usage of the balance of power refers, surprisingly enough, to a factual situation in which competing powers are *not* balanced—to a condition of disequilibrium. It is customary in this connection to introduce the image of the bank balance. . . in which deposits are noticeably larger than withdrawals.

It is widely suspected that many, if not most, statesmen have this conception in mind when they dilate upon the beauties of the balance of power. As Nicholas J. Spykman put it, "The truth of the matter is that states are interested only in a balance which is in their favor. Not an equilibrium, but a generous margin is their objective. . . . The balance desired is the one which neutralizes other states, leaving the home state free to be the deciding force and the deciding voice."[1] . . .

. . . The notion of a *favorable* balance, implying superiority for one side, is frequently encountered in the literature of world politics.

Since balance of power sometimes means equilibrium and sometimes means disequilibrium, it is not too surprising to learn that it sometimes achieves a position of majestic neutrality and consents to mean either one. In this usage, the balance of power becomes the equivalent of "the distribution of power"; just as temperature refers to the thermal situation, whether it be hot or cold, so balance of power refers to the power situation, whether it be balanced or unbalanced. . . .

[1] *America's Strategy in World Politics* (New York: Harcourt, 1942), pp. 21–22.

Balance of Power as a Policy

. . . Another usage . . . treats balance of power as a policy of states or as a principle capable of inspiring the policy of states.

Balance of power is sometimes identified as a policy of promoting the creation or the preservation of equilibrium. This involves recognizing and acting upon the principle that unbalanced power is dangerous. The stronger power may succumb to the temptation to dominate, to oppress, to conquer, to destroy. In a multistate system, the only policy which promises to prevent such behavior is that of confronting power with countervailing power; stability, survival, protection of national rights and interests demand that power be neutralized by equivalent power. In these terms, the balance of power is a policy of prudence. . . .

. . . When Winston Churchill writes that the balance of power is "the wonderful unconscious tradition of British foreign policy," it is evident that he has in mind not the situation of balance but the policy of *balancing*. Balance of power is obviously to be understood as a principle guiding policy toward equilibrating action in such a passage as this: "Properly understood, the balance of power is . . . simply the natural tendency of states to combine, even in advance, against the probable aggressor."[2] . . .

. . . The assertion that states normally seek preponderance for themselves is not usually regarded as incompatible with the generalization that states "play the game" of balance of power, or follow a balance of power policy. . . . Hans J. Morgenthau energetically rebuts the notion that any valid explanatory principle can be found "to replace the balance of power as the guiding principle of American foreign policy,"[3] and then promptly asserts that it has been standard American policy to maintain "unchallengeable supremacy" in the Western Hemisphere (p. 61). The implication is clear that Morgenthau regards such a policy as an expression of the principle of balance of power. Critics of the balance of power also tend to identify that notion with a policy of pursuing military superiority. . . .

Balance of Power as a System

The versatility of the three words, balance of power, is further exhibited in their capacity to denote *systems* of international politics. Perhaps the most common use of the phrase makes balance of power mean not a certain type of power configuration, or a certain precept of policy, but a certain kind of arrangement for the operation of international relations in a world of many states. This usage is made explicit in the innumerable references to "the balance of power system" which dot the literature of international politics. Moreover, references to the mechanics, the instruments, the rules, and the operation of the balance of power provide unmistakable evidence that it is a system which is under consideration.

. . . Charles O. Lerche, Jr., writes that "In operation, the balance of power

---

[2] Paul Scott Mowrer, *Our Foreign Affairs* (New York: Dutton, 1924), p. 252.

[3] *Dilemmas of Politics* (Chicago: University of Chicago Press, 1958), p. 56.

is supposed to arrange matters so that any state which seeks to upset the peace will automatically have ranged against it sufficient power to persuade it of its folly.''[4] . . .

Viewpoints vary considerably regarding the nature of the system which is, or ought to be, identified with the balance of power. Some writers, for instance, stress the automatic or self-regulating character of the balance of power system, while others insist that it is a system wholly dependent upon manipulations carried out by shrewd statesmen. . . .

Enough has been said about the various meanings attached to the terminology of the balance of power to indicate the extreme difficulty of analyzing the concept. . . .

MORGENTHAU AND THE BALANCE OF POWER

Any consideration of the significance of the balance of power in the theory of international relations must include careful attention to the works of Hans J. Morgenthau, perhaps the most important figure in contemporary thought on this subject. . . . It is essential to consider the manner in which he uses the term balance of power and some major implications of his usage.

In beginning Part Four of Morgenthau's book, *Politics Among Nations,* the reader may breathe a sigh of relief to note that this author prefaces his treatment of the balance of power with an explanatory note concerning the meaning which he attaches to it.[5] It is perhaps a little discouraging to learn that he intends to use the term in four different senses: ''(1) as a policy aimed at a certain state of affairs, (2) as an actual state of affairs, (3) as an approximately equal distribution of power, (4) as any distribution of power.'' One wonders why Morgenthau does not adopt four different expressions to convey these four meanings, particularly since he obviously attaches great importance to the balance of power and should therefore wish to write about it with the utmost clarity. But reassurance comes with the promise which follows in Morgenthau's footnote: ''Whenever the term [balance of power] is used without qualification, it refers to an actual state of affairs in which power is distributed among several nations with approximate equality.'' We are on notice that Morgenthau uses balance of power to mean equilibrium, unless he provides indication to the contrary.

Alas, the promise is not fulfilled, and the sense of reassurance was premature. My analysis of Morgenthau's treatment of the balance of power, in *Politics Among Nations* and elsewhere, finds him using the term in a variety of senses, usually without warning signals to indicate that he is departing from the equilibrium usage. . . .

If one usage of the term occurs more frequently than any other in Morgen-

[4] *Principles of International Politics* (New York: Oxford University Press, 1956), p.128.

[5] 3rd ed. (New York: Knopf, 1960), p. 167, n. I. Note that the third edition is used exclusively in this [essay].

thau's works, I would hazard the proposition that it is the one which treats balance of power as a *system*; this, be it noted, is a meaning which Morgenthau does not acknowledge at all in his list of meanings. Time after time this connotation is implied: "the balance of power operates"; "the mechanics of the balance of power"; "the configurations to which the balance of power gives rise"; "the balance of power of that period was amoral rather than immoral."[6] On occasion, he is explicit: ". . . the self-regulatory mechanism of the social forces, which manifests itself in the struggle for power on the international scene, that is, the balance of power."[7] . . .

. . . A notable illustration . . . is provided by Morgenthau's doctrine of the inevitability of the balance of power.

This doctrine is stated repeatedly in Morgenthau's works. It appears in uncompromising form in the following passage.

> The aspiration for power on the part of several nations, each trying either to maintain or overthrow the status quo, leads of necessity to a configuration that is called the balance of power and to policies that aim at preserving it. We say "of necessity" advisedly. For here again we are confronted with the basic misconception . . . that men have a choice between power politics and its necessary outgrowth, the balance of power, on the one hand, and a different, better kind of international relations on the other. It insists that a foreign policy based on the balance of power is one among several possible foreign policies. . . .
>
> It will be shown . . . that the international balance of power is only a particular manifestation of a general social principle to which all societies composed of a number of autonomous units owe the autonomy of their component parts; that the balance of power and policies aiming at its preservation are not only inevitable but are an essential stabilizing factor in a society of sovereign nations. . . .[8]

Morgenthau likens a statesman who does not believe in the idea of balance of power to "a scientist not believing in the law of gravity," and asserts . . . "That a new balance of power will rise out of the ruins of an old balance and that nations with political sense will avail themselves of the opportunity to improve their position within it, is a law of politics for whose validity nobody is to blame."[9] He describes balance of power as "a universal instrument of foreign policy used at all times by all nations who wanted to preserve their independence," and as "a natural and inevitable outgrowth of the struggle for power."[10]

This is strong doctrine, and one ought to understand what Morgenthau is saying before reaching a firm judgment on its validity. In view of the diversity of meanings ascribed to the balance of power in Morgenthau's writings, a preliminary question is in order: *Which* balance of power—balance of power *in what sense*—is alleged to be inevitable?

Presumably, we can discard at once the notion that Morgenthau means to say

[6] *Politics Among Nations*, pp. 173, 175, 189, 190.

[7] *Ibid.*, p. 23. Cf. *In Defense of the National Interest* [New York: Knopf, 1951], p. 41.

[8] *Politics Among Nations*, p. 167. Cf. *Dilemmas of Politics* [Chicago: University of Chicago Press, 1958], p. 41.

[9] *In Defense of the National Interest*, p. 33.

[10] Morgenthau and Thompson, *Principles and Problems of International Politics* [New York: Knopf, 1950], p. 104; *Politics Among Nations*, p. 187.

that in a multistate system some pattern of power relationship always exists. This is a truism—like saying that there will always be *weather* (good or bad, hot or cold) on the earth, or that Mr. X and Mr. Y are inevitably either identical or different in age. There is no evidence that Morgenthau is engaged in anything so insignificant as saying that states are inevitably either equal or unequal in power.

Does Morgenthau mean to say that equilibrium is inevitable? . . .

. . .Can he mean that all states, in the nature of things, must follow the policy of creating and maintaining a situation of balanced power in the international arena? Are states inexorably dedicated to equilibrium? There are intimations of this in Morgenthau's statements of his proposition: The necessity which he recognizes is one which calls for policies aimed at preserving the configuration called the balance of power; he denies that "a foreign policy based on the balance of power" is optional for states; he calls balance of power "a universal instrument of foreign policy."

The supposition, however, that Morgenthau presumes all states to be avid supporters of equilibrium cannot stand. His general theoretical picture of international relations is one of an incessant struggle for power, a struggle in which at least some of the states some of the time are seeking to upset the status quo or even to achieve a power position which makes them complete masters of the world.[11] Note these decisive statements in *Politics Among Nations:*

> . . . all nations actively engaged in the struggle for power must actually aim not at a balance—that is, equality——of power, but at superiority of power in their own behalf. And since no nation can foresee how large its miscalculations will turn out to be, all nations must ultimately seek the maximum of power obtainable under the circumstances. (p. 210).
>
> All politically active nations are by definition engaged in a competition for power of which armaments are an indispensable element. Thus all politically active nations must be intent upon acquiring as much power as they can . . . (p. 396).

Morgenthau's description of the multistate system shows states engaged "in an unending succession of attempts to equalize and, if possible, to surpass the strength of their enemies."[12] Concretely, he readily recognizes the limitless ambition for power which has characterized the great would-be world conquerors.[13] While picturing the United States as a state motivated to uphold equilibrium in Europe, he holds that "In the Western Hemisphere we have always endeavored to preserve the unique position of the United States as a predominant power without rival."[14] Thus, when Morgenthau avers that balance of power is inevitable, he evidently means neither that a situation of equilibrium will always prevail nor that the policies of states will always aim at the creation or preservation of such a situation.

Does he mean that a balance of power *system* is inevitable in a world of states, that given a multiplicity of states, no other system for managing their relationships with each other can possibly be operative? This interpretation is at least plausible,

[11] *Politics Among Nations*, pp. 27–35, 39.

[12] *In Defense of the National Interest*, p. 41.

[13] *Politics Among Nations*, p. 56.

[14] *In Defense of the National Interest*, p. 5.

since we have noted that Morgenthau does on many occasions refer to the balance of power, explicitly, as a system or mechanism. When he deprecates Woodrow Wilson's belief "that the balance of power itself can be abolished together with its instruments, such as alliances,"[15] he seems to be saying that the balance of power is a system which has to be accepted as an inherent characteristic of the world political scene. Presumably this means that states have no choice but to carry on the management of their relationships with each other within a framework of political pluralism—a situation in which states are autonomous power units, maneuvering freely in the absence of a central control agency.

However, this interpretation is belied by the assertion that "Five methods have been developed throughout history to maintain international order and peace: the balance of power, international law, international organization, world government, diplomacy."[16] Balance of power, it appears in this passage, is only one of several systems which can be conceived and put into operation. In this case, it is hardly the inevitable way of doing international business.

The difficulties we have encountered in establishing the meaning of Morgenthau's doctrine of the inevitability of the balance of power lead to the suspicion that we ought to have been examining his usage of another term. Can it be that there are peculiarities in his definition of *inevitability* which, if taken into account, would lead to an understanding of this doctrine?

An incident which has a bearing on this question arises out of Morgenthau's discovery of an "iron law of politics" which requires that states pursue the national interest conceived in terms of power. This position is fundamentally rooted in his general theory of "political realism," with its premise that "politics, like society in general, is governed by objective laws that have their roots in human nature."[17] Morgenthau assumes "that statesmen think and act in terms of interest defined as power," and asserts that "the evidence of history bears that assumption out" (p. 5). Over and over in his writing, this proposition is presented as a law of politics, grounded in a necessity which denies choice to the managers of the affairs of states. Thus, referring to the United States, he says: "We have acted on the international scene, *as all nations must*, in power-political terms.[18] He regards the subordination by a state of its legal obligations to its national interests as an "iron law of international politics," or "a general law of international politics, applicable to all nations at all times" (pp. 144, 147). It should be noted that he establishes a close connection between this proposition and his doctrine concerning balance of power; power politics is lumped with "its necessary outgrowth, the balance of power," in a passage in which he denounces the "misconception" that "men have a choice" regarding them.[19]

Having established this objective law of politics, Morgenthau does some curious things with it. He accuses various American statesmen of having violated it—of having disregarded or even explicitly rejected the national interest as the

---

[15] Morgenthau and Thompson, *Principles and Problems of International Politics,* p. 50.

[16] *Ibid.,* p. 103.

[17] *Politics Among Nations,* p. 4.

[18] *In Defense of the National Interest,* p. 7. Italics mine.

[19] *Politics Among Nations,* p. 167.

foundation of policy, substituting moral principles for national interest.[20] He shatters his assertion that no choice exists by commenting that the debacle of collective security in the Italo-Ethiopian case of 1935 demonstrated the dire results of statesmen's incapacity to decide "whether to be guided by the national interest."[21] He writes one remarkable sentence in which he describes as an "iron law" a precept from which, he thinks, "no nation has ever been completely immune"—which implies that some nations have sometimes been somewhat immune from its operation.[22] Ultimately, he finds it desirable to conclude the volume in which he most often asserts that the pursuit of the national interest defined in power terms is an iron law, with an eloquent sermon exhorting American statesmen to obey that law.[23]

The revelation comes when Morgenthau responds to the obvious criticism of his position. Having been subjected by Robert W. Tucker to the charge that he was inconsistent in regard to his iron laws,[24] Morgenthau retorts that "It ought not to need special emphasis that a principle of social conduct, in contrast to a law of nature, allows of, and even presupposes, conduct in violation of the principle," and accuses his critic of "zeal to find contradictions where there are none."[25]

The cat, so to speak, is out of the bag. Morgenthau does not wish to be interpreted as meaning what he seems to say when he speaks of iron laws and inevitability. . . .

With this revised understanding of the concept of inevitability, we can return to the problem of interpreting Morgenthau's doctrine concerning the necessity of the balance of power. He has said that "the balance of power . . . is the very law of life for independent units dealing with other independent units—domestic or international—that want to preserve their independence. Independent power, in order to be kept in check, must be met by independent power of approximately equal strength."[26] More frequently, he has stated the power objective as either equality or superiority, with the latter regarded as preferable. Perhaps the point comes to this: In a world of multistate power struggle, a state should be basically concerned about its power situation, and do what it can to develop and maintain its power. Its power must be adequate to protect its interests and promote its purposes. Its policy can succeed only if backed by power, and policy aims should be kept in balance with the power resources available or likely to become available to support them. The power of competitors is mortally dangerous to the state; a state can be secure only if it can mobilize, unilaterally or in combination with

---

[20] *In Defense of the National Interest*, pp. 13, 23, 25–29, 114.

[21] *Politics Among Nations*, p. 419.

[22] *In Defense of the National Interest*, p. 144.

[23] *Ibid.*, pp. 239–242.

[24] "Professor Morgenthau's Theory of Political 'Realism'," *American Political Science Review*, March 1952, Vol. 46, pp. 214–224. Cf. the subsequent critique by Benno Wasserman, "The Scientific Pretensions of Professor Morgenthau's Theory of Power Politics," *Australian Outlook*, Vol. 13, March 1959, pp. 55–70.

[25] "Another 'Great Debate': The National Interest of the United States," *American Political Science Review*, December 1952, Vol. 46, p. 962, n. 2.

[26] *Dilemmas of Politics*, [p. 258].

others, power equal or superior to that which might be exercised against it. States may fail to recognize these truths, or they may not be able to meet these requirements successfully, but prudent men will recognize the validity of this analysis of international reality and try to conform to the requirements which it poses.

If this is what Morgenthau means, then it should be noted that the concept of the balance of power is essentially a redundancy in his theory of international politics. It really says that in a power struggle, states must and do struggle for power. A reasonable and dutiful statesman can be expected to recognize that his state must have at least as much power as its probable enemy, or be conquered, and to act accordingly. Conceivably the notion of balance adds one idea: that the statesman should be moderate in his quest for power, lest in trying for too much he precipitate a reaction of fear and hostility, thus defeating his own purposes.

BALANCE OF POWER AS A SYMBOL

Whether or not I have rightly interpreted Morgenthau's doctrine of the inevitability of the balance of power, it is clear that many writers have used the term balance of power not as a definable concept but as a *symbol* of realistic and prudent concern with the problem of power in international relations. This usually takes a negative form: Whoever repudiates the balance of power thereby convicts himself of lamentable disregard for the factor of power. As one pair of textbook writers put it, the alternative to balance of power policy "is to remain poorly armed, without allies, and with no attempt to balance the power of the aggressor state."[27]

This treatment of balance of power as a symbol characterizes a great deal of commentary on Woodrow Wilson. Louis J. Halle describes Wilson as "refusing to accept power as a fact in international relations."[28] John Morton Blum maintains that "Wilson long persisted in the habit of optimistic mind that denied the existence of force as a factor in human affairs," and that he conceived of the League of Nations as "an international political association constructed to preserve peace by substituting a world parliament and law for force."[29] Reinhold Niebuhr observes that "In the case of Wilson, the internationalist outlook was devoid of appreciation of the power-political elements in international relations."[30]

---

[27] [Lenox A. Mills and Charles H. McLaughlin, *World Politics in Transition* (New York: Holt, 1956), p. 109.]

[28] *Civilization and Foreign Policy* (New York: Harper, 1955), p. 49.

[29] *Woodrow Wilson and the Politics of Morality* (Boston: Little, Brown, 1956), pp. 119, 125.

[30] *Christian Realism and Political Problems* (New York: Scribner's, 1953), p. 62. For comparable statements regarding Wilson, see Ernst B. Haas and Allen S. Whiting, *Dynamics of International Relations* (New York: McGraw-Hill, 1956), p. 461; Robert Langbaum, "The American Mind in Foreign Affairs," *Commentary*, April 1957, Vol. 23, p. 303; Robert E. Osgood, *Ideals and Self-Interest in America's Foreign Relations* (Chicago: University of Chicago Press, 1953), p. 191; Arthur S. Link, "Portrait of the President," in Earl Latham, ed., *The Philosophy and Policies of Woodrow Wilson* (Chicago: University of Chicago Press, 1958), p. 19.

These allegations of blindness to the significance of the power factor in international relations are made in the face of the evidence that Wilson spoke and wrote constantly of the need for concerted power to prevent aggression and that he undertook to construct the League of Nations as the instrument for the application of concerted power. It is hard to believe that these scholars are ignorant of this evidence, or that they are parties to a conspiracy to suppress it. I suggest that their statements simply reflect their reaction to the fact that Wilson engaged in a persistent attack upon the balance of power. They associate a favorable attitude toward the idea of the balance of power with a healthy concern for the power factor. Wilson's attitude was unfavorable; therefore, he must have been guilty of a fatuous unwillingness to look the reality of power in the face.

Similarly, Herbert Feis pictures Cordell Hull and his crew of planners for post-World War II international organization as men enthralled by dreams of a world in which power is unimportant; in their view, "Principle, not power, was to hold dominion over the actions of all nations."[31] . . . Feis associates advocacy of international organization and denigration of the balance of power with unwillingness to recognize the significance of the power factor in world affairs; since Hull and his colleagues were involved in the former, Feis assumes that they must have been guilty of the latter.

These cases illustrate the widespread tendency to make balance of power a symbol of realism, and hence of respectability, for the scholar or statesman. In this usage, it has no substantive content as a concept. It is a test of intellectual virility, of he-manliness in the field of international relations. The man who "accepts" the balance of power, who dots his writing with approving references to it, thereby asserts his claim to being a hard-headed realist, who can look at the grim reality of power without flinching. The man who rejects the balance of power convicts himself of softness, of cowardly incapacity to look power in the eye and acknowledge its role in the affairs of states.

---

[31]*Churchill—Roosevelt—Stalin* (Princeton: Princeton University Press, 1957), p. 217.

6

Nuclear Weapons and the Institution of War

JONATHAN SCHELL

In this essay, Jonathan Schell launches a powerful attack not only on nuclear weapons
but also on the institution of war as an instrument of international conflict resolution.
Extrapolating from the destructiveness of thermonuclear weapons, he concludes that
nuclear war is so "senseless" that "violence . . . can no longer be war." Schell is a
staff writer for *The New Yorker* and author of *The Time of Illusion* (1976).

Since July 16, 1945, when the first atomic bomb was detonated, at the Trinity test
site, near Alamogordo, New Mexico, mankind has lived with nuclear weapons in
its midst. Each year, the number of bombs has grown, until now there are some
fifty thousand warheads in the world, possessing the explosive yield of roughly
twenty billion tons of TNT, or one million six hundred thousand times the yield
of the bomb that was dropped by the United States on the city of Hiroshima, in
Japan, less than a month after the Trinity explosion. These bombs were built as
"weapons" for "war," but their significance greatly transcends war and all its
causes and outcomes. They grew out of history, yet they threaten to end history.
They were made by men, yet they threaten to annihilate man. They are a pit into
which the whole world can fall—a nemesis of all human intentions, actions, and
hopes. Only life itself, which they threaten to swallow up, can give the measure
of their significance. Yet in spite of the immeasurable importance of nuclear
weapons, the world has declined, on the whole, to think about them very much.
We have thus far failed to fashion, or to discover within ourselves, an emotional
or intellectual or political response to them. This peculiar failure of response, in
which hundreds of millions of people acknowledge the presence of an immediate,
unremitting threat to their existence and to the existence of the world they live in
but do nothing about it—a failure in which both self-interest and fellow-feeling
seem to have died—has itself been such a striking phenomenon that it has to be
regarded as an extremely important part of the nuclear predicament as this has
existed so far. Only very recently have there been signs, in Europe and in the
United States, that public opinion has been stirring awake, and that ordinary people may be beginning to ask themselves how they should respond to the nuclear
peril. . . .

The widespread belief that a nuclear holocaust would in some sense bring about the end of the world has been reflected in the pronouncements of both American and Soviet leaders in the years since the invention of nuclear weapons. For example, President Dwight Eisenhower wrote in a letter in 1956 that one day both sides would have to "meet at the conference table with the understanding that the era of armaments has ended, and the human race must conform its actions to this truth or die." More recently—at a press conference in 1974—Secretary of State Henry Kissinger said that "the accumulation of nuclear arms has to be constrained if mankind is not to destroy itself." And President Jimmy Carter said in his farewell address . . . that after a nuclear holocaust "the survivors, if any, would live in despair amid the poisoned ruins of a civilization that had committed suicide." Soviet leaders have been no less categorical in their remarks. In late 1981, for example, the Soviet government printed a booklet in which it stated, "The Soviet Union holds that nuclear war would be a universal disaster, and that it would most probably mean the end of civilization. It may lead to the destruction of all mankind." In these and other statements, examples of which could be multiplied indefinitely, Soviet and American leaders have acknowledged the supreme importance of the nuclear peril. However, they have not been precise about what level of catastrophe they were speaking of. . . . No doubt, the leaders have been vague in part because of the difficulty of making reliable predictions about an event that has no precedent. Yet it seems important to arrive, on the basis of available information, at some judgment concerning the likelihood of these outcomes, for they are not the same. Nor, presumably, would the appropriate political response to all of them be the same. The annihilation of the belligerent nations would be a catastrophe beyond anything in history, but it would not be the end of the world. The destruction of human civilization, even without the biological destruction of the human species, may perhaps rightly be called the end of the world, since it would be the end of that sum of cultural achievements and human relationships which constitutes what many people mean when they speak of "the world." The biological destruction of mankind would, of course, be the end of the world in a stricter sense. As for the destruction of all life on the planet, it would be not merely a human but a planetary end—the death of the earth. . . .

Anyone who inquires into the effects of a nuclear holocaust is bound to be assailed by powerful and conflicting emotions. Preeminent among these, almost certainly, will be an overwhelming revulsion at the tremendous scene of devastation, suffering, and death which is opened to view. And accompanying the revulsion there may be a sense of helplessness and defeat, brought about by an awareness of the incapacity of the human soul to take in so much horror. A nuclear holocaust, widely regarded as "unthinkable" but never as undoable, appears to confront us with an action that we can perform but cannot quite conceive. Following upon these first responses, there may come a recoil and a decision, whether conscious or unconscious, not to think any longer about the possibility of a nuclear holocaust. (Since a holocaust is a wholly prospective rather than a present calamity, the act of thinking about it is voluntary, and the choice of not thinking about it is always available.) When one tries to face the nuclear predicament, one feels sick, whereas when one pushes it out of mind, as apparently one must do most of the time in order to carry on with life, one feels well again. But this feeling of well-being is based on a denial of the most important reality of our time, and therefore is itself a kind of sickness. A society that systematically shuts its eyes to an urgent peril to its physical survival and fails to take any steps to save itself cannot be called psychologically well. In effect, whether we think about nuclear weapons or avoid thinking about them, their presence among us makes us sick, and there seems to be little of a purely mental or emotional nature that we can do about it. . . .

The self-extinction of our species is not an act that anyone describes as sane or sensible; nevertheless, it is an act that, without quite admitting it to ourselves, we plan in certain circumstances to commit. . . . Our political and military traditions, . . . with the weight of almost all historical experience behind them, teach us that it is the way of the world for the earth to be divided up into independent, sovereign states, and for these states to employ war as the final arbiter for settling the disputes that arise among them. This arrangement of the political affairs of the world was not intentional. No one wrote a book proposing it; no parliament sat down to debate its merits and then voted it into existence. It was simply there, at the beginning of recorded history; and until the invention of nuclear weapons it remained there, with virtually no fundamental changes. Unplanned though this arrangement was, it had many remarkably durable features, and certain describable advantages and disadvantages; therefore, I shall refer to it as a "system"— the system of sovereignty. Perhaps the leading feature of this system, and certainly the most important one in the context of the nuclear predicament, was the apparently indissoluble connection between sovereignty and war. For without sovereignty, it appeared, peoples were not able to organize and launch wars against other peoples, and without war they were unable to preserve their sovereignty from destruction by armed enemies. (By "war" I here mean only international war not revolutionary war, which I shall not discuss.) Indeed, the connection between sovereignty and war is almost a definitional one—a sovereign state being a state that enjoys the right and the power to go to war in defense or pursuit of its interests.

It was into the sovereignty system that nuclear bombs were born, as "weapons" for "war." As the years have passed, it has seemed less and less plausible that they have anything to do with war; they seem to break through its bounds. Nevertheless, they have gone on being fitted into military categories of thinking. One might say that they appeared in the world in a military disguise, for it has been traditional military thinking, itself an inseparable part of the traditional political thinking that belonged to the system of sovereignty, that has provided those intentional goals—namely, national interests—in the pursuit of which extinction may now be brought about unintentionally, or semi-intentionally, as a "side effect." The system of sovereignty is now to the earth and mankind what a polluting factory is to its local environment. The machine produces certain things that its users want—in this case, national sovereignty—and as an unhappy side effect extinguishes the species.

The ambivalence resulting from the attempt to force nuclear weapons into the preexisting military and political system has led to a situation in which, in the words of Einstein—who was farseeing in his political as well as in his scientific thought—"the unleashed power of the atom has changed everything save our modes of thinking, and we thus drift toward unparalleled catastrophes."As Einstein's observation suggests, the nuclear revolution has gone quite far but has not been completed. The question we have to answer is whether the completion will be extinction or a global political revolution—whether the "babies" that the scientists at Alamogordo brought forth will put an end to us or we will put an end to them. For it is not only our thoughts but also our actions and our institutions— our global political arrangements in their entirety—that we have failed to change. We live with one foot in each of two worlds. As scientists and technicians, we live in the nuclear world, in which whether we choose to acknowledge the fact or not, we possess instruments of violence that make it possible for us to extinguish ourselves as a species. But as citizens and statesmen we go on living in the prenuclear world, as though extinction were not possible and sovereign nations could still employ the instruments of violence as instruments of policy—as "a continuation of politics by other means," in the famous phrase of Karl von Clausewitz, the great philosopher of war. In effect, we try to make do with a Newtonian politics in an Einsteinian world. The combination is the source of our immediate peril. For governments, still acting within a system of independent nation-states, and formally representing no one but the people of their separate, sovereign nations, are driven to try to defend merely national interests with means of destruction that threaten not only international but intergenerational and planetary doom. In our present-day world, in the councils where the decisions are made there is no one to speak for man and for the earth, although both are threatened with annihilation. . . .

. . . Since military action is the one activity through which we deliberately threaten to employ our new mastery over nature to destroy ourselves, nothing could be more crucial to an understanding of the practical dimensions of the nuclear predicament than a precise understanding of what nuclear weapons have done to war, and, through war, to the system of sovereignty of which war has traditionally been an indispensable part. All war is violent, but not all violence is war. War is a violent means employed by a nation to achieve an end, and, like all mere means, is subject to Aristotle's rule "The means to the end are not unlimited, for the end itself sets the limit in each case." The possible ends of war are as varied as the desires and hopes of men, having ranged from the recovery of a single beautiful woman from captivity to world conquest, but every one of them would be annihilated in a nuclear holocaust. War is destructive, but it is also a human phenomenon—complex, carefully wrought, and, in its way, fragile and delicate, like its maker—but nuclear weapons, if they were ever used in large numbers, would simply blow war up, just as they would blow up everything else that is human.

One of the respects in which war is unique among the uses to which mankind's steadily increasing technical skills have been put is that in war no benefit is obtained and no aim achieved unless the powers involved exert themselves to the limit, or near-limit, of their strength. In the words of Clausewitz: "War is an act of violence pushed to its utmost bounds; as one side dictates to the other, there arises a sort of reciprocal action which logically must lead to an extreme." For only at the extremes are victory and defeat—the results of war—brought about.

Even when victory and defeat are not absolute, the terms of the disengagement are determined by the nearness of one side to defeat. In this case, the antagonists, like chess players near the end of the game, see the inevitable outcome and spare themselves the trouble of actually going through the final moves. As Clausewitz writes, "everything is subject to a supreme law: which is the *decision by arms*." Therefore, "all action . . . takes place on the supposition that if the solution by force of arms which lies at its foundation should be realized, it will be a favorable one." For "the decision by arms is, for all operations, great and small, what cash payment is in bill transactions," and "however remote from each other these relations, however seldom the realization may take place, still it can never entirely fail to occur." Nuclear arms ruin war by making the decision by arms impossible. The decision by arms can occur only when the strength of one side or the other is exhausted, or when its exhaustion is approached. But in nuclear "war" no one's strength fails until *both* sides have been annihilated. There cannot be a victor without a vanquished, the collapse of whose military efforts signals the end of the hostilities, permitting the victor to collect his spoils. But when both adversaries have nuclear arms that moment of collapse never comes, and the military forces—the missiles—of both countries go on "fighting" after the countries themselves have disappeared. From the point of view of a power contemplating war in the pre-nuclear world, war appeared to depend on the possession of great strength, since the side that possessed the greater strength had the better chance of being victorious. But when war is seen from the point of view of the nuclear world it becomes clear that as an institution—as the mechanism with which sovereign states settled their disputes—war depended, above all, on weakness: the weakness of the defeated party, whose collapse made the decision by arms (the whole purpose of war) possible. And this weakness, in turn, depended on the presence of certain technical limitations on the ability of mankind in general to avail itself of natural forces for destructive purposes. When science made the energy in mass available to man, the crucial limits were removed, for everybody, forever, and the exhaustion of the defeated party—and so the triumph of the victor—was rendered impossible. War itself has thus proved to be a casualty of the tremendous means that were put at its disposal by science. We are now in a position to see that helplessness has always been the specific product of war, and weakness its essential ingredient. War has never been anything but unilateral disarmament—the disarmament of one side by the other. But now, before the exhaustion of either party can be reached, everyone will be dead, and all human aims—the aims pursued in the "war" and all others—will have been nullified. In a nuclear conflict between the United States and the Soviet Union—the holocaust—not only the adversaries but also the world's bystanders will vanish. In this "war," instead of one side winning and the other losing, it is as though all human beings lost and all the weapons won. Clausewitz writes, "War can never be separated from political intercourse, and if, in the consideration of the matter, this is done in any way, all the threads of the different relations are, to a certain extent, broken, and we have before us a senseless thing without an object." War can, for example, decline into mere looting or banditry or some other form of aimless violence. But, of all the "senseless things" that can ever occur when war's violence (its means) is severed from its political purposes (its ends), a nuclear holocaust is the most senseless. To call this senseless thing "war" is, in fact, simply a misnomer, and to go on speaking of "nuclear war," and the like, can only mislead and confuse us. Thus, while the Soviet Union and the United States are perfectly free to fire their thousands of nuclear weapons at one another, the result would not be war, for no end could be served by it. It would be comprehensive destruction—a "senseless thing." With the invention of nuclear weapons, it became impossible for violence to be fashioned into war, or to achieve what war used to achieve. Violence can no longer break down the opposition of the adversary; it can no longer produce victory and defeat; it can no longer attain its ends. It can no longer be war.

It must be emphasized that what nuclear weapons have ruined is not only "nuclear war" but all war (that is, all war between nuclear powers). "Conventional war," which in fact encompasses everything that deserves to be called war, is ruined because as long as nuclear weapons are held in reserve by the combatants, in accordance with the supposedly agreed-upon rules of some "limited war," the hostilities have not run to that extreme of violence at which the essential helplessness of one side or the other has been produced. If a decision were to be reached while the "defeated" party held potentially decisive means of violence in its possession, then that decision would be not "by arms" but by something else. We have to imagine that this power would accept its defeat while knowing that the use of its bombs would reverse it. A current example illustrates how little willingness there is among nuclear powers to accept such an outcome. For some time, it has been widely believed that the Soviet Union enjoys a preponderance in conventional forces over the NATO powers in Europe, and the United States has reserved for itself the right to resort to nuclear weapons in Europe rather than accept a conventional defeat there. Thus, the United States has already publicly discarded the notion of abiding by any rules of "limited war" if those rules should prove to mean a defeat for the United States. And there is certainly very little reason to suppose that the Soviet Union is any more willing to volunteer for defeat than the United States. That being the likely state of things, there seems little chance that a conventional war between nuclear powers could stay limited. And this means that a conventional war between nuclear powers must not even be begun, since it threatens the same holocaust that the limited use of nuclear weapons threatens. As a practical matter, this rule has up to now been followed by the statesmen of the nuclear world. Disregarding theoretical treatises on the possibility of "limited war" between nuclear powers, including "limited nuclear war," they have held back from any war; thus, in our thirty-six years of experience with nuclear weapons no two nuclear powers have ever entered into even conventional hostilities. The same cannot be said, of course, of hostilities between nuclear powers and non-nuclear powers, such as the Vietnam War or the Soviet-Afghanistan war. These remain possible—although, for reasons that I shall not go into here, they are not, it would seem, profitable.

It is often said that nuclear arms have made war obsolete, but this is a misunderstanding. Obsolescence occurs when a means to some end is superseded by a new and presumably better means—as when it was discovered that vehicles powered by internal-combustion engines were more efficient than vehicles pulled by horses at transporting people and goods from one place to another. But war has not been superseded by some better means to its end, which is to serve as the final arbiter of disputes among sovereign states. On the contrary, war has gone out of existence without leaving behind any means at all—whether superior or inferior—to that end. The more than three decades of jittery peace between the nuclear superpowers which the world has experienced since the invention of nuclear weapons is almost certainly the result of this lack. There is thus no need to "abolish war" among the nuclear powers; it is already gone. The choices don't include war any longer. They consist now of peace, on the one hand, and annihilation, on the other. And annihilation—or "assured destruction"—is as far from being war as peace is, and the sooner we recognize this the sooner we will be able to save our species from self-extermination. . . .

7

On the International Uses of Military Force in the Contemporary World

KLAUS KNORR

In this essay, Klaus Knorr rejects the proposition that military force has lost its utility in contemporary world politics. Given the constancy with which states resort to military force, Knorr concludes that the most important trend is the shift of military conflicts to the Third World. Author of *The Power of Nations* (1975) Knorr is professor emeritus at the Woodrow Wilson School, Princeton University.

In 1965, this author wrote a book (published by Princeton University Press in 1966)—*On the Uses of Military Power in the Nuclear Age*—in which he was one of the first to advance the thesis that the usability and usefulness of military force in interstate relations, compared with previous historical periods, had been diminished by several changes in underlying conditions. . . . [Now] it seems interesting to review this proposition in the light of subsequent writings that greatly amplified it, on the one hand, and in consideration of the actual uses of military power and the preparations for its use that have occurred since, on the other. Do the relevant events of the past decade or so, and what they foreshadow, confirm or disconfirm the thesis and the amplifications it has received? . . .

This theme of the declining value of military forces has been pushed a great deal further in more recent writings. For the sake of economy, I will briefly sum up these opinions and the propositions without attributing them to individual authors.

This new school of thought asserts that international relationships have recently been experiencing, and are still undergoing, a revolutionary transformation in the following terms. First, the nuclear balance of terror, which is assumed to be safely stable, has inhibited any large-scale use of force between powerful states, whose leaders, as rational actors, are completely self-deterred. Second, societies everywhere are now preoccupied with the solution of economic and social problems on which national welfare depends. The fading of serious questions of military security has facilitated this emphasis on domestic priorities over the previous

Reprinted from Klaus Knorr, "On the International Uses of Military Force in the Contemporary World," *Orbis* 21 (Spring 1977), pp. 5–27. Reprinted from *Orbis*, A Journal of World Affairs, by permission of the publisher. Copyright 1977 by the Foreign Policy Research Institute, Philadelphia. Footnotes have been deleted.

stress on defense budgets and military service. Third, rapidly growing international interdependence, particularly economic, has been accompanied by the vigorous growth of transnational forces and organizations, including multinational business corporations, which in turn have undermined the primacy of governmental inter-state behavior in favor of that of private actors and have greatly reduced the significance of state boundaries. Indeed, as many see it, the classic nation-state, in which military sovereignty reposed, is being increasingly hemmed in and dominated by these forces and is probably on the way out. Fourth, contemporary international affairs are more and more devoted to problems—economic, environmental and normative—that generate negotiations in which military power is irrelevant, which are more subject to international economic power, and which in any case increasingly require management by authorities and institutions that transcend national boundaries.

The world, according to this concept, is being shaped by forces and visions that are creating new forms of "international life," in relation to which the realities and teachings of the past are largely, if not wholly, irrelevant. The extent to which the members of this new school assert the presence of novel realities or express a vision of the future is often unclear. They apparently believe they are addressing themselves to an international reality that is in the process of swift and irresistible change and that is evidently escaping from the grim shackles of the premodern world. . . . [The author next cites information on the actual behavior of governments in military matters, including the incidence of their wars, their military expenditures, their military interventions, the number of their military personnel, their arms transfers abroad, and their propensity to contribute to nuclear arms proliferation. These, in conjunction with the general absence of efforts at international arms control and the continuation of military alliances, lead Knorr to observe that there has been substantially little change in the attachment of states to military instruments of foreign policy—eds.]

. . . A firm believer in the thesis that international resort to military force has become and is becoming less useful, possible and relevant can contend that there have been no wars between major powers, that the military conflicts that have taken place have been small-scale, short-lived or both, and that the continued high level of military spending results from the lagging ability of governments to comprehend the real changes that are going on around them or from bureaucratic and special-interest-group politics.

The same evidence can be interpreted differently. . . . [P]rolonged periods without wars between major powers have occurred before, and the number of international military conflicts in recent years has certainly not been small. If many of these conflicts have been on a modest scale, this has been because many of the states involved have modest capabilities that do not permit them to wage war for very long or very far beyond their boundaries. If several of these conflicts have been of extremely short duration, this has been either because . . . the weapons supply, especially of sophisticated imported arms, was quickly exhausted—or because one belligerent proved far superior to the other and achieved quick results. In regard to the persistently high level of military expenditures, it is possible that governments do perceive serious security problems and believe scholarly assertions of a transformed world to be premature. . . .

The frequency of armed conflict in recent years, the rise in global military expenditures and manpower, and the expansion of the international trade in arms does not appear prima facie to support any thesis asserting a secular diminution in the use of force or in the expected utility of military capabilities. If there is a pronounced trend, it expresses a remarkable international shift. Military conflicts have occurred mostly in the Third World, mainly between Third World countries, and this shift is paralleled by the fact that the proportion of world military spending, manpower and weapons imports outside the developed capitalist states has sharply increased.

All this is incontrovertible. Nevertheless, it is arguable that most government behavior in these respects is lagging behind changes in underlying realities. Whether it is or is not we cannot know. But we can subject to critical analysis the components of the theses asserting a decline in the utility of force. To what extent is it true or plausible that the costs of employing force have been rising relative to the gains that may be expected from its use?

The evidence concerning the range and imputed value of expected gains is naturally very poor because motivations are involved. It does seem, though, that the notion of economic gain as a justification for the aggressive use of force is far less in evidence, at least superficially, than it was for millennia prior to World War II. . . .

It would nevertheless be imprudent to disregard or unduly belittle economic motives that might fuel military conflict in the future. Severe shortages of food and raw materials, combined with the attempt of states controlling scarce supplies to exploit such control for economic and political purposes, may well serve to preserve some potential—even if a lesser one relative to other issues—for dangerous conflict. Current moves to extend territorial control over the sea are indicative of this prospect.

The use of force to seize or control territory for reasons of military security, also a traditionally important motive, likewise seems to have lost attraction. Yet it has not disappeared altogether. . . .

. . . [T]he fading importance of some objectives does not mean that there are not other goals that may justify the use of military force. Several other traditional objectives of this kind have lost little, if any, of their urgency or legitimacy, either internationally or domestically. Deterrence of, and defense against, attacks on political or territorial integrity as well as the rescue of citizens facing organized violence abroad fall into this category. Nor is there any lack of grounds on which to justify force for the purpose of revising the status quo. Aside from the Arab-Israeli conflict, which is in some ways unique, the recent military conflicts . . . suggest the contemporary importance of three major issues capable of generating the decision to go to war. One involves disputes over established boundaries that are regarded unjust by one side or the other. A second, sometimes overlapping with the first, is the protection or liberation of ethnically related peoples; that is, ethnic unification or national reunification. The third issue, apparently the one most productive of international conflict in the world today, is intervention in civil strife, either to support or help combat incumbent regimes. The precise objective or combination of objectives no doubt varies from case to case, but ideological commitments and the desire to maintain or extend spheres of influence, or reduce the interest of a rival power, evidently play an important part. Anyhow, contemporary governments do not seem to lack incentives to consider force or to be militarily prepared for executing that option.

Turning to the cost side, the deterrent effect of the nuclear balance of terror has figured as a major reason for speculations about the declining utility of military force. The risk of a nuclear war that would destroy both sides, it is argued, keeps each side from using lesser military force against the other. So long as this balance of terror prevails, the aggressive use of military force is undoubtedly curbed. But if deterrent power is needed for this purpose, that power has extremely high utility as an insurance of self-protection. Moreover, because strategic nuclear reprisal against lesser military attacks, including attacks against allies, is suicidal under these conditions, and because its threat therefore has low credibility, the maintenance of adequate conventional forces for defense also has a great deal of utility. The effective balance of both types of forces accounts for the military stability in Europe in recent decades—provided, of course, that deterrence was needed to stifle the emergence of aggressive designs. The claim that nuclear technology has engendered a decline in the utility of military force can only refer to one thing: namely, fear that a serious conflict might increase the risk of escalation to the strategic nuclear level has restrained adventurism. This consequence, however, will endure only so long as the nuclear balance of terror and that of associated defense capabilities remain solid. The future is by no means certain in this regard. New technological choices or an unreciprocated decay of the will to retaliate or to provide sufficient capabilities for deterrence and defense could upset this balance.

States without nuclear weapons are apparently little, if at all, restrained in their behavior toward states possessing nuclear arms. (The behavior of North Vietnam and North Korea toward the United States is illustrative.) This is so because a powerful moral stigma has become attached to the use of nuclear weapons, especially against a nonnuclear opponent. The magnitude of the expected moral and political costs constrains their use and reduces their utility in these relationships. The fact that states possessing nuclear weapons are thus inhibited from bringing their most effective military technology into play against the vast majority of countries is greatly to the advantage of the latter. It tends to increase the utility of *their* military forces against the nuclear superpowers, thereby making the distribution of military deterrence and defensive power less unequal than it would otherwise be. . . .

Heightened awareness of war's destructiveness, claimed to have greatly increased in recent decades, should lead to greater reluctance to use military power. Indeed, numerous surveys in highly developed countries provide evidence that confirms this awareness of the costs of using military force. . . .

However, there is far less evidence that this sensitivity is equally developed in other parts of the world, specifically in the communist societies and the LDCs. Of course, restricted access to opinions and attitudes in these countries obstructs the assembly of relevant evidence one way or the other. Such evidence is sparse. But it would not be surprising if this awareness were more thinly spread in those societies where some of the conditions that seem to account for its development in the capitalist-democratic nations are absent or nearly so: namely, a strong sensitivity to the destructiveness of war, broad-based higher education, a huge volume of news production and dissemination under conditions of freedom of speech and press, and lively media competition.

Sensitivity to the destructiveness of war has also inspired the new normative restraints that are part of the UN Charter. . . .

The frequency of recent armed conflict in the Third World does not encourage the view that the new norm has attracted more than a shallow adherence. This is not surprising. After all, the prohibition of aggressive warfare in the UN Charter was a Western, particularly an American, idea, and it was lodged in the charter at a time when relatively few Third World states were present—at a time when decolonization had only begun. Given their historical experience, countries in the Third World are primarily anxious about aggression by great powers.

Thus, it is not difficult to be skeptical about the profound systemic transformations that, as a number of writers have proposed, governments will increasingly be compelled to adapt to, and that tend to make war less feasible and relevant. We have already dealt with the consequences believed (with inadequate justification) to stem from the evolution of nuclear arms. The thesis that contemporary societies are primarily preoccupied with solving domestic political, economic and social problems seems to be true by and large. How much of a systemic change this sense of priorities represents is problematical. Moreover, the thesis often associated with this finding—that the forementioned preoccupation has generally caused societies to turn "inward"—is implausible. The economies of the highly developed capitalist countries are far too dependent on one another to encourage this sort of isolationism, and the vast majority of the LDCs seek the solution of their economic problems predominantly through the establishment of a new world economic order. While these are not problems that commend the use of military force as a solution, the historical record does not suggest that other pressing issues cannot come to dominate the agenda and the international behavior of states. In the past, certainly, societies have not rarely been content to devote themselves for considerable periods of time primarily to domestic problems, only to be seized by, or have forced on them, international issues that claimed priority. There are a number of countries whose structure of priorities is largely shaped by international considerations that do not rule out the use of force. . . .

The further thesis that growing international interdependence and the rise of transnational actors and institutions are threatening the demise of the nation-state, to which military sovereignty is attached, thus far has scant claim to validity. The citizens of democratic-capitalist nations have been making greatly increased demands on their national governments. In the communist states, the national governments reign supreme. The Third World is engaged in an intensive effort to establish and strengthen national government. If anything, the nation-state as an institution, long restricted to Western societies, is only now coming into its own in the rest of the world. . . .

One can only conclude, unhappily and disappointingly, that the global picture is far from clear so far as the utility of military force is concerned. The components of this picture do not encourage the prediction that the use and the usefulness of military force are definitely on the decline. What look like considerable changes in parameters are too ambiguous and have been with us for too short a time to permit confident answers to the questions we have raised. The changes on the cost side (actual, probable, possible?) certainly do not establish the disutility of force, and they could not do so even if we accepted the changes as substantial and if their impact were uniform throughout the world. Rational actors, to be sure, will not resort to force unless they expect gains to exceed costs. But aside from the circumstance that deviations from rationality are not unknown among political leaders, there is a powerful subjective element and a great deal of unavoidable guesswork in estimates of costs and gains. All we can argue is this: if cost-increasing factors persist and become less unevenly distributed, then war will become a less likely choice of action statistically speaking. This would be an important change, but such a downgrading effect would be acting only marginally on a historically high level of readiness to consider military options when vital, or seemingly vital, values are at stake. Even if the costs of using force rose substantially, rational actors would be willing to meet them when expected gains have exceeding appeal. The recent behavior of governments in regard to military conflict, both engaging in it and preparing for it, is in line with this judgment.

The conclusion I arrived at more than ten years ago did maintain that the utility of military power was on the decline, but several qualifications were attached. Among them, I noted the uneven global distribution of the relevant changes in parameters. Yet I did not then perceive their importance nearly so much as I do at this time, and I regard my overall assessment now to justify less optimism than I expressed then. The world would seem to contain plenty of state actors for whom the avoidance of violence, including international violence, is not the supreme good; and, as if in recognition of this fact, there are even more actors who still find the aura of military power attractive, if only for reasons of security. I now expect international military conflict and direct foreign intervention in civil wars to continue at a high level, and I expect, too, that the superpowers will have diminishing military influence in the Third World. . . . [T]he military relationship between the Soviet Union and the United States, both on the strategic level and in Europe, . . . depends on the ability of each to maintain solid deterrence. Conflicts in the Third World are likely to remain localized so long as this condition obtains.

It seems to me also interesting that the appreciably more optimistic analyses and predictions that have been offered in more recent years are virtually all the product of scholarship in those societies wherein the new distaste for the use of force is most highly developed. This suggests the possibility that these comforting interpretations suffer from being a bit culture-bound, unless one takes the patronizing view—which seems to be congenial in the West—that revolutionary, systemic transformations have been first generated in the West, that the rest of the world is only lagging behind, and that it is therefore only a matter of time before it catches up.

8
Rethinking Non-Proliferation

HEDLEY BULL

Numerous factors undermine the ability of proponents of nuclear non-proliferation to realize their goal of preventing the spread of nuclear weapons to non-nuclear states. Here, Hedley Bull notes some of the time-specific explanations underlying these arguments, but also explores the tenets of the broader proposition that the principal weakness of a non-proliferation regime is that it "is perceived by a very substantial segment of international society . . . as an instrument of super-power domination." Bull is Montague Burton Professor of International Relations at Oxford University. Among his many publications is *The Anarchical Society* (1977).

. . . The most dramatic blow struck at the NPT [Non-Proliferation Treaty] was the Indian nuclear explosion of May 18, 1974. First, the Indian explosion demonstrates the 'failure' of the Treaty, if we take its central objective to have been to restrict the circle of states that had conducted nuclear explosions at the point it had reached in 1970. Secondly, the Indian explosion provides new incentives for other states to acquire nuclear weapons: Pakistan, for example, perceives the Indian explosion as a threat to its security, Japan views it as diminishing its relative status, and everywhere it is taken to confirm the idea that the spread of nuclear explosive technology is inevitable. Thirdly, India's action has indicated a new route to nuclear proliferation—that of conducting an explosion, and issuing a declaration that it is for peaceful purposes only, while resisting requests for international inspection to authenticate the declaration. Whether or not one takes seriously Indian assurances that no Indian nuclear weapons programme is being planned, this route has been opened up for other states. Fourthly, the Indian action confronts arms control planners with the problem of how to deal with peaceful nuclear explosions (PNEs) conducted by non-nuclear weapon states—a problem that the NPT sought to avoid by laying down, in effect, that nuclear explosions can be peaceful only if they are conducted by nuclear weapon states. Fifthly, by identifying the NPT as part of the system of super-power domination, and successfully defying it in the name of the rights of the underprivileged, India has helped to diminish the legitimacy of the Treaty and to make more respectable further acts of defiance by itself and others.

However, the most important factors working against the NPT would be having their effect even if the Indian nuclear explosion had not taken place. The capacity to make nuclear weapons, which the NPT does little to restrict, is spread-

Reprinted from Hedley Bull, "Rethinking Non-Proliferation," *International Affairs* 51:2 (Spring 1975), pp. 175–181. Reprinted by permission.

ing at an accelerating rate as a consequence of the rapid rise in the number of plutonium power reactors . . . and in the number of countries possessing operable reactors . . .; the decline of the nuclear weapon states' monopoly of uranium enrichment processes; the development of new methods of uranium enrichment, especially gas centrifuge; the availability of reactors of heavy water design, that consume natural rather than enriched, uranium which is widely available; the intensive development in a number of countries of fast breeder reactors that produce more fissionable fuel than they consume; and the declining effectiveness of controls imposed by the exporters of nuclear technology and materials.

The spread of the capacity to make nuclear weapons does not necessarily imply the spread of the will to do so, but a number of recent developments encourage it. The policies of the five nuclear weapon states continue to provide confirmation of the idea—from which the will to proliferate derives—that nuclear weapons are a vital strategic instrument, a vital source of great power status or prestige, or both: one may cite . . . the development by both the United States and the Soviet Union of missiles accurate enough to give some credence to the [idea of nuclear war as an instrument of policy]; the failure of the SALT negotiations . . . to issue in any actual disarmament, or even—with the possible exception of the 1972 ABM Treaty—any restrictions on Soviet-American arms competition of a truly vital nature; and the continued nuclear testing programmes not only of the United States and the Soviet Union but also of China, France and Britain.

For many potential nuclear weapon states the alternative to a nuclear weapons system of their own is reliance upon guarantees of nuclear support from the United States or the Soviet Union. But these guarantees are . . . eroding. The multilateral guarantee which the nuclear weapon state sponsors of the NPT sought to provide through UN Security Council Resolution 255 of June 19, 1968, was of the most feeble kind imaginable, and whatever meaning it had was destroyed when China became a permanent member of the Security Council. The bilateral guarantees of nuclear support, given explicitly or implicitly by the two superpowers not only to their respective allies but also to other clients or associates—one thinks, for example, of the United States' implicit guarantees to Israel and Sweden, and Russia's implicit guarantees to India and certain Arab countries—are still an important factor working against proliferation. But confidence in these guarantees is declining as a consequence of the decay of the American and Soviet alliance systems, the consolidation of Soviet-American detente, and the development of a relationship of mutual nuclear deterrence between China and the Soviet Union, if not yet between China and the United States.

Moreover, the NPT bears the marks of its origins in the mid-1960s when the ability of the United States and the Soviet Union, while working together, to mobilise support for their policies throughout the international political system as a whole was greater than it is now. The principal weakness of the NPT, as a means of controlling nuclear proliferation, is that it is not based upon a consensus of international society as a whole but is perceived by a very substantial segment of international society, especially in the Third World, as an instrument of superpower domination.

It is true that at the end of 1974, 106 states had signed the Treaty and 84 had ratified it. But three of the six states that have conducted nuclear explosions are outside the system. So also are some of the most crucial of the potential nuclear weapon states; the list of non-signatories includes, in addition to India, Israel, South Africa, Brazil, Argentina, Chile, Spain and Pakistan, while the list of states that have signed but not ratified includes Japan, Egypt and Indonesia. If the chief test of a country's attitude towards the NPT is to be whether it accepts, or is willing to protest against, the hegemony of the super-powers, the Treaty is bound to go into decline, for antagonism to this hegemony is one of the most powerful emotions in the world today. An NPT which is regarded by the representatives of half the world's population as simply the instrument of the nuclear weapon Haves in their struggle to maintain their ascendancy over the Have Nots will have as little to contribute to the control of nuclear proliferation as the League of Nations had to contribute to the maintenance of international security when, in the 1930s, it became simply the instrument of Britain and France.

CRITICS OF THE ANTI-PROLIFERATIONIST DOCTRINE

In rethinking this subject one must begin by asking again the fundamental questions. Is the spread of nuclear weapons undesirable—in terms of the interests not of any particular section of international society, but of the world as a whole? And in what sense is control of the spread of nuclear weapons a feasible objective?

The case that may be stated by critics of the anti-proliferationist conventional wisdom is a powerful one.[1] It focuses first of all on the idea that an increase in the number of nuclear weapon decision-makers endangers international peace and security. The 'statistical argument'—that the more such decision-makers there are, the more likely nuclear war will be—ignores differences in the political nature of the decision-makers and the strategic situation in which they find themselves: the acquisition of nuclear weapons by a country that does not threaten others but is itself threatened by a nuclear weapon state may make war less likely, not more. Arguments to the effect that new nuclear weapon states would prove less 'responsible' custodians of the weapons than the existing five (because they would be incapable of adequate safety measures, or because their political conflicts are more impassioned, or because their weapons would be vulnerable) are unproven and when applied to the countries of the Third World, it has been said, are 'modern versions of the doctrines of the white man's burden'.[2]

If the presence of nuclear weapons on both sides in the Soviet-American conflict has helped to preserve peace between the super-powers for a quarter of a century may this not also be true of other conflicts? Are not the protagonists of anti-proliferationist doctrine the same persons who in relation to the conflict be-

---

[1] See especially K. Subrahmanyam: *The Indian Nuclear Test in a Global Perspective*. New Delhi: India International Centre, 1974.

[2] *Ibid.*, p. 11.

tween the super-powers have insisted on the positive role played by the nuclear 'balance of terror'?

The critics focus their attention not only on considerations of international peace and security, which lie at the heart of the anti-proliferationist doctrine, but also on considerations of international justice or equity, which this doctrine leaves out of account. Even if one accepts that the spread of nuclear weapons is likely to endanger peace and security rather than enhance them, the argument for halting it is an argument for consolidating the existing distribution of power.

This is, of course, why the argument appeals to the three original nuclear weapon states and their allies and clients, who provide the bulk of the supporters of the NPT. Behind the doctrine propounded by the super-powers about the general dangers of proliferation to the world, there lurks an awareness of the special dangers to themselves of a shift in the distribution of power. Implicit in their choice of proliferation as the danger to peace and security that must be curbed now—rather than, say, the danger inherent in the growth of their own weapons stockpiles—is the perception that curbs in this area will restrict others and not themselves.

For those who feel that the issues should be assessed in terms of international justice or equity as well as of international peace and security, and who recognise that the former calls for a redistribution not simply of wealth or resources but also of power, as between the main sections of the world community, the anti-proliferationist doctrine will carry no conviction.

All the arguments of the critics may be accepted and yet there is a sense in which the control of nuclear proliferation is desirable in the interests not simply of the existing nuclear weapon states and their clients but of international society as a whole. If selective nuclear proliferation may in some cases serve to enhance international security, this does not mean that the process of proliferation as a whole does so—the process that began with the acquisition of nuclear weapons by the United States and would logically culminate in a world of 150 or so nuclear weapon powers. If the control of nuclear proliferation is not the only or the most important objective of arms control, and the propaganda of the super-powers has exaggerated its urgency, this does not mean that it is not an important objective at all.

The idea that the more states acquire nuclear weapons, the more international security will be strengthened, exaggerates the stability of the Soviet-American relationship of mutual nuclear deterrence, which can in principle be upset and which even while it lasts does not make nuclear war impossible but simply makes it irrational. The idea also wrongly assumes that proliferation would result in the duplication, in other international conflicts, of the kind of relationship of mutual nuclear deterrence that now exists between the two super-powers, rather than relationships in which one party has a nuclear monopoly or superiority over the others.

If the nuclear weapons club in its present membership perpetuates an unjust distribution of power, it has also to be recognised that so also would a club whose membership had been expanded. Perfect international justice with regard to the possession of nuclear weapons can be achieved only by complete nuclear disarmament, or by an international system in which nuclear weapons are available to every state. Since neither of these alternatives can be expected to come about, the world has to accept a situation in which some states have nuclear weapons and some do not. This does not mean that the present line of division is the only possible one, or that some other line of division could not be held to be at least relatively more just.[3] But whatever expansion of the nuclear weapons club takes place, the argument that it is unjust can always be used by those who are left outside.

That nuclear proliferation in general is undesirable is in fact recognised in their actions if not always in their words—even by those powers that have been the strongest opponents of anti-proliferationist doctrine. China has taken the position that whether acquisition of nuclear weapons by a state is good or bad depends on the purposes for which it wants to use them, but this is not a position that sanctions indiscriminate proliferation, and so far it has been used to sanction proliferation only in the case of China itself. France has stated that it will act consistently with the purposes of the NPT, even while remaining outside the Treaty itself, and India—while rejecting the Treaty and resisting any obstacle that might stand in the way of its own weapons option—continues to speak of proliferation as undesirable and of its own policies as serving to check it. None of them has done anything directly to disseminate nuclear explosive technology or material.

The recalcitrant or dissenting states, in other words, do not challenge the doctrine that the spread of nuclear weapons is undesirable, but rather—like the United States, the Soviet Union and Britain before them—seek to show that an exception should be made in their own case. The argument between supporters and opponents of the NPT is not about the desirability or otherwise of non-proliferation but about where the line should be drawn.

In considering how far non-proliferation is feasible it is necessary to distinguish between stopping the spread of nuclear weapons and controlling it. It has never seemed likely at any point in the nuclear era, and it does not seem likely now, that all further proliferation will be stopped. It is simply not credible that one of the most vital strategic and political instrumentalities of the time, which is technically within reach of many states, will remain permanently the monopoly of the few that first developed it. If nuclear weapons should cease to be vital political and strategic instrumentalities—either because arms control understandings have gradually pushed them into the background of international politics, or because new weapons have emerged to displace them—then we may imagine that nuclear proliferation may cease altogether.

But until they do the control of proliferation should include other objectives besides that of stopping it at a given point. It should include attempts to inhibit or discourage proliferation—to ensure that it cannot take place without the surmounting of certain obstacles; to slow the pace of proliferation—so as to gain time in which the limitation of existing nuclear weapons may develop; to absorb the effects of proliferation—to ensure that if it does take place, it does so with the

---

[3] It may be argued, for example, that nuclear weapons would be more justly distributed if all countries in the world enjoyed the protection of one or another nuclear power.

minimum adverse consequences for international security (for example, by seeking to ensure that if two antagonistic powers are acquiring nuclear weapons, a balance is preserved between them, and by seeking to ensure that new nuclear weapon states are incorporated into the structure of arms control agreements); and to set ultimate limits to the process of proliferation. If the argument is correct which leads us to prefer five nuclear weapon states to six, it should also lead us to prefer six to 20 or 50 or more. It may also be important to ensure that nuclear weapons remain the monopoly of the sovereign state, and do not proliferate beyond it to fall into the hands of sub-national or transnational political groups. . . . [The author goes on to advance some recommendations about how safeguards may be established and about how the spread of nuclear weapons capability might be contained—*eds.*]

9

MAD Versus NUTS

SPURGEON M. KEENY, JR., AND WOLFGANG K. H. PANOFSKY

Arguing that "mutual assured destruction, or MAD, is inherent in the existence of large numbers of nuclear weapons," Spurgeon M. Keeny, Jr., and Wolfgang K. H. Panofsky refute the argument that a nuclear utilization targeting strategy (NUTS) will eliminate the essentially MAD character of nuclear war. Keeny has been a scholar-in-residence at the National Academy of Sciences in Washington, D.C., and was deputy director of the U.S. Arms Control and Disarmament Agency from 1977 to 1981. Panofsky is professor of physics at Stanford University and was a member of the General Advisory Committee on Arms Control and Disarmament from 1977 to 1981.

Since World War II there has been a continuing debate on military doctrine concerning the actual utility of nuclear weapons in war. This debate, irrespective of the merits of the divergent points of view, tends to create the perception that the outcome and scale of a nuclear conflict could be controlled by the doctrine or the types of nuclear weapons employed. Is this the case?

We believe not. In reality, the unprecedented risks of nuclear conflict are largely independent of doctrine or its application. The principal danger of doctrines that are directed at limiting nuclear conflicts is that they might be believed and form the basis for action without appreciation of the physical facts and uncertainties of nuclear conflict. The failure of policymakers to understand the truly revolutionary nature of nuclear weapons as instruments of war and the staggering size of the nuclear stockpiles of the United States and the Soviet Union could have catastrophic consequences for the entire world.

Military planners and strategic thinkers for 35 years have sought ways to apply the tremendous power of nuclear weapons against target systems that might contribute to the winning of a future war. In fact, as long as the United States held a virtual nuclear monopoly, the targeting of atomic weapons was looked upon essentially as a more effective extension of the strategic bombing concepts of World War II. With the advent in the mid-1950s of a substantial Soviet nuclear capability, including multimegaton thermonuclear weapons, it was soon apparent that the populations and societies of both the United States and the Soviet Union were mutual hostages. A portion of the nuclear stockpile of either side could inflict on

Reprinted from Spurgeon M. Keeny, Jr., and Wolfgang K.H. Panofsky, "MAD Versus NUTS: Can Doctrine or Weaponry Remedy the Mutual Hostage Relationship of the Superpowers?" *Foreign Affairs* 60 (Winter 1981/82), pp. 287–304. Abridged by permission of Foreign Affairs. Copyright 1982 by the Council on Foreign Relations, Inc.

the other as many as 100 million fatalities and destroy it as a functioning society. Thus, although the rhetoric of declaratory strategic doctrine has changed over the years, mutual deterrence has in fact remained the central fact of the strategic relationship of the two superpowers and of the NATO and Warsaw Pact alliances.

Most observers would agree that a major conflict between the two hostile blocs on a worldwide scale during this period may well have been prevented by the specter of catastrophic nuclear war. At the same time, few would argue that this state of mutual deterrence is a very reassuring foundation on which to build world peace. In the 1960s the perception of the basic strategic relationship of mutual deterrence came to be characterized as "Mutual Assured Destruction," which critics were quick to note had the acronym of MAD. The notion of MAD has been frequently attacked not only as militarily unacceptable but also as immoral since it holds the entire civilian populations of both countries as hostages.[1]

As an alternative to MAD, critics and strategic innovators have over the years sought to develop various war-fighting targeting doctrines that would somehow retain the use of nuclear weapons on the battlefield or even in controlled strategic war scenarios, while sparing the general civilian population from the devastating consequences of nuclear war. Other critics have found an alternative in a defense-oriented military posture designed to defend the civilian population against the consequences of nuclear war.

These concepts are clearly interrelated since such a defense-oriented strategy would also make a nuclear war-fighting doctrine more credible. But both alternatives depend on the solution of staggering technical problems. A defense-oriented military posture requires a nearly impenetrable air and missile defense over a large portion of the population. And any attempt to have a controlled war-fighting capability during a nuclear exchange places tremendous requirements not only on decisions made under incredible pressure by men in senior positions of responsibility but on the technical performance of command, control, communications and intelligence functions—called in professional circles "c^3I" and which for the sake of simplicity we shall hereafter describe as "control mechanisms." It is not sufficient as the basis for defense policy to assert that science will "somehow" find solutions to critical technical problems on which the policy is dependent, when technical solutions are nowhere in sight.

In considering these doctrinal issues, it should be recognized that there tends to be a very major gap between declaratory policy and actual implementation expressed as targeting doctrine. Whatever the declaratory policy might be, those responsible for the strategic forces must generate real target lists and develop procedures under which various combinations of targets could be attacked. In consequence, the perceived need to attack every listed target, even after absorbing the worst imaginable first strike from the adversary, creates procurement "requirements," even though the military or economic importance of many of the targets is small.

In fact, it is not at all clear in the real world of war planning whether decla-

---

[1] See, for example, Fred Charles Iklé, "Can Nuclear Deterrence Last Out the Century?", *Foreign Affairs*, January 1973, pp. 267–85.

ratory doctrine has generated requirements or whether the availability of weapons for targeting has created doctrine. With an estimated 30,000 warheads at the disposal of the United States, including more than 10,000 avowed to be strategic in character, it is necessary to target redundantly all urban areas and economic targets and to cover a wide range of military targets in order to frame uses for the stockpile. And, once one tries to deal with elusive mobile and secondary military targets, one can always make a case for requirements for more weapons and for more specialized weapon designs.

These doctrinal considerations, combined with the superabundance of nuclear weapons, have led to a conceptual approach to nuclear war which can be described as Nuclear Utilization Target Selection. For convenience, and not in any spirit of trading epithets, we have chosen the acronym of NUTS to characterize the various doctrines that seek to utilize nuclear weapons against specific targets in a complex of nuclear war-fighting situations intended to be limited, as well as the management over an extended period of a general nuclear war between the superpowers.[2]

While some elements of NUTS may be involved in extending the credibility of our nuclear deterrent, this consideration in no way changes the fact that mutual assured destruction, or MAD, is inherent in the existence of large numbers of nuclear weapons in the real world. In promulgating the doctrine of "countervailing strategy" in the summer of 1980, President Carter's Secretary of Defense Harold Brown called for a buildup of nuclear war-fighting capability in order to provide greater deterrence by demonstrating the ability of the United States to respond in a credible fashion without having to escalate immediately to all-out nuclear war. He was very careful, however, to note that he thought that it was "very likely" that the use of nuclear weapons by the superpowers at any level would escalate into general nuclear war.[3] This situation is not peculiar to present force structures or technologies; and, regardless of future technical developments, it will persist as long as substantial nuclear weapon stockpiles remain.

Despite its possible contribution to the deterrence of nuclear war, the NUTS approach to military doctrine and planning can very easily become a serious danger in itself. The availability of increasing numbers of nuclear weapons in a variety of designs and delivery packages at all levels of the military establishment inevitably encourages the illusion that somehow nuclear weapons can be applied in selected circumstances without unleashing a catastrophic series of consequences. . . . [T]he recent uninformed debate on the virtue of the so-called neutron bomb as a selective device to deal with tank attacks is a depressing case in

---

[2] The acronym NUT for Nuclear Utilization Theory was used by Howard Margolis and Jack Ruina, "SALT II: Notes on Shadow and Substance," *Technology Review,* October 1979, pp. 31–41. We prefer Nuclear Utilization Target Selection, which relates the line of thinking more closely to the operational problem of target selection. Readers not familiar with colloquial American usage may need to be told that "nuts" is an adjective meaning "crazy or demented." For everyday purposes it is a synonym for "mad."

[3] See Harold Brown, Speech at the Naval War College, August 20, 1980, the most authoritative public statement on the significance of Presidential Directive 59, which had been approved by President Carter shortly before.

point. NUTS creates its own endless pressure for expanded nuclear stockpiles with increasing danger of accidents, accidental use, diversions to terrorists, etc. But more fundamentally, it tends to obscure the fact that the nuclear world is in fact MAD.

The NUTS approach to nuclear war-fighting will not eliminate the essential MAD character of nuclear war for two basic reasons, which are rooted in the nature of nuclear weapons and the practical limits of technology. First, the destructive power of nuclear weapons, individually and most certainly in the large numbers discussed for even specialized application, is so great that the collateral effects on persons and property would be enormous and, in scenarios which are seriously discussed, would be hard to distinguish from the onset of general nuclear war. But more fundamentally, it does not seem possible, even in the most specialized utilization of nuclear weapons, to envisage any situation where escalation to general nuclear war would probably not occur given the dynamics of the situation and the limits of the control mechanisms that could be made available to manage a limited nuclear war. In the case of a protracted general nuclear war, the control problem becomes completely unmanageable. Finally, there does not appear to be any prospect for the foreseeable future that technology will provide a secure shield behind which the citizens of the two superpowers can safely observe the course of a limited nuclear war on other people's territory. . . .

[The authors continue with a discussion of the horrendous consequences of a nuclear war, consequences that point to the conclusions that a nuclear war would be devastating and that each of the two superpowers is inescapably vulnerable to the capacity of the other to destroy it—regardless of who launches the first missile. They then critique the views of those who support the concept of a nuclear war-fighting capability, and especially those advocating the development of theater nuclear forces (TNF) and the associated doctrine that a nuclear war can remain limited. Contending, finally, that the protection of populations against large-scale attack is impossible, they are driven to the conclusion that nuclear utilization theory is indeed NUTs—that it cannot succeed without imperiling civilization as we know it—*eds.*]

. . . [W]e are fated to live in a MAD world. This is inherent in the tremendous power of nuclear weapons, the size of nuclear stockpiles, the collateral damage associated with the use of nuclear weapons against military targets, the technical limitations on strategic area defense, and the uncertainties involved in efforts to control the escalation of nuclear war. There is no reason to believe that this situation will change for the foreseeable future since the problem is far too profound and the pace of technical military development far too slow to overcome the fundamental technical considerations that underlie the mutual hostage relationship of the superpowers.

What is clear above all is that the profusion of proposed NUTS approaches has not offered an escape from the MAD world, but rather constitutes a major danger in encouraging the illusion that limited or controlled nuclear war can be waged free from the grim realities of a MAD world. The principal hope at this time will not be found in seeking NUTS doctrines that ignore the MAD realities but rather in recognizing the nuclear world for what it is and seeking to make it more stable and less dangerous.

10

The Anatomy of International Crises

GLENN H. SNYDER AND PAUL DIESING

The characteristics of international crises are conceptually defined by Glenn H. Snyder and Paul Diesing. Their discussion demonstrates not only the important role that crises play in international affairs, but also their relationship to war and to peace. Snyder and Diesing are professors of political science at the State University of New York at Buffalo. Snyder is the author of *Deterrence and Defense* (1961). Diesing is the author of *Patterns of Discovery in the Social Sciences* (1971).

The term *crisis* has been used in so many different ways, in personal and domestic social contexts as well as in international affairs, that it has no generally accepted meaning. Consequently, we must stipulate a definition. . . .

An international crisis is a sequence of interactions between the governments of two or more sovereign states in severe conflict, short of actual war, but involving the perception of a dangerously high probability of war.

We use the term *sequence of interactions* rather than *situation* because of the ambiguity and emptiness of the latter term. *Sequence of interactions* is more meaningful, first, because it is the kind of interaction going on between the states that gives their relations the character of "crisis" and because the term *interaction* ties in nicely with . . . bargaining. Second, the word *sequence* clearly denotes a span of time and also a certain relatedness between the specific instances of interaction—each instance is affected by the instances just past and by the contemplation of possible following instances.

Note that our definition says nothing about the amount of time covered by a crisis. Most previous analysts have emphasized shortness of decision time as one of the defining conditions of crisis, along with a related sense of urgency. While the notion of urgency is supportable in terms of a sense of danger and risk that the parties feel must be alleviated as soon as possible, short decision time is not a necessary characteristic of crisis. . . .

Quite obviously, a crisis always involves "severe conflict." There is, first, a deep *conflict of interest* between the parties. However, conflict of interest in itself is not sufficient to bring about a crisis. One of the parties must initiate some form of *conflict behavior* in an attempt to resolve the underlying conflict of interest in its favor. Usually, a crisis erupts when one party attempts to coerce the other with threats of violence and the other party resists.

The centerpiece of our definition is "the perception of a dangerously high probability of war" by the governments involved. Just how high the perceived probability must be to qualify as a crisis is impossible to specify. But ordinary usage of the term *crisis* implies that whatever is occurring might result in the outbreak of war. The perceived probability must at least be high enough to evoke feelings of fear and tension to an uncomfortable degree. . . .

. . . [C]rises are between governments who identify each other as enemies or at least potential enemies. . . .

. . . [T]he term *probability of war* excludes war itself from the concept "crisis," although minor forms of violence "short of war" are included as potential instruments of coercive bargaining. In the modern age, when the line between peace and war has become increasingly blurred, it may in some empirical cases be difficult to determine precisely when "crisis violence" becomes transformed into "war." And, as Thomas Schelling has emphasized, war itself, especially limited war, has become increasingly an affair of bargaining, similar in many respects to crisis bargaining.[1] . . .

Finally, the term *probability,* in the loose, subjective sense in which we use it here, suggests the element of *uncertainty,* an element stressed by Thomas Schelling: "The essence of the crisis is its unpredictability."[2] One kind of unpredictability is that arising from the participant's lack of full control over events, the possibility of "things getting out of hand." But even if the parties do have firm control (over their own behavior at least), uncertainty also arises from their very imperfect information about the other party's values and intentions. To a considerable extent it is this element of uncertainty, in both the forms mentioned, that lends to an event its "crisis atmosphere," i.e., to feelings of fear, tension and urgency. If each party *knew* what the other intended to do—in simple terms: yield, stand firm, or fight—and also knew its own intentions in the light of that knowledge, there could be no crisis. Either no coercive challenge would be issued, or, if issued, it would be followed inexorably either by the opponent's capitulation or by war. Even if some length of time occurred between challenge and outcome, it would be characterized not by feelings of "crisis" but by the parties' preparation to do what their values and certain knowledge dictated. Thus, it is largely because of the lack of complete information that crises occur at all. A corollary is that if one of the parties thinks it *does* have accurate information about the other's intentions, the situation does not *become* a crisis for that party until it realizes it has misestimated those intentions or loses confidence in its initial estimate. For example, the Cuban crisis of 1962 did not become a crisis for the Soviet Union until President Kennedy issued the U.S. challenge in a television speech and confounded Soviet expectations. It had already been a crisis for the U.S. government for a week while secret decisions were being made.

Our definition is quite different from those typically employed by students of the effects of crisis on decision-making behavior. A definition of this latter type

---

[1] Thomas C. Schelling, *The Strategy of Conflict* (Cambridge, Mass.: Harvard University Press, 1960), pp. 53–81.

[2] Schelling, *Arms and Influence* (New Haven, Conn.: Yale University Press, 1966), p. 97.

is the one advanced by Charles F. Hermann: "a crisis is a situation that (1) threatens high-priority goals of the decision-making unit, (2) restricts the amount of time available for response before the decision is transformed, and (3) surprises the members of the decision-making unit by its occurrence."[3] While this definition usefully points to certain characteristics of crisis that presumably affect decision making, it obscures the state-to-state interaction aspect of crises, which we regard as fundamental. Only when this aspect is central to the definition do all the dimensions of crisis as an international political phenomenon come into view.[4]

Of course, we do not assert that crises have no effects on the context of internal decision making, or that these effects are not important. For example the feeling of tension that always accompanies a crisis is subjectively felt within states, although it is a consequence of the objective tension between the interests of the states involved. Thus, Edward L. Morse includes in his definition of crisis the notion of "a situation requiring a choice between mutually incompatible but highly valued objectives."[5] That is, a crisis not only is a severe conflict of interests between states but also sets up a sharp conflict of values within the states. Each party faces the uncomfortable choice between preserving its politico-strategic *interests* by standing firm at the risk of war, or ensuring *peace* by sacrificing important interests. It is probably the difficulty and distastefulness of this choice, combined with the quality of uncertainty mentioned above (notably uncertainty about how the other party will choose), and the perception of the possible imminence of war, that produces the general sense of crisis. Moreover the internal value conflict may give rise to an internal struggle between individuals, factions and agencies, each favoring different ways of resolving the conflict along a "hard-soft" continuum. Thus the Morse component is a useful supplement to our own definition because it points to internal effects in a way that links them to the central interaction process between the state adversaries.

So much for the definition of crisis. We turn now to a discussion of how crises fit into the wider pattern of diplomatic-strategic events and to some further characteristics of their "anatomy."

It is useful to conceive of a crisis as an intermediate zone between peace and war. Almost all wars are preceded by a crisis of some sort, although of course not all crises eventuate in war. A crisis is a sort of hybrid condition, neither peace nor war, but containing elements of both and comprising the potential for transformation from peace to war. Thus a study of crisis behavior should cast some light on the age-old problem of the causes of war, especially if we consciously

---

[3] Hermann, ed., *International Crises: Insights from Behavioral Research* (New York: The Free Press, 1972), p. 13.

[4] James L. Richardson has made a similar point in "The Definition of Crisis: A Working Paper" (mimeographed) 1973, p. 9.

[5] Morse's complete definition is "the sudden emergence (whether or not anticipated) of a situation requiring a policy choice by one or more states within a relatively short period of time, a situation requiring a choice between mutually incompatible but highly valued objectives." We exclude the notions of suddenness and short time for decision from our own definition because they are not logically necessary and some empirical crises do not have these qualities. See Morse, "Crisis Diplomacy, Interdependence, and the Politics of International Economic Relations," in Raymond Tanter and Richard H. Ullman, eds., *Theory and Policy in International Relations* (Princeton, N.J.: Princeton University Press, 1973), p. 127.

ask ourselves: under what conditions are crises resolved peacefully and what conditions tend to make them escalate to war? Beyond this, the "intermediate zone" conception highlights an interesting characteristic of crisis behavior: it tends to be a mixture of behavioral elements typical of war and other elements typical of peacetime diplomacy. War in its extreme form is the ultimate form of coercion—the raw, physical clash of armed forces—in a context where the pursuit of objectives in conflict greatly predominates over the pursuit of common interest. Accommodation occurs only in the terminal phase in negotiating the terms of surrender, although in limited war, the parties also tacitly agree during the war about the nature of the limits. Non-crisis peacetime diplomacy, even between adversaries, is generally accommodative; attempts to realize common interests predominate over the use of coercion to win conflicts. Relations between adversaries are colored by some sort of conflict of interest, but conflict behavior takes relatively mild or passive forms: mutual deterrent postures, minor disputes, and so on.

In a crisis, these contrasting types of behavior tend to converge, merging in a complex blend of coercion and accommodation. Diplomacy becomes more actively coercive, and the emotional climate shifts toward greater hostility and fear. Aims center on winning the conflict rather than realizing common interests. When accommodation occurs, it is not "amicable settlement" but "backing down" or "painful compromise," forced by the risk of war. Pressure is exercised not by brute force, as in warfare, but by manipulating the risk of war and the fear of escalation. The risk of violence if one stands his ground is analogous, in function, to the actual violence suffered as one tries to take or hold ground in war. Backdown or facedown are the analogues to defeat or victory. The outcome is determined not by relative physical strength, but by psychological strength—the relative ability of the parties to stand risk. The well-known terms *coercive diplomacy* and *force short of war,* each from a different perspective, express the notion of a blend of peace-like and war-like behavior. The central problem of crisis statesmanship is how to achieve an optimum blend of coercion and accommodation in one's strategy, a blend that will both avoid war and maximize one's gains or minimize one's losses.

How and why do crises occur? What is it that causes conflicts of interests and mild conflict behavior to escalate to the point where war seems possible and a crisis exists? How does one identify the beginning and end of a crisis? Are there more or less regular phases within a crisis, as well as immediate pre-crisis and post-crisis phases, each with its own typical characteristics? Questions such as these seem to call for a phase model of crisis interaction over time, which can be compared with the course of events in actual cases.

Typically, the immediate cause of a crisis is an attempt by one state to coerce another by an explicit or implicit threat of force. The first act of severe coercion may be called the *challenge;* technically it starts the crisis by posing a distinct possibility of war. A challenge is stimulated or motivated by a *precipitant,* of which there are two broad types, external and internal. In the external type, a state perceives an intolerable situation developing in its environment as a result of action by another state or states. It may be intolerable for a variety of reasons: it is threatening to the state's external or internal security, it threatens the state's economic viability or affronts its national dignity and prestige. We may call this the *general* precipitant, which provokes the challenge. There is usually also a *specific* precipitant, a particular and especially provocative act by the opponent that is seen as the "last straw," or perhaps as the pretext for the challenge. . . .

. . . In . . . the Cuban missile crisis of October 1962, the general precipitant was the flow of Russian armaments into Cuba during the summer and early fall, the specific precipitant was the Soviet attempt to deploy long-range missiles, and the challenge was a televised speech by President Kennedy demanding that the missiles be withdrawn.

The identification of specific precipitants is useful in developing a pattern of crisis events, but in most cases little causality should be imputed to them. They function more as convenient occasions for, or as legitimizers of, the challenge than as causes of it. When McGeorge Bundy was asked about the importance of the Communist raid on the Pleiku base in triggering the start of U.S. bombing of North Vietnam, he replied "Pleikus are like streetcars"—one will come along eventually if you wait long enough. The real causes of a crisis challenge are more likely to be found in the general precipitant—the larger and longer-term developments in the challenger's environment that create an intolerable conflict of interest between the challenger and some other states(s).[6] But a full statement of the "causes" of any particular crisis would have to go beyond even the general precipitant, to whatever it was that caused the "intolerable situation" to develop, and this would lead into a host of factors in the general historical background. In short, our "precipitant" does not mean "cause" in any complete sense, but only in a partial proximate sense: those developments that finally caused a developing conflict to boil over into crisis.[7]

We have so far discussed only precipitants external to the challenger; the challenger's interests and values do not necessarily change; they are threatened or violated by the actions of other states or some other outside forces. Another type involves changes internal to the challenger—e.g., changes in the values and perceptions of leaders, or of the balance of power between factions within the regime, or a change of the regime itself. In these cases, the state's leaders come to perceive opportunities for change by coercion and place a high value on such change. The purpose of the challenge that starts the crisis is to revise the status quo to the state's advantage, not to preserve it against the efforts of others to change it, as in the first type.

Examples of such an internal precipitant may be seen in the crises of the 1930s in Europe. Although many Germans no doubt were dissatisfied with the boundaries of Germany as drawn by the Versailles treaty, it was only after Hitler came to power, with his special values and perception of the external environment, that a series of crises occurred. The external environment was not changing to Ger-

---

[6] The Cuban missile crisis is a notable exception to this statement. There was more real causality in the specific precipitant—the introduction of Soviet missiles into Cuba—than in the general precipitant, defined as Soviet military aid to Cuba in general.

[7] We are indebted to Robert Jervis and Lawrence Finkelstein for the point made in this paragraph, and to Jervis for the Bundy comment. The latter is quoted in Townsend Hoopes, *The Limits of Intervention* (New York: David McKay, 1969), p. 30.

many's disadvantage; it became "intolerable" and was challenged because of changes within Germany that produced an expansionist foreign policy. . . .

In some cases the crisis arises out of a combination of external and internal precipitants. An example would be the Berlin crisis of 1958. To a considerable degree, Khrushchev's challenge was motivated by factors internal to the Communist bloc: the weakness of the East German government and the perception by the Soviet leadership that getting the Western powers out of West Berlin and/or gaining the formal recognition of the German Democratic Republic would both strengthen East Germany and give the Soviet Union a great diplomatic triumph. However, there was also a degree of external precipitation in the anti-Communist propaganda, espionage, and subversive activity that the Soviets perceived to be emanating from West Berlin, and perhaps also in the rearmament of West Germany and the U.S. deployment of tactical nuclear weapons on West German territory.

In a broad sense, almost every crisis would have a mixed precipitant, since with the external stimulus, it is certain of the challenger's values and perceptions that impel him to react. With the internal stimulus, the shift in the internal perspectives of the challenger tends to focus his attention on some aspect of the external environment that presents an opportunity for gain. Thus, the external–internal distinction refers in most cases to a preponderance of motivation one way or the other.

Once a challenge is given, it must be *resisted* by the challenged party in order for a crisis to occur. If the victim were to cave in immediately, there would be no crisis. Sometimes resistance is immediate, overt, and clear: a vigorous "no" is issued to the challenger's demand. Sometimes it is more diffuse, consisting of an absence of official response to the challenge, a defiant outcry in the press and public opinion, simple continuance of an activity that the challenger has demanded be stopped, or perhaps a quiet increase in military readiness. Even in the barely conceivable case of neither clear nor diffuse signals of resistance, a crisis will generally be perceived to exist as a consequence of the challenge alone, since it will be clear both to the immediate parties and to outside observers that important interests of the victim have been threatened, and that he therefore can be *expected* to resist, at least initially.

The resister is not only resisting but also deterring. That is, besides saying "no" to the challenger's demands, he is also explicitly or implicitly threatening to fight if the challenger carries out his threat. It may also be said that the issuance of the challenge constitutes a kind of failure of deterrence for the resister—a failure to deter coercive action against itself.[8]

The collision of challenge and resistance produces a *confrontation,* which is the core of the crisis. The confrontation may continue for a short or fairly long

---

[8] Alexander George and Richard Smoke have clearly explained and demonstrated that deterrence is a complex, multilevel phenomenon. The theory of deterrence began at the level of deterring strategic nuclear attack, then was extended downward to the deterrence of limited war. George and Smoke, in *Deterrence in American Foreign Policy: Theory and Practice* (New York: Columbia University Press, 1974) have developed a valuable theory of how deterrence operates at "lower" levels of conflicts—i.e., in crisis-prevention and crisis resolution.

time (from days to months) and is characterized by high or rising tension and predominantly coercive tactics on both sides, each standing firm on its initial position and issuing threats, warnings, military deployments, and other signals to indicate firmness, to undermine the other's firmness, and generally to persuade the other that he must be the one to back down if war is to be avoided.

There may be several peaks of tension of varying intensity during the confrontation phase, each centering perhaps on a particular issue, or perhaps following an especially severe and provocative coercive act. At these peaks, the likelihood of war appears to rise, and the feelings of anxiety associated with tension become more intense.

In general, there are three possible outcomes of the confrontation phase: war, capitulation by one side, or negotiated or tacit compromise. If it is war, the crisis is over, as we define it, and the parties move into a different type of interaction. If it is capitulation or compromise, the confrontation is followed by a *resolution* phase during which the details of settlement are arranged, and accommodative tactics—bids, concessions, settlement proposals—become preponderant over coercive behavior, although the latter may not entirely disappear. This phase will involve capitulation by one party if the other has clearly established its dominance of resolve during the confrontation phase; it will involve compromise if neither has established such dominance and both mutually decide to retreat from the brink to avoid disaster. In the former case, "accommodation" often includes some sort of minor facesaving concessions by the victor to allow the loser to rationalize his yielding; in the latter case, accommodation will require some hard bargaining, with one or both sides making displays of determination and mild coercive moves somewhere along the road toward settlement. Accommodation may settle both the crisis and the underlying conflict of interest; or it may only settle the crisis, leaving the conflict of interest unresolved or only partially resolved. There usually is a fairly clear breakpoint between the two phases of confrontation and resolution, resulting from the recognition by one or both sides that further coercive and countercoercive tactics based on the initial challenge–resistance positions will either be unsuccessful or too dangerous, or both.

Figure 1 summarizes our model of crisis phases. The solid horizontal lines represent the degree of "tension" or intensity of conflict behavior. It is low or mild up to the challenge–resistance point, when it rises above the "crisis threshold" (long dotted line). It varies in intensity during the confrontation phase, then either sharply increases with the transition to war, or falls back to something approximating the pre-crisis level during or following the resolution phase.

The pattern we have just sketched probably fits a majority of crises, but there are also many variations, and some totally different types. Alexander George has emphasized that crises are heavily context-dependent[9] and their political contexts may differ greatly. First, to examine the way a crisis begins, our phase model has

[9] Alexander F. George, David K. Hall and William R. Simons, *The Limits of Coercive Diplomacy* (Boston: Little-Brown, 1971), p. 217. Our phase model is adapted from a similar one by Charles Lockhart in his "A Bargaining Conceptualization of International Crises," Center for International Conflict Studies, State University of New York at Buffalo (mimeographed), April 1970.

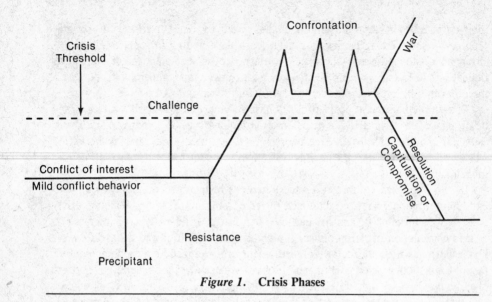

Figure 1.   **Crisis Phases**

an aura of deliberateness about it; the challenger who starts the crisis does so deliberately in an attempt to coerce another party. But are there also *accidental* crises, the parties "stumbling into" a confrontation through a series of actions that neither expected to reach crisis proportions? We find no examples in our sample where the challenge move is accidental, and by definition it hardly could be. . . . However, the idea of an accidental crisis seems to connote something more than surprise at being challenged; it implies that both protagonists get drawn into a confrontation by contextual factors beyond the control of either. This would seem to be best exemplified by two major powers being dragged into a crisis by the actions of their clients or allies. For example, the Soviet–U.S. "alert crisis" in the fall of 1973 was precipitated by actions of the Arabs and Israelis. There are elements of accident surrounding the beginning of other crises: e.g., the assassination at Sarajevo was "accidental" from the point of view of the highest officials, at least, of the Serbian government. But the *general* precipitant—the Serbian agitation within Austria–Hungary—was hardly accidental, nor was the Austrian response. In general, while elements of accident, surprise, chance, and imperfect control are often present in our cases, we find no clear example of a crisis beginning entirely by accident, and, in all cases, elements of deliberateness predominate over elements of inadvertence, even though the deliberateness may be premised in very inaccurate perceptions of the situation.

A different type of crisis from the coercive bargaining type portrayed in our model is what might be called the "war scare" or "security dilemma" crisis. Here, tension arises not because one party makes a coercive demand upon another but because one or both parties begin to fear that the other is about to attack. Typically, the parties are already in a fairly high state of hostility and tension. Then one side takes some action that looks like preparation to attack, the other side reacts with partial mobilization, the first side responds with further measures, which confirm the second side's fears and cause it to mobilize further, etc. The preparedness measures are undertaken not to bring coercive pressure upon the opponent but simply to be ready to defend against a possible attack. But the defensive measures on both sides self-confirm each side's fears that the other is preparing an attack, in the familiar dynamics of the security dilemma. . . . Since typically in these cases neither side intends to attack or coerce the other, they are, in a sense, "illusory" crises; yet they are still crises by our definition. . . .

11

The Politics of International Terrorism

ANDREW J. PIERRE

In this article, Andrew J. Pierre argues that international terrorism is likely to remain endemic to world politics. In part that conclusion is based on the pessimistic judgment that "the politics of international terrorism are such that many countries are . . . more willing to condone than to condemn it." Pierre is a senior fellow at the Council on Foreign Relations and author of "Arms Sales: The New Diplomacy," which appears earlier in this book.

International terrorism is a new, growing and increasingly important phenomenon in present-day world politics. Hardly a week now goes by without the hijacking of an airplane across national boundaries, or the kidnaping of a diplomat or foreign businessman, or some other violent incident in the name of a political cause. . . .

. . . To give an approximate idea of the growth of international terrorism, in the twenty years before 1969 there was an average of five hijackings per year; in the early 1970s the average was over sixty annually. The [1970–1975 period] witnessed more than 500 major acts of international terrorism including over sixty-five kidnapings with international ramifications.

There is nothing new about terrorism per se. The term first came into modern usage during the Reign of Terror in revolutionary France. It commonly refers to the threat of violence and the use of fear to coerce, persuade or gain public attention. Terror has been used by ideologies of both the Right and the Left, by the former to repress a population and by the latter to win self-determination and independence. Terror has been used by governments as an instrument of state as well as by guerrillas or insurgents as an instrument of subversion.[1]

Reprinted from Andrew J. Pierre, "The Politics of International Terrorism," *Orbis* 19 (Winter 1976), 1251–1269. Reprinted from *Orbis: A Journal of World Affairs* by permission of the publisher. Copyright 1976 by the Foreign Policy Research Institute, Philadelphia.

[1] The best theoretical work on terrorism remains E. V. Walter, *Terror and Resistance: A Study of Political Violence* (New York: Oxford University Press, 1969). Most other studies only touch on terrorism in the context of internal conflict or guerrilla war. See, for example, J. Bowyer Bell, *The Myth of the Guerrilla* (New York: Alfred Knopf, 1971); Robert Moss, *The War for the Cities* (New York: Coward, McCann and Geoghegan, 1972); Harry Eckstein, *Internal War* (New York: Free Press, 1964). "State terrorism" is discussed in Barrington Moore, Jr., *Terror and Progress in the U.S.S.R.* (Cambridge, Mass.: Harvard University Press, 1954). For two recent studies, see Richard Clutterbuck, *Living with Terrorism* (London: Faber and Faber, 1975) and Brian Jenkins, *International Terrorism: A New Mode of Conflict* (Los Angeles, Calif.: California Seminar on Arms Control and Foreign Policy, Research Paper No. 48, 1975).

The concept of *international* terrorism is more difficult to endow with a universally accepted definition. In this analysis it will refer to acts of violence across national boundaries, or with clear international repercussions, often within the territory or involving the citizens of a third party to a dispute. Thus it is to be distinguished from *domestic* terrorism of the sort that has taken place in Ulster, the Soviet Union or South Africa. Admittedly, the line is often thin between terror which is essentially domestic and that possessing a clear international character.

International terrorism is usually, though not exclusively, political in intent and carried out by nongovernmental groups, although they may receive financial and moral support from nation-states. Many of the Palestinian Liberation Organization (PLO) terrorist activities have taken place outside the boundaries of Israel, have been financed or abetted by some Arab states, and have affected nationals of third countries. Most of the victims have been innocent bystanders, such as . . . tourists machine-gunned in the waiting room of [an] airport. . . . Targets are often selected because of their connection to a foreign state, i.e., diplomats and foreign businessmen, or because they have become symbols of international interdependence, such as airlines with overseas routes or multinational corporations.

Due to its international character, this form of terrorism is of particular concern to the world community. Repressive or violent activities totally within national boundaries may be of real and valid concern, but they are obviously less amenable to pressure and change through international action by means of diplomacy or law. Moreover, the motivations of international terrorists are often related to the world community and public opinion abroad. . . .

It is unlikely that international terrorism is a passing and transitory phenomenon. The trend toward the weakening of central authority in governments, the rise in ethnic and subnational sentiments, and the increasing fractionalization of the global political process point toward its growth as a form of political protest and persuasion. Classic balance of power diplomacy is of little utility in dealing with it, for violent acts of small groups of people, or individuals, are difficult for governments to control. International terrorism is likely to continue and to expand because in the minds of many of its perpetrators it has proven to be "successful."

Technological change and growth account for much of the new strength and disruptive capacity of terrorist groups. Television gives the terrorist instant access to the world's living rooms, thereby enabling him to draw global attention to his cause. The mobility offered by the modern jet aircraft allows him to strike at will almost anywhere in the world and then move on to safe asylum. Hence, advances in technology have made it possible for a large society to be directly affected by a small band of terrorists.

Yet the increasing frequency of international terrorism is only beginning to be understood and has thus far received relatively little sustained, analytic attention. We are at the rudimentary stages of learning to cope with it. In this article we will examine the response to international terrorism as it has evolved in the practice of governments, at the United Nations where it has been identified as a major item of international concern, and through the processes of international law. Policy suggestions will be made for the future. But first, in order to understand him better, we must look at what it is that moves and motivates the terrorist.

ONE MAN'S TERRORIST IS ANOTHER MAN'S "FREEDOM FIGHTER"

There is no simple explanation for the causes of international terrorism, nor is there common agreement on its purposes and ends. Perceptions about the legitimacy of the means vary dramatically. What to one man is an outrageous act of lawlessness and immorality . . . appears to another as an unfortunate but necessary step toward achieving a political goal rooted in existing or perceived injustice and deprivation. As we will see later, these differing perceptions have been transformed into the diverging attitudes of governments at the United Nations and elsewhere.

Motivations for international terrorism vary from case to case and are often complex, but their roots can be discerned in one or more of the following profiles:

(1) The terrorist is dedicated to a political goal which he sees as one of transcendent merit. The aim of the *fedayeen* (Arabic for "self-sacrificers") has been to gain political salience for the Palestinian cause. By making their goal appear viable to the Arab world, they have received financial and political assistance from Moslem states that support, or feel compelled to support, their cause. The Tupamaros in Uruguay and the People's Revolutionary Army (ERP) in Argentina have sought popular support through the widespread use of terrorist tactics that induce the government to react harshly and therefore appear oppressive in its response.[2]

(2) The terrorist seeks attention and publicity for his cause. The world becomes his stage as contemporary media enable him to dramatize his goals effectively and attempt to win over public opinion. A display of determination and devotion to the cause focuses world attention upon it and may induce sympathy. In an age seemingly lacking in heroics, a cause for which an individual is prepared to sacrifice his life appears to some as worthy of support. Without the flamboyant terrorist acts of recent years the Palestinian issue would probably have remained relatively neglected and would be ranked lower on the international agenda than it is today. In this sense the PLO has achieved considerable success.

(3) The terrorist aims to erode support for the established political leadership or to undermine the authority of the state by destroying normality, creating uncertainty, polarizing a country, fostering economic discord and generally weakening the fabric of society. Attacks on foreign business firms, such as multinational corporations and their executives in Latin America, have forced them to reduce or close down their operations, as in the case of IBM and the Ford Motor Company, thereby creating unemployment and fanning discontent among the population that can be channeled into activities against the government. Attacks on civil aircraft and in the lounges of airports have sought to reduce air travel and tourism to Israel through psychological disruption and the spread of fear. Sometimes the intent is to provoke a government to ill-judged measures of repression that will alienate public opinion.

[2] See Maria Esther Gilio, *The Tupamaro Guerrillas* (New York: Saturday Review Press, 1972); Jack Davis, *Political Violence in Latin America* (London: International Institute for Strategic Studies, Adelphi Paper No. 85, 1972); Robert Moss, *Urban Guerrilla Warfare* (London: International Institute for Strategic Studies, Adelphi Paper No. 79, 1971).

(4) The terrorist's actions can be a measure of deep frustration when there is no legitimate way to redress grievances. It may be an act of desperation when a political impasse has been reached. As such, terrorism can be a sign of fundamental weakness as well as of momentary strength. Zeal and determination often compensate for an inherent position of weakness, for not having full backing for one's political aims. At the same time terrorism can be perceived as a patriotic deed. Palestinian perpetrators of terrorism—those who survive—return home as heroes to their people.

(5) The terrorist may seek to liberate his colleagues in foreign jails. Aircraft hijacking appears to be an especially popular way of securing the release of prisoners. . . .

(6) Finally, the terrorist may desire money so as to buy arms and finance his organization. Some claim that they want to distribute food and shelter to the poor and needy. The kidnaping of foreign executives for ransom has become endemic in Latin America in recent times. Because corporations are willing, if forced, to pay substantial amounts to secure the release of their executives or avoid the sabotage of their plants, terrorism can be lucrative. Such companies as Amoco, Peugeot and Pepsico are reported to have paid large ransoms to terrorists in Argentina. Some de. ᵔands are for perceived just causes, while some, as in Mexico, can take on the form of banditry. Sometimes appearance is deceptive: at the Bank of America in Beirut a representative of Douglas Aircraft was shot by ordinary bank robbers posing as *fedayeen*.[3]

Modern society has become highly vulnerable to the terrorist deed. The crowded environment of the urban metropolis presents a "soft" target. Mass disruption of ordinary activities could be readily achieved through tampering with the electrical grid system, or by poisoning or polluting a city's water supply. In case of a more limited aim, the new sealed-window office building is subject to chemical and biological contamination through the air ventilation system. Poisonous powder on subway tracks can spread noxious germs throughout parts of a city. Such activities could be highly successful in generating mass fear and social disintegration.

Technology is making efficient tools available to terrorists. Ingenious timing and detonating devices are increasing the capacity for selective violence. Particularly worrisome is the prospect of civilian airliners being shot at by portable hand-held surface-to-air missiles as they land at or take off from airports. . . . Another danger is terror by mail—on one occasion the secretary of the defense attaché at the British Embassy in Washington was maimed by a letter-bomb.

The risk of nuclear materials being stolen and used by terrorist groups is also to be taken seriously. The growth in use of nuclear reactors to generate electrical power will yield large amounts of fissionable materials in the form of plutonium that can be used to manufacture nuclear explosives or weapons with relative ease. Should terrorists succeed in diverting such materials to their purposes, not to

---

[3] Fascinating insights into the terrorist's frame of mind are to be found in a "minimanual" written by Carlos Marighella, a Brazilian terrorist, five months before he was killed in an ambush. For extracts see *Survival*, March 1971, pp. 95–100.

speak of the real possibility of stealing nuclear weapons, they would acquire fearsome means with which to threaten communities and governments.[4]

Clearly, the vulnerability and fragility of contemporary society, in combination with the availability of sophisticated technology, increases the potential for disruptive activities. Moreover, modern communication aids the terrorist in his search for publicity by making possible detailed, on-the-spot coverage of his acts even when they occur in remote parts of the world. His ability to count on the media to dramatize and instantaneously inform the world of his activities—and thereby his cause—should not be underrated as a stimulus and an incentive.

COPING WITH INTERNATIONAL TERRORISM

Dealing with terrorism has become a problem of some magnitude and urgency, and is increasingly recognized as a challenge to the community of nations. Yet the political dynamics of international terrorism make coping with it an extremely difficult and subtle task. The need will not be limited to responding to terrorism or deterring it with the threat of punishment. Of equal importance—some would argue, far greater—is the need to prevent it by treating its underlying root causes.

This is the clear lesson of the debate on terrorism in the United Nations. Following the tragedy at the Munich Olympics, Secretary-General Kurt Waldheim asked the Twenty-seventh General Assembly to consider "measures to prevent international terrorism and other forms of violence which endanger or take innocent human lives or jeopardize fundamental freedoms." The Assembly agreed to his request, but amended it to include "the study of the underlying causes of those forms of terrorism and acts of violence which lie in misery, frustration, grievance and despair and which cause some people to sacrifice human lives, including their own, in an attempt to effect radical changes."

Debate in the Sixth Committee of the General Assembly and in a specially appointed thirty-five-state Ad Hoc Committee on International Terrorism brought out wide divergencies in perceptions of the problem. The principal interest of many of the developing countries was to avoid anything that could be used to suppress, or deny the legitimacy of, national liberation movements. Because many member-states had themselves been born out of rebellion and revolution, it was argued that condemnation of others who might be following similar courses, e.g., Palestinians, would be wrong and incongruous. This view was widely shared by African and Arab as well as many Asian countries. Some insisted that any consideration of international terrorism must begin with the condemnation of "state terrorism" as practiced by governments. Thus the Syrian Arab Republic said it was convinced "that the main cause of violence is the colonialist and imperialist policies and practices, as well as the crimes, of racist regimes against peoples."[5]

---

[4] For the best exposition of this problem, see Mason Willrich and Theodore B. Taylor, *Nuclear Theft: Risks and Safeguards* (Cambridge, Mass.: Ballinger Press, 1974).

[5] United Nations General Assembly, 27th Session, Ad Hoc Committee on International Terrorism, A/AC. 160/2, p. 16.

The principal proposal placed before the United Nations has been an American draft of a "Convention for the Prevention and Punishment of Certain Acts of International Terrorism." Wisely, the convention is narrowly drawn and does not attempt to deal with all acts of terrorism. In no way does it cover domestic terrorism designed to alter the political order within a single country. Rather, it focuses on the "export" of violence to third countries and innocent parties, undertaken by persons who kill, seriously assault or kidnap other persons in such a manner as to commit an offense of "international significance." According to Article I, it would be limited to acts in which each of four separate conditions apply: The act is committed or takes effect outside the territory of a state of which the alleged offender is a national; is committed or takes effect outside the territory of the state against which the act is directed; is committed neither by nor against a member of the armed forces of a state in the course of military activities; and is intended to damage the interest of or obtain concessions from a state or an international organization.[6] It would therefore not apply to acts of terrorism committed by a "freedom fighter" struggling within his country in a war of national liberation, but would be pertinent to most of the major international terrorist incidents of recent times.

Despite its limited approach, the convention failed to receive general support at the United Nations. The more radical view, most often espoused by African and Arab governments, held that terrorism was part of the struggle for national liberation and the right of self-determination, and therefore should not be considered an international offense. This argument was also made by Yasir Arafat in his speech at the UN when he equated his struggle with that of George Washington against the British colonialists. Moderate countries acknowledged the need to address the problem but emphasized the necessity to deal with long-term solutions and the grievances that lead to terrorism. Even West European governments were reluctant to take action. Debate within the United Nations has thus far led to no productive results. Experience suggests that while the majority of countries in the world body acknowledge the danger spreading terrorism poses for international order, the politics of international terrorism are such that many countries are still more willing to condone than to condemn it. . . .

[The author next turns his attention to efforts to bring specific types of international terrorism, such as aerial piracy or the kidnaping of diplomats, under legal control. He concludes this portion of the discussion with a generally pessimistic assessment of the prospects for combating terrorism through the mechanism of legal conventions—*eds.*]

WHAT IS TO BE DONE?

The remedies for international terrorism sought at the United Nations and through international legal conventions, though commendable, are of only limited utility. The problem is not so much one of law as one of politics. The evidence suggests

---

[6] United Nations General Assembly, 27th Session, Sixth Committee, A/C.6/L., p. 850.

that there are a substantial number of states, or groups within them, that view terrorism as an acceptable answer to perceived oppression—or feel politically restrained from saying otherwise—and are therefore prepared to condone it. Because international terrorism is a form of political violence and ultimately requires political solutions, an effective response must come to terms with its political dimensions. Steps for coping with terrorism will therefore need to include both *measures of prevention* and *measures of deterrence*. Only through a combination of the two, consciously pursued in parallel, can we hope to reduce and eventually eliminate this spreading epidemic.

Prevention would require giving more attention than we now do to economic, social and political grievances and sources of frustration. Individuals are more likely to turn to violence if they lose hope, if life seems not worth living, and if the "system" appears to be unresponsive to legitimate protest. Prevention would attempt to eradicate the conditions that spawn terrorism by looking for long-term solutions. It would seek to find and strengthen common interests, and constructively channel remaining discontent. At a minimum, it would seek to offer alternative, nonviolent forms of protest. . . .

Prevention, however, is a long-term process that must be continuously pursued. In the short run, measures of *deterrence* are more likely to be effective in coping with international terrorism. There are a number of specific measures that should now be undertaken by nations acting in concert.

First, and most important, acts of terrorism, especially those involving random killing, should not continue to go unpunished. Although hard data are not available, it is quite clear that . . . terrorists have been repeatedly set free by governments in Western Europe and the Middle East. . . .

Second, deterrence would be enhanced if specific sanctions were imposed against countries that shelter hijackers and saboteurs of planes by granting safe asylum. These could include a suspension of commercial air traffic to countries that let hijackers off scot free, or a boycott of their airliners by withholding permission to land. Since the ICAO [International Civil Aviation Organization] has failed to take effective action, this could be accomplished by a series of bilateral accords providing for extradition or prosecution, using the Cuban-American agreement as a model. If a consensus could be reached that countries protecting hijackers will be boycotted by civil aviation, and that hijackers will be punished, a major step would be taken toward deterring this form of terrorism.

Related to this is the question of the availability of aircraft in response to terrorist demands for transportation out of a country and the granting of landing rights for refueling purposes. It has become the custom of terrorists to expect that they can flee by demanding a plane and a crew. This should now be reversed, with governments agreeing among themselves, and publicly declaring beforehand, that they will not provide aircraft for the use of terrorists or even temporary landing rights. . . .

Third, countries that believe in the need to control international terrorism should cooperate on practical precautionary steps that might be undertaken together. Chief among these is the sharing of intelligence data and other information about terrorist organizations, their membership, structure, leaders, motivations, and so on. The United States has established a cabinet-level committee and appointed a Special Assistant to the Secretary of State for Combating Terrorism. His activities involve both contingency planning and coordinating action once a terrorist incident develops; . . . other countries, including West Germany, have now established similar offices. Like-minded governments should be encouraged to set up bureaus for this purpose and develop cooperation among them. Technological aids, such as devices for improving airport security throughout the world, should also be shared. Nations possessing atomic reactors should tighten existing precautions to safeguard against the theft or diversion of nuclear materials. Some international cooperation along this line is already in progress, but it should be broadened and deepened. Most important, the states that share a common perception of the dangers of international terrorism should act now to concert their efforts, without waiting for the agreement of all member-states of the United Nations.

This intergovernmental cooperation is especially important in light of increasing evidence of transnational linkages between terrorist groups with varied purposes, even located in different continents. Such collaboration often exists to facilitate the flow of arms and information. The Japanese Red Army, for instance, has established ties with the PLO, and in Europe it has had contacts with a number of terrorist groups. . . . International linkages of this type can be of considerable practical significance to terrorist organizations in increasing their outreach and effectiveness. Although one cannot yet speak of a "brotherhood" of terrorists, . . . a number of "networks" have been uncovered. They should be combated through international cooperation among as many countries as possible. In this manner the very internationalism of terrorist movements might contribute to their undoing.

Fourth, the communications media have a special responsibility in taking care not to encourage acts of terrorism and violence by giving them undue publicity. Such acts often possess a particular aspect of sensationalism designed to attract public attention out of proportion to the real importance of the event. Terrorism is usually directed at the watching audience, rather than the real victims. Although, obviously, newsworthy incidents of terrorism cannot and should not be suppressed, television and the press must avoid being manipulated by terrorists for their own advantage. This suggests a need for restraint and prudence by the Fourth Estate in its reportage of terrorism.

Fifth, in regard to American policy, we might re-examine our present blanket "no ransom" policy in dealing with international terrorism. After the Khartoum incident President Nixon firmly stated that the United States would not pay ransom, reasoning that "the nation that compromises with the terrorist today could well be destroyed by terrorism tomorrow." But the evidence is hardly available or clear that this would be the case, and the analogy between political terrorism and ordinary criminal blackmail ("extortion breeds extortion") may be somewhat misleading. If a Boeing 747 filled with 350 American citizens was about to be blown up, would Washington still refuse to buy their safety? If the chairman of the Senate Foreign Relations Committee was kidnaped . . . , would the U.S. government not be willing to release a few foreign terrorists, or urge another government to give in to such terrorist demands? . . .

Finally, the community of states should seek as broad a consensus as possible establishing that acts of international terrorism—especially indiscriminate violence when the victims are innocent third parties sitting in planes, walking the streets or resting at home—are, regardless of motive, beyond acceptable norms of behavior. It should be made clear that when the terrorist deliberately inflicts death and destruction on the innocent, rather than on the enemy, he is crossing an ethical threshold and committing a crime against humanity as a whole. Even if political reasons dim the prospects for a UN convention on the "export" of terrorism, or early ICAO action on hijacking is unlikely, it should be possible to create a moral climate that will help to deter random violence. . . .

Responding successfully to international terrorism will require both the balm of prevention and the sting of deterrence. It will involve piecemeal coping rather than comprehensive solution. The enduring difficulty will be to reconcile the imperatives of international order and safety with the legitimate grievances that give rise to despair and violence. Moral dilemmas will abound.

We must be prepared to accept the fact that terrorism could become a new form of warfare. With the increasing availability of relatively small and inexpensive means of destruction, a handful of men could have an enormous impact upon states and societies anywhere. Some countries might even prefer to arm and use terrorists to pursue their foreign policy objectives, rather than accept the stigma of direct and visible involvement in a conflict with another state. They might view terrorist activities as a continuation of warfare by other and more effective means, in which the constraints applying to conventional warfare under accepted standards of international behavior and law could be conveniently disregarded. Thus terrorism could be intentionally used to instigate an international incident, to provoke an enemy, to carry out acts of sabotage, or to incite a repressive reaction against a group in a country.

Terrorism is a relatively inexpensive and efficient way of doing a great deal of harm, and doing it without the political embarrassment that can be attached to many overt state actions. In some ways, therefore, it could become an alternative to conventional wars—not necessarily an undesirable step. It is not too early to think creatively about arms control—in the political sense—for international terrorism. Should terrorism continue to grow, as appears likely, it will enter the mainstream of world politics. Then, even more than today, it will present a major political, legal, arms-control and, perhaps above all, moral challenge to us all.

Part TWO

Discord and Collaboration

States necessarily must direct their attention and resources toward the quest for security, for the threat of war is an ever-present danger in an anarchical society. Issues relating to arms and influence therefore occupy a prominent place on the foreign policy agendas of nation-states, and the pursuit of national security—defined especially in terms of military policy and strategy—seems in today's insecure world to constitute the very essence of international politics. Hence the issues treated in Part I of *The Global Agenda* appropriately command central importance.

Compelling as this realist perspective is, it is at best a caricature of international politics if it fails to acknowledge the broad range of issues and objectives that motivate states' behavior, even in their quest for security. The "high politics" of peace and security entails both issues and strategies that lie beyond arms and war, deterrence, and the raw exercise of influence. It also includes activities of states that often have little or nothing to do with armaments or the threat of war.

Indeed, contrary to the Hobbesian perspective of some observers, international politics is not exclusively a "war of all against all." States are not normally straining at the leash to attack one another. Nor do they allocate the bulk of their time, on a day-to-day basis, to planning the use of force against their perceived adversaries. The texture of world politics is shaped by more varied national interests and activities.

Part II of *The Global Agenda* directs attention to issues and perspectives that involve some of the routine and continuing interactions of states as they seek to promote their national interests. No assumption is made that under normal conditions relations among states are conducted without conflict. Conflict is endemic to all those relations—like politics, it is unavoidable. But we *can* assume that the manner in which states usually respond to conflicts includes activities that do not involve the threat or use of force.

By extension, this way of looking at international politics in Part II begins with the assumption that states respond not only to a perceived need for power, but also to a perceived need for order. Accordingly, inter-state interaction is characterized by both cooperation and conflict, by collaboration as well as discord. Nation-states seek a stable international environment, and therefore seek and support not just a strong defense, but common institutions, rules, and procedures that contribute to the creation of a more orderly world. In short, states engage in cooperation as well as conflict to realize their preferred objectives.

What factors influence whether amity or enmity will dominate the pattern of interaction among states? Clearly, there are many. Underlying all of them, it may be argued, are states' perceptions of reality. Reality is partially subjective—what states perceive it to be—and consequently actions are influenced strongly by images of reality as well as by objective facts. Whether states see the world as fearful and hostile or perceive it as holding out opportunities for collaboration to realize preferred futures will influence the postures they assume toward global issues and their reactions to the challenges and options those issues present. How states view the world will thus shape their perspectives on the issues composing the global agenda.

In our first selection in Part II, "Deterrence, the Spiral Model, and Intentions of the Adversary" by Robert Jervis, the author introduces the logic of images and perceptions as an approach to understanding the pattern of discord and collaboration in world affairs. Jervis' commentary on the problems of "high politics" begins with the assumption that "differing perceptions of the other state's intentions often underlie policy debates." Debate over deterrence theories in the United States are exemplary, Jervis observes, because such debates often center on disagreements about the Soviet Union's intentions. To illustrate this tendency and to demonstrate the cogency of the perceptual perspective, Jervis discusses how not just deterrence but nearly all global issues depend to a considerable extent on the accuracy of actors' perceptions for their resolution. The pronounced propensity of nations to *misperceive* the motives of their adversaries does not augur well for the peaceful management and resolution of disputes. The study of international issues deserves to be informed, for this reason, by the perspective offered by analysts of images and belief systems.

The cogency and urgency of this perspective take on concreteness in the case of relations between the United States and the Soviet Union. Successful management of the East-West conflict, which remains today, as throughout most of the post–World War II era, perhaps *the* most threatening global contest, is all the more important because of the enormous capacity for nuclear destruction now in the hands of the United States and the Soviet Union. Yet the probability of discord remains high, and the possibilities for cooperation questionable, because of the perceptions and misperceptions that the superpowers maintain of one another.

This thesis is elaborated by the eminent statesman and scholar George F. Kennan, in "Soviet-American Relations: The Politics of Discord and Collaboration." Kennan examines the persistent discord in Soviet-American relations by tracing its roots to the legacy of misunderstanding and misperception that has punctuated the entire record of United States–Soviet relations since the Bolshevik revolution in 1917. Focusing on the policy reaction of the United States to the Soviet Union, Kennan captures the extent to which mistaken images may produce missed opportunities for conflict reduction in world politics. His conclusions hold out the hope and belief that, despite the antagonisms between the superpowers, efforts to devise a world in which they can live together are not doomed to failure— that out of threats and conflict mutually beneficial collaboration may emerge, especially if statesmen adopt the appropriate vision.

One way the superpowers have sought collaboratively to reduce tensions is through negotiated arms control agreements. Arms control and disarmament efforts have a long if not very encouraging history. When successful, they have contributed to a dampening of the risks that weapons themselves contribute to political conflict, and, therefore, in the eyes of some observers, to the reduced probability of war. A willingness to engage in and abide by arms control agreements thus constitutes one means by which states can collaborate in order to enhance their security.

In the contemporary period, SALT (Strategic Arms Limitations Talks) represents the most ambitious attempt by the superpowers to bring the level of their strategic weapons under control. Opposition to the SALT process and agreements that arose among domestic groups in the United States and, presumably, in the Soviet Union renders the future of arms control problematic (and illustrates the fragile underpinnings of arms control endeavors as an approach to the management of strategic weapons). Barry M. Blechman puts the future of this issue into perspective by addressing the question "Do Negotiated Arms Limitations Have a Future?" His conclusions—that the best hope for arms limitations rests on the fact that countries have real interests in reaching them, but that the prospects for pursuing them tend to be undermined by the inclination of states to expect too much from them—demonstrate that the ability of states to find satisfactory solutions to their common problems may be significantly colored by domestic political considerations. Because not all politically influential domestic groups share the same vision of reality, the desirability of states' collaborating to resolve the issues that their own actions help to create may not be matched by the ability of foreign policy decision makers to accomplish that task.

The potential for either discord or collaboration is illustrated vividly by another mechanism of statecraft: alliances. Coalitions and the alliances that formalize them are voluntary associations created to enable allies to collaborate among themselves for defense against those with whom they are in conflict. Today, because of the destructiveness of nuclear weapons, the political role of alliances, that of making more credible the commitment of one state to the defense of others, is perhaps more important than their strictly military function, that of aggregating power. Thus, as "latent war communities" they are inherently and simultaneously institutions for conflict and for cooperation. Their successful management is, therefore, necessarily an important issue in world politics.

Two essays in *The Global Agenda* bring perspective to issues surrounding alliance maintenance. The first, "Coalition Dynamics: The Western Alliance" by Stanley Hoffman, examines the dynamics of coalition formation and maintenance within the North Atlantic Treaty Organization (NATO), the principal alliance linking the United States to the defense of Western Europe. Hoffmann lucidly demonstrates how problems within the Western alliance stem from a cluster of deeply entrenched divisions—historical, geographical, and domestic. Their nature and magnitude suggest that they are unlikely to disappear in the immediate future.

Similarly, in "Coalition Dynamics: The Soviet Union and Eastern Europe," Alvin Z. Rubinstein finds that discord exists between the Soviet Union and its European allies, much as differences exist within the Western alliance. Unlike NATO, however, the Warsaw Pact is a hierarchical bloc structure with the Soviet Union its undisputed hegemonic power. Rubinstein emphasizes that the Soviet position in Eastern Europe is a purposeful one that Soviet leaders will maintain by force if necessary. At the same time, he argues that the management of intra-bloc relations is significantly affected by Soviet domestic considerations and by Eastern European ethnic nationalism tinged by strong anti-communist and anti-Russian sentiments. As in the case of NATO, issues within the Soviet domain can be expected to persist.

Thus far, the selections in Part II have stressed issues that orbit the East-West conflict. Of equal importance and timeliness are those that center on the North-South conflict between the "core" and the "periphery"—between the rich countries of the First World and the poor countries of the Third World. In an illuminating survey of the multiple issues that crowd the agenda on this axis of world politics, Stephen D. Krasner addresses the topic of "What the Third World Wants and Why." His analysis of the Third World's quest for the creation of a new international regime—one that would give Third World countries greater opportunities to compete for status and wealth with the relatively advantaged states—indicates that most of the aspirations that animate the less developed countries relate to their desire to escape the constraints imposed by what they perceive as an international economic system that makes them dependent on others (namely the rich countries). The analysis underscores the extent to which perspectives on international economic and political issues are often intertwined on today's global agenda.

Problem-solving in international affairs requires the creation of effective institutions to cope with global issues. The United Nations represents perhaps the greatest hope, and most bitter disappointment, for meeting these needs. In "The United Nations and World Politics," Secretary-General of the United Nations Javier Perez de Cuellar turns a critical eye toward the institution his Secretariat manages and assesses its potential for carrying out the multiple missions its Charter assigns it. The Secretary-General's perspective on the world organization is a particularly useful one, for it frames well the problems and prospects of the United Nations in a global environment where nation-states remain the principal actors, and where disputes between states have a greater impact on international institutions than those institutions have on the management and resolution of these conflicts.

The international system's capacity for both discord and collaboration is exhibited by yet another of its structural features: its legal system. In "Is It Law or Politics? The Role of International Law and Its Limitations," Louis Henkin casts into perspective a diversity of viewpoints regarding the functions international law performs in world affairs. He concludes that, despite its limitations (many of which are exaggerated by those uninformed about its principles and procedures), international law succeeds in adequately performing the functions states have assigned it, not the least of which is maintenance of the order, stability, and predictability that states prize.

At the zenith of interstate collaboration is the possibility that formerly separate (and competitive) states will integrate—that is, voluntarily join together to become new, larger, independent decision-making entities in world affairs. Hopes for this peaceful and collaborative path to the creation of new forms of world governance were raised by economic and political developments in Western Europe during the 1950s, when the European Coal and Steel Community and later the European Economic Community, or Common Market, were created. There emerged, accordingly, two perspectives on the integration process: transactionalism and neo-functionalism. Donald J. Puchala contrasts these theories with actual experiences over the past three decades and provides a useful critique of each. His observations provide a useful analysis of the reasons why some of the expectations of integration theorists were not realized, but why the propositions driving them retain their relevance today.

Will issues relating to integration processes dominate the global agenda of the future? Or will the tendency toward fragmentation command more attention? It is to these divergent trends and their implications that K. J. Holsti brings insight in the concluding selection of Part II of *The Global Agenda*. Using the ubiquitous concept of "interdependence" as a background, Holsti astutely notes in "Interdependence, Integration, and Fragmentation" how the future will be shaped by the interaction of divergent trends: one toward closer ties between states, the other toward fragmentation as states and sub-national groups within them recoil from the consequences of these links. Whether discord or collaboration will be greater or lesser ingredients in the future of world politics will be influenced considerably by the rapidity and direction these divergent trends take. Furthermore, the collective responses of individual nation-states to the issues these trends pose both now and for the future will affect nations' capacities to realize the security that in the world of "high politics" is at stake.

12

Deterrence, the Spiral Model, and Intentions of the Adversary

ROBERT JERVIS

In this essay, Robert Jervis theorizes about the role that misperceptions of an adversary's intentions play in contributing to international conflict. Particularly important is his treatment of psychological images as they relate to the dynamics of inter-state conflict. Jervis is professor in the department of political science and the Institute of War and Peace Studies at Columbia University. Author of *The Logic of Images in International Politics* (1970), he is well-known for his writing on the role of perceptions and misperceptions in international politics.

TWO VIEWS OF INTERNATIONAL RELATIONS AND THE COLD WAR

Differing perceptions of the other state's intentions often underlie policy debates. In the frequent cases when the participants do not realize that they differ on this crucial point, the dispute is apt to be both vituperative and unproductive. This has been the case with much of the debate in the United States over deterrence theories and policies. Although the arguments have been couched in terms of clashing general theories of international relations, most of the dispute can be accounted for in terms of disagreements about Soviet intentions. . . .

Deterrence

For our purposes we need not be concerned with the many subtleties and complexities of deterrence theory, but only with the central argument that great dangers arise if an aggressor believes that the status quo powers are weak in capability

Reprinted from Robert Jervis, *Perception and Misperception in International Politics* (Princeton: Princeton University Press, 1976), pp. 58–76. Copyright © 1976 by Princeton University Press. Excerpt reprinted by permission of Princeton University Press. Some footnotes have been deleted; others have been renumbered to appear in consecutive order.

or resolve. This belief will lead the former to test its opponents, usually starting with a small and apparently unimportant issue. If the status quo powers retreat, they will not only lose the specific value at stake but, more important in the long run, will encourage the aggressor to press harder. . . .

To avoid this disastrous situation, the state must display the ability and willingness to wage war. It may not be able to ignore minor conflicts or to judge disputes on their merits. Issues of little intrinsic value become highly significant as indices of resolve. Thus even though President Kennedy had ordered American missiles out of Turkey before the Cuban missile crisis, he would not agree to remove them as the price for obtaining Soviet cooperation. Many conflicts resemble the game of "Chicken," and, in such a game, Thomas Schelling argues, "It may be safer in the long run to hew to the center of the road than to yield six inches on successive nights, if one is really going to stop yielding before being pushed onto the shoulder. It may save both parties a collision."[1] . . .

The state must often go to extremes because moderation and conciliation are apt to be taken for weakness. Although the state may be willing to agree to a settlement that involves some concessions, it may fear that, if it admits this, the other side will respond, not by matching concessions, but by redoubled efforts to extract a further retreat. . . .

The fear that concessions may be taken by the other as indicating that the state can be beaten at the game of Chicken also inhibits the state from making overtures that might end a conflict. . . . President Johnson believed that the most telling argument against halting the bombing of North Vietnam was that this action might lead the North to conclude that American resolve was weakening. Even civility is dangerous because it is often misinterpreted by aggressors. . . .

This does not mean that the state should never change its position. At times superior power must be recognized. Legitimate grievances can be identified and rectified, although care must be taken to ensure that the other side understands the basis on which the state is acting. In other cases, fair trades can be arranged. And at times concessions will have to be made to entice the other to agree. But while carrots as well as sticks are to be employed, the other's friendship cannot be won by gratuitous concessions. . . .

The other side of this coin is that, if the distribution of power is favorable, firmness can check aggression. The combination of the high cost of a war, the low probability that the aggressor can win it, and the value the aggressor places on retaining what he has already won will lead even a minimally rational state to refrain from an expansionist attack. And it will not strike in the mistaken belief that the first side is planning aggression because it knows that the latter is defensive. Thus once it realizes that the defender cannot be bullied, the other side will try to increase its values by peaceful and cooperative means. . . .

In this view, the world is tightly interconnected. What happens in one interaction influences other outcomes as each state scrutinizes the others' behavior for indications of interests, strengths, and weaknesses. As the German foreign min-

---

[1] "Uncertainty, Brinkmanship, and the Game of 'Chicken,' " in Kathleen Archibald, ed., *Strategic Interaction and Conflict* (Berkeley: Institute of International Studies, University of California, 1966), p. 87.

ister said during the Moroccan crisis of 1905, "If we let others trample on our feet in Morocco without a protest, we are encouraging a repetition of the act elsewhere."[2] As we will discuss below, this view often rests on the belief that the other side's aims are unlimited. . . .

The Spiral Model

The critics of deterrence theory provide what seems at first to be a contrasting general theory of international influence. The roots of what can be called the spiral model reach to the anarchic setting of international relations. The underlying problem lies neither in limitations on rationality imposed by human psychology nor in a flaw in human nature, but in a correct appreciation of the consequences of living in a Hobbesian state of nature. In such a world without a sovereign, each state is protected only by its own strength. Furthermore, statesmen realize that, even if others currently harbor no aggressive designs, there is nothing to guarantee that they will not later develop them. . . .

The lack of a sovereign in international politics permits wars to occur and makes security expensive. More far-reaching complications are created by the fact that most means of self-protection simultaneously menace others. . . .

. . . [A]rms procured to defend can usually be used to attack. Economic and political preparedness designed to hold what one has is apt to create the potential for taking territory from others. What one state regards as insurance, the adversary will see as encirclement. This is especially true of the great powers. Any state that has interests throughout the world cannot avoid possessing the power to menace others. For example, as Admiral Mahan noted before World War I, if Britain was to have a navy sufficient to safeguard her trading routes, she inevitably would also have the ability to cut Germany off from the sea.[3] Thus even in the absence of any specific conflicts of interest between Britain and Germany, the former's security required that the latter be denied a significant aspect of great power status.

When states seek the ability to defend themselves, they get too much and too little—too much because they gain the ability to carry out aggression; too little because others, being menaced, will increase their own arms and so reduce the first state's security. Unless the requirements for offense and defense differ in kind or amount, a status quo power will desire a military posture that resembles that of an aggressor. For this reason others cannot infer from its military forces and preparations whether the state is aggressive. States therefore tend to assume the worst. The other's intentions must be considered to be co-extensive with his capabilities.

[2] Quoted in E. L. Woodward, *Great Britain and the German Navy* (Oxford: Clarendon Press, 1935), p. 84. During the Seven Years' War the French foreign minister had a similar perception of Russia although the two countries were allied. See L. Jay Oliva, *Misalliance* (New York: New York University Press, 1964), p. 98. For the argument that most deterrence theorists have overestimated the degree of interdependence among conflicts because they have overstressed the importance of resolve and paid insufficient attention to each side's interest in the issue at stake, see Robert Jervis, "Bargaining and Bargaining Tactics," in J. Roland Pennock and John Chapman, eds., *Nomos*, vol. 14: *Coercion* (Chicago: Aldine Atherton, 1972), pp. 281–83.

[3] Cited in Bernard Brodie, *War and Politics* (New York: Macmillan Co., 1973), p. 345.

What he can do to harm the state, he will do (or will do if he gets the chance). So to be safe, the state should buy as many weapons as it can afford.

But since both sides obey the same imperatives, attempts to increase one's security by standing firm and accumulating more arms will be self-defeating. . . .

These unintended and undesired consequences of actions meant to be defensive constitute the "security dilemma" that Herbert Butterfield sees as that "absolute predicament" that "lies in the very geometry of human conflict. . . . [H]ere is the basic pattern for all narratives of human conflict, whatever other patterns may be superimposed upon it later." From this perspective, the central theme of international relations is not evil but tragedy. States often share a common interest, but the structure of the situation prevents them from bringing about the mutually desired situation. This view contrasts with the school of realism represented by Hans Morgenthau and Reinhold Niebuhr, which sees the drive for power as a product of man's instinctive will to dominate others. As John Herz puts it, "It is a mistake to draw from the universal phenomenon of competition for power the conclusion that there is actually such a thing as an innate 'power instinct.' Basically it is the mere instinct of self-preservation which, in the vicious circle [of the security dilemma], leads to competition for ever more power."[4]

Arms races are only the most obvious manifestation of this spiral. The competition for colonies at the end of the nineteenth century was fueled by the security dilemma. Even if all states preferred the status quo to a division of the unclaimed areas, each also preferred expansion to running the risk of being excluded. The desire for security may also lead states to weaken potential rivals, a move that can create the menace it was designed to ward off. For example, because French statesmen feared what they thought to be the inevitable German attempt to regain the position she lost in World War I, they concluded that Germany had to be kept weak. The effect of such an unyielding policy, however, was to make the Germans less willing to accept their new position and therefore to decrease France's long-run security. Finally, the security dilemma can not only create conflicts and tensions but also provide the dynamics triggering war. If technology and strategy are such that each side believes that the state that strikes first will have a decisive advantage, even a state that is fully satisfied with the status quo may start a war out of fear that the alternative to doing so is not peace, but an attack by its adversary. And, of course, if each side is aware of the advantages of striking first, even mild crises are likely to end in war. This was one of the immediate causes of World War I, and contemporary military experts have devoted much thought and money to avoiding the recurrence of such destabilizing incentives.

If much of deterrence theory can be seen in terms of the game of Chicken, the spiral theorists are more impressed with the relevance of the Prisoner's Dilemma. Although they realize that the current situation is not exactly like the Prisoner's

[4] Herbert Butterfield, *History and Human Relations* (London: Collins, 1951), pp. 19–20; Wolfers, *Discord and Collaboration* (Baltimore: Johns Hopkins Press, 1962), p. 84; John Herz, *Political Realism and Political Idealism* (Chicago: University of Chicago Press, 1959), p. 4.

Dilemma because of the unacceptable costs of war, they believe that the central characteristic of current world politics is that, if each state pursues its narrow self-interest with a narrow conception of rationality, all states will be worse off than they would be if they cooperated. Not only would cooperation lead to a highler level of total benefits—and this is of no concern to a self-interested actor—but it would lead to each individual actor's being better off than he would be if the relations were more conflictful. States are then seen as interdependent in a different way than is stressed by the theorists of deterrence; either they cooperate with each other, in which case they all make significant gains, or they enter into a conflict and all suffer losses. A second point highlighted by the Prisoner's Dilemma is that cooperative arrangements are not likely to be reached through coercion. Threats and an adversary posture are likely to lead to counteractions with the ultimate result that both sides will be worse off than they were before. . . . [S]tates must employ and develop ingenuity, trust, and institutions if they are to develop their common interests without undue risks to their security.

PSYCHOLOGICAL DYNAMICS

. . . Contemporary spiral theorists argue that psychological pressures explain why arms and tensions cycles proceed as if people were not thinking. Once a person develops an image of the other—especially a hostile image of the other—ambiguous and even discrepant information will be assimilated to that image. . . . [P]eople perceive what they expect to be present. If they think that a state is hostile, behavior that others might see as neutral or friendly will be ignored, distorted, or seen as attempted duplicity. This cognitive rigidity reinforces the consequences of international anarchy.

Although we noted earlier that it is usually hard to draw inferences about a state's intentions from its military posture, decision-makers in fact often draw such inferences when they are unwarranted. They frequently assume . . . that the arms of others indicate aggressive intentions. So an increase in the other's military forces makes the state doubly insecure—first, because the other has an increased capability to do harm, and, second, because this behavior is taken to show that the other is not only a potential threat but is actively contemplating hostile actions.

But the state does not apply this reasoning to its own behavior. A peaceful state knows that it will use its arms only to protect itself, not to harm others. It further assumes that others are fully aware of this. As John Foster Dulles put it: "Khrushchev does not need to be convinced of our good intentions. He knows we are not aggressors and do not threaten the security of the Soviet Union." . . .[5]

In fact, others are not so easily reassured. . . . Herbert Butterfield catches the way these beliefs drive the spiral of arms and hostility:

[5] Quoted in Richard Nixon, *Six Crises* (Garden City, N.Y.: Doubleday, 1962), p. 62.

It is the peculiar characteristic of the . . . Hobbesian fear . . . that you yourself may vividly feel the terrible fear that you have of the other party, but you cannot enter into the other man's counter-fear, or even understand why he should be particularly nervous. For you know that you yourself mean him no harm, and that you want nothing from him save guarantees for your own safety; and it is never possible for you to realize or remember properly that since he cannot see the inside of your mind, he can never have the same assurance of your intentions that you have. As this operates on both sides the Chinese puzzle is complete in all its interlockings and neither party can see the nature of the predicament he is in, for each only imagines that the other party is being hostile and unreasonable.[6]

Because statesmen believe that others will interpret their behavior as they intend it and will share their view of their own state's policy, they are led astray in two reinforcing ways. First, their understanding of the impact of their own state's policy is often inadequate—i.e. differs from the views of disinterested observers—and, second, they fail to realize that other states' perceptions are also skewed. Although actors are aware of the difficulty of making their threats and warnings credible, they rarely believe that others will misinterpret behavior that is meant to be more compatible with the other's interests. Because we cannot easily establish an objective analysis of the state's policy, these two effects are difficult to disentangle. But for many purposes this does not matter because both pressures push in the same direction and increase the differences between the way the state views its behavior and the perceptions of others. . . . .

The psychological dynamics do not, however, stop here. If the state believes that others know that it is not a threat, it will conclude that they will arm or pursue hostile policies only if they are aggressive. For if they sought only security they would welcome, or at least not object to, the state's policy. Thus an American senator who advocated intervening in Russia in the summer of 1918 declared that if the Russians resisted this move it would prove that "Russia is already Germanized."[7] . . .

When the state believes that the other knows that it is not threatening the other's legitimate interests. disputes are likely to produce antagonism out of all proportion to the intrinsic importance of the issue at stake. Because the state does not think that there is any obvious reason why the other should oppose it, it will draw inferences of unprovoked hostility from even minor conflicts. Thus the belief that the Open Door policy was in China's interest as well as in America's made the United States react strongly to a Chinese regime that disagreed. If, on the other hand, each side recognizes that its policies threaten some of the other's values, it will not interpret the other's reaction as indicating aggressive intent or total hostility and so will be better able to keep their conflict limited.

The perceptions and reactions of the other side are apt to deepen the misunderstanding and the conflict. For the other, like the state, will assume that its adversary knows that it is not a threat. So, like the state, it will do more than increase its arms—it will regard the state's explanation of its behavior as making

---

[6] Butterfield, *History and Human Relations,* pp. 19–20.

[7] Quoted in Peter Filene, *Americans and the Soviet Experiment, 1917–1933* (Cambridge, Mass.: Harvard University Press, 1967), p. 43.

no sense and will see the state as dangerous and hostile. When the Soviets consolidated their hold over Czechoslovakia in 1948, they knew this harmed Western values and expected some reaction. But the formation of NATO and the explanation given for this move were very alarming. Since the Russians assumed that the United States saw the situation the same way they did, the only conclusion they could draw was that the United States was even more dangerous than they had thought. As George Kennan put the Soviet analysis in a cable to Washington:

> It seemed implausible to the Soviet leaders, knowing as they did the nature of their own approach to the military problem, and assuming that the Western powers must have known it too, that defensive considerations alone could have impelled the Western governments to give the relative emphasis they actually gave to a program irrelevant in many respects to the outcome of the political struggle in Western Europe (on which Moscow was staking everything) and only partially justified, as Moscow saw it, as a response to actual Soviet intentions. . . . The Kremlin leaders were attempting in every possible way to weaken and destroy the structure of the non-Communist world. In the course of this endeavor they were up to many things which gave plenty of cause for complaint on the part of Western statesmen. They would not have been surprised if these things had been made the touchstone of Western reaction. But why, they might ask, were they being accused precisely of the one thing they had *not* done, which was to plan, as yet, to conduct an overt and unprovoked invasion of Western Europe? Why was the imputation to them of this intention being put forward as the rationale for Western rearmament? Did this not imply some ulterior purpose . . . ?[8]

. . . This perspective leads to speculation about possible Soviet perceptions of the American alert at the end of the 1973 Arab-Israeli war. The alert was justified by the claim that the Russians were threatening to send troops to Egypt. If this was a real danger, the American response may have been appropriate. But if Russia was not seriously contemplating this measure, an unfortunate misunderstanding would have been produced.[9] For in this case Russia probably would have assumed that the United States knew that there was no danger. Why, then, she would ask herself, did the United States mobilize? Either because she had militant plans of her own or because she wanted to humiliate Russia by later claiming that her vigorous actions had made Russia retreat. This inference could be avoided only if Russia realized that the United States had overestimated the challenge she was posing. . . .

The explication of these psychological dynamics adds to our understanding of international conflict, but incurs a cost. The benefit is in seeing how the basic security dilemma becomes overlaid by reinforcing misunderstandings as each side comes to believe that not only is the other a potential menace, as it must be in a setting of anarchy, but that the other's behavior has shown that it is an active enemy. The inability to recognize that one's own actions could be seen as menacing and the concomitant belief that the other's hostility can only be explained by its aggressiveness help explain how conflicts can easily expand beyond that

[8] *Memoirs*, vol. 2: *1950–1963* (Boston: Little, Brown, 1972), pp. 335–36. Kennan also stresses the ideologically rooted Soviet predispositions to see Western aggressiveness.

[9] Ray Cline, who was Director of Intelligence and Research in the State Department when these events occurred, argues that the evidence available to him did not indicate that the Soviets were going to intervene. "Policy Without Intelligence," *Foreign Policy* 17 (Winter 1974–75), 132–33.

which an analysis of the objective situation would indicate is necessary. But the cost of these insights is the slighting of the role of the system in inducing conflict and a tendency to assume that the desire for security, rather than expansion, is the prime goal of most states. . . . [S]piral theorists, like earlier students of preju- dice, stereotypes, and intergroup relations, have given a psychological explanation for perceptions of threat without adequate discussion of whether these perceptions are warranted. . . .

. . . For a variety of reasons, many of which have been discussed earlier, nations' security requirements can clash. While an understanding of the security dilemma and psychological dynamics will dampen some arms-hostility spirals, it will not change the fact that some policies aimed at security will threaten others. To call the incompatibility that results from such policies "illusory" is to misun- derstand the nature of the problem and to encourage the illusion that if the states only saw themselves and others more objectively they could attain their common interest. . . .

13

Soviet-American Relations: The Politics of Discord and Collaboration

GEORGE F. KENNAN

In this article, George F. Kennan interprets the broad historical record of Soviet-American relations as one punctuated by misunderstandings and missed opportunities for reconciliation. Although recognizing the threat the Soviet Union poses to the United States, he concludes that the best explanation for shifts in United States policy toward the Soviet Union is to be found, not in changes in the nature of the Soviet regime or its foreign policy behavior, but in the responses of the American professional political establishment to the pressures of influential lobbies and minorities at home. Kennan is professor emeritus at the Institute for Advanced Study at Princeton University. Former United States ambassador to the Soviet Union and Yugoslavia, he is one of the leading Western scholars of Russian affairs. *The Nuclear Delusion* (1982) is among the most recent of his many books and articles.

The second Russian revolution of 1917 (actually not a "revolution" but the Bolshevik–Communist seizure of power in the two greatest Russian cities) took place in the highly confused international atmosphere of the final year of World War I. It was followed by a three-year period of even greater confusion in Russian internal affairs, marked by such things as the Russian civil war, the Allied intervention, the Russo-Polish war of 1920, and a famine. It was not until 1921 that things sorted themselves out sufficiently to make it clear that the Communists were at least firmly installed throughout most of the former empire and to confront the American government with the necessity of clarifying its attitude toward the newly established Communist regime.

For the next twelve years—Republican years, all of them—the policy adopted in Washington was a simple one: no diplomatic recognition; no official relations at all. The principal reasons for this attitude were two. The first was the refusal of the Soviet regime to accept any obligation to meet the debts of previous Russian regimes or the claims arising from the Soviet nationalization of foreign properties in Russia. The second was the resentment engendered by the world revolutionary pretensions of the Soviet regime. After 1923, the promotion of world revolution gradually ceased, to be sure, to be the prime motivation of Soviet foreign policy. But the inflammatory rhetoric remained. So did the intensive efforts at instigation, support, and manipulation of Communist activities in other countries. The shameless hypocrisy with which the Communist Party leaders attempted to deny responsibility for these activities, pretending that the Communist International was something over which they, in their governmental positions, had no control, was offensive to much American opinion, as was also the scarcely concealed contempt and hostility for all "capitalist" countries which rang through so much official Soviet rhetoric. In all of this were to be found the reasons for the decade-long denial of American diplomatic recognition to the Soviet regime.

Franklin Roosevelt, coming into office in 1933, soon changed the American policy. The change was explained by two facets of his thinking. He cared very little, in the first place, about the reasons that had animated his Republican predecessors in matters of policy toward the Soviet Union. The trouble over "debts and claims" disturbed him only insofar as he felt himself obliged to respond to congressional pressures along that line. Nor did the activities of the Communist International bother him much. Politician and pragmatist that he was, he was well aware of the political insignificance of Soviet-inspired radical activities in the United States ("Stamp out Trotskyism in Kansas" was a flaming headline in the *Daily Worker* one day in the early thirties). What seemed to him more important was the shadows of German national socialism and Japanese militarism rising on the horizon—both so offensive to influential segments of American opinion. It seemed to FDR that Americans had a bond in this respect with the Soviet leaders, who had their own reasons for fearing these emerging political forces. This bond, he thought, could be usefully developed by the establishment of diplomatic relations with the Soviet regime. So, at the end of 1933, after skillfully placating American opinion with the smoke screen of the largely meaningless exchanges of diplomatic notes known as the "Litvinov agreements," he proceeded to "recognize Russia": that is, to send an ambassador to Moscow, and to receive a Soviet one in Washington, thus establishing the formal diplomatic relationship that has endured to the present day.

During the initial years of this new relationship—the remaining years of the 1930s—the experiment of mutual diplomatic representation was not a particularly successful one. At the moment when relations were established, the Soviet leaders had been assailed by fears that the Japanese might be preparing to attack Russia's eastern provinces. This had accounted for some of their conciliatory disposition at that time. It soon became apparent, however, that the danger was less urgent than they had thought, and their enthusiasm for the new relationship declined. Little came of the rosy assurances embodied in the Litvinov agreements. Initially welcomed with an unusual show of cordiality, the new American Embassy in Moscow soon fell victim to the routine treatment of isolation, clandestine observation, and avoidance of all but the most perfunctory official contact to which foreign diplomatic representatives have traditionally been subjected in Moscow. The mission came to serve, in those years of the 1930s, primarily as a place where a group of young American Foreign Service officers learned a few things about Russia and went through that unique schooling by means of which the Soviet government has contrived, over a period of half a century, to educate and to graduate from their period of service in Moscow one class after another of embittered diplomats, sending them out into the world to preach vigilance against the wiles and pretenses of Soviet policy.

The years immediately following American recognition were marked in the Soviet Union by the fearful and indescribable orgy of official terror and brutality known as "the purges." Their effect on the Soviet–American relationship was mixed. On those Americans who lived in Moscow at the time, the effect was one of utter and enduring horror coupled with a profound conviction that any regime capable of perpetrating such monstrous cruelties against its own people, and indeed against itself, was to be dealt with only at arm's length and with the utmost circumspection. That Franklin Roosevelt ever fully understood the nature and significance of these nightmarish events is doubtful. He appears never wholly to have departed, even in those terrible years, from his conviction that Stalin was probably really not such a bad fellow at heart, that what was needed to set him on the right track was a bit more relaxed treatment—a bit less suspicion and more cordiality than a snobbish upper-class American plutocracy (as FDR saw it) had been inclined to concede. Roosevelt seems never fully to have understood the limitations that rest upon the possibilities for intimacy or friendship with people who have a great deal of blood on their hands. This failure of understanding was to some extent shared by much of the remainder of the American liberal community. A greater shock was received by that community, actually, with the news of the conclusion of the German–Soviet Non-Aggression Pact, in 1939. Mistreatment of the Soviet population was one thing (much could be excused in the name of the Revolution), but that the Soviet Union, which for years had held itself out as the greatest opponent of German nazism and had encouraged others to go even further in that stance, should now have turned around and suddenly, after highly conspiratorial preparations, made a cynical deal with Hitler at the expense of the Poles and the Baltic peoples was a great blow not only to pro-Soviet liberal circles in the United States but to many Communists, there and elsewhere, as well.

Yet all this abruptly changed again when, in 1941, both the Soviet Union and the United States found themselves (involuntarily) at war with Nazi Germany. The "Russians" became, almost overnight, our great and good allies. The image of Stalin changed instantly from that of the "crafty giant" Churchill once correctly described to that of a benevolent hero of the resistance to Hitlerism. War psychology, to which the American public is no less prone than any other, at once led to the discovery of previously unknown virtues in a regime that was also now at war with America's principal military enemy. Considering that the Soviet Union was absorbing some 80 percent of the Nazi war effort while we and our Western allies were, up to 1944, unable even to mount a second front, the American official community (and particularly the military leadership) generally felt that the most important thing was to "get on" (that was the term then commonly used) with Moscow, politically and propagandistically as well as in point of military aid. In these circumstances, nothing was too good, in 1942 and 1943, for our valiant Soviet allies. Anyone who in those years attempted to remind others that Soviet ideas about the postwar future might be seriously in conflict with our own was sternly admonished that in wartime we Americans did not "take our eyes off the ball''—the ball being, in this instance, the earliest possible total defeat of Germany. Gone, now, were the resentments over Soviet aspirations for world revolution. Soviet demands, advanced by Stalin during the war, for the westward extension of the boundaries of the Soviet Union were accepted by Britain, and silently (though not happily) acquiesced to by the United States.

In the ensuing years of 1944 and 1945, other far-reaching concessions were made. The bitter implications of Soviet behavior at the time of the Warsaw uprising were largely ignored. There must be no attempt, while hostilities were in progress, to discuss realistically with our Soviet allies the sordid questions of the political arrangements that should prevail in Central and Eastern Europe when the war was over. Such discussions, it was insisted, might be destructive of the wartime intimacy; matters of this nature were to be taken care of, after the termination of hostilities, by general political collaboration among the United States, Britain, the Soviet Union, and—at FDR's insistence—Chiang Kai-shek's China.

It is small wonder that in the face of such wishful and unrealistic attitudes there was, in the immediate post-hostilities period, a rude awakening and disillusionment. There is no need to recount the details. Soviet leaders, partially confused by the official pro-Soviet American rhetoric of the wartime years and misled by the ease with which they had obtained Western agreement to the extension of their borders and the ruthless consolidation of their political domination in the occupied areas, were somewhat dizzy with success. They were not sure how far they would be permitted to go. Their dreams ran to the acquisition of a dominant political position in Germany and the remainder of Western Europe. They had no thought of trying to achieve this by force of arms. Their thoughts were rather of political devices such as acquiring a share of the control over the Ruhr, taking advantage of the strong positions of the French and Italian Communist parties, exploiting Soviet military-control powers in Berlin and Vienna, and penetrating Western labor-union, intellectual, and student movements. They had, after all, been encouraged to expect an extensive withdrawal of American forces and of American involvement in European affairs when the war was over. This, they thought, would create a serious political vacuum; the rest might be accomplished, or so it was hoped, by the clever, ruthless exploitation of the political cards they now held in their hands.

Actually, those cards were not so strong as the Soviet leaders supposed. This was at once revealed by the Marshall Plan initiative, in 1947–1948, which wholly frustrated any dreams of the political takeover of Western Europe. The remaining Soviet efforts of the 1940s, outstandingly the crackdown on Czechoslovakia and the mounting of the Berlin blockade, were defensive in inspiration—attempts to play Moscow's last major political cards in anticipation of what they saw looming before them: a new division of power across the European continent.

These attempts reflected no Soviet desire for a full-fledged military showdown, or even for a division of the continent into opposing military alliances. It is entirely possible that had the Western European countries, while resisting the Berlin blockade, continued to concentrate steadily on Europe's economic and political recovery, Stalin, whose country had the most pressing need for at least several years of peaceful reconstruction, would have been prepared to make extensive compromises—compromises that would at least have obviated the necessity for such a military division of the continent. But the Western Europeans, conditioned by the experience of centuries to see any serious international tension as the forerunner of a war, immediately interpreted the existing evidence of Soviet political recalcitrance as a menace of invasion. And we Americans, always high-mindedly disinclined to make compromises with evil (except, of course, in our own domestic politics), were disinclined to go in for any political deals with what was rapidly coming to be seen as "the enemy." Thus the North Atlantic Treaty Organization came into existence, to be responded to, in its turn, by the Warsaw Pact. And thus the decision to take Western Germany into NATO, and to re-arm it, produced the inevitable countermeasures with respect to East Germany. These developments, together with the revelation, in 1949, of a Soviet nuclear capability, followed by the Korean War (the origins and purposes of which were seriously misinterpreted in the West), laid a firm and unshakable foundation for the militarization of the American attitude toward the Soviet problem that has been the dominant feature of American diplomacy ever since.

This might be a good place to pause and note the full import of the changes that by the end of the 1940s had come over the American-Soviet relationship. The factors that had been the determining ones in the early years of the relationship had been either removed or greatly weakened. The problem of what was once called "debts and claims" had been eclipsed by the traumatic experiences of World War II, and was rapidly falling victim to the tendency of international life that so often causes "insoluble" problems, if allowed to remain long enough unsolved, gradually to lose their significance. And as for "world revolution": the Comintern, once the symbol of all that Americans objected to in Soviet policy, had by this time been formally abolished. It had been Stalin's custom, in any case, to use the subservient foreign Communist parties as instruments for the support of Soviet foreign policy rather than as vehicles for the serious promotion of revolution. With the abolition of the Comintern Moscow's relations with those foreign parties, previously channeled through the Comintern, had been turned over partly to the Soviet secret police, which used them for espionage and for other forms of its chartered skulduggery, and partly to a section of the apparatus of the Soviet Central Committee, to which was given the unpleasant task of holding the hands of the foreign Communist leaders and assuring their continued subservience while preventing them from either unduly influencing or embarrassing Soviet policy-makers. In these circumstances, no informed person, either in the Soviet Union or elsewhere, any longer took seriously Moscow's theoretical and rhetorical commitment to world revolution.

With these issues out of the way, the relationship was now destined to be shaped primarily by two factors: one old, one new.

The old factor was what might be called the substructure of tensions, misunderstandings, irritations, and minor conflicts flowing from the great disparity between the two political systems, not only in ideology but, even more important, in traditions, habits, customs, and methodology. This factor had never been absent at any time since the founding of the Soviet regime (indeed, to some extent it had been present in the czarist period as well). It continued to weigh upon the Soviet–American relationship in the postwar years, even in the post-Stalin period, almost as heavily as it had before the war. It must be regarded as a permanent burden on the relationship, probably never to be wholly overcome, certainly not to be importantly mitigated in any short space of time.

The new factor was the military and geopolitical situation arising from the circumstances of the war and its aftermath: a situation destined, as it turned out, to overshadow all other aspects of the relationship in intensity, in endurance, and in gravity—gravity for the two countries and for the world at large.

Prior to World War II, the respective military situations and interests of the two powers had not constituted a significant factor in their relations. The Soviet Union was then not a competitor or a threat to the United States in naval power; the same thing applied, the other way around, when it came to land power. By the end of the 1920s, the Soviet Union had acquired, to be sure, a formidable land army (in the Russian tradition)—an army that was already the greatest, numerically, in the world. But the two countries were so widely separated—in the West by the Atlantic Ocean and the intervening powers of Europe, in the East by the Pacific Ocean plus China and Japan—that there was no consciousness on either side of a serious military rivalry.

With the conclusion of World War II, all that changed. The final stages of military operations had enabled the Soviet Union to overcome the communications-poor barrier of the territory between the Baltic and Black seas which had historically separated Central and Western Europe from the Russian armies. The traditional military power of Russia, now represented by the Soviet Union, had been projected into the heart of Europe, where there was nothing to oppose it at the time but a number of Western European peoples either shattered by the recent Hitlerian occupation or militarily exhausted or both. This Western Europe was unable to restore either its political self-confidence or its capacity for self-defense without American support. And the absence of any realistic agreement among the victors on a political future for the defeated Germany, or indeed for Central and Eastern Europe generally, left Soviet and American military forces confronting each other across a line through the middle of North-Central Europe—a line never originally meant to become the central demarcation of a divided Europe but destined, as we now know, to remain just that for at least several decades into the future.

This major geopolitical displacement marked a fundamental change in the Soviet–American relationship. It did not, as many seem to have supposed, render either necessary or inevitable a war between the two powers—then or at any other time. But it injected into the relationship a new factor: an immediate military proximity, made all the more delicate and dangerous insofar as it was superimposed upon the permanent substructure of friction referred to above. If, before the war, Washington had dealt with the Soviet Union primarily as a revolutionary political force, it was now obliged to deal with it as a traditional military great power, suddenly and unexpectedly poised on the very edge of America's own newly acquired sphere of political–military interest.

And this new geopolitical relationship was burdened by several further complications—all new, all serious.

The end of the war, in the first place, had left the United States with little in the way of military manpower (in view of its precipitous demobilization) but with a bloated military superstructure, and particularly with an expanded apparatus for military planning, for which use now had to be found. With Germany and Japan out of the way, there was need of a new prospective opponent with relation to whose military personality a new American military posture could be designed. The Soviet Union was the obvious, indeed the only plausible, candidate.

It is said that Woodrow Wilson was shocked to learn, in 1915, that the Army War College was studying plans for wars against other countries. The story, sometimes cited as an example of Mr. Wilson's naiveté, seems to be the somewhat distorted version of a real episode. But it is suggestive of a historically significant reality. When a military planner selects another country as the leading hypothetical opponent of his own country—the opponent against whom military preparations and operations are theoretically to be directed—the discipline of his profession obliges him to endow that opponent with extreme hostility and the most formidable of capabilities. In tens of thousands of documents, this image of the opponent is re-created, and depicted in all its implacable formidability, until it becomes hopelessly identified with the real country in question. In this way, the planner's hypothesis becomes, imperceptibly, the politician's and the journalist's reality. Even when there is *some* degree of substance behind the hypothesis, what emerges is invariably an overdrawn and distorted image.

And so it has been in the case of the Soviet Union, with the result that what began as a limited political conflict of interests and aspirations has evolved into a perceived total military hostility; and what was in actuality a Soviet armed-forces establishment with many imperfections and many limitations on its capabilities has come gradually to be perceived as an overpowering paragon of military efficiency, standing at the beck and call of a political regime consumed with no other purpose than to do us maximum harm. This sort of distortion has magnified inordinately, in the public eye, the dimensions of what was initially a serious political problem, and has created, and fed, the impression that the problem is one not to be solved otherwise than by some sort of a military showdown.

A second complication—and a tremendous one—has been the addition of nuclear weaponry to the arsenals of the two powers, and their competition in the development of it. This form of weaponry, with its suicidal and apocalyptic implications, has thrown such uncertainty and confusion into the whole field of military planning, and has aroused such extreme anxieties and such erratic reactions on the part of the public, that it has come close to obscuring the real political, and even military, conflicts of interest between the United States and the Soviet Union behind a fog of nuclear fears, suspicions, and fancied scenarios.

Finally, there was one other effect, this time political, of the outcome of World War II that must also be noted. In the two decades before the war, the western borders of the USSR were essentially those of the old Grand Duchy of Muscovy. They corresponded, in a rough way, to the real ethnic line between those who might be called "Russians" (Little and Great) and those to whom that term could not properly be applied. The wartime extension of the Soviet borders far to the west, together with the acquisition and consolidation of a Soviet hegemony over all of Eastern, and parts of Central, Europe, brought into the Soviet orbit a number of non-Russian nationalities—some formerly included in the czarist empire, some not—very much against the will of a great many of their members, especially those who fled and found refuge in the United States. The result was to add materially to those existing American political factions (some highly vocal and not without political influence) that were animated by a burning hatred of the Soviet Union and were anxious to enlist the political and military resources of the United States for the destruction of the Soviet empire.

In order that this new proximity of Soviet and American forces, together with its various complications, might be removed, and a more normal and less dangerous situation created in Central and Eastern Europe, three sorts of agreements would have been necessary between the United States and its allies, on the one hand, and the Soviet Union and (for formality's sake) its allies, on the other.

One would have been an agreement to assure the extensive retirement of both Soviet and American forces from the center of Europe. The Soviet side would never have agreed to this except on the condition that the Germany thus freed from the forces of the two powers should be a neutralized and disarmed one, not in alliance with the United States. But this was a condition that the Western powers, for their part, were never prepared even to consider; and with the rearming of West Germany and the consolidation of its position as a member of NATO, all practical possibility for meeting this requirement passed, in any case. This precluded, as early as the first years of the 1950s, and has precluded ever since, any effective agreement over the German problem.

The second essential agreement would have been one assuring the extensive dismantling of the Soviet hegemony in Eastern Europe—i.e., the concession to the Eastern European governments of a full freedom of action including at least the right to change their social systems at will. To this, too, Moscow would never have agreed in the absence of a settlement of the German problem.

The third agreement would have been one outlawing nuclear weapons and assuring their removal from the arsenals of all countries, first and foremost those of the United States and the Soviet Union. However, such has been the commitment of the United States government to nuclear weaponry as an indispensable component of its defense force that there has never been a time since 1950 when that government would have been prepared to consider its complete outlawing. The problem was subsequently further complicated by the proliferation of nuclear weapons into the hands of several other governments; so that today, the level of the largest of these peripheral arsenals constitutes the floor beneath which the nuclear arsenals of the two leading nuclear powers could in any case not be expected to sink.

In these circumstances, there has never been any conceivable basis for a one-time, general settlement of the military–political stalemate that World War II produced. It would obviously require some major alteration in the entire balance of power—some drastic internal breakdown or some new and overpowering external involvement of one side or the other—to make possible, even theoretically, any immediate untying of this knot. The peaceful resolution of this problem is conceivable today only under the benevolent influence of the passage of time, supported by such efforts as mere men can make to promote a greater measure of background confidence and understanding between the governments involved.

Given this situation, the best that men of good will were able to do over the two decades following the death of Stalin was to tinker around the edges of this unresolved and (for the moment) unresolvable military–political deadlock, trying, wherever opportunity seemed to present itself, to narrow the area to which the disagreements applied or to reduce their dangerousness (for dangerous they were and are) in other ways. This a number of these men did; and their successes, while always limited and modest, were more numerous and in some instances more extensive than many today recall.

In Khrushchev's time, there was, outstandingly, the negotiation of the Austrian peace treaty—a product of Khrushchev's own relative good will plus the patient efforts of several excellent Western negotiators, among them our own ambassador, Llewellyn Thompson, to whose exceptional skills and insights Europe probably owes more than to those of any American of his time. This happily removed one strategically placed European country from the arena of Soviet–American conflict. In addition, there was the signing of the first nuclear-test-ban treaty, in 1963; and there were several early arrangements in the field of cultural exchange.

The ensuing Brezhnev era saw, of course, the spectacular summitry of Messrs. Nixon and Kissinger, marking the successful conclusion of a whole series of agreements in a number of fields—cultural, scientific, technological, and military—culminating in the first SALT agreement of 1972 and the initiation of negotiations for the second one. A number of these agreements proved valuable in one degree or another, and some might have yielded even greater positive results had they been given a longer period of trial and a bit more commitment from the American side. They were supplemented, of course, by the West German–Soviet agreements concluded around the same time, largely under the leadership of Willy Brandt—agreements that, among other things, gave to the western sectors of Berlin, for the first time, reasonably dependable communications with the remainder of West Germany, and thus alleviated one of the greatest, and least necessary, of the dangers of the postwar period.

These were, I reiterate, modest and limited gains. Their real significance was obscured, rather than enhanced, by the overdramatization to which they were often subjected, under the misleading heading of "détente." The Soviet–American relationship continued, of course, to be burdened at all times by the permanent substructure of friction. But the results of all these efforts to mitigate the prevailing tensions and to improve the atmosphere of Soviet–American relations were on balance positive, so much so that the record of achievement up to 1974 provided in itself no reason why they should not have been continued—rather the contrary.

This, however, was not to be. As we all know, the latter part of 1974 witnessed, together with the Watergate scandal, the beginning of a deterioration of

Soviet–American relations that has lasted [into the early 1980s]—a deterioration in which many of the achievements of the preceding years have been destroyed.

The deterioration was inaugurated by the Jackson-Vanik amendment to the 1974 Trade Reform Act—an amendment that had the effect of knocking out the Soviet–American trade agreement already negotiated in 1972 and of denying to the Soviet Union the concession of the normal customs treatment the agreement provided. Since then, there has been nothing but one long and dreary process of retrogression: rapidly declining trade; neglect or abandonment of cultural-exchange arrangements; throttling down of personal contacts; failure of ratification of the second SALT agreement; reckless acceleration of the weapons race; demonstrative tilting toward Communist China; angry polemic and propagandistic exchanges, all culminating in the shrill denunciations and various anti-Soviet "sanctions" of the Carter and Reagan administrations. Of the list of constructive principles agreed upon eight years ago [1974] by Nixon and Brezhnev for the future peaceful and productive shaping of the relationship, not one is left that Mr. Nixon's successors have not denounced or abandoned, or both.

How is this sudden turnabout to be explained? The search for the answers to that question is a revealing exercise.

Was there, perhaps, some change in the nature of the Soviet regime with which we were dealing —some change that, alone, would have warranted a drastic departure from previous American policy? Not at all. On the contrary: the Brezhnev regime was marked expressly by an extraordinary steadiness and consistency of behavior. The entire personality of the Soviet structure of power, as distinct from the Soviet society, has shown very little alteration, in fact, since the first years of the post-Stalin epoch.

Was it perhaps that the men who conducted American policy in the years prior to 1974 were naive, or affected by pro-Soviet sympathies, or for some other reason blind to the negative sides of the Soviet personality and behavior? Again, the answer is no. These men were perfectly well aware of the negative aspects of the political regime with which they were dealing. They simply considered that in the light of the prevailing military–political stalemate, there were limits to the usefulness of heroic gestures of petulance and indignation over these various disagreements, whereas it might be useful to take advantage of whatever opportunities seemed to present themselves for the mitigation of existing tensions in ways not adverse to American interests. Their efforts were often, admittedly, experimental. Not all were fully expected to work out; but most of them did. And the gains were considered to be worth whatever minor sacrifices or concessions were involved.

Was it, then, that American public opinion had revolted against the policies pursued in earlier years? Here, too, the answer is no. There was at all times, of course, a hard-line faction, or cluster of factions, not very large but violent in its opinions, that opposed any and every form of negotiation or compromise with Moscow, and looked to military intimidation, if not to the actual use of force, as the only means through which anything useful could be accomplished in relations with the Soviet Union. This faction had always existed; and it had recently been strengthened by new flurries of interest in some quarters in the Soviet "dissidents" and in the human-rights question. But the bulk of the American people had seemed to accept with understanding, if not with enthusiasm, these various efforts to diminish tension and to narrow the dangers of the military–political standoff. Even many of those who were not convinced initially of the usefulness of such efforts were willing to see them given a try by people—namely, the various American statesmen and diplomats in question—who, they thought, knew more, or ought to know more, about the problem of Soviet–American relations than they themselves did, and who deserved a certain initial margin of confidence. This, plainly, was an instance in which people were inclined, by and large, to respond to political leadership; and there is no apparent reason to suppose that if that leadership had wished to continue to conduct, and to explain, the sort of policy that had prevailed prior to 1974, it would have failed to continue to enjoy an adequate measure of public acquiescence.

If one asks those who have presided over this process of deterioration why they viewed it as necessary or desirable, one receives a variety of answers. There was the human-rights problem; there were the restrictions on Jewish emigration; there were the expansionist tendencies of the Soviet regime with relation to the Third World; there was Afghanistan; there was the Jaruzelsky take-over in Poland; there was, above all, the continued Soviet military buildup.

There is some degree of substance in most, if not all, of these charges, but not very much, particularly if taken in relation to Soviet policies prior to that benchmark of 1974. Certainly, there was no change in Soviet behavior in any of these respects drastic enough to justify a change in American policy as abrupt and drastic as the one that took place.

Human rights? The policies applied in the mid-1970s and since in this respect have been no more severe than in the preceding decades, and have actually been far more lenient than anything Russia knew in the Stalin era, when this was scarcely an issue in Soviet–American relations at all.

The treatment of Jews, and the problem of Jewish emigration? In proposing their trade amendment, Jackson and Vanik chose a moment when Jewish emigration was running at the highest rate since at least the 1950s. There was no reason to conclude that, barring this effort, it would not have continued at this rate, or possibly even have increased. Nor would the amendment appear to have been in any way useful to the people on whose behalf it was ostensibly advanced. On the contrary, it would seem to have set Jewish emigration back by some five years.

Soviet "adventurism" in the Third World? I know of no evidence that Soviet efforts to gain influence with Third World regimes were any more extensive in the 1970s, or since, than they were in earlier periods of Soviet history. Least of all is it evident that they were any more successful. The methods had indeed been changing—but changing in a direction (namely, the generous export of arms and advisers) that made them depressingly similar to some of our own.

Afghanistan? Yes, of course: a crude, bungled operation; an obvious mistake of Soviet policy, with origins not entirely dissimilar to those of our own involvement in Vietnam. But not one that impinged directly on American interests, particularly if it be considered that the alternative might have been the growing influence of a Khomeini type of violently anti-American Moslem fanaticism in that part of the world. And one no more serious in its consequences than the absorption of Outer Mongolia into the Soviet sphere of interest in the 1920s, or of Tibet into Communist China at a later date, both changes to which the United States found it possible to accommodate itself without violent repercussions on the bilateral relations with the respective countries.

Poland? Yes, indeed, a tragic situation, the product of a long series of mistakes—many, though not all, on the Soviet side. But this was not a situation that was suddenly created at the end of the 1970s; nor was it worse then than in earlier years. The fact is that Moscow, after being publicly warned by our government on dozens of occasions in 1980 not to intervene militarily in Poland, actually refrained from intervening, and was punished anyway. The theory offered as justification for this—that Jaruzelsky undertook his crackdown on Moscow's orders and would not have done so in the absence of those orders—rests, so far as I am aware, solely on conjecture. And the resulting situation, while indeed onerous and even dangerous, is less so than it was a year ago, and no more so than the situation that prevailed in earlier decades.

Finally, the Soviet arms buildup? Yes, a reality, no doubt— some of it exaggerated by calculated leaks from Western military establishments, but another portion of it real enough, and parts of it, such as the mounting of the SS-20s in the western districts of the USSR, unnecessary and foolish. But this, too, did not begin in 1974, nor has the United States government done all that it could to prevent or discourage the buildup. It was, after all, we, and not the Soviet government, who declined to ratify the second SALT treaty. There was no reason why that agreement should not have been ratified (we are, after all, finding it possible to observe its provisions); and no reasons why negotiations for further such agreements could not have been put in hand long ago and with a much greater evidence of enthusiasm than the Reagan Administration has evinced. In the welter of mistakes, misconceptions, and fixations that has led to the present arms race, both sides have their hearty share of the blame; but there was never any reason why negotiations for the tempering and overcoming of this dangerous competition should not have gone forward, as they did in earlier years, without detriment to the remaining fabric of Soviet–American relations.

These points concerning the recent deterioration of relations are mentioned here because they illustrate a situation of great importance, the significance of which seems hardly to have been noted on this side of the water. This is that the fluctuations of official American attitudes and policies with relation to the Soviet Union would appear to have been responsive only in minor degree, if at all, to changes in the nature of the problem that country has presented for American statesmanship. The Soviet Union with which we declined to have relations in the 1920s was not greatly different from that which we found it possible to recognize in 1933. The Stalin regime that aroused our indignation during the Non-Aggression Pact period was precisely the same as that in which we came to discern so many virtues during the war. This latter, in its turn, was no different from the one that we discovered, at the end of the 1940s, to be a great danger to us and to the free world in general.

There was, indeed, a certain real change in the nature of the regime by virtue of the transition from Stalin to Khrushchev in the years 1953 to 1957; and this, as we have seen, was taken advantage of by American statesmen in the ensuing years. But again, the Brezhnev that Messrs. Nixon and Kissinger did such extensive business with was very much the same as the one with whom subsequent American statesmen found it impossible to collaborate at all. There were, of course, over this entire period, important gradual changes in Soviet society and even in the relations between people and regime; but these changes were not pronounced in the structure of power itself, and even less so—except in the transition from the Stalin era to the succeeding ones—in the problem that this structure of power presented for the outside world. Yet American attitudes and policies were subject to abrupt, and sometimes drastic, alterations.

All this would seem to indicate that the motivations for American policy toward the Soviet Union from the start have been primarily subjective, not objective, in origin. They have represented for the most part not reactions to the nature of a certain external phenomenon (the Soviet regime) but rather the reflections of emotional and political impulses making themselves felt on the internal American scene. And these impulses would appear to have been not of American public opinion at large (for that opinion, good-humoredly tolerant but reserved and noncommittal, has exhibited no such violent fluctuations) but of the professional political establishment. This is explicable, perhaps, to the extent that policy toward the Soviet Union has been a partisan political issue; but this has been true only to a limited extent. More important would seem to have been the momentary violence of feeling on the part of politically influential lobbies and minorities to whose pressures the politicians of the moment were inclined to pander or defer.

However that may be, the record of American policy toward the Soviet Union over the six and a half decades of the existence of that body politic gives the impression that it was not really the nature of any external problem that concerned us but rather something we were anxious to prove to ourselves, about ourselves.

It is, surely, not unreasonable to point out that this state of affairs is not adequate as a response to the problem that the Soviet Union actually presents. Indeed, it holds great dangers for this country and for others as well. The problem presented by the need for a continued peaceful co-existence on the same planet of the Soviet Union and the United States is one that would challenge even the highest resources of this country for analysis, for it must be dealt with in ways conducive not just to American national interest in the narrow sense but to peace among the various great powers—a condition without which no American interest of any sort can be served. Vital prerequisites for the successful policy of a great power are stability and consistency. Even our allies cannot be helped by a policy that lacks these qualities. If there was ever a time in the history of this country when there was no place for the sort of self-conscious posturing, and the sort of abrupt changes of concept, that have marked our reaction to Soviet power in recent decades, that time is now.

. . . With a nuclear-weapons race increasingly out of control now staring us in the face—confronted as we are with accumulations of modern weapons, nuclear and otherwise, of such monstrous destructiveness that their detonation (and weapons have a way of being detonated in the end) could well put an end to civilization—we can no longer afford to address to the problem of Soviet–American relations anything less than the best, in the way of sobriety, objective analysis, steadiness, thoughtfulness, and practicality of purpose, that our society can produce. There is not much more time for the recognition of this fact to penetrate the national consciousness. . . .

14

Do Negotiated Arms Limitations Have a Future?

BARRY M. BLECHMAN

In this article, Barry M. Blechman argues that the SALT (Strategic Arms Limitations Talks) process, which linked the United States and the Soviet Union in a mutual effort to reduce strategic arms during the 1970s, was pursued by both superpowers because it was in their interests to do so. Eventually, however, domestic groups within the United States came to oppose arms limitation because it promised more than it could deliver. Blechman concludes that only a realistic understanding of the meaning of arms limitation will produce meaningful results. Blechman is Vice President of the Roosevelt Center for American Policy Studies. An assistant director of the United States Arms Control and Disarmament Agency from 1977 through 1979, he was the first head of its policy planning staff.

[The author begins with a survey of the disappointing results of Soviet–American arms control negotiations during the Carter administration. He notes that the troubled fate of the second SALT agreement between the United States and the Soviet Union, the SALT II treaty signed by the superpowers in 1979 but never approved by the United States Senate, symbolized the apparent, and perhaps fatal, defeat of negotiated arms limitation agreements—*eds.*]

. . . Surveying the connection between U.S.-Soviet relations and the progress of arms negotiation over the past ten years, it is worth recalling the words of Vladimir S. Semyonov, who began the Soviet presentation at the first session of the Strategic Arms Limitation Talks in 1969:

> The government of the U.S.S.R. attaches great importance to the negotiations on curbing the strategic arms race. *Their positive results should undoubtedly contribute both to improvement in Soviet-American relations and in the consolidation of universal peace.*[1]

Thus, at the very outset of the talks, the concept which eventually was to break the back of the SALT process was recognized formally: linkage, the idea that progress toward arms limitation would lead to progress in other aspects of U.S.-Soviet relations and, conversely, its corollary, that cooperation (or lack of

Reprinted from Barry M. Blechman, "Do Negotiated Arms Limitations Have A Future?" *Foreign Affairs* 59 (Fall 1980), pp. 102–125. Abridged by permission of Foreign Affairs. Copyright 1980 by the Council on Foreign Relations, Inc. Originally prepared for the National Security Affairs Institute, National Defense University. Some footnotes have been deleted; others have been renumbered to appear in consecutive order.
[1] *The New York Times,* November 18, 1969, p. A16 (italics added).

cooperation) in other aspects of U.S.-Soviet relations would facilitate (or hamper) movement in arms negotiations. Both the United States and the Soviet Union have been ambivalent about "linkage." Each has stressed or de-emphasized "linkage" when it was in its own interest to do so. In the end, however, the concept took firm root in the American political system and, as a result, imposed a heavier burden on the talks than they could possibly bear; indeed, the notion implied a model of U.S.-Soviet relations which was strongly opposed by a variety of groups with powerful voices in national security decision-making.

Given their ideological origins, it would be surprising if Soviet commentators did not stress interrelationships between negotiated arms limitations and broader accommodation between the United States and the Soviet Union. From a Marxist theoretical perspective, the source of all conflict is economic and by extension political, stemming fundamentally from the existence of historically antagonistic social systems. To a Marxist theorist, the basic premise of arms control—that weapons in themselves contribute to the risk of war—is sophistry. Conflict results from the necessary clash of opposing social forces. The alleviation of conflict, therefore, can only result from broad political accommodation. By making preexisting settlements specific and legally binding, arms limitation agreements can strengthen political accommodations but they can never force new arrangements; they are the "practical embodiment" of détente, not its cause. . . .

For the most part, however, the close linkage between movement in broader political relations and progress in arms limitations which would seem to be dictated by Soviet theory has not proved to be important in practice. Most notably, in 1972 the Soviets completed SALT I as scheduled, despite the United States' mining of Haiphong and other North Vietnamese ports on the eve of the summit (an act which trapped or damaged a number of Soviet-flag merchant ships). More recently, the Soviets . . . vigorously protested U.S. attempts to link progress in arms negotiation to the curtailment of Soviet military activities in Africa, Cuba and South Asia.

To be sure, Soviet forbearance did not result either from devotion to the cause of arms limitation or from a rejection of their Marxist heritage in favor of historic American pragmatism. What did happen was that the stream of world events and the dictates of Soviet internal politics were such that the Brezhnev regime found pursuit of SALT very much in its interest, despite continued erosion of the broader context of U.S.-Soviet relations. . . .

In the United States, the experience has been just the opposite. The American theory of arms control would isolate such negotiations from politics. In theoretical terms, arms limitation talks should be viewed as technical exercises, directed at constraining the risks which weapons themselves add to existing political conflicts. As those espousing arms control made no pretense of solving political conflicts through the negotiations they proposed, they saw no relationship (other than that artificially instilled by politicians) between progress or lack of progress in settling underlying sources of conflict and progress or lack of progress in arms negotiations. Indeed, they accepted international tensions as inevitable and saw arms limitation talks simply as one way to manage their more dangerous consequences.

In practice, however, the United States has closely linked movement in arms control with broader political accommodation with the Soviet Union. Specifically, successive U.S. Administrations, perhaps reluctantly, have frequently concluded that there could not be movement in arms talks unless or until the Soviet Union modified its international behavior so as not to pose military challenges to Western interests. Examples are legion. The start of the talks, for example, planned for 1968, was delayed by the occupation of Czechoslovakia. In 1976, completion of the Vladivostok accord was deferred because of Soviet military involvement in Angola. And, despite its public protestations to the contrary, as early as 1978 the Carter Administration's positions in SALT and other arms negotiations were strongly influenced by the deterioration of U.S.-Soviet relations, punctuated by such events as the Soviet military involvement in the Horn of Africa and the East German and Cuban roles in the Shaba incident in Zaïre.

This sensitivity on the part of American policymakers should be expected in a democratic political system. Policies—especially innovative policies that run counter to traditional ways of doing business[2]—cannot be sustained without substantial political constituencies. SALT suffered more from rising uneasiness among the American populace about Soviet military power and Soviet assertiveness than from any deficiencies of its own. Never mind that SALT was the one policy instrument that conceivably could place limits on Soviet forces. The concept that prevailed in the public's mind extended the basic premise of linkage (i.e., that progress in arms control could facilitate progress in broader relations) to an assertion that if arms control was worth pursuing, it would result in broader accommodation. Since there was no evidence of such a broad accommodation, the argument ran, then obviously arms control was at least not serving its purposes and probably, in some mysterious way, was itself contributing to the problem. . . .

In effect, the SALT talks became a weathervane of U.S.-Soviet relations, the centerpiece and primary symbol of a certain model of that relationship. As such, the talks were criticized by, indeed contributed to, the creation of a coalition of dedicated opponents who fought both the treaties and the process which led to them, as much for what they implied for U.S.-Soviet relations as for whatever specific limitations they did or did not impose on American and Soviet nuclear weapons.

The 1972 treaty which placed severe limitations on antiballistic missile (ABM) systems is the key factor here. By agreeing not to deploy weapons that could create the illusion of a capability to defend against a major nuclear attack, the two nations formally recognized the probability that each would suffer unprecedented destruction in the event of a major nuclear exchange. Thus, they accepted the necessity for a certain degree of cooperation in their relations and implicitly set limits on their competition. This is not to say that they agreed to get along with one another, to end the rivalry, or anything like that; far from it. Still, they did establish a formally recognized mutual need to stop the competition from getting

---

[2] One is reminded here of former Arms Control and Disarmament Agency Director Paul Warnke's characterization of arms control as "an unnatural act."

out of hand, to avoid confrontations that could contain a real danger of nuclear war.

The ABM treaty is thus a central element in the quest for cooperative U.S.-Soviet relations. The continuing SALT process supported the viability of the ABM treaty; limits on defensive weapons probably cannot be sustained in the presence of a wide-open offensive weapons race. SALT thus came to symbolize America's acceptance of the need to get along with the Soviet Union. Additionally, by linking the United States and the U.S.S.R. in a cooperative venture reserved for them and no other nations, SALT set the two superpowers apart from all other states—even America's allies.

To many Americans these postures are wrong, both morally and in terms of U.S. security interests. They believe that the United States must seek to change Soviet society and, that to do so, it must remain in a state of tension with the Soviet government. They argue that if it is isolated, the Soviet state eventually will crack of its own internal contradictions—nationalities problems, economic failures, corruption, the natural yearnings of individuals for freedom, and so forth. This means that the United States should seek to construct a wall of implacable hostility around the U.S.S.R., a political-cum-military alliance among the nations of Western Europe, Japan, China and others in the Third World. Only America can galvanize such an alliance, it is argued, and to do so the United States must avoid bilateral agreements or even bilateral negotiations, as these imply permanent acceptance of the Soviet regime and accord legitimacy to it. The ABM treaty, the SALT II treaty, and the SALT process itself—to say nothing of other arms negotiations—are thus seen to undermine the long-run objective of causing fundamental change in Soviet society.

Obviously, opponents of arms limitations typically find it in their interest not to articulate this line of reasoning; they prefer to debate technical points in the treaty itself, arguing that they support arms control in the abstract, but that a better deal should have been made. The reasons for this stance are clear: the specter of unfettered and open-ended competition with the Soviet Union, including a relatively high risk of confrontation and nuclear war, is not one likely to find substantial political support over the long term. . . .

It is widely believed in the United States that nuclear weapons can play only a small and tightly circumscribed role in foreign policy. Because of the tremendous risks they imply, the standard argument proceeds, nuclear weapons (meaning nuclear threats) can be utilized only for narrow and quite specific purposes. First and foremost, they serve to deter nuclear attacks on, or coercion of, the United States itself. Additionally, it is believed, the U.S. nuclear umbrella can be extended to a few other nations—primarily the industrialized democracies. And that, more or less, is that. It is true that beginning in the early 1970s some officials began to speak of additional purposes for nuclear weapons, as when discussing limited nuclear options, but this was strictly in a reactive context, to offset the presumed political consequences of growth in Soviet nuclear capabilities.

Some argue, however, that the *threat* of nuclear war should be integrated more centrally into U.S. foreign policy; nuclear strength could be translated into political clout in a positive and assertive way. Indeed, some would maintain that this has already occurred, and continues to occur, regardless of our declaratory stance. Ever since World War II, they argue, nuclear weapons in fact have provided the one trump card in the U.S. hand. From the two bombs dropped on Japan, to nuclear threats, implicit or explicit, during the Berlin blockade, Korean War, Quemoy crisis, Cuban missile crisis, and 1973 Middle East war, as well as other more uncertain occasions, the United States turned to the threat of its nuclear arsenal, when push came to shove, to protect its own security and the security of its friends and allies.

Faced with the impossibility, in a democracy, of sustaining over the long haul conventional forces large enough to match those of the Soviet Union—this reasoning continues—the United States will likely confront this necessity again. . . .

To the extent that the United States must rely on nuclear weapons, it is argued, agreements which seek to enshrine strategic nuclear parity as a permanent condition of U.S.-Soviet relations are misguided; rather, the United States must turn its resources and technology to the quest for strategic superiority. Not that success in this goal is seriously contemplated; none but the most naïve believe that such an end is attainable. Nonetheless, the argument runs, by placing itself formally in a posture of seeking nuclear superiority the United States would be demonstrating a willingness to manipulate the risk of nuclear war for political objectives, thus lending credibility to the nuclear threats implicit in its foreign policy. In short, only in an environment of wide-open U.S.-Soviet nuclear competition can the United States' *necessary reliance* on nuclear weapons to underpin its foreign policy be supported successfully.

An element uniting these two underlying strands of argumentation against SALT—implications for U.S.-Soviet relations and for the role of nuclear weapons in foreign policy—is that those adhering to these viewpoints cannot be satisfied by any changes in the specific content of agreements. From their perspectives, the adverse implications of SALT can be erased only when the very process of seeking arms limitation comes to an end, and its meager products are dismantled. . . .

The theory of "arms control" is based on the rather modest notion that decisions to acquire certain types or quantities of weapons can aggravate political conflicts and thereby *in themselves contribute to the risk of war*. This is not to say that weapons decisions are a primary or even secondary cause of conflict; only that such decisions are one factor which influences the relative probabilities that political conflicts are resolved peacefully, remain unsettled, or result in war. It is assumed that one nation's weapons decisions are perceived and interpreted by other states, and that these judgments influence the latters' assessments of the potential military threat to their security, the likelihood that their adversaries intend to make use of that potential, and what weapons or military actions in response are necessary on their own part. Thus the initial decision and the decisions which follow affect both the "stability" (a key word) of the military balance and of broader political relations among nations, as well as the risk of war. Conversely, the theory continues, these adverse effects can be reduced, or at least contained, both through unilateral decisions to avoid deployments of "destabilizing" weapons and, more important, through international negotiations on agreements to mutually avoid deploying certain types of weapons or to place other types of agreed mutual limitations on weaponry.

Thus, at its root, "arms control" offers a technically oriented approach to arms limitations with a modest set of objectives. It accepts conflict among nations as an inevitable part of contemporary international politics and views military force as a necessary (and legitimate) instrument of national policy. It views negotiated limitations on armaments solely as a means of containing the risks and costs of political conflict. "Arms control" and military programs are seen as two sides of the same coin, both being means of enhancing the nation's security.

The limited objectives of arms control flow from its recognition of the fundamental political basis of international conflict, and its acceptance that essentially technical discussions about weapons can only reflect, not initiate, political accommodation. In the usual formulation, three goals are mentioned: (a) to reduce the risk of war; (b) to reduce the cost of preparing for war; and (c) to reduce the cost of war should it occur. In all three, however, success can come only at the margin. The purpose is not to abolish war, but to diminish the risk that war would occur. The objective is not to turn all swords into plowshares, but to create conditions wherein some resources which otherwise might be used to prepare for war can instead be utilized for peaceful purposes.

As this modest theoretical construct (of interest chiefly to a handful of defense intellectuals and military specialists) was transformed into a national political issue, however, these objectives and even the ultimate promise of arms control were sharply revised. Essentially, the nation's political leaders found in arms control a convenient means of satisfying popular demands resulting both from international circumstances and certain fundamental strands of opinion long present in the nation's psyche. These latter—*inter alia*, anti-militarism, with its concomitant desire to minimize defense spending, and an aversion to power politics, especially a fear of foreign entanglements—had dominated the nation's foreign policies (except for a few short-lived periods) until the Second World War. They remain important determinants of certain basic American perspectives on world affairs, and can become more or less so depending on events. For convenience, I will refer to those whose attitudes on world affairs are dominated by these sorts of concerns as the "disarmament constituency." Readers should be clear, however, that this shorthand refers to a far larger group than that small minority which actively supports true disarmament.

In the late 1950s and early 1960s, concerns of the "disarmament constituency" concentrated largely on nuclear weapons. . . . Ten years later, in the late 1960s, the concerns of the disarmament constituency were far broader, its demands more strident, and its political clout far more impressive. Twenty years later, in the late 1970s, as memories of Vietnam faded, as increasing Soviet assertiveness revitalized old fears of Russian imperialism, and as events in Africa and Southwest Asia demonstrated anew the potential utility of military power, attitudes which motivate the disarmament constituency [were] subsumed by other concerns.

For those 20 years, however, American political leaders found in arms control a pragmatic means of satisfying the demands of this constituency—at least for a while. . . .

Regardless of who was President, . . . the implicit promise was that the arms control process would continue, and that each stage would have more ambitious goals. In this way, the disarmament constituency could accept tentative and modest early measures; political support was exchanged for the promise of more ambitious undertakings in the future.

It is surprising that this deal survived as long as it did. The premises upon which it was based simply could not be fulfilled, and evidence to that effect soon became apparent. After all, the 1963 Limited Test Ban Treaty did not soon result in a comprehensive end to nuclear testing. Treaties in the 1960s to demilitarize the Antarctic, outer space, and the seabed were not soon followed by progress toward demilitarization of regions in which the threat of military conflict was more pertinent. And, most important, the SALT I Interim Agreement on Offensive Weapons did not quickly lead to more significant constraints on nuclear weapons as had been promised.

It took the SALT II Treaty, however, for the bargain finally to come unstuck. SALT II would place many important restraints on U.S. and Soviet nuclear weapons, restraints which could significantly stabilize the nuclear competition and the balance of strategic forces, thereby contributing to a lower risk of nuclear war. Its features in this regard—limits on the number of warheads on strategic missiles, limits on the introduction of new types of land-based missiles, a special subceiling on the number of land-based missiles with multiple warheads, and others—were readily recognizable to the specialist in arms control. However, the importance of these things was not nearly so apparent to the general public, nor to most politicians. What the latter looked for were the obvious—the signs of progress toward disarmament, toward fulfillment of the promise attributed to arms control 20 years before. And these did not exist. The treaty would cause only slight reductions in Soviet nuclear forces, and, in fact, would ratify an increase in U.S. forces. The treaty would not end weapons modernization, and thereby permit budget reductions—far from it. It would allow an acceleration of U.S. strategic programs and thereby larger expenditures on strategic forces. For all these reasons, the treaty disappointed the disarmament constituency. . . .

If efforts to negotiate limits on arms are to succeed in the future, policymakers will have to choose between two alternatives. They can define, structure and pursue these efforts along the lines of the original concept of arms control, seeking modest objectives, and enlisting the support of those elements of the government, industry, labor, and the scientific community which are most personally and directly concerned with nuclear weapons; or they can continue to blur the distinction between arms control and disarmament, seeking to reinvigorate that wider political constituency whose roots lie in considerations of religion, morality and the fundamental American antipathy to military power. The latter approach can succeed, however, only if the products of negotiations are more dramatic than those recently delivered. If this wider constituency is to be rebuilt, the benefits of agreements will have to be apparent, on their merits, to a large popular audience. As there is little basis in either the history of arms negotiations or in more recent developments in U.S.-Soviet relations to believe that such dramatic results are at all feasible, a return to the original concept of arms control is clearly warranted. . . .

. . . [I]f arms control is to be revived, policymakers and political opinion leaders should be forthright about the modest potential of even successful negotiations. Arms talks can reduce the risk of war, but not abolish war. Arms talks can reduce the cost of preparing for war, but the burden of military preparations will remain high as long as the international political system remains in its present form. Agreements that result from arms negotiations are not stepping stones to peace; at best, they can accomplish specific things in the context of continuing international political conflict.

In concrete terms, this means that the first step must be to rewrite and substantially narrow the arms control agenda. What is needed most is a clear set of priorities: a firm sense of what is important and what is trivial. . . .

[At this point Blechman argues in favor of a limited arms control agenda focused on Europe, a revitalization of United States–Soviet strategic weapons negotiations, and a shift from bilateral United States–Soviet negotiations to multilateral forums—*eds.*]

If negotiated arms limitations are to have a future, they need to return to the more limited concept which originally characterized arms control. In this heterogeneous world of sovereign nations, there are real conflicts—over land, over economic rights, over religious and political values. And there are real villains in this world as well—individuals dedicated to the aggrandizement of themselves, their friends, their nations, even at the expense of others, and even at grave risk of war. Weapons are not the cause of these conflicts, they are their reflection. Discussions about weapons cannot solve these conflicts; they can—and even then only at certain times—contain their effects.

In another sense, given the rhetoric of confrontation which now characterizes U.S.-Soviet exchanges, even this modest agenda may appear naïve. An acceptance of a return to more tense U.S.-Soviet relations, however, need not include the abandonment of efforts to contain the military competition at its most dangerous points. Given the extraordinary uncertainties of nuclear war and the unprecedented potential of nuclear weapons for destruction, containing the effects of political conflict, reducing the risk of war—even if only modestly—could be a crucial accomplishment. . . .

15

Coalition Dynamics: The Western Alliance

STANLEY HOFFMANN

The North Atlantic Treaty Organization (NATO) and the Warsaw Pact (Warsaw Treaty Organization) have been the principal alliances linking the United States and the Soviet Union, respectively, to their European allies. Neither has been free of intra-coalition differences. Stanley Hoffmann emphasizes that the persistent divisions within the NATO alliance are not transient phenomena but are deeply rooted in geography, history, domestic politics, and national character. Hoffmann is Douglas Dillon Professor of the Civilization of France at Harvard University and chairman of Harvard's Center for European Studies. Among his many publications is _Primacy or World Order: American Foreign Policy Since the Cold War_ (1978).

A number of factors have led, in the past couple of years, to an acute sense of crisis among the members of the Atlantic Alliance and to heightened tensions within it.[1] . . . Clearly, the three fundamental considerations are: a new awareness of the fact that the world has become a single strategic stage, and that the security of the members of the Alliance can be threatened by events occurring outside its geographic area, especially in the Middle East and Persian Gulf region; the unfavorable evolution of the military balance in Europe, because of the relentless modernization of Soviet conventional forces and of the development of new Soviet middle-range nuclear weapon systems that are both mobile and highly precise; and the collapse of the Soviet–American détente.

In this essay, I will concentrate on what I deem essential: the different reactions to these events within the Alliance, and the causes of these divergences. . . .

NUANCE AND THE NEW CONSENSUS

It is important, in analyzing the current drift, to diagnose correctly the nature and the limits of transatlantic discord.

Reprinted from Stanley Hoffman "The Western Alliance: Drift or Harmony?" _International Security_ 6 (Fall 1981), pp. 105–125, by permission of The MIT Press, Cambridge, Massachusetts. © 1981 by the President and Fellows of Harvard College and the Massachusetts Institute of Technology. Some footnotes have been deleted; others have been renumbered to appear in consecutive order.

[1] See "Reflections on the Present Danger" and "The Crisis in the West," _New York Review_, March 6, 1980, and July 17, 1980; also see the author's "Europe and the New Orthodoxy," _Harvard International Review_, December 1980/January 1981.

It is not, in the first place, a simple matter of disagreement between Americans and West Europeans. Western European opinion covers a whole range of attitudes, not only *within* each country (the same would be true of the United States) but *among* governments. Today, the official position of Britain is closer to that of the Reagan Administration than is the position of the Bonn government; yet another gap exists between the major three West European powers and some of the smaller European members of NATO. . . .

Disagreement centers *not* on the existence of a renewed Soviet threat to Western security interests; in this respect, the divergences over the response to the Soviet invasion of Afghanistan are actually less profound than the split in the Alliance in October 1973, when many Europeans refused to view the October War between Israel, Egypt, and Syria as a confrontation between Washington and Moscow, as Kissinger saw and wanted them to see it. By contrast, in 1980, all the Allies deemed Soviet behavior in Kabul unacceptable.

There are, in academia and among public officials on both sides of the Atlantic, two different conceptions of Soviet behavior; both can be found in varying degrees in every country of the Western Alliance. To simplify, I would call one the *essentialist* view; it stresses the radically *different* nature of the Soviet system (either because of its imperial essence, or, more usually, because of its revolutionary one). In a manner comparable to George Kennan's in 1946-1947, the essentialist view describes the Soviet Union as an inextricable mix of power and ideology on the march, driven to paranoia because its whole rationale is the assumption of external hostility, and to expansion because its survival depends on the elimination of its enemies (within as well as abroad). Thus, it is a system with which no mutual gains or lasting cooperation are possible. The West is condemned either to endure inexpiable conflict with that system (the "harder" version of this conception), or to practice perpetual containment of it (Kennan's early notion, or Raymond Aron's formulation, "to survive is to win").

The other view of Soviet behavior describes it as relentlessly opportunistic. Ideology is important to Moscow as a world map (drawn around the "correlation of forces") and as a method of domestic legitimation, but not as a compass. This view puts greater emphasis on the similarity between Soviet behavior and the behavior of other great powers in history; on past experiences as the roots of paranoia and expansion; and on the cumulative effect of gradual changes within the Soviet Union and of transformations of the international system. It is, in short, a more empirical approach, paying greater attention to the context of decisions. Finally, it attaches greater importance to internal difficulties, as a way of placing external behavior in perspective. Accordingly, the second of these views prescribes a mix of containment and search for agreements as a means to induce Moscow to behave in a more "responsible" way.

Among policymakers, one finds agreement on a number of key factors: There is an increased Soviet threat because of the Soviet arms build-up, which gives the Soviet Union both dangerous new military options in Europe and the ability to project its power abroad. . . . That threat is made more dangerous still by a perceived Soviet determination to exploit opportunities in the third world (hence the key issue of third world "destabilization"). A third source of agreement focuses on the threat posed by Moscow's perceived unwillingness to interpret détente in a non-conflictual way. This consensus points to Moscow's insistence that détente means neither a reduction of ideological conflict nor an end to attempts at changing the "correlation of forces" by support of "national liberation" or "progressive" forces. Finally, all members agree that what is dangerous, and could become explosive, is the mix of Soviet domestic weaknesses and external reliance on military might as the main instrument of Soviet policy.

For their part, the Allies are in general agreement on the need to improve the military preparedness of NATO (as exemplified by the long-range defense program) and to meet the threat of new Soviet theater nuclear forces with, for instance, NATO's December 1979 TNF decision, and comparable French policies.

There are, however, important *nuances and disagreements* that divide allied officials; they center on five issues.

The United States, since 1978-1979 and especially after Afghanistan, has moved away from that more complex worldview that sees the East-West conflict as only one corner of the tapestry, and the conflict itself as manageable through the pursuit of both containment and détente policies (arms control, economic agreements, occasional diplomatic cooperation). Gaining ground in American policy is a view of the world that is intensely bipolar and conflictual. That view either relegates to the back burner issues that are not reducible to the bipolar contest (as the New International Economic Order), or analyzes those issues (such as human rights, turbulence in Central American countries, Africa or the Middle East) in East-West terms. The Soviet Union is to be dealt with, according to this conception, from a position of strength and in the context of explicit linkages subordinating agreements to good behavior. Even in France and England—where a stern view of Soviet expansionism and a highly critical one of President Carter's vacillations have dominated public opinion during the past several years—there is considerable unease about so bipolar a view. For whenever bipolarity is most intense, the freedom of maneuver of European states is minimal. The newly conflictual approach of American policymakers is similarly discomforting. . . . Such a confrontational stance is seen as provocative, possibly dangerous, and there is considerable skepticism about the effectiveness of explicit linkages.

The [Reagan] Administration reflects far more than a newly militant public opinion: It reflects neo-nationalism; a desire to restore American pride and prestige; a will to put an end to humiliation; a determination to restore American leadership; a conviction that Soviet daring and Alliance drift can be explained by past American failures to lead. Many West European statesmen welcome the promise of a new American consistency and clarity of purpose; the same individuals nevertheless wonder whether the . . . American Administration is aware that a *number* of factors act to prevent a simple return to the days of American hegemony. Among those factors, several are particularly pronounced—changes in the respective economic power of the two sides of the Atlantic; the progress of the European Nine (now Ten) in political cooperation; the rise of new middle powers in the developing world, and the desire of third world countries for independence. More bluntly, at a time when Washington seems to see only the challenge of Moscow on the geopolitical map, the West European leaders see a multiplicity of problems: Moscow, to be sure; but also the various troubles and conflicts in the different parts of the third world; the specific crisis of Poland (a case in which some West Europeans believe that there is, or ought to be, a possibility of finding interests common to them, the Poles, *and* the Soviets); the difficulties that too aggressive an American policy could create; and the need to protect from internal tensions and external pressures the West European enterprise itself, a delicate construction whose progress requires a stable environment.

The Reagan Administration, although its domestic economic priorities are the curtailment of inflation and the increase in productive investment as a way of restoring American industrial supremacy, has given to the military budget a priority that may well detract from both goals. It could be highly inflationary; and by reinforcing the drive to cut the non-military expenditures, thus reducing the savings capacity of many victims of such cuts, and by giving a clear priority to defense industries, it could divert from and delay the indispensable industrial "redeployment." Meanwhile, the West European countries are all giving priority to their own internal economic difficulties. Since they do not have the political ability to dismantle the social services of the post-war welfare state (or would provoke major social explosions if they tried), and since most of them have been hit by the second oil shock much harder than by the first (and harder than has the United States), their margin for maneuver is very narrow, and the limits within which they can increase their defense expenditures are very strict. They have to explain to Washington that such an increase at the expense of their economic health and social stability would be senseless—just when the Americans explain that economic recovery and military preparedness must go hand in hand.

There is also disagreement about the precise nature of the Soviet threat, and therefore about the desirable response. Washington emphasizes the Soviet military menace: Moscow's arms machine is doubly dangerous, insofar as it can "cover" Soviet non-military expansion (by making a Western military response more risky) *as well as* encourage those in the Kremlin to use direct military action, as in Afghanistan; hence America's determination to reply in kind, to restore a "margin of safety" and to build a military presence in the Middle East. West European leaders deem the Soviet build-up dangerous *primarily* because it makes non-military destabilization, or destabilization by proxy, safer for Moscow, whereas in the past the West often responded with the use of force (e.g., Lebanon, Vietnam, etc.). The Soviets' emphasis is now on opportunities in the third world rather than on direct aggression. Hence the Europeans' preference for a more nuanced response; on the one hand, the Allies endorse a restoration of global military balance, but with less emphasis on the need for specific military balances, and with a plea for prudence in deployments; some deployments, they argue, could actually be counterproductive and destabilizing, as in the Middle East. Instead, they recommend a greater willingness and ability to play the *politics* of each area (which requires a certain decentralization of roles: France in Africa, West Germany in Turkey, a European role for the resolution for the Palestinian issue, and for a resumption of the North-South dialogue). In short, the foreign policy priorities and preferred methods of pursuing them are not identical on both sides of the Atlantic.

There is finally disagreement about the degree to which, and the way in which, the outside world can influence the explosive mix of Soviet power and weakness. In the United States, there is a tendency to deem Soviet intentions irrelevant, to focus only on the effects (actual and potential) of Soviet moves, to dismiss détente as having been a failure since it placed no significant restraint on Soviet behavior, and to characterize détente as indivisible (and therefore dead).[2] West European leaders believe that even if Soviet intentions are (inevitably) mixed and the effects of Soviet policies clearly bad, the West has the ability to affect Soviet calculations at the margin, by a combination of clear advance warnings . . . *and* preservation of the "dialogue" and of those aspects of the Soviet–West European détente that have proven beneficial to all sides. This is the basis of the European tendency to declare détente divisible, and of warnings to the United States not to seek military superiority or confrontation.

AMERICAN-EUROPEAN AND INTRA-EUROPEAN RELATIONS: CENTRIFUGAL FORCES

What are the reasons for these divergences? Although they concern the key issue of coping with Soviet challenge, they actually do not have much to do with differences in evaluating Soviet behavior. They result from geography, history, domestic politics, and national character (or political culture).

Geography: The Fundamental Factor of Divergence

When the United States contemplates the security of West Europe, it sees a choice between emphasizing deterrence (i.e., extended deterrence, through a credible threat of nuclear retaliation) and emphasizing defense. Should a strategy resting on mutual assured destruction appear implausible, war-fighting strategies (conventional *or* nuclear, concentrating on counterforce) are conceivable. West Europeans have only the luxury of discomfort. Mutual assured destruction always seemed to them hardly compatible with extended deterrence: MAD stresses a counter-city strike, while extended deterrence requires the ability to strike Soviet military targets first if necessary; indeed, . . . MAD was one of the incentives for the building of the French *force de frappe*. But at present, the credibility of extended deterrence is being undermined by Soviet advances and advantages in theater nuclear forces: the main function of the SS-20 and Backfire may well be one of the counter-deterrence, making a Soviet conventional thrust in Europe possible, by placing NATO before the unholy dilemma of either fighting a defensive conventional battle or else taking a nuclear initiative that would expose NATO's conventional targets *and* nuclear installations to retaliatory destruction by the Soviet theater nuclear forces, or even expose America's vulnerable land-based missiles to a

[2] See Robert W. Tucker, "The Purposes of American Power," *Foreign Affairs*, Volume 59, Number 2 (Winter 1980/81), pp. 241–274.

Soviet strike.[3] Moreover, as prestigious and knowledgeable an American as Henry Kissinger, in September 1979, proclaimed that it would be a mistake for the allies to believe that extended deterrence was still credible. But a purely conventional defense of West Europe has always been unwelcome to the West Europeans, since it would mean devastation (given the certainty of a Soviet invasion: NATO does not aim at striking first). And scenarios of actual nuclear war-fighting, whether in the form of . . . limited nuclear options, in that of PD-59's [i.e., the Carter administration's Presidential Directive 59—*eds.*] emphasis on counterforce targets, or in that of integrated war fighting strategies for NATO,[4] seem like extermination compounded. In this respect, the new Soviet ability to strike West European military targets with precision, i.e., to resort to (geographically) limited nuclear war for actual fighting purposes, is coupled with this growing American tendency to doubt the credibility of deterrence (whether in its MAD or in its extended versions), and this emphasis on the need for war-fighting capabilities, if only in order to match Soviet strategic doctrines that appear to envisage fighting and winning nuclear wars. The two combine to provoke, in various European countries and parties, a new wave of quasi-pacifism.[5] Hence, a desire to get out of an insane world, a tendency to withdraw altogether: what is sometimes (wrongly) called scandinavization. . . . This explains why many West European leaders insist so strongly, both on the need to contain the risk of actual nuclear war through arms control . . ., and on the need to deal with Moscow not only by military containment and confrontation but by détente.

Geography also explains the different attitudes of the United States and of West European leaders toward Eastern Europe. As was already clear during World War II, the United States never had a truly distinct policy toward Eastern Europe. . . . To West Europeans, Eastern Europe is not a Soviet *glacis* but a wound— and this is especially true for West Germany *vis-à-vis* East Germany; this is another reason to try to save what the West European-Soviet détente has achieved— to provide the only breath of fresh air coming into the East European cage, the only opportunity for wide contacts between the *frères séparés*.

History as a Source of Divergence

In Western relations with Moscow, there have been two separate détentes, resting on two separate sets of wagers. The West European-Soviet détente came first. De Gaulle was its initiator; then came West Germany. On the basis of the recognition of the territorial status quo, the West Europeans made a bet on the dynamic

---

[3] See Pierre Lellouche, "Introduction Générale," in *La Securité de l'Europe dans les Années 80* (Paris: Institut Français des Relations Internationales, 1980). See also the author's "New Variations on Old Themes," *International Security*, Volume 4, Number 1 (Summer 1979); and Lellouche's "Europe and her Defense," *Foreign Affairs*, Volume 59, Number 4 (Spring 1981), pp. 813–834.

[4] See Richard Burt, "L'Alliance Atlantique et la Crise Nucléaire Cachée," in Lellouche (ed.), *La Securité de l'Europe.*

[5] Josef Joffe, "European-American Relations: The Enduring Crisis," *Foreign Affairs,* Volume 59, Number 4 (Spring 1981), pp. 835–851.

transformation of the East, and on a possible decrease of their defense effort as a result; the Soviets bet on receiving benefits from economic links, and on a decrease of American influence in West European political systems. The results, clearly, were mixed; but the Soviets did obtain economic benefits (as did the West), and changes were achieved in Eastern Europe—some, as in the case of the Berlin agreement, with Soviet consent, others, despite Soviet resistance, through the dynamics of greater openness (as in Poland). The Soviet-American détente of the early 1970s corresponded, on the American side, to Kissinger's complex theory of linkages and networks, and, on the Soviet side, to the hope of achieving thereby a formal recognition of military equality and political condominium, a consolidation of the Soviet system through American economic and technological aid, and a demobilization of America abroad, leading to advances for the "progressive" forces. By 1979, both sides, not so strangely, felt cheated: the United States, by Soviet moves in the third world and by the Soviet arms drive; the Soviet Union, by the failure to receive the aid expected, by the American rejection of duopoly (especially in the Middle East), by evidence of new moves to strengthen NATO, and by America's and Japan's *rapprochement* with China. Today, West European leaders often tend to believe that the balance sheet in Europe is rather unfavorable to Moscow: the momentum of détente has "destabilized" Poland and, to some extent, East Germany. And the Berlin and Helsinki agreements, by keeping the Central Front quiet, facilitate the redeployment of American forces toward the Middle East. But Americans are skeptical; they believe that insofar as Eastern Europe is destabilized, the Soviets will as usual resort to brutal repression, and that détente in Europe has doubly served the Soviets. It has made, they believe, defense efforts politically more difficult for the West European members of NATO, and above all, it has given West European governments such a stake in preserving trade with the East that they become far too accommodating to Moscow in political and military affairs. Moscow pursues a two-track policy—economic cooperation with Western Europe, and political and military expansion. Both tracks serve Soviet power. But Western Europe finds it difficult to object to and counter the second of these pursuits out of fear that too strong an anti-Soviet stand on the strategic-diplomatic chessboard could jeopardize the economic gains of that burgeoning relationship.

In relations with the third world, the United States has a tendency to militarize issues, partly because of disillusionment with economic assistance, partly because of difficulties and even disasters encountered in the manipulation of domestic politics abroad. West Europeans have had, on the whole, disastrous military experiences in the days of decolonization, but look at their economic deals with third world countries (e.g., the Lomé agreements) with some pride, and they have had some great successes in dealing with the politics of troubled countries (e.g., the British in Zimbabwe).

History has also opened an important gap of experience between the United States, with its post-war quasi-monopoly of decision in the Alliance, and the West Europeans' quasi-abdication. With the exception of France under the Fifth Republic, responsibility for security is seen as a NATO (i.e., a largely American), more than a national or European responsibility. . . . The proper function of the European entity is seen as the development of Europe as a civilian power: this reinforces the interest in trade relations (with the East in particular), and feeds the indifference, in the smaller countries, to military issues. And whereas the United States does not want to accept the Soviet Union as an equal superpower (except in the military realm), the Europeans have an old experience of dealing with Russia as a (difficult) partner in the game of nations.

Domestic Politics and the Breach

In the United States the constituency for détente has always been limited (a small part of the business and intellectual communities). The majority of the public has been skeptical; most of the debate in the post-war era has only been over how best to resist Soviet expansion. In Western Europe, foreign policy has played a far more important and variable role in domestic political battles and the Soviet Union has not·been the only, or even the dominant factor. In Britain, the Labor left expresses a deep desire to concentrate on domestic reform, a resentment of the outside world of NATO, the United States, and Europe, and an old unilateralist and pacifist dream. In West Germany, some of the same feelings can be found in fragments of the SPD and FDP. The hope for more contacts with the *other* Germans in the East, if not for reunification, is an added element—one that is often exaggerated, but carefully watched, in France, where some always suspect . . . *Ostpolitik* to be a nationalist prelude to a reunification strategy. In France, the left's dislike of power politics, its preference for arbitration and disarmament, and its distaste for U.S. "imperialism" have been a notable feature of the political landscape. . . . In Italy, foreign policy has always been a weapon in domestic political maneuvers, a movable symbol of internal alignments and realignments.

Domestic differences thus aggravate the effects of an unfortunate geography and a humiliating history for the Europeans. America's native tendency is, perhaps not isolation, but self-concern: to redress the balance, and to jerk Americans away from their concentration on domestic issues, U.S. officials must often engage in overkill and sound a global alarm—in 1947 as in 1980. West European political systems are the victims of a "tyranny from the outside": either because of the presence of powerful Communist parties, or because of a constant battle between domestic demands and foreign policy needs in countries with limited means. For the Nine, building the EEC has been a partial answer to that competition. In turn, the European construction leads to tension with the United States: first, because it can best proceed when the outside world places no demands on the members of the Community . . . ; secondly, because, in an effort to compensate for its internal cleavages and multiple deadlocks with the *fuite en avant* of "political (i.e., foreign policy) cooperation," the European community finds compelling reasons to define stands different from Washington's. All of this, then, tends to give to American policies an arrow-like quality, and to the Europeans' the aspect of a highly complex piece of clockwork.

National Character and the Breach

Finally, there are factors of political culture that should not be neglected in such an analysis; they result in three lines of cleavage within the Atlantic Alliance.

The first could be called simplicity *vs.* complexity. Americans prefer simple policies to complex ones. When complications had to be introduced into the anti-communist policy of containment, it was mainly for pragmatic reasons: the costs of purely military approaches (as in China in 1948-1949), for instance, and the defection from Moscow of a communist country (Tito's Yugoslavia). Détente, as I have tried to show elsewhere,[6] was partly "sunk" by widespread resistance toward a mixed policy of rewards and punishments; first, it had to be oversold, and when it appeared to have failed, a formidable reaction set in. A complex policy toward China, in the 1970s, always threatened to "tilt," becoming an overly enthusiastic "China card" policy. . . . West European statesmen have some skepticism toward simplicity. Their historical experience is both that of the balance of power, with its nuances, shifts, and switches, and that of the disasters caused by Europe's own "terrible simplifiers" in the twentieth century.

Secondly, attitudes toward conflict are not the same on both sides of the Atlantic. Many Americans still dream of ultimate harmony—a pleasant dream—but show a terrible rage against those who seem to block it (like the Jacobins of the French Revolution, who also tended to believe that the obstacles to the dream were not the nature of things, but evil human beings). Recall, for instance, Truman's or Carter's reaction when they felt bullied and duped by Moscow. Against such human obstacles, force is a legitimate instrument; and Americans sometimes project on others the idea that force is a privileged tool on behalf of one's mission. Robert Legvold[7] has shown how Soviet strategic literature looks at *America* as a creature of force, while Americans, of course, believe that the *Soviets* put force at the center of their policy; each side sees itself as merely reacting to the threat of the other. In 1980, as in 1950, many in America saw in a local military aggression—by North Korea then, by Russia in Afghanistan—a possible prelude to a generalized use of force. And American discussions of policy have been almost obsessively focused on the nightmare scenarios of Minuteman vulnerability, and on the threat of Soviet aggression in the Persian Gulf. The West Europeans look at international affairs less as a duel with swords, more as a game played with a whole range of cards; they are more concerned with the overall correlation of forces than with the balance (or imbalance) of military force; and they are more Clausewitzian, i.e., more interested in the variety of ways in which force can serve political objectives.

The United States is still (or again) in the throes of "exceptionalism"—the belief in the unique mission of America. This tends to promote a peculiar kind of

---

[6] *Primacy or World Order* (New York: McGraw Hill, 1979), Chapter 2; "Requiem," *Foreign Policy,* Number 42 (Spring 1981).

[7] "The Soviet Union and the Political Significance of Military Power," to be published in a forthcoming book edited by Uwe Nerlich.

insecurity: the need to ask oneself at every moment if one still is number one, if one is up to the task, faithful to the mandate. It also makes it difficult for Americans to understand experiences different from their own—social revolutions for instance—and it makes them want to project abroad the experiences that have made America great—free enterprise, political democracy. A sense of mission makes sharing responsibility—not only with an evil power, but with allies—equally difficult. The politics of Western Europe are not those of exceptionalism but those of survival. When the Cold War intensifies, dangers for survival and for political autonomy increase, giving rise to the two tendencies of either wanting to opt out altogether (which often prevails among those far from power) or else of working to improve the atmosphere—pleading for summits and negotiations, thus often exposing European statesmen to the charge of being naive and of playing right into Moscow's hands, of helping Moscow's attempt to lull Europeans to sleep and to estrange them from Washington.

These three lines of cleavage cumulatively amount to different conceptions of stability. In the United States, stability means preserving the *status quo;* it means a world in which the Soviets eschew subversion, the exploitation of revolutionary opportunities, the support of revolutionary forces—a world in which peaceful change becomes the norm. The West Europeans assuredly hope for a moderation of Soviet behavior, a stabilization of the world when (as at present) things have gone out of kilter. But they have no real expectation of preserving the *status quo* all over: they expect less and they demand less—they would, on the whole, be happy if the inevitable (and, often, inevitably violent) changes occur in such a way that the vital interests and values of the West are not destroyed in the process. . . .

[Hoffmann continues with a set of prescriptions for closing the breach between the United States and its Western allies. Included in the discussion is consideration of the means necessary to enhance European security and of the role that Europeans might play in extra-NATO affairs—*eds.*]

CONCLUSION

The biggest threat to the Alliance today is not the Soviet menace, however serious its military dimensions and global its scope may be. The gravest threat lies in the centrifugal potential of the present situation: an America that tries to reassert its leadership with a militantly and almost obsessively anti-Soviet worldview; a German ally increasingly unhappy about American trends and eager to preserve opportunities for agreement with Moscow; a France that, in the wake of the May [1981] elections [which brought the Socialist party to power], will be feeling its way in the realm of foreign policy, under the wait-and-see scrutiny of its European neighbors and the United States, and will most probably continue to try, somewhat acrobatically, both to maintain the Franco–German entente that is the motor of European cooperation, and to restore a Franco–American entente at a moment when the Soviet–French one appears sterile, and the Washington–Bonn one a bit frayed; a Britain that favors both a close American alliance and European political cooperation, yet suffers from serious internal weaknesses that affect its performance in Europe and on the world stage; an Italy absorbed in the morose contemplation of its stalemated politics; and the smaller European nations tempted to drift to neutralism.

Both the Alliance *and* the European enterprise are threatened by these developments. And yet, we cannot return to the days when strong American leadership either succeeded in rallying most of the West Europeans, or provoked a collective European resistance that was good for European unification without being dangerous for NATO. This is why a major effort at political compromise, strategic integration, and institutional innovation is needed. Nothing short of that will serve the purpose of further European cooperation, and preserve the transatlantic alliance. But it will require a drastic turn away from American unilateralism, and a new European willingness not merely to claim but to play a world role—starting with defense at home.

16

Coalition Dynamics: The Soviet Union and Eastern Europe

ALVIN Z. RUBINSTEIN

In this essay, Alvin Z. Rubinstein surveys the post–World War II record of Soviet relations with Eastern Europe. Noting the willingness of Soviet leaders to use force, if necessary, to maintain Soviet dominance in Eastern Europe, Rubinstein shows that the nature and sources of the divisions among the socialist countries are such that force is not likely to remove them. Author of *Soviet Policy Toward Turkey, Iran, and Afghanistan* (1982), Rubinstein is professor of political science at the University of Pennsylvania.

Since 1945, the lodestar of the Soviet Union's European policy has been strategic control of Eastern Europe in order to prevent that territory from ever again serving as a springboard for an invasion of the Soviet Union. Stalin's postwar objectives were relatively clear-cut: to eliminate Western influence from Eastern Europe and concomitantly to establish Moscow's hegemony, and to develop a belt of submissive Communist regimes whose leaders governed at Moscow's discretion and depended for their survival on Soviet troops. From 1945 to 1953, the Soviet Union's Draconian policy toward Eastern Europe was unmistakably Stalin's handiwork.

His successors, however, were faced with more subtle challenges; to preserve yet decentralize their empire; to obtain Western acceptance of the permanence of Soviet domination over Eastern Europe; and to expand Soviet power without jeopardizing the security of the USSR or its imperial system. They soon discovered that preserving an empire is more difficult than acquiring one. Not only do the techniques of rule differ from those of revolution, but the price of empire may prove so high that it weakens the structure of power within the metropolitan country itself. Over the years, Stalin's successors alternated reform and repression in a never-ending search for a mix that extended the range of permissible autonomy within a framework that ensured loyalty, stability, and strategic control. . . .

Reprinted from Alvin Z. Rubinstein, *Soviet Foreign Policy Since World War II: Imperial and Global* (Cambridge, Mass.: Winthrop Publishers, 1981), pp. 72–92. Copyright © 1981 by Little, Brown and Company (Inc.). Reprinted by permission. Some notes have been deleted; others have been renumbered to appear in consecutive order.

DE-STALINIZING THE EMPIRE

On August 9, 1953, Premier G. M. Malenkov spoke of the government's intention to allocate more resources to satisfy consumer needs. He alluded to a departure from the previous hostility toward the West, though simultaneously he used the occasion to inform the world that the United States was "not the only possessor of the hydrogen bomb."

The "de-Stalinization" process that reached its apogee at the CPSU's twentieth congress in February 1956 developed slowly, varying in degree and scope from country to country but following a common pattern. Amnesties were proclaimed, forced collectivization was halted, price cuts on consumer staples were instituted, the more oppressive features of the labor and criminal codes were changed, and the arbitrary power of the secret police was curbed. The aim was to "return to Leninism." In Eastern Europe, those who were too closely identified as Stalinists were gradually replaced by national Communists, that is, those Communists who were popularly regarded as defenders of the country's interests against unreasonable exploitation by and abject subservience to the Soviet Union. Party and government apparatuses were separated, and economic reforms were introduced.

In another major policy reversal, Moscow decided on a reconciliation with Tito. . . . [In June 1956] Moscow formally acknowledged the principle of "many roads to socialism," which was to serve as the doctrinal basis for granting greater measures of autonomy to the members of the Soviet bloc.

The errant Tito's return to the fold was a necessary step in the reconstitution of the formal unity of the Communist world. . . . Improved Soviet-Yugoslav relations "harmonized with the then current Soviet policy of attaining cooperation with the respectable socialist parties of the West, demonstrating to the world Moscow's reasonableness and flexibility, and of encouraging neutralist tendencies in the free world by demonstrating that the USSR was not a threat against which an unaligned country needed to seek protection by joining the other bloc."[1] The Soviet-Yugoslav second honeymoon, however, lasted only until late 1956, when, in the aftermath of the Hungarian revolution, Moscow's temporary turn from diversity to bloc unity and neo-Stalinism alienated Belgrade. But this time, unlike in 1948, the quarrel did not result in a rupture.

Khrushchev's determination to carry out far-ranging reforms at home and to place Soviet-East European relations on a more truly fraternal basis required improved relations with the Western countries. Accordingly, in the spring of 1955, over the objections of Molotov and others, Khrushchev agreed to a peace treaty with Austria, thus reversing Moscow's previous insistence on linking the treaty with a settlement of the German problem. The treaty, signed on May 15, ended the four-power occupation and committed Austria to a policy of permanent nonalignment with either bloc. It was significant because it marked the first voluntary Soviet withdrawal from an entrenched position in the center of Europe. . . .

Moscow's previously unchallenged authority in the Communist world was seriously shaken as a consequence of what was perhaps the most spectacular event in Soviet politics of the post-Stalin period: Khrushchev's secret speech at the CPSU's twentieth congress in February 1956, denouncing Stalin's crimes and self-deification. An outgrowth of the struggle for power among the Kremlin oligarchs, the speech had a powerful effect on the course of developments in Eastern Europe, China, and the world Communist movement. It immediately set in motion in Eastern Europe additional pressures for changes that gathered momentum and threatened to unhinge the Soviet empire.

The twentieth congress would have been important even without Khrushchev's speech against Stalin because of the significant doctrinal shifts that affected the Kremlin's approach to world affairs. Khrushchev affirmed the Leninist thesis of the irreconcilability of capitalism and communism, but stated that war between the two systems "is not fatalistically inevitable." The emergence of the "world camp of socialism" (and by implication its possession of nuclear weapons) enabled the forces for peace in the world to find a champion and to rebuff would-be aggressors; the USSR's possession of nuclear weapons would deter any would-be capitalist aggressor, and if "all anti-war forces" cooperated with the Soviet camp, "the greater the guarantees that there will be no new war." Khrushchev also formally embraced the Titoist thesis that there are many roads to socialism, thereby providing doctrinal approval for diversity or polycentrism in the Communist world and a theoretical basis for closer cooperation not only with Yugoslavia but also with the socialist parties of Western Europe. Moscow hoped that this position would also lead to better relations with the new nations and nationalist movements of the Third World. Third, Communists in capitalist countries were encouraged to seek power, where and when possible, through parliamentary means.

In bringing Soviet foreign-policy perceptions and guidelines into line with emerging international realities, Khrushchev greatly disturbed the Chinese, who saw in his stress on peaceful coexistence and efforts to effect a limited détente with the United States a downgrading of the Sino-Soviet alliance, a shift in Soviet foreign-policy priorities and methods, and a possible shelving of Beijing's quest for international recognition and for the overthrow of the Koumintang regime on Taiwan. But the disruptive effects of de-Stalinization were most apparent in Eastern Europe. An unwary Kremlin had unwittingly released turbulent anti-Russian, anti-Communist, and nationalist currents. The result was the most substantial uprising against Soviet rule ever witnessed. Shaking the very foundations of the Soviet empire, it led to a Stalinist revival and to serious reconsiderations of ways in which to ensure the permanence of Soviet strategic gains in Eastern Europe and avoid the perils of liberalization.

Riots broke out in Poznan, Poland, in June 1956. Sparked by Khrushchev's revelations, smoldering resentment of a decade of economic exploitation and Soviet domination flared into open denunciations of the Moscow-controlled government. The Poles' traditional hatred of Russia made for a volatile political situation. The Kremlin, realizing the gravity of the situation, grudgingly made concessions. . . . (Notwithstanding its greater independence in internal affairs, Poland remains inevitably influenced in important foreign-policy decisions by its powerful Communist neighbor, if only because friendship with the USSR is Poland's ultimate guarantee against the possibility of another Soviet-German "understanding" at its expense, as in 1939. Soviet troops in East Germany and in

Poland, as well as Poland's deep-rooted fear of the claims of a revived, united, expansionist Germany to the territories east of the Oder-Neisse line that are now incorporated into Poland, are Moscow's levers to assure that nation's continued adherence to the Soviet bloc.)

Events in Hungary took a violent and tragic turn. Matyas Rakosi, a confirmed Stalinist and longtime party boss of Hungary, was deposed in June 1956, and his successor, Ernö Gero, was not up to the challenge of mounting popular pressure for change. On October 23, revolution erupted in Budapest. Anti-Communist and anti-Soviet, it threatened the entire Soviet position in Central Europe. Moscow could not find a political solution as it had in Poland because the Hungarians wanted full independence and their party leadership had lost control of the situation. The rebels wanted to disband the Communist party, leave the Warsaw Pact organization, and liquidate all vestiges of Soviet rule. Confronted with the imminent loss of Hungary and possible disintegration elsewhere in Eastern Europe, Moscow hurled 250,000 troops and 5000 tanks against the Hungarians on November 4, after it violated a truce that betrayed key Hungarian military leaders and delivered them into Soviet hands. Where negotiation had failed, brute force and deceit succeeded.

. . . As the Soviet steamroller crushed the Hungarians, the West watched, helpless to intervene for fear of precipitating World War III. This moment of truth for the West tragically confirmed what Raymond Aron has described as "the unwritten law of the atomic age": that the Soviet Union can do as it pleases within its sphere of influence without fear of retaliation. And Hungary is part of that sphere.

But the Kremlin learned several bitter lessons. First, Soviet control in Eastern Europe can be preserved *only* if backed by the Red Army. Military force, not ideology, is the effective cement for cohesion. Second, nationalism remains strong, even among avowed Communists, and in Eastern Europe it is permeated with an anti-Russian tinge. Third, authority once weakened cannot easily be reimposed. Fourth, a prerequisite for the continued political and military adherence of East European countries to the Soviet-dominated Warsaw Pact military alliance is Soviet acceptance of a substantial measure of economic, cultural, and political autonomy in those countries.

Strategically, control of Eastern Europe plays a key role in Soviet military thinking about the defense of the USSR; and Moscow will undoubtedly resist any attempt, either by the West or by the region's members, to dislodge its military influence and control. . . .

On the other hand, Eastern Europe can no longer be considered an unquestioned asset to the Kremlin. The area represents a material drain on Soviet resources; the reliability of East European troops remains a continual question; and East European nationalism, a force too often slighted in the West, greatly complicates the process of Soviet rule. The intervention in Hungary cost Moscow heavily among influential West European intellectuals and in the consequent agonizing reappraisals that occurred in Western Communist parties. African and Asian leaders expressed varying degrees of disappointment, but the remoteness of Hungary to them blunted their concern and indignation. They were far more outraged over the British, French, and Israeli attack on Egypt, a country only recently emerged from colonialism and one with which they felt intimate emotional ties. Moreover, Soviet leaders, unlike their Western counterparts, who must contend with an influential public opinion, could simply ignore the protests. What the 1956 crises in Eastern Europe (and the 1968 crisis in Czechoslovakia) have shown is that the Soviet Union regards Eastern Europe as vital to its national security and that it is prepared to use force if necessary to preserve its hegemony there. . . .

COURTING BELGRADE

. . . During the years 1958 to 1961, the Soviet-Yugoslav controversy centered on four main points. First, the Yugoslavs maintained that the USSR as well as NATO was responsible for the Cold War and the division of the world into rival blocs. Second, they insisted on the unqualified right of each Communist state to determine its own course toward socialism. Third, they accused Moscow of continuing Stalinist practices and of having developed into a bureaucratic state that kept "strengthening in all fields of social life" instead of withering away in accordance with Marxist-Leninist theory. And fourth, the League of Yugoslav Communists' party program claimed for Yugoslavia a democratic and socialist evolution that Moscow could not accept or allow to go ideologically unchallenged. The Soviet leadership denounced the Yugoslavs for "assisting imperialism" and deviating from the position taken by the Communist parties of other socialist countries, applied economic and political pressure, but stopped far short of military threats or another break.

. . . The continuing deterioration of Soviet relations with China in the 1960s gave impetus to better relations with Yugoslavia. However, the Soviet invasion of Czechoslovakia in August 1968 triggered Yugoslavia's deepest anxieties over Soviet intentions in Eastern Europe, and the Soviet-Yugoslav relationship has fluctuated ever since. Moscow has found the Yugoslav position congenial on many issues, such as the convening of the Conference on Security and Cooperation in Europe (CSCE), the establishment of a nuclear-free zone in the Balkans, the admission of the two Germanies to the United Nations, the condemnation of U.S. policy in Southeast Asia and the Middle East, and the need for disarmament. However, on other issues of core concern to each, for example, on the issue of Soviet authority in Eastern Europe and the world Communist movement, on the policy of nonalignment, and on nonintervention in the internal affairs of socialist countries, their disagreement persists.

Throughout the 1970s, Soviet-Yugoslav relations were generally good: Tito and Brezhnev exchanged visits, disagreed without rancor on bloc politics, Eurocommunism, and China, and encouraged expanded economic ties. Moscow carefully avoided overt threats, though after the 1968 Czechoslovak crisis Belgrade took firm steps to improve its defenses against attack from the east. However, with the death of Tito in May 1980, Soviet-Yugoslav relations enter a period of new uncertainty. A Soviet invasion is always a possibility that cannot be dismissed, since the Kremlin covets permanent military access to the Mediterranean and an end to Yugoslavia's irritating type of national communism, but Moscow is unlikely to bite on such a tough nut. Facing its own succession problem, Moscow is apt to practice patience and await promising opportunities for affecting Yugoslav developments. Through a combination of pressure and accommodation, it will prod the Yugoslav leadership in an attempt to nudge Belgrade closer to the Soviet position on bloc and world issues. Soviet temptation will be a function of Yugoslavia's internal cohesion: the more the post-Tito republic party oligarchs satisfactorily negotiate their differences and sustain national unity, the less the Kremlin will be tempted to intervene, and vice versa.

After the tumultuous events of 1956, Moscow's policy toward Eastern Europe underwent a number of important changes that have dominated its approach since then. First, Moscow accommodated to East European nationalism by granting substantial domestic autonomy to indigenous Communist elites. . . .

Second, the USSR readjusted its economic relations with Eastern Europe. It gave the East Europeans concessionary rates on imports of some Soviet raw materials and extended long-term credits without visible political strings. Third, it accepted expanded economic and cultural links between Eastern Europe and the West, though it did caution bloc members against using "their relations with capitalist countries at the expense of other fraternal countries."

By the time Khrushchev was deposed in October 1964, Soviet policy toward Eastern Europe had changed considerably. From the one-sided and callous exploitation of the Stalin era, it had moved to a more businesslike and sophisticated economic give-and-take. From day-to-day control by pro-Moscow satraps and resident KGB procurators, it had changed to allow considerable autonomy to national Communists in managing their internal affairs, as long as there was no threat to the Communist character of the regime or its loyalty to the USSR. And from imposed conformity to Soviet norms in all things Soviet policy had grown to tolerate diversity in most areas. From a classic type of colonial system, the Soviet–East European bloc has evolved into an imperial system, in which the center places greatest importance on strategic and military control rather than on economic exploitation or cultural conformity.

The duumvirate of Leonid Brezhnev and Alexei Kosygin altered the style— the ebullience of Khrushchev was replaced by the deliberateness of Brezhnev— but not the substance of Khrushchev's policy. They . . . followed the trail he marked to preserve Soviet hegemony in Eastern Europe. Confronted with intensifying nationalism in Eastern Europe, worsening relations with China, and the end of the myth of international Communist solidarity, the Soviet leaders . . . tried to improve relations with the West and find a formula for asserting their authority within the bloc. . . .

INTERVENTION IN CZECHOSLOVAKIA

In January 1968 a combination of disgruntled Stalinists and reformers ousted Antonin Novotny, Moscow's man in Prague, as general secretary of the Czechoslovak Communist party, and brought in Alexander Dubcek. Long a loyal party bureaucrat, Dubcek became the rallying figure for all factions and groups seeking to liberalize Czechoslovak society and to assert a greater autonomy in domestic affairs. By mid-February, liberalization was occurring so rapidly that the skepticism among the population at large changed to hopeful anticipation. By late spring, the air of freedom intoxicated the country. Dubcek and the reformers spoke of a parliament free from party control; they rehabilitated the victims of the Stalinist past, began to rid the party and trade unions of the front men for Moscow, and eliminated censorship. Ludvik Svoboda replaced Novotny as president. In the Central Committee, the Dubcek group was in control. Democratization flowered. From early February to August 1968, Czechoslovakia experienced a rebirth of political, cultural, and social freedom. The secret police were stripped of their arbitrary powers; links to the Soviet KGB apparatus were exposed; criticisms of the past and proposals for the future were aired with a candor and passion that disturbed the oligarchs of Byzantine communism in Moscow.

The "Prague spring" lasted until August 21. In the early hours of that day, Soviet troops invaded Czechoslovakia. As in Hungary in 1956, Moscow responded with overwhelming force to a perceived threat to its strategic military position in Central Europe. Joined by Polish, East German, Hungarian, and Bulgarian (but not Romanian) troops in order to give the intervention a Warsaw Pact imprimatur, the Red Army quickly occupied the country.

From the very beginning, Moscow was exposed and discredited by its own lies. It said that Soviet troops were sent at the request of party and government officials, but Svoboda, Dubcek, and other leaders denied this allegation. It claimed to have acted to forestall an insidious effort at counterrevolution, but the collapse in late August of its initial efforts to install pro-Soviet puppets showed that what was in jeopardy in Czechoslovakia was Soviet domination, not socialism. It resorted to anti-Semitism to tarnish all Czech reformers, a few of whom were Jewish, but abandoned this ploy when it became counterproductive.

The Soviet justification for the invasion of Czechoslovakia appeared in *Pravda* on September 26, 1968. Quickly dubbed the Brezhnev Doctrine, it proclaimed the inherent right of the Soviet Union to intervene anywhere in the socialist world to preserve socialism. While reaffirming the principle of many roads to socialism, it insisted that no action "should do harm either to socialism" in the country or party involved "or to the fundamental interests of other socialist countries and of the entire working-class movement which is striving for socialism. This means that each Communist party is responsible not only to its own people but also to all the socialist countries and to the entire Communist movement." Moreover, the article warned, though every Communist party is free "to apply the basic principles of Marxism-Leninism," it is not free to depart from those principles or to adopt a "nonaffiliated" attitude toward the rest of the socialist community; and though self-determination is each nation's right, it cannot be applied in a way that would weaken the socialist community. World socialism "is indivisible and its defense is the common cause of all Communists." In defending socialism, Moscow proclaimed that it would be the sole judge and jury of when the limits of permissible autonomy had been exceeded, and that it would act accordingly.

In proceeding as they did, Soviet leaders demonstrated the paramountcy of

Eastern Europe in their thinking about the defense of the Soviet Union. They used force even at the risk of jeopardizing many of their policy goals—for example, détente with the United States, including prospects for an agreement limiting strategic delivery systems; the weakening of NATO; and the support of foreign Communists, many of whom publicly condemned the Soviet aggression against an ally and fellow-Communist country. The reasons for the invasion may help us project probable Soviet policy in the future.

What may have been the most important single catalyst was the domestic situation in the Soviet Union. The ethnic and racial diversity of the USSR has a profound effect on Soviet politics and policymaking, though given the secrecy shrouding Soviet foreign-policy decision-making, it is often difficult to adduce this in specific instances. The Russians, who constitute no more than 52 percent of the approximately 260 million Soviet people, have had trouble for more than three-hundred years with the 42 million Ukrainians, the second largest nationality group. Of all the peoples in Eastern Europe, the Czechs and Slovaks are regarded by Ukrainians as the nearest to them in tradition and culture. The Kremlin may well have been afraid that the virus of Czechoslovak liberalization would find a congenial breeding ground in the national consciousness of the Ukrainians and stimulate demands in the Ukrainian SSR for extensive reform. After all, if the Slavs and fraternal Communists of Czechoslovakia were permitted democratization, why not those of the Soviet Union? . . .

A second major consideration in the Soviet decision to invade Czechoslovakia was the pressure of the military to safeguard the Soviet position in Central Europe against possible erosion; strategic imperatives transcended political risks. The Czech suggestion in July 1968 that the Warsaw Pact be revised raised the specter of another Hungarian crisis. The military argued that Czechoslovakia was too centrally placed geographically for Moscow to let it go neutralist or succumb to instability. . . . East German leaders strongly supported the Soviet military, arguing that if Czechoslovakia continued to liberalize, to open her economy to Western investment, and to follow her own way in dealing with the Federal Republic of Germany, as Romania had, the net result would be a severe weakening of the GDR, Moscow's ally in orthodoxy and most important economic partner. Finally, it is also possible that Soviet intelligence had assured the Politburo that the Czechs would not fight and that the affair could be handled swiftly and satisfactorily if massive power were applied.

Thus for both domestic and strategic reasons, Moscow acted in Czechoslovakia as it had in Hungary twelve years earlier. The USSR showed that control over East European real estate is nonnegotiable—that its policy is based on the axiom "What's mine is mine; what's yours is negotiable." It will use force to preserve its imperial system intact. Though seeking better relations with Western Europe, it will not tolerate any erosion of its strategic hold over a contiguous Communist country; nor will considerations of prestige among foreign Communist parties deter it from expeditiously suppressing national Communists who exceed Moscow's guidelines for autonomy.

In Moscow's behavior we see again the dominance of Russian national and imperial interests over the needs and wishes of Communist parties abroad. Different political constellations in control in the Kremlin at any given time may be prepared to accept lesser or greater parameters of autonomy, but the ultimate determination of what is permissible is Moscow's prerogative. Eastern Europe cannot divest itself completely of Soviet influence; geography, the reliance of the "new class" in Eastern Europe on the protective power of the Red Army, growing dependency on imports of Soviet energy, and the realities of international relations preclude such a situation. By keeping fears of a West German revanche alive, particularly among the Poles and East Germans, Moscow ensures their military dependence. Should any of the East European regimes show signs of assuming an anti-Soviet, anti-Communist stance, Moscow would presumably feel impelled to act militarily once again to preserve its perceived vital interests. Its velvet glove contains an iron fist. To paraphrase what the Mexican dictator Porfirio Diaz once said of Mexico and the United States: "Poor Eastern Europe, so far from God, so close to the Soviet Union." . . .

INSTITUTIONALIZING SOVIET HEGEMONY

To stabilize its imperial position in Eastern Europe and promote bloc cohesion and integration, the Soviet Union increasingly relies on a number of multilateral institutions, most notably the Warsaw Treaty Organization (WTO), more commonly referred to as the Warsaw Pact, and the Council for Mutual Economic Assistance (Comecon). The Warsaw Pact was created on May 14, 1955, the day before the signing of the Austrian state treaty. Moscow decided that it needed a formal alliance binding the bloc together. In shifting from an exclusive reliance on bilateralism to a heavy emphasis on multilateralism, it was motivated by several aims. The first and most immediate, given the imminence of the treaty with Austria, was to find a way to legitimize the continued presence in Hungary and Romania of the Soviet troops that had been justified until then on the basis of assuring lines of communication for Soviet occupation forces in Austria. The second, after Moscow had failed to prevent the FRG's [West Germany's] rearmament and formal entry into NATO on May 9, 1955, was to carry through on its previously announced intention to have Soviet-bloc countries "take common measures for the organization of armed forces and their commands," and to create a counterpart to NATO. Third, Moscow wanted an effective instrument for safeguarding its interests in the area.

From the beginning, political objectives were paramount—witness that the first joint military exercises were not held until late 1961. The WTO's Political Consultative Committee, responsible for coordinating all but purely military matters, was inactive in the early years, but took on added importance after the 1968 Czech crisis. In November 1976, it established a committee of Foreign Ministers and a Unified Secretariat in order to improve "the mechanism of political collaboration."

Though formally a military alliance protecting the bloc against external threats, the Warsaw Pact mainly serves an intrabloc policing function. . . . The pact is also used by Moscow to pressure a reluctant member to go along with the consensus view, to persuade bloc members to join with it in isolating a dissident member (for instance, excluding Albania from participation because of its pro-Beijing policies from 1961 to 1978), to rebut Chinese accusations that the USSR is a disintegrating rather than integrating influence within the Communist world, and to encourage a sense of common interest among the members.

The military objectives of the Warsaw Pact, though subordinate, are substantial. They include organizing Eastern Europe as a defensive buffer zone against a possible invasion from the West, extending the Soviet air defense system as far west of the Soviet homeland as possible, serving as an offensive prod against NATO in the event of a war in Europe, creating military forces loyal to the Communist regimes, and promoting bloc unity through standardization of weaponry, tactical coordination, and interlocking command structures. . . .

In its quest for improved military effectiveness and integration, the Soviet Union finds Romania a persistently troublesome stumbling block. Since 1966, when he proposed that the position of commander-in-chief of Warsaw Pact forces be rotated and that the East European members be consulted on decisions affecting the use of nuclear weapons, Ceausescu has moved steadily to reduce Romania's participation. Not only did he refuse to join the invasion of Czechoslovakia and publicly condemn the action as a "flagrant transgression" and contradiction "to the fundamental standards concerning relations that must reign among socialist countries and among Communist parties and of generally recognized principles of international law," but since 1972 he has withdrawn from joint military maneuvers and has had Romanian representatives at WTO meetings maintain a relatively inactive role. . . .

Moscow has so far acted with remarkable restraint. It permits Romania to prevent full military integration because there is no serious NATO force on the "southern tier" Balkan flank and also because it has no fear of liberalization occurring in Romania, where Ceausescu runs a Stalinist-type society. For the moment, imposing a greater degree of military cohesion would only jeopardize the long-term viability of the alliance. So Moscow continues to be patient.

The Soviet leadership has also been unsuccessful in its periodic efforts to persuade members to amend the Warsaw treaty to include non-European states, for example Mongolia. All these complications raise the ultimate question concerning the Warsaw Pact: How reliable would the East European forces be in the event of a war in Europe? A great deal would depend on the kind of war and the circumstances under which it begins. However, judging by the USSR's difficulties in fashioning agreement on basic issues, the thin crust on which the legitimacy of Communist regimes stands, the pervasive suspicion of Moscow that permeates public perceptions in Eastern Europe, and the unwillingness of Soviet leaders to decrease their force levels significantly in the area, the pact's future must be a matter of continuing concern in the Kremlin. . . .

Moscow has used Comecon to promote economic integration, and thereby political stability, in the Soviet bloc. Originally established in January 1949 as a symbolic facade to parallel the Marshall Plan, the Council for Mutual Economic Assistance was for many years a moribund organization. Under Stalin, there was no necessity for a regional organization; the USSR was in physical control and preferred to maximize its exploitation on a bilateral basis. It felt no need to legitimize the Soviet–East European economic relationship.

Starting under Khrushchev in 1955, Comecon went through a period of gradual upgrading: information was pooled, economic agreements were placed on a five-year instead of a one-year basis, and an atmosphere of bargaining replaced that of acquiescence. . . . In institutional terms, Comecon came of age in the 1960s, but actual integration has proceeded very slowly. . . .

In July 1971 Comecon adopted a twenty-year blueprint for integration, albeit within the existing sovereign nation-state system. Moscow is serious about the comprehensive program and insists that it be accorded the status of a multilateral treaty. The program postulates cooperation in drafting five-year economic plans, joint planning, a convertible ruble for making commercial transactions in the bloc easier, pooling of research and productive capacities, cost-sharing for the development of energy resources, and raising the standard of living of less-developed members. However, fundamental problems continue, such as the absence of a supranational authority, the reliance on consensus-building, and the indefiniteness in the statutes about implementing recommendations.[2] . . . Before Soviet-bloc integration can match Western Europe's, Moscow will have to overcome Eastern Europe's suspicion that integration will weaken their national sovereignties and bring a new, disguised form of Soviet interference; regional differences in levels of economic development and each country's desire to industrialize; the desire to insulate national economies from disruptive price competition; and the persistence of political over economic factors in shaping policies toward Comecon.

How stable is Soviet rule in Eastern Europe? Notwithstanding the impressive array of military, economic, political, and ideological arrangements that Moscow uses to perpetuate its strategic control, it must remain very watchful. As one wit observed, the Soviet Union is the only Communist country surrounded by hostile Communist states. The centrifugal forces—nationalism, neorevisionist national communism, slothful economies that consume more than they produce, sociocultural alienation, demands for human rights in accordance with the provisions of the 1975 Helsinki Conference on Security and Cooperation in Europe, and the weakening ideological vigilance of increasingly nationalistic party elites—are a constant worry. On the other hand, Moscow can look with some confidence to the centripetal forces to keep Eastern Europe securely in the Soviet orbit.

First and most unequivocally, the presence of approximately thirty Soviet divisions in East Germany, Poland, Hungary, and Czechoslovakia acts as a constant reminder of the limits of Moscow's tolerance of dissidence, of its capacity to settle any crisis with dispatch. Not only has the USSR shown its readiness to use force if need be to suppress threats to "socialism," but the nations of Eastern Europe know that no help will come from the West. Militarily, Moscow has a free hand to maintain hegemony over the bloc. The constraints on its use of force are internal and bloc-derived.

Second, and of growing importance, Eastern Europe's dependence on Soviet energy and raw materials has increased enormously, and its more active participation in Comecon may well be the sine qua non for continued Soviet assistance. Ever since the energy crisis exploded on the international scene in the mid-1970s, Eastern Europe's economic situation has worsened. Except for Romania, the area is energy poor. By contrast, the USSR is the world's largest producer of oil and natural gas. Since 1975, Moscow has begun to raise the prices of oil and raw materials; it is no longer willing to give its East European partners concessionary benefits. Moscow has told the East Europeans that if they want assured supplies in the future, they must invest in the development of Soviet resources or look elsewhere. No longer will the Soviet Union play the role of a colony to Eastern Europe. . . .

Third, the fears of the individual East European leaderships bind them to a policy of friendship with the Soviet Union. The Poles' phobia is of another Soviet-German deal at their expense; the GDR worries about a Rapallo-type accord between Moscow and Bonn; Romania dreads an imposed return of its part of Transylvania to Hungary, and so on. Discord among nationalities, a potentially explosive brew, lends credence to the Soviet Union's claim that its policy contributes to the maintenance of peace and stability in Eastern Europe.

Fourth, a generation of party-military-secret-police cadres has acquired a stake in the political status quo. They know their regimes ultimately depend on Moscow's friendship, and therefore they pay ritualistic tribute to Marxist-Leninist internationalism to mollify the Kremlin. At the same time, they try to mobilize popular support in order to obtain internal acceptance of their authoritarian regimes.

Finally, there is that least reliable unifying cohesive, ideology — or Moscow's interpretation of what it is at any given moment. It legitimizes Soviet policies, but cannot be counted on for inoculative potency against the virus of nationalism or polycentric communism. When applied to domestic issues, ideology is in many respects nothing more than a fig leaf, a flimsy cover for pretended unity, not a guide to problem-solving or political bargaining within the bloc.

Eastern Europe is destined to remain the USSR's Achilles' heel. Soviet leaders would prefer to prevent crises and not have to suppress them. While recognizing and wishing to avoid the prohibitive costs of a return to Stalinist methods, they must at the same time minimize the contradictions of policies established by Khrushchev—decentralization, diversity, and consumerism, which contain within them the seeds of rampant nationalism, incipient anticommunism, and cynicism toward ideology. Their policy is geared toward reinforcing mutual dependencies and transmuting them into a genuine interdependency that will assure Soviet strategic interests and promote bloc cohesion. Barring serious instability in the USSR, there is no real threat on the horizon to the preeminent Soviet position in Eastern Europe.

NOTES

1. U.S. Department of State, *Soviet Affairs Notes*, no. 224 (July 28, 1958) (Washington, D. C.), 3.
2. See George Ginsburgs, "Unification of Law in the Socialist Commonwealth: The Implications of the 20-Year Comprehensive Programme of Economic Integration," in Donald D. Barry, et al. (eds.), *Codification in the Communist World* (Leiden: A. W. Sijthoff, 1975), 123–144.

17

North and South: What the Third World Wants and Why

STEPHEN D. KRASNER

In this article, Stephen D. Krasner argues that Third World countries seek to restructure international regimes—international institutions, rules, principles, and norms—a goal firmly lodged in the comparatively weak international and domestic positions of Third World leaders, in the opportunities for regime change presented by existing international organizations in a period when United States influence has waned, and in the pervasive belief in the ideology of dependency shared by Third World elites. Dependency, Krasner notes, attributes the persistent underdevelopment of Third World countries "to the workings of the international economic system rather than the indigenous characteristics of their own societies." Krasner is professor of political science at Stanford University. Author of *Defending the National Interest* (1978), he has written extensively in the area of international political economy.

INTRODUCTION

Developing countries have pursued many objectives in the international system. Some objectives have been purely pragmatic, designed to enhance immediate economic well-being. However, the most publicized aspects of North-South relations, global bargaining over the restructuring of international regimes, cannot be understood in strictly economic or instrumental terms. By basically changing principles, norms, rules, and procedures that affect the movement of goods and factors in the world economy, the Third World can enhance not only its economic well-being but also its political control. The emphasis the South has given to fundamental regime change is a manifestation of four basic factors: the international weakness of virtually all developing countries; the domestic weakness of virtually all developing countries; the systemic opportunities offered by the international institutions which were created by a hegemonic power [the United States] now in decline;

Reprinted from Stephen D. Krasner, "Transforming International Regimes: What the Third World Wants and Why," *International Studies Quarterly* 25 (March 1981), pp. 119–148, 161–173. Reprinted by permission of the publisher. Some footnotes have been deleted; others have been renumbered to appear in consecutive order. Bibliographical references not included in the excerpt have been deleted.

AUTHOR'S NOTE: I would like to thank Richard Baum, Peter Gourevitch, Robert Jervis, Peter Katzenstein, Peter Kenen, Robert Keohane, John Ruggie, Arthur Stein, and the editors of the *International Studies Quarterly*. Without their help the arguments presented here would have been far less satisfactory. John Kroll provided very able assistance in analyzing the data on tax structures.

and the pervasive acceptance of a belief system embodying a dependency orientation.

At the international level all states are accorded formal equality as sovereigns: The underlying power capabilities of states establish no presumptive differentiation with regard to certain basic rights, especially sole legitimate authority within a given geographic area. At the same time, the present international system is characterized by an unprecedented differentiation in underlying power capabilities between large and small states. Never have states with such wildly variant national power resources coexisted as formal equals. Very weak states can rarely hope to influence international behavior solely through the utilization of their national power capabilities. For them, regime restructuring is an attractive foreign policy strategy, because it offers a level of control over states with much larger resources that could never be accomplished through normal statecraft grounded in dyadic [bilateral] interactions.

The rigidity and weakness of domestic economic and political structures in developing countries is a second factor that has made basic regime change important for the Third World. With the exception of a small number of countries, the economies of the Third World are dominated by agricultural and primary sectors with low levels of factor mobility. Vulnerability is high because it is difficult to adjust to external changes. Political systems are also weak; the state cannot manipulate those resources that might lessen the impact of pressures emanating from the international environment. International regimes can limit external vacillations or automatically provide resources to compensate for deleterious systemic changes.

The third element accounting for the prominence of a basic regime change strategy is the set of opportunities offered by the character of post-World War II international organizations. These organizations have offered opportunities that made Third World programs more feasible and effective. The Third World has been able to turn institutions against their creators. Such developments are likely to afflict any set of regimes created by a hegemonic power. This power establishes institutions to legitimate its preferred norms and principles, but legitimation can only be effective if the institutions are given independence and autonomy. This autonomy can then be used by weak states to turn the institutions to purposes and principles disdained by the hegemonic power.

Affecting both domestic incentives and international opportunities in the Third World's quest for a new international economic order has been a belief system associated with theories of dependency. This intellectual orientation has been a critical factor, accounting not only for some of the Third World's success, but also for its extraordinary unity on questions associated with regime transformation. Even economically successful developing countries with flexible domestic structures and conservative political regimes have not broken with the Group of 77. In an atmosphere pervaded by *dependencia* perspectives, such a break could undermine a regime's position with domestic elements. No Third World state openly endorses the norms and principles of international liberalism, even if some of them adopt its rules and procedures. The ideological hegemony enjoyed by the United States at the conclusion of World War II has totally collapsed, and the alternative world view presented by dependency analyses has forged the South into a unified bloc on questions related to fundamental regime change.

THE VARIETY OF THIRD WORLD GOALS

The emphasis in this essay on weakness, vulnerability, and the quest for control is not meant to imply that LDCs are uninterested in purely economic objectives. Third World states have pursued a wide variety of goals. These include economic growth, international political equality, influence in international decision-making arenas, autonomy and independence, the preservation of territorial integrity from external invasion or internal fragmentation, the dissemination of new world views at the global level, and the maintenance of regime stability (Wriggens, 1978: 37-39; Rothstein, 1979: 3). They have used a wide variety of tactics to promote these objectives, including commodity organizations, regional coalitions, universal co-alitions, alliances with major powers, local wars to manipulate major powers, irregular violence, bilateral economic arrangements, regulation of multinational corporations, nationalization of foreign holdings, foreign exchange manipulation, and international loans.

This essay does not review all aspects of Third World behavior. It concentrates on an area where political objectives associated with control have been highly salient—Third World efforts to enhance power through the transformation and construction of international regimes. By building or altering international institutions, rules, principles, and norms, weaker countries can both ameliorate the vulnerability imposed by their lack of national material-power capabilities and their weak domestic political structures, and increase resource flows.

Third World political behavior, like all political behavior, can be divided into two categories: relational power behavior which accepts existing regimes, and meta-power behavior which attempts to alter regimes. Relational power refers to the ability to change outcomes or affect the behavior of others in the course of explicit political decision-making processes. Meta-power is the capacity to structure the environment within which decisions are made. This structuring can involve the manipulation of institutional arrangements, norms, and values (Baumgartner and Burns, 1975). Relational power behavior accepts the existing rules of the game; meta-power behavior attempts to alter those rules. . . .

Most studies of international politics have implicitly emphasized relational power because they deal with war and the use of force. In this arena, meta-power considerations are of limited import because institutional restraints, norms, and rules are weak. . . . War outcomes are determined by the relative national material capabilities for the actors involved: what resources are nominally under the jurisdiction of the state, and how well the state is able to mobilize and efficiently deploy these resources.

In issue areas other than the use of force, however, regimes have been more salient. . . . Wars involve relational power strategies based on national power capabilities; nonbelligerent issue areas are susceptible to meta-power strategies designed to alter regimes.

Third World states are interested in employing both relational power and meta-power. Proposals for regime change, voiced by the less developed countries, reflect an effort to exercise meta-power. The objective of these proposals, of which the program associated with the New International Economic Orders (NIEO) is the most recent and salient, is to transform the basic institutional structures, norms, principles, and rules that condition the international movement of goods, services, capital, labor, and technology. Such transformation is particularly attractive because the ability of Third World states to accomplish their objective solely through the exercise of relational power is limited by the exiguity of their national material-power capabilities. These alone could not resolve the vulnerability problem of poorer states.

Most Third World proposals for regime change have been made in international organizations. Debates within these organizations have been concerned with institutional structures, norms, and rules, not just the transfer of resources. . . .

THIRD WORLD MOTIVATIONS

Third World demands for regime restructuring cannot be seen in any simple way as a reflection of economic failure. During the postwar period the overall rate of growth of developing areas has been faster than that of industrialized countries. Trade patterns have become more diverse with regard to partners and commodities. Indicators of social well-being, including life expectancy, infant mortality, and literacy, have dramatically increased in many areas. The economic performance of the South during the postwar period has been better than that of the industrialized countries during the nineteenth century.

However, the South continues to suffer from an enormous gap in power capabilities at the international level and from social rigidity and political weakness at the domestic level. Creating new regimes that reflect Southern preferences is one way to deal with these structural weaknesses.

International Structures

There have always been small states in the modern international system. Before the industrial revolution, however, there was little variation in levels of economic development. With regard to per capita income, the richest country was only about twice as well off as the poorest at the beginning of the nineteenth century. Now, the richest countries are 80 to 100 times better off than the poorest. The combination of small size and underdevelopment has left many Third World states in an unprecedentedly weak position. . . .

In 1830, the ratio of the GNPs of the largest state, Russia, to the smallest state for which figures are available, Denmark, was 41:1. In 1970, the ratio of the national incomes of the largest state, the United States, and the smallest, the Maldives, was 97,627:1. By 1970, 34% of the states in the international system had national incomes that were less than one thousandth that of the United States and 72% had national incomes less than one hundredth of the U.S. figure. These are staggering disparities. In 1970, the Third World as a whole accounted for only 11% of world GNP (Leontief, 1977: 8).

With the exception of China, there is no Third World country that can lay claim to great power status. However, the GNP of the United States is 5.64 times larger than China's. Countries proffered as regional hegemonic powers do not have impressive national power capabilities. In the mid-1970s, the GNPs of India and Brazil (the two largest in the Third World after China) were about the same as those of Spain and Poland; Iran's (and this before the Khomeini regime) rivalled Belgium's; Saudi Arabia and Nigeria had GNPs about equal to those of Denmark and Finland.

There is little prospect for fundamental change in the foreseeable future. . . .

Thus, if attention is focused on the GNP gap between the North and South, the situation of Third World countries is bleak. Few can hope to challenge even medium to small size industrialized countries in the area of aggregate economic activity. Even with rapid rates of economic growth, the absolute gap is now so large that it cannot be closed in the foreseeable future.[1]

Using GNP figures as a measure of power capability has the advantages of easy comparability and accessibility; however, it also has the disadvantage of obscuring potential variations in power capabilities across different issue areas. Yet, even at a disaggregated level, there is little evidence that Third World countries can act effectively by utilizing only their national material resources. In the area of raw materials cartelization efforts have failed—with the exception of oil—although coffee exporting states have had sporadic success in pushing up prices by buying in London and New York, and copper producers in withholding stock from the market. The fundamental problem for the exporters of primary commodities is that there is a high temptation to cheat on any cartel scheme, because the marginal rewards of additional revenues for Third World governments strapped for resources are very high (Krasner, 1974). With regard to trade in manufactures, Third World exporters depend far more on Northern markets than industrialized countries do on manufactured goods from the South. Northern countries have import competing industries capable of producing the same products, while the South does not have alternative markets. With regard to bank lending, large Third World debtors, especially Mexico and Brazil, have secured some leverage through the consequences of default. While this has given them continued access to credit markets, it has not enabled them to alter the basic nature of credit relations or to keep interest rates down.[2] Smaller debtors carrying heavy burdens are rolling over their old debt but having difficulty securing new loans.

---

[1] The condition for beginning to close the absolute gap is that the ratio of the growth rate of the smaller country to the growth rate of the larger exceed the ratio of the GNP of the larger country to the GNP of the smaller. In the mid-1970s even the fastest growing LDCs, such as Korea and Brazil (which were growing four times faster than most industrialized countries), did not meet this condition for the United States, although they did for most European countries.

[2] Brazil has recently been paying spreads of up to 1.5% above LIBOR while industrialized countries have been securing spreads of 0.5% or less even though the Euro-dollar market is flush with new deposits from oil-exporting states.

There are two major exceptions to these comments about Third World national power capabilities in specific-issue areas. The first is OPEC, where the combination of excess financial resources and inelastic demand has enabled Third World countries to raise prices eightfold in nominal terms over the last seven years. The second is national control of multinational corporations. Many developing countries have excluded MNCs from certain sectors, nationalized or unilaterally altered the concessions of petroleum and hard mineral corporations, and limited the ownership share of foreign nationals either generally or in specific industries (UN, 1978: 19–24). . . . However, the pressure that can be exercised by host countries is limited by the ability of firms to relocate in more hospitable countries.[3]

Aside from oil and domestic regulation of MNCs, few Third World states have any ability to alter their international environment solely through the use of national material-power capabilities. Their small size and limited resources, even in specific-issue areas, is the first condition that has led them to attempt the fundamental alteration of international regimes. Conventional statecraft based upon national material attributes is unlikely to reduce vulnerabilities. A meta-political strategy designed to alter rules, norms, and institutions offers an attractive alternative, if only by default.

Domestic Structures

The second condition that has driven Third World states to attempt a transformation of international regimes is the weakness of their own domestic societies and political systems. The international weakness of most developing states, as indicated by their small aggregate output in comparison with that of industrialized states, suggests that they cannot directly influence the international system. It also suggests that they will be subject to external forces that they cannot change. Small states are usually more heavily involved in the world economy. In 1973, trade (exports plus imports) was equal to 37% of GNP for developing countries, 29% for industrialized countries. In the same year, 48 out of 87 LDCs had trade proportions greater than 50% (International Bank for Reconstruction and Development, 1976: Table 3).

Although small states, as a rule, are more heavily involved in the world economy, state size does not determine internal capacity to modulate the pressures emanating from an uncertain international environment. A small, adaptable state could adjust to many regime structures. Such a state could accept its lack of influence at the international level but remain confident of its ability to deal with environmental disturbances over a wide range of international rules, norms, and institutions. . . .

Social Rigidity. At early stages of development, countries lack the capability to absorb and adjust to external shocks. This incapacity is produced by rigidities inherent in traditional structures. In an elegant analysis concerned with problems

---

[3] For an excellent review of Third World power capabilities with conclusions similar to these see Smith (1977).

of national dependence, Jowitt (1978) elaborates five characteristics of a traditional or status society. First, a status society is based upon exclusive corporate groups, which lock individuals within a rigid structure. Second, social action is determined by personal rather than impersonal norms. Different individuals are treated in different ways because of ascriptive characteristics. Third, the division of labor in the society is based on assignment to specific ascriptive groups. An individual's economic activity is permanently established by his group membership. Fourth, the ontology of the society stresses the concrete and discrete. General principles that can be applied to a wide range of situations are eschewed. Fifth, the world is seen composed of "concrete and discrete elements—that is, indivisible units—economic, social, cultural, and political resources are seen as being finite and immobile rather than expanding and flexible." By contrast, modern societies are market rather than status-based. Interactions are governed by impersonal norms of action. The individual and the nuclear family, rather than the corporate group, are the building blocks of the society (Jowitt, 1978: 7–10).

Modern societies are less vulnerable to external changes because their factors are more mobile. Better-trained workers can perform a wider variety of tasks. More-developed capital markets can more readily reallocate investment resources. It is easier for an industrial worker to move from one factory to another than for a peasant to shift from one crop to another, much less move from agrarian to industrial employment. In his seminal study of the power aspects of international trade, Hirschman (1945: 28) argues that "the inherent advantage with respect to all these aspects of the mobility of resources lies overwhelmingly with the great manufacturing and trading countries as opposed to countries in which agriculture or mining predominates."

The transition from traditional to modern society is taking place in the Third World, but it is a slow and difficult process. It is not unidirectional or irreversible, as events in Iran and Cambodia demonstrate. Most developing countries are still in what Chenery (1979: 18, 29) has called the early phase of the transition from a traditional to a modern economy which occurs at per capita income levels from $200 to $600 (in 1976 dollars). In this phase, societies are vulnerable to external shock. Most employment is still in agriculture. Cross-national data indicate that, on average, industrial output does not exceed agricultural output until per capita incomes of $800 are reached, and that industrial employment does not exceed agricultural employment until per capita income is $1600.

. . . Almost 50% of the developing countries for which figures are available have at least four times as many workers in agriculture as in industry. Most Third World countries have not moved very far along the path from tradition to modernity. While there is considerable variation among the countries of the Third World, a very sharp cleavage still exists between industrialized and developing countries.

Political Weakness. The rigidity of the social and economic structure in developing countries is reflected in the political system. Most central political institutions in the Third World are weak. The state is often treated as but one more compartmentalized unit. Its ability to extract resources from the society is limited. Efforts to combine diverse social and material units are likely to be frustrated by the compartmentalized nature of the society. Economic activity that takes place outside the market cannot be effectively tapped by the government.[4] Often the state is unable to resist pressure from powerful society groups. Low levels of skill and education make it difficult to formulate effective economic policies. Under conditions of social mobilization and low levels of political institutionalization, the likely outcome is political decay rather than political development (Huntington, 1968). The state is rarely able to adjust domestic structures in ways that would lessen the deleterious consequences of external changes.

The situation of most Third World states can be illuminated by contrasting it with that of small industrialized countries. The small developed countries have little control over the international environment. Although they have generally placed more emphasis on international organizations and international norms than larger states, they have not made regime transformation a major aspect of their foreign policies. At least in part, this is because small industrialized countries are much better able to adjust to external shocks. . . .

 . . . [T]he political systems of . . . small European states are characterized by dense policy networks which fuse the public and the private sectors. These networks integrate all groups within the society. They facilitate communication and prevent stalemate. The political organization of the small states has allowed them to enjoy the economic benefits of full participation in the international economy, while insulating their domestic social structures from the disruptive consequences that would ensue from uncontrolled external perturbation.

Tax Structures. Tax structures offer the opportunity to illustrate differences between the political capabilities of industrialized and developing countries. Tax collection is generally a good indicator of the ability of the state to extract resources from its own society.[5] Developing countries collect a smaller proportion of their GNPs than industrialized states and rely more heavily upon trade taxes; the level of state revenue is, therefore, more subject to international economic vicissitudes. . . .

Government revenues are but one indicator of the impact of the world economy on particular states. . . . One of the persistent complaints of Third World countries has been that they suffer from substantial trade fluctuation. While the vacillations in trade experienced by developing countries have declined, they are still much larger than those affecting industrialized countries. The Third World has argued that these vacillations inhibit their economic growth. However, no empirical substantiation has been found for this claim. One study even reveals a

---

[4] See Ardant (1975) for a discussion of the importance of the market for European fiscal development.

[5] The most glaring exceptions to this generalization are levies imposed by oil-exporting and some other resource-producing countries on multinational corporations. The centralized structure of resource extraction industries makes them easy targets even for weak states.

The calculations in this section are based on United Nations, *Statistical Yearbook*, Public Finance Tables for total government revenue, total government expenditures, and trade revenues; National Account and Gross Domestic Product Tables for gross domestic product; International Monetary Fund, *International Financial Statistics* for consumer price indices, imports and exports; World Bank, *World Bank Atlas*, 1977 for per capita GNP.

positive relationship between export instability and economic growth (Knudsen and Parnes, 1975: 7-15).

While vacillations in trade may not be related to economic growth, they are related to the state's ability to extract revenue. Political leaders can be more sensitive to threats to their command over resources that can be used for immediate political purposes than they are to threats to the long-term economic growth prospects of their countries. Third World disaffection with the trading regime may be rooted in the weak domestic political structures of LDCs which necessitate reliance on trade taxes.

The NICS vs OPEC

There is one major exception to these generalizations about weak political and rigid social structures in Third World countries. The newly industrializing countries, or NICs, have been able to adjust effectively to the international environment. Singapore, Hong Kong, Taiwan, South Korea, and Brazil have adopted aggressive export-oriented strategies. In Hong Kong the private market has acted effectively in a laissez-faire situation. In the other NICs the government has been more active. In Korea and Brazil for instance, the state explicitly decided to promote export-oriented growth and move away from protectionism in the early 1960s. Despite domestic pressure, both were able to maintain lower effective exchange rates, a precondition for international export competitiveness. Through the 1970s, the NICs were able to adjust to restrictions imposed by industrialized nations by developing new product lines and diversifying their exports (Krueger, 1978: ch. 2; Yoffie, 1980). For the period 1970-1976, Korea's exports grew at an annual average rate of 31.7%, Taiwan's at 16.2%, Brazil's at 10.3%, Hong Kong's at 8.6% and Singapore's at 14.1%. The average rate of export growth for low-income countries for the same period was −0.4%, for all middle-income LDCs (the category into which the NICs fall) 3.8%, and for industrialized countries 7.8% (International Bank for Reconstruction and Development, 1978: Tables 2 and 6).

The NICs are one of the two groups of dramatic success stories with regard to economic growth, or at least transfers, in the postwar period. The other is oil-exporting states. If purely economic considerations are used to explain the behavior of developing countries, the difference in foreign policy orientations of countries in these two groups is difficult to understand. Both the NICs and the OPEC countries have dramatically benefited from the present system. While none of the NICs have taken a leading role in the South's efforts to restructure international regimes, a number of OPEC countries have been at the forefront of the Third World movement. Algeria and Venezuela have taken leading roles in the Group of 77. Iraq, Libya, and now Iran are hardly devotees of the existing global order.

While the NICs and OPEC countries are comparable with regard to income growth and export earnings, their vulnerabilities to changes in the international economy are dramatically different. The NICs are moving toward flexible economic structures and strong political systems capable of adjusting to shifts in the external environment. The OPEC countries now enjoy enormous bargaining power as a result of the inelastic demand for petroleum and the low opportunity costs of controlling supplies for the surplus OPEC states. However, few OPEC countries would be able to adjust to alterations in bargaining power. Their domestic factors are immobile. Their political structures are weak. The international radicalism of some OPEC countries is not compatible with a conventional orientation which explains the disaffection of developing countries as a manifestation of their lack of economic success.

Domestic structural weakness, a manifestation of traditional social norms, and political underdevelopment, together become a second factor that makes international regime transformation attractive for almost all Third World countries. The external environment is inherently threatening even in the absence of any direct effort by more powerful states to exercise leverage. International regimes controlled by developing countries can mitigate the exposure of developing areas to systemically generated changes. They offer some control in a situation where the lack of domestic adjustment capacity precludes effective cushioning against external shocks.

SYSTEMIC OPPORTUNITIES

Demands for regime restructuring have occupied a dominant place in North-South relations, not simply because this approach could compensate for the international and domestic weakness of Third World states, but because the postwar system offered developing countries a setting in which to pursue this strategy: The prominence given to metapolitical goals has been a function of opportunities as well as needs. The postwar liberal regime, especially the importance that it accorded to international organizations, provided the Third World with forums in which to press their demands. . . .

In the postwar period, the Third World has made international organizations a centerpiece of its demands for regime change. The South has succeeded in dominating the agendas of all major multifunctional universal organizations. The North has been compelled to respond rather than initiate. Convening an international conference places an issue on the agendas of Northern states. Position papers have to be prepared. Voting positions must be determined (Wriggins, 1978: 113).

Debates and resolutions presented at international forums have altered norms, rules, and procedures in a variety of ways favored by developing countries. Various resolutions have endorsed 0.7% of GNP as a target for concessionary capital transfers from the North to the South. While this norm is more honored in the breach, it is still held up as a goal that has been accepted by the North as well as the South. . . . In the immediate postwar period there was no accepted international norm for the level of aid, and policies were unilaterally set by donors.

In the area of trade, developing countries have used GATT [General Agreement on Trade and Tariffs] to legitimate concessional treatment. During the 1960s, the industrialized countries agreed to institute a generalized system of preferences that would eliminate tariffs on some products from developing countries. The nontariff barrier codes and revisions to the GATT Articles of Agreement negotiated during the Tokyo Round provide for special and differential treatment for developing countries, although more symmetrical behavior is expected as countries reach higher stages of development. These changes are a fundamental break with the two central norms of the postwar trading order: nondiscrimination and reciprocity. The South has enshrined new principles emphasizing development and equity, not just secured exceptions from the old liberal rules.

Southern pressure exercised at international forums has secured acceptance of the principle that major parts of the global commons are the common heritage of mankind. Developing countries have made claims on radio frequencies and outer space, even though they do not now have the technical capability to utilize them. Mining activity in the deep seabed will be controlled by an international authority and revenues from the exploitation of manganese nodules will be taxed to provide assistance to the South. Some developing countries have called for the internationalization of Antarctica, although their ability to press this claim has been impeded by the lack of a suitable international forum (Petersen, 1980: 401-402). The common heritage of mankind is radically different from the prevailing principles before the 1960s, which recognized the right of a state to claim unutilized areas that it could occupy or develop.

Even in the area of monetary affairs, that bastion of postwar conservatism, the South has had some success, at least within the regimes' formal institutional manager, the IMF. While LDCs did not get an aid link with SDRs [Special Drawing Rights, popularly known as "paper gold"], they did get an allocation based on quotas. The industrialized nations had originally wanted virtually to exclude developing countries. The partial use of IMF gold sales to establish a Trust Fund (which makes loans to developing countries with few conditions at concessional interest rates) is a form of international taxation for aid. The Fund has begun to liberalize its conditions for stand-by agreements. In an international environment, in which the scope and growth of Fund activities will depend in part on continuing willingness of developing countries to use its resources, the organization has moved to change its rules and procedures if not its basic principles.

In general the institutional structure has become more responsive to the South. By using its voting majority in the General Assembly, the South has been able to create new institutions, especially UNCTAD and UNIDO, which represent its interests. Even in established forums, where votes are not equally divided, the South has changed voting power and decision-making procedures. Mutual veto voting arrangements for major decisions now prevail in all international financial institutions, including the Fund. In the Inter-American Development Bank, the largest of the regional lending institutions, and in the United Nations Development Program the Third World has a majority of votes. In the newest international financial institution, the International Fund for Agricultural Development, votes are equally divided between OPEC countries, non-oil developing countries, and industrialized countries.

Thus, in a variety of issue areas the South has been able to alter principles, norms, rules, and procedures. It is difficult to imagine similar success in the absence of institutional structures that provided automatic access for developing countries. By taking advantage of the autonomy that the hegemonic power, the

United States, was compelled to confer on international organizations during the period of regime formation at the conclusion of World War II, Third World countries have been able to alter regime characteristics during the period of American hegemonic decline. The relationship between underlying national power capabilities and regime characteristics has become increasingly incongruent.

BELIEF SYSTEMS

While vulnerabilities that arise from domestic and international weakness provide the impetus for Third World demands—and international organizations the opportunity to realize them—the form and unity of these goals have been shaped by the pervasive acceptance of dependency orientations. Most developing countries have explicitly accepted arguments that attribute their underdevelopment to the workings of the international economic system rather than the indigenous characteristics of their own societies. The belief system has been endorsed, not only by individual states, but by international organizations close to the Third World, such as UNCTAD and the UNDP, as well as by important groups with claims to speak for the North as well as the South.[6] Individual states may reject dependency prescriptions in practice but even the most conservative lack a belief system to offer in its stead.

The dependency orientation serves important functions for Third World states both internationally and domestically. At the international level, dependency arguments have provided a unifying rationale for disparate Southern demands. Calls for special and differential treatment are justified by the contention that the South has been treated unjustly in the past. Existing norms and rules are rejected as inherently exploitative. A coherent intellectual orientation has been particularly important because of the strategy of using international organizations to promote meta-political goals. In such arenas the ability to define issues and control the agenda is critical. Such initiatives are facilitated by a widely shared and internally consistent analytic framework.

Dependency perspectives are also linked to domestic political conditions in Third World countries. Given the limitations on effective state action, foreign policy is an attractive way to build support. Prominence in universal coalitions can enhance a Third World leader's domestic position. Castigating the North can rally bureaucratic, military, and popular elements. The structure of international organizations affords Third World statesmen an opportunity to play on the world stage, a platform which they could not mount if they had to rely solely on the domestic power capabilities of their countries. Even if their activity is perceived as a minor walk-on part by more powerful countries, an effective leader may transform it into a major role for domestic political consumption (Wriggins, 1978: 40; Korany, 1976: 86; Good, 1962: 7).

Third World leaders who follow such a course must find ideological arguments

---

[6] An important example is the report of the Brandt Commission (Independent Commission on International Development Issues 1980).

that resonate with their domestic populations. The most accessible themes reject existing international regimes. For most countries in Asia and Africa, if not Latin America, the central historical event is decolonization. Anticolonialism and nationalism are widely accepted values endorsed by virtually all groups in the Third World (Packenham, 1973: 41; Good, 1962: 5; Rothstein, 1977: 75-76, 110; Nettl, 1968: 591). Dependency arguments are widely diffused. A Third World leader who opts for enhancing support through international behavior will reject existing rules, norms, and institutions. . . .

The belief system of dependency is a key factor in explaining the exceptional unity maintained by the Third World in its quest for a New International Economic Order. Despite the substantial diversity that exists among developing countries with respect to economic and political structures, there have been no outright defections from the Group of 77. This unity is not the result of log-rolling. The NIEO program would disproportionately benefit a small number of countries heavily involved in the export of raw materials or manufactures. In some cases, such as policy toward OPEC, a strategy of alliance with the industrialized countries would be more in accord with Third World economic interests. However, attacking OPEC and pointing to differences among Third World states would contradict the basic analytic conclusion of the dependency perspective. Since this viewpoint is widely accepted within developing countries, not just voiced at international forums, it is difficult for even highly developed Third World countries with conservative regimes to break with the rest of the South and endorse the liberal order. The attitude of Third World states toward calls for regime transformation has only ranged from strident advocacy to passive acquiescence. It has not included outright rejection or alliance with the North. . . .

[The author here uses Mexico to illustrate the arguments elaborated above. He notes in particular that, despite Mexico's impressive economic performance in the 1960s and 1970s, Mexican leaders were major critics of the existing international order—*eds.*]

CONCLUSION

The countries of the Third World have not simply sought higher levels of resource transfer. They have wanted to restructure international regimes. In some cases they have succeeded. The New International Economic Order is the successor of SUNFED, and the First and Second Development Decades. It will be followed by other programs with different names but the same import—control, not just wealth. The NIEO, and its antecedents and probable successors, cannot be understood through analogies to reform efforts within national politics such as the labor union, consumer, welfare, and civil rights movements in the United States. These were movements based upon shared norms; the South rejects the liberal norms of the American-created postwar system. They were movements content to share power within existing structures; the South wants effective control over new structures.

The demands of the South are a function of the profound international and domestic weakness of most Third World states. These demands may temporarily abate but they will not disappear. Since most states of the South cannot hope to garner the national resource capabilities needed to assert effective control in the international system, they will continue to press for international institutions and norms that can offer them some control over the international environment. In the pursuit of this goal, they will enjoy some success by taking advantage of institutional structures that were created by the powerful to serve their own purposes. In this, and other ways, the power of hegemonic states is dissipated by the very structures they have created.

REFERENCES

ARDANT, G. (1975) "Financial policy and economic infrastructure of modern states and nations," pp. 164-242 in C. Tilly (ed.) The Formation of National States in Western Europe. Princeton, NJ: Princeton Univ. Press.

BAUMGARTNER, T. and T. R. BURNS (1975) "The structuring of international economic relations." Int. Studies Q. 19 (June): 126-159.

CHENERY, H. (1979) Structural Change and Development Policy. New York: Oxford Univ. Press.

GOOD, R. C. (1962) "State-building as a determinant foreign policy in the new states," in L. W. Martin (ed.) Neutralism and Nonalignment. New York: Praeger.

HIRSCHMAN, A. O. (1945) National Power and the Structure of Foreign Trade. Berkeley: Univ. of California Press.

HUNTINGTON, S. P. (1973) "Transnational organizations in world politics." World Politics 25 (April): 333-368.

————— (1968) Political Order in Changing Societies. New Haven, CT: Yale Univ. Press.

International Bank for Reconstruction and Development (1980) World Tables. Baltimore: Johns Hopkins Univ. Press.

————— (1978) World Development Report. Washington, DC: IBRD.

————— (1977) World Bank Atlas. Washington, DC: IBRD.

————— (1976) World Tables. Baltimore: Johns Hopkins Univ. Press.

International Monetary Fund (various years) International Financial Statistics. Washington, DC: IMF.

JOWITT, K. (1978) The Leninist Response to National Dependence. Berkeley, CA: Institute of International Studies.

KNUDSEN, O. and A. PARNES (1975) Trade Instability and Economic Development: An Empirical Study. Lexington, MA: D. C. Heath.

KORANY, B. (1976) Social Change, Charisma and International Behavior: Toward a Theory of Foreign Policy-making in the Third World. Leiden: A. W. Sijthoff.

KRASNER, S. D. (1974) "Oil is the exception." Foreign Policy 14 (Spring): 68-83.

KRUEGER, A. O. (1978) Foreign Trade Regimes and Economic Development: Liberalization Attempts and Consequences. Cambridge, MA: Ballinger.

LEONTIEF, W., P. CARTER, and P. A. PETRI (1977) The Future of the World Economy. New York: Oxford Univ. Press.

NETTL, J. P. (1968) "The state as a conceptual variable." World Politics 20 (July) 559-592.

PACKENHAM, R. A. (1973) Liberal America and the Third World. Princeton, NJ: Princeton Univ. Press.

PETERSON, M. J. (1980) "Antarctica: the last great land rush on earth." Int. Organization 34: 377-404.

ROTHSTEIN, R. L. (1979) Global Bargaining: UNCTAD and the Quest for a New International Economic Order. Princeton, NJ: Princeton Univ. Press.

——— (1977) The Weak in the World of the Strong: The Developing Countries in the International System. New York: Columbia Univ. Press.

SMITH, T. (1977) "Changing configurations of power in North-South relations since 1945." Int. Organization 31 (Winter): 1-27.

United Nations (1978) "Transnational corporations in world development: a reexamination." E/C.10/38, March 20.

——— (various years) Statistical Yearbook. New York: UN.

WRIGGINS, W. H. (1978) "Third World strategies for change: the political context of North-South interdependence," in W. H. Wriggins and G. Adler-Karlsson, Reducing Global Inequities. New York: McGraw-Hill.

YOFFIE, D. (1980) The Advantages of Adversity: Weak States and the Politics of Trade. Ph.D. dissertation, Stanford University.

18

The United Nations and World Politics

JAVIER PEREZ de CUELLAR

Each year the secretary-general of the United Nations makes a report on the work of the organization that effectively represents his personal statement on global issues. In his first annual report, Secretary-General Javier Perez de Cuellar departed from the tradition of summarizing the UN's role in coping with world problems. Instead, he addressed problems with the United Nations itself. In discussing what member states ought to do to make the United Nations more effective, the secretary-general focuses clearly on the UN's shortcomings as an instrument for conflict management and resolution and as a mechanism for the improvement of global welfare. Perez de Cuellar is secretary-general of the United Nations.

The past year has seen an alarming succession of international crises as well as stalemates on a number of fundamental international issues. The United Nations itself has been unable to play as effective and decisive a role as the Charter certainly envisaged for it. Therefore, in this, my first annual report to the General Assembly, I shall depart from the usual practice of surveying the broad range of the work of the United Nations; instead I shall focus on the central problem of the Organization's capacity to keep the peace and to serve as a forum for negotiations. I shall try to analyse its evident difficulties in doing so, difficulties related to conflicts between national aims and Charter goals and to the current tendency to resort to confrontation, violence and even war in pursuit of what are perceived as vital interests, claims or aspirations. The general international divisions and disorder which have characterized the past year have unquestionably made it even more difficult than usual for the Organization to be, as it was intended to be, a centre for harmonizing the actions of nations in the attainment of common ends.

The problems faced by the United Nations in fulfilling its mission derive in large measure from the difficulties which Governments appear to have in coming to terms, both within and outside the Organization, with the harsh realities of the time in which we live. This question is, of course, highly relevant to the use, misuse or non-use of the United Nations as an instrument for peace and rational change.

I am of the view that we now have potentially better means to solve many of the major problems facing humanity than ever before. For this reason I retain, in

Reprinted from Javier Perez de Cuellar *Report of the Secretary-General on the Work of the Organization 1982* (New York: United Nations, 1982).

the last analysis, a sense of optimism. This basic optimism, however, is tempered by our apparent inability to make adequate use of these means. Instead we sometimes appear still to be in the grip of the dead hand of a less fortunate past. As a result we often lack the vision to differentiate between short-term advantage and long-term progress, between politically expedient positions and the indispensable objective of creating a civilized and peaceful world order. While such attitudes do not affect the validity of the ideals of the Charter, they seriously impair the proper utilization of the machinery of the United Nations for the purposes for which it was set up.

We live today in the presence of a chilling and unprecedented phenomenon. At the peak of world power there exist enough nuclear weapons to destroy life on our planet. It seems evident that nothing worthwhile would survive such a holocaust, and this fact, above all else, contains the nuclear confrontation—for the time being at least.

In the middle level of world power there exist vast quantities of sophisticated, so-called conventional weapons. . . . These weapons are, by comparison with those of former times, immensely destructive, and they are actually being used. They are also the objects of a highly profitable international trade.

At yet another level we have the poverty of a vast proportion of the world's population—a deprivation inexplicable in terms either of available resources or of the money and ingenuity spent on armaments and war. We have unsolved but soluble problems of economic relations, trade, distribution of resources and technology. We have many ideas and plans as to how to meet the growing needs of the large mass of humanity, but somehow such human considerations seem to take second place to the technology and funding of violence and war in the name of national security.

It is for these reasons that our peoples, especially the young, take to the streets in their hundreds of thousands in many parts of the world to proclaim their peaceful protest against the existing situation and their deep fear of the consequences of the arms race and nuclear catastrophe. Who can say that these gentle protesters are wrong or misguided? On the contrary, they recall us to the standards and the duties which we set ourselves in the Charter of the United Nations. The States Members of this Organization should not ignore the significance of what they are trying to say.

What in reality is the role and the capacity of the United Nations in such a world? Our Charter was born of six years of global agony and destruction. I sometimes feel that we now take the Charter far less seriously than did its authors, living as they did in the wake of a world tragedy. I believe therefore that an important first step would be a conscious recommitment by Governments to the Charter.

Certainly we have strayed far from the Charter in recent years. Governments that believe they can win an international objective by force are often quite ready to do so, and domestic opinion not infrequently applauds such a course. The Security Council, the primary organ of the United Nations for the maintenance of international peace and security, all too often finds itself unable to take decisive action to resolve international conflicts and its resolutions are increasingly defied or ignored by those that feel themselves strong enough to do so. Too frequently the Council seems powerless to generate the support and influence to ensure that its decisions are respected, even when these are taken unanimously. Thus the process of peaceful settlement of disputes prescribed in the Charter is often brushed aside. Sterner measures for world peace were envisaged in Chapter VII of the Charter, which was conceived as a key element of the United Nations system of collective security, but the prospect of realizing such measures is now deemed almost impossible in our divided international community. We are perilously near to a new international anarchy.

I believe that we are at present embarked on an exceedingly dangerous course, one symptom of which is the crisis in the multilateral approach in international affairs and the concomitant erosion of the authority and status of world and regional intergovernmental institutions. Above all, this trend has adversely affected the United Nations, the instrument that was created specifically to prevent such a self-destructive course. Such a trend must be reversed before once again we bring upon ourselves a global catastrophe and find ourselves without institutions effective enough to prevent it.

While I do not propose here to review in detail specific situations and developments, it is, of course, my deep concern about them which leads me to examine the underlying deficiencies of our present system. The tragedy of Lebanon and the imperative need to resolve the problem of the Middle East in all its aspects, including the legitimate rights of the Palestinians and the security of all States in the region; the war between Iran and Iraq; the political situation relating to Afghanistan; the prevailing convulsion of Central America; questions relating to Kampuchea; painful efforts to reach a settlement in Cyprus; the situation in Western Sahara and in the Horn of Africa—these and other potential conflict situations, although often differing widely in their nature, should all be responsive to a respected international system for the peaceful settlement of disputes. Even in the sudden crisis over the Falkland/Malvinas Islands, despite the intensive negotiations which I conducted with the full support and encouragement of the Security Council and which endeavoured to narrow the differences between the parties, it nevertheless proved impossible in the end to stave off the major conflict.

Yet in all of these cases, all of the parties would have gained immeasurably in the long run from the effectiveness of a system for the peaceful settlement of disputes. In the case of Namibia we now see some signs of the possibility of a solution after many setbacks. Let us hope that this will prove a welcome exception to the general rule. But the lesson is clear—something must be done, and urgently, to strengthen our international institutions and to adopt new and imaginative approaches to the prevention and resolution of conflicts. Failure to do so will exacerbate precisely that sense of insecurity which, recently, cast its shadow over the second special session of the General Assembly devoted to disarmament. Despite present difficulties, it is imperative for the United Nations to dispel that sense of insecurity through joint and agreed action in the field of disarmament, especially nuclear disarmament.

I must mention here some of the other main sides of our work. There is the promotion and protection of human rights throughout the world. . . . There are the great humanitarian challenges, often involving large numbers of refugees and displaced persons, whose plight in many parts of the world is the tragic reflection of political strife and economic distress. There is the grave and as yet unsolved problem of *apartheid*. There is, furthermore, the whole spectrum of issues related to social and economic development, which so vitally affect both present conditions and future prospects. . . .

In our endeavour to carry out this extremely wide and demanding range of tasks, a fundamental requirement is the continued dedication, integrity and professionalism of the international civil service. I expect the highest standards from the staff of the Secretariat and, for my part, am determined to protect their independence and to ensure that performance and merit are the essential criteria for professional advancement. . . .

It seems to me that our most urgent goal is to reconstruct the Charter concept of collective action for peace and security so as to render the United Nations more capable of carrying out its primary function. It was the lack of an effective system of collective security through the League of Nations that, among other factors, led to the Second World War. Although we now face a vastly changed world situation, Governments in fact need more than ever a workable system of collective security in which they can have real confidence. Without such a system, Governments will feel it necessary to arm themselves beyond their means for their own security, thereby increasing the general insecurity. Without such a system, the world community will remain powerless to deal with military adventures which threaten the very fabric of international peace, and the danger of the widening and escalation of local conflicts will be correspondingly greater. Without such a system there will be no reliable defence or shelter for the small and weak. And without such a system all of our efforts on the economic and social side, which also need their own collective impetus, may well falter.

There are many ways in which Governments could actively assist in strengthening the system prescribed in the Charter. More systematic, less last-minute use of the Security Council would be one means. If the Council were to keep an active watch on dangerous situations and, if necessary, initiate discussions with the parties before they reach the point of crisis, it might often be possible to defuse them at an early stage before they degenerate into violence.

Unfortunately there has been a tendency to avoid bringing critical problems to the Security Council, or to do so too late for the Council to have any serious influence on their development. It is essential to reverse this trend if the Council is to play its role as the primary world authority for international peace and security. I do not believe that it is necessarily wise or responsible of the Council to leave such matters to the judgement of the conflicting parties to the point where the Council's irrelevance to some ongoing wars becomes a matter of comment by world public opinion.

In recent years the Security Council has resorted increasingly to the valuable process of informal consultations. However there is sometimes a risk that this process may become a substitute for action by the Security Council or even an excuse for inaction. Along the same line of thought, it may be useful for the Council to give renewed consideration to reviewing and streamlining its practices and procedures with a view to acting swiftly and decisively in crises.

Adequate working relations between the permanent members of the Security Council are a *sine qua non* of the Council's effectiveness. Whatever their relations may be outside the United Nations, within the Council the permanent members, which have special rights and special responsibilities under the Charter, share a sacred trust that should not go by default owing to their bilateral difficulties. When this happens, the Council and therefore the United Nations are the losers, since the system of collective security envisaged by the Charter presupposes, at the minimum, a working relationship among the permanent members. I appeal to the members of the Council, especially its permanent members, to reassess their obligations in that regard and to fulfil them at the high level of responsibility indicated in the Charter.

There is a tendency in the United Nations for Governments to act as though the passage of a resolution absolved them from further responsibility for the subject in question. Nothing could be further from the intention of the Charter. In fact resolutions, particularly those unanimously adopted by the Security Council, should serve as a springboard for governmental support and determination and should motivate their policies outside the United Nations. This indeed is the essence of the treaty obligation which the Charter imposes on Member States. In other words the best resolution in the world will have little practical effect unless Governments of Member States follow it up with the appropriate support and action.

Very often the Secretary-General is allotted the function of following up on the implementation of a resolution. Without the continuing diplomatic and other support of Member States, the Secretary-General's efforts often have less chance of bearing fruit. Concerted diplomatic action is an essential complement to the implementation of resolutions. I believe that in reviewing one of the greatest problems of the United Nations—lack of respect for its decisions by those to whom they are addressed—new ways should be considered of bringing to bear the collective influence of the membership on the problem at hand.

The same consideration applies to good offices and negotiations of various kinds undertaken at the behest of the Security Council. Very often a Member State or group of Member States with a special relationship to those involved in such negotiations could play an extremely important reinforcing role in promoting understanding and a positive attitude.

In order to avoid the Security Council becoming involved too late in critical situations, it may well be that the Secretary-General should play a more forthright role in bringing potentially dangerous situations to the attention of the Council within the general framework of Article 99 of the Charter. My predecessors have done this on a number of occasions, but I wonder if the time has not come for a more systematic approach. Most potential conflict areas are well known. The Secretary-General has traditionally, if informally, tried to keep watch for problems likely to result in conflict and to do what he can to pre-empt them by quiet diplomacy. The Secretary-General's diplomatic means are, however, in themselves quite limited. In order to carry out effectively the preventive role foreseen for the Secretary-General under Article 99, I intend to develop a wider and more systematic capacity for fact-finding in potential conflict areas. Such efforts would naturally be undertaken in close co-ordination with the Council. Moreover, the Council itself could devise more swift and responsive procedures for sending good offices missions, military or civilian observers or a United Nations presence to areas of potential conflict. Such measures could inhibit the deterioration of conflict situations and might also be of real assistance to the parties in resolving incipient disputes by peaceful means.

Peace-keeping operations have generally been considered to be one of the most successful innovations of the United Nations, and certainly their record over the years is one of which to be proud. They have proved to be a most useful instrument of de-escalation and conflict control and have extended the influence of the Security Council into the field in a unique way. I may add that United Nations peace-keeping operations have traditionally shown an admirable degree of courage, objectivity and impartiality. This record, which is a great credit to the Organization, is sometimes overlooked in the heat of partisanship.

The limitations of peace-keeping operations are less well understood. Thus when . . . a peace-keeping operation is overrun or brushed aside, the credibility both of the United Nations and of peace-keeping operations as such is severely shaken.

It is not always realized that peace-keeping operations are the visible part of a complex framework of political and diplomatic efforts and of countervailing pressures designed to keep the peace-keeping efforts and related peace-making efforts effective. It is assumed that the Security Council itself and those Member States in a position to bring influence to bear will be able to act decisively to ensure respect for decisions of the Council. If this framework breaks down, as it did for example in Lebanon last June [1982], there is little that a United Nations peace-keeping force can by itself do to rectify the situation. Indeed in such circumstances it tends to become the scapegoat for the developments that follow.

Peace-keeping operations can function properly only with the co-operation of the parties and on a clearly defined mandate from the Security Council. They are based on the assumption that the parties, in accepting a United Nations peace-keeping operation, commit themselves to co-operating with it. This commitment is also required by the Charter, under which all concerned have a clear obligation to abide by the decisions of the Council. United Nations peace-keeping operations are not equipped, authorized, or indeed made available, to take part in military activities other than peace-keeping. Their main strength is the will of the international community which they symbolize. Their weakness comes to light when the political assumptions on which they are based are ignored or overridden.

I recommend that Member States, especially the members of the Security Council, should again study urgently the means by which our peace-keeping operations could be strengthened. An increase in their military capacity or authority is only one possibility—a possibility which may well give rise in some circumstances to serious political and other objections. Another possibility is to underpin the authority of peace-keeping operations by guarantees, including explicit guarantees for collective or individual supportive action.

In recent months, two multinational forces were set up outside the framework of the United Nations to perform peace-keeping tasks, because of opposition to United Nations involvement either within or outside the Security Council. While understanding the circumstances which led to the establishment of these forces, I find such a trend disturbing because it demonstrates the difficulties the Security Council encounters in fulfilling its responsibilities as the primary organ for the maintenance of international peace and security in the prevailing political conditions.

We should examine with the utmost frankness the reasons for the reluctance of parties to some conflicts to resort to the Security Council or to use the machinery of the United Nations. The fact is that the Council too often finds itself on the sidelines at a time when, according to the Charter, its possibilities should be used to the maximum. Allegations of partisanship, indecisiveness or incapacity arising from divisions among Member States are sometimes invoked to justify this side-tracking of the Council. We should take such matters with the utmost seriousness and ask ourselves what justifications, if any, there are for them and what can be done to restore the Council to the position of influence it was given in the Charter.

This last problem also applies to other organs of the United Nations and brings me to the question of the validity and utility of the United Nations as a negotiating forum. We have seen, in the case of the law of the sea for example, what remarkable results can be achieved in well-organized negotiations within the United Nations framework, even on the most complex of issues and even though there was no unanimous agreement. On the peace and security side, the Security Council has shown and continues to show that it is often capable of negotiating important basic resolutions on difficult problems. The General Assembly also has to its credit historic documents negotiated in that organ and in its subsidiary organs, not only on the political but also on the economic and social side.

But in spite of all this I am concerned that the possibilities of the United Nations, especially of the Security Council, as a negotiating forum for urgent international problems are not being sufficiently realized or used. Let us consider what is perhaps our most formidable international problem—the Middle East. It is absolutely essential that serious negotiations on the various aspects of that problem involve all the parties concerned at the earliest possible time. Far too much time has already elapsed, far too many lives and far too many opportunities have been lost, and too many *faits accomplis* have been created.

I feel that the Security Council, the only place in the world where all of the parties concerned can sit at the same table, could become a most useful forum for this absolutely essential effort. But if this is to be done, careful consideration will have to be given to what procedures, new if necessary, should be used and what rules should govern the negotiations. I do not believe that a public debate, which could well become rhetorical and confrontational, will be enough. Other means will have to be used as well if negotiations on such a complex and deeply rooted problem are to have any useful outcome. . . .

A related question to which we should give more consideration concerns what are productive and what are counter-productive approaches to the different aspects of our work. Obviously, a parliamentary debate may generate rhetoric, and sometimes even a touch of acrimony. But negotiations and the resolution of urgent problems require a different approach. Debate without effective action erodes the credibility of the Organization. I feel that in the United Nations, if we wish to achieve results, we must make a more careful study of the psychological and political aspects of problems and address ourselves to our work accordingly. It is insufficient to indulge in a course of action that merely tends to strengthen extreme positions.

The United Nations . . . has survived a period of unprecedented change in almost all aspects of human life. The world of [today] is vastly different from that of 1945, and that difference is reflected in the United Nations. In other words, the Organization has had to adapt to new circumstances to a quite unexpected extent. But it is not enough for the United Nations merely to reflect change or conflict. The Organization was intended to present to the world the highest common denominator of international behaviour and, in doing so, to develop a binding sense of international community. It was to that end that Governments drafted and ratified the Charter. Amid the various perils that now threaten the orderly progress of humanity, I hope that we can rally once again to the standards of the Charter, beginning with the peaceful settlement of disputes and steadily branching out towards the other objectives of that prophetic document.

Finally let me appeal to all Governments to make a serious effort to reinforce the protective and pre-emptive ring of collective security which should be our common shelter and the most important task of the United Nations. The will to use the machinery of the Charter needs to be consciously strengthened, and all Governments must try to look beyond short-term national interests to the great possibilities of a more stable system of collective international security, as well as to the very great perils of failing to develop such a system. . . .

Member States will, I hope, understand if I end this report on a personal note. Last year I was appointed Secretary-General of this Organization, which embodies the noblest hopes and aspirations of the peoples of the world and whose functions and aims under the Charter are certainly the highest and most important ever entrusted to an international institution. This year, time after time we have seen the Organization set aside or rebuffed, for this reason or for that, in situations in which it should, and could, have played an important and constructive role. I think this tendency is dangerous for the world community and dangerous for the future. As one who has to play a highly public role in the Organization, I cannot disguise my deep anxiety at present trends, for I am absolutely convinced that the United Nations is indispensable in a world fraught with tension and peril. Institutions such as this are not built in a day. They require constant constructive work and fidelity to the principles on which they are based.

We take the United Nations seriously when we desperately need it. I would urge that we also seriously consider the practical ways in which it should develop its capacity and be used as an essential institution in a stormy and uncertain world.

19

Is It Law or Politics? The Role of International Law and Its Limitations

LOUIS HENKIN

In this essay, Louis Henkin disputes the widespread belief that international law is irrelevant to international politics. Noting that law is crucial to the conduct of routine international interactions, Henkin argues that states act in accordance with legal precepts because it is in their interest to do so. Author of *Foreign Affairs and the Constitution* (1972), Henkin is Hamilton Fish Professor of Law and Diplomacy at Columbia University.

. . . The layman tends to think of domestic law in terms of the traffic policeman, or judicial trials for the thief or murderer. But law is much more and quite different. . . . [I]n domestic society law includes the scheme and structure of government, and the institutions, forms, and procedures whereby a society carries on its daily activities; the concepts that underlie relations between government and individual and between individuals; the status, rights, responsibilities, and obligations of individuals and incorporated and non-incorporated associations and other groups, the relations into which they enter and the consequences of these relations. . . .

In relations between nations, too, one tends to think of law as consisting of a few prohibitory rules (for instance, that a government may not arrest another's diplomats) or the law of the U.N. Charter prohibiting war. Readers may think of law as including major treaties, such as those of Utrecht, Vienna, Paris, or Versailles. But international law, too, is much more and quite different. Although there is no international "government," there is an international "society"; law includes the structure of that society, its institutions, forms, and procedures for daily activity, the assumptions on which the society is founded and the concepts which permeate it, the status, rights, responsibilities, obligations of the nations which comprise that society, the various relations between them, and the effects of those relations.* Through what we call foreign policy, nations establish, main-

Reprinted from Louis Henkin, *How Nations Behave* (New York: Columbia University Press, 1979), pp. 13–26, 88–92, 337–339. Reprinted by permission of the publisher. Endnotes have been deleted.

* I do not include here that which nations do merely from habit, custom, "convention." I refer to *law*, to behavior as to which there is—on the part of the actor, the victim, and others—a sense of obligation, and a sense of violation when it fails. Between law and non-law the line is, of course, sometimes uncertain. . . .

tain, change, or terminate myriads of relations; law—more or less primitive, more or less sophisticated—has developed to formalize these relationships, to regulate them, to determine their consequences. A major purpose of foreign policy for most nations at most times is to maintain international order so that they can pursue their national interests, foreign and domestic. That order depends on an "infrastructure" of agreed assumptions, practices, commitments, expectations, reliances. These too are international law, and they are reflected in all that governments do.

To move from the abstract, consider some of the "givens" of international relations. First, they are relations between nations (states.)* The nation is the principal unit. All the forms of intercourse, all the institutions, all the terms even, depend on the existence of "nations." . . . That political society is based on the nation is not commonly seen as involving either policy or law; ordinarily, nationhood is the unspoken assumption of political life. But the nation ("state") is not only a political conception; it is also a fundamental legal construct with important consequences. Statehood—who is and shall be a state—has been one of the major political issues of our day. The legal concept of statehood is crucial, of course, when the character of an entity as a state is itself in issue. It figured in Soviet insistence on U.N. membership for Outer Mongolia, as well as in continued recognition by the United States of governments-in-exile for the Baltic republics incorporated by the U.S.S.R. It was raised when Palestine was partitioned and Israel created and underlies the recent claims of Palestinians to a state of their own. It was entangled in the question of Chinese representation in the United Nations and still bedevils the future of Taiwan. The "nation" has been in issue in differences over recognition of divided countries and their membership in international organizations—China, Korea, Vietnam, Germany. The legal concept and consequences of nationhood underlie the explosion of "self-determination" which ended Western colonialism and transformed the map of the world, and have troubled even the new nations, *e.g.*, Biafra, Bangladesh. It still deeply troubles Cyprus, and also Kashmir. It has given new significance to the problem of the "micro-state" or "mini-state."

Relations between nations generally begin with "housekeeping arrangements," including recognition and establishment of diplomatic relations. That these involve law (*e.g.*, in regard to recognition, sovereign, and diplomatic immunities) is commonly known, but the importance of this law for foreign policy is commonly depreciated. In fact, this law is basic and indispensable, and taken for granted because it rarely breaks down. The newest of nations promptly adopts it and the most radical scrupulously observes it. The occasional exception con-

---

* While international society today recognizes other entities—intergovernmental and other international organizations (the United Nations, the International Committee of the Red Cross), national and multinational companies with major transnational activities, even individual human beings—these are normally of concern only when, and because, their actions and the effects of their actions spill over national boundaries. Even to the extent that the individual has become a "subject" of international law, it is *international law* he is a subject of. Even the new concern for the human rights of individuals finds expression to date only through treaties and practice between nations, or through organizations of nations or bodies created by nations. . . .

firms the obvious, that there would be no relations with a nation that regularly violated embassies and abused diplomats. There are also the special cases when "housekeeping" becomes important policy: whether to recognize Communist China and seat its representatives in the United Nations were major questions for many nations, and the United States did not resolve them for many troubling years. The importance of these questions depends on legal concepts of recognition (or U.N. representation), on legal definitions of "state" and "government"; it reflects, too, the failure of law to develop clear distinctions between accepting the effective existence of a government, "recognizing" a government, and maintaining relations with it. Law does not determine the policy of governments on these issues, but it directs whatever actions might be taken and limits the choices available to governments. . . .

The relations of one nation with another, as soon as they begin, are permeated by basic legal concepts: nationality, national territory, property, torts, contracts, the rights and duties and responsibilities of states. These do not commonly figure in major policy doctrines, nor do they commonly occupy the attentions of diplomats. They too are taken for granted because they are rarely in issue. The concept of territory and territorial sovereignty is not prominent in foreign policy; but every foreign policy assumes the integrity and inviolability of the national territory, and any intentional violation would probably lead to major crisis. Territorial disputes are still with us, on several frontiers in Latin America and Africa, in Kashmir, between China and India, and China and Russia, over Gibraltar, in the Sahara, between Israel and its neighbors. Contemporary international relations were long troubled by other "territorial" issues turning on law: for example, the reach of the territorial sea, the continental shelf and coastal state authority for other purposes; innocent and less-than-innocent passage, and free transit through international straits; the right to broadcast inland, to dig for oil and gas, or to fish for food or pearls in coastal waters. Foreign policy takes for granted that nations observe the territorial airspace of others, but planes have been shot down in incidents leading to diplomatic tensions, to United Nations debates, to judicial proceedings. . . .

Related to territoriality is the concept of internal sovereignty. Except as limited by international law or treaty, a nation is master in its own territory. That principle is fundamental, and commonly observed. Yet it is in issue whenever there is a claim that internal action violates international law. It figures in disputes about nationalization of alien properties and about violations of human rights. It is proclaimed by South Africa, and challenged by many nations, in regard to *apartheid*.

The concepts of property lie deep in international relations. Property rights are taken for granted in all international trade and finance. When a vessel plies the seas, the assumption is that others will observe the international law prohibiting interference with free navigation, recognizing rights of ownership in property, forbidding torts against persons and property. The United States went to war in 1917, in part because it thought this law was being violated to its detriment. . . .

. . . Because there is this law [on the treatment of foreign nationals] (and because it is largely observed), there is tourism and foreign investment; and consular activity and "diplomatic protection" are a common, friendly, continuous part of international intercourse.

Not least, by far, are particular prohibitions of the law deriving from the basic concepts, such as those designed to protect the independence of nations against various forms of intervention. Accusations of intervention are common fare; to refrain from "intervention" is a tenet of foreign policy for many nations.

Law is also essential to foreign policy and to diplomacy in that it provides mechanisms, forms, and procedures by which nations maintain their relations, carry on trade and other forms of intercourse, resolve differences and disputes. There is international law in the establishment and operation of missions and in communications between governments, in the writing of contracts and other commercial paper, in oil concessions, in tariffs and customs practices, in the registry of vessels, the shipment of goods, the forms of payment, in all the intricacies of international trade and finance. There is law in and about the variety of international conferences. International organization—from the United Nations to the Universal Postal Union—involves legal concepts, and different organizations have contributed substantial law. For settling disputes, the law provides diplomats with claims commissions, arbitration bodies, mediators and conciliators, even courts.

For foreign policy, perhaps the most important legal mechanism is the international agreement, and the most important principle of international law is *pacta sunt servanda*: agreements shall be observed. This principle makes international relations possible. The mass of a nation's foreign relations involve innumerable agreements of different degrees of formality. The diplomat promotes, develops, negotiates, implements various understandings for various ends, from establishing diplomatic relations to trade, aid, allocation of resources, cultural exchange, common standards of weights and measures, to formal alliances affecting national security, cease-fire and disengagement, arms control, and a regime for outer space. The diplomat hardly thinks of these arrangements and understandings as involving law. He does assume that, if agreement is reached, it will probably be observed; if he did not, he would not bother to seek agreement. No doubt, he thinks that nations generally observe their undertakings because that is "done" in international society and because it is generally in the interest of nations to do so. That is law, the lawyer would say. . . .

In our times, there flourishes a type of international agreement that has added new dimensions to foreign policy and international law. Much of contemporary international law consists of new arrangements, often among large numbers of nations, to promote cooperation for some common aim. In this category one might place the various intergovernmental organizations and institutions, universal or regional—the United Nations, the World Bank and the Monetary Fund, the FAO, UPU, ITU and the IAEA, OECD, GATT, the International Coffee Agreement and UNCTAD, NATO and the European Economic Community, the OAS and OAU or the anticipated International Sea-bed Authority—as well as bilateral aid agreements. . . .

These programs for cooperation figure prominently in the foreign policy of many nations. The political officers who develop and maintain these policies may not think of them as creating or involving law—until issues arise involving alleged violations or differences in the interpretation of agreements. But the law supports these arrangements even—or especially—when there are no issues, when they run as intended. The foreign policy involved in these arrangements depends on as-sumptions, habits, practices, and institutions that derive their vitality from their quality as law and international legal obligation.

Law reflected in the assumptions, concepts, institutions, and procedures of international society is not the kind of international law one commonly thinks about because it does not, on its face, direct governments how to behave. But, in fact, all law is intimately related to national behavior. Even that "submerged" law molds the policies of governments. The concept of the nation determines that the United States has relations with Canada, not with Quebec. The concept of territoriality means that the United States can do largely as it likes within the United States, but is sharply restricted in what it can do outside. There are clear prohibitions in the basic legal concepts, in the rights and duties they imply: terri-toriality, property, tort imply that the United States cannot, at will, invade or violate the territory or seize the property of another nation. Freedom of the seas means that one nation cannot prevent the vessels of others from going their way. Contracts and agreements are not to be broken. Even organizations for cooperative welfare, though commonly distinguished from traditional law of "abstention," impose obligations on members which they must "abstain" from violating: they may not interfere with the international mails; they must pay budget assessments to the FAO. These organizations have also promoted common procedures and minimum standards of national behavior, *e.g.*, in regard to labor, or the treatment of refugees, or basic human rights even for a nation's own citizens.

There is also the law which aims directly at controlling behavior. Governments may not arrest accredited diplomats or deny basic justice to foreign nationals. I have mentioned, and shall discuss the law forbidding intervention in the internal affairs of other nations. . . .

International relations and foreign policy, then, depend on a legal order, op-erate in a legal framework, assume a host of legal principles and concepts which shape the policies of nations and limit national behavior. If one doubts the signif-icance of this law, one need only imagine a world from which it were absent—approximately a situation in which all nations were perpetually in a state of war with each other. There would be no security of nations or stability of govern-ments; territory and airspace would not be respected; vessels could navigate only at their constant peril; property—within or without any given territory—would be subject to arbitrary seizure; persons would have no protection of law or of diplo-macy; agreements would not be made or observed; diplomatic relations would end; international trade would cease; international organizations and arrangements would disappear. . . .

THE LIMITATIONS OF INTERNATIONAL LAW

The student of foreign affairs may grant, if the lawyer insists, that the law implied in international society gives some direction to national policies and places some limitations on how nations behave. But he remains skeptical of the influence of law as it is commonly and more narrowly conceived, of that law which seeks to control the conduct of nations within the framework of the society of nations. . . .

The tendency to dismiss international law reflects impressions sometimes summed up in the conclusion that it is not really law because international society is not really a society: the world of nations is a collection of sovereign states, not an effective body politic which can support effective law. . . .

The society of nations has no effective law-making body or process. General law depends on consensus: in principle, new law, at least, cannot be imposed on any state; even old law cannot survive if enough states, or a few powerful and influential ones, reject it. New universal law, then, can come about only through long, gradual, uncertain "accretion" by practice and acquiescence, or through multilateral treaties difficult to negotiate and more difficult to get accepted. Law is also slow and difficult to clarify, or amend, or repeal. The law is therefore haphazard and static. As concerns customary law in particular, there is often uncertainty and little confidence as to what it is. The law is also inadequate, for many important actions and relations remain unregulated. There are important disorders—for example, the arms race or the oil embargo—which are not subject to law. In the absence of special undertakings, nations may engage in economic warfare, may boycott, even starve each other. And law has not achieved a welfare society: there is no law requiring social and economic assistance by the very rich to the very poor, or providing community relief even to the starving.

Also lacking is an effective judiciary to clarify and develop the law, to resolve disputes impartially, and to impel nations to observe the law. The International Court of Justice does not satisfy these needs. Its jurisdiction and procedures are starkly insufficient: jurisdiction requires the consent of the parties, and few consent to it; only a minority of nations have accepted the Court's compulsory jurisdiction. . . . Nations still prefer the flexibility of diplomacy to the risks of third-party judgment. . . .

The greatest deficiency, as many see it, is that international society lacks an executive authority with power to enforce the law. There is no police system whose pervasive presence might deter violation. The society does not consider violations to be crimes or violators criminals, and attaches no stigma which might itself discourage violation. Since nations cannot be made to observe rules and keep promises, they will not do so when they deem it in their interest not to do so. . . .

In sum, to many an observer, governments seem largely free to decide whether to agree to new law, whether to accept another nation's view of existing law, whether to comply with agreed law. International law, then, is voluntary and only hortatory. It must always yield to national interest. . . .

These depreciations of international law challenge much of what the international lawyer does. Indeed, some lawyers seem to despair for international law until there is world government or at least effective international organization. But most international lawyers are not dismayed. Unable to deny the limitations of international law, they insist that these are not critical, and they deny many of the alleged implications of these limitations. If they must admit that the cup of law is half-empty, they stress that it is half-full. They point to similar deficiencies in many domestic legal systems. They reject definitions (commonly associated with the legal philosopher John Austin) that deny the title of law to any but the command of a sovereign, enforceable and enforced as such. They insist that despite inadequacies in legislative method, international law has grown and developed and changed. If international law is difficult to make, yet it is made; if its growth is slow, yet it grows. If there is no judiciary as effective as in some developed national systems, there is an International Court of Justice whose judgments and opinions, while few, are respected. The inadequacies of the judicial system are in some measure supplied by other bodies: international disputes are resolved and law is developed through a network of arbitrations by continuing or *ad hoc* tribunals. National courts help importantly to determine, clarify, develop international law. Political bodies like the Security Council and the General Assembly of the United Nations also apply law, their actions and resolutions interpret and develop the law, their judgments help to deter violations in some measure. If there is no international executive to enforce international law, the United Nations has some enforcement powers and there is "horizontal enforcement" in the reactions of other nations. The gaps in substantive law are real and many and require continuing effort to fill them, but they do not vitiate the force and effect of the law that exists, in the international society that is.

Above all, the lawyer will insist, critics of international law ask and answer the wrong questions. . . . The fact is, lawyers insist, that nations have accepted important limitations on their sovereignty, that they have observed these norms and undertakings, that the result has been substantial order in international relations. . . .

IS IT LAW OR POLITICS?

. . . That nations generally decide to act in accordance with law does not change the voluntary character of these decisions. Nations act in conformity with law not from any concern for law but because they consider it in their interest to do so, and fear unpleasant consequences if they do not observe it. . . .

Much of international law resembles the civil law of domestic society (torts, contracts, property); some of it is analogous to "white collar crimes" (violations of antitrust or other regulatory laws, tax evasion) sometimes committed by "respectable" elements. Like such domestic law, international law, too, has authority recognized by all. No nation considers international law as "voluntary." If the system is ultimately based on consensus, neither the system nor any particular norm or obligation rests on the present agreement of any nation: a nation cannot decide that it will not be subject to international law; it cannot decide that it will not be subject to a particular norm, although it may choose to risk an attempt to have the norm modified; surely, it cannot decide to reject the norm that its international undertakings must be carried out. Like individuals, nations do not claim a right to disregard the law or their obligations, even though—like individuals—they may sometimes exercise the power to do so. International society does not recognize any right to violate the law, although it may not have the power (or desire) to prevent violation from happening, or generally to impose effective communal sanction for the violation after it happens.

In arguments that international law is voluntary there lies also a common confusion about the relation of law to "policy." The two are often contrasted, suggesting that law is obligatory while policy is voluntary. In fact, law and policy are not in meaningful contrast, and their relation is not simple, whether in domestic or international society. All law is an instrument of policy, broadly conceived. Law is not an end in itself: even in the most enlightened domestic society it is a means—to order, stability, liberty, security, justice, welfare. The policies served by law are sometimes articulated—in a constitution, in statutory preambles, in legislative pronouncements, in the opinions of the courts; often these policies are tacit, and commonly assumed. International law, too, serves policy, and the policies are not too different from the domestic: order and stability, peace, independence, justice, welfare. . . .

Much is made of the fact that, in international society, there is no one to compel nations to obey the law. But physical coercion is not the sole or even principal force ensuring compliance with law. Important law is observed by the most powerful, even in domestic societies, although there is no one to compel them. In the United States, the President, Congress, and the mighty armed forces obey orders of a Supreme Court whose single marshal is unarmed.

Too much is made of the fact that nations act not out of "respect for law" but from fear of the consequences of breaking it. And too much is made of the fact that the consequences are not "punishment" by "superior," legally constituted authority, but are the response of the victim and his friends and the unhappy results for friendly relations, prestige, credit, international stability, and other interests which in domestic society would be considered "extra-legal." The fact is that, in domestic society, individuals observe law principally from fear of consequences, and there are "extra-legal" consequences that are often enough to deter violation. . . .

Law, I sum up, is a major force in international relations and a major determinant in national policy. Its influence is diluted, however, and sometimes outweighed, by other forces in a "developing" international society. Failure to appreciate the strengths and weaknesses of the law underlies much misunderstanding about it and many of the controversies about its significance. "Realists" who do not recognize the uses and the force of law are not realistic. "Idealists" who do not recognize the law's limitations are largely irrelevant to the world that is. Those who resist new law because of general skepticism about international law or the expectation that others will not abide by it, or from a reluctance to see their own government limited by it, may frustrate their own nation's interest, including its interest in general welfare and greater order in international relations. . . .

Today, extremes of "realism" or "idealism" about law are rare. The lawyer may sometimes place too much faith in law. The diplomat or policy-maker too often errs on the side of skepticism. He resists persuasion as to the desirability of some new undertaking—from inertia, from undue confidence in his diplomacy, from a desire for "flexibility" and the avoidance of commitment. He sees in *laissez faire* the benefits of freedom for his country; he tends not to see the disadvantages to his country in the unbridled freedom of others. (He sees, for example, security in his country's weapons, not the security that might come from controlling the armaments of others.) Skepticism may also affect governmental attitudes toward existing law, exaggerate the need or benefit of violation, and underrate the advantage to the national interest of law observance in general and of keeping a particular norm or obligation.

The important questions that divide the lawyer and the diplomat today are not whether and why law is insufficiently effective, or whether in a very different world—the distant hope of some for more-or-less world government—law would be more effective. In its extreme form, the question is whether, admitting the inadequacies of international society, law really matters—whether it makes sense for nations to bother with law, to depend on it, to uphold it, to seek its extension.

To me, the answer is clear. In the society we have, international law sustains what order we have and promises better. There is bound to be controversy about its application and interpretation, but that does not vitiate its significance or effectiveness. Nor is law destroyed by the fact that it is sometimes violated, even by the fact that it is sometimes hypocritically invoked by the violators. (We do not reject scripture merely because the devil may cite it.) In regard to the law against force, there is no longer any doubt about its validity, its desirability, its necessity. The question is whether men and nations will live by it or will violate it and be destroyed. . . .

International society "works"; at least it "muddles through." There has been no big war and there are cogent reasons to hope that there will be none. There has been progress beyond wildest hopes in giving peoples independence—the national analogue to individual liberty. There is a spreading law of human rights. There has been some recognition of responsibility for general welfare. . . . From there to a welfare society is a long road, as it has been in national societies; but if wars can be avoided, progress toward a more just welfare society is a reasonable expectation. . . .

20

The Integration Theorists and the Study of International Relations[1]

DONALD J. PUCHALA

In this essay, Donald J. Puchala weaves together the various strands of thinking about international integration. Arguing that it is useful to distinguish between integration theory and integration studies, he concludes that "the findings of the integration theorists . . . are, in retrospect, less important than their broader contributions to the contemporary study of international relations." Puchala is professor and director of the Institute of International Studies at the University of South Carolina. Among his many publications is *The Global Political Economy of Food* (co-edited with Raymond F. Hopkins, 1979).

When the intellectual history of twentieth-century social science is written, there is likely to be at least one chapter on "the study of international integration." Somewhere in that chapter there may be a rather long, but not especially prominent, footnote that will explain how a series of events in Western Europe after World War II prompted two generations of scholars to proliferate abstract explanations of what was happening.[2] It will further tell how the European experience and forthcoming explanations inspired some of these scholars to ask whether what was happening on the Old Continent was also happening elsewhere.[3] The early consensus among these scholars was to label the phenomenon under consideration "international integration" (although, as it turned out, there was little consensus about what this label meant). Under the influence of the prevailing social "scientism" of the 1950s and 1960s, newly generated abstractions about international integration were clustered and elevated to the status of "integration theories."[4] There ensued a prolonged debate among scholars concerning the power and accuracy of the various theories, and schools of analysis consequently emerged, all mutually critical and highly self-critical as well, and each claiming exclusive insight, almost as in the parable of the blind men and the elephant.[5]

As this debate among theorists gathered momentum, and indeed as it was beginning to yield some imaginative efforts to "integrate" integration theory,[6] whatever had been happening in Western Europe apparently stopped happening. It stopped happening elsewhere as well, and to the intellectual embarrassment of scholars involved, integration theory offered no satisfactory explanation for these turns of events.[7] At this juncture some suggested that the so-called integration

This essay was written especially for this book.

185

theories were probably not theories at all but simply *post hoc* generalizations about current events. Others suggested that the integration theories had been moralizations and utopian prescriptions only. Still others held that they were accurate generalizations, but that since they were addressed to explaining time-bound, nonrecurrent events, they were prone to obsolescence as theories.[8]

INTEGRATION THEORIES

It is true that integration theories formulated during the 1950s and 1960s did not provide complete answers to the theorists' main question: *Within what environment, under what conditions, and by what processes does a new transnational political unit peacefully emerge from two or more initially separate and different ones?* The theories had to be incomplete because the cases available for investigation—the Western European Common Market, Latin American and African customs unions and various other regional ventures—were themselves incomplete. Little could therefore be learned about processes leading to an end state because no end states were attained. It was supposed that integration would ultimately produce something like a nation-state or multinational federation, but empirically there was no way to tell. History could have been mined for more cases, and it was to a certain extent, but this left other unanswerable questions about the comparability of conditions across eras.[9]

The main point of this paper is that the findings of the integration theorists specifically concerning international political unification are, in retrospect, less important than their broader contributions to the contemporary study of international relations. This point will be elaborated in a moment. However, the integration theories per se should not be dismissed out of hand, because they reveal a good deal about the process of peaceful international merger. We will therefore examine these first before taking up their implications. Most of the lasting work was done within the intellectual confines of two distinct theoretical schools, transactionalism and neo-functionalism, led by two American political scientists, Karl W. Deutsch and Ernst B. Haas, respectively.

Transactionalism

Karl Deutsch's approach to the study of international integration came to be labeled *transactionalism* because members of the theoretical school tested propositions concerning community formation among peoples by examining frequencies of intra- and inter-group transactions.[10] However, Deutsch's most direct statements concerning international integration are set forth in *Political Community and the North Atlantic Area*, written in collaboration with colleagues at Princeton University between 1952 and 1956.[11] Here Deutsch specifies that integration is to be distinguished from amalgamation, in that the former has to do with the formation of communities, and the latter with the establishment of organizations, associations, or political institutions. Communities are groups of people who have attributes in common, who display mutual responsiveness, confidence, and esteem, and who self-consciously self-identify. A minimum condition of community is a shared expectation among members that their conflicts will be peacefully resolved.[12] This minimum community is called a security community.[13]

International communities may be either amalgamated or pluralistic. If amalgamated, the community would look very much like a federation or nation-state, with institutions of central government regulating the internal and external relations of an integrated population. (A fully amalgamated community would in fact be indistinguishable from a federation or nation-state.) By contrast, the pluralistic international community is a population integrated into at least a security community, but politically fragmented into two or more separate sovereign states. Typical of the various kinds of international communities would be the thirteen American states in 1781, as an example of a newly amalgamated international community, Americans and Canadians at present, as an example of a pluralistic international community, and the Benelux Union, as an example of an entity intermediate between a pluralistic and an amalgamated community.

It should be underlined that for the transactionalists, both integration and amalgamation are quantitative concepts. Both are to be measured with regard to degree or intensity and both range along continua that extend from incipience to fulfillment. Notably, this gives rise to an almost infinite variety of entities defined by the combination of their degrees of integration and amalgamation. Many of these exist empirically. What is fascinating here is that the behavioral properties of the various entities created by combination of integration and amalgamation tend to differ markedly with regard to both their internal and their external relations. Compare, for example, differences in internal and external relations between Scotland, the United Kingdom, the British Empire, and the British Commonwealth of Nations, each of which can be located at a different integration-amalgamation intersect. What is theoretically challenging is to determine precisely the behavioral properties of the various bi-variately defined entities, and to explain whether and exactly why variations in behavior relate to varying degrees of integration and amalgamation in combination.

Deutsch and his colleagues took up this theoretical challenge by nominally distinguishing between amalgamated and pluralistic communities (and implicitly between amalgamated and pluralistic non-communities). But the more refined theorizing suggested by the quantitative conceptualization of amalgamation and integration never reached fruition in either Deutsch's work or that of his students, because the metrics that would permit accurate assessment of degrees of amalgamation and integration could not be devised. Operationalization proved insuperable.[14] "Integration," for example, is in one sense an attitudinal phenomenon having to do in the broadest way with people's degrees of feelings of "we-ness." In another sense, integration is a process of attitudinal change that creates or culminates in such feelings of "we-ness." In neither sense is "integration" readily observable or measurable, except perhaps in the very limited number of very recent cases where mass opinion data are available, accurate, and appropriate.[15]

Amalgamation similarly defies precise quantification, partly because it has no precise definition. Deutsch defines it as "the formal merger of two or more independent units into a larger unit, with some type of common government after amalgamation.''[16] But what does "formal merger" mean in an operational sense, and how does one know it when one sees it? A number of historical cases, and all of the contemporary ones, intuitively suggest that "formal merger" tends to take place in piecemeal fashion, one institution or one institutionalized task at a time. But, empirically, it remains extremely difficult to determine whether there is more of it or less of it in evidence[17] in particular cases at particular times. These became crucial concerns for the analysis of Western European unification during the 1960s, and a considerable effort was invested in index construction, with the result that "amalgamation" became "institutionalization," which then became a multivariate concept embodying degrees of authority, scope of authority, and resources available to authorities. Measures of institutionalization were then questioned as indices of amalgamation because they ignored "political system" attributes on the input side.[18] Amalgamation then became the "coming into being of a political system" as this was variously defined by leading theorists in comparative politics.[19] Indicators and metrics were sought for degrees of political socialization, interest articulation, demand and support, and the like. By this time "amalgamation" operationally defined had become a matrix of attributes. But their indicators tended to vary in different directions at different rates in different contexts and hence to render confusing (and fruitless) any attempts to devise composite measures of amalgamation. Of course, too, as soon as one moved from contemporary cases to historical ones, measurement problems were exacerbated by data problems.

None of this is to suggest that the methodological problems generated in attempts to operationalize and measure integration and amalgamation should detract from the heuristic value of the concepts. Even rather primitive measurement, at the level of nominal typology or simple dichotomy, often opens the way to productive research and theorizing. As alluded to above, in terms of Deutsch's concepts, we can develop an interesting typology by distinguishing between integrated and non-integrated international communities, and between amalgamated and non-amalgamated ones. From this classification, we get four entities: (1) state systems (non-integrated and non-amalgamated), (2) empires (non-integrated but amalgamated), (3) pluralistic security communities (integrated but non-amalgamated), and (4) amalgamated security communities (integrated and amalgamated). The first two have been the foci of traditional research and theorizing in international relations for many years; number 4 was the particular object of integration theorizing, and number 3 is the threshold for a number of recent departures in international relations theory discussed later in this paper.

Examining the amalgamated security community and the forces that produce and maintain it is tantamount to examining international political unification. For Deutsch, as for others, the principal empirical focus for the investigation of the amalgamated security community was the Western Europe of the Six. Here his work and that of his students and colleagues was directed toward ascertaining the existence of a security community among the peoples of the Six, ascertaining the degree of political amalgamation in evidence, and projecting both integration and amalgamation into the future in order to draw conclusions about European unification. Deutsch's most ambitious efforts at analyzing developments in Western

Europe appear in his book with Merritt, Macridis, and Edinger, *France, Germany and the Western Alliance*.[20]

Aside from their substantive importance as attempts to better understand the course of European unification, these exercises were also a test of a developmental model of political unification devised by Deutsch and initially contained in his work on nationalism.[21] In this model, international political unification, or the coming into being of amalgamated security communities, is a phenomenon similar to the coming into being of nation-states. Therefore, what one would observe at the international level as political unification occurs is comparable to what one would observe at the national level when nation-states are born. First, functional links develop between separate communities. Such ties in trade, migration, mutual services, or military collaboration prompted by necessity or profit generate flows of transactions between communities and enmesh people in transcommunity communications networks. Under appropriate conditions of high volume, expanding substance, and continuing reward, over extended periods of time, intercommunity interactions generate social-psychological processes that lead to the assimilation of peoples, and hence to their integration into larger communities. Such assimilatory processes are essentially learning experiences of the stimulus-response variety.[22] Once such community formation has taken place, the desires of members and the efforts of the elites may be directed toward institutionalizing, preserving, and protecting the community's integrity and distinctiveness and regulating transactions through the establishment of institutions of government. In overview, then, the model posits that political unification—national or international—consists in moving first from communities to community, and then from community to state. This follows from initial functional link, increased transaction, social assimilation, community formation, and ultimately political amalgamation. Integration therefore precedes amalgamation; sentimental change precedes institutional change; social change precedes political change. At the core of this formulation rests the assumption that peaceful change in international relations has its origins in the perceptions and identification of people.

As an *integration theory*, in the sense that the term is being used in this paper, Deutsch's formulation is valuable in that it focuses attention on international community formation during unification. This sentimental dimension is largely ignored in other integration theories.[23] Deutsch's formulations allow for a number of possible end-products, as noted, but to the extent that international political unification is under investigation, the postulated end-product looks like a nation-state, and attaining this implies that both integration and amalgamation have occurred, most likely in sequence.

For all its elegance and intuitive promise, Deutsch's developmental model of the unification process has some rather serious shortcomings. For one thing, the conditions under which people in newly integrated communities will or will not initiate drives for political amalgamation are never specified. Therefore, one cannot predict future amalgamation from evidence of present integration. The relationship between integration and amalgamation is certainly not causal. Otherwise the pluralistic community could never exist for any length of time. But there is a contingency link between the two that is never exactly specified in either

Deutsch's work or that of his students. In short, the motivational dynamics are missing from Deutsch's process model, and this opens a serious gap.[24]

Political dynamics are similarly missing from Deutsch's model and this too seriously affects its explanatory and predictive power. The underemphasis on political dynamics—that is, decision-making, organizational behavior, coalition behavior, and so on—in the Deutsch model is essentially a level-of-analysis problem. His formulation makes statements about people's attitudes and sentiments, individually and in the aggregate, and it also makes statements about governments' policies (that is, to amalgamate or not). Therefore, as far as the theory informs us, we can believe that changes in people's attitudes and sentiments may prompt changes in governments' policies. This is reasonable, but not very helpful. What remains undisclosed is how, when, and why changes at the social-psychological level are converted into changes at the governmental level. There are no social or political structures or processes in Deutsch's integration models—no groups or classes (except elites and masses, and even these are seldom differentiated analytically), no decision makers, no decisions, very little voluntaristic behavior, and no politics. Without these social-political variables the Deutsch model forces unguided inferential leaps of considerable magnitude.

These criticisms of Deutsch's model of political unification suggest that it is incomplete, not inaccurate. Its strengths lie precisely in the fact that its explanatory and predictive power can be improved through further research into clearly definable problems. Much could be accomplished, for example, by filling the gap between integration and amalgamation with some of the neo-functionalists' findings (explained below) concerning the politics of unification, the conditions for "spillover," and the influence of international bureaucracies. If political structure and dynamics were added in this manner the power of the model would be greatly enhanced. Similarly, the gap between integration and amalgamation could be further filled by modeling the motivational dynamics of the unification process from the findings of the literatures of ideology and integration, liberal and Marxist political economy, domestic politics and integration, and the management of interdependence.[25]

Neo-functionalism

As contemporaries, Karl Deutsch and Ernst Haas exchanged relatively few insights concerning international integration because their foci of analytical attention and conceptual vocabularies were very different. Where Deutsch paid scant attention to the role of international institutions during political unification, Haas dwelt upon this. Moreover, Deutsch's concepts and analytical vocabulary came largely from communications theory and his earlier work on nationalism, whereas Haas drew some of his concepts from David Mitrany's functionalism,[26] created many of his own, and wrote using a vocabulary tailored for his specific purposes. It also appeared for a time that Deutsch and Haas differed rather fundamentally on a principal causal relationship in the political unification process. As noted, Deutsch saw the mutual identification of peoples or "community" preceding, and creating favorable conditions for, institutional amalgamation. But Haas' work, by contrast, suggested that institutional amalgamation precedes and leads to community because effective institutionalization at the international level invites a refocusing of people's political attentions and a shifting of their loyalties. Community among peoples, Haas contended, follows sometime after these political and cultural shifts have occurred.[27]

Research ultimately stilled much of the controversy about the sequencing of community formation and institutional amalgamation, as both turned out to be more complex than either Deutsch or Haas supposed, and each partially caused the other in homeostatic fashion.[28] Moreover, while it may have appeared to contemporaries that Haas and Deutsch and their respective colleagues were laboring in separate intellectual vineyards, reviewing their work a decade later reveals striking complementarities in their ideas and findings. Most important, Haas explained the political dynamics of international institutionalization and policy-making and consequently linked the learning and assimilatory experiences that Deutsch observed in community formation to the political-decisional processes that occurred as governments decided to amalgamate.

Haas' work, contained in *The Uniting of Europe* and in a series of articles that refined his theory,[29] came to be called *neo-functionalism* partly, we would suppose, because it was a revision of Mitrany's work and partly because it generalized about the behavior of people like Jean Monnet and Walter Hallstein who called themselves "neo-functionalists."[30] In his book Haas sought to determine the extent to which the architects of European unity were correct in assuming that they could move from piecemeal international mergers in particular sectors, such as coal and steel, to ultimately arrive at the fullblown political union of formerly separate nation-states. Even more ambitiously, in his articles Haas sought to determine whether there were general conditions and dynamics in functional amalgamation that could set integration into motion anywhere.

Haas discovered that there is an "expansive logic" in sector integration that operates, under appropriate conditions, to continually extend the range of activities under international jurisdiction. Therefore, once the international amalgamation process is initiated it could, again under appropriate conditions, "spill over" to broaden and deepen the international policy realm until ultimately most functions normally performed by national governments were transferred to international authorities. This happens because each functional step toward greater international authority sets into motion political processes that generate demands for further steps. At each step, and in the face of demands for new ones, national governments are forced to choose between surrendering additional autonomy or refusing to do so and risking the collapse of their initial effort at sectoral amalgamation. At higher levels of amalgamation, where many sectors have been internationalized, further movement comes to require major cessions of national autonomy, but, at these levels, failure to move forward, or sliding backward, may also impose great costs. Neo-functionalism posits that, other things being equal, political pressures mounted at key decision points will cause governments to choose to move toward greater amalgamation.

Spillover follows from several causes, all having to do with the politicization of issues in pluralistic societies. First, because modern industrial societies are highly interdependent it is impossible to internationalize one functional sector, say, steel production, without affecting numerous other sectors, as for example mining, transport, and labor organization and representation. Because other sectors are affected and because elites within them are organized to bring pressure on national governments, their concerns become subjects of international discussion and questions arise about granting further authority to international agencies to handle matters in affected cognate sectors. At such points governments must decide to either grant the extended international authority or court failure in the initial sector integration. If the balance of perceived rewards and penalties favors moving toward greater amalgamation, as it frequently does, governments will grant extended authority to international agencies.

Sometimes spillover follows from failures to appreciate the true magnitude or implications of tasks assigned to international agencies, so that initial conservative grants of authority prove unfeasible and must be extended. For example, when Western European attempts to promote free trade in pharmaceutical products began, the European Commission was empowered only to ask national governments to remove obstacles like tariffs. But before the free flow of pharmaceuticals could be fully facilitated it proved necessary to involve the Commission in everything pertaining to the drug industry, up to and including the education of pharmacists.[31] Then too, international bureaucrats can, and do, deliberately engineer links among tasks and sectors in efforts to enhance their own authority and to push toward the complete political unification of countries to which they are committed.[32]

Haas and his colleagues uncovered considerable evidence of spillover in the progressive integration of the European Communities during the 1960s, but very little elsewhere. In fact, in most other regions, "functional encapsulation" was the most frequent result of sector amalgamation, as no expansion of international authority followed initial grants.[33] As a result Haas was prompted to elaborate and enrich his theory by specifying conditions under which spillover would and would not occur. Most important among these was societal pluralism, which contributed to the politicization of integration issues that forced governmental decisions at pivotal points. Also crucial were the nature of sectors selected for amalgamation, links between international and national bureaucracies, prevailing incremental styles in national and international decision-making, and general value complementarity among national elites.[34]

The great strength of Haas' work was his accurate portrayal of international integration as an intensely political phenomenon. It has to do with numerous political actors, pursuing their own interests, pressuring governments, or, if they are governments, pressuring one another to negotiate toward international policies that are collectively beneficial because they are individually beneficial for all concerned. Like politics more generally, the politics of international integration is a game of bargaining—tugging, hauling, log-rolling, and horse-trading that eventuates in transnationally applicable policies. A distinctive element in the politics of integration, however, is that there are always some actors who perceive that they cannot accept diminutions of national prerogative and others who insist that they will not accept the undoing of amalgamation already attained. Therefore the fate of the union itself is a constant political consideration.

Neo-functionalism naturally had some weaknesses. For one thing, the theory is limited in applicability. It concerns only international mergers that proceed in sectoral fashion, and only under appropriate conditions. In addition, it says little about the initiation of the amalgamation process. On this the neo-functionalists are as sketchy as the transactionalists. Surely, if political forces and processes drive amalgamation once it is underway, they must also have something to do with first steps. Yet neo-functionalism offers little insight into the politics of this matter. With regard to the progressive merger of sectors, moreover, neo-function-alism never produced a complete process model. The spillover dynamic is stipulated and conditioning factors are inventoried, but these factors are not related to the dynamic directly or clearly enough to show the "whens," "hows," and "whys" of their speeding, slowing, starting, or stopping effects. Some of the neo-functionalist theorists were moving toward such sophisticated modeling about the time that the effort began to peter out.[35]

The neo-functionalist effort to understand and model international integration stalled about the time that Western European movement toward greater unity encountered difficulties in the 1970s. By this time, a number of other potentially promising regional schemes in East Africa, West Africa, Central America, the Caribbean, and Latin America had also collapsed. Cases for investigation by students of international integration were therefore vanishing and this was happening before any had reached the end-state of political union that the theorists aspired to explain. At this point Haas pronounced integration theory obsolete.[36] He concluded that with some effort the theories could be improved, but he questioned the worth of making the effort, given the unlikelihood of significant international political unification during the remainder of our century. Though Haas' notice about the demise of Western European integration was exaggerated, his sense that integration theorizing had run its course was largely correct.

INTEGRATION STUDIES AND THE DISCIPLINE OF INTERNATIONAL RELATIONS

I began this essay by relegating the efforts of twenty years of formal theorizing about international integration to the status of a "footnote" to intellectual history because in a broader and more meaningful context explaining political unification was neither the most enduring nor the most significant accomplishment of the integration theorists. To understand why this is so we must make two distinctions, first between the *theories* of the integrationists and their *philosophies*, and second between *integration theory*, as represented by the generalizations of the transactionalists, neo-functionalists and others, and *integration studies* as represented by the full range of concerns, questions, observations and findings of all of those scholars who undertook to discover in the broadest sense "what was happening" within customs unions, common markets and other regional associations.

The Attainability of Peace

Though the integration theorists differed in their approaches and foci of attention and at times questioned one another's findings, their philosophies, or the values that prompted them to try to better understand international unification, were similar. Most fundamentally, the integration theorists sought to explain the conditions and dynamics of peaceful change in international relations. They were convinced that lasting peace and peaceful change were attainable, that integration processes were somehow involved in accounting for these, and that to shed light on the causes and conditions of peace was the principal goal of the study of international relations.

But, in their assumptions about the promise in international collaboration and the attainability of peace, the integration theorists, in the 1960s, were a small minority among students of international relations. Their works were injected into a scholarly community preoccupied with questions of strategic balancing in a world dominated by cold warfare. It was therefore the integrationists, and almost the integrationists alone among American scholars, who kept alive an idealism that made peace worth studying because it was assumed to be attainable. The assumption was not a flight of idealistic fancy, because the integrationists' subject matter demonstrated that peaceful change could take place and that peace could last.

The Challenge to Political Realism

The integrationists' studies also demonstrated that the legitimate and theoretically significant subject matter of international relations was more extensive, varied, and complex than allowed for in the disciplinary paradigm that prevailed during the first two postwar decades. Students of international integration probed into realms of postwar international relations where productive collaboration among governments was actually taking place—regional theaters, customs unions, and common markets. The patterns of behavior turned up by their research not only enlightened the understanding of integration, but also shook a number of orthodox assumptions about the nature of international relations. According to conventional wisdom in the discipline of International Relations at that time, much of the behavior and many of the outcomes and events that the integrationists were reporting *either were not supposed to happen or were not supposed to be very consequential if and when they did happen.* That is, from the very beginning of their investigations in the early 1950s students of integration were making observations and reporting discoveries that directly contradicted the prevailing political realist or "power politics" paradigm of the discipline of International Relations.[37] With emphases on conflict and coercion, states as unitary actors, and state security as an end, this paradigm conditioned the philosophical assumptions of scholars and their research priorities in studying international relations from the early 1940s onward. By the 1950s, with the eclipse of early idealism about the United Nations, political realism also became the prevailing paradigm for the study of international organization, thus leaving integration studies as a distinct, rather isolated, philosophically unorthodox subculture within International Relations. As Table 1 shows, there was no place in political realist thinking for the kinds of findings that the integrationists were making. For one thing, in the 1950s and early 1960s the integrationists were virtually alone in holding that international collaboration for welfare ends was an important aspect of contemporary international relations. They were also alone in arguing that, in terms of quantity and intensity, such collaboration was something new in the post–World War II world.

Of course the new findings of the integrationists were no more representative of the total substance of international relations than were the more traditional ones of the realists. But they were valid findings arrived at by focusing upon cases of collaborative behavior. For example:

- widespread and consequential collaboration does occur in international relations;
- supranationality is both practicable and practiced in international relations;
- international pursuits of welfare ends tend often to be highly, or more highly, politicized than international pursuits of security ends;
- transnationally organized non-governmental organizations are consequential actors in international relations;
- transgovernmentally linked bureaucrats and officials coordinate foreign policies and foreign policy-making;
- interdependence constrains states' autonomy and it complicates determinations of relative power;
- to the extent to which they serve welfare ends, the domestic and foreign policies of modern states, both industrialized and less developed, are integrally and inextricably linked.

Because these new findings were valid, they opened the way and lent academic legitimacy to the study of international cooperation at a time when the world seemed engulfed in all-pervading, protracted conflict, and when the discipline of International Relations seemed fixed in the notion that conflict was the beginning and the end of its subject matter. Although it was not clearly articulated until the 1970s, integration studies in the 1950s and 1960s embodied the conceptual elements of an alternative disciplinary paradigm that contrasted sharply with the *Weltanschauung* of political realism. Later this came to be labeled post-realism.[38] In the light of this, it is small wonder that integrationist writings were greeted with incredulity by the more realist-oriented, whose frequent criticisms were either that politics within common markets were basically competitions for national power, like all international politics, or that they were not really politics at all but technocratic dealings of little international political consequence.[39] Interestingly, and ironically, at the time that the findings of integration studies were raising serious questions about the assumptions of political realism, the integrationists were so engaged in intellectual conflict with one another that they largely ignored what their work was doing to their discipline.[40]

Enlightened by twenty years of hindsight, and cognizant of recent developments in the study of international relations, one can say with some confidence that the lasting impact of the study of international integration was the confrontation with disciplinary orthodoxy that it fomented in the 1950s and 1960s. This is its contribution to the history of social science. Moreover, once the study of international collaboration was legitimized and highlighted by the integrationists,

Table 1   The Realist Paradigm and Integrationist Findings

Assumptions of Political Realism as Applied to International Relations	Findings of Integration Studies in the 1950s and 1960s	Impacts on the Discipline of International Relations
(1) States and nation-states are the only consequential actors in international relations, and therefore the study of international relations should be focused upon the motives and behavior of states and nation-states or their representatives. Other actors exist but they are consequential only as agents or instruments of states.	(1) States and nation-states are not the only consequential actors in international relations. Indeed, some outcomes in international relations can be understood only in terms of the motives and behavior of international public organizations and bureaucracies, formal and *ad hoc* coalitions of officials transnationally grouped, transnationally organized non-governmental associations, multinational business enterprises, international social classes, and other actors traditionally deemed inconsequential.	(1) Orthodoxy was brought into question, and theoretical and empirical inquiries were initiated that led eventually to theories of transnational relations.
(2) International relations result from foreign policies directed toward enhancing national security, defined in terms of military might and territorial and ideological domain. Other goals are pursued by international actors, but these are "low politics" and hence command little priority in foreign policy and are of little consequence to international relations.	(2) International relations result from foreign policies directed toward enhancing national welfare defined in terms of per capita income, employment, and general well-being. The importance which governments attach to such goals and the domestic penalties and rewards surrounding their attainment or sacrifice render their pursuit "high politics."	(2) Orthodoxy was brought into question and theoretical analyses were initiated that led to the emergence and prominence of international political economy as a central disciplinary concern.

(3) International relations are fundamentally conflict processes played out in zero-sum matrices, i.e. all significant outcomes take the form of aggrandizement for one actor or coalition at the expense of other actors or coalitions. Conflict is the international mode.

(4) Influence in international relations follows from the application of power defined as military or economic capability, actual or potential. Coercion is the modal means to influence.

(3) International relations are fundamentally collaborative processes played out in positive sum matrices, i.e. all significant outcomes take the form of realizing and distributing rewards among collaborating actors or coalitions. Cooperation is the international mode.

(4) Influence in international relations follows from the manipulation of bonds of interdependence that connect actors. Persuasion is the modal means to influence.

(3) Orthodoxy was brought into question and theoretical and empirical inquiries were initiated that led to the emergence and prominence of bargaining theory as applied to international relations.

(4) Orthodoxy was brought into question and theoretical and empirical inquiries were initiated that led ultimately to theories of interdependence.

Source: From R.L. Merritt and Bruce M. Russett (eds.), *From National Development to Global Community* (London: George Allen and Unwin, 1981), p. 149. Reprinted by permission.

research and theorizing spread rapidly beyond problems of unification and into cognate areas that produced several of the literatures currently at the center of the study of international relations. Indeed, many of those researchers who began by seeking insights into political unification found in their case-study materials wealths of new and interesting information about occurrences in subject areas that came eventually to be called transnational and transgovernmental relations, international political economy, international regimes, interdependence, linkage politics, political and economic development, and more. Together, these cognate fields constitute *integration studies*—investigations into peaceful transnational problem-solving. Integration studies remain relevant, alive, well, and quite vibrant in the 1980s because the integrationists' earlier curiosities about international collaboration via transnational processes within settings of interdependence have become central concerns of International Relations.[41]

INTEGRATION STUDIES
AND INTERNATIONAL PLURALISM

In recent years integration studies have come to focus on the nature and problems of what Karl Deutsch called the "pluralistic security community." The term "pluralistic security community" is rather cumbersome and is therefore not much used in the literature of international relations, but the entity it identifies has been the object of a good deal of investigation. This has been especially the case since the late 1960s when the European Communities settled into a mode of relationship where the states and peoples constituted neither a politically unified and culturally assimilated unit nor a traditional unintegrated international state system. In fact, Western Europe has become a pluralistic security community—a cluster of non-warring peoples in an arena of peaceful conflict resolution among governments. What is even more interesting is that by the 1970s it was not only the Western Europeans who constituted a pluralistic security community, but also the Europeans and the North Americans, the North Americans and the Japanese, the Japanese and the Europeans, in fact more or less the entire "trilateral" world. Here states remain separate and sovereign, but peoples share a degree of mutual identification that gives their official and unofficial relations a special quality.

Matters conventionally called "managing interdependence," "North-North" problems or "OECD" problems, or the like, have to do fundamentally with understanding relations among those peoples who have ceased to expect or prepare for war among themselves, but who nevertheless are so closely bound politically and economically that their relationships generate constant friction, which must be diplomatically handled in the common interest. Current research is focused upon how peaceful problem-solving is accomplished in internationally pluralistic settings and in the absence of authoritative regulatory institutions.[42] How are foreign policies coordinated in the absence of central coordinators? How are "prisoners' dilemma" situations avoided in the setting of decentralized adjustment? How, in fact, is adjustment managed so that frictions do not preclude or cancel rewards promised by collaboration? Numerous policy-prescriptive inquiries into these questions are being directed toward setting guidelines to improve the workings of pluralistic international communities and toward the end of making such communities more durable.

But there are also more fundamental questions about pluralistic international communities that need to be confronted and answered. When, where, and why do such entities form? How durable are they, and what affects this durability? Under what conditions do they deteriorate? Methodologically, how are we to observe the emergence of such communities, what indexes their durability, and what signals their deterioration? Except for the fascinating study of the Anglo-American security community by Russett and the fine doctoral dissertation on the same subject by Richard Storatz, very little research has been directed toward answering these questions in theoretical terms.[43] And yet they are crucial to understanding the foundations of the international relations of the contemporary Western world! We presently have no theory of international pluralism; Deutsch and other integration theorists left this work unfinished and no one has carried it forward.

Whatever the future of integration theory, integration studies and their progeny in transnational relations and interdependence studies will likely remain prominent in international relations into the foreseeable future. So too will the "post-realist" paradigm that integration studies thrust upon the discipline. Whether peaceful problem-solving and peaceful change will ever become prevailing features of international relations is uncertain. But they have apparently become more frequent in our part of the twentieth century. If understanding these better could have anything to do with further increasing their frequency, then there is much to be said for heightening our understanding.

NOTES

1. This paper is a considerably revised version of my "Integration Theory and the Study of International Relations," published in *From National Development to Global Community: Essays in Honor of Karl W. Deutsch,* Richard L. Merritt and Bruce M. Russett, eds. (London: Allen & Unwin, 1981), pp. 145–164.
2. See, for example, Ernst B. Haas, *The Uniting of Europe: Political, Social and Economic Forces, 1950–1957* (Stanford: Stanford University Press, 1958); Ernst B. Haas, "International Integration: The European and the Universal Process," *International Organization,* Vol. 15, no. 3 (Summer 1961), pp. 366–392; Leon N. Lindberg and Stuart A. Scheingold, *Europe's Would-Be Polity: Patterns of Change in the European Community* (Englewood Cliffs, N.J.: Prentice-Hall, 1970).
3. Ernst B. Haas and Philippe C. Schmitter, "Economics and Differential Patterns of Political Integration: Projections About Unity in Latin America," *International Organization,* Vol. 18, no. 4 (Autumn 1964), pp. 705–737; Philippe C. Schmitter, "Central American Integration: Spillover, Spill-Around or Encapsulation?" *Journal of Common Market Studies,* Vol. 9, no. 1 (September 1970), pp. 1–48; Joseph S. Nye, Jr., "East African Economic Integration," in *International Political Communities: An Anthology* (Garden City, N.Y.: Doubleday/Anchor Books, 1966), pp. 405–436; and Andrzej Korbonski, "Theory and Practice of Regional Integration: The Case of COMECON," *International Organization,* Vol. 24, no. 4 (Autumn 1970), pp. 942–977.

4. For a comparative sampling of these theories, see Leon N. Lindberg and Stuart A. Scheingold, eds., *Regional Integration: Theory and Research* (Cambridge, Mass.: Harvard University Press, 1971); Charles Pentland, *International Theory and European Integration* (N.Y.: Free Press, 1973); Roger D. Hansen, "Regional integration: Reflections on a Decade of Theoretical Efforts," *World Politics,* Vol. 21, no. 2 (January 1969), pp. 242–271; Ronn D. Kaiser, "Toward the Copernican Phase of Regional Integration Theory," *Journal of Common Market Studies,* Vol. 10, no. 2 (March 1972), pp. 207–232; *Pour l'Etude de l'Integration Europeenne* (Montreal, Que.: Université de Montreal, Centre d'Etudes et de Documentation Europeennes, 1977), pp. 3–91; and Marie-Elisabeth de Bussy, Helene Delorme, and Françoise de la Serre, "Approches theoriques de l'integration europeenne," *Revue Française de Science Politique,* Vol. 20, no. 3 (June 1971), pp. 615–653.

5. Donald J. Puchala, "Of Blind Men, Elephants and International Integration," *Journal of Common Market Studies,* Vol. 10, no. 3 (March 1972), pp. 267–284.

6. See, for example, Pentland, *International Theory and European Integration;* and Lindberg and Scheingold, eds., *Regional Integration.*

7. Ernst B. Haas, "The Uniting of Europe and the Uniting of Latin America," *Journal of Common Market Studies,* Vol. 5, no. 4 (June 1967), pp. 315–343.

8. Ernst B. Haas, "Turbulent Fields and the Theory of Regional Integration," *International Organization,* Vol. 30, no. 2 (Spring 1976), pp. 173–212; and Ernst B. Haas, *The Obsolescence of Regional Integration Theory* (Berkeley, Calif.: University of California, Institute of International Studies, 1975).

9. See Karl W. Deutsch et al., *Political Community and the North Atlantic Area: International Organization in the Light of Historical Experience* (Princeton, N.J.: Princeton University Press, 1957); Robert A. Kann. *The Hapsburg Empire: A Study in Integration and Disintegration* (N.Y.: Praeger, 1957); Raymond E. Lindgren, *Norway-Sweden: Union, Disunion and Scandinavian Integration* (Princeton, N.J.: Princeton University Press, 1959).

10. Donald J. Puchala, "International Transactions and Regional Integration," *International Organization,* Vol. 24, no. 4 (Autumn 1970), pp. 732–764.

11. Deutsch et al., op. cit.

12. Ibid., pp. 5–7.

13. The concept "security community" was introduced by Richard W. Van Wagenen in his *Research in the International Organization Field: Some Notes on a Possible Focus* (Princeton, N.J.: Princeton University, Center for Research on World Political Institutions, 1952).

14. For attempts at such operationalization, see Donald J. Puchala, "Patterns in West European Integration," *Journal of Common Market Studies,* Vol. 9, no. 2 (December 1970), pp. 117–142; Donald J. Puchala, "Integration and Disintegration in Franco-German Relations, 1954–1965," *International Organization,* Vol. 24, no. 2 (Spring 1970), pp. 183–208; and Leon N. Lindberg, "Political Integration as a Multidimensional Phenomenon Requiring Multivariate Measurement," *International Organization,* Vol. 24, no. 4 (Autumn 1970), pp. 649–731.

15. Karl W. Deutsch et al., *France, Germany and the Western Alliance: A Study of Elite Attitudes on European Integration and World Politics* (N.Y.: Charles Scribner's Sons, 1967); Ronald A. Inglehart, "Ongoing Changes in West European Political Cultures," *Integration,* Vol. 1, no. 4 (1970), pp. 250–273; Ronald A. Inglehart, "Public Opinion and Regional Integration," *International Organization,* Vol. 24, no. 4 (Autumn 1970), pp. 764–795; Ronald A. Inglehart, "Cognitive Mobilization and European Identity,"

Comparative Politics, Vol. 3, no. 1 (October 1970), pp. 45–70; Donald J. Puchala, "The Common Market and Political Federation in Western European Public Opinion," *International Studies Quarterly,* Vol. 14, no. 1 (March 1970), pp. 32–59.

16. Deutsch et al., *Political Community and the North Atlantic Area,* p. 6.
17. Lindberg and Scheingold, eds., *Regional Integration;* Puchala, "Patterns in West European Integration"; Karl W. Deutsch, "Integration and Arms Control in the European Political Environment: A Summary Report," *American Political Science Review,* Vol. 60, no. 2 (June 1966), pp. 354–365.
18. James A. Caporaso, *The Structure and Function of European Integration* (Pacific Palisades, Calif.: Goodyear, 1974).
19. Gabriel A. Almond, "Introduction: A Functional Approach to Comparative Politics," in *The Politics of the Developing Areas,* ed. Gabriel A. Almond and James S. Coleman (Princeton, N.J.: Princeton University Press, 1960), pp. 3–64; and David Easton, *A Systems Analysis of Political Life* (New York: Wiley, 1965).
20. Deutsch et al., *France, Germany, and the Western Alliance.*
21. Karl W. Deutsch, *Nationalism and Social Communication: An Inquiry into the Foundations of Nationality* (Cambridge, Mass., and N.Y.: M.I.T. Press and John Wiley & Sons, 1953); and Puchala, "International Transactions and Regional Integration."
22. Donald J. Puchala, "The Pattern of Contemporary Regional Integration," *International Studies Quarterly,* Vol. 12, no. 1 (March 1968), pp. 38–64.
23. The work of Amitai Etzioni is an exception; see his *Political Unification : A Comparative Study of Leaders and Forces* (N.Y.: Holt, Rinehart & Winston, 1965).
24. Peter J. Katzenstein takes important steps toward filling this gap in his *Disjoined Partners: Austria and Germany Since 1815* (Berkeley, Calif.: University of California Press, 1976); Cf. also, Katzenstein, "Domestic Structures and Political Strategies: Austria in an Interdependent World," in Merritt and Russett, eds., op. cit., pp. 252–278.
25. Joseph S. Nye, Jr., *Pan-Africanism and East African Integration* (Cambridge, Mass.: Harvard University Press, 1965); Richard N. Cooper, *The Economics of Interdependence: Economic Policy in the Atlantic Community* (N.Y.: McGraw-Hill, 1968); Johan Galtung, *The European Community: A Superpower in the Making* (Oslo: Universitetsforlaget; London: Allen & Unwin, 1973); and Robert Keohane and Joseph S. Nye, Jr., *Power and Interdependence: World Politics in Transition* (Boston: Little, Brown, 1977).
26. David Mitrany, *A Working Peace System* (Chicago: Quadrangle Books, 1966).
27. Ernst B. Haas, "The Challenge of Regionalism," in *Contemporary Theory in International Relations,* Stanley Hoffmann, ed. (Englewood Cliffs, N.J.: Prentice-Hall, 1960), pp. 223–240.
28. Lindberg and Scheingold, op. cit., Chs. 3, 8, and 9.
29. See Haas, "International Integration: The European and the Universal Process"; Haas and Schmitter, op. cit.; and Haas, "The Uniting of Europe and the Uniting of Latin America."
30. See Walter Hallstein, *Europe in the Making* (N.Y.: Norton, 1972), pp. 24–28, 292–303.
31. Donald J. Puchala, "Domestic Politics and Regional Harmonization in the European Communities," *World Politics,* Vol. 27, no. 4 (July 1975), pp. 496–520.
32. Leon N. Lindberg, *The Political Dynamics of European Economic Integration* (Stanford: Stanford University Press, 1963), pp. 284–285.
33. Philippe C. Schmitter, "Central American Integration."

34. Ernst B. Haas and Philippe C. Schmitter, op. cit.

35. Joseph S. Nye, Jr., *Peace in Parts: Integration and Conflict in Regional Organization* (Boston: Little, Brown, 1971), pp. 21–107.

36. See Haas, *The Obsolescence of Regional Integration Theory,* and Haas, "Turbulent Fields and the Theory of Regional Integration."

37. Robert O. Keohane and Joseph S. Nye, Jr., "Interdependence and Integration,"in *Handbook of Political Science,* Fred I. Greenstein and Nelson Polsby, eds. (Reading, Mass.: Addison-Wesley, 1975) Vol. 8, pp. 363–414; Keohane and Nye, *Power and Interdependence*, pp. 3–62; Donald J. Puchala and Stuart I. Fagan, "International Politics in the 1970s: The Search for a Perspective," *International Organization,* Vol. 28, no. 2 (Spring 1974), pp. 247–266.

38. Puchala and Fagan, op. cit., pp. 247–250.

39. Stanley Hoffmann, "Obstinate or Obsolete? The Fate of the Nation-State and the Case of Western Europe," in *International Regionalism,* Joseph S. Nye, Jr., ed. pp. 177–231; Stanley Hoffmann, "Europe's Identity Crisis: Between Past and America," *Daedalus,* Vol. 93, no. 4 (Fall 1964), pp. 1244–1297; Raymond Aron, *Peace and War: A Theory of International Relations,* (Garden City, N.Y.: Doubleday, 1966), pp. 21–176, 643–666; Hans J. Morgenthau, *Politics Among Nations: The Struggle for Power and Peace,* 4th ed. (N.Y.: Alfred A. Knopf, 1967), pp. 511–516.

40. Ernst B. Haas, "The Challenge of Regionalism"; Karl W. Deutsch, "Towards Western European Integration: An Interim Assessment," *Journal of International Affairs,* Vol. 16, no. 1 (1962), pp. 89–101; Ronald A. Inglehart, "An End to European Integration?" *American Political Science Review,* Vol. 61, no. 1 (March 1967), pp. 91–105; and William E. Fisher, "An Analysis of the Deutsch Sociocausal Paradigm of Political Integration," *International Organization,* Vol. 23, no. 2 (Spring 1969), pp. 254–290.

41. Keohane and Nye, "Interdependence and Integration."

42. Theoretical development in the field of international "regime" studies is very promising in this regard. Cf., Stephen D. Krasner, ed., *International Regimes,* a special issue of *International Organization,* Vol. 36, no. 2 (Spring 1982).

43. Bruce M. Russett, *Community and Contention: Britain and America in the Twentieth Century* (Cambridge, Mass.: M.I.T. Press, 1963); Richard Storatz, "Anglo-American Relations: A Theory and History of Political Integration," unpublished doctoral dissertation, Department of Political Science, Columbia University, 1981.

21
Interdependence, Integration, and Fragmentation

K. J. HOLSTI

Integration and fragmentation are divergent trends apparent in contemporary world politics. In this essay, K. J. Holsti argues that while most scholarship has focused on how increased interaction may lead to interdependence and integration, fragmentation is an equally plausible consequence. Holsti is professor of political science at the University of British Columbia. He is author of *International Politics: A Framework for Analysis* (1983), from which the first selection in this book was extracted.

Observers of contemporary international relations have used a variety of terms to capture the essential characteristics of global interaction and politics. Many have emphasized détente, dependency, neo-colonialism, or the development of multipolarity. . . . [M]ost would argue that *interdependence* is the most pervasive and fundamental result of rapidly growing *transaction* rates between societies. . . .

Few have argued that another prominent feature of our world is disintegration and international fragmentation. The dramatic growth of means of transportation, communication, and exchange of goods, money, and ideas has helped bring about an unprecedented "interconnectedness"[1] between societies. It has thus been fashionable for commentators to claim that in these circumstances, the "shrinking world" has superseded nationalism. Nationalism reached its zenith in nineteenth century Europe and in the anticolonial movements of this century; to most observers, it is now declining as an international phenomenon.[2]

This view is largely incorrect either as a description of current reality or as a prediction for the future. Analysts have been so impressed by growing interdependence that they have ignored a simultaneous or parallel process that results in increased international fragmentation: This chapter argues, and provides some evidence, that while transactions between societies have indeed grown dramatically throughout this century, nationalism, separatism, and international dis-integration have also been prominent. . . . [I]ntegration and dis-integration or fragmentation are taking place concurrently, and in some cases the latter is the consequence of, or reaction to, "too much" interdependence or integration. . . .

Reprinted from K. J. Holsti, "Change in the International System: Interdependence, Integration, and Fragmentation," in Ole R. Holsti, Randolph M. Siverson, and Alexander L. George, eds., *Change in the International System* (Boulder, Colo.: Westview Press, 1980), pp. 23–53. Reprinted by permission of Westview Press. Copyright © 1980 by Westview Press, Boulder Colorado. Some footnotes have been deleted; others have been renumbered to appear in consecutive order.

. . . To my knowledge, no major approach to international relations theory has emphasized the prominence of nationalist behavior as an important characteristic of the contemporary international system. And only a few have examined the nature and sources of autonomy-seeking behavior at the foreign policy level.[3] The glitter and dazzle of growing interdependence have caused a degree of myopia in both academic speculation and diplomatic rhetoric. When we examine the popular contemporary portraits of the international system, it becomes easier to understand why nationalist phenomena have received so little attention. . . .

THE WORLD AS A SYSTEM OF TRANSNATIONAL RELATIONS

Many authors have rejected the image of international politics as a game played by sovereign, impermeable states. They argue that the archaic conception of power politics does not take into account the fundamental consequences of modern technology, the close interconnection between domestic and foreign policy, and the permeability of societies to outside forces. To accommodate the new facts of international life, the world must be seen as a system of patterned interaction in which the main units of action are individuals and a variety of functional groups, as well as national and subnational government units. . . . This view seems based on an assumption that as interactive processes grow and expand, as people increasingly interact across state frontiers, they will be more prone to adjust their differences rather than resort to lethal violence which might destroy the system. A further assumption holds that as technology increases the opportunities (some imply necessity, rather than opportunity) for interaction, people, groups, and states will want to take advantage of them and will seldom suffer losses from so doing. . . .

The systems metaphor has the advantage of placing the state in a setting that is broader than the traditional one in which only diplomats, heads of state, and military forces interact. We are alerted to the importance of subnational foreign policies, to the influence of international organizations, and to the role of transnational groups that have an impact on states and societies. Multinational corporations (MNCs) and terrorist groups are obvious examples. But except for studies on the economic and political impacts of MNCs on developing countries, little attention has been directed to the efforts of many governments to control, reduce, and sometimes even to eliminate the influence of transnational groups and processes on their societies and politics. While the growth of transnational organizations may appear inevitable, it is by no means inevitable that governments will merely "adapt" to them. Some will perceive them as threats to a variety of national values and will deal with them accordingly, even at considerable economic cost. Attempts to enlarge autonomy, to reduce external penetration, and to control transnational organization may involve the construction of national "moats." . . .

THE WORLD OF INTERDEPENDENCE

Interdependence, of course, is not an approach, framework for analysis, or metaphor distinct from those discussed above; indeed, the image of a global system, in which profuse transnational relations take place, implies a high degree of interconnectedness among a variety of units. If there is no connection, there is no system. Global interconnectedness has certain sources (technology, transportation, and communication), it can be measured by looking at transactions, and it leads to sensitivity and vulnerability, where conditions in country A become critically influenced by decisions, trends, and events in countries B . . . X. . . .

. . . [W]e often hear that the *world* is increasingly interdependent, as if growing interconnectedness affected everyone the same way. Once we begin looking at pairs of states rather than at regional or global trends, however, the realities of great differentials in vulnerability, dependency, influence, and coercive capacity become much more apparent. The world may indeed be more interdependent, but that fact has not radically altered the position of, for example, Czechoslovakia or Chile when they attempted to break away from the hegemony of the Soviet Union and the United States. If anything, the extensive interconnection between the client states and their mentors prevented the former from achieving policymaking autonomy and generated conflict, not mutual tolerance or empathy.

Statements such as "the world is increasingly interdependent" are generally nonilluminating except in the banal sense that what people do today has greater impact on others abroad than was the case six centuries ago. Even if the comment contains some face validity, it can be applied with complete accuracy only to the relations between the industrial countries and possibly between them and members of the Organization of Petroleum Exporting Countries (OPEC). . . .

The argument that increased interdependence is likely to reduce international conflict is also open to serious question.[4] As diplomatic relations in Africa have grown more complex, the number of diplomatic quarrels appears to have increased. It would be well to recall also that the marked growth of European interconnectedness and interdependence throughout the nineteenth and twentieth centuries did not prevent the outbreak of the two most destructive wars in human history. To sum up: the fact of increasing interconnectedness is undoubtedly correct. Its consequences remain problematical, however. Increased transaction flows can lead to dependency, exploitation, conflict, and violence as well as to more collaboration and mutual knowledge. To find out the actual consequences of interconnectedness, one must examine pairs of states and avoid the ecological fallacy of arguing that a system property pervades the relationships in all dyads.[5] The *patterns* and *qualities* of transactions are more important than quantities and growth rates. Nationalist policies, secession, and international fragmentation and/ or dis-integration are likely to occur exactly in situations typified by asymmetrical patterns of sensitivity and vulnerability, unequal exchange, unidirectional flows, and attempts by the strong to penetrate the political, economic, and cultural life of the weak.

THE WORLD OF INTEGRATION

Few postwar diplomatic developments have excited as much intellectual enthusiasm as has the regional integration of Western Europe. . . . [I]ntegration theorists have undertaken a massive cumulative effort to explain why formerly independent units come together to create supranational bodies. While the movement for European unification gave the impetus to the inquiry, most of the theories and models of integration have been developed with an eye to universal application. This body of literature has sought to identify necessary and sufficient conditions for integration, has developed techniques for measuring degrees of integration, and has speculated at great length on which variables explain what aspects of the integration process. . . .

. . . While research on integration has generally followed many canons of scientific inquiry, there is little question that authors have been "for" integration—hence the problem has been approached in a particular way, namely locating the necessary and sufficient conditions for *successful* integration. Conditions militating *against* integration—particularly political opposition to integration—have received little attention.

Why the great concern—or hope—for political amalgamation? Most authors implicitly, and sometimes explicitly, assume that integration reduces international conflict. Hence, to study integration is to study the conditions of peace. Although this notion borders on a tautology, it is ultimately the search for peace that has justified the extensive intellectual endeavor. . . . Integration, however defined, is thus the ultimate answer to the problem of war. Why should we assume that decreasing the number of sovereignties decreases the incidence of lethal violence?

The most obvious answer is that people who share a common identity and political loyalties do not quarrel as often or as lethally as those who are separated by language, ethnic, religious, and political frontiers. . . . Integration theory rests squarely upon the old idea that the better people know each other the more they will like each other. This "birds of a feather flock together" thesis is a critical normative dimension in much of the literature, one which is more often assumed than demonstrated. . . .

. . . While there are forces creating demands for more integration (and interdependence) there are also those that are pushing in the direction of dis-integration, resisting further integration, and promoting international fragmentation. Ours is still an age of nationalism despite technology—and sometimes because of it.

Others have made the observation that processes leading to increased interdependence and fragmentation may occur simultaneously.[6] But is there a connection between the two processes? My argument is that in some cases, dis-integration and fragmentation are *responses* to asymmetrical integration and to certain profiles of transactions in dependent and interdependent relationships. They are the reactions of those who see greater interconnectedness not in terms of greater opportunities or benefits, but rather as resulting in inequitable distribution of rewards or as posing threats to national, ethnic, language, or religious identity. In brief, the "shrinking world" may result not in greater consensus and internationalism, but in heightened nationalism and drives to extend or protect autonomy.

Five general types of policies resulting in international dis-integration or fragmentation can be outlined. Governments or groups claiming governmental status may:

1. Terminate practices of joint policymaking, problem solving, or policy coordination; they may also withdraw from, or reduce participation in, institutions having supranational characteristics.
2. Construct mechanisms systematically to reduce or terminate the free flow of goods, people, funds, and ideas between two or more societies. Those fearing absorption or loss of autonomy attempt to reduce external penetration of their government, economy, and society by building walls to reduce access. In its extreme form, it can be termed isolationism.
3. Alter asymmetrical relationships by significantly diversifying external contacts, building regional coalitions, or entering into regional integration schemes as a way of escaping domination by a hegemon.
4. Organize, at the national level, a secessionist movement which seeks to secure or protect autonomy by establishing independent statehood.
5. Resist further integration but not seek to dis-integrate or secede. This would be a marginal category.

. . . [G]overnments may pursue several of the policies simultaneously. Whether singly or in combination, the underlying objective is to create more distance between governments and societies and/or to gain national control over transnational processes. In the . . . nationalist behaviors in Canada and Burma in recent years, . . . the results of greater transaction flows and increased interdependence (or dependency) were not those predicted in most of the literature. The inexorable forces of interdependence in these cases did not result in more integration, more mutual empathy and understanding, or less international conflict. If anything, the reverse was the case.

Canada–United States

No two separate societies in the world better fulfill the assumed necessary conditions to amalgamate politically than do those of the United States and Canada. For most of this century these two countries have constituted a pluralistic security community, where no military forces have been arrayed against each other and where no government has contemplated the use of force to resolve bilateral conflicts. . . .

. . . While Canada and the United States would not score as high on Nye's integration indicators[7] as would the EEC members, by the mid-1960s the two countries indulged in considerable policy consultation and coordination. One could argue that if the trends of the 1950s and 1960s had been allowed to continue, a fully integrated continental economy would have emerged by the 1980s or 1990s, and if the spillover hypothesis was correct, this would subsequently lead to political integration.

Such predictions were, of course, the problem. By the mid-1960s, many Canadians were becoming increasingly concerned that if natural market forces were allowed to continue between the two countries, Canada eventually would be *absorbed* by the United States. Although the scope and breadth of transactions between the two societies was unparalleled in the world, the flows were basically asymmetrical. Hence, many Canadians came to regard them as threatening to Canadian culture and identity, and ultimately to political autonomy. What a neutral observer (particularly a theorist of integration) might see as an extraordinarily rich relationship in terms of empathy, shared values and transactions, many Canadians came to see as overextensive U.S. penetration into Canadian society.[8]

Whether or not one sympathizes with various manifestations of Canadian nationalism, it is not difficult to understand why a negative response to asymmetrical transaction structures would arise. For example, on the average during the 1960s, Americans owned or controlled 55 percent of Canada's manufacturing capacity, constituting more than 20 percent of Canada's GNP; over 90 percent of the theaters (which refused to show Canadian films); and virtually the entire retail trade industry. In the same period, more than 70 percent of unionized Canadians belonged to U.S. labor organizations. With a majority of the Canadians living within the broadcast range of U.S. television stations, most Canadians were watching U.S. material most of the time. The Canadian entertainment industry, with its market only 10 percent that of the United States, could not compete successfully. Although Canadian newspapers and magazines were locally owned, virtually all news of the outside world came via United Press International (UPI) and Associated Press (AP), or from *Time* magazine. Finally, in many Canadian universities, some departments were heavily staffed by Americans, and in more than one instance U.S. department heads would hire fellow nationals without even looking for qualified Canadians.

Under these circumstances—as well as the Canadians' view of the Vietnam War and domestic disturbances in the United States—Canadian nationalists were able to select from a wide menu of issues and argue that if trends in economics, communication, education, and culture were allowed to continue, Canada would eventually lose what remained of its political autonomy. . . .

Between 1968 and 1973 the Canadian federal government—reacting to, rather than leading, public opinion—instituted a variety of measures to alter the pattern or structure of transactions and to halt certain integrative trends. This included a notable decline in the use of some of the many Canadian-U.S. institutions for policy coordination. At the cultural level, the Canadian Radio and Television Commission imposed minimum Canadian content requirements on all broadcasting facilities; developed a set of regulations forcing advertisers to produce their commercials in Canada rather than importing them from the United States; and required Canadian broadcasting companies to divest themselves of U.S. ownership to the 20 percent level. The Canadian secretary of state's office placed considerable pressure on U.S.-owned theater chains to show Canadian films. It also acted several times to prevent U.S. firms from buying out Canadian publishers. After years of debate the Canadian federal government also set up a foreign investment review board with the task of assuring that foreign investment and takeover bids of existing Canadian companies would bring "significant benefits" to Canada.

Starting in 1972 the government also reorganized its policymaking procedures with the United States. Its general philosophy was to create a more "arms length" approach, to accept higher levels of conflict with the United States, and to impose more central control over transgovernmental relations.[9] The days of the "special relationship" and "good partner" diplomacy came to an end. Moreover, the Canadian government politely turned down U.S. proposals to establish more institutions for policy coordination and joint problem solving. The political atmosphere in Ottawa and the country was such that any proposals smacking of "continentalism" (the Canadian expression for arrangements containing integrationist characteristics) were quietly rejected. A detailed Economic Council of Canada study on trade between the two countries, which emphasized the economic gains accruing to the country from a free trade arrangement, never saw the light of public or parliamentary debate.

At the level of foreign policy, the Canadian government set out to diversify its diplomatic and trade contacts as a means of reducing Canada's vulnerability to U.S. economic decisions, such as Nixon's import surcharge and dollar devaluation in August 1971. The major thrust of the program was to use the EEC and Japan as counterweights to the overwhelming trade reliance upon the United States.

Measures to reduce penetration and to reverse integrationist arrangements were not confined to the federal government level. Many provincial governments passed legislation prohibiting the sale of crown lands to nonresidents and a few even considered banning sales of private property to foreigners. The Canadian trade union movement began systematically untying itself from U.S. organizations: by the mid-1970s more than one-half of Canada's unionized labor belonged to independent Canadian unions; a decade earlier the figure had been only 30 percent. The universities agreed upon regulations requiring all academic positions to be advertised in Canada, and a number of departments unofficially began to give preference to Canadian applicants.

Taken together, all these policies were designed, sector by sector, to monitor and control, or alter the profile of Canadian-U.S. transactions, to build up local institutions more effectively to compete with Americans, and to erect filters or screens on some forms of U.S. penetration such as private investment. Programs were also designed to create more distance in diplomacy, to turn the border into a reality as far as cultural relations were concerned, and in a few cases to abandon or modify certain Canadian-U.S. arrangements and institutions that contained integrated characteristics. The policies represent a combination of types 1, 2, 3, and 5 listed earlier. The Canadian case shows clearly the linkage between increased transaction flows, interdependence (or dependence), and the rise of nationalism. Although the United States and Canada share many attributes and still engage in unparalleled quantities of transactions, there is undeniably greater "distance" between the two countries today than there was a decade ago.

Burma

Burma is an example of an even more extreme reaction to foreign penetration and asymmetrical interdependence. From 1963 to 1966, the Burmese government constructed an extensive set of mechanisms to reduce foreign penetration and to establish a greater degree of policy-making autonomy.[10]

The U Nu government, from 1948 until its overthrow in 1962 by the military, generally opened up the country to a number of foreign influences and adopted the typical strategy of development through foreign tutelage, learning from others, seeking foreign investment and aid, and importing modern technology.

The military regime under General Ne Win adopted exactly the opposite approach: total autarchy and isolation, with development achieved through self-reliance. Burma is an extreme case, of course, but it does illustrate how the typical postcolonial pattern of contacts between industrial and developing countries can lead to a fear of being overly penetrated and ultimately losing all cultural and political autonomy. . . .

. . . In Ne Win's judgment, Burma could not achieve true independence if Burmese politicians and civil servants took their political (cold war) cues, their consumption habits, their cultural values, and their life aspirations from others. Interdependence (or as the Burmese would define it, overdependence) thus led to an extreme, almost xenophobic response. Isolationism seeks not just to create greater "arm's length" from a former or actual hegemon, but to reduce *all* contacts with the outside world to a bare minimum.

Many have argued that isolationism is no longer feasible in today's interdependent world. Indeed, if growth in national wealth is the criterion of national success or failure, isolationism in most cases—including Burma—leads to economic decay. But as theorists of interdependence and integration seldom acknowledge, economics is not everything. Other values—in the Burmese case, national pride and fear of loss of autonomy—are also relevant. Economic gains may be forsaken in order to maximize other values. . . .

SECESSIONIST MOVEMENTS AND INTERNATIONAL FRAGMENTATION

International fragmentation may result also from the myriad of contemporary secessionist movements. There are no collected longitudinal data on the incidence of secessionist movements during this century, so it is not possible to determine whether or not there are trends. Nevertheless, ethnically based nationalism is highly visible today and is not confined to the developing nations. . . .

If increased interdependence is supposed to create bonds of community between peoples and societies, why does the search for autonomy and separateness continue at the national and international levels? Several hypotheses might be advanced.[11]

The necessary condition for most secessionist movements is the existence of more than one ethnic language or religious community occupying the same state territory. This condition exists in a majority of the world's states. Connor writes that of 132 states (in the late 1960s), only 12, or 9 percent, can be described as basically homogenous in ethnic makeup. In 32 states, the largest single ethnic group does not comprise even 50 percent of the population, and in 53 states, the population is divided into more than five significant groups.[12] In such nations increased communications between ethnic, language, or religious groups may underline uniqueness, cause greater group solidarity, promote stereotypic thinking, and ultimately increase intergroup cleavages. Connor[13] has argued that the optimistic predictions about the results of increasing social communication are taken from the U.S. or European nineteenth century experience and are not borne out in other milieus. In many developing countries, the first extensive contacts between minority groups and central government authorities or the dominant cultural communities lead to conflict, not assimilation. Leaders of many secessionist movements are not those who have remained isolated; on the contrary, most have had considerable experience with the majority population and central government agents.[14] They have rejected offers to assimilate and even to share political power, and chosen the path of armed struggle for independence. Increased communication has fostered separatism, not integration. Contrary to much popular thinking on interdependence and political development, we might hypothesize that the faster the rate of growth of communication between distinct social groups or societies, the greater the probability that autonomy-preserving or -seeking behavior will result.[15]

A second avenue for exploration would focus on the *profile of social transactions* between groups or states. . . . [W]here transactions are highly asymmetrical and contacts between societies involve unidirectional penetration, perceptions of nonmilitary threats (e.g., threats to autonomy, continued independence, cultural survival, religious purity, and the like) are likely to arise, resulting in demands for controlling international transactions and instituting policies to establish greater "distance" between groups within a state, or between states. When some see their community or society has become highly penetrated by outsiders—even by good friends—common knowledge, broad communication, and empathy are not likely to prevent demands from protecting or reestablishing autonomy. The Quebec independence movement grew apace as French-speaking Canadians were required to speak English in English-Canadian firms, as the flow of non-French-speaking European immigrants into the province continued to rise, and as the birth rate of French-Canadians continued to decline. The nationalists drew the obvious conclusions from these trends: if allowed to continue, French language and culture in North America would no longer exist after several generations. Few in Quebec could ignore these facts, even if they were bilingual, felt national loyalty to Canada, conducted extensive transactions with English-Canadians, and "understood" them. Quebecois have argued that the flow of transactions and communications, increasing throughout the 1960s, was predominantly in one direction: from English-Canada into Quebec. While Anglophone Canadians were worrying about the U.S. "threat," Quebecois were worrying, not about Yankees, but about Anglophone Canadians. The parallel in each language group's concern with autonomy and cultural preservation is striking. . . .

A third line of explanation would emphasize hardheaded economic calculations: dis-integrative and secessionist movements are likely to arise when certain groups perceive that they are not receiving an adequate and/or fair share of economic gains, resulting from interdependence, or are paying an inequitable share of government or supranational burdens. The East African Community dissolved in 1977 over disagreements on both costs and rewards.[16] Small secessionist movements in western Canada argue that Alberta and British Columbia pay taxes to the federal government way out of proportion to the services they receive from Ottawa.[17] Finally, Chile withdrew from the Andean Pact after 1974 because the Pinochet regime did not want to apply the restrictions on foreign investment called for in the treaty.

Fourth, demands for dis-integration or secession may arise where loss of decisionmaking autonomy has become intolerable. Interdependence and integration exact a high cost in freedom of choice. The reasons for collaborative undertakings and integration are no doubt compelling—particularly maximizing joint gains—but frequently some are going to believe that supranational policymaking bodies do not take into account sufficiently the unique needs of certain partners. The Canadian attempt to return to a more classical diplomatic relationship with the United States was in part formulated on the grounds that use of joint institutions locked Canada into agendas set in the United States and induced a presumption of collaborative behavior that mitigated against the vigorous pursuit of Canadian national objectives.

Finally, the doctrine of self-determination, a genuine transnational ideology or value, has become one of the most important sources of political legitimacy, the most potent propaganda symbol used to raise the consciousness (and conscience) of both nationals and foreign audiences. A national liberation movement, no matter how authoritarian its leadership and bloody its tactics, can obtain significant international attention, sympathy, and occasionally material support by portraying itself as fighting a colonial regime or seeking to obtain independence for a distinct ethnic, language, or religious group. In the early twentieth century, the notion of self-determination was closely linked to democratic principles. Its application to the defeated powers after World War I was based on the assumption that the new states would adopt reasonably pluralist political institutions. Today, in contrast, a national liberation movement does not have to establish democratic credentials in order to claim legitimacy. Merely to speak in the name of a minority is usually sufficient. Thus, as long as there are states whose boundaries do not coincide with ethnic divisions, we can expect to see the continued development of secessionist movements, invoking the doctrine of self-determination to justify their struggles.

CONSEQUENCES

If we acknowledge that nationalism continues to be a potent force in national and international politics, and that increased interdependence may foster nationalism and instability as well as integration and harmony, what consequences can we expect in terms of the structure and processes of the international system? At first glance, the prevalence of secessionist movements might suggest that the number of sovereign units in the system will continue growing, with perhaps as many as 200 members in the United Nations by the end of the century. If such were to be the case, the system would be numerically one of the largest since the early spring and autumn period during the Chou dynasty in China of the eighth century B.C. Many of the microstates would be highly dependent upon outsiders for economic and defense support, but they would still possess voting power in international organizations. Since many of the new states would come from the developing areas, we would expect them to lend additional weight to the LDCs on north-south issues. The industrial countries would thereby become an even smaller minority in global organizations, maintaining influence primarily by the size of their financial contributions rather than by their numbers. We could predict as well that if the number of violent secessionist movements continues to grow, new arenas of international conflict would appear, as the major powers would likely involve themselves either to promote the forces of national liberation or to protect the territorial integrity of the mother nation—as the Soviets and the French have done in Ethiopia and the Congo.

Numerous predictions about the consequences of increasing the size of the international system by about 25 percent over the next decades could be made, but for such an exercise to be worthwhile there must be a reasonable probability that the predicted trend will in fact occur. Despite the universal popularity of the self-determination principle and the widespread sympathy secessionist movements manage to generate abroad, experience of the past suggests that many of the movements will not succeed in obtaining full independence. Whatever their sympathies, most governments have opted for the principle of territorial integrity over minority independence when confronted with the choice.[18] The ethnic rebellions in Burma have been continuing for almost three decades, with little probability of ultimate success, and with little outside support. In Biafra, the Congo, the Ogaden, and elsewhere, most foreign governments have ended up on the side of the central authorities in their contests with secessionist movements.[19] In the United Nations, members have voted consistently to emphasize that the principle of self-determination applies to territories and not to peoples. For example, during the fifteenth session of the General Assembly the members strongly supported a resolution that stated: "Any attempt at the partial or total disruption of the national unity and territorial integrity of a country is incompatible with the purposes and principles of the United Nations Charter."[20]

With the possible exception of Quebec, secessionist movements in the industrial countries seem to have few possibilities for obtaining full independence. Both local arrangements involving greater autonomy and protection of ethnic, language, or religious traditions, and/or repression seem more likely outcomes. In brief, the probabilities of a significant increase—say 25 percent—in the number of new states are quite low. . . . Domestic instability and occasional insurrection remain distinct possibilities, but dramatic increases in the rate of international fragmentation appear unlikely.

The incidence of international dis-integration or more "moat-building" foreign policies in the future remains problematic. Weak and vulnerable societies involved in highly asymmetrical relationships no doubt find strategies of self-sufficiency and autarchy politically, if not economically, appealing, if only to break down dependency and to reduce foreign penetration of their institutions. On the other hand, development strategies such as those pursued by Saudi Arabia and the shah's Iran, where extensive foreign investment and penetration are accepted, may have greater appeal because of the visible and rapid economic results. The lack of research on isolationist and autarchic impulses makes it difficult to predict which types of societies, under which sorts of domestic and international conditions, will attempt to disengage themselves by turning inward.

Certainly the Canadian relationship vis-à-vis the United States finds few counterparts in Western Europe. There, the small members of the EEC appear content with their lot, and new members will join the organization soon. Even though we may expect to find considerable opposition to *major* moves in the direction of political unification the Norwegian vote must be interpreted as an aberration rather than as a symptom of general European malaise about protecting cultural identity or political autonomy. In Eastern Europe dis-integration takes the form of our marginal category, that is, resistance to further integration. Compared to the North Atlantic Treaty Organization (NATO), the Warsaw Treaty Organization has achieved more integration, particularly in standardization of weapons and command structure. But there has been little evidence of "spillover" from security arrangements to other spheres, and Soviet attempts to establish a permanent economic division of labor in the region have been resisted. While there has been some movement toward establishing integrated institutions, the centrifugal forces in Eastern Europe remain vigorous.[21]

In the remainder of the world, regional economic integration schemes enjoy varying fortunes. Some, like the Central American Common Market, have significantly increased regional trade, but serious problems of benefit distribution remain. The Andean Pact, on the other hand, has failed to enhance the mutual trade of the signatories, and Chile has withdrawn from the organization. The Caribbean Free Trade Association (CARIFTA) has barely succeeded in reducing its members' dependency on the United States and Britain, and also faces problems of benefit distribution and the distrust of the smaller members toward Jamaica and Guyana.[22] Some of the regional organizations in Africa rest on similarly shaky foundations. The East African Community, probably the most advanced integrative scheme in the developing world, with prospects of even greater successes in the future, collapsed in 1977.

CONCLUSION

This excursion into the international ramifications of modern nationalism has been undertaken in an attempt to compensate for some of the distortions found in contemporary conceptions of the international system, as well as in much current diplomatic rhetoric. Themes such as a "shrinking world," "growing interdependence," "regionalism," or "international system" often imply inevitable processes leading to desirable outcomes, affecting all equally. While there are undoubted benefits accruing to human societies from their greater interconnectedness, there are costs that must be considered as well. . . . Weak, vulnerable societies and communities are not likely to favor schemes of economic or political integration if they predict that their implementation will lead to extensive foreign penetration, inequitable distribution of costs and rewards, and submerging of local lifestyles. To argue abstractly that integration increases the possibilities of peace is not likely to make much impact on those who see their language, religion, customs, or occupations threatened by foreign penetration.

The statistics demonstrating increased transaction flows throughout most of the world cannot be denied. But as this essay has sought to underline, this growth can have numerous consequences, not all of which contribute to international peace and stability or integration. An accumulating body of evidence suggests that in many instances as interconnectedness increases, so does nationalism (in the sense of more "moat-building"), and interethnic and international conflict. If our conceptions of the international system are to be reasonably consistent with realities, we must not confuse the European with a universal experience, assume that the consequences of increased communications are always positive, or argue that processes that are developing primarily among the industrial states extend to other areas of the world as well. This is not to argue that the manifestations of nationalism outlined previously lead to desirable consequences either. Ultimately the costs and gains of integration or fragmentation can only be assessed according to one's value preferences. But before that debate can be launched, the international relations scholarly community must at least recognize that nationalism is a persisting phenomenon, one that has not been done in by the advent of supersonic aircraft, large trade volumes, and international television. . . .

ACKNOWLEDGMENTS

I am grateful for the many useful comments and suggestions offered by Peter Busch, David Haglund, Ole Holsti, Roff Johannson, Robert Keohane, Saadia Touval, and John Wood.

NOTES

1. Alex Inkeles uses the term to signify transactions and interactions between societies in "The Emerging Social Structure of the World," *World Politics* 27 (July 1975):467–495.
2. Walker Connor, "Self-Determination: The New Phase," *World Politics* 20 (October 1967):45; Zbigniew Brzezinski, *Between Two Ages* (New York: Viking Press, 1970), esp. p. 275. A notable exception to this view is Robert O. Keohane and Joseph S. Nye, Jr., *Power and Interdependence: World Politics in Transition* (Boston: Little, Brown and Co., 1977), esp. p. 4.
3. Richard Cooper, "Economic Interdependence and Foreign Policy in the Seventies," *World Politics* 24 (January 1972):159-181; Connor, "Self-Determination: The New Phase"; Arnfinn Jorgensen-Dahl, "Forces of Fragmentation in the International System: The Case of Ethno-nationalism," *Orbis* 19 (Summer 1975): 652–674; and the argument that interdependence is now giving way to a new mercantilism, Gregory Schmid, "Interdependence Has Its Limits," *Foreign Policy* 21 (Winter 1975–1976):188–197.
4. He predicts increased incidence of crises and conflict resulting from interdependence. Other newer writings on interdependence also acknowledge that interdependence and

conflict do not necessarily vary in the same direction. See Keohane and Nye, *Power and Interdependence*, chap. 5, pp. 8–11.

5. [K. J. Holsti, "A New International Politics? Diplomacy in Complex Interdependence," *International Organization* 32 (Spring 1978):520.]

6. See Geoffrey Goodwin, "The Erosion of External Sovereignty," in [Ghita Ionescu, ed., *Between Sovereignty and Integration* (London: Croom Helm, 1974)]. Robert Gilpin has discussed the causal relationship between increased integration and the rise of economic nationalism in the smaller party in "Integration and Disintegration in the North American Continent," *International Organization* 28 (Autumn 1974):851–874. Anti-integrationist tendencies are acknowledged in Ernst B. Haas, "Turbulent Fields and the Theory of Regional Integration," *International Organization* 30 (Summer 1976):185, 195–196.

7. [Joseph S. Nye, Jr., *Peace in Parts: Integration and Conflict in Regional Organizations* (Boston: Little, Brown and Co., 1971), chaps. 2, 3.]

8. The increase of Canadians' perceptions of threat emanating from U.S. presence–particularly economic–in Canada is clearly revealed in public opinion polls. For example, in 1964, 46 percent of the respondents believed there was enough U.S. investment in the country. In 1978, the figure had risen to 69 percent. See *Vancouver Sun*, 12 August 1978, p. D-1. Responding to the question, "Do you think the Canadian way of life is, or is not being too much influenced by the United States?" 39 percent replied in the affirmative in 1961, and 53 percent in 1966. See John H. Sigler and Dennis Goresky, "Public Opinion on United States-Canadian Relations," in Annette B. Fox, Alfred O. Hero, and Joseph S. Nye, Jr., eds., *Canada and the United States: Transnational and Transgovernmental Relations* (New York: Columbia University Press, 1974), pp. 64–65.

9. The most comprehensive treatment of Canadian policy formulation to alter the pattern of Canadian-U.S. relations is by John Kirton, *The Conduct and Co-ordination of Canadian Government Decisionmaking Towards the United States* (Ph.D. diss., The Johns Hopkins University, 1977).

10. A detailed description of Burma's isolationist strategy and an attempt to explain the reasons it was chosen is in K. J. Holsti, *Why Nations Realign: Foreign Policy Restructuring in the Postwar World*, forthcoming, chap. 7.

11. A thorough discussion of the preconditions and necessary conditions for the rise of secessionist movements is in John R. Wood, "Toward A Theory of Secession" (Paper presented to the American Political Science Association meetings, New York, September 1978). Only a few of the conditions that are relevant both to secession and international dis-integration are discussed here. Multiethnicity is an important source of disintegration only at the national level.

12. Walker Connor, "Nation-building or Nation-destroying?" *World Politics* 24 (April 1972):320–321.

13. Ibid., pp. 346–348.

14. Jorgensen-Dahl, "Forces of Fragmentation," p. 664.

15. In a statistical study of secessionist movements, Church and his colleagues demonstrate a positive relationship between degrees of social mobilization and separatism. Social mobilization, of course, involves a notable increase in communication flows. Roderick Church et al., "Ethnoregional Minorities and Separatism: A Cross-National Analysis," mimeo (1978), pp. 20–21.

16. See Nye, *Peace in Parts,* p. 33.

17. The Quebec government has used data to demonstrate that the province has done poorly in terms of taxes and government benefits under confederation. This argument rationalizes separation and is not a cause of it.

18. Various considerations underlying external powers' generally conservative stance regarding support for secessionist movements are discussed in Wood, "Toward a Theory of Secession," pp. 26–27.

19. The successful breakaway of East Pakistan, with Indian assistance, is the significant exception to the generalization.

20. Cited in Jorgensen-Dahl, "Forces of Fragmentation," p. 669.

21. Cf. Paul Marer, "Prospects for Integration in Eastern Europe: The Council for Mutual Economic Assistance," in Jan F. Triska and Paul M. Cocks, eds., *Political Development in Eastern Europe* (New York: Praeger Publishers, 1977), pp. 256–274.

22. R. S. Milne, "Impulses and Obstacles in Caribbean Political Integration: Academic Theory and Guyana's Experience," *International Studies Quarterly* 18 (September 1974):291–316.

Politics and Markets

During recent years the global agenda has included issues relating to international trade protectionism, balance-of-payments adjustments, and international monetary instability. These have been matched on the domestic agendas of many nations with issues relating to inflation, unemployment, and economic stagnation. The two sets of issues are not unrelated. Under conditions of global interdependence—defined as a condition of *mutual sensitivity* and *mutual vulnerability*—decisions made in one nation often have important implications and consequences for other nations. Efforts to control inflation at home, for example, can affect the value of national currencies used for international trade and capital transactions, which in turn may affect different nations' balance-of-payments positions, that is, the state of their financial transactions with the rest of the world.

Interdependence, by blurring the distinctions between foreign policy and domestic policy and between foreign security policy and foreign economic policy, raises important questions about the problems that have long dominated world politics. Traditionally, issues relating to economics have been regarded as matters of *low politics*. While the *high politics* of peace and security issues engaged the attention of nations' policy-making elites, the *low politics* of more routinized international economic affairs could be left to the lower-level bureaucrats. Today, as controversies over the distribution of wealth and the processes and institutions that govern it affect everyone, transnational economic issues are among the most important political issues on the global agenda, and they now compete with traditional national security issues for the attention of top-level elites.

The term *political economy* highlights the intersection of politics and economics, which have developed increasingly tight links as the world has grown more interdependent economically. The term draws attention to the facts that economic linkages between nations affect their political affairs, and that the nature of their political ties influences their economic exchanges. Thus politics (the exercise of power and influence) and economics (the distribution of material wealth) have a reciprocal impact on each other.

The *high-politics, low-politics* distinction has always been over-drawn, perhaps, but the complexity and urgency of political economy issues— fueled by the expansion of world trade since World War II and the globalization of production and finance via multinational corporations and banks—are now more apparent than ever. Thus it is no exaggeration to argue that some of the most important issues on the global agenda are affected by the interplay of political and economic forces, and that an answer to the classic political question—Who gets what, when, and how?—must be sought in this interplay. Political economy thus provides a conceptual focus designed to accommodate the complex realities of the contemporary global environment.

As noted, the issues on the global agenda that comprise the political economy issue-area are numerous. It is not surprising, therefore, that a number of analytical perspectives compete with one another in an effort to bring insight and meaning to them. It is useful to begin with a discussion of some of these contending perspectives and schools of thought. Robert Gilpin does this admirably in the first essay in Part III, "Can the Interdependent World Political Economy Survive? Three Perspectives on the Future." Gilpin evaluates the merits and limitations of three paradigms or approaches to understanding international political economy. These are the liberal, Marxist, and economic nationalist schools of thought. The first sees the future affected most by challenges to the nation-state posed by increasing economic interdependence and technological advances; it is termed the *sovereignty-at-bay* model. The second envisions the future influenced most by the continuing struggle between haves and have-nots in a hierarchical system that, consistent with Marxist thought, is seen as inherently exploitive; it is termed the *dependencia* model to emphasize the pattern of inequality and dependency that this view ascribes to the international political economy. This perspective, like the liberal one, emphasizes the role of multinational corporations in the world political economy. The third, by contrast, sees the future determined primarily by the way in which nation-states pursue their national interests; appropriately, it is labeled the *mercantilist* model. Not only does Gilpin's essay usefully describe and evaluate these alternative perspectives, it also offers some inviting propositions about the implications of interdependence for the world's future.

The meaning and consequences of interdependence are explored systematically by Robert O. Keohane and Joseph S. Nye, Jr., in "Complex Interdependence, Transnational Relations, and Realism: Alternative Perspectives on World Politics." Seeing political realism, the classic model of international affairs, as no longer able to depict adequately current realities, Keohane and Nye sketch the parameters of an alternative paradigm, *complex interdependence,* which incorporates as well elements of the *transnational relations* perspective. In contrast to the state-centric realist perspective, complex interdependence draws attention to the role that non-state actors, such as international organizations and multinational firms and banks, play in shaping the contours of contemporary world politics. It also challenges the realists' view of the centrality of military power in states' foreign policies, arguing instead that, for some actors on some issues, military power is relatively irrelevant. These provocative ideas, which have commanded considerable attention in recent years, provide the reader not only with competing views of world politics, but also with insight into why "issue politics" have assumed such importance in world affairs.

The multinational corporation is perhaps the most salient and controversial non-state actor in today's global political economy. Its nature and role are assessed in "The Multinational Corporation in World Politics," written by the editors of *The Global Agenda.* In it, Kegley and Wittkopf summarize data about transnationally organized business enterprises, with a focus on their economic power and global reach. They also examine controversies regarding the impact of MNCs on host states, the political activities in which MNCs are often alleged to be engaged, and their long-run impact on world politics.

No analysis of the world political economy would be complete without a consideration of the global market system through which states conduct their economic exchanges. Capitalism at the international level, it can be argued, rests on both economic and political foundations. And while some observers may be uncomfortable with this thesis, all must acknowledge that today's global economy is profoundly influenced by the way the international political system has evolved historically, and that the positions of nation-states in the contemporary world economy have been strongly affected by how economic and political forces have combined over time to shape rates of capital accumulation and economic growth.

The so-called "world-system" perspective, advanced by Immanuel Wallerstein and his many followers, has gained popularity because of its ability to generate insight into contemporary conditions through analyses of the evolution of the world's political economy through many centuries to the present. Wallerstein introduces the central ideas encapsulated in the world-system perspective in his essay, "The Future of the World Economy: A World-System Perspective." Wallerstein spells out the reasons for his belief that the structural contradictions of the world's capitalist economy are destined to undermine its survival. His conclusion—that we are witnessing a historic world transition from capitalism to socialism—will alarm some (and cheer others). But regardless of how his prediction is greeted, the theoretical basis for the prophecy raises important questions about the structural foundations upon which the capitalist system rests and around which the global political system has been built.

A major conclusion of the world-system perspective is that, within the world political economy as currently structured, no ascendant state—no matter how powerful or resourceful—can maintain hegemonic status permanently. That is, once a state rises to the apex of the system's hierarchy, history suggests it then begins an inevitable descent.

Has the United States, the hegemonic power of the post–World War II international political economy, started down that slope? Will the characteristics inherent in the world capitalist system assure the deterioration of America's power?

If answers to these questions are ambiguous, the changing role of the United States in the world political economy is not, as shown by C. Fred Bergsten in "The United States and the World Economy." Bergsten's survey of a wide spectrum of trends provides incontrovertible evidence that American dependence on the world economy has grown dramatically, but that at the same time the ability of the United States to manage world economic events has declined precipitously. Against the background of dependence on the world economy beyond the nation's historic experience, the United States will be faced with a number of critical if complex policy issues in the future. Because the United States remains the single largest economy in the world today, its responses to these issues will shape not only its own future world but that of many others as well.

It is axiomatic that the United States alone does not have the power to steer world economic conditions in a favorable direction. Like others in a voluntary exchange system in which the purchase of goods and services is, in principle, a product of free choice, and in which the welfare of all is dependent on the actions of each, the United States will benefit—or suffer—from the kinds of trade practices that all states pursue. Hence, international trade policy in a system that relies on market mechanisms is a central issue on the global agenda. Appropriately, Raymond Vernon discusses a wide range of international trade policy issues in "International Trade Policy in the 1980s: Prospects and Problems." Recognizing the critical role of the United States in creating trade policies for the future, Vernon's assessment emphasizes the need for a strong international trade regime, and for changes in some of the principles of the prevailing regime to which states voice allegiance in their policy pronouncements.

The international *regime* to which Vernon (and others in this volume) alludes is often defined as a collection of rules, norms, and procedures that members of a political system support in order to regularize behavior and to resolve issues that surface on their common agendas. Thus a *regime* can be thought of as an institutionalized system of cooperation. With the tightened links that now bind nation-states and other, non-state actors together in the world political economy, the regime concept has commanded interest because, presumably, empirically identifiable regimes play a crucial role in the peaceful management of international relations. Regime analysis has accordingly become part of the analysis of interdependence and political economy, and it is not accidental that all three concepts have simultaneously gained increased attention intellectually.

Does regime analysis offer a meaningful perspective on the issues catalogued in this section of *The Global Agenda?* Susan Strange, author of "Regime Analysis in the Study of International Political Economy: A Critique," submits the regime concept to scrutiny and finds it wanting. Not only does Strange find the regime concept imprecise; she also concludes it distorts reality as much as it illuminates it. If these and other criticisms of the regime concept are valid, they raise serious questions about our analytical tools and suggest the need for identifying alternative perspectives from which to view global issues. We respond to that need in Part IV of *The Global Agenda*, where the focus on the issues of *low politics* shifts from politics and markets to politics and ecology.

22

Can the Interdependent World Political Economy Survive? Three Perspectives on the Future

ROBERT GILPIN

In this essay, Robert Gilpin summarizes and critically analyzes three perspectives on international political economy: the liberal, Marxist, and mercantilist/nationalist. He utilizes these comparative assessments to reflect on the probable future course of international economic relations. Gilpin is professor of politics and international affairs at Princeton University. His publications include *War and Change in World Politics* (1981).

Edward Hallet Carr observed that "the science of economics presupposes a given political order, and cannot be profitably studied in isolation from politics."[1] Throughout history, the larger configurations of world politics and state interests have in large measure determined the framework of the international economy. Succeeding imperial and hegemonic powers have sought to organize and maintain the international economy in terms of their economic and security interests.

From this perspective, the contemporary international economy was the creation of the world's dominant economic and military power, the United States. At the end of the Second World War, there were efforts to create a universal and liberal system of trade and monetary relations. After 1947, however, the world economy began to revive on the foundations of the triangular relationship of the three major centers of noncommunist industrial power: the United States, Western Europe, and Japan. Under the umbrella of American nuclear protection and connected with the United States through military alliances, Japan and Western Europe were encouraged to grow and prosper. In order to rebuild these industrial economies adjacent to the Sino-Soviet bloc, the United States encouraged Japanese growth, led by exports, into the American market and, through the European

Reprinted from Robert Gilpin, "Three Models of the Future," *International Organization* 29 (Winter 1975), pp. 37–60 by permission of The MIT Press, Cambridge, Massachusetts. © 1975 by the Regents of the University of Wisconsin System. Some footnotes have been deleted; others have been renumbered to appear in consecutive order.

[1] Edward Hallet Carr, *The Twenty Years' Crisis 1919-1939* (London: Macmillan and Co., 1951), p. 117.

Economic Community's (EEC) common external tariff and agricultural policy, also encouraged discrimination against American exports.

Today, the triangular relationship of the noncommunist industrial powers upon which the world economy has rested is in disarray. The signs of decay were visible as early as the middle 1960s, when President John F. Kennedy's grand design failed to stem the coalescence of an inward-looking European economic bloc and to achieve its objective of an economic and political community extending from Scandinavia to Japan and pivoted on the United States.

Believing that the world trading and monetary system was operating to America's disadvantage, the administration of Richard Nixon took up the challenge with a completely different approach. On 15 August 1971, former President Nixon announced a new foreign economic policy for the United States. In response to the first trade deficit since 1893 and to accelerating attacks on the dollar, the president imposed a surcharge on American imports, suspended the convertibility of the dollar, and took other remedial actions. Subsequently the dollar was devalued twice (December 1971 and February 1973); the world moved toward a system of flexible exchange rates; and intense negotiations were initiated to create a new international monetary and trading system.

A new economic policy was necessary for several reasons. The United States believed an overvalued dollar was adding significantly to its unemployment rate.[2] American expenditures abroad for military commitments, foreign direct investment, and goods and services required, in the 1970s, greater outlays of foreign exchange than the United States could earn or wished to borrow. The US rapprochement with China, its moves toward détente with the Soviet Union, and President Nixon's announcement of the New Economic Policy appeared to signal the end of the political order that American economic and military supremacy had guaranteed; this political order had been the foundation for the post–World War II world economy. All these policy initiatives were efforts to adjust to the growing economic power of America's partners, Europe and Japan, and to the growing military power of its primary antagonist, the Soviet Union. In terms of the present article, these economic and political changes raised the question of whether the interdependent world economy could survive in the changing political environment of the 1970s and beyond.

In this brief article I make no attempt to give a definitive answer to this question. Rather, my purpose is to present and evaluate three models of the future drawn from current writings on international relations. These models are really representative of the three prevailing schools of thought on political economy: liberalism, Marxism, and economic nationalism. Each model is an amalgam of the ideas of several writers who, in my judgment (or by their own statements), fall into one or another of these three perspectives on the relationship of economic and political affairs.

Each model constitutes an ideal type. Perhaps no one individual would subscribe to each argument made by any one position. Yet the tendencies and as-

---

[2] C. Fred Bergsten, "The New Economics and U.S. Foreign Policy," *Foreign Affairs* 50 (January 1972): 199–222.

sumptions associated with each perception of the future are real enough; they have a profound influence on popular, academic, and official thinking on trade, monetary, and investment problems. One, in fact, cannot really escape being influenced by one position or another.

Following the presentation of the three models, I present a critique that sets forth the strengths and weaknesses of each. On the basis of this critique, I draw some general conclusions with respect to the future of . . . international relations. . . .

THE SOVEREIGNTY-AT-BAY MODEL

I label the first model *sovereignty at bay,* after the title of Raymond Vernon's influential book on the multinational corporation.[3] According to this view, increasing economic interdependence and technological advances in communication and transportation are making the nation state an anachronism. These economic and technological developments are said to have undermined the traditional economic rationale of the nation state. In the interest of world efficiency and domestic economic welfare, the nation state's control over economic affairs will continually give way to the multinational corporation, to the Eurodollar market, and to other international institutions better suited to the economic needs of mankind.

Perhaps the most forceful statement of the sovereignty-at-bay thesis is that of Harry Johnson–the paragon of economic liberalism. Analyzing the international economic problems of the 1970s, Johnson makes the following prediction:

> In an important sense, the fundamental problem of the future is the conflict between the political forces of nationalism and the economic forces pressing for world integration. This conflict currently appears as one between the national government and the international corporation, in which the balance of power at least superficially appears to lie on the side of the national government. But in the longer run economic forces are likely to predominate over political, and may indeed come to do so before the end of this decade. Ultimately, a world federal government will appear as the only rational method for coping with the world's economic problems.[4]

Though not all adherents of the sovereignty-at-bay thesis would go as far as Johnson, and an interdependent world economy is quite conceivable without unbridled scope for the activities of multinational corporations, most do regard the multinational corporation as the embodiment par excellence of the liberal ideal of an interdependent world economy. It has taken the integration of national economies beyond trade and money to the internationalization of production. For the first time in history, production, marketing, and investment are being organized on a global scale rather than in terms of isolated national economies. The multinational corporations are increasingly indifferent to national boundaries in making decisions with respect to markets, production, and sources of supply.

The sovereignty-at-bay thesis argues that national economies have become en-

---

[3] Raymond Vernon, *Sovereignty at Bay* (New York: Basic Books, 1971).

[4] Harry G. Johnson, *International Economic Questions Facing Britain, the United States, and Canada in the 70's,* British-North American Research Association, June 1970, p. 24.

meshed in a web of economic interdependence from which they cannot easily escape, and from which they derive great economic benefits. Through trade, monetary relations, and foreign investment, the destinies and well-being of societies have become too inexorably interwoven for these bonds to be severed. The costs of the ensuing inefficiencies in order to assert national autonomy or some other nationalistic goal would be too high. The citizenry, so this thesis contends, would not tolerate the sacrifices of domestic economic well-being that would be entailed if individual nation states sought to hamper unduly the successful operation of the international economy.

Underlying this development, the liberal position argues, is a revolution in economic needs and expectations. Domestic economic goals have been elevated to a predominant position in the hierarchy of national goals. Full employment, regional development, and other economic welfare goals have become the primary concerns of political leadership. More importantly, these goals can only be achieved, this position argues, through participation in the world economy. No government, for example, would dare shut out the multinational corporations and thereby forgo employment, regional development, or other benefits these corporations bring into countries. In short, the rise of the welfare state and the increasing sensitivity of national governments to the rising economic expectations of their societies have made them dependent upon the benefits provided by a liberal world-economic system.

In essence, this argument runs, one must distinguish between the creation of the interdependent world economy and the consequences of its subsequent dynamics.[5] Though the postwar world economy was primarily a creation of the United States, the system has since become essentially irreversible. The intermeshing of interests across national boundaries and the recognized benefits of interdependence now cement the system together for the future. Therefore, even though the power of the United States and security concerns may be in relative decline, this does not portend a major transformation of the international economy and political system.

The multinational corporation, for example, is now believed to be sufficiently strong to stand and survive on its own. The flexibility, mobility, and vast resources of the corporations give them an advantage in confrontations with nation states. A corporation always has the option of moving its production facilities elsewhere. If it does, the nation state is the loser in terms of employment, corporate resources, and access to world markets. Thus the multinationals are escaping the control of nation states, including that of their home (source) governments. They are emerging as sufficient powers in their own right to survive the changing context of international political relations.

On the other hand, it is argued that the nation state has been placed in a dilemma it cannot hope to resolve.[6] It is losing control over economic affairs to

---

[5] Samuel Huntington, "Transnational Organizations in World Politics," *World Politics* 25 (April 1973): 361.

[6] Edward Morse, "Crisis Diplomacy, Interdependence, and the Politics of International Economic Relations," *World Politics* 24, supplement (Spring 1972): 123–50.

transnational actors like the multinational corporation. It cannot retain its traditional independence and sovereignty and simultaneously meet the expanding economic needs and desires of its populace. The efforts of nation states to enhance their security and power *relative* to others are held to be incompatible with an interdependent world economy that generates *absolute* gains for everyone. In response to the growing economic demands of its citizens, the nation state must adjust to the forces of economic rationality and efficiency.

In the contemporary world, the costs of disrupting economic interdependence, of territorial conquest, and of risking nuclear warfare are believed to be far greater than any conceivable benefits. The calculus of benefits and risks has changed, and "the rational relationship between violence as a means of foreign policy and the ends of foreign policy has been destroyed by the possibility of all-out nuclear war."[7] In contrast to the nineteenth century, the cost of acquiring territory is viewed as having simply become too great. In the contemporary world, there is more to be gained through economic cooperation and an international division of labor than through strife and conflict. Thus, in the opinion of Saburo Okita, formerly president of the Japan Economic Research Center, the exercise of force for economic gain or to defend economic interests is an anachronism:

> We are living in a century when such military action is no longer viable. To build up military power just to protect overseas private property is rather absurd in terms of cost-benefit calculations. The best course for the Government in case of nationalization or seizure of overseas private Japanese assets is to compensate Japanese investors directly in Japan rather than to spend very large amounts of money to build up military strength.[8]

Just as the nuclear revolution in warfare now inhibits the exercise of military power, the revolution in economic relations now inhibits the national exercise of economic power by increasing the cost. Advances in transportation and communications have integrated national economies to the point where many believe it is too costly to threaten the severance of economic relations in order to achieve particular political and economic goals. Economically as well as militarily in the contemporary world, nations are said to be mutually deterred from actions that would disrupt the interdependent economy. This mutual vulnerability of necessity limits and moderates the economic and political struggle among nation states. It provides the necessary minimum political order where the multinational corporations of all the major industrial powers can flourish and bring benefits to the whole of mankind.

The sovereignty-at-bay view also envisages a major transformation of the relationships among developed and underdeveloped countries. The multinational corporations of the developed, industrial economies must not only produce in each other's markets, but the locus of manufacturing industry will increasingly shift to

---

[7] Hans Morgenthau, "Western Values and Total War," *Commentary*, October 1961, p. 280.
[8] Quoted in *New York Times Magazine*, 29 October 1972, p. 58.

underdeveloped countries.[9] As the economies of developed countries become more service oriented, as their terms of trade for raw materials continue to deteriorate, and as their labor costs continue to rise, manufacturing will migrate to lesser-developed countries. United States firms already engage in extensive off-shore production in Asia and Latin America. Western Europe has reached the limits of importing Mediterranean labor, which is the functional equivalent of foreign direct investment. Japan's favorable wage structure and undervalued currency have eroded. With the end of the era of cheap energy and of favorable terms of trade for raw materials, the logic of industrial location favors the underdeveloped periphery. Increasingly, the multinational corporations of all industrial powers will follow the logic of this manufacturing revolution. Manufacturing, particularly of components and semiprocessed goods, will migrate to lesser-developed countries.

This vision of the future has been portrayed most dramatically by Norman Macrae, in an issue of *The Economist,* who foresees a world of spreading affluence energized perhaps by "small transnational companies run in West Africa by London telecommuters who live in Honolulu?"[10] New computer-based training methods and information systems will facilitate the rapid diffusion of skills, technologies and industries to lesser-developed countries. The whole system will be connected by modern telecommunications and computers; the rich will concentrate on the knowledge-creating and knowledge-processing industries. More and more of the old manufacturing industries will move to the underdeveloped world. The entire West and Japan will be a service-oriented island in a labor-intensive global archipelago. Thus, whereas the telephone and jet aircraft facilitated the internationalization of production in the Northern Hemisphere, the contemporary revolution in communications and transportation will encompass the whole globe.

"The logical and eventual development of this possibility," according to management consultant John Diebold, "would be the end of nationality and national governments as we know them."[11] This sovereignty-at-bay world, then, is one of voluntary and cooperative relations among interdependent economies, the goal of which is to accelerate the economic growth and welfare of everyone. In this model, development of the poor is achieved through the transfer of capital, technology, and managerial know-how from the continually advancing developed lands to the lesser-developed nations; it is a world in which the tide of economic growth lifts all boats. In this liberal vision of the future, the multinational corporation, freed from the nation state, is the critical transmission belt of capital, ideas, and growth.

[9] John Diebold, "Multinational Corporations–Why be Scared of Them?," *Foreign Policy,* no. 12 (Fall 1973): 79–95.

[10] "The Future of International Business," *The Economist,* 22 January 1972.

[11] Diebold, p. 87.

THE DEPENDENCIA MODEL

In contrast to the sovereignty-at-bay vision of the future is what may be characterized as the *dependencia* model.[12] Although the analysis underlying the two approaches has much in common, the dependencia model challenges the partners-in-development motif of the sovereignty-at-bay model. Its Marxist conception is one of a hierarchical and exploitative world order. The sovereignty-at-bay model envisages a relatively benevolent system in which growth and wealth spread from the developed core to the lesser-developed periphery. In the dependencia model, on the other hand, the flow of wealth and benefits is seen as moving—via the same mechanisms—from the global, underdeveloped periphery to the centers of industrial financial power and decision. It is an exploitative system that produces affluent development for some and dependent underdevelopment for the majority of mankind. In effect, what is termed transnationalism by the sovereignty-at-bay advocates is considered imperialism by the Marxist proponents of the dependencia model.

In the interdependent world economy of the dependencia model, the multinational corporation also reigns supreme. But the world created by these corporations is held to be far different from that envisaged by the sovereignty-at-bay school of thought. In the dependencia model the political and economic consequences of the multinational corporation are due to what Stephen Hymer has called the two laws of development: the law of increasing firm size, and the law of uneven development. The law of increasing firm size, Hymer argues, is the tendency since the Industrial Revolution for firms to increase in size "from the *workshop* to the *factory* to the *national* corporation to the *multidivisional corporation* and now to the multinational corporation."[13] The law of uneven development, he continues, is the tendency of the international economy to produce poverty as well as wealth, underdevelopment as well as development. Together, these two economic laws are producing the following consequence:

> . . . a regime of North Atlantic Multinational Corporations would tend to produce a hierarchical division of labor within the firm. It would tend to centralize high-level decision-making occupations in a few key cities in the advanced countries, surrounded by a number of regional sub-capitals, and confine the rest of the world to lower levels of activity and income, i.e., to the status of towns and villages in a new Imperial system. Income, status, authority, and consumption patterns would radiate out from these centers along a declining curve, and the existing pattern of inequality and dependency would be perpetuated. The pattern would be complex, just as the structure of the

[12] The literature on dependencia, or underdevelopment, has now become legend. One of the better statements of this thesis is Osvaldo Sunkel, "Big Business and 'Dependencia': A Latin American View," *Foreign Affairs* 50 (April 1972): 517–31. For an excellent and critical view of the dependencia thesis, see Benjamin J. Cohen, *The Question of Imperialism–The Political Economy of Dominance and Dependence* (New York: Basic Books, 1973), chapter 6.

[13] "The Multinational Corporation and the Law of Uneven Development," in *Economics and World Order–From the 1970's to the 1990's,* ed. Jagdish Bhagwati (New York: The Macmillan Co., 1972), p. 113 and passim.

corporation is complex, but the basic relationship between different countries would be one of superior and subordinate, head office and branch office.[14]

In this hierarchical and exploitative world system, power and decision would be lodged in the urban financial and industrial cores of New York, London, Tokyo, etc. Here would be located the computers and data banks of the closely integrated global systems of production and distribution; the main computer in the core would control subsidiary computers in the periphery. The higher functions of management, research and development, entrepreneurship, and finance would be located in these Northern metropolitan centers. "Lower" functions and labor-intensive manufacturing would be continuously diffused to the lesser-developed countries where are found cheap pliable labor, abundant raw materials, and an indifference to industrial pollution. This global division of labor between higher and lower economic functions would perpetuate the chasm between the affluent northern one-fifth of the globe and the destitute southern four-fifths of the globe.

The argument of the dependencia thesis is that the economic dependence of the underdeveloped periphery upon the developed core is responsible for the impoverishment of the former. Development and underdevelopment are simultaneous processes; the developed countries have progressed and have grown rich through exploiting the poor and making them poorer. Lacking true autonomy and being economically dependent upon the developed countries, the underdeveloped countries have suffered because the developed have a veto over their development:

> By dependence we mean a situation in which the economy of certain countries is conditioned by the development and expansion of another economy to which the former is subjected. The relation of interdependence between two or more economies, and between these and world trade, assumes the form of dependence when some countries (the dominant ones) can expand and be self-sustaining, while other countries (the dependent ones) can do this only as a reflection of that expansion, which can have either a positive or negative effect on their immediate development.[15]

Though this particular quotation refers to trade relations, much of the dependence literature is addressed to the issue of foreign direct investment. In content, most of this literature is of a piece with traditional Marxist and radical theories of imperialism. Whether because of the falling rate of profit in capitalist economies or the attraction of superprofits abroad, multinational corporations are believed to exploit the underdeveloped countries. Thus, Paul Baran and Paul Sweezy see the multinationals necessarily impelled to invest in lesser-developed countries.[16] Constantine Vaitsos has sought to document the superprofits available to American corporations in Latin America.[17] The message conveyed by this literature is that

[14] Ibid., p. 114.

[15] Quoted in Cohen, pp. 190–91.

[16] *Monopoly Capital–An Essay on the American Economic and Social Order* (New York: Monthly Review Press, 1966).

[17] Constantine Vaitsos, "Transfer of Resources and Preservation of Monopoly Rents," Economic Development Report No. 168, Development Advisory Service, Harvard University, 1970. (Mimeographed.)

the imperialism of free investment has replaced the imperialism of free trade in the contemporary world.

THE MERCANTILIST MODEL

A key element missing in both the sovereignty-at-bay and the dependencia models is the nation state. Both envisage a world organized and managed by powerful North American, European, and Japanese corporations. In the beneficial corporate order of the first model and the imperialist corporate order of the second, there is little room for nation states, save as servants of corporate power and ambition. In opposition to both these models, therefore, the third model of the future–the mercantilist model–views the nation state and the interplay of national interests (as distinct from corporate interests) as the primary determinants of the future role of the world economy.[18]

According to this mercantilist view, the interdependent world economy, which has provided such a favorable environment for the multinational corporation, is coming to an end. In the wake of the relative decline of American power and of growing conflicts among the capitalist economies, a new international political order less favorable to the multinational corporation is coming into existence. Whether it is former President Nixon's five-power world (US, USSR, China, the EEC, and Japan), a triangular world (US, USSR, and China), or some form of American-Soviet condominium, the emergent world order will be characterized by intense international economic competition for markets, investment outlets, and sources of raw materials.

By *mercantilism* I mean the attempt of governments to manipulate economic arrangements in order to maximize their own interests, whether or not this is at the expense of others. These interests may be related to domestic concerns (full employment, price stability, etc.) or to foreign policy (security, independence, etc.).

This use of the term *mercantilism* is far broader than its eighteenth-century association with a trade and balance-of-payments surplus. The essence of mercantilism, as the concept is used in this article, is the priority of *national* economic and political objectives over considerations of *global* economic efficiency. The mercantilist impulse can take many forms in the contemporary world: the desire for a balance-of-payments surplus; the export of unemployment, inflation, or both; the imposition of import and/or export controls; the expansion of world market shares; and the stimulation of advanced technology. In short, each nation will pursue economic policies that reflect domestic economic needs and external political ambitions without much concern for the effects of these policies on other countries or on the international economic system as a whole.

---

[18] See, for example, David Calleo and Benjamin Rowland, *America and the World Political Economy* (Bloomington, Ind.: Indiana University Press, 1973). Mercantilism is also the real theme of Ernest Mandel's *Europe vs. America–Contradictions of Imperialism* (New York: Monthly Review Press, 1970).

The mercantilist position in effect reverses the argument of the liberals with respect to the nature and success of the interdependent world economy. In contrast to the liberal view that trade liberalization has fostered economic growth, the mercantilist thesis is that several decades of uninterrupted economic growth permitted interdependence. Growth, based in part on relatively cheap energy and other resources as well as on the diffusion of American technology abroad, facilitated the reintroduction of Japan into the world economy and the development of a closely linked Atlantic economy. Now both cheap energy and a technological gap, which were sources of rapid economic growth and global interdependence, have ceased to exist.

International competition has intensified and has become disruptive precisely because the United States has lost much of its technological lead in products and industrial processes. As happened in Britain in the latter part of the nineteenth century, the United States no longer holds the monopoly position in advanced technologies. Its exports must now compete increasingly on the basis of price and a devalued dollar. As was also the case with Great Britain, the United States has lost the technological rents associated with its previous industrial superiority. This loss of industrial supremacy on the part of the dominant industrial power threatens to give rise to economic conflict between the rising and declining centers of industrial power.

From the mercantilist perspective, the fundamental problem of modern international society has been how to organize an industrial world economy. This issue arose with the spread of industrialism from Great Britain and the emergence of several competing capitalist economies in the latter part of the nineteenth century. In the decades prior to the First World War, the issue of how to organize a world economy composed of several competing industrial economies was at the heart of international politics. The resulting commercial and imperial struggle was a major factor in the subsequent outbreak of the First World War.

The issue was never resolved during the interwar period. During the Second World War, the organization of the world economy was regarded, at least in the United States, as a central question for the postwar era. Would it be a universal liberal system or a fragmented system of regional blocs and preference arrangements? With the outbreak of the cold war and the undisputed hegemony of the United States over other capitalist economies, however, the issue faded into the background. Former President Nixon's 15 August 1971 speech signaled to mercantilist writers that with the easing of the cold war the issue has once again moved to the fore.

These mercantilist writers tend to fall into the two camps of malevolent and benign mercantilism. Both tend to believe the world economy is fragmenting into regional blocs. In the wake of the relative decline of American power, nation states will form regional economic alliances or blocs in order to advance their interests in opposition to other nation states. International trade, monetary arrangements, and investment will be increasingly interregional. This regionalization of economic relations will replace the present American emphasis on multilateral free trade, the international role of the dollar, and the reign of the American multinational corporation.

Malevolent mercantilism believes regionalization will intensify international economic conflict. Each bloc centered on the large industrial powers–the United States, Western Europe, Japan, and the Soviet Union–will clash over markets, currency, and investment outlets. This would be a return to the lawlessness and beggar-thy-neighbor policies of the 1930s.

Benign mercantilism, on the other hand, believes regional blocs would stabilize world economic relations.[19] It believes that throughout modern history universalism and regionalism have been at odds. The rationale of regional blocs is that one can have simultaneously the benefits of greater scale and interdependence and minimal accompanying costs of economic and political interdependence. Though the material gains from a global division of labor and free trade could be greater, regionalism is held to provide security and protection against external economic and political forces over which the nation state, acting alone, has little influence or control. In short, the organization of the world economy into regional blocs could provide the basis for a secure and peaceful economic order.

Benign mercantilism derives from the view of John Maynard Keynes and other Englishmen who were highly critical of an increasingly interdependent world economy. The loss of national self-sufficiency, this more benign view of mercantilism holds, is a source of economic-political insecurity and conflict.[20] Liberalism, moreover, is detrimental to national cultural and political development. Therefore, this benign mercantilist position advocates a regionalization of the world economy as the appropriate middle road between a declining American-centered world economy and a global conflict between the capitalist economies. An inevitable clash between industrial economies can be prevented through the carving out of regional spheres of influence and the exercise of mutual self-restraint among them.

In the opinion of benign mercantilism, the thrust of much domestic and international economic policy, especially since the end of the First World War, has in fact been away from interdependence. Nations have placed a higher priority on domestic stability and policies of full employment than on the maintenance of international links; they have sought to exert national control over their monetary and other economic policies. This is what the Keynesian revolution and its emphasis on management of the domestic economy is said to be all about. The same desire for greater latitude in domestic policy underlies the increasing popularity today of flexible over fixed exchange rates and the movement toward regional blocs. Mercantilists point out that in many industrialized economies there is, in fact, a renewed questioning of whether the further benefits of trade liberalization and interdependence are worth the costs. Interdependence accentuates domestic economic adjustment problems as economic instabilities in one economy spill over into others. It causes labor dislocations, may accentuate inequalities of income distribution, and makes national planning more difficult. In short, according to

[19] Calleo and Rowland.

[20] This paradox is analyzed by Eugene Staley, *World Economy in Transition* (New York: Council on Foreign Relations, 1939), chapter 6, especially p. 15.

these mercantilists, the world has reached the limits of interdependence and loss of national self-sufficiency.

A CRITIQUE OF THE THREE MODELS

In this section of the article, I evaluate the three models and draw from each what I consider to be important insights into the nature of contemporary international economic relations. This critique is not meant to cover all the points of each model but only those most directly relevant to this essay.

Sovereignty at Bay

Fundamentally, the sovereignty-at-bay thesis reduces to a question of interests and power: Who has the power to make the world economy serve its interests? This point may be best illustrated by considering the relationship of the multinational corporation and the nation state. In the writings I identified with the sovereignty-at-bay thesis, this contest is held to be most critical.

On one side of this contest is the host nation state. Its primary source of power is its control over access to its territory, that is, access to its internal market, investment opportunities, and sources of raw material. On the other side is the corporation with its capital, technology, and access to world markets. Each has something the other wants. Each seeks to maximize its benefits and minimize its costs. The bargain they strike is dependent upon how much one wants what the other has to offer and how skillfully one or the other can exploit its respective advantages. In most cases, the issue is how the benefits and costs of foreign investment are to be divided between the foreign corporation and the host economy.

The sovereignty-at-bay thesis assumes that the bargaining advantages are and always will be on the side of the corporation. In contrast to the corporation's vast resources and flexibility, the nation state has little with which to bargain. Most nation states lack the economies of scale, indigenous technological capabilities, or native entrepreneurship to free themselves from dependence upon American (or other) multinational corporations. According to this argument, the extent to which nation states reassert their sovereignty is dependent upon the economic price they are willing to pay, and it assumes that when confronted with this cost, they will retreat from nationalistic policies.

In an age of rising economic expectations, the sovereignty-at-bay thesis rests on an important truth: A government is reluctant to assert its sovereignty and drive out the multinational corporations if this means a dramatic lowering of the standard of living, increasing unemployment, and the like. But in an age when the petroleum-producing states, through cooperation, have successfully turned the tables on the multinational corporations, it becomes obvious that the sovereignty-at-bay thesis also neglects the fact that the success of the multinational corporation has been dependent upon a favorable political order. As this order changes, so will the fortunes of the multinationals.

This political order has been characterized by an absence of unity on the part of the economies that have been host to American and other corporations. The divisions between and within the host countries themselves, and the influence of the American government, left the host countries with little power to bargain effectively or to increase their relative benefits from foreign investments in their countries. Thus, in the case of Canada, the competition between the provinces and particularly between English Canada and Quebec greatly weakened Canada's position vis-à-vis American investors. Similarly, nationalistic competition for investment has weakened attempts, such as the Andean Pact, that have tried to develop a common policy toward foreign corporations. But the importance of political factors in the overseas expansion of American corporations may be best illustrated by the case of Western Europe and Japan.

American corporations coveted both the Japanese and Western European markets; they have been able to establish hundreds of subsidiaries in the latter but only a few in the former. The reason for this difference is largely political. Whereas the former has one central government controlling access to Japan's internal market of 100 million population, six (now nine) political centers have controlled access to the European Common Market. By interposing itself between powerful American corporations and intensely competitive Japanese firms that desired American capital and technology, the Japanese government has been able to prevent the latter from making agreements not desired by the government. As a consequence, the Japanese home market has been protected as the almost exclusive domain of Japanese industry. American firms have had, therefore, a strong incentive to license their technology to the Japanese or to form corporate arrangements in which the American firms were no more than a minor partner.

What the Japanese succeeded in doing was to break up the package of capital, technology, and entrepreneurship that foreign direct investment entails. The Japanese did not need the capital; they got the technology without managerial control by American corporations; entrepreneurship remained in the hands of Japanese. This Japanese example of untying the package and obtaining the technology, and in many cases the capital, required for development without loss of control has become an inspiration for economic nationalists in Latin America, Canada, and elsewhere.

In Western Europe, on the other hand, an American firm denied the right to establish a subsidiary in one Common Market country has had the option of trying another country and thereby still gaining access to the whole Market. Moreover, the strong desire of individual European countries for American investment has enabled American corporations to invest on very favorable terms. In certain cases, the firms have followed a divide-and-conquer strategy. Denied permission by President de Gaulle to invest in France, General Motors established in Belgium one of the largest automobile assembly plants in the Common Market. Through this route, the corporation gained access to the French market as well as to other European markets.

In response to this situation, de Gaulle sought to obtain West German cooperation against American investment in EEC countries. Together these two most powerful of the Six could dictate a policy the others would be forced to accept. Through the instrumentality of the Franco-German Friendship Treaty of 1963, therefore, de Gaulle sought to form a Bonn-Paris axis directed against American hegemony in Western Europe.

Although there was sentiment in West Germany favorable to taking measures to limit the rapidly growing role of American subsidiaries in EEC countries, the West German government refused to take any action that might weaken the American commitment to defend Western Europe. The United States government not only reminded the West Germans that a continued American military presence was dependent upon West German support of measures to lessen the American balance-of-payments deficit, but it also pressured West Germany to increase its military purchases from the United States and to avoid competitive arrangements with France. Largely as a result of these American pressures, the Friendship Treaty was, in effect, aborted. The first serious counteroffensive of the nation state against the multinational corporation collapsed. It is clear, however, that the outcome of this tale would have been altogether different if West Germany had desired greater military and economic independence from the United States. In short, the American corporate penetration of the European Common Market has been dependent upon the special security relationship of the United States and West Germany.

One could extend this type of analysis for the whole of American overseas investment. American investment in the Middle East, Africa, Latin America, Canada, and elsewhere has benefited from America's dominant position in the world. This position is now seriously challenged not only by the Soviet Union but by Japan, Western Europe, China, the Arabs, and Brazil in Latin America. Throughout these areas, economic nationalism is on the rise, threatening American investments and the income they bring to the United States. The thrust of this attack has been to break up the package of capital, technology, and management in order to acquire the first two without the third; the goal is greater local control through joint ventures, nationalization, and other policies. While the host countries are unlikely to "kill off" the American multinational corporations, they will increasingly make them serve local interests. This in turn will undoubtedly make direct investment abroad less attractive to American corporations.

A reversal of fortunes has already been seen in the case of the oil multinationals. The significance of the offensive by the oil-producing states against the large international oil companies is not merely that the price of oil to the United States and to the rest of the world has risen but also that the United States may lose one of its most lucrative sources of investment income. The oil crisis and Arab oil boycott which followed the 1973 Arab-Israeli war was a profound learning experience for Europe, Japan, and even the United States. The oil boycott and the behavior of the oil multinationals set into motion a series of events that cannot help but transform national attitudes and policies toward the oil multinationals. The sudden appreciation of how vulnerable governments were to the policies of the oil multinationals and how far their "sovereignty" had been compromised awakened them to the inherent dangers of overdependence on the corporations and their policies. . . .

. . . [W]hen the multinationals were perceived as no longer supportive of the national interests of the United States, there was a reassertion of national sovereignty.

The case of oil and the oil multinationals is perhaps unique. Yet it does suggest that nation states have not lost their power or their will to act when they believe the multinational corporations are threatening their perceived national interests and sovereignty. The experience of the oil boycott and the role of the multinationals in carrying it out reveal the extent to which the operators and the success of these corporations have been dependent upon American power. With the relative decline of American power and the rise of governments hostile to American interests and policies, this case history at least raises the question of how the weakening of the Pax Americana will affect the status of other American multinational corporations throughout the world.

Dependencia

The weakness of the dependencia, or ultraimperialism, model is that it makes at least three unwarranted assumptions. In the first place, it assumes much greater common interest among the noncommunist industrial powers–the United States, Western Europe, and Japan–than is actually the case. Secondly, it treats the peripheral states of Asia, Africa, Latin America, Canada, and the Middle East solely as objects of international economic and political relations. Neither assumption is true. As the first assumption is considered in more detail in the next section, let us consider the second for a moment.

After nearly two centuries, the passivity of the periphery is now past. The Soviet challenge to the West and the divisions among the capitalist powers themselves have given the emerging elites in the periphery room for maneuver. These nationalist elites are no longer ignorant and pliable colonials. Within the periphery, there are coalescing centers of power that will weigh increasingly in the future world balance of power: China, Indonesia, India, Iran, Nigeria, Brazil, and some form of Arab oil power. Moreover, if properly organized and led, such centers of power in control over a vital resource, as the experience of the Organization of Petroleum Exporting Countries (OPEC) demonstrates, may reverse the tables and make the core dependent upon the periphery. For the moment at least, a perceptible shift appears to be taking place in the global balance of economic power from the owners of capital to the owners of natural resources.[21]

The third unwarranted assumption is that a quasi-Marxist theory of capitalist imperialism is applicable to the relationship of developed and lesser-developed economies today. Again, I illustrate my argument by considering the role of the multinational corporation in the lesser-developed countries, since its allegedly exploitative function is stressed by almost all dependencia theorists.

The dependencia theory undoubtedly has a good case with respect to foreign direct investment in petroleum and other extractive industries. The oil, copper, and other multinationals have provided the noncommunist industrial world with a plentiful and relatively cheap supply of minerals and energy. The dramatic reversal of this situation by the oil-producing countries in 1973-74 and the steady rise

---

[21] See C. Fred Bergsten, "The Threat From The Third World," *Foreign Policy,* no. 11 (Summer 1973): 102–24.

of prices of other commodities support the contention that the producing countries were not getting the highest possible price and possibly not a just price for their nonrenewable resources. But what constitutes the just price for a natural endowment that was worthless until the multinationals found it is not an easy issue to resolve.

With respect to foreign direct investment in manufacturing, the case is far more ambiguous. Even if technological rents are collected, does the foreign corporation bring more into the economy in terms of technology, capital, and access to world markets than it takes out in the form of earnings? The research of Canadian, Australian, and other economists, for example, suggests that it does. They find no differences in the corporate behavior of domestic and foreign firms; on the contrary, foreign firms are given higher marks in terms of export performance, industrial research and development, and other economic indicators. Nonetheless, it would be naive to suggest that no exploitation or severe distortions of host economies have taken place.

On the other hand, it may not be unwarranted to suggest that a strong presumption exists for arguing that in terms of economic growth and industrial development, foreign direct investment in *manufacturing* is to the advantage of the host economy. A major cause of foreign direct investment is the sector-specific nature of knowledge and capital in the home economy.[22] In order to prevent a fall in their rate of profits through overinvesting at home or diversifying into unknown areas, American corporations frequently go abroad to guard against a lower rate of profit at home rather than because the superprofits abroad are attractive. Insofar as this is true, and there is sufficient evidence to warrant its plausibility, foreign direct investment benefits both the corporation and the host economy at a cost to other factors of production in the home economy. Thus, though the Marxists may be right in saying that there is an imperative for capitalism to go abroad, the effect is not to exploit but to benefit the recipient economy–a conclusion, by the way, that Marx himself would have accepted.[23]

While it is true that, in general, lesser-developed countries are economically dependent upon developed countries, the conclusions to be drawn from this fact are not self-evident. Are the countries underdeveloped because they are dependent, as dependencia theorists assume, or are they dependent because they are underdeveloped? China is underdeveloped, but it is not dependent upon any external power (though one could argue a historical case). As Benjamin Cohen has pointed out, the critical question is whether the poor are worse off economically because of this dependence.[24] Does dependence upon the developed countries entail a new loss, or foreclose opportunities of greater benefit to the economy of the undeveloped country? While the opportunity to exploit may be there, is it exercised? These are empirical questions to which no general answers can be given.

[22] This point is developed in US Congress, Senate Committee on Labor and Public Welfare, *The Multinational Corporation and the National Interest* (report prepared for the Committee), 93rd Cong., 1st sess., 1973, Committee print.

[23] Karl Marx, "The Future Results of British Rule in India," in *Karl Marx on Colonialism and Modernization,* ed. Shlomo Avineri (Garden City, N.Y.: Doubleday, 1968), pp. 125–31.

[24] Cohen, chapter 6.

Whether foreign direct investment is exploitative or beneficial depends on the type of investment, its terms, and the policies of the recipient economy itself.

The dependencia argument that foreign direct investment by multinational corporations preempts the emergence of an indigenous entrepreneurial middle class and creates a situation of technological dependence provides a clue to what is the central concern of dependence theory. Though most frequently couched solely in economic terms, the concepts of underdevelopment and dependence are more political than economic in nature. They involve an assessment of the political costs of foreign investment. They refer both to the internal political development of the recipient country and its external relations. As one of the better dependence theorists has put it, the problem "is not so much growth, i.e., expansion of a given socio-economic system, as it is 'development,' i.e., rapid and fundamental politico-socio-economic transformation."[25] In other words, foreign direct investment fosters an international division of labor that perpetuates underdevelopment and politico-economic dependencia.

This distinction between *growth* and *development* is crucial.[26] Economic growth is defined by most development economists simply as an increase in output or income per capita; it is essentially a positive and quantitative concept. The concepts of development and underdevelopment as used by dependence theorists are primarily normative and qualitative; they refer to structural changes internal to the lesser-developed economy and in external relations with the developed world. Dependencia theory really calls for a change in the current international division of labor between the core and the periphery of the international economy, in which the periphery is a supplier of raw materials and whose industries are branch plants of the core's multinational corporations.

Whatever its economic merits, the dependencia model will continue to generate opposition against the structure of the contemporary world economy and the multinational corporation throughout the underdeveloped periphery of the world economy. As these peripheral societies grow in power, one can anticipate that they will undertake initiatives that attempt to lessen their dependence upon developed countries.

Mercantilism

It seems to me that mercantilists either ignore or ascribe too little significance to certain primary facts. Although the relative power of the United States has declined, the United States remains the dominant world economy. The scale, diversity, and dynamics of the American economy will continue to place the United States at the center of the international economic system. The universal desire for access to the huge American market, the inherent technological dynamism of the American economy, and America's additional strength in both agriculture and

[25] This distinction is developed by Keith Griffin, *Underdevelopment in Spanish America* (Cambridge, Mass.: The M.I.T. Press, 1969), p. 117.

[26] For a more detailed analysis of the distinction, see J. D. Gould, *Economic Growth in History* (London: Methuen and Co., 1972), chapter 1.

resources–which Europe and Japan do not have–provide a cement sufficient to hold the world economy together and to keep the United States at its center.[27]

Furthermore, the United States can compensate for its loss of strength in one issue area by its continued strength in another. For example, the American economic position has indeed declined relative to Europe and Japan. Yet the continued dependence of Europe and Japan on the United States for their security provides the United States with a strong lever over the economic policies of each.

Thus, the fundamental weakness of the mercantilist model is the absence of a convincing alternative to an American-centered world economy. Western Europe, the primary economic challenger to the United States, remains internally divided; it is as yet unable to develop common policies in such areas as industry and energy or with respect to economic and monetary union. It is merely a customs union with a common agricultural policy. Moreover, like Japan, it continues to be totally dependent upon the United States for its security. As long as both Europe and Japan lack an alternative to their military and economic dependence on the United States, the mercantilist world of regional blocs lacks credibility.

The so-called energy crisis has affirmed this assessment. In the first place, the Arab oil boycott revealed the fragility of European unity. Threatened with the loss of vital supplies of Middle Eastern oil, every nation fended for itself. But subsequently, despite their reluctance, both Europe and Japan participated in the American-sponsored Washington energy conference. The American purpose in calling the conference was in part to reinforce its Middle Eastern diplomacy. But the purpose was also to reassert America's influence over its allies and to forestall policies such as competitive currency depreciation, creation of new trade barriers, and bilateral deals that would tend to fragment the world economy. No doubt, too, as the French and others charge, the United States hoped to find a solution to the energy crisis that did not threaten the position of the American oil multinationals.

Calling for cooperation from its European and Japanese allies, the United States reminded them that their security still rested on American goodwill. Moreover, in the event of a conflict over oil, America's economic weapons were far superior. Thus chastened and reminded where power continued to rest, all but the French fell into line. For the time being at least, the United States demonstrated that it retained sufficient power to maintain intact an American-centered world economy.

Yet sufficient tensions and conflicts of interests remain within this world economy to prevent one from dismissing so quickly the mercantilist thesis. Undoubtedly, the interstate conflict that will be the most vexing is the growing demand and competition for raw materials, particularly petroleum. The loss of energy self-sufficiency by the United States and the growth in demand for petroleum and other raw materials **have** already shifted the terms of trade against developed economies, and commodity prices have become major factors in world inflation. In the longer term, these changes have put the industrial powers in competition for these

[27] A forceful statement of this position is Raymond Vernon's "Rogue Elephant in the Forest: An Appraisal of Transatlantic Relations," *Foreign Affairs* 51 (April 1973): 573–87.

limited resources. They are also competing for export markets in order to finance these vital imports and for the capital the oil-producing states now have to invest. Thus, whereas in the past America's virtual control over the noncommunist world's supply of petroleum was a source of unity, today the United States is struggling with other industrial powers to insure its own position in a highly competitive environment.

In fact, one witnesses in the contemporary world the reemergence of the neo-Malthusian and Social Darwinist fears that swept industrial society and were so disruptive in the latter part of the nineteenth century. A common factor in the several imperialisms that burst forth after 1880 and fragmented the world economy was the growing fear of the potential consequences of exclusion from resources and markets. With expanding populations and productive industries believed to be dependent on foreign sources of food and raw materials, the insecurity of European states was magnified by the loss of their former relative self-sufficiency. The paradox of an interdependent world economy is that it creates sources of insecurity and competition. The very dependence of one state on another and the necessity for access to external markets and sources of raw materials cause anxieties and suspicions that exacerbate international relations.

The other reason for believing that there may be some validity in the mercantilist vision of the future is the weakening of political bonds between the United States, Western Europe, and Japan. During the height of the cold war, the foreign economic policies of these three countries were complementary. Potential conflicts over economic matters were subordinated to the necessity for political unity against the Soviet Union and China. The United States encouraged export-led growth and accepted anti-American trade discrimination in order to enable Japan and Europe to rebuild their shattered economies. Reciprocally, Japan and Europe supported the international position of the dollar. Through foreign direct investment, American corporations were able to maintain their relative share of world markets. Neither the Europeans nor the Japanese challenged America's dominant position with respect to the industrial world's access to vital raw materials, particularly Middle Eastern petroleum.

Until the early 1970s, the political benefits of this arrangement were regarded as outweighing the economic costs to each partner. With the movement toward détente and with the revival of the European and Japanese economies, however, the political benefits have receded in importance and the concern over costs has increased. As a consequence, the United States and its industrial partners now desire reforms of the world's trading and monetary systems that would enable each to pursue its own particular set of interests and to limit that of the others. For example, the United States has proposed reforms of the trade and monetary systems that would limit the ability of the Europeans and the Japanese to run up huge trade surpluses. Europe and Japan, for their part, desire to preserve this scope and to limit the privileges of the United States as world banker.

Regardless of the outcome of the negotiations over the future of the international monetary system, one thing is certain: whatever privilege is retained by the dollar will not be sufficient to enable the United States to behave as it has in the past. Gone are the days when the United States could run an immense balance-of-payments deficit in order to support foreign commitments, to buy up foreign assets, and at the same time pursue a full employment policy at home. It will no longer be able to expand overseas at a relatively low cost to the American standard of living. Having already lost its technological superiority and technological rents, the United States will have to finance its economic and military position abroad through currency devaluation and a current account surplus. Thus the cost of any effort to maintain US political and economic hegemony will bear upon the American people themselves. The weight and popular appreciation of this cost will profoundly alter American attitudes toward America's world role and toward its European and Japanese allies. These changes in political interests and perceptions cannot but help to push the world in a mercantilistic direction. . . .

CONCLUSION

In conclusion, what does this redistribution of world power imply for the future of the interdependent world economy? Today, the liberal world economy is challenged by powerful groups (especially organized labor) within the dominant economy; the dominant economy itself is in relative decline. With the decline of the dominant economic power, the world economy may be following the pattern of the latter part of the nineteenth century and of the 1930s and may be fragmenting into regional trading and monetary blocs. This would be prevented, of course, if the United States, as it is presently trying to do, were to reassert its waning hegemony over Western Europe, Japan, and the rest of the noncommunist world economy.

In the wake of the decline of American power and the erosion of the political base upon which the world economy has rested, the question arises whether the wisest policy for the United States is to attempt to reassert its dominance. May not this effort in the areas of trade, money, investment, and energy exacerbate the conflicts between the United States, Western Europe, and Japan? If so, a future that could be characterized increasingly by benign mercantilism could well be transformed into its more malevolent relative. If this were to happen, the United States and its allies would be the losers.

This admonition suggests that the United States should accept a greater regionalization of the world economy than it has been wont to accept in the past. It implies greater representation and voice for other nations and regional blocs in international economic organizations. While such a policy of retrenchment would no doubt harm the interests of American corporations and other sectors of the American economy, the attempt to hold on to rather than adjust to the shifting balance of world power could be even more costly for the United States in the long run.

In a world economy composed of regional blocs and centers of power, economic bargaining and competition would predominate. Through the exercise of economic power and various trade-offs, each center of the world economy would seek to shift the costs and benefits of economic interdependence to its own advantage. Trade, monetary, and investment relations would be the consequence of negotiations as nation states and regional blocs sought to increase the benefits of interdependence and to decrease the costs. This in fact has been the direction of the evolution of the international economy, from a liberal to a negotiated system, since the rise of large and rival economic entities in the latter part of the nineteenth century.

Therefore, debate and policy planning today should not focus on economic independence or dependence but on the nature and consequences of economic interdependence. Economic interdependence may take many forms; it may affect the welfare of nations in very different ways. Some will emphasize security; others, efficiency, low rates of inflation, or full employment. The question of how these benefits and costs will be distributed is at the heart of the increasingly mercantilistic policies of nation states in the contemporary world.

23

Complex Interdependence, Transnational Relations, and Realism: Alternative Perspectives on World Politics

ROBERT O. KEOHANE AND JOSEPH S. NYE, JR.

In this essay, Robert O. Keohane and Joseph S. Nye, Jr., compare realism and complex interdependence as alternative perspectives on world politics. They argue that, because both perspectives are idealized versions and visions of political reality, most situations in world politics will fall somewhere between the two. Keohane is professor of political science at Brandeis University. Nye is professor of government at Harvard University. The excerpts here are from two of the best-known of their many writings on transnational relations and interdependence.

One's assumptions about world politics profoundly affect what one sees and how one constructs theories to explain events. We believe that the assumptions of political realists, whose theories dominated the postwar period, are often an inadequate basis for analyzing the politics of interdependence. The realist assumptions about world politics can be seen as defining an extreme set of conditions or *ideal type*. One could also imagine very different conditions. In this chapter, we shall construct another ideal type, the opposite of realism. We call it *complex interdependence*. After establishing the differences between realism and complex interdependence, we shall argue that complex interdependence sometimes comes closer to reality than does realism. When it does, traditional explanations of change in international regimes become questionable and the search for new explanatory models becomes more urgent.

For political realists, international politics, like all other politics, is a struggle for power but, unlike domestic politics, a struggle dominated by organized violence. In the words of the most influential postwar textbook, "All history shows that nations active in international politics are continuously preparing for, actively involved in, or recovering from organized violence in the form of war."[1] Three

Reprinted by permission from Robert O. Keohane and Joseph S. Nye, Jr., *Power and Interdependence: World Politics in Transition* (Boston: Little, Brown, 1977), pp. 23–37, copyright © by Little, Brown and Company (Inc.); and Joseph S. Nye, Jr., and Robert O. Keohane, "Transnational Relations and World Politics: An Introduction," in Robert O. Keohane and Joseph S. Nye, Jr., eds., *Transnational Relations and World Politics* (Cambridge, Mass.: Harvard University Press, 1972), pp. ix–xxix, copyright ©1971 by the President and Fellows of Harvard College.

assumptions are integral to the realist vision. First, states as coherent units are the dominant actors in world politics. This is a double assumption: states are predominant; and they act as coherent units. Second, realists assume that force is a usable and effective instrument of policy. Other instruments may also be employed, but using or threatening force is the most effective means of wielding power. Third, partly because of their second assumption, realists assume a hierarchy of issues in world politics, headed by questions of military security: the "high politics" of military security dominates the "low politics" of economic and social affairs.

These realist assumptions define an ideal type of world politics. They allow us to imagine a world in which politics is continually characterized by active or potential conflict among states, with the use of force possible at any time. Each state attempts to defend its territory and interests from real or perceived threats. Political integration among states is slight and lasts only as long as it serves the national interests of the most powerful states. Transnational actors either do not exist or are politically unimportant. Only the adept exercise of force or the threat of force permits states to survive, and only while statesmen succeed in adjusting their interests, as in a well-functioning balance of power, is the system stable.

Each of the realist assumptions can be challenged. If we challenge them all simultaneously, we can imagine a world in which actors other than states participate directly in world politics, in which a clear hierarchy of issues does not exist, and in which force is an ineffective instrument of policy. Under these conditions—which we call the characteristics of complex interdependence—one would expect world politics to be very different than under realist conditions.

We will explore these differences in the next section of this chapter. We do not argue, however, that complex interdependence faithfully reflects world political reality. Quite the contrary: both it and the realist portrait are ideal types. Most situations will fall somewhere between these two extremes. Sometimes, realist assumptions will be accurate, or largely accurate, but frequently complex interdependence will provide a better portrayal of reality. Before one decides what explanatory model to apply to a situation or problem, one will need to understand the degree to which realist or complex interdependence assumptions correspond to the situation.

THE CHARACTERISTICS OF COMPLEX INTERDEPENDENCE

Complex interdependence has three main characteristics:

1. *Multiple channels* connect societies, including: informal ties between governmental elites as well as formal foreign office arrangements; informal ties among nongovernmental elites (face-to-face and through telecommunications); and transnational organizations (such as multinational banks or corporations). These channels can be summarized as interstate, transgovernmental, and transnational relations. *Interstate* relations are the normal channels assumed by realists. *Transgovernmental* applies when we relax the realist assumption that states act coher-

ently as units; *transnational* applies when we relax the assumption that states are the only units.

2. The agenda of interstate relationships consists of multiple issues that are not arranged in a clear or consistent hierarchy. This *absence of hierarchy among issues* means, among other things, that military security does not consistently dominate the agenda. Many issues arise from what used to be considered domestic policy, and the distinction between domestic and foreign issues becomes blurred. These issues are considered in several government departments (not just foreign offices), and at several levels. Inadequate policy coordination on these issues involves significant costs. Different issues generate different coalitions, both within governments and across them, and involve different degrees of conflict. Politics does not stop at the waters' edge.

3. Military force is not used by governments toward other governments within the region, or on the issues, when complex interdependence prevails. It may, however, be important in these governments' relations with governments outside that region, or on other issues. Military force could, for instance, be irrelevant to resolving disagreements on economic issues among members of an alliance, yet at the same time be very important for that alliance's political and military relations with a rival bloc. For the former relationships this condition of complex interdependence would be met; for the latter, it would not.

Traditional theories of international politics implicitly or explicitly deny the accuracy of these three assumptions. Traditionalists are therefore tempted also to deny the relevance of criticisms based on the complex interdependence ideal type. We believe, however, that our three conditions are fairly well approximated on some global issues of economic and ecological interdependence and that they come close to characterizing the entire relationship between some countries. . . .

Multiple Channels

A visit to any major airport is a dramatic way to confirm the existence of multiple channels of contact among advanced industrial countries; there is a voluminous literature to prove it.[2] Bureaucrats from different countries deal directly with one another at meetings and on the telephone as well as in writing. Similarly, nongovernmental elites frequently get together in the normal course of business, in organizations such as the Trilateral Commission, and in conferences sponsored by private foundations.

In addition, multinational firms and banks affect both domestic and interstate relations. The limits on private firms, or the closeness of ties between government and business, vary considerably from one society to another; but the participation of large and dynamic organizations, not controlled entirely by governments, has become a normal part of foreign as well as domestic relations.

These actors are important not only because of their activities in pursuit of their own interests, but also because they act as transmission belts, making government policies in various countries more sensitive to one another. As the scope of governments' domestic activities has broadened, and as corporations, banks, and (to a lesser extent) trade unions have made decisions that transcend national boundaries, the domestic policies of different countries impinge on one another more and more. Transnational communications reinforce these effects. Thus, foreign economic policies touch more domestic economic activity than in the past, blurring the lines between domestic and foreign policy and increasing the number of issues relevant to foreign policy. Parallel developments in issues of environmental regulation and control over technology reinforce this trend.

Absence of Hierarchy among Issues

Foreign affairs agendas–that is, sets of issues relevant to foreign policy with which governments are concerned–have become larger and more diverse. No longer can all issues be subordinated to military security. As Secretary of State Kissinger described the situation in 1975:

> progress in dealing with the traditional agenda is no longer enough. A new and unprecedented kind of issue has emerged. The problems of energy, resources, environment, population, the uses of space and the seas now rank with questions of military security, ideology and territorial rivalry which have traditionally made up the diplomatic agenda.[3]

Kissinger's list, which could be expanded, illustrates how governments' policies, even those previously considered merely domestic, impinge on one another. The extensive consultative arrangements developed by the OECD, as well as the GATT, IMF, and the European Community, indicate how characteristic the overlap of domestic and foreign policy is among developed pluralist countries. The organization within nine major departments of the United States government (Agriculture, Commerce, Defense, Health, Education and Welfare, Interior, Justice, Labor, State, and Treasury) and many other agencies reflects their extensive international commitments. The multiple, overlapping issues that result make a nightmare of governmental organization.[4]

When there are multiple issues on the agenda, many of which threaten the interests of domestic groups but do not clearly threaten the nation as a whole, the problems of formulating a coherent and consistent foreign policy increase. In 1975 energy was a foreign policy problem, but specific remedies, such as a tax on gasoline and automobiles, involved domestic legislation opposed by auto workers and companies alike. As one commentator observed, "virtually every time Congress has set a national policy that changed the way people live . . . the action came after a consensus had developed, bit by bit, over the years, that a problem existed and that there was one best way to solve it."[5] Opportunities for delay, for special protection, for inconsistency and incoherence abound when international politics requires aligning the domestic policies of pluralist democratic countries.

Minor Role of Military Force

Political scientists have traditionally emphasized the role of military force in international politics. . . . [F]orce dominates other means of power: *if* there are no constraints on one's choice of instruments (a hypothetical situation that has only been approximated in the two world wars), the state with superior military force will prevail. If the security dilemma for all states were extremely acute, military force, supported by economic and other resources, would clearly be the dominant source of power. Survival is the primary goal of all states, and in the worst situations, force is ultimately necessary to guarantee survival. Thus military force is always a central component of national power.

Yet particularly among industrialized, pluralist countries, the perceived margin of safety has widened: fears of attack in general have declined, and fears of attacks *by one another* are virtually nonexistent. France has abandoned the *tous azimuts* (defense in all directions) strategy that President de Gaulle advocated (it was not taken entirely seriously even at the time). Canada's last war plans for fighting the United States were abandoned half a century ago. Britain and Germany no longer feel threatened by each other. Intense relationships of mutual influence exist between these countries, but in most of them force is irrelevant or unimportant as an instrument of policy.

Moreover, force is often not an appropriate way of achieving other goals (such as economic and ecological welfare) that are becoming more important. It is not impossible to imagine dramatic conflict or revolutionary change in which the use or threat of military force over an economic issue or among advanced industrial countries might become plausible. Then realist assumptions would again be a reliable guide to events. But in most situations, the effects of military force are both costly and uncertain.[6]

Even when the direct use of force is barred among a group of countries, however, military power can still be used politically. Each superpower continues to use the threat of force to deter attacks by other superpowers on itself or its allies; its deterrence ability thus serves an indirect, protective role, which it can use in bargaining on other issues with its allies. This bargaining tool is particularly important for the United States, whose allies are concerned about potential Soviet threats and which has fewer other means of influence over its allies than does the Soviet Union over its Eastern European partners. The United States has, accordingly, taken advantage of the Europeans' (particularly the Germans') desire for its protection and linked the issue of troop levels in Europe to trade and monetary negotiations. Thus, although the first-order effect of deterrent force is essentially negative–to deny effective offensive power to a superpower opponent–a state can use that force positively–to gain political influence.

Thus, even for countries whose relations approximate complex interdependence, two serious qualifications remain: (1) drastic social and political change could cause force again to become an important direct instrument of policy; and (2) even when elites' interests are complementary, a country that uses military force to protect another may have significant political influence over the other country.

In North-South relations, or relations among Third World countries, as well as in East-West relations, force is often important. Military power helps the Soviet Union to dominate Eastern Europe economically as well as politically. The threat of open or covert American military intervention has helped to limit revolutionary changes in the Caribbean, especially in Guatemala in 1954 and in the Dominican Republic in 1965. Secretary of State Kissinger, in January 1975, issued a veiled warning to members of the Organization of Petroleum Exporting Countries

(OPEC) that the United States might use force against them "where there is some actual strangulation of the industrialized world."[7]

Even in these rather conflictual situations, however, the recourse to force seems less likely now than at most times during the century before 1945. The destructiveness of nuclear weapons makes any attack against a nuclear power dangerous. Nuclear weapons are mostly used as a deterrent. Threats of nuclear action against much weaker countries may occasionally be efficacious, but they are equally or more likely to solidify relations between one's adversaries. The limited usefulness of conventional force to control socially mobilized populations has been shown by the United States failure in Vietnam as well as by the rapid decline of colonialism in Africa. Furthermore, employing force on one issue against an independent state with which one has a variety of relationships is likely to rupture mutually profitable relations on other issues. In other words, the use of force often has costly effects on nonsecurity goals. And finally, in Western democracies, popular opposition to prolonged military conflicts is very high.[8]

It is clear that these constraints bear unequally on various countries, or on the same countries in different situations. Risks of nuclear escalation affect everyone, but domestic opinion is far less constraining for communist states, or for authoritarian regional powers, than for the United States, Europe, or Japan. Even authoritarian countries may be reluctant to use force to obtain economic objectives when such use might be ineffective and disrupt other relationships. Both the difficulty of controlling socially mobilized populations with foreign troops and the changing technology of weaponry may actually enhance the ability of certain countries, or nonstate groups, to use terrorism as a political weapon without effective fear of reprisal.

The fact that the changing role of force has uneven effects does not make the change less important, but it does make matters more complex. This complexity is compounded by differences in the usability of force among issue areas. When an issue arouses little interest or passion, force may be unthinkable. In such instances, complex interdependence may be a valuable concept for analyzing the political process. But if that issue becomes a matter of life and death—as some people thought oil might become—the use or threat of force could become decisive again. Realist assumptions would then be more relevant.

It is thus important to determine the applicability of realism or of complex interdependence to each situation. Without this determination, further analysis is likely to be confused. Our purpose in developing an alternative to the realist description of world politics is to encourage a differentiated approach that distinguishes among dimensions and areas of world politics—not (as some modernist observers do) to replace one oversimplification with another.

THE POLITICAL PROCESSES OF COMPLEX INTERDEPENDENCE

The three main characteristics of complex interdependence give rise to distinctive political processes, which translate power resources into power as control of outcomes. . . . [S]omething is usually lost or added in the translation. Under conditions of complex interdependence the translation will be different than under realist conditions, and our predictions about outcomes will need to be adjusted accordingly.

In the realist world, military security will be the dominant goal of states. It will even affect issues that are not directly involved with military power or territorial defense. Nonmilitary problems will not only be subordinated to military ones; they will be studied for their politico-military implications. Balance of payments issues, for instance, will be considered at least as much in the light of their implications for world power generally as for their purely financial ramifications. McGeorge Bundy conformed to realist expectations when he argued in 1964 that devaluation of the dollar should be seriously considered if necessary to fight the war in Vietnam.[9] To some extent, so did former Treasury Secretary Henry Fowler when he contended in 1971 that the United States needed a trade surplus of $4 billion to $6 billion in order to lead in Western defense.[10]

In a world of complex interdependence, however, one expects some officials, particularly at lower levels, to emphasize the *variety* of state goals that must be pursued. In the absence of a clear hierarchy of issues, goals will vary by issue, and may not be closely related. Each bureaucracy will pursue its own concerns; and although several agencies may reach compromises on issues that affect them all, they will find that a consistent pattern of policy is difficult to maintain. Moreover, transnational actors will introduce different goals into various groups of issues.

Linkage Strategies

Goals will therefore vary by issue area under complex interdependence, but so will the distribution of power and the typical political processes. Traditional analysis focuses on *the* international system, and leads us to anticipate similar political processes on a variety of issues. Militarily and economically strong states will dominate a variety of organizations and a variety of issues, by linking their own policies on some issues to other states' policies on other issues. By using their overall dominance to prevail on their weak issues, the strongest states will, in the traditional model, ensure a congruence between the overall structure of military and economic power and the pattern of outcomes on any one issue area. Thus world politics can be treated as a seamless web.

Under complex interdependence, such congruence is less likely to occur. As military force is devalued, militarily strong states will find it more difficult to use their overall dominance to control outcomes on issues in which they are weak. And since the distribution of power resources in trade, shipping, or oil, for example, may be quite different, patterns of outcomes and distinctive political processes are likely to vary from one set of issues to another. If force were readily applicable, and military security were the highest foreign policy goal, these variations in the issue structures of power would not matter very much. The linkages drawn from them to military issues would ensure consistent dominance by the overall strongest states. But when military force is largely immobilized, strong states will find that linkage is less effective. They may still attempt such links, but in the absence of a hierarchy of issues, their success will be problematic.

Dominant states may try to secure much the same result by using overall economic power to affect results on other issues. If only economic objectives are at stake, they may succeed: money, after all, is fungible. But economic objectives have political implications, and economic linkage by the strong is limited by domestic, transnational, and transgovernmental actors who resist having their interests traded off. Furthermore, the international actors may be different on different issues, and the international organizations in which negotiations take place are often quite separate. Thus it is difficult, for example, to imagine a militarily or economically strong state linking concessions on monetary policy to reciprocal concessions in oceans policy. On the other hand, poor weak states are not similarly inhibited from linking unrelated issues, partly because their domestic interests are less complex. Linkage of unrelated issues is often a means of extracting concessions or side payments from rich and powerful states. And unlike powerful states whose instrument for linkage (military force) is often too costly to use, the linkage instrument used by poor, weak states—international organization—is available and inexpensive.

Thus as the utility of force declines, and as issues become more equal in importance, the distribution of power within each issue will become more important. If linkages become less effective on the whole, outcomes of political bargaining will increasingly vary by issue area.

The differentiation among issue areas in complex interdependence means that linkages among issues will become more problematic and will tend to reduce rather than reinforce international hierarchy. Linkage strategies, and defense against them, will pose critical strategic choices for states. Should issues be considered separately or as a package? If linkages are to be drawn, which issues should be linked, and on which of the linked issues should concessions be made? How far can one push a linkage before it becomes counterproductive? For instance, should one seek formal agreements or informal, but less politically sensitive, understandings? The fact that world politics under complex interdependence is not a seamless web leads us to expect that efforts to stitch seams together advantageously, as reflected in linkage strategies, will, very often, determine the shape of the fabric.

The negligible role of force leads us to expect states to rely more on other instruments in order to wield power. . . . [L]ess vulnerable states will try to use asymmetrical interdependence in particular groups of issues as a source of power; they will also try to use international organizations and transnational actors and flows. States will approach economic interdependence in terms of power as well as its effects on citizens' welfare, although welfare considerations will limit their attempts to maximize power. Most economic and ecological interdependence involves the possibility of joint gains, or joint losses. Mutual awareness of potential gains and losses and the danger of worsening each actor's position through overly rigorous struggles over the distribution of the gains can limit the use of asymmetrical interdependence.

Agenda Setting

Our second assumption of complex interdependence, the lack of clear hierarchy among multiple issues, leads us to expect that the politics of agenda formation and control will become more important. Traditional analyses lead statesmen to focus on politico-military issues and to pay little attention to the broader politics of agenda formation. Statesmen assume that the agenda will be set by shifts in the balance of power, actual or anticipated, and by perceived threats to the security of states. Other issues will only be very important when they seem to affect security and military power. In these cases, agendas will be influenced strongly by considerations of the overall balance of power.

Yet, today, some nonmilitary issues are emphasized in interstate relations at one time, whereas others of seemingly equal importance are neglected or quietly handled at a technical level. International monetary politics, problems of commodity terms of trade, oil, food, and multinational corporations have all been important during the last decade; but not all have been high on interstate agendas throughout that period.

Traditional analysts of international politics have paid little attention to agenda formation: to how issues come to receive sustained attention by high officials. The traditional orientation toward military and security affairs implies that the crucial problems of foreign policy are imposed on states by the actions or threats of other states. These are high politics as opposed to the low politics of economic affairs. Yet, as the complexity of actors and issues in world politics increases, the utility of force declines and the line between domestic policy and foreign policy becomes blurred: as the conditions of complex interdependence are more closely approximated, the politics of agenda formation becomes more subtle and differentiated.

Under complex interdependence we can expect the agenda to be affected by the international and domestic problems created by economic growth and increasing sensitivity interdependence . . . . Discontented domestic groups will politicize issues and force more issues once considered domestic onto the interstate agenda. Shifts in the distribution of power resources within sets of issues will also affect agendas. During the early 1970s the increased power of oil-producing governments over the transnational corporations and the consumer countries dramatically altered the policy agenda. Moreover, agendas for one group of issues may change as a result of linkages from other groups in which power resources are changing; for example, the broader agenda of North-South trade issues changed after the OPEC price rises and the oil embargo of 1973-74. Even if capabilities among states do not change, agendas may be affected by shifts in the importance of transnational actors. The publicity surrounding multinational corporations in the early 1970s, coupled with their rapid growth over the past twenty years, put the regulation of such corporations higher on both the United Nations agenda and national agendas.

Politicization—agitation and controversy over an issue that tend to raise it to the top of the agenda—can have many sources, as we have seen. Governments whose strength is increasing may politicize issues, by linking them to other issues. An international regime that is becoming ineffective or is not serving important issues may cause increasing politicization, as dissatisfied governments press for change. Politicization, however, can also come from below. Domestic groups may become upset enough to raise a dormant issue, or to interfere with interstate bargaining at high levels. In 1974 the American secretary of state's tacit linkage of a Soviet-American trade pact with progress in detente was upset by the success of domestic American groups working through Congress to link a trade agreement with Soviet policies on emigration.

The technical characteristics and institutional setting in which issues are raised will strongly affect politicization patterns. In the United States, congressional attention is an effective instrument of politicization. Generally, we expect transnational economic organizations and transgovernmental networks of bureaucrats to seek to avoid politicization. Domestically based groups (such as trade unions) and domestically oriented bureacracies will tend to use politicization (particularly congressional attention) against their transnationally mobile competitors. At the international level, we expect states and actors to "shop among forums" and struggle to get issues raised in international organizations that will maximize their advantage by broadening or narrowing the agenda.

Transnational and Transgovernmental Relations

Our third condition of complex interdependence, multiple channels of contact among societies, further blurs the distinction between domestic and international politics. The availability of partners in political coalitions is not necessarily limited by national boundaries as traditional analysis assumes. The nearer a situation is to complex interdependence, the more we expect the outcomes of political bargaining to be affected by transnational relations. Multinational corporations may be significant both as independent actors and as instruments manipulated by governments. The attitudes and policy stands of domestic groups are likely to be affected by communications, organized or not, between them and their counterparts abroad.

. . .

Another way of looking at transnational interactions, and of distinguishing them from interstate interactions, is to refer to a diagram that we found useful in thinking about the subject. The classic paradigm of interstate politics, depicted in figure 1, focuses on governments as the agencies through which societies deal politically with each other. Interstate politics is conceptually distinguished from, although linked indirectly to, domestic politics; transnational interactions are ignored or discounted. Governments may, however, interact through intergovernmental organizations; thus, this is included in the classic paradigm.

The additional lines drawn in figure 2 indicate what we mean by transnational interactions. For each of the interactions represented by these lines at least one of the actors is neither a government nor an intergovernmental organization. The point can be made somewhat differently by referring to J. David Singer's distinction between two ways in which individuals and organizatons in a given society

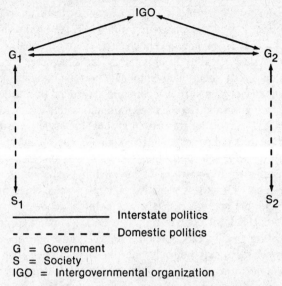

Figure 1.   **A State-Centric Interaction Pattern**

can play roles in world politics: 1) They may participate as members of coalitions that control or affect their governments or 2) they may play direct roles vis-à-vis foreign governments or foreign societies and thus bypass their own governments. Only the second type of behavior is transnational by our definition.

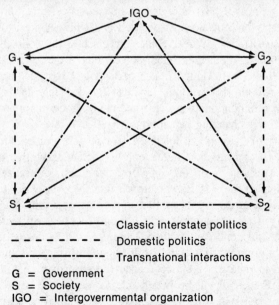

Figure 2.   **Transnational Interactions and Interstate Politics**

. . .

Thus the existence of multiple channels of contact leads us to expect limits, beyond those normally found in domestic politics, on the ability of statesmen to calculate the manipulation of interdependence or follow a consistent strategy of linkage. Statesmen must consider differential as well as aggregate effects of interdependence strategies and their likely implications for politicization and agenda control. Transactions among societies–economic and social transactions more than security ones–affect groups differently. Opportunities and costs from increased transnational ties may be greater for certain groups–for instance, American workers in the textile or shoe industries–than for others. Some organizations or groups may interact directly with actors in other societies or with other governments to increase their benefits from a network of interaction. Some actors may therefore be less vulnerable as well as less sensitive to changes elsewhere in the network than are others, and this will affect patterns of political action.

The multiple channels of contact found in complex interdependence are not limited to nongovernmental actors. Contacts between governmental bureaucracies charged with similar tasks may not only alter their perspectives but lead to transgovernmental coalitions on particular policy questions. To improve their chances of success, government agencies attempt to bring actors from other governments into their own decision-making processes as allies. Agencies of powerful states such as the United States have used such coalitions to penetrate weaker governments. . . . They have also been used to help agencies of other governments penetrate the United States bureaucracy.[11] . . .

The existence of transgovernmental policy networks leads to a different interpretation of one of the standard propositions about international politics–that states act in their own interest. Under complex interdependence, this conventional wisdom begs two important questions: which self and which interest? A government agency may pursue its own interests under the guise of the national interest; and recurrent interactions can change official perceptions of their interests. As a careful study of the politics of United States trade policy has documented, concentrating only on pressures of various interests for decisions leads to an overly mechanistic view of a continuous process and neglects the important role of communications in slowly changing perceptions of self-interest.[12]

The ambiguity of the national interest raises serious problems for the top political leaders of governments. As bureaucracies contact each other directly across national borders (without going through foreign offices), centralized control becomes more difficult. There is less assurance that the state will be united when dealing with foreign governments or that its components will interpret national interests similarly when negotiating with foreigners. The state may prove to be multifaceted, even schizophrenic. National interests will be defined differently on different issues, at different times, and by different governmental units. States that are better placed to maintain their coherence (because of a centralized political tradition such as France's) will be better able to manipulate uneven interdependence than fragmented states that at first glance seem to have more resources in an issue area.

Role of International Organizations

Finally, the existence of multiple channels leads one to predict a different and significant role for international organizations in world politics. Realists in the tradition of Hans J. Morgenthau have portrayed a world in which states, acting from self-interest, struggle for "power and peace." Security issues are dominant; war threatens. In such a world, one may assume that international institutions will have a minor role, limited by the rare congruence of such interests. International organizations are then clearly peripheral to world politics. But in a world of multiple issues imperfectly linked, in which coalitions are formed transnationally and transgovernmentally, the potential role of international institutions in political bargaining is greatly increased. In particular, they help set the international agenda, and act as catalysts for coalition-formation and as arenas for political initiatives and linkage by weak states.

Governments must organize themselves to cope with the flow of business generated by international organizations. By defining the salient issues, and deciding which issues can be grouped together, organizations may help to determine governmental priorities and the nature of interdepartmental committees and other arrangements within governments. The 1972 Stockholm Environment Conference strengthened the position of environmental agencies in various governments. The 1974 World Food Conference focused the attention of important parts of the United States government on prevention of food shortages. The September 1975 United Nations special session on proposals for a New International Economic Order generated an intragovernmental debate about policies toward the Third World in general. The International Monetary Fund and the General Agreement on Tariffs and Trade have focused governmental activity on money and trade instead of on private direct investment, which has no comparable international organization.

By bringing officials together, international organizations help to activate potential coalitions in world politics. It is quite obvious that international organizations have been very important in bringing together representatives of less developed countries, most of which do not maintain embassies in one another's capitals. Third World strategies of solidarity among poor countries have been developed in and for a series of international conferences, mostly under the auspices of the United Nations.[13] International organizations also allow agencies of governments, which might not otherwise come into contact, to turn potential or tacit coalitions into explicit transgovernmental coalitions characterized by direct communications. In some cases, international secretariats deliberately promote this process by forming coalitions with groups of governments, or with units of governments, as well as with nongovernmental organizations having similar interests.[14]

International organizations are frequently congenial institutions for weak states. The one-state-one-vote norm of the United Nations system favors coalitions of the small and powerless. Secretariats are often responsive to Third World de-

Political Processes Under Conditions of Realism and Complex Interdependence

	Realism	Complex Interdependence
Goals of actors	Military security will be the dominant goal.	Goals of states will vary by issue area. Transgovernmental politics will make goals difficult to define. Transnational actors will pursue their own goals.
Instruments of state policy	Military force will be most effective, although economic and other instruments will also be used.	Power resources specific to issue areas will be most relevant. Manipulation of interdependence, international organizations, and transnational actors will be major instruments.
Agenda formation	Potential shifts in the balance of power and security threats will set the agenda in high politics and will strongly influence other agendas.	Agenda will be affected by changes in the distribution of power resources within issue areas; the status of international regimes; changes in the importance of transnational actors; linkages from other issues and politicization as a result of rising sensitivity interdependence.
Linkages of issues	Linkages will reduce differences in outcomes among issue areas and reinforce international hierarchy.	Linkages by strong states will be more difficult to make since force will be ineffective. Linkages by weak states through international organizations will erode rather than reinforce hierarchy.
Roles of international organizations	Roles are minor, limited by state power and the importance of military force.	Organizations will set agendas, induce coalition-formation, and act as arenas for political action by weak states. Ability to choose the organizational forum for an issue and to mobilize votes will be an important political resource.

mands. Furthermore, the substantive norms of most international organizations, as they have developed over the years, stress social and economic equity as well as the equality of states. Past resolutions expressing Third World positions, sometimes agreed to with reservations by industrialized countries, are used to legitimize other demands. These agreements are rarely binding, but up to a point the norms of the institution make opposition look more harshly self-interested and less defensible.

International organizations also allow small and weak states to pursue linkage strategies. In the discussions on a New International Economic Order, Third World states insisted on linking oil price and availability to other questions on which they had traditionally been unable to achieve their objectives. . . . [S]mall and weak states have also followed a strategy of linkage in the series of Law of the Sea conferences sponsored by the United Nations.

Complex interdependence therefore yields different political patterns than does the realist conception of the world. ([The preceding table] summarizes these differences.) Thus, one would expect traditional theories to fail to explain international regime change in situations of complex interdependence. But, for a situation that approximates realist conditions, traditional theories should be appropriate. . . .

[NOTES]

1. Hans J. Morgenthau, *Politics Among Nations: The Struggle for Power and Peace*, 4th ed. (New York: Knopf, 1967), p. 36.
2. See . . . Edward L. Morse, "Transnational Economic Processes," in Robert O. Keohane and Joseph S. Nye, Jr. (eds.), *Transnational Relations and World Politics* (Cambridge, Mass.: Harvard University Press, 1972).
3. Henry A. Kissinger, "A New National Partnership," *Department of State Bulletin*, February 17, 1975, p. 199.
4. See the report of the Commission on the Organization of the Government for the Conduct of Foreign Policy (Murphy Commission) (Washington, D.C.: U.S. Government Printing Office, 1975), and the studies prepared for that report. See also Raymond Hopkins, "The International Role of 'Domestic' Bureaucracy," *International Organization* 30, no. 3 (Summer 1976).
5. *New York Times*, May 22, 1975.
6. For a valuable discussion, see Klaus Knorr, *The Power of Nations: The Political Economy of International Relations* (New York: Basic Books, 1975).
7. *Business Week*, January 13, 1975.
8. Stanley Hoffmann, "The Acceptability of Military Force," and Laurence Martin, "The Utility of Military Force," in *Force in Modern Societies: Its Place in International Politics* (Adelphi Paper, International Institute for Strategic Studies, 1973). See also Knorr, *The Power of Nations*.
9. Henry Brandon, *The Retreat of American Power* (New York: Doubleday, 1974), p. 218.
10. *International Implications of the New Economic Policy*, U.S. Congress, House of Representatives, Committee on Foreign Affairs, Subcommittee on Foreign Economic Policy, Hearings, September 16, 1971.

11. For a more detailed discussion, see Robert O. Keohane and Joseph S. Nye, Jr., "Transgovernmental Relations and International Organizations," *World Politics* 27, no. 1 (October 1974): 39-62.

12. Raymond Bauer, Ithiel de Sola Pool, and Lewis Dexter, *American Business and Foreign Policy* (New York: Atherton, 1963), chap. 35, esp. pp. 472–75.

13. Branislav Gosovic and John Gerard Ruggie, "On the Creation of a New International Economic Order: Issue Linkage and the Seventh Special Session of the UN General Assembly," *International Organization* 30, no. 2 (Spring 1976): 309–46.

14. Robert W. Cox, "The Executive Head," *International Organization* 23, no. 2 (Spring 1969): 205–30.

24
The Multinational Corporation in World Politics

CHARLES W. KEGLEY, JR., AND EUGENE R. WITTKOPF

In this essay, Charles W. Kegley, Jr., and Eugene R. Wittkopf provide empirical information on the global reach and economic power of multinational corporations (MNCs), examine the complaints lodged against MNCs, and assess the role of MNCs in propelling the transformation of world politics. Kegley is professor of government and international studies at the University of South Carolina. Wittkopf is professor of political science at the University of Florida. Together they have written *American Foreign Policy: Pattern and Process* (1982).

Investment by individuals of one country in the economic system of another country is not new. Since World War II, however, the volume of direct investment abroad through transnationally organized business enterprises has grown substantially.[1] The term *multinational corporation* (MNC) is popularly used to describe the instrumentality of this transnational phenomenon, which has resulted in the internationalization of production. The impact of this development is suggested by the estimate that by the year 2000 half or more of all industrial production in the world will be accounted for by a relative handful of MNCs (Heilbroner, 1977). And its pace is suggested by the growth of American-based multinational corporations. One study has shown that the number of foreign subsidiaries of 187 United States-based MNCs grew from just over 2,000 in 1950 to nearly 8,000 by 1967, roughly a fourfold increase in less than two decades (Vaupel and Curhan, 1969: 123). This parallels the increase in the number of IGOs [international governmental organizations] and INGOs [international nongovernmental organizations] the world has witnessed since World War II—all three of which have grown more rapidly than the number of nation-states.

The remarkable rise in the overseas activities of businesses whose parent corporations are located elsewhere is one reason why the multinational corporation has commanded attention. Indeed, the term *multinational corporation* often

Reprinted from Charles W. Kegley, Jr., and Eugene R. Wittkopf, *World Politics: Trend and Transformation* (New York: St. Martin's, 1981), pp. 129–141. Copyright © 1981 by St. Martin's Press and reprinted by permission of the publisher. Footnotes have been renumbered to appear in consecutive order.

[1] The Commission on Transnational Corporations (1978: 36) reports that direct foreign investment grew from $105 billion in 1967 to $158 billion in 1971 and $287 billion in 1976. The 1976 level represents more than an 80 percent increase above the level existing only five years earlier.

evokes strong emotional responses, suggesting that the MNC has become more than simply the agent of a global system of production. May it have become so powerful and its tentacles so far-reaching that it has undermined the ability of nation-states to control their own fates? Indeed, is it possible that MNCs are undermining the very foundations of the present international system?

THE GLOBAL REACH AND ECONOMIC POWER OF MULTINATIONALS

What is a multinational corporation? Definitions differ (see Feld, 1979), but they converge on the notion of a business enterprise organized in one society with activities abroad growing out of direct investment (as opposed to portfolio investment through shareholding). Typically they are hierarchically organized and centrally directed (Jacobson, 1979). Thus "a distinctive characteristic of the transnational organization is its broader-than-national perspective with respect to the pursuit of highly specialized objectives through a central optimizing strategy across national boundaries" (Huntington, 1973).

The initiation of the European Economic Community (EEC) in 1958 gave impetus to this form of business organization. Because the six EEC members anticipated a common external tariff wall around their customs union, it made economic sense for American firms to establish production facilities in Europe. That way they could remain competitive by selling their wares as domestic products rather than foreign imports with their added tariff costs.[2]

Table 1 indicates how extensive this form of business organization has become. Nearly 10,400 business firms (based in nineteen First World nations) have at least one foreign affiliate in one or more host countries.[3] (*Host country* refers to the country in which the operations of a company owned or controlled by a parent firm headquartered in another country are carried on.) The United States, Britain, and West Germany account for over half of these companies, the United States alone for more than a quarter. Although the growth of transnational corporations is a global phenomenon, "the major part of all transnational business is

[2] The reasons for direct investments overseas are more complex than this simplified explanation suggests. The product-cycle theory is one example. According to this view, overseas expansion is essentially a defensive maneuver designed to forestall foreign competitors and hence to maintain the global competitiveness of domestically based industries. The theory views MNCs as having an edge in the initial stages of developing and producing a new product, and then having to go abroad to protect export markets from foreign competitors that naturally arise as the relevant technology becomes diffused or imitated. In the final phase of the product cycle "production has become sufficiently routinized so that the comparative advantage shifts to relatively low-skilled, low-wage, and labor-intensive economies. This is now the case, for example, in textiles, electronic components, and footwear" (Gilpin, 1975). See this source and especially Vernon (1971) for an elaboration of the product-cycle theory. Noteworthy is Gilpin's (1975) conclusion after examining several theories of foreign direct investment: "The primary drive behind the overseas expansion of today's giant corporations is maximization of corporate growth and the suppression of foreign as well as domestic competition."

[3] *Transnational* rather than *multinational* is perhaps a more descriptive term for these firms, since many have affiliates in only one host country. Only 54 percent of the 10,373 firms shown in Table 1 have affiliates in two or more host countries, and less than 20 percent have affiliates in six or more (Commission on Transnational Corporations, 1979: 8).

Table 1 Business Firms With One or More Foreign Affiliates by Number of Host Countries and Third World Host Regions, 1977

Location of Parent Firms	Number of Firms with Foreign Affiliates in One or More Developed or Developing Countries	Number of Firms with Foreign Affiliates in Developing Countries				
		Total	In Western Hemisphere only	In Africa only	In Asia only	In More than One of the Three Regions
United States of America	2,783	1,197	522	53	130	492
United Kingdom	1,598	639	97	102	176	264
Germany, Federal Republic of	1,404	316	134	29	57	96
Switzerland	852	109	48	6	11	44
Netherlands	600	104	28	10	18	48
France	564	246	36	125	19	66
Canada	432	121	77	9	12	23
Japan	380	225	46	5	77	97
Belgium	320	90	16	49	2	23
Australia	323	181	11	1	150	19
Italy	249	58	23	9	7	19
Sweden	258	63	27	3	5	28
New Zealand	167	58	2	—	55	1
Denmark	132	22	7	4	4	7
Norway	116	15	4	—	5	6
Spain	79	34	22	4	3	5
Austria	54	11	3	1	5	2
Finland	52	7	4	2	—	1
Portugal	10	6	2	3	1	—
Total	10,373	3,502	1,109	415	737	1,241

Source: Commission on Transnational Corporations, "Supplementary Material on the Issue of Defining Transnational Corporations," U.N. Doc. E/C.10/58, United Nations Economic and Social Council, March 23, 1979, pp. 8, 11.

Table 2 **Countries and Corporations Ranked According to Size of Annual Product, 1978**

Rank	Economic Entity	$(billions)	Rank	Economic Entity	$(billions)
1	United States	2,117.89	51	Algeria	22.29
2	Soviet Union	965.52	52	Colombia	21.79
3	Japan	836.16	53	Thailand	21.79
4	Germany, West	587.70	54	IBM	21.08
5	France	439.97	55	GENERAL ELECTRIC	19.65
6	China, People's Rep.	424.62	56	Portugal	19.54
7	United Kingdom	281.09	57	Libya	18.96
8	Italy	218.32	58	UNILEVER	18.89
9	Canada	216.09	59	GULF OIL	18.07
10	Brazil	187.19	60	Kuwait	18.04
11	Spain	128.92	61	Pakistan	17.53
12	Poland	128.33	62	CHRYSLER	16.34
13	Netherlands	117.19	63	Egypt	15.52
14	Australia	113.83	64	Israel	15.30
15	India	112.66	65	New Zealand	15.27
16	Germany, East	95.49	66	ITT	15.26
17	Belgium	89.52	67	Chile	15.18
18	Sweden	84.75	68	PHILIPS' GLOEILAMPENFABRIEKEN	15.12
19	Mexico	84.15	69	STANDARD OIL (IND.)	14.96
20	Switzerland	76.05	70	Malaysia	14.54
21	Czechoslovakia	71.32	71	Hong Kong	14.05
22	Saudi Arabia	63.31	72	SIEMENS	13.86
23	GENERAL MOTORS	63.22	73	VOLKSWAGENWERK	13.33
24	EXXON	60.33	74	TOYOTA MOTOR	12.77
25	Austria	52.72	75	RENAULT	12.72
26	Yugoslavia	52.34	76	Morocco	12.61

27	Turkey	51.75	77	ENI	12.57
28	Denmark	50.41	78	Korea, North	12.53
29	Argentina	50.25	79	FRANCAISE DES PÉTROLES	12.51
30	Indonesia	48.82	80	Peru	12.44
31	Nigeria	45.72	81	ATLANTIC RICHFIELD	12.30
32	ROYAL DUTCH/SHELL GROUP	44.04	82	DAIMIER-BENZ	12.09
33	FORD MOTOR	42.78	83	HOECHST	12.07
34	Korea, South	42.46	84	United Arab Emirates	11.44
35	South Africa	40.94	85	BAYER	11.39
36	Venezuela	40.71	86	Ireland	11.21
37	Norway	38.50	87	SHELL OIL	11.06
38	Romania	38.17	88	U.S. STEEL	11.05
39	Hungary	36.86	89	NESTLÉ	11.00
40	MOBIL	34.74	90	BASF	10.73
41	Finland	32.38	91	PEUGEOT-CITROËN	10.62
42	Greece	30.53	92	E.I. DUPONT de NEMOURS	10.58
43	TEXACO	28.61	93	MATSUSHITA ELECTRIC INDUSTRIAL	10.02
44	Bulgaria	28.45			
45	BRITISH PETROLEUM	27.41	94	NISSAN MOTOR	9.75
46	China, Rep. of	23.93	95	NIPPON STEEL	9.52
47	Philippines	23.25	96	WESTERN ELECTRIC	9.52
48	STANDARD OIL OF CALIF	23.23	97	CONTINENTAL OIL	9.46
49	NATIONAL IRANIAN OIL	22.79	98	MITSUBISHI HEAVY INDUSTRIES	9.20
50	Iraq	22.72	99	THYSSEN	9.18
			100	HITACHI	9.15

Source: *World Bank Atlas* (Washington, D.C.: World Bank, 1979), pp. 12 *et passim*; *Fortune*, 100 (August 13, 1979), 208.
23

located in the developed areas of North America, Western Europe, and Japan"
(Modelski, 1979).

The preference for the First World is implied by the data in Table 1. Somewhat less than half of the British and American firms have Third World affiliates, while fewer than a quarter of the German firms have them. The difference between the United States and Britain on one hand, and Germany on the other, reflects differences in their historic patterns of global involvement. Overall, only a third of the more than 10,000 firms referenced in Table 1 have affiliates in the Third World.

The dominance of the United States in the network of multinationals is especially apparent from an examination of the economic characteristics of MNCs. In 1976, 54 percent of the 411 industrial firms comprising the Billion Dollar Club (sales of at least $1 billion) were American. The closest competitors to the United States were Japan and Britain, with 12 and 10 percent respectively (Commission on Transnational Corporations, 1979: 14). Among the leading firms were the giants of American industry—Exxon, General Motors, Ford Motor, Texaco, Mobil, Standard Oil of California, Gulf Oil, IBM, General Electric, and International Telephone and Telegraph. But the dominance extends to banking as well. In 1976 Bankamerica Corporation and Citicorp were the two largest banks in the world, with 494 foreign affiliates and combined assets in excess of $135 billion. Japan accounted for twelve of the fifty largest banks in the world while the United States accounted for only ten, but the assets of the American banks outstripped the Japanese, $348 billion to $318 billion (Commission on Transnational Corporations, 1978: 215–216).

The importance of these economic characteristics is illustrated in Table 2, which intersperses billion-dollar-or-more firms with nations ranked by the size of their gross national product. The results show that (in 1978) General Motors and Exxon outranked all but twenty-two nation-states. Among the top fifty entries, multinationals account for only nine, but in the next fifty, thirty-two are multinationals.

The spread of their activity and the potency of their economic potential are two important reasons MNCs have commanded so much attention. Furthermore, the attention has been relatively greater on the part of Third World nations, since MNCs are generally more important in developing nations' overall GNP and in their most advanced economic sectors. Third World views of MNCs have also been more charged emotionally, since these predominantly Northern-based economic giants are frequently seen through the nationalistic eyes of the newly independent nations as agents of neocolonialism.

Let us examine briefly three general complaints lodged against multinational corporations: that they have an adverse impact on host nations; that they engage in illegitimate political activity; and that they are beyond national control and thus are undermining the territorial nation-state.

IMPACT ON HOST NATIONS

Multinational corporations have been important transmission belts for the diffusion of technology and managerial know-how across national boundaries. For the home countries of MNCs this movement is often alleged to have occurred at great cost. MNCs are charged with shifting productive facilities abroad to avoid demands of powerful labor unions for higher wages. According to this view, the practice of moving from industrially advanced countries to industrially backward countries, where labor is cheap and unions weak or nonexistent, is the cause of structural unemployment in the advanced countries, because capital is more mobile than labor.

If home countries have incurred costs, have others realized benefits? From one perspective, the movement of capital and production from the First World to the Third has produced net gains for the latter:

> For all the talk (and the reality) of imperialist domination, most of the underdeveloped nations want domestic foreign investment, European and/or American, for a variety of reasons. The multinationals pay higher wages, keep more honest books, pay more taxes, and provide more managerial know-how and training than do local industries. Moreover, they usually provide better social services for their workers, and certainly provide fancy career opportunities for a favored few of the elite. They are, in addition, a main channel through which technology, developed in the West, can filter into the backward nations. To be sure, the corporations typically send home more profits than the capital that they originally introduce into the "host" country; but meanwhile that capital grows, providing jobs, improving productivity, and often contributing to export earnings.[4] (Heilbroner, 1977: 345–346)

From another Third World perspective, however, the costs associated with the multinational firm have been excessive. "The capital, jobs and other benefits they bring to developing economies are recognized, but the terms on which these benefits come are seen as unfair and exploitative and as robbing the new nations of their resources"(Cutler, 1978).

One of the costs is technology dependence. Technology imported from the North impedes local development: what is transferred to the Third World is often not appropriate to the local setting, and the spread effects of industrial activity within developing nations in particular are limited. In addition, because MNCs seek to maximize profits for shareholders, who more often than not reside in the parent state rather than in the host state, capital is not reinvested in the country where production occurs but instead finds its way to someone else's hands. Moreover, the returns are often excessive. In 1965–1968, for example, profit on American direct foreign investment in the First World averaged 7.9 percent, but in the Third World it averaged over 17 percent (Spero, 1977: 198; compare Drucker, 1974).

MNCs benefit in other ways as well. Critics argue that profits represent only a small part of the effective return to parent companies. "A large part of the real return comes from licensing fees and royalties paid by the subsidiary to the parent

---

[4] Underdeveloped nations themselves have begun to spawn multinational firms. *Fortune* magazine's 1978 list of the 500 largest industrial corporations outside the United States showed 34 companies headquartered in the developing world, a figure 48 percent higher than the previous year (Heenan and Keegan, 1979: 102). Thus the multinational corporation, long regarded by its opponents as the unique instrument of capitalist oppression against the impoverished world, could prove to be the tool by which the impoverished world builds prosperity. . . . Third World multinationalism, only yesterday an apparent contradiction in terms, is now a serious force in the development process (Heenan and Keegan, 1979: 109).

for the use of technology controlled by the parent'' (Spero, 1977). Parent companies admittedly have to absorb the research and development costs of the technology used abroad by others.

> What the critics contend is that subsidiaries in underdeveloped countries pay an unjustifiably high price for technology and bear an unjustifiably high share of the research and development costs. The monopoly control of technology by the multinational corporation enables the parent to exact a monopoly rent from its subsidiaries. And the parent chooses to use that power to charge inordinately high fees and royalties to disguise high profits and avoid local taxes on those profits. (Spero, 1977: 198)

The "transfer" pricing mechanism is another device used by multinationals that can effectively increase their profits while minimizing their tax burdens. The raw, semiprocessed, or finished materials produced by a parent's subsidiaries located in different countries are in effect traded among the subsidiaries. Since the same company is sitting on both sides of the transaction, the sales or "transfer" prices of these import-export transactions can be manipulated so as to benefit the parent firm.

> Some firms do this as objectively as they can, without regard to tax considerations. But there are also some who exercise this discretion so as to minimize their global taxes and maximize their after-tax earnings. Since tax rates vary around the world, they accomplish this by recording profits in jurisdictions where taxes are relatively low. (Cutler, 1978: 11)

The net effect is increased capital flow from South to North. Poverty is said to be the primary product (Müller, 1973–1974).

In sum, the multinational corporation, while conferring some benefits on host states, may do so only at great cost.[5] Critics of the MNC argue, in fact, that the MNC has had a negative effect on developing nations' growth prospects. Joan Edelman Spero has conveniently summarized the arguments of the critics:

> Multinational corporations often create highly developed enclaves which do not contribute to the development of the larger economy. These enclaves use capital-intensive technology which employs few local citizens; acquire supplies from abroad, not locally; use transfer prices and technology agreements to avoid taxes; and send earnings back home. In welfare terms the benefits of the enclave accrue to the home country and to a small part of the host population allied with the corporation. (Spero, 1977: 199)

POLITICS AND MULTINATIONAL CORPORATIONS

The charges often lodged against multinational corporations are not confined to the adverse effects they allegedly exert on Third World development prospects. They also extend to the involvement of MNCs in local political affairs.

Perhaps the most notorious instance of a multinational corporation's interven-

---

[5] The economic consequences of the activities of multinational corporations are not, of course, altogether discernible. The effects show country-by-country variations and assessments do not point to consensus. Charles Kindleberger (1969), for instance, contends that despite the monopolistic and exploitative tendencies of MNCs, multinationals in the aggregate have, paradoxically, expanded competition and enhanced world economic efficiency.

tion in the politics of a host state occurred in Chile in the early 1970s. There, International Telephone and Telegraph (ITT) attempted to protect its interests in the profitable Chiltelco telephone company by preventing Salvador Allende, a Marxist, from being elected president and then exercising political power effectively. ITT's efforts to undermine Allende included giving monetary support to his political opponents and attempting to induce the American government to launch a program designed to disrupt the Chilean economy once Allende was elected.

Multinationals have also used bribery to influence key foreign officials. The extent of such activity by American firms was unearthed in the aftermath of the Watergate scandal in the United States in the early 1970s. The Securities and Exchange Commission and later a congressional inquiry disclosed improper foreign payments totaling more than $100 million made by 100 American firms (Cutler, 1978: 18).

The Chilean ITT case and the bribery scandals of the 1970s suggest that MNCs have a capacity to undertake their own private foreign policies. The efforts probably less often involve direct political action or bribery than they do legitimate lobbying of the host government's legislators and advertising "to influence the climate of ideas" (Nye, 1974). Regardless of the particular form, however, such private political activity "contravenes the traditional assumption of world politics that governments deal with governments and that citizens or corporations affect governments of other countries indirectly through policies they press upon their own government. But . . . citizens and corporations are also affecting the governments and politics of other countries by dealing with them directly, quite apart from the activities of their home governments" (Nye, 1974). Such transnational activity may not be unique to MNCs, but the global reach and potential economic power of MNCs give added significance to their activities.

In addition to direct political roles, multinationals indirectly serve as instruments through which national governments pursue their objectives. The United States, for example, has sought to use the foreign affiliates of American-based multinationals to extend into other jurisdictions its policies regarding trade embargoes against other nations (Nye, 1974). Similarly, the governments of the Organization of Petroleum Exporting Countries effectively used the multinational oil companies in 1973-1974 to achieve OPEC's goal of using oil as a political weapon against the West. Multinationals have also been used to enhance American intelligence-gathering capabilities in other societies. In these cases it almost seems that the multinational corporation is the captive of governments.

On the other hand, multinational corporations often lobby their home governments for policies that back the MNCs in disputes with host governments. The Hickenlooper amendment, which stipulates that American foreign aid will be cut off from any country that nationalizes American overseas investments without just compensation, is an example of home-state support of multinationals' overseas activities. More generally, multinational corporations facilitated creation of the liberal multilateral trading system supported as a policy objective by the United States since World War II, and multinationals in turn have helped shape the specific policies regarding trade and taxes that contributed to the realization of that goal. In this sense, MNCs may help governments decide what their objectives are.

CONTROLLING MULTINATIONAL CORPORATIONS

It is clear that multinationals have become important actors in world politics in the sense that decisions critical to nation-states are now made by entities over which those nations may not have control. This, in fact, and not the question of expatriated earnings, is the heart of the question of ownership or control of MNCs so central to Third World perceptions of these corporate giants. "Most host governments believe that foreign owners will subordinate the interests of the host nation to their own international interests and that they will be less amenable than local owners to the host government's views" (Cutler, 1978). But the question of control is not confined to the Third World, for the international interests of multinational firms are not necessarily more compatible with the interests of home governments than with those of the hosts.

The potential long-run importance of multinational corporations for the transforming world political order is vividly depicted by Richard J. Barnet and Ronald E. Müller:

> The global corporation is the most powerful human organization yet devised for colonizing the future. By scanning the entire planet for opportunities, by shifting its resources from industry to industry and country to country, and by keeping its overriding goal simple—worldwide profit maximization—it has become an institution of unique power. The World Managers are the first to have developed a plausible model for the future that is global. They exploit the advantages of mobility while workers and governments are still tied to particular territories. For this reason, the corporate visionaries are far ahead of the rest of the world in making claims on the future. In making business decisions today they are creating a politics for the next generation. (Barnet and Müller, 1974: 363)

Whether the "corporate visionaries" will succeed in creating a better, more humane, and just world is questioned. "For some, the global corporation holds the promise of lifting mankind out of poverty and bringing the good life to everyone. For others, these corporations have become a law unto themselves; they are mini-empires which exploit all for the benefit of a few" (Gilpin, 1975b).

Those who view the MNC favorably see national competitiveness giving way to a supranational world order in which welfare issues will be of more importance than narrow ideological or security contests. Because the MNC knows no national boundaries, and because its interests are disrupted by national aggressiveness and militarism, the MNC from this perspective is characterized as a "peacemonger" (Ewing, 1974).

Those more negatively disposed toward MNCs maintain that because of their desire for political stability in order to realize maximum profits, they will often deal with repressive political regimes and "powerfully oppose the kinds of revolutionary upheavals that in many backward areas are probably the essential precondition for a genuine modernization" (Heilbroner, 1977). Furthermore, multinationals may be the agents of a worldwide spread of economic benefits, but the distribution of these benefits is not even. Hence, multinationals perpetuate and deepen global inequality. And because they threaten national autonomy, *all* countries are challenged by the rise of independent, transnationally organized corporations.

> According to this view, the diminution of the role of the nation-state would signal a new feudalism rather than healthy progress. Kings and corporate barons will engage in conflicts and coalitions, but the serfs of the world will suffer. The real global divisions will not be among nations, but between a world city knit together by transnational elites and the diverse but intense parochialisms of the world countryside. The decline of the nation-state would not be a sign of health but a sign of disaster: "a sound international order cannot be built on the wreckage of nation-states." The nation-state provides the internal order and sense of political community that underlie democratic institutions, and there is little prospect that our political norms can be adapted to keep pace with the evolution of powerful and autonomous transnational corporations playing an increasingly political role. (Nye, 1974: 167)

Optimists and pessimists may differ in their evaluations of the ultimate consequences of the rise of multinational corporations,[6] but they share the view that if nation-states are to manage these corporate giants they will have to devise new transnational institutions of their own capable of controlling a phenomenon that presently operates outside national and international legal and political jurisdictions. . . .

REFERENCES

BALL, GEORGE W. (ed.) (1975) *Global Companies: The Political Economy of World Business*. Englewood Cliffs, N.J.: Prentice-Hall.

BARNET, RICHARD J. and RONALD E. MÜLLER. (1974) *Global Reach: The Power of the Multinational Corporations*. New York: Simon and Schuster.

BERGSTEN, C. FRED, THOMAS HORST, and THEODORE MORAN. (1978) *American Multinationals and American Interests*. Washington, D.C.: Brookings Institution.

Commission on Transnational Corporations. (1979) "Supplementary Material on the Issue of Defining Transnational Corporations," UN Doc. E/C.10/58, United Nations Economic and Social Council (March 23). New York: United Nations.

———. (1978) *Transnational Corporations in World Development: A Re-Examination*. UN Doc. E/C.10/38, United Nations Economic and Social Council (March 20). New York: United Nations.

CUTLER, LLOYD N. (1978) *Global Interdependence and the Multinational Firm*. Headline Series 239 (April). New York: Foreign Policy Association.

DRUCKER, PETER F. (1974) "Multinationals and Developing Countries: Myths and Realities," *Foreign Affairs* 53 (October): 121–134.

EWING, DAVID W. (1974) "The Corporation as Peacemonger," pp. 150–157 in Peter A. Toma, Andrew Gyorgy, and Robert S. Jordan (eds.), *Basic Issues in International Relations*. Boston: Allyn and Bacon.

FELD, WERNER J. (1979) *International Relations: A Transnational Approach*. Sherman Oaks, Calif.: Alfred.

[6] For elaborations on the prospective significance of multinationals, see Barnet and Müller (1974), Bergsten et al. (1978), Ewing (1974), Heilbroner (1977), Nye (1974), Vernon (1971), and the essays in Ball (1975) and Modelski (1979).

GILPIN, ROBERT. (1975) *U.S. Power and the Multinational Corporation*. New York: Basic Books.

HANRIEDER, WOLFRAM F. (1978) "Dissolving International Politics: Reflections on the Nation-State," *American Political Science Review* 72 (December): 1276–1287.

HEENAN, DAVID A., and WARREN J. KEEGAN. (1979) "The Rise of Third World Multinations," *Harvard Business Review* 57 (January–February): 101–109.

HEILBRONER, ROBERT L. (1977) "The Multinational Corporation and the Nation-State," pp. 338–352 in Steven L. Spiegel (ed.), *At Issue: Politics in the World Arena*. New York: St. Martin's.

HUNTINGTON, SAMUEL P. (1973) "Transnational Organizations in World Politics," *World Politics* 25 (April): 333–368.

JACOBSON, HAROLD K. (1979) *Networks of Interdependence*. New York: Knopf.

KEOHANE, ROBERT O., and JOSEPH S. NYE. (eds.) (1971) "Transnational Relations and World Politics," *International Organization* 25 (Summer): 329–758.

KINDLEBERGER, CHARLES P. (1969) *American Business Abroad*. New Haven: Yale University Press.

MANSBACH, RICHARD W., YALE H. FERGUSON, and DONALD E. LAMPERT. (1976) *The Web of World Politics*. Englewood Cliffs, N.J.: Prentice-Hall.

MODELSKI, GEORGE. (ed.) (1979) *Transnational Corporations and World Order*. San Francisco: Freeman.

MÜLLER, RONALD. (1973–1974) "Poverty is the Product," *Foreign Policy* 13 (Winter): 71–103.

NYE, JOSEPH S., JR. (1974) "Multinational Corporations in World Politics," *Foreign Affairs* 53 (October): 153–175.

———, and ROBERT O. KEOHANE. (1971) "Transnational Relations and World Politics: An Introduction," *International Organization* 25 (Summer): 329–349.

SPERO, JOAN EDELMAN. (1977) *The Politics of International Economic Relations*. New York: St. Martin's.

VAUPEL, JAMES W., and JOAN P. CURHAN. (1969) *The Making of Multinational Enterprise: A Sourcebook of Tables Based on a Study of 187 Major U.S. Manufacturing Corporations*. Boston: Division of Research, Graduate School of Business Administration, Harvard University.

VERNON, RAYMOND. (1971) *Sovereignty at Bay*. New York: Basic Books.

VOLGY, THOMAS J. (1974) "Reducing Conflict in International Politics: The Impact of Structural Variables," *International Studies Quarterly* 18 (June): 179–210.

25

The Future of the World-Economy: A World-Systems Perspective

IMMANUEL WALLERSTEIN

In this essay, Immanuel Wallerstein examines cyclical patterns in the modern world characterized as a capitalist world-economy. The nexus between politics and economics in the world-system perspective is underscored by Wallerstein's contention that the basic economic mechanisms of the capitalist world-economy operate in a space characterized by the absence of an overarching international political authority. Wallerstein is professor of sociology at the State University of New York at Binghamton and author of *The Modern World-System I* (1974) and *The Modern World-System II* (1980).

We are fond of temporal contrasts (the future and the past, the new and the old)–as well as temporal disjunctures–(the present, the crisis, the transition). But time is a social reality, not a physical one. And our visions of time (or rather of spacetime) both reflect the social system of which they are a part, and in a very basic way are constitutive of those systems.

We cannot discuss what we think to be the future of the modern world-system unless we come to some agreement about which past it is to which we are referring. For me, the answer has become increasingly clear. The modern world is a capitalist world-economy, and this capitalist world-economy came into existence in Europe somewhere between 1450 and 1550 as a mode of resolving the "crisis of feudalism" that had shaken this same Europe in the period 1300-1450.

It came into existence as a mode of repressing the increasingly successful ability that the European work-force had demonstrated, during the period of crisis, to withhold surplus from the seigniorial and urban patriarchal strata who had appropriated it under the feudal system. From this perspective, the capitalist system that replaced the feudal system proved marvelously adept. The period from 1450 to 1600 registered a dramatic fall in the real income of Europe's direct producers and, with the constant widening of the geographic scope of the world-economy, this process of polarization (and therefore, in the old-fashioned phrase, of absolute immiserization) has never ceased to expand since. This can be empirically demonstrated, *provided* one measures the polarization in terms of the world-economy as a whole and not in terms of particular states.

Reprinted from Immanuel Wallerstein, "The Future of the World-Economy," in Terence K. Hopkins and Immanuel Wallerstein, eds., *Processes of the World-System* (Beverly Hills, Calif.: Sage Publications, 1980), pp. 167–180; © 1980 Sage Publications, Inc., with permission.

In order to appreciate the real changes which are occurring today and which may occur in the future, we must assess what are the structural mechanisms by which the system has up to now reproduced itself, and what are the structural contradictions by which it has up to now undermined itself. I shall however do this somewhat briefly, as I wish to concentrate on the organizational responses of the oppressed strata, the politics of the antisystemic movements that have grown up in the course of the historical development of the capitalist world-economy. For it is these movements which themselves represent a principal nexus of both the undermining and the reproduction of the system.

All systems are both structure and change, have both cycles and trends. Intelligent analysis must always be wary of emphasizing the one at the expense of the other—of seeing only repetitive patterns, of discovering always what is "new." For much of the "new" has always been there, and the repetitions, such as they are, are spiral in character.

The basic economic mechanisms of the capitalist world-economy derive from the fact that the absence of an overarching political structure renders it likely that those producers who seek to operate on the imperative of ceaseless accumulation of capital will drive from competition, over the long run, those who would operate economic enterprises on any other normative principle. This means that producers/entrepreneurs tend to make their production and investment decisions in terms of what will optimize the medium-run likelihood of individual profit.

The basic contradiction of the capitalist system is found in the disjuncture of what determines supply and what determines demand. World production decisions are made on an individual basis. The sum of the activities of the individual producers/entrepreneurs constantly increases world production, which means that continued profitability for all is necessarily a function of an *expanding* world demand. However, expanding world demand is not a function of the decisions of the individual producers/entrepreneurs. If anything, the sum of their individual decisions, insofar as they press individually to reduce costs of their factors of production (and hence to reduce labor costs), serves actually to diminish world demand. World demand is fundamentally determined by a set of preexisting political compromises within the various states that are part of the world-economy, and which more or less fix for medium-run periods (circa fifty years) the modal distribution of income to various participants in the circuit of capital. This phenomenon often is discussed under such names as the existence of different "historic levels of wages." Wage-levels are indeed based on historic factors, but they are far from unchanging on that account.

An economic system in which world supply expands more or less continuously but world demand remains relatively fixed for medium periods of time is bound to create a cyclical pattern of production. Empirically the capitalist world-economy has in fact known such cycles of expansion and contraction since its beginning (that is, for at least 500 years). The most important of these cycles seems to be the expansion-stagnation cycle of 40–55 years that is often called the Kondratieff cycle.

In the stagnation phase of the cycle, precipitated by the excess of world production over world demand, individual entrepreneurs seek to maintain their own relative share of profit (or even expand it) either by expanding production, or by reducing costs (through reducing wages or through technological advance that increases productivity), or by reducing competition, or by some combination of these three methods. One of the many ways of reducing costs is to shift the locus of production to lower wage-zones (from city to country, or from core to peripheral zone both within states and within the world as a whole). Along with this goes pressure to redirect global flows of labor ("outward" from core toward periphery, rather than "inward" from periphery toward core, as occurs in expansion phases).

While individual entrepreneurs and individual geographic areas may benefit precisely because of stagnation, globally the effect is perceived as a squeeze, one felt on the one hand by weaker entrepreneurs (who face bankruptcy amidst the concentration of capital), and on the other hand by those segments of the world labor force previously steadily employed as wage workers. This latter group is unevenly distributed worldwide. Wherever wage workers are found in sufficient numbers, acute class struggles become the visible outgrowth of the stagnation phase. Wherever segments of the petty bourgeoisie are dispossessed because of the effects of stagnation, they join in the acute social conflict.

Over the period of this stagnation phase, the acute class struggles in the various states usually lead to a reopening of the previous historic compromises that had resulted in the existing distributions of appropriated surplus. In addition, semiperipheral zones are able to achieve either higher prices for their goods or a higher proportion of the world market, and thus retain larger segments of world surplus.

There results a redistribution of surplus—more to the bourgeoisie of semiperipheral zones, and more to parts of the labor force of core areas—which effectively expands world monetary demand enough to revive the inherent expansionist tendencies of the capitalist world-economy.

However, as a result of this redistribution of surplus, the world bourgeoisie, and particularly that segment located in the old core areas, is faced with a diminution of its share of world surplus, unless it takes two kinds of crucial countermeasures: technological advances which lead to temporary (but significant) superprofits deriving from temporary monopolies; and expansion of the outer boundaries of the world-economy to incorporate new zones of low-cost, not fully proletarianized, workers.

In this cyclical mechanism, we can see the pressures that lead to the creation and reinforcement of the four basic institutions of the capitalist world-economy: the states; classes; ethno/national status-groups; households. We shall briefly indicate the function of each.

It is by reinforcing and utilizing the state machineries of the states in which they are domiciled that entrepreneurs/producers can best increase their ability to profit, given the vagaries of the market, especially during the stagnation phase, both vis-à-vis other entrepreneurs and vis-à-vis the working classes. The consequent pressure to strengthen the efficacy of state machineries is not countered by working-class pressure in an opposite direction. Far from being antistate per se, the working classes of a given state in their struggle with the bourgeoisie of that state equally seek to strengthen the particular state machinery (whether their tactics are reformist or revolutionary), however much they are politically opposed to the domination of the existing regime by bourgeois elements. Hence, over time, and particularly in periods of stagnation, state machineries, in *all* parts of the world have in fact been systematically articulated and strengthened. This does not mean, however, that the initial difference between the greater state strength of core areas and the lesser state strength of peripheral zones has been diminished. Quite the contrary, despite the fact that all states have grown stronger in relation to internal forces, and there has been an overall trend to the ever-clearer institutionalization of a well-defined interstate system (which has reached its ideological culmination in the formation of the United Nations based on the formal insistence on sovereign equality), there has nonetheless also been an ever-increasing polarization of the strength of states.

The states are not the only institutions thus created by the operations of the world-economy. Classes are also created. Indeed, Marx's original insight that the operation of the capitalist system created two clear and polarized classes is in fact affirmed and not disconfirmed by the evidence. Whereas, originally, the multiplicity of social arrangements meant that the vast majority of households were in part of their activities the appropriated, and in another part the appropriators, hence both "proletarian" and "bourgeois," the slow but steady commodification of the work-force as well as of the managerial sectors has in fact diminished the "social veil" that blurred class structure. Most households today fall clearly into either a category which is receiving in *all* segments of its total income less than the social product it is creating (and hence is objectively proletarian) or into a category which is receiving a part of the global surplus product in all segments of its total income (and hence is objectively bourgeois).

What is important for our purposes is to note two things. This objective clarification, or lifting of the social veil, is in fact the product of the periodic stagnation phases and the consequent pressures on both entrepreneurs and workers. And the needs of both groups, especially insofar as they have wanted to manipulate state structures, have led to increasing class consciousness at both the state and the world level, initially historically of the bourgeoisie and then later of the proletariat.

The creation of classes is matched by the creation and recreation of the multitude of status groups (whether the lines are national, ethnic, racial, religious, or linguistic) as a mode by which sectors of the bourgeoisie and of the proletariat assert short-run interests amidst the cyclical rhythms of the world-economy. In the times of economic squeezes (the B-phases), groups seek extraeconomic legitimation for monopolistic hoarding of privileges (such as employment, education, etc.). In the times of expansion (the A-phases), upper- and middle-status groups seek to preclude the potential decline of market advantage by encrusting access to position through legislating cultural specifications of rights; or lower-status groups pursue class objectives in status-group garb in those situations in which working-class terminology has been preempted by middle-status groups. In all these instances, a renewed emphasis on status-group distinctions helps advance the interests of specific segments of the world-economy. When all is said and done, status-group formation, like state activity, serves as a mode of constraining and constricting both market and class forces in favor of some group or groups who would otherwise lose out in the medium run.

Finally, we should not ignore the fact that the capitalist world-economy has organized its bourgeoisie and its proletariat into income-pooling households of particular kinds. Despite the vaunted individualism of capitalist ideology, the members of classes and status groups are not individuals but these households. And these households too are creations of the world-economy in that the boundaries of the real economic units are the result of pressures upon kin and coresidential groups to expand and contract their boundaries in specific ways in order to produce the necessary labor-force at appropriate wage-levels in specific zones of the world-economy.

In particular, the so-called "extended family," which is often in fact not a purely kin group, is a created structure that optimizes the furnishing of part-life-time wage labor at below the minimum wage, by attaching such laborers to income pools fed by surplus value created by other members of the pool (or by themselves at other moments of time) to the benefit of the employer of the wage laborer. Conversely, the so-called "nuclear family," which may also be not a purely kin group, optimizes the creation of monetary demand, by reducing the proportion of consumption goods not obtained via the market. The contradictory pressures of the world economic forces create a cyclical pattern wherein household structures vary according to economic zone and to expansion-stagnation phases.

The periodic cyclical stagnations of the world-economy have been essentially resolved by a combination of three mechanisms. First, some producers have utilized advances in technology to create new and/or more efficiently produced commodities which would enable them to successfully challenge other producers who had previously dominated particular commodity markets. This provided new, so-called "dynamic" sectors of production. Secondly some segment of households which were previously "extended" and receiving only a small proportion of their life-time income from wage sources have found themselves dislocated, expropriated, or otherwise forced to become "proletarianized," that is, to become more fully dependent on the wage labor market for life-time household income. For those that survived the process of forced transition, this in fact has meant an increase in money income (if not at all necessarily an increase in real income). Thirdly, new direct producers have been incorporated into the world-economy, on its former "frontiers." These newly incorporated direct producers formed new pools of low-cost, part-time wage labor; they were of course also productive of new supplies of raw materials for world industrial production necessary for the new expansion phase of the world-economy.

Of the three mechanisms—technological change, proletarianization, incorporation—most writers refer to the first one as the most linear of all processes in the capitalist world-economy. In fact, the contrary is true, if one analyzes technology not as an autonomous process but in terms of its impact on the structure of the world-system as such. More than other mechanisms, the impact of technological change is the most cyclical and the least secular. Let me explain. What technological advance has accomplished above all is that it has regularly permitted one set of entrepreneurs to compete successfully with other entrepreneurs. This has had two consequences. The specific nature of the high-profit, high-wage commodities has repeatedly changed in favor of those in which the new technology has been invested. Particular commodities that were previously in this category have shifted downward in terms of overall profitability, and consequently in the attached wage structures. Secondly, the physical locus of the most "dynamic" sectors has also regularly changed—both within state boundaries and across state boundaries.

Hence, both the list of commodities involved in unequal exchange and the geographical location of core and peripheral economic processes have constantly shifted over time, without however transforming to any significant extent the world-wide structure of unequal exchange based on the axial division of labor. At first, wheat was exchanged against textiles; later textiles against steel; today steel against computers *and wheat*. Once Venice was a core zone and England semi-peripheral; later Britain was core and the northern states of the United States semiperipheral; still later the United States was a core zone and Russia or Japan or many others semiperipheral; and tomorrow? In this way, technological advance has created a situation of constant geopolitical restructuring of the world-system, but has it *directly* undermined its viability? I suspect not.

It is rather in the two other cyclical processes—the reorganization of house-hold structures and the incorporation of new zones into the world-economy—that I find the working-out of the essential contradictions of capitalism as a world-system, contradictions that are bringing about the contemporary systemic crisis in which we are living. Each time a segment of world household structures has been reorganized, the relative number of what we may call proletarianized households has grown as a proportion of the world labor force. Each time new zones have been incorporated into the ongoing production processes of the world-economy, the proportion of global land and population that is a real part of the operations of the capitalist world-economy has risen. But proportions inevitably have a limit. Their maximum is 100%. Ergo, these two mechanisms—proletarianization and incorporation—which serve to permit the regular renewal of expansion of the cap-italist system also are its own undoing. Their success renders less likely their future utility as renewal mechanisms. This is one way to translate operationally the concept of the contradictions of capitalism as a system. These secular trends result from the basic contradiction of combining the anarchy of production with the social determination of demand.

The growing economic constraints produced by the secular trends precisely generate at the political level the rise of the antisystemic movements who are acting as the crucial social intermediary of global systemic change. These anti-systemic movements have taken two generic forms since their emergence as im-portant forces in the nineteenth century. These two forms are the social movement and the national movement.

While rural worker and urban poor discontent have been a constant of the system, and have periodically resulted in jacqueries and food riots, it was not until the relative concentration of proletarianized households in the core countries of the capitalist world-economy in the nineteenth century that the social movement emerged in the form of labor unions, socialist parties, and other kinds of workers' organizations. The social movement emphasized the growth of the polarity bourgeois/proletarian and called for a basic transformation of the system of inequality. *Ad interim,* however, the particular movements organized to obtain partial or total state power to advance the interests of the proletariat. The *Communist Manifesto,* for example, clearly exemplified this dual approach: on the one hand, the call for fundamental restructuring; on the other, the pursuit of *ad interim* objectives en route.

While the search of weaker states for greater strength has also been a constant of the system, it was not until the reorganization of the interstate system that followed on the Napoleonic wars and the subsequent Holy Alliance—with the increasing drive for culturo-linguistic as well as religious homogenization—that the peripheral and semiperipheral zones of Europe took up the banner of nationalism. The national movement emphasized the growth of the polarity core/periphery and called for a basic transformation of the system of inequality. *Ad interim,* however, the particular movements called for a somewhat stronger national entity (shifting from being an assimilated zone to being an autonomous zone, from a colony to an independent entity, from a weak state to a stronger state). 1848 was the Springtime of the Nations as well as the year of the *Communist Manifesto.*

Both the social movement and the national movement have had breathtaking careers since 1848. The social movement has spread from core to semiperiphery and periphery. Today there is hardly a corner of the earth that has not been touched by such movements. Conversely, the national movement, having swept the semiperipheral and peripheral zones of the world, has now reached the core, with the new explosion of political ethnicities in Western Europe and North America.

In the process of the social movement spreading from core to periphery and the national movement from periphery to core, the two movements have in fact rallied each other in two ways. First, they began their history in the nineteenth century as ideological rivals. But today, there is scarcely a social movement which is not nationalist, and there are few national movements which are not socialist. The confluence is not perfect, but it is great enough to argue that a social movement that is not nationalist and a national movement that is not socialist is suspect as a fraud to large segments of the world population. Secondly, and even more fundamentally, the two world movements have followed a similar trajectory. The initial ambiguity—the search for equality on the one hand via fundamental transformation and on the other hand via *ad interim* solutions—has revealed itself as being not an ideological option subject to the change of individual or even collective will but as being the result of a structural pressure of the world-system as such.

The capitalist world-economy is precisely a system in which the basic economic processes are located in a zone far larger than that of any political authority, and hence these processes are not *totally* responsive to the set of political decisions of any state—even to those of a hegemonic state; *a fortiori* to those of a state in the periphery. Yet, the mechanisms that are most easily manipulable are these same state structures of limited power, especially precisely for antisystemic movements. Hence both the social movement and the national movement almost necessarily have to seek medium-run gain via the control (or partial control) of a given state structure. Yet to achieve this control, they strengthen these state structures, which in turn reinforces the operations of the interstate system and thereby of capitalism as a world-system. The dilemma is not a minor one.

I should like to view this dilemma too as acting itself out historically in the form of a cycle and a trend. The cycle is very simple and has been widely observed, most often cynically. It is described in the following manner: The movements have emerged and asserted revolutionary objectives. They have succeeded and achieved power. Once in power, they have effectuated changes, which were however less fundamental than previously sought. Having compromised, they have thereupon been accused of "betrayal" or "revisionism." Finally, Thermidor has been imposed either by counterrevolution or by inner transformation of the movement. The adepts, such as survive, have been disillusioned, and for the next generation what had been revolutionary slogans became ideological and oppressive myths.

Is this simple cycle what has in fact historically happened? Only partially. It is true of course that the Social-Democrats of nineteenth-century Europe seemed to have followed such a path when they came to (partial) power in the early twentieth century. It is true that one could make a similar case for the various Communist parties, most prominently first that of the U.S.S.R., then that of China. And it is true that every anticolonial revolution has seemed to fit the pattern.

But are we telling the whole story? I think not. There has been first of all the impact of the initial mobilizations. Many particular movements were total failures, but those that succeeded did so because, over a period of time, they were able to create organizational structures of some kind that were able to mobilize their prospective audiences in three concentric circles of intensity: an inner circle of dedicated cadres, a middle circle of activists, an outer circle of sympathizers. The very process of creating these structures over time itself had major consequences for the political structure of the world-system, and first of all in terms of the political *rapport de forces* in the particular state in question.

For such movements to come to even partial power in given states represented a *conquest* of power, whose very achievement resulted not only in the specific reforms subsequently enacted but in shifts in collective mentality which were themselves continuing political facts. Nor are the "reforms" themselves to be lightly condemned. They may have seemed paltry next to the aspirations, but is this the appropriate measure? Should they not be seen rather as a mechanism, and a rather successful one, of slowing down the galloping polarization of the world-system as a whole, thereby preserving the material possibilities for anti-systemic activity? From this point of view, such "revolutions" have in fact been neither "false" nor without effect. But they have to be sure been "recuperated" in the sense that the achievement of state power has forced the movements sooner or later to conform to the norms of the interstate system and, more than they wished, to the law of value underlying the operations of the capitalist world-economy.

The fact is that, however radical the reforms that have been initiated by any such movement, these movements have discovered that no single state structure can enact a transformation either of the interstate system or of the world-economy, and there is no simple way in which the rest of the world can be wished away. A given state led by a given movement can attempt to "secede" from the politico-economic structures of the world-system. The Cambodia of Pol Pot has perhaps been the most dramatic example of such an attempt. But quite apart from whether this was at all a desirable tactic in terms of the results, it has become quite clear that it was not a feasible tactic, since the rest of the world-system was simply not prepared to let it happen—even for such a minor segment of the globe as Cambodia. Everywhere, the reality has been that the fact that a movement proclaims the unlinking of a state's productive processes from the integrated world-economy has never in fact accomplished the unlinking. It may have accomplished temporary withdrawal which, by strengthening internal production and political structures, enabled the state to improve its relative position in the world-economy. In this case, it has merely meant that, de facto, particular relative prices were imposed in fact on particular exchanges, such that—within the proclaiming state—some gained and some lost. But this is of course how the capitalist world-economy has always operated. Hence the logic of Mao Tse-tung's position on the continuing class struggle within states undergoing "socialist construction" is impeccable. The only issue is what to do about it.

Here we must return to the movements. The arrival at partial or total state power has meant always partial compromise. And in many cases, it has eventually meant total compromise, given movements having ceased altogether to be anti-systemic movements. But we must view these movements historically. After the phase of mobilization came the phase of compromised power for an antisystemic movement. Compromised power was not at all the same as total abandonment of antisystemic objectives. It was this fact of a phase of compromised power that created the spiral effect, and turned what seemed to be a cyclical phenomenon into a secular trend of the world-system as a whole.

The achievement of power by given movements has had two important consequences beyond whatever reforms such movements were able to enact in particular states. These movements have, first of all, quite clearly served as inspiration and reinforcement for analogous neighboring movements, particularly at the very beginning of their phase of achieved power. One cannot imagine the political history of the twentieth century without taking into account this spread effect. Mobilization has bred mobilization, and the success of one has been the source of hope of the other. Secondly, the success of the one has created more political space for the other. Each time an antisystemic movement has come to partial or total power, it has altered the balance of power of the interstate system such that there has been more space for other antisystemic movements.

But if the coming to power of one movement gave both inspiration and space to others, should not the inevitable compromising in which movements in power engage have reduced both the inspiration and the space? Not at all, because the operations of the world-system are more complex than such a simple symmetry would suggest. The movements that have come later have not only been inspired; they have been instructed. They have learned that part of the world political struggle for them involves putting pressure on these movements in power, these movements who have compromised but whose internal strength depends in part on a maintenance of the continuity of ideology. The mobilizing movements have not hesitated to play upon this social reality and force these movements in power to "compromise" less than they would otherwise be inclined—extracting the space and even the inspiration they need from now reluctant partners.

Hence what seems like a simple upward-downward cycle of the political effect of antisystemic movements turns out on closer inspection to have been an upward-downward-upward thrust. If one cumulates such threefold thrusts across the world-economy and over time, one can quickly see that there would be, has been, a secular upward trend of the overall strength of antisystemic movements in the capitalist world-economy over the past 150 years, despite all the "recuperative" political mechanisms which exist within the system. This is why the prophets of doom are to be found not among antisystemic forces but rather among the defenders of the system. The importance of antisystemic movements is not in the reforms they achieve or in the regimes they establish. Many of these regimes are in fact parodies of their stated objectives. The importance of these movements is in terms of the changes they bring about in the world-system as a whole. They transform not primarily the economics but rather the politics of the capitalist world-economy. Joined with the more narrowly socioeconomic trends previously described, this secular increase of the strength of antisystemic movements undermines the viability of the world-system.

In the light of this analysis, let us look at the contemporary conjuncture. Worldwide, the downward turning point of the post-Second World War Kondratieff cycle was either 1967 or 1973. (It is hard to tell at such short historical distance.) If we take it at 1967, which for the moment seems to me the more plausible, we can see the accentuation of worldwide class struggle that occurred in the very early moments of this B-phase. The shakiness of world markets for the products of core countries (these products being essentially too numerous for world demand) was signaled by the end of the period where the U.S. dollar anchored the world monetary system. All over the world, in various forms, there came to be a squeeze on total social expenditure—reflected both in household spending patterns and in state and other collective "fiscal crises."

Social unrest was immediately visible. In China, there was an acute internal struggle known as the Cultural Revolution. In Czechoslovakia, a social movement within the Communist party led to the Dubček reforms, implying changes not only internally but in the whole relationship of eastern European states to the U.S.S.R. In the West, 1968–1969 was the high point of the antiauthoritarian uprisings by students and workers, which was combined in many countries with an intensification of the political demands of the ethno-nationalist movements within them, as well as a new "nationalism" in the social movement (e.g., Eurocommunism).

The weakening of the financial solvency and political stability of the core states meant that the United States could no longer offer efficacious opposition in Southeast Asia, or Portugal in Africa, to the persistent struggle of the nationalist movements in these areas. In 1973, the oil-producing states took advantage of the changed world economic situation to increase dramatically the price of their crucial product. The result of course was not only to reallocate distribution of world surplus, but to constrain world production. (It is for this reason that political opposition to OPEC in the core states has only been nominal.) In a number of peripheral areas, the world economic squeeze was felt in the form of acute famines, which cleared some rural zones of producers, forcing many of the survivors into a marginalized existence in urban areas. (This involves also a reduction in world agricultural production, to the benefit of the mechanized agrobusiness of certain core areas.)

This first outburst of political struggles in the current world stagnation seems to have been contained—reversal of the Cultural Revolution, the Soviet invasion of Czechoslovakia, the suppression of the various so-called radical movements in North America and Western Europe, the "socialist wars" in Southeast Asia, the pressures for " internal settlements" in southern Africa, the recycling of OPEC money. On the other hand, this B-phase is far from over. Relatively high unemployment rates, further fiscal crises, even perhaps an acute price crash are still to be expected throughout the 1980s.

One state in which further acute social unrest is likely is the United States which must go through a widespread income readjustment as a result of its relative decline vis-à-vis other core states. Acute class struggles that will center on the demands of Blacks and Spanish-speakers will probably result. This will be especially true if the United States increases its support to white settler interests in southern Africa. We may perhaps see similar acute struggles within the U.S.S.R. The need to keep the lid on wages in order for Soviet products to compete in the world market may lead to migrations of Moslem/Asian populations to industrial zones and thus to accentuated de facto ethno-class stratification, which may in turn force class tensions there, as in the United States, to take on ethnic forms in the tight years ahead.

In the many semiperipheral zones in the world, the internal pressures created by the desire of each to profit from the conjuncture will lead many of them to have internal explosions. Wherever they occur, the explosion will of course eliminate that particular state from the race the semiperipheral states are conducting with each other, and in which there can only be one or two who gain substantially. Iran was the first such explosion, but explosions similar in effect if not in form are not to be ruled out in such diverse zones as China, India, South Africa, Brazil.

Finally, we are witnessing a major reshuffling in the interstate system. The reconciliation of China with the United States, and even more significantly with Japan, may be matched in the years to come by equally spectacular revisions of alliances. For example, I would not rule out a German-Soviet entente.

Finally, I expect the world-economy to take a marked upturn once again in the 1990s. The result of the turmoil and the realignments will in fact have been, as before, to increase world demand to a point high enough to stimulate a further expansion of world production. There will probably be significant cost-saving technological inventions, possibly centering on the provision of energy. There will be significant further "proletarianization," deriving on the one hand from the impact of the displacement of "traditional" industrial enterprises to semiperipheral areas and on the other hand from the reinforcement of wage-income-dependent household structures in the core. This further change in core household structures will be effectuated by a vast increase in the tertiary sector, the continuing entry of women into the full-time wage-labor force, and the redefinition of social roles sought by the various antisexist and antiracist movements. We shall probably enter the year 2000 to the renewed hosannas of the rosy-eyed optimists of capitalist apologetics. This will be particularly true if we survive the critical 1980s without any serious interstate war.

And yet underneath, both the structural contradictions of capitalism and the antisystemic movements it has bred in such force will continue to eat away at the entrails of the system. The details are impossible to predict, but the broad pattern is clear. We are living in the historic world transition from capitalism to socialism. It will undoubtedly take a good 100–150 years yet to complete it, and of course the outcome is not inevitable. The system may yet see several periods of remission. There may come again moments where capitalism will seem to be in bloom. But in a comparison of life-cycles of social systems, the modern world-system can be seen to be in a late phase. What will replace it will surely not be utopia. But with the end of this peculiar moral aberration that capitalism has represented, a system in which the benefits for some have been matched by a greater exploitation for the many than in all the prior social systems, the slow construction of a relatively free and relatively egalitarian world may at last begin. This it seems to me, and only this, is likely to permit each individual and the species to realize their potential.

26

The United States and the World Economy

C. FRED BERGSTEN

In this article, C. Fred Bergsten explores the heavy dependence of the United States on the world economy. Bergsten notes that the ability of the United States to direct the course of international economic transactions has eroded—an erosion complicated by the dual and incompatible needs of the United States to support liberal trade practices and to protect its domestic market from foreign imports. Bergsten is director of the Institute for International Economics. Recent among his numerous publications is *The World Economy in the 1980s* (1980).

The United States has become heavily dependent on the world economy. Over 20 percent of U.S. industrial output is now exported. One of every six U.S. manufacturing jobs produces for export. Two of every five acres of U.S. farmland produce for export. Almost one-third of the profits of American corporations derive from their exports and foreign investments. Imports meet more than one-half of U.S. demand for 24 of the 42 most important industrial raw materials.

All these ratios have been rising rapidly. The share of trade in the U.S. gross national product (GNP) has doubled during the past decade. The cost of oil imports alone rose from $3 billion in 1970 to over $80 billion today. For many of the largest U.S. companies, more than 50 percent of profits and/or sales are international.

Changes in the international economic position of the United States are now so important that they can dominate even our huge domestic economy over particular periods of time. The weakening of the dollar in the foreign exchange market during 1977–78 probably added at least two percentage points to U.S. inflation, pushing it into double-digit territory. From 1978 to 1980, 60 percent of the modest increase in U.S. GNP resulted from a dramatic improvement in the trade balance—with exports growing at twice the rate of world trade for all three years. Conversely, a sharp decline in the trade balance more than accounted for the decline in GNP during the second and third quarters of 1981, the starting point of our latest recession.

International economic developments have thus become critically important to the United States. Jobs, growth, price stability, and economic security in the United States all depend substantially on events abroad and the interaction with

Reprinted from C. Fred Bergsten, "The United States and the World Economy," *The Annals of the American Academy of Political and Social Science* 460 (March 1982), pp. 11–20, © 1982 by the American Academy of Political and Social Science, with permission.

them of internal economic developments and policies. The United States is no longer a self-contained continent, but rather an integral component of a deeply interdependent global economy.

DECLINING INFLUENCE

At the same time that the United States has become more dependent on the world economy, its ability to dictate the course of international economic events has declined markedly. This is primarily because of the reduction in the relative weight of the United States in the global economic system, as other countries have risen to positions of greater influence: Europe from the late 1950s; Japan from the 1960s; the Organization of Petroleum Exporting Countries (OPEC) from the early 1970s; and a number of other advanced developing countries (ADCs) more recently.

As late as 1950, the United States accounted for 50 percent of the gross world product; that ratio has now been cut in half. The level of U.S. trade is only about 12 percent of the world total and one-third that of the European Communities (ECs), which function jointly on trade matters; U.S. exports of manufactured goods are less than those of Germany alone. The international monetary reserves of the United States are less than seven percent of the global aggregate; they are considerably less than those of Saudi Arabia and Germany, and about the same as Japan or France—with gold valued at the old official price, per official U.S. practice. Even the international role of the dollar, though still far greater than that of any other national currency, has declined considerably since 1977.

The decline in the objective power of the United States in world economic affairs has been accelerated by the politics of international economic management. The European countries have banded together in the EC on trade matters and increasingly in the monetary and other areas as well. The oil-producing countries formed OPEC. The developing countries organized the Group of Seventy-Seven and related groups to enhance their policy impact. The United States must now deal with several relatively cohesive groups of nations, which can translate their underlying economic strength into effective bargaining positions and political salience.

Another key development that has contributed to the erosion of U.S. international economic power, and in fact that of all national governments, is the emergence of major nonnational actors in the international economic process. The multinational corporations now account for perhaps $2 trillion of offshore production. Private international banking arrangements and the so-called Eurocurrency markets recycle the bulk of the OPEC surpluses, now running at about $100 billion annually. So private entities, often operating outside the direct control of any government, have reduced sovereign power in general and that of the United States in particular.

To be sure, a widely perceived weakening of the performance of the U.S. economy itself has contributed to the decline of U.S. power. The dollar remained under pressure throughout the 1960s, and underwent three major depreciations in the 1970s. U.S. inflation has exceeded that of several other major countries for extended periods of time. U.S. productivity growth has fallen sharply. Until the late 1970s, there was a steady erosion of the U.S. share of world export markets.

International security developments have also contributed to the erosion of U.S. economic hegemony. During the cold war period of the 1950s and early 1960s, the alliance structures of both East and West were extremely rigid and hierarchical. The constantly perceived threat of open hostilities rendered alliance members largely subservient to the alliance leaders. Even the European countries and Japan, let alone developing countries, were severely constrained from challenging U.S. economic—as well as military or political—preferences. The onset of detente, however, presaged an erosion of other countries' security dependence on the United States and thus enabled them to challenge its dominance more frequently in all aspects of international relations.

THE SCISSORS EFFECT

Hence the United States has simultaneously become much more dependent on the world economy and much less able to dictate the course of international economic events. The global economic environment is more critical for the United States and is less susceptible to its influence. One result is that international economic policy must be assigned a much higher priority in U.S. policymaking. Another is that the formulation and implementation of that policy must be conducted with much greater skill and subtlety than ever before.

In this situation, however, the United States is not without major assets. It is still the largest single country in virtually every category of economic activity. Its markets for goods and capital, in particular, give it enormous leverage. The dollar still finances well over one-half of world trade. The continued role of the United States as the leader of the non-Communist world's security system still carries major, if often intangible, implications for international economic negotiations. So the United States can still promote its international economic intents effectively, if less bluntly than in the past.

At least two new domestic trends, however, make it more difficult for the United States to carry out an effective international economic policy in support of these interests. One is budgetary; in an era of declining federal support for traditional domestic programs such as food stamps and educational loans, it is extremely difficult—if not impossible—to obtain increased, or even undiminished, appropriations for key international programs. Concessional foreign assistance, including U.S. contributions to the multilateral lending agencies such as the International Development Association, are hit the hardest. But funding adequate to meet international needs also becomes difficult for such programs as the Export-Import Bank, which finances a significant portion of U.S. exports; the World Bank, which is of great importance to the economic health of the developing countries, the fastest growing markets in the world for U.S. exports; trade adjustment assistance, which cushions the impact of increased imports on U.S. firms and workers and thus supports a liberal trade policy; and even U.S. participation in the International Monetary Fund, which manages the international monetary system and is thus central to the functioning of the entire global economy.

A second, more subtle, constraint derives from the sharply greater impact of international events on the U.S. economy. As already described, these developments increase the opportunities for U.S. exports, investment earnings, and the like and thus have major positive effects on our economy. At the same time, however, the increased U.S. exposure to import competition and export competition in third markets can often produce pressures of two types: protectionist pressures to restrict trade and reduce at least the pace of the increased U.S. exposure to international economic events, and neomercantilist pressures to subsidize exports and otherwise promote U.S. sales and earnings abroad. In a world where governments of most countries intervene significantly in international economic events, there will be constant pressures on the United States to do so as well.

Indeed, the current situation presents a major challenge to the fundamental premise on which U.S. international economic policy has traditionally been based. Historically, the United States has done abroad as it has done at home—regarding taxation, antitrust, the extension of government credit, morality issues—human rights, bribery, and antiboycott—and many others. Most other countries, however, have operated on a fundamentally different premise: do abroad what is necessary to get the business. The inevitable clash between the two philosophies has often left the United States at a competitive disadvantage.

From a U.S. perspective, the costs involved were largely acceptable during periods when external events had little impact on the domestic economy and/or when U.S. power was sufficient to force others to accept its standards. Neither condition holds today, however, as indicated at the outset. Hence questions must be raised as to whether the United States must change its traditional premises in the light of such dramatic changes in circumstance. To put it another way, should the United States "fight 'em or join 'em" in heavier government intervention in international economic affairs and in competing abroad through methods more akin to those pursued by others?

SPECIFIC ISSUES

These questions cannot be answered in the abstract, so we now turn to some of the most important issues facing the United States in the international economic area. The problems described next cover a wide spectrum: international monetary concerns, trade, energy, and investment. We ignore a host of specific issues that are also quite important, especially regarding specific trade issues—such as steel and automobile imports, and export supports such as credit and tax incentives. The issues considered here, however, do indicate both the breadth of the international economic area and the depth of its impact on the United States.

In the monetary area, at least two major problems exist. One centers on the recycling process, through which the financial surpluses accumulated by the OPEC countries are channeled—largely via the private financial markets—to the countries, both industrialized and developing, whose balance of payments deficits mirror those OPEC surpluses. The issue is whether this process will continue to function smoothly, and whether the costs involved in it are sustainable over the longer run.

The oil exporters, primarily those in the Persian Gulf, have now acquired about $400 billion of liquid reserves, and the total is rising steadily. On the other side of the equation, the external debt of the developing countries is approaching $500 billion. About 75 percent of these flows have been intermediated through the private banking system, sharply raising its liabilities to a small number of depositors and raising its claims on a somewhat larger, though still fairly concentrated, number of debtors.

Two primary questions arise. First, what is the probability that one or more debtor countries will become unable or unwilling to maintain their repayment obligations within the bounds of politically tolerable economic growth at home, even on negotiated rescheduling terms? Poland has already come very close to formal default. There was widespread concern in late 1980 about Brazil, the largest debtor of all. A radical change of government could lead to debt repudiation, as was initially threatened by the revolutionary regime in Iran. Theoretically, debtor countries will lose much of their incentive to keep repaying—in order to keep new loans coming in—when their repayments begin to exceed the level of their inflows.

The second recycling issue is whether the several tiers of possible defensive mechanisms would hold in the face of any such threat to the maintenance of normal credit and repayment arrangements, and what the consequences would be if they did not. Would an individual bank be able to recoup lost deposits via the interbank market? Would access to central banks obviate any risk of a liquidity crisis caused by nonrepayment? Could the solvency of a major bank be jeopardized, or does the combination of prudent bank management plus tighter regulatory supervision preclude such a risk? Who would accept responsibility for the foreign branches and subsidiaries of multinational banking groups, or for truly international banks with no single parent? Could central banks cope effectively with the exchange market consequences of a major default? Are debt rescheduling arrangements sufficiently flexible to ward off more drastic action? Could failure at any of these stages cause important problems for any national banking system, or the international monetary mechanism as a whole?

Simply to ask these questions is to suggest their potentially enormous implications for both the United States and the world economy as a whole. The collapses of Herstatt and Franklin National in 1974 represented an extremely mild version of what could happen in this area. Nothing less than the stability of both the international system and our domestic banking arrangements could be challenged by a series of defaults by major debtor countries and a failure of the existing institutional mechanisms to respond adequately. Any such financial disruption could of course create enormous difficulties for the economy, at both the domestic and the international levels.

A second key monetary question also affects trade and investment flows very directly: Is the system of flexible exchange rates working satisfactorily to achieve effective international adjustment of the inevitable differences that emerge almost continuously among the different national economies? In principle, exchange-rate flexibility promotes adjustment by altering the price relationships among national currencies, the most important single international factor in determining the allocation of trade flows and the locus of production in many industries. A country with high inflation restores its competitive position through a decline in the international value of its currency, at the cost of less command over goods and services produced abroad, while a country with low inflation reaps real income benefits from a steady strengthening of its currency and thus greater command over foreign products.

The problem, in practice, is that the exchange-rate mechanism seems to be substantially overshooting the levels that would maintain equilibrium relationships among the major countries. In one sense, this is not surprising; all markets, such as those for equities and commodities, tend to overshoot frequently. But the exchange rate is the most important single price for most countries, and a disequilibrium exchange rate can have major costs—by eroding competitiveness and destroying jobs in the case of overvaluation, by driving up the price of imports and accelerating inflation in the case of undervaluation.

The current situation of the United States is a dramatic case in point. From late 1978 through mid-1981, the dollar rose by a trade-weighted average of 25 percent against the other major currencies and by 50 percent against the German mark and some other Western European currencies. During this period, however, U.S. prices rose as fast as those in the other countries, on average, and rose faster than in Germany and Japan. Hence the international price competitiveness of the U.S. economy eroded substantially; major firms reported declines of 40-50 percent in their export orders, and imports rose rapidly in several key industries, such as steel. As a result, the United States experienced sizable costs in terms of lost production and employment. In fact, the resultant decline in the U.S. trade balance more than explained the entire drop in U.S. GNP during the second and third quarters of 1981, pushing the economy into its latest recession.

Moreover, an overvalued dollar and the subsequently inevitable deterioration of the U.S. trade balance have major implications for U.S. trade policy. The postwar record strongly suggests that such a situation is much more likely than high unemployment, or any other single variable, to trigger domestic pressures to restrict imports into the United States. Thus a whole range of problems, ranging well beyond the monetary issues per se, are raised by this overshooting of the exchange rates.

Several aspects of U.S. policy itself were of major importance in pushing the dollar into such an overvalued state in 1981 and cannot be blamed on international monetary arrangements. Nevertheless, the system of flexible exchange rates has translated these and other recent developments into disequilibria as great as existed during the last years of the Bretton Woods system of fixed exchange rates in the late 1960s and early 1970s, which then collapsed. Serious questions must therefore be raised about the stability and efficiency of the current regime, and whether it can be modified to promote better U.S. and global objectives.

Turning to trade more directly, a pair of interrelated major questions arises. On the one hand, even ignoring the temporary—it is hoped—exchange-rate problem just described, is there a steady drift—both in the United States and else-where—away from the open trading system that has heretofore characterized the postwar period? If so, should that trend be arrested? If so, how can that be done?

On the other hand, there is the closely related question of how the industrial-ized countries can adjust to the steadily increasing competitive pressure from the ADCs—Korea, Taiwan, Brazil, and in fact much of East Asia and Latin America. These countries' share of world industrial production and exports has been rising significantly for a decade or so, and seems likely to continue to do so for at least the remainder of this century. In the contemporary world of modest economic growth and huge OPEC-induced payments deficits, however, such intensified competition is bound to generate significant counterpressures from industries and workers whose livelihoods are threatened as a result. For public policy, the issue is further complicated by the fact that these same countries are the fastest-growing markets for our exports and, in many cases, the largest debtors to our banks; hence restrictions on their trade would also cost us business and would add to the financial risks previously outlined.

Nevertheless, this structural trend toward growing ADC competition adds to the pressures for a retreat from the relatively open trading system of the past 30 years. Such a retreat would add to world inflationary pressures, slow growth fur-ther, and have potentially severe consequences for the development prospects of the poorer countries. Important foreign policy problems would emerge as well, straining relations among the industrialized countries as well as along the North-South axis.

The international dimensions of the energy issue are, of course, enormous. In addition to its financial consequences, already discussed, the United States and—to a much greater extent—the other industrial countries and most developing countries remain heavily dependent on oil imports to fuel their economies and to protect their national security. Short of war, the world has never before experi-enced an economic shock of the magnitude of the 16-fold rise in the price of oil over the past 10 years. The adjustment to that shock has severely retarded eco-nomic growth in virtually all oil-importing countries.

At present, however, two major developments may offer some hope for sta-bilizing the situation for the medium-term future at least. On the one hand, there is substantial downward pressure on the world oil price due to slow economic growth in the oil-importing countries, to the continued impact of higher prices and national conservation policies in reducing energy demand per unit of output, and to increasing production in a number of non-OPEC countries. This implies that the continued anxiety of consumers, born of the two momentous shocks of the 1970s, may be increasingly matched by anxiety on the part of at least some key producers. Such a "balance of uncertainty" is a necessary ingredient for mean-ingful producer-consumer cooperation on any international commodity issue, and may now be developing in the energy area.

At the same time, OPEC has finally reunified its pricing structure and begun—out of necessity, given the market situation just described—to seek to coordinate the production policies of its members. Meanwhile, the industrialized oil-import-ing countries continue to seek to organize their efforts through the International

Energy Agency. There may thus be an institutional basis for pursuing an effort to achieve long-term stability of the energy situation within the more balanced market situation that has now come to exist.

In principle, some such arrangement would clearly be desirable. Energy is the most important single sector of the international economy, yet it is one of only two major areas—investment is the other—where there exists no global institutional arrangement to support stability and multilateral cooperation. The search for such arrangements must certainly rank high on the agenda for international economic policy, with central economic and security concerns of the United States and of most other countries at stake in the process.

A final area for consideration is international investment. The value of offshore production by multinational firms, of which close to one-half is American, is now approaching $2 trillion—roughly the level of international trade itself. Yet here, as in energy, there exist no international rules of the game or institutional arrangements that seek to maintain an environment conducive to optimizing global economic welfare and harmony among nations.

Partly as a result, problems in the investment area are growing rapidly and threatening to disrupt the relatively open environment that has prevailed during most of the postwar period. The primary cause is the increasing sophistication with which host countries, in pursuit of their own economic and social objectives, are now manipulating the firms. Far from concerns about "sovereignty at bay" or the "global reach" of the multinationals, host-country governments in fact employ a blend of policies to harness the companies: investment incentives, to lure the firms inside their borders in the first place; and performance requirements, such as minimum export quotas and local content rules, to assure the desired impact of the resultant production. The companies benefit sufficiently from the incentives to accept the requirements, and a working alliance is forged between the two.

In some senses, such developments are acceptable or even desirable. Incentives may be needed to channel foreign investment to some, particularly poorer, countries; some home countries themselves in fact offer incentives to their firms to invest in such locations. Performance requirements, in some cases, may simply counter oligopoly conditions in an industry—as when the parent company forbids a particular subsidiary to export at all. Furthermore, although both practices are widespread, there is a substantial difference in degree as to their prevalence across industries, where the high-technology firms can best resist and the natural-resource firms are most susceptible, and across countries in terms of their ability to achieve their purposes.

The growing problem, however, is that the increased use of these devices tends to shift a rising share of world production—taking with it jobs, technology, capital, exports, and the like—from home to host countries without clear economic justification. The inevitable reactions in home countries may take the form of emulating what is being done elsewhere, direct retaliation, or both. In either case, one can readily envisage a scenario of "investment wars" not unlike the "trade wars" of an earlier period.

In the United States, the complexity of the impact of these developments on outward foreign investment is compounded by the growing level of inward direct investment as foreign firms increasingly exploit the attractiveness of virtually the only unregulated market in the world. This two-way flow, which is eminently healthy in both economic and political terms, highlights the disparities between U.S. nonintervention in the process and the active engagement of others, notably, neighbors Canada and Mexico. The search for a "General Agreement on Tariffs and Trade (GATT) for investment," or some sort of international arrangement to limit the intervention of governments in this process, is thus a major policy concern for the 1980s.

CONCLUSION

Each of the preceding issues illustrates the central point suggested at the outset of this article: the critically important, and rapidly growing, role of international economic events on the domestic economy of the United States. Each also illustrates the complexities involved for the United States in pursuing its policy objectives.

International economic policy will thus be among the most vital, and at the same time the most difficult, responsibilities of U.S. officials in the years to come. . . .

27

International Trade Policy in the 1980s: Prospects and Problems

RAYMOND VERNON

In this essay, Raymond Vernon evaluates the potential for change in the international trade regime, with special attention to the critical role played by the United States. His comparative analysis of the probable trade policies of the major economic powers is pessimistic about the possibility of restoring support for open markets and reducing barriers to trade. Vernon is Clarence Dillon Professor of International Affairs in the department of government at Harvard University. His extensive writings on international economic relations include *Sovereignty at Bay* (1971).

The past thirty years have seen a remarkable reduction in the trade barriers that once existed among the world's principal trading states. The tariff rates of the advanced industrialized countries, for instance, have been cut to about one-quarter of their previous levels. The import licensing schemes that were in effect in all but a few of these countries in the early 1950s have long since been dismantled. More recently, those countries have made a promising start on nontariff trade barriers in the form of a series of negotiated codes. In recent years, too, even a few of the developing countries have taken steps to reduce their import restrictions.

Yet, despite these remarkable developments, there is everywhere a sense of foreboding. There is a widespread expectation that the world is in for a period of protectionism as states respond to a reduction in their growth rates by closing their borders to foreign goods. So far, to be sure, the prospect does not seem to have materialized (at least not in any acute form), but the expectation persists. The need to understand the basis of that expectation, as well as the probability of its realization, is also strong.

U.S. POLICY

The policies of the United States are particularly critical in assessing the future. In decades past, this country served as the principal energizer and organizer of projects for the reduction of trade barriers, as in the formation of the General

Reprinted from Raymond Vernon, "International Trade Policy in the 1980s: Prospects and Problems," *International Studies Quarterly* 26 (December 1982), pp. 483–510. Reprinted by permission of the publisher. Some footnotes have been deleted; others have been renumbered to appear in consecutive order. Bibliographical references not included in the excerpt have been deleted.

Agreement on Tariffs and Trade (GATT) in 1948, and in the succession, in the following decades, of giant tariff negotiation sessions. . . .

The United States has been committed to open competitive markets and nondiscrimination among its trading partners. Its trade policies over the past thirty or forty years, when viewed as a whole, seem remarkably stable. At the same time, when viewed in detail, those policies have appeared riddled with inconsistency and contradiction. . . .

U.S. actions in the field of international trade . . . have been the product of two distinct processes. One of these has been based on the bedrock preferences of the country; it has created a succession of international negotiations that have served as action-forcing events to produce a fairly continuous decline in import restrictions over the past three or four decades. The other has been a succession of unilateral acts on the part of the United States, restrictive in nature, which have represented the sporadic successes of special interest groups in achieving their objectives through one or another of the various avenues for political action that the system characteristically provides. The 1980s could generate either pattern of behavior. . . .

The Unites States came out of the [Second World War] with a profoundly changed perception of its place in the world economy. The conduct of the war had required the marshaling of various elite groups into the government service—business executives, labor leaders, and academics, among others. . . . This group shared one common perception: They assumed that if an effective international economic system were to be restored in the world, the United States would have to take the lead in fashioning it. . . .

The widespread assumption that the United States was the indispensable leader in any movement to reestablish an effective international economic order was, of course, wholly consistent with the economic facts of the immediate postwar period. If the United States presented any problem for the international economic system at the time, it was the threat that its overbearing dynamism might prevent the achievement of an equilibrium in world trade (Kindleberger, 1950). Out of these attitudes and perceptions came the leadership of the United States in sponsoring an International Trade Organization and its offshoot, the General Agreement on Tariffs and Trade (GATT). These same forces were instrumental in generating five large-scale tariff negotiations between 1947 and 1956 that drastically reduced the world's tariff levels. . . .

The commitment of the U.S. body politic to the concept of open markets and nondiscriminatory treatment in world trade survived the 1950s, but the support for that commitment meanwhile underwent some critical changes. By 1962, the leadership role of the United States was beginning to be questioned. The American dollar was no longer quite so impregnable. The country's exports still exceeded its imports, but the trend had grown uncertain. At the same time, high levels of foreign aid and foreign military expenditures were adding to the burden of the dollar.

More important was a decline in the relative importance of the U.S. economy. Between 1950 and 1960, U.S. exports dropped from about 50% of the exports of all advanced industrialized countries to less than 25% of the group's total. Further, the European Economic Community (EEC) was emerging as an economic unit equal to the United States in aggregate output and in exports. The possibility that European and Japanese producers might reduce the technological lead of American industry began to be realized. . . .

. . . The brief period of U.S. hegemony over Europe, it was evident, was rapidly coming to a close.

After 1962, the continuation of trade liberalization policies by the United States, therefore, could no longer be attributed quite so strongly to the imperialist perceptions of its leadership and its related concern for the global system as a whole. Instead, continuation rested to a considerable extent on a growing perception in some quarters of the United States that a return to protectionism in world markets would harm their immediate interests. In 1950, U.S. merchandise exports had amounted to only 6.2% of the final sales of U.S. goods. By 1960, the figure had risen to 7.6%. In later years, it was destined to grow to much higher figures—for instance, to 9.1% in 1970 and 19.1% in 1980. Part of the rise, to be sure, could be attributed to the growing export of agricultural products. But with such products excluded from the export totals, the relative importance of the remaining exports still rose rapidly between 1950 and 1980, growing from 4.5% to 12.7% of final sales of U.S. goods.

Most significant of all, perhaps, was the rapid multinationalization of U.S. firms. In 1957, the foreign manufacturing affiliates of firms in the United States had recorded sales amounting to less than 6% of all the country's shipments of manufactured products; but by 1965, the figure was above 9% and in 1976, would rise to 18%.[1]

Of course, firms that develop a multinational structure cannot automatically be counted on to throw their weight against protectionism. Some multinationals prefer open markets for their international operations, especially those that have adopted a strategy of scattering the production of their required components and intermediate products across a number of different countries. Other multinationals, however, rely on high import duties or on other import restrictions to protect their foreign subsidiaries; this is particularly the case, for instance, for subsidiaries that are producing for markets in developing countries. Still, the industries that have been most consistently protectionist in outlook, notably textiles and steel, have been dominated by national, not multinational, firms. Moreover, there is some direct evidence that multinational enterprises as a group tend to give greater support to a regime of open world markets than would national firms similarly situated (Hedlund and Otterbeck, 1977: 155–162; Perlmutter, forthcoming).

Nevertheless, despite the growth of multinational enterprises in the U.S. economy, individual industries in increasing number have pushed for some form of special protection for their products. The number of escape clause investigations completed by the U.S. Tariff Commission (now the U.S. International Trade Commission) reflected those increased pressures, rising from two or three per year in the 1960s to twelve in 1976 and thirteen in 1977.[2] The quickened tempo of protectionist efforts appeared also in an increase in petitions to secure counter-

---

[1] Calculated from various published studies of the U.S. Department of Commerce. For evidence of the link between multinational structure and international transactions see Vernon (1971: 16).

[2] From annual reports of the U.S. Tariff Commission and the U.S. International Trade Commission.

vailing, or antidumping, duties on imports, as well as in the increased number of special trade bills before the Congress.

Despite the growing obstacles, the general direction of U.S. trade policy has been maintained. However, with each renewal of the legislation that authorized the president to alter U.S. tariffs as a result of international negotiations, a succession of ingenious provisions has been added that increases the capacity of interest groups to secure special consideration (Balassa, 1978: 409-436). So far, to be sure, these provisions have not been very effectively exploited. . . .

Still, domestic industries continue to look for ways to increase their ability to threaten or block foreign imports; indeed, with the enactment of the 1979 Trade Act, so many devices of this sort have been created as to raise serious questions about whether the main lines of United States trade policy can still prevail.

THE POLICIES OF OTHER COUNTRIES

The decline in the leadership position of the United States has left a vacuum. Neither the New International Economic Order of the developing countries, nor the network of trade agreements spawned by the Europeans, nor the growing strength of the Japanese offers much promise of filling the leadership role.

The Developing Countries

Throughout the past three decades, the developing countries of the world have resisted the blueprint for an open world trading system epitomized by the GATT. Instead, the developing countries have been groping for some alternative, so far not very well specified, that would curb the political and economic power of the advanced countries and more fully reflect their own interests.

Nevertheless, because the United States and other advanced industrialized countries saw themselves at first as shaping a world trading system, they were eager to include the developing countries in any global trade organization, even if the commitments of those countries, for the time being, were trivial or nonexistent. Various exemptive clauses in the GATT, when applied in combination, effectively relieved developing countries of any significant trade-liberalizing obligations. In practice, even when a developing country applied discriminatory or restrictive trade measures in obvious violation of the GATT's provisions, no serious efforts were made to enforce the agreement. At the same time, having opted out of their GATT obligations, the developing countries had no real influence over the pace and direction of negotiations in the GATT. Nevertheless, as the advanced industrialized countries progressively reduced their tariffs and other import barriers in successive rounds of negotiations, the nondiscrimination clauses of the GATT served to ensure that the liberalization measures were extended to the developing countries as well (Balassa, 1980).

The developing countries made numerous efforts to generate trade commitments among themselves that would lie alongside the network of GATT commitments. But none of these projects made much of a mark (Business International

Corp., 1977; Hazlewood, 1979; Abangwu, 1975; and Ramasaran, 1978). The only trade-liberalizing undertakings sponsored by the developing countries that were successful in any substantial degree were projects that extracted special trade concessions from the advanced industrialized countries (Spero, 1981: 197-216). One such undertaking was the so-called Generalized System of Preferences sponsored by the UN Conference on Trade and Development (UNCTAD).

Still, as industries in the developing countries have grown and matured, some of these countries have shifted their trade policies toward the encouragement of exports. As part of that shift, the early propensity of most of these countries to restrict imports without limit has given way to a more eclectic approach. At the same time, however, the attachment of developing countries to the GATT continues to be tenuous and equivocal, more akin to the role of observers than of committed participants. Accordingly, when developing countries have taken steps toward trade liberalization, these have been the result mainly of their unilateral decisions, not of commitments under the GATT. For the present, there is nothing in the offing to suggest that the developing countries will prove willing to accept new obligations in world trade.

The Europeans

Europe's relationship to the GATT system has always been more ambivalent and reserved than that of the United States. The success of the first few tariff negotiations under the GATT, undertaken soon after the end of World War II, said very little about the real attitudes of Europeans toward trade liberalization. These early negotiations were being conducted at a time when the United States was helping to finance the recovery of Western Europe, and when import licensing, rather than tariffs, was the means by which most European countries controlled imports.

By the early 1960s, however, the European Economic Community had come into existence. Its six original members were in the process of creating the customs union and common agricultural policy that were the core of the arrangement. From that time forward, two things became clear. The European Community would pursue a trade policy that was much more eclectic than that of the United States, highly liberal in some sectors and highly protectionist in others. And in that context, despite the participation of its members in the GATT, it would feel free to deviate from the principle of nondiscrimination to any extent that its interests required.

As far as most European states were concerned, they had little choice during the postwar period but to maintain open borders with respect to a considerable part of their trade. Under the benign influence of the European Recovery Program following World War II, these countries had managed to develop extensive economic ties with one another, reflected in extraordinarily high levels of foreign trade. The eclectic quality in their trade policies, however, stemmed from the fact that their interest in maintaining open borders was based heavily on parochial or regional factors rather than on global considerations.

According to conventional wisdom, the survival of the Community rests mainly on a critical bargain between Germany and France (Curtis, 1965: 23, 194-200; Marjolin, 1981: 36-54). One element in that bargain is an undertaking to create a highly protected area for agricultural products, in deference to France's aspirations to displace North America from the grain markets of Europe; the other is an undertaking to follow a liberal trade policy with respect to manufactured goods, in accordance with Germany's desire to push its products in world markets. That basic element of the original bargain seems to have persisted through the decades of the 1960s and 1970s.

Another set of forces has been operating to keep the European community on a liberal trade course, namely, the intimate linkages of its members to various sets of countries outside the community. . . .

The upshot has been that consistency of principle has been much less important in the trade policies of the Community and its member states than in the policies of the United States. . . .

These differences in style between the United States and Europe reflect differences in their patterns of governance as well as differences in their perceptions of role. During much of the postwar period, the United States saw itself as a leader of the noncommunist world and saw important advantages in retaining its leadership; Europe, on the other hand, viewed its interests in terms that were much more particularistic and more narrowly defined, and, accordingly, much less concerned with the problems of building and strengthening a global system. This European view persisted into the 1980s, dampening any expectation that Europe would take the lead in any new global initiatives in the trade field.

The Japanese

Japan's heavy stake in the maintenance of open competitive markets, coupled with the country's growing economic strength, raises the possibility that Japan might assume a leadership role in protecting what is left of the principles of the GATT. But on closer examination that possibility does not appear very strong. Japan's internal political process inhibits it from taking strong initiatives in the foreign trade field. Even if those internal difficulties could be overcome, other countries would find it hard to accept Japan's leadership in any major initiative involving international trade.

Japan began the postwar era with special economic ties to the United States, a relationship first created during the six years of military occupation immediately following World War II. During the occupation, Japan faithfully played the role of the subjugated state and ward, adopting without protest a series of radical reforms imposed by the conquering state, including redistribution of the land, creation of a labor movement, renunciation of the right to rearm, and "democratization" of political processes.[3] Meanwhile, the relatively benign U.S. attitude toward Japan, which rested at first on complex cultural factors, was strengthened by the advent of the Cold War and by hostilities in Korea.

---

[3] The strong cultural factors that allowed the United States and Japan comfortably to assume their respective roles are nicely summarized in Destler (1976: 114-119).

When the occupation ended, the United States continued to act as Japan's guardian and mentor for a little while longer. By 1952, the United States was sponsoring Japan's membership in various international bodies, notably including the GATT, the International Monetary Fund, and the World Bank. And in 1964, the United States promoted Japan's membership in the Organization for Economic Cooperation and Development (OECD).

Although Japan was admitted into various global organizations in the two decades following the end of the war, a number of countries continued to look on Japan's performance in world markets with special misgivings. In the 1950s, European countries were slow to end their discrimination against Japan's goods, despite Japan's adherence to the GATT (Hanabusa, 1979: 2-3). The U.S. government's pressure on Japan to restrict "voluntarily" the export of some of its textile items is well known.

Japan's early experiences, therefore, were hardly calculated to inspire confidence in the GATT system. . . .

By the 1970s, Japan had obviously succeeded, for the time being, in overcoming the obstacles that lay in its way for securing needed raw materials and penetrating foreign markets. Accordingly, the state was gradually becoming convinced that it must support an open competitive market system.[4] Moving at a rate that often seemed maddeningly glacial in the eyes of other governments, Japan formally suspended most of the licensing requirements and other special restrictions that had previously encumbered the importation of foreign goods and the investment of foreign capital.[5] By 1982, the government was engaged in an ambitious process of dredging out some especially resistant practices, such as the use of elaborate inspection schemes, meticulous classification systems, and forbidding health and safety requirements that were serving to block the importation of foreign products (Anonymous, 1982: 6, 10-13).

A considerable debate continues over whether a system of informal restrictions still exists in Japan that tends to reduce the liberalizing effect of the official measures. But there is no doubt that a major change in Japanese practices had in fact occurred. The movement was all the more significant because Japan continued to be the target of discriminatory trade measures, as embodied in "voluntary export agreements" or in overt import quotas on the part of several important countries, including the United States and various European states.

The oil crisis of the past decade has threatened Japan's support for an open trading system but has not reversed it. In light of Japan's perceptions of its special vulnerability with respect to raw materials, its reaction to the oil crisis was bound to be strong and singleminded. . . . In an effort to diversify its sources of supply, Japan has been diligently attempting to expand its trade with China and the USSR. Moreover, it has been developing government-to-government arrangements in raw materials with Mexico, Iraq, and other countries. Such arrangements implicitly encourage preferential dealings between the parties concerned.

---

[4] Numerous studies exist on trade disputes between Japan and other countries, analyzing such disputes from the differing viewpoints of the various disputants. In addition to Tasca (1980) and Hanabusa (1979), see, for instance, Weil and Glick (1979) and U.S. Controller-General (1980).

[5] The relatively unrestrictive character of Japan's formal system of trade restrictions is suggested by data in Cao (1980: 97).

As in the case of a number of other countries, including France and Germany, Japan thus finds itself in a position of trying to live within two quite distinctive systems of trade. So far, fortunately, the inherent contradiction between the GATT-sponsored system and the system of government-conducted trade has not reached very significant proportions. If it does, the market economies may have to consider jointly how the two systems of trade can be reconciled; otherwise, what is left of the principle of nondiscrimination in trade will be imperiled.

In any future negotiations over the direction of the world trading system, Japan is likely to support the continuation of an open trading regime, fearing that any other regime would make it the target for more flagrant discriminatory measures. But Japan's concern with the vulnerability of its economy will inhibit it from making strong commitments in any direction and hence limit its capacity to play a leadership role. At the same time, however, Japan is likely to be less passive and acquiescent in multilateral negotiations than it has been in the past (MITI, 1980). In recent years, some Japanese commentators have questioned whether Japan should continue to follow a "tradesman's policy," that is to say, a policy of accommodating to all economic pressures without responding to any principles other than survival itself (Amaya, 1980; Sase, 1980; Nukazawa, 1980). These discussions may eventually bring Japan's role in the shaping of a new international regime more into line with her economic power.[6] But for the time being, they will not overcome Japan's deep-seated sense of caution when approaching issues of international trade.

FUTURE POLICIES

Starting Assumptions

Robert Marjolin, looking back on thirty years of the evolution of Europe's Common Market, said sadly, "The time for grand designs is over, at least for a while, until circumstances change and the existing order is shaken again" (1980: 77). His observation could apply to trade policies on a global scale as well. For the present, one can only hope to protect and conserve some of the extraordinary openness in international markets that has been achieved in the past three decades. Even to achieve this modest objective, however, will be difficult.

One change that may support the objective is the great increase in the importance of foreign trade and foreign investment interests in the economies of most countries. But it will be imperiled by many countries' increased determination to reduce the impact that the increasing openness of their economies has generated and to limit the rate of adjustment demanded of their industries. In addition, there has been a change in the nature of existing barriers to trade, from relatively transparent tariffs and quotas to less visible subsidies, administrative practices, and

---

[6] Illustrations of the new quality of Japanese participation in global economic issues are found, for instance, in numerous documents of the Tripartite Commission, and in the Wise Men's Report . . . [Japan-U.S. Economic Relations Group, 1981], where Japanese contributors have been increasingly explicit in their stated preferences. See also Hosomi (1978) and Tanaka (1980).

procurement policies. Finally, there has been a weakening in the concept of un-conditional most-favored-nation treatment as the norm for international trade. I assume these trends will not be reversed in the 1980s; therefore, they should be viewed as constraints in the formulation of policy for this period.

I make one other critical assumption based on the history outlined earlier. Both the United States and Japan require the action-forcing discipline of a prospective international negotiation in order to maintain an open trading system. Such pres-sures seem needed to focus the diverse elements in each country on a general policy that transcends narrower group interests. Otherwise, the internal political process in the United States will generate restrictive measures in response to those narrower interests, while the internal process of Japan will produce near immobil-ity.

With these starting assumptions, policymakers in the United States and else-where will have to address a series of linked questions: If the content of the global trade agreements of the past no longer suffices, what is the direction in which new agreements should move? If the most-favored-nation principle is losing its force, what is to take its place? And, if the United States is no longer in a position to assert its leadership in the formulation of global trade proposals, what kind of process can be envisaged that will produce such proposals?

Scope and Substance

The direction in which global trade agreements are heading became fairly obvious in the last giant negotiating session of the GATT, the so-called Multilateral Trade Negotiations (MTN) that were completed in Geneva in 1979. With tariffs reduced to tolerable levels, the ascendant problems in the 1970s included the prolif-eration of public subsidies in all their obvious and subtle forms: governments' demands on selected enterprises (usually foreign owned) in their territories that the enterprises should limit their imports and increase their exports, the procure-ment practices of state entities, and the unilateral application of quotas by import-ing countries.

These problems have proven much more varied, much less transparent, and much more deeply embedded in domestic programs than the fixing of tariff rates.[7] Accordingly, both the formulation and the enforcement of agreements in these fields are much more difficult than agreements to freeze or reduce existing tariff rates. They demand more trust among the contracting parties and a better fact-finding, conciliating, and adjudicating apparatus than the 100-member GATT can be expected to provide. Not surprisingly, therefore, it has proved impossible to reach agreement on some of these subjects in the GATT context.

Even with appropriate sponsorship, one can anticipate only a limited number of countries reaching agreement on these difficult subjects. The complexity of these areas is illustrated by the supplemental negotiations that became necessary to implement the 1979 Geneva agreement on governmental procurement. Al-

---

[7] For a description of export credit programs illustrative of these points, see The Economist (1981: 78).

though the agreement was limited, in the first instance, to a small number of countries, Japan and the United States nevertheless found it necessary to elaborate the agreement in much greater detail for its application between them (Yoshimine, 1981: 75-77). Until many other governments widen the circle by joining in—a most unlikely development—the government procurement code establishes preferential rights within a small group of countries.

The question raised by this illustration is whether or not we have reached a point at which selective discrimination may generate more open international markets than the rule of nondiscrimination could produce. In some circumstances, as the rules of the GATT recognize, this may well be the case. GATT's tolerance of customs unions, free trade areas, and similar preferential arrangements acknowledge this point; although arrangements of this sort sometimes have the effect of diverting trade from efficient outside sources to less efficient inside sources, they are justified since they reduce the level of protection among the participants themselves.

Understandably, however, some members of the GATT, including Japan and the United States, have resisted the possibility of a more uninhibited recognition of the right of GATT members to apply discriminatory trade measures, especially when these are clearly restrictive.[8] The reasons for American and Japanese hesitation are fairly evident. Even though the United States has violated the rule of nondiscrimination from time to time, it has had trouble envisaging a coherent world trading system without such a rule. From the Japanese viewpoint, the danger of legitimizing restrictive preferences and discrimination in international trade lies in Japan's risk of being the first victim. But both these arguments have been losing their force as preferential arrangements have been proliferating under other names. In a world of second-best choices, international agreements based on the principle of nondiscrimination may no longer be possible on any significant scale; the question then is whether or not international agreements with preferential provisions can be made to produce results that are superior to inaction.

The possibilities for using preferential agreements as action-forcing occasions for trade liberalization are illustrated by the various liberalizing codes that were adopted in the 1979 GATT agreements. But the possibilities are illustrated also by the 1981 imbroglio over Japanese exports of automobiles to the United States. Predictably, the preference of the United States has been to cheat on the GATT's rule of nondiscrimination by forcing Japan to restrain "voluntarily" its exports to the U.S. market. If, instead, the U.S. restrictions on Japanese cars were forthrightly acknowledged, there would also be the possibility of acknowledging Japan's right to preferential compensation. For instance, one could envisage a bilateral agreement between the United States and Japan that imposed a temporary restraint on U.S. imports of Japanese cars but that was offset by a temporary preference in the importation of other Japanese manufactured products.

The introduction of extensive preferential provisions in bilateral and multilateral trade agreements among the advanced industrialized countries in the GATT

---

[8] The question has been debated repeatedly in the GATT and was the center of an inconclusive negotiation in the recently completed MTN agreements. See Merciai (1981).

would force a reexamination of various other aspects of the GATT structure, including the smoldering issue of "graduation." This is the question of whether or not the "newly industrializing countries" of the GATT, such as Brazil, India, and Korea, should now be obliged to assume some of the agreement's obligations in addition to being entitled to its rights (Frank, 1979). It is worth noting that if any group of GATT countries enters into preferential agreements that the developing countries choose not to join, the developing countries will find themselves disadvantaged in the first instance. At the same time, however, if preferential agreements were more widely legitimated, Brazil might still hope for access to the markets of the advanced countries through bilateral agreements. For example, if Brazil failed to adhere to a GATT code, the United States might still exchange equivalent rights and obligations with Brazil in a bilateral agreement.

There should be no illusions about the pattern of trade relations that would emerge from agreements of the sort just described. At times, preferential measures that are liberalizing in nature can be made to endure for a while: Witness the twenty-year record of the European Economic Community. But by and large, preferential measures of trade liberalization that are based on agreements among a limited group of countries risk being restrictive. All that can be said in favor of such measures is that they are superior to the alternative, when the alternative appears to be unilateral measures of restriction. Eventually, a return to a global approach in the development of international trade relations will be indispensable. Meanwhile, the problem is to stem or reverse the threat that inertia, accompanied by piecemeal measures of restriction imposed unilaterally by individual countries, may sharply reduce the openness of international markets. . . .

REFERENCES

ABANGWU, G. C. (1975) "Systems approach to regional integration." J. of Common Market Studies 13, 1/2: 116-133.

AMAYA, N. (1980) "Grumblings of a shop-clerk of Japan, a tradesman's country." Translated from Bungei Shunju (March).

——— (1978) "Japan's system of distribution under scrutiny." World Economy 1 (April): 219-326.

Anonymous (1982) "Government making all-out effort to remove non-tariff barriers." J. of Japanese Trade and Industry 1, 2.

BALASSA, B. (1980) "The Tokyo Round and the developing countries." World Bank Staff Working Paper No. 370. Washington, DC: World Bank.

Business International Corp. (1977) Operating in Latin America's Integrating Markets: ANCOM, CACM, CARICOM, LAFTA. New York: BIC.

CAO, A. D. (1980) "Non-tariff barriers to U.S. manufactured exports." Columbia J. of World Business 15 (Summer): 93-102.

CURTIS, M. (1965) Western European Integration. New York: Harper & Row.

DESTLER, I. M. [ed.] (1976) Managing an Alliance. Washington, DC: Brookings Institution.

The Economist (1981) "The high cost of export credit." (February 14): 78.

EPSTEIN, L. D. (1967) Political Parties in Western Democracies. New York: Praeger.

FRANK, I. (1979) "The 'graduation' issue for IDCs." J. of World Trade Law 13 [July-August]: 289-302.

HANABUSA, M. (1979) Trade Problems Between Japan and Western Europe. New York: Praeger.

HAZLEWOOD, A. (1979) "The end of East African community: what are the lessons for regional integration schemes?" Common Market Studies 18 September: 40-58.

HEDLUND, G. and OTTERBECK, L. (1977) The Multinational Corporation, the Nation-State and Trade Unions: A European Perspective. Kent, OH: Kent Univ. Press.

HOSOMI, T. (1978) "Japan's changing perception of her role in the world economy." World Economy 1 January: 135-148.

Japan-U.S. Economic Relations Group (1981) Report ("The Wise Men's Report"). Tokyo and Washington, D.C. (January).

KINDLEBERGER, C. P. (1950) The Dollar Shortage. New York: John Wiley.

MARJOLIN, R. (1981) "Europe in search of its identity," in Council Papers on International Affairs. New York: Council on Foreign Relations.

MERCIAI, P. (1981) "Safeguard measures in GATT." J. of World Trade Law 15 (January-February): 41-66.

Ministry of International Trade and Industry [MITI] (1978) "The vision of MITI policies in the 1980s." March 18. MITI Information Service.

NUKAZAWA, K. (1980) "Whither Japan's foreign economic policy? Straws in the wind." World Economy 1 (February): 467-480.

PERLMUTTER, H. V. (forthcoming) "The multinational firm and the future." Annals of the American Academy of Political and Social Sciences.

RAMSARAN, R. (1978) "CARICOM: The Integration Process in Crisis." J. of World Trade Law 12, 3 [May-June]: 208-217.

SASE, M. (1980) "Rejection of 'tradesman's nation' argument." Translated from Bungei Shunju (April).

SMITH, T. (1981) The Pattern of Imperialism. New York: Cambridge Univ. Press.

SPERO, J. (1981) The Politics of International Economic Relations. New York: St. Martin's.

TANAKA, N. (1980) "The increasingly complex Japan-U.S. relationship." Econ. Eye 1 (September): 23-25.

TASCA, D. [ed.] (1980) U.S.-Japanese Economic Relations: Cooperation, Competition, and Confrontation. Elmsford, N.Y.: Pergamon.

U.S. Comptroller General (1980) "U.S.-Japan trade: issues and problems." Report of the Comptroller General of the United States, September 20. Washington, DC: General Accounting Office.

VERNON, R. (1971) Sovereignty at Bay. New York: Basic Books.

WEIL, F. A. and N. D. GLICK (1979) "Japan—is the market open?" Law and Policy in Int. Business 11.3: 894-902.

YOSHIMINE, T. (1981) "Settlement finally reached for NTT procurement issue." Business Japan 3: 75-77.

YOSHINO, M. (1975) Marketing in Japan: A Management Guide. New York: Praeger.

28

Regime Analysis in the Study of International Political Economy: A Critique

SUSAN STRANGE

Regime analysis has gained popularity among students of international political economy as a way of accounting for the rules and principles subscribed to by parties linked in interdependent relationships. In this article, Susan Strange reviews the assumptions inherent in what she suspects may be an intellectual fad and provides a challenging critique that both illuminates the phenomena regime analysis seeks to explain and questions the cogency of its logic. Strange is Montague Burton Professor of International Relations at the London School of Economics and Political Science. Her publications include *The International Politics of Surplus Capacity* (edited with Roger Tooze, 1981).

. . . [T]his . . . article . . . queries whether the concept of regime is really useful to students of international political economy or world politics; and whether it may not even be actually negative in its influence, obfuscating and confusing instead of clarifying and illuminating, and distorting by concealing bias instead of revealing and removing it.

It challenges the validity and usefulness of the regime concept on five separate counts. . . . The five counts . . . are first, that the study of regimes is, for the most part a fad, one of those shifts of fashion not too difficult to explain as a temporary reaction to events in the real world but in itself making little in the way of a long-term contribution to knowledge. Second, it is imprecise and woolly. Third, it is value-biased, as dangerous as loaded dice. Fourth, it distorts by over-emphasizing the static and underemphasizing the dynamic element of change in world politics. And fifth, it is narrowminded, rooted in a state-centric paradigm that limits vision of a wider reality. . . .

FIVE CRITICISMS OF THE CONCEPT OF REGIMES
A Passing Fad?

. . . [C]oncern with regimes may be a passing fad. A European cannot help making the point that concern with regime formation and breakdown is very much an American academic fashion. . . .

Reprinted from Susan Strange, *"Cave! Hic Dragones:* A Critique of Regime Analysis," *International Organization* 36 (Spring 1982), pp. 479–496, by permission of The MIT Press, Cambridge, Massachusetts. © 1982 by the World Peace Foundation and the Massachusetts Institute of Technology. Footnotes and bibliographical references have been deleted.

. . . [T]he fashion for regime analysis may not simply be . . . a rehash of old academic debates under a new and jazzier name—a sort of intellectual mutton dressed up as lamb—so that the pushy new professors of the 1980s can have the same old arguments as their elders but can flatter themselves that they are breaking new ground by using a new jargon. It is also an intellectual reaction to the objective reality. . . .

Imprecision

. . . "Regime" is yet one more woolly concept that is a fertile source of discussion simply because people mean different things when they use it. . . .

Experience with the use of . . . woolly words warns us that where they do not actually mislead and misrepresent, they often serve to confuse and disorient us. "Integration" is one example of an over-used word loosely taken to imply all sorts of other developments such as convergence as well as the susceptibility of "integrated" economies to common trends and pressures. . . .

. . . "[R]egime" is used to mean many different things. In the Keohane and Nye formulation ("networks of rules, norms and procedures that regularize behavior and control its effects") it is taken to mean something quite narrow—explicit or implicit internationally agreed arrangements, usually executed with the help of an international organization—even though Keohane himself distinguishes between regimes and specific agreements. Whereas other formulations emphasize "decision-making procedures around which actors' expectations converge," the concept of regime can be so broadened as to mean almost any fairly stable distribution of the power to influence outcomes. In Keohane and Nye's formulation, the subsequent questions amount to little more than the old chestnut, "Can international institutions change state behavior?" The second definition reformulates all the old questions about power and the exercise of power in the international system. So, if—despite a rather significant effort by realist and pluralist authors to reach agreement—there is no fundamental consensus about the answer to [the] question, "What is a regime?", obviously there is not going to be much useful or substantial convergence of conclusions about the answers to the other questions concerning their making and unmaking.

Why, one might ask, has there been such concerted effort to stretch the elasticity of meaning to such extremes? I can only suppose that scholars, who by calling, interest, and experience are themselves "internationalist" in aspiration, are (perhaps unconsciously) performing a kind of symbolic ritual against the disruption of the international order, and do so just because they are also, by virtue of their profession, more aware than most of the order's tenuousness.

Value Bias

The third point to be wary of is that the term regime is value-loaded; it implies certain things that ought not to be taken for granted. As has often happened before in the study of international relations, this comes of trying to apply a term derived from the observation of national politics to international or to world politics.

Let us begin with semantics. The word "regime" is French, and it has two common meanings. In everyday language it means a diet, an ordered, purposive plan of eating, exercising, and living. A regime is usually imposed on the patient by some medical or other authority with the aim of achieving better health. A regime must be recognizably the same when undertaken by different individuals, at different times, and in different places. It must also be practised over an extended period of time; to eat no pastry one day but to gorge the next is not to follow a regime. Nor does one follow a regime if one eats pastry when in Paris but not in Marseilles. Those who keep to a diet for a day or two and abandon it are hardly judged to be under the discipline of a regime.

Based on the same broad principles of regularity, discipline, authority, and purpose, the second meaning is political: the government of a society by an individual, a dynasty, party or group that wields effective power over the rest of society. Regime in this sense is more often used pejoratively than with approval— the "ancien regime," the "Franco regime," the "Stalin regime," but seldom the "Truman" or "Kennedy" regime, or the "Attlee" or "Macmillan," the "Mackenzie King" or the "Menzies" regime. The word is more often used of forms of government that are inherently authoritarian, capricious, and even unjust. Regimes need be neither benign nor consistent. It may be (as in the case of Idi Amin, "Papa Doc" Duvalier or Jean-Bedel Bokassa) that the power of the regime is neither benign nor just. But at least in a given regime, everyone knows and understands where power resides and whose interest is served by it; and thus, whence to expect either preferment or punishment, imprisonment or other kinds of trouble. In short, government, rulership, and authority are the essence of the word, not consensus, nor justice, nor efficiency in administration.

What could be more different from the unstable, kaleidoscopic pattern of international arrangements between states? The title (if not all of the content) of Hedley Bull's book, *The Anarchical Society,* well describes the general state of the international system. Within that system, as Bull and others have observed, it is true that there is more order, regularity of behavior, and general observance of custom and convention than the pure realist expecting the unremitting violence of the jungle might suppose. But by and large the world Bull and other writers describe is characterized in all its main outlines not by discipline and authority, but by the absence of government, by the precariousness of peace and order, by the dispersion not the concentration of authority, by the weakness of law, and by the large number of unsolved problems and unresolved conflicts over what should be done, how it should be done, and who should do it.

Above all, a single, recognized locus of power over time is the one attribute that the international system so conspicuously lacks.

All those international arrangements dignified by the label regime are only too easily upset when either the balance of bargaining power or the perception of national interest (or both together) change among those states who negotiate them. In general, moreover, all the areas in which regimes in a national context exercise the central attributes of political discipline are precisely those in which corresponding international arrangements that might conceivably be dignified with the title are conspicuous by their absence. There is no world army to maintain order. There is no authority to decide how much economic production shall be public and how much shall be privately owned and managed. We have no world central bank to regulate the creation of credit and access to it, nor a world court to act as the ultimate arbiter of legal disputes that also have political consequences. There is nothing resembling a world tax system to decide who should pay for public goods—whenever the slightest hint of any of these is breathed in diplomatic circles, state governments have all their defenses at the ready to reject even the most modest encroachment on what they regard as their national prerogatives.

The analogy with national governments implied by the use of the word regime, therefore, is inherently false. It consequently holds a highly distorting mirror to reality.

Not only does using this word regime distort reality by implying an exaggerated measure of predictability and order in the system as it is, it is also value-loaded in that it takes for granted that what everyone wants is more and better regimes, that greater order and managed interdependence should be the collective goal. . . .

Too Static a View

The fourth [problem] to beware is that the notion of a regime—for the semantic reasons indicated earlier—tends to exaggerate the static quality of arrangements for managing the international system and introducing some confidence in the future of anarchy, some order out of uncertainty. In sum, it produces stills, not movies. And the reality, surely, is highly dynamic, as can fairly easily be demonstrated by reference to each of the three main areas for regimes considered in this collection [i.e., the special issue of *International Organization* in which this and other essays on regime analysis were first published]: security, trade, and money.

For the last thirty-five years, the international security regime (if it can be so called) . . . has not been derived from Chapter VII of the U.N. Charter, which remains as unchanged as it is irrelevant. It has rested on the balance of power between the superpowers. In order to maintain that balance, each has engaged in a continuing and escalating accumulation of weapons and has found it necessary periodically to assert its dominance in particular frontier areas—Hungary, Czechoslovakia, and Afghanistan for the one and South Korea, Guatemala, Vietnam, and El Salvador for the other. Each has also had to be prepared when necessary (but, fortunately, less frequently) to engage in direct confrontation with the other. And no one was ever able to predict with any certainty when such escalation in armaments, such interventions or confrontations were going to be thought necessary to preserve the balance, nor what the outcome would be. Attempts to "quick-freeze" even parts of an essentially fluid relationship have been singularly unsuccessful and unconvincing, as witness the fate of the SALT agreements, the European Security Conference, and the Non-Proliferation Treaty.

In monetary matters, facile generalizations about "the Bretton Woods regime" abound—but they bear little resemblance to the reality. It is easily forgotten that the original Articles of Agreement were never fully implemented, that there was a long "transition period" in which most of the proposed arrangements were put on ice, and that hardly a year went by in the entire postwar period when some substantial change was not made (tacitly or explicitly) in the way the rules were applied and in the way the system functioned. Consider the major changes: barring the West European countries from access to the Fund; providing them with a multilateral payments system through the European Payments Union; arranging a concerted launch into currency convertibility; reopening the major international commodity and capital markets; finding ways to support the pound sterling. All these and subsequent decisions were taken by national governments, and especially by the U.S. government, in response to their changing perceptions of national interest or else in deference to volatile market forces that they either could not or would not control.

Arrangements governing international trade have been just as changeable and rather less uniform. Different principles and rules governed trade between market economies and the socialist or centrally planned economies, while various forms of preferential market access were practiced between European countries and their former colonies and much the same results were achieved between the United States and Canada or Latin America through direct investment. Among the European countries, first in the OEEC [Organization for European Economic Cooperation] and then in EFTA [European Free Trade Area] and the EC [European Community], preferential systems within the system were not only tolerated but encouraged. The tariff reductions negotiated through the GATT were only one part of a complex governing structure of arrangements, international and national, and even these (as all the historians of commercial diplomacy have shown) were subject to constant revision, reinterpretation, and renegotiation.

The trade "regime" was thus neither constant nor continuous over time, either between partners or between sectors. The weakness of the arrangements as a system for maintaining order and defining norms seems to me strikingly illustrated by the total absence of continuity or order in the important matter of the competitive use of export credit—often government guaranteed and subsidized—in order to increase market shares. No one system of rules has governed how much finance on what terms and for how long can be obtained for an international exchange, and attempts to make collective agreements to standardize terms (notably through the Berne Union) have repeatedly broken down.

The changeable nature of all these international arrangements behind the blank institutional facade often results from the impact of the two very important factors that regime analysis seems to me ill-suited to cope with: technology and markets. Both are apt to bring important changes in the distribution of costs and benefits, risks and opportunities to national economies and other groups, and therefore to cause national governments to change their minds about which rules or norms of behavior should be reinforced and observed and which should be disregarded and changed. . . .

Since the chain of cause and effect so often originates in technology and markets, passing through national policy decisions to emerge as negotiating postures in multilateral discussions, it follows that attention to the end result—an international arrangement of some sort—is apt to overlook most of the determining factors on which agreement may, in brief, rest.

The search for common factors and for general rules (or even axioms), which is of the essence of regime analysis, is therefore bound to be long, exhausting, and probably disappointing. . . .

State-centeredness

The final but by no means least important warning is that attention to these regime questions leaves the study of international political economy far too constrained by the self-imposed limits of the state-centered paradigm. It asks, what are the prevailing arrangements discussed and observed among governments, thus implying that the important and significant political issues are those with which governments are concerned. Nationally, this is fairly near the truth. Democratic governments have to respond to whatever issues voters feel are important if they wish to survive, and even the most authoritarian governments cannot in the long run remain indifferent to deep discontents or divisions of opinion in the societies they rule. But internationally, this is not so. The matters on which governments, through international organizations, negotiate and make arrangements are not necessarily the issues that even they regard as most important, still less the issues that the mass of individuals regards as crucial. Attention to regimes therefore accords to governments far too much of the right to define the agenda of academic study and directs the attention of scholars mainly to those issues that government officials find significant and important. . . .

Thus regime analysis risks overvaluing the positive and undervaluing the negative aspects of international cooperation. It encourages academics to practice a kind of analytical *chiaroscuro* that leaves in shadow all the aspects of the international economy where no regimes exist and where each state elects to go its own way, while highlighting the areas of agreement where some norms and customs are generally acknowledged. It consequently gives the false impression (always argued by the neofunctionalists) that international regimes are indeed slowly advancing against the forces of disorder and anarchy. Now it is only too easy, as we all know, to be misled by the proliferation of international associations and organizations, by the multiplication of declarations and documents, into concluding that there is indeed increasing positive action. The reality is that there are more areas and issues of nonagreement and controversy than there are areas of agreement. . . .

Moreover, many of the so-called regimes over which the international organizations preside turn out under closer examination to be agreements to disagree. The IMF amendments to the Articles of Agreement, for example, which legitimized the resort to managed floating exchange rates, are no more than a recognition of states' determination to decide for themselves what strategy and tactics to follow in the light of market conditions. To call this a "regime" is to pervert the language. So it is to call the various "voluntary" export restrictive arrangements bilaterally negotiated with Japan by other parties to the GATT "a multilateral regime." Since 1978 the Multi-Fibre "Agreement," too, has been little more, in effect, than an agreement to disagree. Similarly, UNESCO's debate on freedom and control of information through the press and the media resulted not in an international regime but in a bitter agreement to disagree.

One good and rather obvious reason why there is a rather large number of issues in which international organizations preside over a dialogue of the deaf is simply that the political trend within states is towards greater and greater intervention in markets and greater state responsibility for social and economic conditions, while the major postwar agreements for liberal regimes tended the other way and bound states to negative, noninterventionist policies that would increase the openness of the world economy.

In a closely integrated world economic system, this same trend leads to the other aspect of reality that attention to regimes obscures, and especially so when regimes are closely defined . . . as being based on a group of actors standing in a characteristic relationship to each other. This is the trend to the transnational regulation of activities in one state by authorities in another, authorities that may be, and often are, state agencies such as the U.S. Civil Aeronautics Authority, the Department of Justice or the Food and Drug Administration. There is seldom any predictable pattern of "interaction" or awareness of contextual limitations to be found in such regulation.

[A] OUTLINE OF A BETTER ALTERNATIVE

My alternative way of analyzing any issue of international political economy, which is likely to avoid some of these [problems], involves extending Charles Lindblom's useful clarifying work on *Politics and Markets* to the world system. Whether one chooses to apply it to sectors of the world economy or to the structures of that system, it suggests many much more open-ended and value-free questions about the relationship between authorities and markets and about the outcomes of their interaction than does regime analysis.

It thus allows serious questions to be posed for research or discussion about any issue, whether they are of interest to governments or not. Moreover, it does not take markets as part of the data, but accepts that they are creations of state policies—policies that affect transactions and buyers and sellers, both directly and indirectly, through the part played by markets in shaping basic structures of the world system such as the security structure, the production structure, the trade and transport structure, the credit and money structure, the communication and knowledge structure, and (such as it is) the welfare structure.

It involves asking a series of questions, none of which in any way prejudges the answers. It is therefore equally adaptable to the concerns and interests of conservatives and radicals, to scholars far to the right or far to the left, or to those who want only to move more freely in the middle ground between extremes.

Not only does it liberate inquiry from the procrustean limits set by ideology, it also breaks the confining limits set when regime analysis identifies an international regime with the existence of a particular international agency or bureaucracy. Patients often abandon a regime but do not feel it necessary to eliminate the doctor; international institutions are seldom wound up, however useless. Indeed, the continued existence of the "doctors" on the international scene and the fairly widespread abandonment of regular regimes by the "patients" seems to me precisely what has been happening in the international political economy in the latter half of the 1970s. There has been a rather marked shift from multilateral arrangements around which actors' expectations (more or less) converged toward bilateral procedures, negotiations, and understandings. . . .

Part
FOUR

Ecology and Politics

Some years ago T. S. Eliot lamented poetically that the world would end not with a bang but a whimper. The nuclear sword of Damocles, which hangs by the slenderest of threads, continues to threaten a fiery and shattering apocalypse. The quest for security in an insecure world thus continues unabated. A growing number of challenges broadly conceived as ecological now also threaten that the final cataclysm will occur more by accretion than by design or accident, but with results no less fatal. Whether nation-states and other world political actors will prove able to cope effectively with these challenges is problematic.

Part IV of *The Global Agenda* examines various issues and perspectives composing the politics of the ecological problematique. *Ecology* in this context refers to the relationship between humans and their physical and biological environments. The importance of ecological issues in world politics derives from the combination of world population growth and technological developments that has placed increasing strains on the earth's delicate life-support systems. Food and resource scarcities are no longer uncommon, and they can be expected to grow. Technological innovations that propel modern industrialization permit new and more efficient use of environmental resources. They also result in pollution and other forms of environmental degradation of waterways, land masses, and the atmosphere that threaten the global habitat future generations will inherit. The global commons, resources such as the oceans, the seabed, the radio spectrum, and outer space, previously regarded as the common heritage of mankind, are now capable of exploitation by the technologically sophisticated, who may seek to deny them to others.

The range of global political issues encompassed by the ecological agenda

315

is broad and, like issues of peace and security and economic interactions, complex. The critical importance of ecological issues is perhaps less well recognized, however. Most of us have been socialized by parents, peers, educators, and policy makers to the view that international politics is concerned fundamentally with issues of war and peace. And we tend to think of war and peace in terms of armies marching or diplomats conferring. Incorporating in this image a concern for the economic dimensions of global conflict is not difficult, for questions relating to the distribution of material wealth touch us all. For most, however, ecological issues are more remote. Unless we are touched directly by an issue, such as the disposal of toxic chemical waste or spent nuclear fuel, or atmospheric contamination in the form of acid rain, or soil erosion due to strip mining or deforestation, ecological issues seem so future-oriented as to be of little immediate relevance. And in the councils of government, the future generally has no constituency.

Compelling as our traditional views of world politics may be, an adequate understanding of the agenda of contemporary world politics must include consideration of ecological issues and the perspectives that have been offered on them. In part this is because such issues bear directly on issues of war and peace. A global environment characterized by resource scarcities may invite the classic kinds of inter-state conflict—and war—that once characterized competition over territory. Even comparatively abundant but unevenly distributed resources may create global conflicts if they lead to a level of dependence on foreign sources of supply that is perceived as a threat to national security, as has happened with oil. If population growth and resource scarcities also portend, as some have argued, that there are limits to growth, and that the consumption patterns of the past necessary to support the standards of living to which at least the Western world has become accustomed must be curtailed in the future, questions of equity and justice, already so prominent on the North-South axis of the global political agenda, will become magnified. And if resource scarcities and a drive to preserve present living standards compel those with the technological ability to "mine" the global commons also to claim sovereign jurisdiction over them, the stage will be set for the kinds of jurisdictional disputes around which so much of history has turned. Richard J. Barnet has pointed out the importance of these issues to people and to nations with the observation that "Whoever controls world resources controls the world in a way that mere occupation of territory cannot match."

At a broader level, the importance of ecological issues is indicated by the fact that the survival of the human species is contingent upon the world's ability to summon the political will to devise policies that can preserve the earth's carrying capacity, on which life itself is dependent. The future of all people and nations is thus affected by how these issues are addressed, and the world that our children and their children will inherit will be profoundly affected by the choices made today. While some of these choices might appropriately be made by nation-states acting alone, others may not. Acid rain knows no boundaries. Nuclear contamination of the atmosphere threatens many nations. Climatological changes induced by fossil fuel consumption, and destruction of the protective ozone layer caused by other abuses, imperil all. Concerted international collaborative efforts are required to deal with these and the many other ecological issues on the global agenda.

Ecopolitics is a concept used by some analysts to stress the relationship between world political and ecological issues. Our first essay in Part IV of *The Global Agenda,* "The Ecological Perspective on International Politics" by Harold and Margaret Sprout, introduces the multifaceted nature of this relationship in a hungry, crowded, environmentally stressed world. The Sprouts emphasize that the ecological perspective takes into account explicitly the interrelatedness in international politics of political communities with one another and with their environment. The milieu in which international intercourse occurs is, according to this outlook, governed to an unprecedented degree by interdependence. This interdependence is real, even if some are unaware of it. And that reality can render the international milieu potentially fatal, the authors warn, if actors fail to appreciate the dangers and their dependence on each other for devising solutions to the ecological risks confronting all. A poisoned atmosphere, an overly exploited earth, pollution of the oceans, abuse of the planet's ecosystem— these are the issues that if not resolved may make the earth uninhabitable. Urging us to take a broad view of these realities, the Sprouts recommend that statesmen and students of world politics alike be cognizant of the interrelatedness of things under conditions of global interdependence. Implicit in this perspective is the belief that environmental afflictions cannot be managed by states independently, that states must act in concert to arrest the environmental deterioration caused by population growth and technological advances. That technology cannot save us, and that further technological innovation, in the absence of means to contain its negative effects, might actually exacerbate the dangers, are also beliefs implicit in the perspective they so forcefully advance.

In "Energy and Security," Joseph S. Nye, Jr., illustrates the connection between the uneven distribution and emergent shortages of valued resources and the traditional national security concerns of nation-states. Nye focuses on the policy predicament the United States faces as it seeks to ensure its energy security. Although the urgency of this issue seemed to dissipate in the early 1980s as a combination of conservation measures and global recession eased worldwide demand for oil, Nye's analysis leads us to be cautious about assuming that the vulnerabilities to which the United States allowed itself to become exposed no longer threaten its security. The wisdom of caution is reinforced by the cogency of Nye's distressing argument that there are no "quick fix" solutions to the long-run energy needs of the United States. And, in an interdependent world, the inability of the United States to come to grips with these problems threatens not only the United States, but also the entire Western world. Hence, the security of the United States and others might be jeopardized by an inability to appreciate the risks and to mount a program designed for the long run.

Nye's analysis serves to describe how a single resource issue, such as access to oil, may dominate America's and the world's future. It also brings concreteness to the view that ecological issues are important and are profoundly linked to and influenced by political choices. Lester R. Brown builds on this argument, but takes it in a radically different direction. He contends in "Redefining National Security" that the whole concept of national security requires reconsideration and revision. Finding the traditional concept much too narrow, Brown advises that it be broadened to include more than merely military matters. Indeed, he finds many developments arising from and related to ecological stresses more threatening to nations' security than military challenges. These include those stemming from population growth, the gap between the world's rich and poor, food shortages, and the like—the kinds of non-military problems for which military approaches are inappropriate and perhaps dysfunctional. Arguing that such issues are inherently multilateral, in that they involve more than one country, Brown concludes that such challenges to national security necessitate coordinated international responses. However, since governments are not well prepared to cope with non-military threats to national security, and given the disproportionate resources they now devote to military matters, movement toward a conception of national security as the same as global security faces formidable odds.

The search for solutions to global ecopolitical issues must begin with the construction of an accurate image of the state of the global environment. The world cannot solve its problems until it recognizes them for what they are, until it devises an objective "definition of the situation." It was to that end that the United States government sought to monitor systematically global environmental trends and to make predictions about their long-term consequences. The result of that effort was a voluminous inventory entitled *The Global 2000 Report to the President*. In an excerpt from that report,"Entering the Twenty-First Century," we are provided with a summary of the documented evidence that points to many alarming ecological developments that seem destined to influence the global agenda throughout the remainder of this century and into the next.

The ecopolitical issues crowding the global agenda invite heated debate among all affected parties. Not surprisingly, therefore, prescriptions promising solutions abound. Among the most well-known analogies that imply strategies for coping with environmental stresses and preventing ecological overshoot are the so-called "tragedy of the commons" and "lifeboat ethics" metaphors. Marvin S. Soroos describes these metaphors and then subjects them to critical analysis in "Coping with Resource Scarcity: A Critique of Lifeboat Ethics." He finds both devoid of sympathy for the victims, who would, according to the prescription for "intrinsic responsibility" implied by both, be sacrificed in order to enhance the well-being of those already comparatively well off, and who themselves place a disproportionate burden on the global carrying capacity. Moreover, a strategy of enforced self-reliance risks inviting terrorism and sabotage as tactics of retaliation by those threatened with victimization. As an alternative, Soroos recommends a regulated commons system which builds on the premise that "the future [ecological] welfare of all societies is closely intertwined." However we may react to this globalist recommendation, the costs and benefits associated with alternative prescriptions for preserving the global carrying capacity deserve serious scrutiny, for how and if the ecological issues on the global agenda are resolved will be influenced strongly by today's political choices.

In "The International State of Nature and the Politics of Scarcity," William Ophuls directs his attention to a related set of issues on which humankind's ability to manage its common problems depends—the ability of nations to bring ecological problems under control given the structural characteristics of the international system. His perspective is not unique; his conclusion not singular in its pessimism. For Ophuls finds that the challenge of scarcity is more likely to precipitate conflict than it is to stimulate greater international cooperation. The absence in the international system of either higher law or higher authority and the persistence of the principle of sovereignty encourage struggle and pursuit of narrow self-interest, not collaboration. It may be a system crying out for recognition that under prevailing circumstances the future of each depends on the future of all, Ophuls observes, but it is nonetheless a system that in the short run rewards those who "help themselves" at the expense of others. The danger, Ophuls warns, is that all will likely suffer.

This pessimistic prognosis draws attention to the fact that the ecological problematique is profoundly affected by the nature of contemporary international society. During recent years a number of "world order" and "futurology" studies have been undertaken to discover the conditions most conducive to the maintenance of world order and international stability, with a view toward designing preferred alternative futures. Antony J. Dolman, in his essay "Alternative Views of a World in Crisis," summarizes the intellectual roots and operating assumptions of many of these world order analyses. The world views expressed in them are then surveyed in order to provide the reader with an understanding of the contribution that world order studies bring to an understanding of international relations. Dolman's essay thus encapsulates a broad spectrum of thought, and advances a series of propositions that bear directly on the prospects for a more orderly and just world.

Part IV of *The Global Agenda* concludes with an original and insightful essay on how issues relating to environmental politics might be meaningfully analyzed. Concentrating attention on one dimension of the global commons, "non-land" resources, the author, James N. Rosenau, asks in "New Non-land Resources as Global Issues" whether the attributes of these issues are sufficiently novel to require new concepts and new perspectives to render them understandable. Answering in the affirmative, Rosenau shows how the resources extractable from outer space and the seabed, and the issues relating to communication through radio frequencies and to climate modification techniques, pose problems that are likely to set them apart, in terms of the way they are processed, from "traditional" issues that remain largely within the competence of national governments, and even from the newer "interdependence" issues that are only partially within their scope. The pressures for new mechanisms for coping with conflict that are exerted by the advent of these non-land resource issues in the realm of low politics represent a serious global challenge. For alongside those global issues that demand global remedies, there remain operative the issues of high politics that reinforce the inclination of states to address them autonomously, without the assistance of but in competition with others.

Perhaps it was this duality of our age—the persistence of the competitive state-system alongside the compelling need for global cooperation—that led former U.S. Secretary of State Henry A. Kissinger to note that "We are stranded between old conceptions of political conduct and a wholly new conception, between the inadequacy of the nation-state and the emerging imperative of global community." If indeed the world is undergoing a fundamental transformation requiring a fundamental reordering, then the future will be shaped by the world's capacity to address adaptively the issues that presently divide it, and to act in concert to manage peacefully the challenges that confront communal destiny. The perspectives and postures assumed by every citizen on planet earth have meaning for which direction the world will take, toward progress or toward destruction.

29

The Ecological Perspective on International Politics

HAROLD SPROUT AND MARGARET SPROUT

In this essay, Harold and Margaret Sprout describe the elements of the ecological perspective on international politics. They note that, contrary to popular usage, "environmental" and "ecological" are not synonymous. Instead, the ecological perspective "envisages international politics as a *system of relationships* among *interdependent, earth-related* communities." Authors of *The Context of Environmental Politics: Unfinished Business for America's Third Century* (1978), the Sprouts extensively broadened awareness of and understanding about man-milieu relationships.

. . . . What does [the ecological perspective] entail? How does it differ from other ways of viewing and comprehending the international scene? . . .

. . . . Academic rhetoric as well as journalese is studded with [ecological] language—ecology, ecosystem, ecological crisis, ecological influences, and many other such expressions. . . . More often than not, it appears that the adjective *ecological* has simply displaced the older adjective *environmental*. . . . [C]oncepts of *environment* and of *environmental relationships* are part of an ecological frame of thinking. But ecology is not synonymous with environmentalism and includes much besides the idea of environmental relationships.

From earliest history, men have been speculating about the ways in which their lives and fortunes are affected by conditions prevailing upon the earth, especially their niche of the earth. Philosophers and historians have attributed the rise and decline of civilizations and cultures, and of hegemonies and other regimes of power and influence, to the geographic layout of lands and seas, to variations of climate, to the distribution of fertile land and of minerals upon and beneath the surface, to periodic famines and epidemics, to other natural catastrophes, to technological innovations, to forms of government, to human avarice, corruption and mismanagement, and to other environing conditions and events. Indeed, some idea of environment and some theory of human relations to environment are part-and-parcel of every serious discussion of human affairs.

Propositions regarding the quality of life achievable in particular environments, propositions regarding the ways by which individuals and communities adapt to environing conditions or try to modify them, and (in the specific context of international relations) propositions regarding the effects of these interactions

Reprinted from Harold Sprout and Margaret Sprout, *Toward a Politics of the Planet Earth* (New York: Van Nostrand Reinhold Company, 1971), pp. 13–31. Copyright © 1971 by Van Nostrand Reinhold Company. Reprinted by permission of the publisher.

on the vitality of national communities and on the distribution of power and influence over the earth are plainly among the concerns of an ecological viewpoint and mode of inquiry and analysis.

There is a tendency, we repeat, to assume that this is all that an ecological viewpoint entails. But that is a mistake! . . .

. . . [T]he ecological way of seeing and comprehending envisages international politics as a *system of relationships* among *interdependent, earth-related* communities that share with one another an *increasingly crowded planet* that offers *finite* and *exhaustible* quantities of *basic essentials* of human well-being and existence. Despite an appearance of abundance in a few countries, food and other essentials are in chronic short supply in many more countries, and the earth as a whole is being denuded, depleted, and polluted at rising rates that portend, unless arrested and reversed, a progressively degraded future for most of mankind, and the somber possibility of irreversible catastrophe for all. . . . [I]t will require major changes in values, attitudes, economic practices, and styles of living, accompanied by massive changes in the allocation of goods and services, and concerted international cooperation of a scope and on a scale only dimly imagined as yet, if the earth is to continue to be a congenial habitat.

SOME ECOLOGICAL CONCEPTS

The starting point of ecologically focused thinking is the simple proposition that some organism, or population of organisms, is surrounded, or encompassed—that is, environed—by some set of conditions in ways that are significant for the present and future of the individual or population in question. We thus have three central concepts: *organisms, environment,* and *interrelationships.* But note carefully—the focus is neither on the behavior or state of the individual or population per se nor on the properties of the environment per se. The focus is on individual or population *interacting with the environment* in patterns that constitute a *system,* more specifically an *ecosystem.* . . .

. . . In the vocabulary of environmental biology . . . , a population of organisms living within a specified geographic space and interacting with other organisms and nonliving matter constitutes a *biotic community,* or ecosystem. The complex of things, living and nonliving, to which a particular population's well-being and survival are linked, constitutes that population's *habitat*—a near synonym for environment, but with stronger territorial connotation. Running through these terms is the concept of an *interrelated-interdependent whole.* This concept is the very essence of the ecological perspective and mode of thinking. . . .

This way of viewing human communities, or ecosystems, directs attention to side effects, by-products, and chains of interaction. It contrasts *in toto* with the narrower engineering perspective that focuses on discrete tasks (for example, building faster automobiles or more lethal missiles) without regard to the side effects that may ramify throughout the community. . . .

Social scientists often, perhaps generally, envisage a community as a population living in a specific geographic area and *exhibiting substantial self-awareness of common identity and concerns.* This is the sense in which most political theorists speak of community. In other contexts, however, *community may denote simply a population whose members are interrelated with one another and with their habitat in ways that are judged to be significant to the population's well-being or survival.* In the first instance, psychic self-awareness is the essence of the concept; if absent, no community exists. In the second, such self-awareness is not essential. Significant interrelatedness is the essential condition. This is substantially the sense in which environmental biologists appear to conceive of an ecological community, or ecosystem.

The distinction here is between *cognition of interrelatedness* and *condition of interrelatedness.* From the ecological perspective the latter is always significant; the former may be, but not necessarily. . . .

Of course, a sense of community, or at least self-awareness of interrelatedness and resulting mutual concerns, may be an essential condition of achieving effective action to deal with the consequences of interrelatedness. But, we repeat, it is the condition of interrelatedness that justifies, from the ecological perspective, the judgment that an ecosystem exists even in the absence of widespread internal recognition thereof. . . .

There may be very little firm evidence that a *sense of community* extending beyond the national polity is spreading. But that does not affect in the slightest the empirical reality of the *condition of interrelatedness* that increasingly characterizes larger regions and indeed the planet as a whole. In this sense, we repeat, the earth has become a single ecosystem, the component elements of which become more complexly and more tightly interdependent with every passing year. . . .

FROM ADAPTATION TO MANIPULATION TO CRISIS

. . . [T]he ecological perspective finds no credible ground whatever for the engineer's faith in the omnipotence of the new technological man. The ecological perspective points unequivocally to the imperative need to recast our thinking about the relations of man and man and of man and nature.

The exponential growth of population, itself a by-product of advancing technology, adds severity and urgency to the spreading and worsening erosion of the earth-based human habitat. Not only have populations acquired more efficient tools wherewith to exploit the earth and its subhuman inhabitants; there are ever more humans to do the exploiting and in the process to deplete the nonhuman environment, to accumulate rising mountains of debris, to poison soil, water, and air, and otherwise to degrade their habitat.

Stated more generally, *the greater the concentration of population and/or the higher the level of industrial technology available to a population, the more extensive has been the environmental deterioration.* It has been asserted, for example, that each American accounts for more toxic wastes poured into rivers and oceans than a thousand Asians. Similar orders of magnitude differentiate American pollution of air, and probably also of land, from pollutions attributable to most countries in the Third World. The resulting state of affairs in some of the richest societies, above all in the United States, can be characterized as the *crisis of affluent squalor*. It is a crisis with many dimensions and ramifications. At the political level, it is a crisis in the sense that it will require radically altered priorities and vast reallocation of resources to block the final phase of the secular trend from adaptive accommodation to manipulative exploitation to progressive despoliation towards eventual catastrophe as worldwide and perhaps as terminal as a full-blown war waged with the most destructive weapons.

INTERRELATEDNESS AND INTERDEPENDENCE

The secular trend toward ever greater mastery over nature has entailed a corresponding *increase of interrelatedness*. Interrelatedness has become the predominant characteristic of our era. It is especially evident in unanticipated and undesired side effects of all kinds of undertakings. The makers and users of motor vehicles, for example, do not desire or intend to pollute the atmosphere and produce scarcely tolerable congestion in the cities and along the highways—but these are none the less by-products of the mobility that modern Americans and others value so highly.

Moreover, interrelatedness is no respecter of sovereignty and jurisdictional boundaries. American and Russian scientists and engineers who tested the early hydrogen bombs manifestly did not intend to poison the atmosphere of other countries—but that was what occurred in varying degrees throughout the world. Americans may not intend to instigate discontent when they travel over the earth and reside in foreign countries—but the psychological impact of their comparative affluence has not been less socially disruptive because unintended.

The ecological principle here is as simple as its operation is inexorable: *Any substantial change in one sector of an ecosystem is nearly certain to produce significant, often unsettling, sometimes severely disruptive, consequences in other sectors. . . .*

VALUES AND PRIORITIES

. . . We suggest that the most elemental values of all are those associated with biological existence: level of health and length of life. In more specifically ecological terms, but still in the context of a world community, or ecosystem, these values can be summed up as the need *to make the earth a reasonably safe and salubrious place to live, not only for ourselves but also for our descendants, and not only for one or a few nations but for all. . . .*

Much remains to be learned about the ways in which ideas about environmental quality are formed—and re-formed in response to changing conditions. There is plenty of evidence that hundreds of millions of people still tolerate fatalistically a milieu that undermines health and shortens life. There is also evidence that even the most "advanced" populations adjust to environmental deterioration, and come in time to recall only dimly that conditions were ever any better.

Moreover, environmental ignorance is colossal even within the countries where environmental deterioration has received most attention. It is doubtful, for example, whether any but the tiniest minority of Americans, chiefly professional ecologists and a scattering of other experts and educated lay conservationists, believe as yet that conditions are sufficiently menacing to justify drastic remedies. It is still more doubtful whether any substantial number of Americans believe the experts who insist that continuation of present trends could render the earth uninhabitable within two or three generations. Such a possibility is simply beyond the comprehension of most people. Still, there are indications of mounting anxiety that may in time quicken the currently feeble and largely ineffective remedial and preventive actions by government and industry.

However defined, any prescribed environmental standard is a complex of public or societal values. These are public in the sense that their cost is spread more or less widely and their benefits are presumptively available to all or most members of the community. Environmental norms tend also to represent long-range values, since there is likely to be considerable time lag before restorative or protective actions show readily discernible benefits. Moreover, actions to improve environmental quality are apt to curtail both personal freedom and privileged access to goods and services. Finally, where environments are deeply eroded from long exploitation, abuse, and neglect, as is notoriously the case in the United States and to varying degrees in many countries, the estimated cost of arrears alone runs to astronomical sums with the prospect of additional heavy annual outlays for future protective maintenance. . . .

For these and other reasons, public authorities in virtually all countries have been chronically tardy in coming to recognize environmental quality as a value of high priority. More often than not it has required fear of imminent catastrophe, or even experience of catastrophe, to convert environmental crises into political crises, with no assurance even then of adequate continuing protection. In short, *a pervasive feature of the deepening and spreading environmental crisis is its disruptive threat to long-standing priorities and consequently its potential impact on the allocation of resources. . . .*

. . . Yet as previously emphasized, we are encumbered with an archaic, fragmented international system of jurisdiction and authority that survives from an era *when the human population of the earth was not one but many.*

How to cope with the diverse, cumulatively enormous, and still proliferating human capabilities to alter the conditions of subsistence upon this planet is becoming the central problem of international politics, just as these same changes and transformations are moving to the center of the stage in nations, provinces, and cities all over the world.

30

Energy and Security

JOSEPH S. NYE

In this essay, Joseph S. Nye describes the political and economic forces that caused a major restructuring of the international oil regime during the 1970s. Writing from the perspective of American energy policy, he notes that the world's largest consumer of oil remains vulnerable to market and non-market oil-supply disruptions, which could produce disastrous consequences throughout the Western world. Nye is professor of government at Harvard University, and was an assistant secretary of state during the Carter administration. Among his many publications is *Peace in Parts* (1971).

When the seventies began, Americans imported 3.5 million barrels of oil a day, about one quarter of our needs. The price was about $2 per barrel and we were the largest oil producer in the world. Three years earlier, we had easily foiled an attempted oil embargo triggered by the June War. But by the end of that distressing decade, we were importing 8.5 million barrels per day—nearly half our needs—at fifteen times the price charged only a few years before, and domestic oil production was in decline. The painful 1973 Arab oil embargo seemed to have taught us nothing when the Iranian Revolution curtailed production in 1979. President Carter did not exaggerate when he called the situation "a clear and present danger to our national security."

Today, nearly two-fifths of the oil consumed by the free world's economy is vulnerable to terrorism, accident, warfare, and extortion. The sudden loss of Persian Gulf oil for a year could stagger the world's economy, disrupt it, devastate it, like no event since the Great Depression of the 1930s. The Congressional Budget Office estimates that the loss of Saudi Arabian oil for a year would cost the United States $272 billion, increase the unemployment rate 2 percent, and boost the already worrisome inflation rate by 20 percentage points. And costs to our allies would be even greater. According to another estimate, a 9 million barrel per day cutback of Saudi oil for a year would slash our GNP 5 percent, the European GNP 7 percent, and the Japanese GNP 8 percent. The loss of *all* Persian Gulf oil would cut our GNP 13 percent; Europe's, 22 percent; and Japan's, 25 percent (Congressional Budget Office 1980; Rowen 1980; see also Department of Energy 1980). Of course, these estimates are only approximations, and they could

Reprinted from Joseph S. Nye, "Energy and Security," in David A. Deese and Joseph S. Nye, eds., *Energy and Security* (Cambridge, Mass.: Ballinger Publishing Company, 1981), pp. 3–22. Copyright 1981, Ballinger Publishing Company. Some footnotes have been deleted; others have been renumbered to appear in consecutive order. Bibliographical references not cited in the excerpt have been deleted.

be overstated. But even if they are twice as high as they should be, the potential economic costs of major supply interruptions are clearly terrifying.

So is the threat to our foreign policy. Since the end of World War II, American strategy has focused on the defense of Europe and Japan, the two greatest concentrations of economic power outside the United States and the Soviet Union. The prosperity and strength of the democratic alliance has been central to the postwar balance of power. But today this balance could be upset by the stress and strain that energy security problems pose to Western prosperity and the solidarity of our alliances. The vulnerable and volatile Middle East is outside the scope of our formal alliance frameworks. Moreover, coordination of domestic economic and energy policies among democracies with different interests is bound to be particularly difficult.

In fact, differences in our allies' vulnerability to energy disruptions present the Soviets—and others—with better opportunities to disrupt Western alliances than direct military threats. Europeans and Japanese, for example, might respond positively to Soviet offers to guarantee energy supplies, even though we would argue that such steps would legitimize Soviet influence over these regions' economic lifeline. Western policy toward Israel shows a similar tendency to reflect different degrees of economic exposure to Arab wrath. Other foreign policy costs include the temptation to trade sensitive nuclear technology for oil supplies—witness Italy's relations with Iraq—and the problems of managing the world economy as well as preserving stability in crucial but economically fragile allies such as Turkey when oil prices rise precipitously. These foreign policy costs are not susceptible to numerical statement, but their magnitude can be judged by speculating about the resources that we would spend to avoid them.

Our concern about military security leads us to spend $150 billion yearly on military forces, the largest part of which is devoted to strengthening the North Atlantic Treaty Organization (NATO). Important as these expenditures are, the probability of Soviet tanks rolling across the North German plain is much lower than the likelihood of an interruption of oil supplies stemming from various conflicts in the Middle East. Yet our energy plans and our diplomatic strategy do not reflect those probabilities. We are far less prepared for an energy emergency than for a military attack.

In the face of our growing exposure to these economic, political, and military dangers, we Americans have not yet risen to the challenge. "Consider this anomaly," noted *The Washington Post* early in 1980. "The president and a great many more Americans are prepared to talk openly of war to secure the oil routes out of the Gulf. But neither the president nor many others are ready to impose a tax on gasoline to diminish imports that, everyone agrees, constitute a clear and present danger to the national security" (*The Washington Post* 1980). Yes, the president did propose a modest import fee, but it was rejected by the Congress. The sad truth is that many government actions taken after 1973—domestic price controls for instance—have actually made our situation worse. Unwilling to allow rising prices to benefit some Americans while penalizing others, we have squabbled among ourselves and followed policies that have let our society's burden grow. Our dependence on oil imports increased 25 percent between 1973 and 1979, and our overall energy security diminished. We *talked* the high rhetoric of energy security but our policies belied our words.

Why have we not done better? Our policy performance reflected public attitudes and misunderstandings. For one thing, the public has persistently refused to believe in an oil shortage. In 1979, "as gasoline lines grew longer, the belief that the energy crisis is contrived became more prevalent." In February 1980, 41 percent of Gallup poll respondents believed the United States was self-sufficient in energy, and other polls showed the public expecting solar and nuclear energy to replace oil as the principal sources of energy in six to ten years (Schneider 1980: 153–156).

These attitudes reflect reality in an odd, distorted way. It is true that the energy problem is not one of absolute shortage. Even conservative estimates maintain that Saudi Arabia and Kuwait have reserve-to-production ratios of fifty to seventy-five years. And domestic alternative energy sources can be developed well within that time. Thus, in July 1973, the London *Economist* labeled the problem a "phony oil crisis" (*The Economist* 1973). Many eminent economists argued that the 1973 oil price rises would solve themselves by constraining demand and calling forth additional supply that would lead to the collapse of OPEC. A Nobel Laureate predicted that the cartel could not last at prices above $10 per barrel. If the world had no friction or politics, all might be right.

These unrealistic views infected our policy in the mid-seventies. Our diplomacy focused on negotiating a $7 per barrel price *floor* to protect alternative energy sources against falling oil prices. We pressed Saudi Arabia to moderate prices by holding auctions and increasing its productive capacity toward 20 million barrels per day, even though this would make us more dependent on the Persian Gulf. And we did little to increase our military posture. Instead, we began talks on Indian Ocean arms control. American political-military policy and energy policy were poorly related. The "Vietnam Syndrome" had its effect, but we also listened too much to economists who told us that international energy policy would take care of itself.

It didn't. So today—nearly a decade after the first warning signals—we still need a coherent policy for energy security. But devising a strategy and thinking about energy as a security problem is not as simple as it first seems; any judgment about security is necessarily complex. Security is a matter of degree, and how much insurance one needs in order to feel secure is a function of the probability of the threatening event and the magnitude of the potential damage. Damages can be defined narrowly, in terms of survival, or broadly, in terms of a whole range of values including welfare, independence, status, and power. We generally speak of national security as the absence of threat to a broad range of values in addition to survival. Indeed, some national security policies, such as our possession of nuclear weapons, may increase the risk to simple survival in order to deter threats to our other values. Similarly, energy security is only part of national security; in some circumstances we would risk energy supplies for other values we consider part of our national security.

Looking back at American policies for energy security in the 1970s, we are struck by two strong ironies. First, we talked about energy security, but some of the policies that followed the talk actually made us more insecure. Second, we acted as though government controls at home and market forces abroad would solve our energy security problems when the opposite was closer to the truth. We failed to recognize the changing realities of world politics that eroded the international regime that once governed oil transactions. In the 1970s, our energy security policies reflected an under-reliance on economic remedies domestically and an over-reliance on them internationally. The first step toward sound policies for the 1980s must be a better understanding of the international political context.

THE DECLINE OF THE INTERNATIONAL OIL REGIME

In 1970, world oil was still generally governed by a loose international regime which might be described as "guided laissez-faire." It had two essential characteristics. First, price and production decisions were made largely by major international oil companies for their own commercial reasons. Second, the major powers—particularly the United States and Britain—occasionally intervened diplomatically to guarantee these companies access to oil. . . . With few exceptions, these governing arrangements were stable and accepted. There seemed to be no real alternative.

As a result of this regime, oil prices and production levels tended to reflect supply and demand conditions in major consumer countries rather than oil's expected long-term scarcity value or the political interests of producing countries. As low-cost Middle East oil became more plentiful in the postwar period, most of the difference in value between its low production cost and the high price of alternative energy sources went to consumers in the form of low and declining oil prices.

Under these favorable conditions, the United States and other major consuming nations devoted little time or attention to developing a coherent energy security policy. Even Europeans and Japanese, with a longer tradition of thinking about oil as a security problem, were lulled into increasing their dependence on Middle East oil. Supply seemed assured by a Pax Americana that was enforced by occasional diplomatic assurances and by antitrust measures promoting a modicum of effective competition.

But dramatic changes were in the offing. By the end of the 1970s, prices and production levels were being set by producer governments rather than by the international oil companies, and for political as well as commercial motives. These decisions were difficult to predict because they did not follow stable or recognizable rules. Now, producers rather than consumers were capturing a large part of the difference between the low costs of production and the higher costs of possible replacements for Middle East oil. Increasingly constrained international oil companies found that their assured access to crude oil under predictable long-term contracts had diminished. Moreover, guarantees of access and oversight of price and production decisions had become widely regarded as absolute sovereign prerogatives of producer governments.

Why did such a remarkable change occur over the course of a decade? Basically, because of longer term trends in the underlying structure of power. In 1960, six of the thirteen present OPEC members were colonies or protectorates, and the key straits of Hormuz, Aden, and Malacca were under European control. As decolonization proceeded, Western dominance of the producing countries diminished. The rise of nationalism in the producer countries also made Western intervention more controversial and costly—witness events in Iran in 1953 and 1979.

In military terms, the British withdrawal from the Persian Gulf in 1971 was a major turning point. America's reaction to the Vietnam War made it certain that the United States would neither replace the British, as it had in the Eastern Mediterranean in 1947, nor fully counter increasing Soviet military capabilities in the area. Instead, the United States sought to fill the power vacuum in the Gulf by building up the Shah of Iran as the local leviathan. This policy allowed policing of the Gulf "without any American resources" (Kissinger 1979: 1265). At least in terms of annual budgets, it seemed we were buying energy security on the cheap; but the fall of the Shah eventually revealed the true costs to America's energy security policy.

In addition to these general political and military changes, were changes in the structure of power in the oil issue. A turning point came with the loss of the American oil surplus after 1971. U.S. production peaked, and America's dependence on imports began to increase. The power to balance the market in a time of crisis passed from the United States to OPEC, particularly Saudi Arabia. No longer did America have the spare capacity to supply its allies when oil flows were interrupted for political reasons, as it had at the time of the Suez Crisis in 1956 and the June War in 1967.

The relative power of the oil companies and of the producer governments also shifted radically. Consistent with longer standing patterns in the relations between multinational corporations and less developed countries, original bargains became obsolete and contracts "renegotiable" as the host countries gradually developed their indigenous capabilities. This trend was accelerated by the entry of new independent oil firms into the world oil markets in the fifties and sixties. Eager to gain access to crude oil, their competition with the established majors increased the options and enhanced the bargaining power of the producer country governments.

Initially, the increased production by the new entrants forced the price of oil down, and producer governments tried to maintain revenue levels by increasing production. Ironically, in 1959, the United States reacted to the falling prices by imposing protectionist quotas that exacerbated the problem of glut in world markets, increased the resentment of producer governments, and contributed to the creation of OPEC. But it was not until the oil market tightened for other reasons that OPEC proved effective in raising prices.

The developments of the 1970s occurred in three major steps, with political events acting as catalysts in the political-economy education of the producer countries. At the beginning of the seventies, the closing of the Suez Canal and the destruction of a pipeline allowed the new revolutionary regime in Libya to capitalize on its geographical location and the weak position of the independent companies by extracting a price increase. Libya's success in turn triggered a similar demand upon the major oil companies by Persian Gulf producers. Eager for political harmony, the U.S. government did not support the companies (Sampson 1975). In this first halting step toward today's energy market, the Middle East producers learned that they could threaten the major oil companies with nationalization and shutdown without incurring serious penalties from the Western powers.

The second step was larger. Resentful of America's resupply of Israel during the October 1973 Arab-Israeli war, Arab producers cut production 25 percent. Although OPEC had planned to increase prices 70 percent to reflect the tightening markets caused by increased U.S. imports, the embargo and cutback had unexpected success. It created a scarcity and panic in world markets which drove prices for marginal quantities to extraordinary levels and allowed Iran to lead the other OPEC states in a 400 percent increase over prewar prices (Penrose 1975: 50). Essentially, the political catalyst of war taught oil producers the value of cutbacks and indicated that the long-run price of oil might be much higher than they had believed.

This lesson was reinforced by the third step—the Iranian Revolution in 1979—which curtailed oil production and showed that even uncoordinated cutbacks can have large effects on price. In addition, some producers concluded that exceedingly high oil revenues had helped erode the Shah's regime and that production cutbacks might make domestic political as well as economic sense.

The result is that control over prices, production, and, to an increasing extent, distribution channels, has largely passed to OPEC countries. Historically, OPEC price increases have generally reflected market tightness more than the accompanying political rhetoric suggests, but economic motives are hardly the only considerations that influence OPEC behavior. Although economics can tell us a lot about demand in energy markets, it tells us only part of the story about supply in a world of sovereign states. Production decisions are made on a national basis and often reflect domestic political conflicts and decisions about matters as diverse as development plans, desirable social trends, and external events. For example, following the Camp David Agreement of 1979, Saudi Arabia's political decision to reduce production to 8.5 million barrels per day contributed greatly to the market's turbulence. Earlier, the Saudi's had helped replace Iranian oil in the market so their reversal shook assumptions about future production levels. A panic buildup of stocks in a tight market resulted, driving prices to record levels (see Stobaugh and Yergin 1980 and Nissen 1980).

Production decisions are also affected by prior investments in capacity that may reflect earlier domestic political considerations. It appears that Saudi slowness in developing capacity a few years ago may have been designed to avoid U.S. pressure for higher production, which would have been embarrassing in intra-Arab politics. Current reported Saudi efforts to increase capacity toward 12 million barrels per day might be interpreted as an effort to regain pre-eminence in oil markets. But we do not fully know the determinants of Saudi behavior. Revenue needs and foreign policy positions provide clues, but it may be that oil production decisions really reflect shifts in coalitions within the royal family or efforts to minimize the family's sense of domestic and international political pressure.

Nor can we be certain about the domestic politics of other producing states. Reserves and revenue needs are only part of the political story. Mexican production, for example, should probably increase on the basis of economic needs, but rates of increase reflect internal politics. In fact, Mexicans worry that too rapid growth of oil exports will create inflation and a high-priced industrial structure unable to export other goods and unable to ease their massive unemployment problem. Similar political arguments over economically and socially desirable production levels occur in such developed allies as Norway and Britain.

A few years ago it was widely assumed that OPEC production would climb toward 40 million barrels per day in the 1980s, and that tight markets would not be a problem until the latter half of the decade. Current conventional wisdom, expressed in the International Energy Agency (IEA) and elsewhere, says otherwise: that OPEC production will not rise much above the late 1970s level of 30 million barrels per day and that it may even be lower. The IEA sees growing demand encountering lowered OPEC production with a national gap of 2 million barrels per day in 1985 and 5 million barrels per day in 1990 (International Energy Agency 1980). Even if these predictions of a tightening market prove wrong, a softer market would not remove the danger of production cutbacks due to revolutions, accidents, or sabotage beyond the producer's control. If we again ignore the political fact that production decisions are controlled by the producer governments, we may be condemned to repeating the costly cycle of disruption raising prices; high prices causing reduced consumption; prices softening; crisis; and severely disruptive price increases again. Faced with risk and uncertainty about production decisions, we should be skeptical about all projections and carry plenty of insurance!

In summary, the loose regime that once governed the oil market broke down in the 1970s under the influence of catalytic political events and long-term shifts of power, not because of OPEC's formation or because of market forces alone. The chances of our creating a regime that is more satisfactory to us will be very low so long as we consumers remain politically divided, militarily weak, and economically dependent on unstable oil-producing states. For the foreseeable future, our world is one of political uncertainty with unpredictable prices, renegotiable contracts, and the lurking threat of disruptive interruptions. . . .

[Nye here notes a number of pitfalls to avoid in designing an effective American energy policy. We pick up with his admonition to avoid thinking that ensuring energy security will be an easy task, a point the author treats in detail—*eds*.]

A final pitfall in thinking about energy security is imagining that there is some easy way to solve our problems. Unfortunately, the broad issue of energy security will be with us well into the coming decade or longer. During the past ten years, proposals have been made to invade the oil fields, "break" OPEC, nationalize the oil companies, set up a new international organization, produce synthetic fuels, and so forth. None of these proposals is a complete and realistic solution. Although some could be vital elements of a long-term strategy, others merely divert our attention.

DRAMATIC POLITICAL ALTERNATIVES

Attractive though they might at first appear, the quick fixes and dramatic political solutions all suffer from flaws.

Political-Military Coercion

Given the political limits of the international market, some analysts have urged that we take over the Persian Gulf oilfields (see, for example, Tucker 1975). They argue that the global (and national) costs of continued acquiescence to cartel price rises are so high that they merit a change in our frame of reference—that they justify military intervention, or "internationalization."

The political and economic costs of such a remedy, however, are likely to be extremely high. First, the risk of destroying the oil infrastructure through fighting or sabotage could *create* one of the major costly disruptions that good energy security policy is supposed to avert. Second, there is little prospect for establishing the international legitimacy of what would inevitably be characterized as a new colonial occupation. Our foreign policy could be severely disrupted. Third, unless the situation approaches what Kissinger termed "strangulation," it is uncertain how long the American public would support any occupation, particularly if less questionable alternatives had not been attempted first. How many lives are worth a few minutes saved in a gasoline line?

Nevertheless, an enhanced defense posture in the Middle East is certainly a good energy investment. The ability to deter Soviet intervention and to protect quickly those who ask for our assistance are important assets in the complex diplomacy of oil. But force alone is not a sufficient strategy.

"Break OPEC"

Some analysts believe that efforts to break OPEC are appropriate, given the enormous gap between the cost of producing Persian Gulf oil and what they consider its artificially maintained cartel price. A variety of cartel-busting schemes have been suggested, ranging from food-export embargoes to governmental purchasing in sealed-bid auctions (House of Representatives 1979).

There are several problems with this "solution." Today, OPEC is not the basic cause of high prices. OPEC as an organization has never succeeded in controlling production rates; that is in the sovereign control of producer states. The fundamental problem is that cheap oil is scarce and concentrated within the borders of a very few states while alternatives to oil are expensive and take time to exploit. Producers have learned the benefits of oligopolist pricing and limiting production; successful oligopoly behavior does not require organization. It is unlikely that producers would forget this lesson even if OPEC disappeared tomorrow.

According to some estimates, at current high prices key Persian Gulf countries could cut production by some 40 percent without bringing their revenues below the value of their current imports. Saudi Arabia is the key country because it can by itself *increase* its revenues by *reducing* production. Yet in 1979, Saudi Arabia produced more than its stated target and sold its oil for less than its OPEC partners. It is an odd cartel whose members produce more than their revenue needs in order to dampen their partners' price rises.

In a tight market, a sealed-bid auction is unlikely to result in lower prices. On the contrary, if such producers as Saudi Arabia retaliated by refusing to bid, such a device might result in *higher* prices. Similarly, efforts to embargo or to limit food shipments would fail in the face of alternative sources of food supplies. And they might well trigger expensive retaliation.

Efforts to "break OPEC" are likely to be costly in other ways as well. They would almost certainly cause friction with our European allies and Japan, who feel too vulnerable to engage in such economic brinksmanship. In particular, exacerbating the already burdened U.S.–Saudi relationship would be costly to our foreign policy as well as to our energy security.

Government Control of Purchasing

While efforts to "break OPEC" may not work, it is sometimes argued that consumers could at least organize to reduce the producers' ability to use the multinational oil companies as their "tax collectors." According to this line of reasoning, government control of oil purchasing would make it more difficult for producer countries to play off one company against another to bid up prices, and would bring the full bargaining power of our government to bear directly on oil price decisions. After all, government-to-government dealings are increasing in oil markets; even our allies have government corporations. We must follow suit to keep our position of power in the game.

One could postulate stronger and milder variants of this approach. A sole government purchasing corporation would strengthen the buyer's power, but it would mean the creation of another large government bureaucracy subject to various domestic political pressures. A competing government import corporation without exclusive import powers could serve as a yardstick for the performance of other importers, and it would provide an instrument in countries where we wish to bring a U.S. government presence to the bargaining table. A still milder variant would leave purchasing in the hands of existing companies but would require them to receive approval from the secretary of energy before they paid more than a designated price.

None of these approaches would appear to have much effect on price when markets are tight, nor would they enhance security of supply. France, for example, did not obtain significantly more or cheaper oil in 1979 as a result of its government-to-government purchasing deals. In a tight market, why should the bargaining power of a consumer government be much greater than that of a private corporation when producer governments have such enormous leeway to control price by altering production? Suppose the corporation or the secretary of energy declared that no oil should be purchased above a given price, and some key producers "conserve" production rather than sell at that price. Faced with greater domestic political concern about supply than price, would consumer governments cut back demand accordingly? More likely they would raise the designated price to ensure supply.

It is true that a government corporation could bring nonoil considerations to bear in a manner that private corporations cannot, but such linkages are a two-way street. We might find that producers would link sensitive political issues, such as the Middle East peace process, to the details of oil negotiations in a manner that reduced our diplomatic flexibility and bargaining power—hardly a gain for energy security, broadly defined. The burden of proof must rest with those who believe that the marginal price benefits that might result from governmental negotiations with weak producers would be greater than the potential foreign policy costs of angering stronger producer states willing to cut back production. Moreover, whatever price benefits we stood to gain from across-the-board government purchasing might as easily be made without the same risks by selective diplomatic jawboning.

We should also be cautious about following the example of other nations in this regard. As home base for the largest number of international oil companies, we have more influence and information than any other consumer country. And although it may be true that the proportion of oil sold through the thirty-four companies that support the IEA emergency oil-sharing plan has diminished from 90 to 60 percent of the total markets, it does not follow that we should encourage the trend toward government-to-government purchases. It is not clear how much oil must flow through the companies to ensure enough market flexibility to defeat selective embargoes and make the IEA sharing system work, but it would not help to weaken such an important buffer. Consumer country coordination in a crisis is important, but it does not require government purchasing.

In sum, it is easier to identify significant potential costs than it is to find significant gains to energy security through government control of purchasing.

International Collective Bargaining

One can imagine a smooth, long-term transition from cheap oil to more expensive energy alternatives that would benefit both consumers and producers. Given the long lead times for alternatives and the opportunities for price gouging during periods of political uncertainty, the real price of oil during the eighties may be pushed higher than the long-term price. This development could reduce the long-term revenues of producer states; create uncertainty for their development planning; and, by destabilizing the world economy, threaten the value of their new investments. Politically, a stable world economy enhances the security of producers who depend on an unprovoked and reliable West. It also reduces the economic sources of political instability in the oil-importing developing countries. A consumer-producer dialogue might well help nations concentrate on issues of long-term mutual interest.[1]

---

[1] For a recent proposal, see Ian Smart (1980: 22–29); also *North–South*, the report of the Brandt Commission (Brandt et al. 1980).

Such a dialogue might seek two- or three-year intergovernmental agreements to stabilize the oil market. For example, OPEC and IEA countries would agree on production targets and consumption limits (at first separately, and then in joint bargaining) which would allow for modest real price rises over the decade. A band of prices might be established for the duration of the agreement. OPEC countries would agree to maintain sufficient spare capacity to keep prices within the agreed range. They would cut production (or permit consumers to increase demand) if prices threatened to fall below a designated minimum. If additional inducements were needed to ensure adequate production levels, consumers might index assets, offer assurances of assistance, and allow new OPEC industries access to their home markets. Special credit or aid provisions might be established for oil-importing developing countries. In fact, representatives of such countries might participate in the bargaining sessions.

The number of problems and questions that have to be solved should make us cautious about embarking on such a course: *Could we keep the agenda focused on energy?* Given the politics of the Middle East and the strong bargaining position of the producers, we might find ourselves unable to keep certain awkward political issues off the table. If developing countries were to participate, we might find ourselves reenacting sterile North–South debates, but with much higher stakes than in the United Nations. We need to be sure we can control the Pandora's Box effect before we start down the path to serious international collective bargaining.

Is a reasonable bargain likely? At modest prices, the economic interests of OPEC's surplus producers who lean toward conservation diverge from those of producers who are interested in maximizing revenues. Large price increases, which maximize revenues and allow painless production cutbacks, tend to reconcile that division. Would OPEC countries be able to agree to a bargain that meant higher production and lower prices than the market would otherwise allow? Or would the process of collective bargaining help OPEC members act again in concert—but at a higher price? Given the weak bargaining position of the consumers, they would have a poor chance of negotiating that price down.

Is OPEC cohesive enough to keep any bargain it makes? Thus far, OPEC countries have been unwilling to limit their separate sovereign control over production decisions because it is their major source of power. They compete for power within the oil arena, and they reserve the right to use oil as a weapon in wider political games. Considering the politics of oil and the domestic instability of many OPEC governments, how credible would an OPEC promise to increase production be if political advantage could be gained from a shortfall?

Would the benefits exceed the costs? International collective bargaining would give consumers a formal framework for debating production and price decisions that are now almost entirely in OPEC hands. What is such a framework worth? If collective bargaining were achieved only at the cost of OPEC solidarity on higher prices, the risks of the new framework could be greater than the benefits. Special instruments such as indexing could prove very costly, particularly if the precedent were to spread.

This is not to argue that conversations with producer states are not useful, or that restoration of an international regime is not a worthy long-term goal. Various bilateral and multilateral discussions are essential. But the time is not ripe for fruitful collective bargaining. The balance of power is too imbalanced. Efforts to reconstruct a satisfactory regime under current circumstances are unlikely to be fruitful unless they are part of a larger strategy to enhance energy security. . . .

STEPS IN THE RIGHT DIRECTION

Painful though it was, we learned some important lessons from the interruption of the Iranian oil supply. In April 1979, we began the gradual decontrol of domestic oil prices that will end the subsidization of imports. We also finally seem to have learned the folly of excessive dependence on the Persian Gulf, for at the Tokyo Summit of June 1979 we began work on government agreements to set ceilings on imports. And the double shock of the Shah's fall and the Soviet invasion of Afghanistan led to steps to repair our military posture in the area.

There is still a long way to go. Even with decontrol, oil industry sources project declines in domestic oil production during the 1980s, and we will be hard pressed to meet our goal of cutting imports in half by 1990 (Exxon Company 1979; Duncan 1980). At the current rate, our Strategic Petroleum Reserve will not be filled for *two decades*. Moreover, even if we are successful in reducing our own dependence, our allies will remain vulnerable to interruptions of supply.

A successful energy security strategy will have to focus on preventing interruptions and alleviating their damage in the short term while reducing Western vulnerability over the course of the eighties. To execute this strategy will require better integration of political-military policy, domestic energy policy, and international energy policy than we have achieved in the past. . . .

REFERENCES

BRANDT, WILLY, et al. 1980. *North–South*. Report of the Brandt Commission. Cambridge, Mass.: MIT Press.

BROWN, WILLIAM, and HERMAN KAHN. 1980. "Why OPEC is Vulnerable." *Fortune* (July 14): 67–68.

Congressional Budget Office. 1980. "The World Oil Market in the 1980s: Implications for the United States." Washington: Government Printing Office.

Department of Energy. 1980. "The Energy Problem: Costs and Policy Options." Policy and Evaluation Staff Working Paper, Draft, March 12.

DUNCAN, CHARLES. 1980. "Posture Statement before Committee on Science and Technology, House of Representatives." Washington, January 31.

The Economist. 1973. "The Phony Oil Crisis: A Survey." (July 7): Supplement, pp. 1–42.

Exxon Company, U.S.A. 1979. *Energy Outlook, 1980–2000*. December.

House of Representatives. 1979. "Alternatives to Dealing with OPEC." Hearings before a Subcommittee of the Committee on Government Operations, June 20. Washington: Government Printing Office.

International Energy Agency. 1980. (80) 9 Paris, June 9. Mimeographed press release.

KISSINGER, HENRY. 1979. *The White House Years*. Boston: Little, Brown.

NISSEN, DAVID. 1980. "OPEC Oil Pricing." Chase Manhattan Bank. Mimeo.

PENROSE, EDITH. 1975. "The Development of Crisis." *Daedalus* 104 (Fall).

ROWEN, HENRY. 1980. "Western Economies and the Gulf War." *Wall Street Journal* (October 2).

SAMPSON, ANTHONY. 1975. *The Seven Sisters*. New York: Viking Press.

SCHNEIDER, WILLIAM. 1980. "Public Opinion and the Energy Crisis." In *The Dependence Dilemma*, edited by Daniel Yergin. Cambridge, Mass: Harvard Center for International Affairs.

SMART, IAN. 1980. "Communicating with the Oil Exporters: The Old Dialogue and the New." *Trialogue* 22 (Winter).

STOBAUGH, ROBERT, and DANIEL YERGIN. 1980. "Energy: An Emergency Telescoped." *Foreign Affairs* 58, no. 3.

TUCKER, ROBERT. 1975. "Oil: The Issue of American Intervention." *Commentary* 59 (January): 21–31.

The Washington Post. 1980. Editorial. January 28.

31
Redefining National Security

LESTER R. BROWN

In this essay, Lester R. Brown argues that threats to national security are no longer adequately conceptualized as simply military. Noting that "threats to security may now arise less from the relationship of nation to nation and more from the relationship of man to nature," Brown concludes that governments generally are ill-equipped to monitor non-military threats to security. He also argues that coping with global crises that know no national boundaries will require coordinated international responses. Brown, a widely published and noted authority on global resources, is president of the Worldwatch Institute.

The term "national security" has become a commonplace expression, a concept regularly appealed to. It is used to justify the maintenance of armies, the development of new weapons systems, and the manufacture of armaments. A fourth of all the federal taxes in the United States and at least an equivalent amount in the Soviet Union are levied in its name.

The concern for the security of a nation is undoubtedly as old as the nation state itself, but since World War II the concept of "national security" has acquired an overwhelmingly military character. Commonly veiled in secrecy, considerations of military threats have become so dominant that other threats to the security of nations have often been ignored. Accumulating evidence indicates that new threats are emerging, threats with which military forces cannot cope.

The notion that countries everywhere should be prepared to defend themselves at all times from any conceivable external threat is a relatively modern one. As recently as 1939, for example, the United States had a defense budget of only $1.3 billion. Prior to World War II, countries mobilized troops in times of war instead of relying on a large permanent military establishment.

The policy of continual preparedness has led to the militarization of the world economy, with military expenditures now accounting for 6 percent of the global product. Worldwide, the military claims of national budgets exceed health-service appropriations. Most countries spend more on "national security" than they do on educating their youth. The development of new, "more effective" weapons systems now engages fully a quarter of the world's scientific talent.

World military expenditures in 1976 reached an estimated $350 billion, a sum

Reprinted from Lester R. Brown, *Redefining National Security*, Worldwatch Paper 14, October 1977. Copyright by Worldwatch Institute, 1977. Some footnotes have been deleted; others have been renumbered to appear in consecutive order.

I am indebted to my colleague Frank Record for his assistance with the research for this paper.

that exceeds the income of the poorest one-half of humanity. At the current rate of weapons procurement, two days of world expenditures on arms equal the annual budget of the United Nations and its specialized agencies. Thirty million men and women in their prime productive years are under arms today.[1] . . .

The overwhelmingly military approach to national security is based on the assumption that the principal threat to security comes from other nations. But the threats to security may now arise less from the relationship of nation to nation and more from the relationship of man to nature. Dwindling reserves of oil and the deterioration of the earth's biological systems now threaten the security of nations everywhere.

National security cannot be maintained unless national economies can be sustained, but, unfortunately, the health of many economies cannot be sustained for much longer without major adjustments. All advanced industrial economies are fueled primarily by oil, a resource that is being depleted. While military strategists have worried about the access of industrial economies to Middle Eastern oil, another more serious threat, the eventual exhaustion of the world's oil supplies, has been moving to the fore. If massive alternative sources of energy are not in place when the projected downturn in world oil production comes some 15 years hence, crippling economic disruptions will result.

While the oil supply is threatened by depletion, the productivity of the earth's principal biological systems—fisheries, forests, grasslands, and croplands—is threatened by excessive human claims. These biological systems provide all food and all the raw materials for industry except minerals and petrochemicals. In fishery after fishery, the catch now exceeds the long-term sustainable yield. The cutting of trees exceeds the regenerative capacity of forests almost everywhere. Grasslands are deteriorating on every continent as livestock populations increase along with human population. Croplands too are being damaged by erosion as population pressures mount. Failure to arrest this deterioration of biological systems threatens not only the security of individual nations but the survival of civilization as we know it.

The deterioration of the earth's biological systems is not a peripheral issue of concern only to environmentalists. The global economy depends on these biological systems. Anything that threatens their viability threatens the global economy. Any deterioration in these systems represents a deterioration in the human prospect.

As the seventies [progressed] these new threats [became] more visible. During the decade, food shortages . . . led to temporary rises in death rates in at least a dozen countries. Indeed, the lives lost to the increase in hunger may [have exceeded] the combat casualties in all the international conflicts of the [preceding] two decades.

Global food insecurity and the associated instability in food prices have become a common source of political instability. The centuries-old dynasty in Ethiopia came to an end in 1974 not because a foreign power invaded and prevailed but because ecological deterioration precipitated a food crisis and famine. In the summer of 1976 the Polish Government was badly shaken by riots when it sought to raise food prices closer to the world level. In 1977, the riots that followed official attempts to raise food prices in Egypt came closer to toppling the government of President Anwar Sadat than has Israeli military power.[2]

The need for countries to confront these threats and to address them cooperatively suggests that the military's role in securing a nation's well-being and survival is relatively less important than it once was. At the same time, protecting and securing the future of a nation by strengthening international cooperation, developing alternative energy sources, and producing adequate food supplies are escalating in importance. . . .

[At this point Brown discusses threats to national security growing out of developments relating to energy, the deterioration of biological systems, climate modification, global food production and distribution, and economic issues— *eds.*]

The military threat to national security is only one of many that governments must now address. The numerous new threats derive directly or indirectly from the rapidly changing relationship between humanity and the earth's natural systems and resources. The unfolding stresses in this relationship initially manifest themselves as ecological stresses and resource scarcities. Later they translate into economic stresses—inflation, unemployment, capital scarcity, and monetary instability. Ultimately, these economic stresses convert into social unrest and political instability.

National defense establishments are useless against these new threats. Neither bloated military budgets nor highly sophisticated weapons systems can halt the deforestation or solve the firewood crisis now affecting so many Third World countries. Blocking external aggression may be a relatively simple matter compared with arresting the deterioration of local ecological systems.

The new threats to national security are extraordinarily complex. Ecologists understand that the deteriorating relationship between four billion humans and the earth's biological systems cannot continue. But few political leaders have yet to grasp the social significance of this unsustainable situation.

Analyzing and understanding the nature and scale of these new threats to national security will challenge the information-gathering and analytical skills of governments. Unfortunately, the decision-making apparatus in most governments is not organized to balance threats of a traditional military nature with those of ecological and economic origins. Many political leaders perceive the new threats to security dimly, if at all. Intelligence agencies are organized to alert political leaders to potential military threats, but there is no counterpart network for warning of the collapse of a biological system. Military strategists understand the nature of military threats. Energy analysts understand the need to shift from oil to alternative energy sources, and ecologists understand the need to arrest ecological deterioration. But few individuals are trained or able to weigh and evaluate such a diversity of threats and then to translate such an assessment into the allocation of public resources that provides the greatest national security.

If military threats are considered in isolation, military strength of adversaries or potential adversaries can be measured in terms of the number of men under arms, the number and effectiveness of tanks, planes, and other military equipment, and (where the superpowers are concerned) the number of nuclear warheads and delivery missiles. Given the desire to be somewhat stronger than one's opponents, those fashioning the military budget can argue precisely and convincingly for a heavy commitment of public resources to the manufacture of weapons.

Non-military threats to a nation's security are much less clearly defined than military ones. They are often the result of cumulative processes that ultimately lead to the collapse of biological systems or to the depletion of a country's oil reserves. These processes in themselves are seldom given much thought until they pass a critical threshold and disaster strikes. Thus, it is easier in the government councils of developing countries to justify expenditures for the latest-model jet fighters than for family planning to arrest the population growth that leads to food scarcity. Likewise, in industrial societies vast expenditures on long-range missiles are easier to obtain than the investments in energy conservation needed to buy time to develop alternative energy sources.

The purpose of national security deliberations should not be to maximize military strength but to maximize national security. If this latter approach were used, public resources would be distributed more widely among the many threats to national security—both the traditional military one and the newer, less precisely measured ones.

The purpose of this paper is not to argue for specific military budget cuts. Rather it is to suggest that profound new threats to the security of nations are arising and that these need to be fully considered along with the traditional ones. Only then can national security be optimized. . . .

Lags in reordering budgetary allocations to confront the new threats to national security are glaring. In 1977, global research expenditures on arms research [were] six times those for energy research, but all nations might be far more secure if this ratio were reversed. Even though a 3-percent annual population growth rate in a Third World country (which translates into a 19-fold increase in a century) can destroy a country's ecological system and social structure more effectively than a foreign adversary ever could, expenditures on population education and family planning are often negligible or nonexistent. Countries will expend large sums on tanks and planes to defend their territorial sovereignty but nothing to conserve the soil on which their livelihoods depend.

A scarcity of vital resources such as oil or grain could lead to intense competition among countries for supplies, a competition that could easily escalate into military conflict. Competition between Iceland and Great Britain over the North Atlantic cod fisheries, between India and Bangladesh over the waters of the Ganges, and between Mexican and U.S. workers for jobs in the United States all manifest the new threats to national economic security posed by scarcity.

The continuing focus of governments on military threats to security may not only exclude attention to the newer threats, but may also make the effective address of the latter more difficult. The heavy military emphasis on national security can absorb budgetary resources, management skills, and scientific talent that should be devoted to the new non-military threats. Given the enormous investment required to shift the global economy from oil to alternative energy sources, one might well ask whether the world could afford the sustained large-scale use of military might of the sort deployed in World Wars I and II. Indeed, the absurdity of the traditional view is pointed out by science-fiction writer Isaac Asimov: "Even a non-nuclear war cannot be fought because it is too energy-rich a phenomenon." We cannot afford such extravagance, contends Asimov, "and are going to have to use all our energy to stay alive" with none "to spare for warfare."[3] In effect, there simply may not be enough fuel to operate both tanks and tractors. At some point governments will be forced either to realign priorities in a manner responsive to the new threats or to watch their national security deteriorate.

The scientific talent required to make the energy transition and to prevent the destruction of biological systems is enormous. The all-out mobilization that circumstances call for entails, among other things, shifting part of that one-fourth of the world's scientific talent now employed in the military sector to the energy sector. At a time when oil reserves are being depleted, developing new energy systems may be more essential to a nation's survival than new weapons systems.

Apart from the heavy claim on public resources, the continuing exorbitant investment in armaments contributes to a psychological climate of suspicion and mistrust that makes the cooperative international address of new threats to the security of nations next to impossible. Conversely, a reduction in military expenditures by major powers would likely lead to a more cooperative attitude among national governments.

In a world that is not only ecologically interdependent but economically and politically interdependent as well, the concept of "national" security is no longer adequate. Individual countries must respond to global crises because national governments are still the principal decision-makers, but many threats to security require a coordinated international response. The times call for efforts to secure the global systems on which nations depend. If the global climatic system is inadvertently altered by human activity, all countries will be affected. If the international monetary system is not secure, all national economies will suffer. If countries do not cooperate and preserve oceanic fisheries, food prices everywhere will rise. But political leaders have yet to realize that national security is meaningless without global security.

In some situations, countries could be drawn together into a variety of cooperative efforts to cope with shared problems. The Soviet need for assured access to U.S. grain, for example, . . . led to a five-year U.S.-Soviet grain agreement, and to strengthened economic ties between the two superpowers. Similarly, Middle Eastern oil-exporting countries have turned to Western banks for assistance in the management of their vast financial reserves.

In the late twentieth century the key to national security is sustainability. If the biological underpinnings of the global economic system cannot be secured, then the long-term economic outlook is grim indeed. If new energy sources and systems are not in place as the oil wells begin to go dry, then severe economic disruptions are inevitable. . . .

. . . Neither individual security nor national security can be sensibly considered in isolation. In effect, the traditional military concept of "national security" is growing ever less adequate as nonmilitary threats grow more formidable.

NOTES

1. Ruth Leger Sivard, *World Military and Social Expenditures 1977* (Leesburg, Virginia: WMSE Publications, 1977).
2. Jack Shepherd, *The Politics of Starvation* (Washington, D.C.: Carnegie Endowment for International Peace, 1975); Flora Lewis, "A Feeling of Crisis is Rising in Poland," *New York Times,* September 19, 1976; "Egypt Suspends Price Increases as Riots Worsen," *New York Times,* January 20, 1977.
3. "Dr. Asimov: The Future is No Fun," *Washington Star,* April 27, 1975.

32

Entering the Twenty-first Century

© GLOBAL 2000 REPORT

The interrelated environmental threats and their possible consequences for life in the twenty-first century are clearly documented in this excerpt from *The Global 2000 Report to the President*. The complete *Global 2000 Report* is a massive document containing the United States government's first systematic attempt to examine the relationships among global trends and to make projections about their long-term consequences. The study concludes unambiguously that to avoid future disasters, hard political choices must be made today.

. . . The world in 2000 will be different from the world today in important ways. There will be more people. For every two persons on the earth in 1975 there will be three in 2000. The number of poor will have increased. Four-fifths of the world's population will live in less developed countries. Furthermore, in terms of persons per year added to the world, population growth will be 40 percent *higher* in 2000 than in 1975.

The gap between the richest and the poorest will have increased. By every measure of material welfare the [*Global 2000*] study provides—per capita GNP and consumption of food, energy, and minerals—the gap will widen. For example, the gap between the GNP per capita in the LDCs and the industrialized countries is projected to grow from about $4,000 in 1975 to about $7,900 in 2000. Great disparities within countries are also expected to continue.

There will be fewer resources to go around. While on a worldwide average there was about four-tenths of a hectare of arable land per person in 1975, there will be only about one-quarter hectare per person in 2000. . . . By 2000 nearly 1,000 billion barrels of the world's total original petroleum resource of approximately 2,000 billion barrels will have been consumed. Over just the 1975-2000 period, the world's remaining petroleum resources per capita can be expected to decline by at least 50 percent. Over the same period world per capita water supplies will decline by 35 percent because of greater population alone; increasing competing demands will put further pressure on available water supplies. The world's per capita growing stock of wood is projected to be 47 percent lower in 2000 than in 1978.

The environment will have lost important life-supporting capabilities. By

Reprinted from *The Global 2000 Report to the President*, Vol. I: Entering the Twenty-first Century. (Washington, D.C.: U.S. Government Printing Office, 1980), pp. 39–42. Footnotes have been deleted.

2000, 40 percent of the forests still remaining in the LDCs in 1978 will have been razed. The atmospheric concentration of carbon dioxide will be nearly one-third higher than preindustrial levels. Soil erosion will have removed, on the average, several inches of soil from croplands all over the world. Desertification (including salinization) may have claimed a significant fraction of the world's rangeland and cropland. Over little more than two decades, 15-20 percent of the earth's total species of plants and animals will have become extinct—a loss of at least 500,000 species.

Prices will be higher. The price of many of the most vital resources is projected to rise in real terms—that is, over and above inflation. In order to meet projected demand, a 100 percent increase in the real price of food will be required. To keep energy demand in line with anticipated supplies, the real price of energy is assumed to rise more than 150 percent over the 1975-2000 period. Supplies of water, agricultural land, forest products, and many traditional marine fish species are projected to decline relative to growing demand at current prices, which suggests that real price rises will occur in these sectors too. Collectively, the projections suggest that resource-based inflationary pressures will continue and intensify, especially in nations that are poor in resources or are rapidly depleting their resources.

The world will be more vulnerable both to natural disaster and to disruptions from human causes. Most nations are likely to be still more dependent on foreign sources of energy in 2000 than they are today. Food production will be more vulnerable to disruptions of fossil fuel energy supplies and to weather fluctuations as cultivation expands to more marginal areas. The loss of diverse germ plasm in local strains and wild progenitors of food crops, together with the increase of monoculture, could lead to greater risks of massive crop failures. Larger numbers of people will be vulnerable to higher food prices or even famine when adverse weather occurs. The world will be more vulnerable to the disruptive effects of war. The tensions that could lead to war will have multiplied. The potential for conflict over fresh water alone is underscored by the fact that out of 200 of the world's major river basins, 148 are shared by two countries and 52 are shared by three to ten countries. Long standing conflicts over shared rivers such as the Plata (Brazil, Argentina), Euphrates (Syria, Iraq), or Ganges (Bangladesh, India) could easily intensify.

Finally, it must be emphasized that if public policy continues generally unchanged the world will be different as a result of lost opportunities. The adverse effects of many of the trends discussed in this Study will not be fully evident until 2000 or later; yet the actions that are necessary to change the trends cannot be postponed without foreclosing important options. The opportunity to stabilize the world's population below 10 billion, for example, is slipping away; Robert McNamara, [former] President of the World Bank, has noted that for every decade of delay in reaching replacement fertility, the world's ultimately stabilized population will be about 11 percent greater. Similar losses of opportunity accompany delayed perceptions or action in other areas. If energy policies and decisions are based on yesterday's (or even today's) oil prices, the opportunity to wisely invest scarce capital resources will be lost as a consequence of undervaluing conservation and efficiency. If agricultural research continues to focus on increasing yields through practices that are highly energy-intensive, both energy resources and the time needed to develop alternative practices will be lost.

The full effects of rising concentrations of carbon dioxide, depletion of stratospheric ozone, deterioration of soils, increasing introduction of complex persistent toxic chemicals into the environment, and massive extinction of species may not occur until well after 2000. Yet once such global environmental problems are in motion they are very difficult to reverse. In fact, few if any of the problems addressed in the Global 2000 Study are amenable to quick technological or policy fixes; rather, they are inextricably mixed with the world's most perplexing social and economic problems.

Perhaps the most troubling problems are those in which population growth and poverty lead to serious long-term declines in the productivity of renewable natural resource systems. In some areas the capacity of renewable resource systems to support human populations is already being seriously damaged by efforts of present populations to meet desperate immediate needs, and the damage threatens to become worse.

Examples of serious deterioration of the earth's most basic resources can already be found today in scattered places in all nations, including the industrialized countries and the better-endowed LDCs. For instance, erosion of agricultural soil and salinization of highly productive irrigated farmland is increasingly evident in the United States, and extensive deforestation, with more or less permanent soil degradation, has occurred in Brazil, Venezuela, and Colombia. But problems related to the decline of the earth's carrying capacity are most immediate, severe, and tragic in those regions of the earth containing the poorest LDCs.

Sub-Saharan Africa faces the problem of exhaustion of its resource base in an acute form. Many causes and effects have come together there to produce excessive demands on the environment, leading to expansion of the desert. Overgrazing, fuelwood gathering, and destructive cropping practices are the principal immediate causes of a series of transitions from open woodland, to scrub, to fragile semiarid range, to worthless weeds and bare earth. Matters are made worse when people are forced by scarcity of fuelwood to burn animal dung and crop wastes. The soil, deprived of organic matter, loses fertility and the ability to hold water— and the desert expands. In Bangladesh, Pakistan, and large parts of India, efforts by growing numbers of people to meet their basic needs are damaging the very cropland, pasture, forests, and water supplies on which they must depend for a livelihood. To restore the lands and soils would require decades—if not centuries—*after* the existing pressures on the land have diminished. But the pressures are growing, not diminishing.

There are no quick or easy solutions, particularly in those regions where population pressure is already leading to a reduction of the carrying capacity of the land. In such regions a complex of social and economic factors (including very low incomes, inequitable land tenure, limited or no educational opportunities, a lack of nonagricultural jobs, and economic pressures toward higher fertility) underlies the decline in the land's carrying capacity. Furthermore, it is generally believed that social and economic conditions must improve before fertility levels will decline to replacement levels. Thus a vicious circle of causality may be at work. Environmental deterioration caused by large populations creates living conditions that make reductions in fertility difficult to achieve; all the while, continuing population growth increases further the pressures on the environment and land.

The declines in carrying capacity already being observed in scattered areas around the world point to a phenomenon that could easily be much more widespread by 2000. In fact, the best evidence now available—even allowing for the many beneficial effects of technological developments and adoptions—suggests that by 2000 the world's human population may be within only a few generations of reaching the entire planet's carrying capacity.

The Global 2000 Study does not estimate the earth's carrying capacity, but it does provide a basis for evaluating an earlier estimate published in the U.S. National Academy of Sciences' report, *Resources and Man*. In this 1969 report, the Academy concluded that a world population of 10 billion "is close to (if not above) the maximum that an *intensively managed* world might hope to support with some degree of comfort and individual choice." The Academy also concluded that even with the sacrifice of individual freedom and choice, and even with chronic near starvation for the great majority, the human population of the world is unlikely to ever exceed 30 billion.

Nothing in the Global 2000 Study counters the Academy's conclusions. If anything, data gathered over the past decade suggest the Academy may have underestimated the extent of some problems, especially deforestation and the loss and deterioration of soils.

At present and projected growth rates, the world's population would rapidly approach the Academy's figures. If the fertility and mortality rates projected for 2000 were to continue unchanged into the twenty-first century, the world's population would reach 10 billion by 2030. Thus anyone with a present life expectancy of an additional 50 years could expect to see the world population reach 10 billion. This same rate of growth would produce a population of nearly 30 billion before the end of the twenty-first century.

Here it must be emphasized that, unlike most of the Global 2000 Study projections, the population projections assume extensive policy changes and developments to reduce fertility rates. Without the assumed policy changes, the projected rate of population growth would be still more rapid.

Unfortunately population growth may be slowed for reasons other than declining birth rates. As the world's populations exceed and reduce the land's carrying capacity in widening areas, the trends of the last century or two toward improved health and longer life may come to a halt. Hunger and disease may claim more lives—especially lives of babies and young children. More of those surviving infancy may be mentally and physically handicapped by childhood malnutrition.

The time for action to prevent this outcome is running out. Unless nations collectively and individually take bold and imaginative steps toward improved social and economic conditions, reduced fertility, better management of resources, and protection of the environment, the world must expect a troubled entry into the twenty-first century.

33

Coping with Resource Scarcity: A Critique of Lifeboat Ethics

MARVIN S. SOROOS

"The tragedy of the commons" and "lifeboat ethics" are popular metaphors commonly used to examine policy alternatives for coping with ecological stresses. Marvin S. Soroos critically evaluates the policy prescriptions flowing from the metaphors, both popularized by Garrett Hardin. Among other things, Soroos observes how ecological stresses derive as much from overconsumption among developed countries as from overpopulation among developing countries. Soroos is associate professor of political science at North Carolina State University. Among his publications is *The Global Predicament* (edited with David W. Orr, 1979).

The rapid growth of the world's population in recent decades has aroused concern of impending global food and resource scarcities. These anxieties became especially salient during the 1970s following the publication of an influential report to the Club of Rome entitled *The Limits to Growth*, which warned of "a rather sudden and uncontrollable decline in both population and industrial capacity" within the next 100 years if current trends in world population, industrialization, pollution, food production, and resource depletion continued unchanged (Meadows et al., 1972: 23). Shortly after the report was issued, two overlapping international episodes made it appear that perhaps we had already entered into an era of scarcity. One was the so-called "energy crisis," triggered by a temporary oil embargo in 1973 combined with a quadrupling of the price of oil by OPEC in 1973–1974, which drew attention to the world's dependence on dwindling reserves of petroleum concentrated in the politically unstable Middle East. The other was a shortfall in world food production, known as the "world food crisis" of 1972–1974, which was attributable to a combination of factors, among which were unfavorable weather conditions in several important and widely dispersed food growing areas, scarcities of fertilizer caused by the oil embargo, and the collapse of the anchovy fishery off the west coast of Latin America.

This is a substantially revised and updated version of "The Commons and Lifeboat as Guides for International Ecological Policy," which appeared in the *International Studies Quarterly*, Vol. 21, No. 4, December 1977, pp. 647–674.

These developments provoked extensive discussion about what adjustments must be done to cope with global food and resource scarcities. In this article, we shall critically consider the solution proposed by biologist Garrett Hardin. In his widely read and discussed writings, Hardin presents a prescriptive theory of ecological politics which leads him to conclude that the United States should withhold food assistance to the poor and hungry people of the less developed regions in the interest of restraining the rapid population growth that has been taking place in these areas. In doing so, Hardin challenges widely held principles of equity and justice. The impact of Hardin's writings is in part attributable to colorful analogies he uses in presenting his theories. The lesson of "the tragedy of the commons" has become a stock concept in ecological politics. Hardin's more recent theory of "lifeboat ethics" was received by a responsive audience of foreign-aid-weary Americans who look upon rapid population growth trends in the Third World as the primary ecological peril of our times. Due to their relative simplicity, such analogies are often more readily comprehended and analyzed than the actual world in its complexity. Simplification can, however, result in an incomplete or distorted understanding of the nature of the problems being analyzed.

Recently, the problem of scarcity has seemed less compelling. Better than average world harvests during the late 1970s and early 1980s have alleviated the food shortages of earlier years. Moreover, OPEC's successes in raising oil prices tenfold during the 1970s provoked serious efforts to conserve energy and encouraged new suppliers to enter the market bringing about an oil glut on international markets that has forced prices downward. Long-term trends suggest, however, that this period of relative abundance will be a temporary reprieve. Within the decade it is not unlikely that we will again be confronted with global scarcities and will be addressing the issues that Garrett Hardin has raised.

The essay that follows will explain and critically analyze some of Hardin's theories of social ecology, focusing particularly on the doctrine of "lifeboat ethics." First, however, the reader may benefit from a brief summary of the analogies and how Hardin incorporates them into his theories.

THE TRAGEDY OF THE COMMONS

In his essay entitled "The Tragedy of the Commons," Hardin (1968, 1972) refers to the commons systems used centuries ago in English villages to illustrate a fundamental problem of ecological politics. Under the commons system, a village pasture is held as publicly owned property subject to the following rules: (1) each herdsman of the village may pasture as many cattle as he wishes, and (2) the gains resulting from the grazing of cattle accrue entirely to the individual herdsman.

The commons system is a satisfactory arrangement until the capacity of the pasture is reached, at which point additional cattle deplete the grasses and eventually render the pasture worthless for grazing purposes. Ironically, the rules of the commons encourage overgrazing, given that the payoff from the animal goes to its owner exclusively, whereas the entire community divides the accompanying costs in the form of damage to the pasture. Thus, the cost/benefit calculation of each villager dictates adding to his personal herd, even with the knowledge that his actions will accelerate the destruction of the pasture.

Several policy options may be implemented in an effort to conserve the pasture. First, attempts may be made to preserve the commons system by urging villagers to voluntarily limit the size of their herds in the interests of the community. Hardin has little confidence in an approach that relies upon social conscience because of the likelihood that irresponsible villagers will continue adding to their herds. Not only would the efforts of the socially minded villagers to conserve the pasture be counteracted, but they would be taken advantage of by the less scrupulous members of the community. Anticipating the futility of their sacrifices, potentially responsible villagers may decide to add to their herds in order to benefit as much as possible from the remaining grasses.

A second and more promising alternative would also maintain the commons arrangement. Conservation would not depend on volunteerism, however, but on the coercive enforcement of regulations that limit the number of cattle each herdsman may graze.

Two other policy alternatives would discard the commons scheme. A socialist system places both the pasture and the cattle under community ownership with the proceeds from the village herd being divided among the residents based on criteria such as equality or need. A potential drawback of the socialist system derives from the appointed managers' lack of incentive for practicing conservation. Typically, managers are rewarded for high levels of production in the short run, but personally bear only a very small proportion of the long-range costs to the community of an ecological overshoot.

Hardin reacts favorably to a fourth alternative in which the pasture is divided into enclosed sections that become the private property of individual herdsmen. The owner is the sole recipient of profits accruing from grazing cattle on his section and bears all costs resulting from any overgrazing. What makes this "private enterprise" system attractive to Hardin is the incorporation of intrinsic responsibility, an arrangement in which those who make decisions also bear the consequences of their actions. Hardin sees intrinsic responsibility as a more effective inducement to conservation than the "contrived responsibility" of the regulated commons in which threats of penalty or punishment coercively induce compliant behaviors (Hardin, 1972: 101–118).

Several situations display some key elements of the "tragedy of the commons." One of the best examples is the demise of a number of important ocean fisheries, which historically were open to harvesting by the fishermen of any nation for individual profit on a first-come, first-served basis. The use of the atmosphere and oceans for the disposal of pollutants is an example of the overuse of a common resource, not by taking something out of it, but by using it as a sink for harmful wastes. Likewise, a couple's decision to give birth to more and more children who will consume the resources of their community could be likened to a herdsman adding cattle to the village pasture.

LIFEBOAT ETHICS

The "Tragedy of the Commons" analysis has generally been quite well received. In contrast, Hardin's (1974a, 1974b, 1977, 1981) later application of selected elements of the commons theory to world population and food problems in his works on "lifeboat ethics" has provoked considerable controversy (Lucas and Ogletree, 1976; Kothari, 1981–1982).

In an article entitled "Living on a Lifeboat," Hardin (1974b: 561–562) metaphorically places the people of each nation on a lifeboat adrift at sea. Americans are portrayed by 50 occupants of a lifeboat having an estimated capacity of 60. One hundred swimmers, forced from the overcrowded boats of the poor countries, surround the American raft, pleading to be allowed to board.

Hardin identifies three policy alternatives that the fortunate occupants of the American lifeboat may exercise. First, all the swimmers from the overcrowded lifeboats may be pulled aboard, an option that parallels the unrestricted commons arrangement. The "tragedy" occurs when too many climb aboard, causing the lifeboat to sink and drowning both the original and the newly boarded occupants. As Hardin expresses it—"complete justice, complete catastrophe." Second, ten may be admitted to fill up the boat to its capacity of 60, an alternative that has the drawback of sacrificing the margin of safety. How to make a nondiscriminatory decision on which 10 of the 100 swimmers will be allowed aboard is also a problem inherent in the second option. Hardin prefers the third alternative which would deny access to all of the swimmers, thereby leaving them to drown, while preserving the American standard of living for present and future generations. Under the third alternative, he treats the lifeboats of each nation in a manner analogous to a sectioning of the village pasture into private plots. Intrinsic responsibility is incorporated by making the occupants of each lifeboat solely accountable for their survival in the same way that the welfare of the individual herdsman is directly dependent upon how he manages his section of the pasture.

The alternatives available to the occupants of the American lifeboat parallel three types of international food policies. Allowing all swimmers to board is analogous to an attempt to provide food assistance to all of the world's hungry people, either unilaterally or through the contributions to a world food bank. The option of taking on a few swimmers is comparable to policies that concentrate available food assistance on a selected group of countries, while the hungry of other countries are left to starve. The third possibility of allowing no swimmers to board corresponds to a policy of providing no food assistance, leaving it up to the residents of each country to provide for themselves.

Hardin (1974b: 562) is critical of the food assistance to hungry peoples that would be provided under the first two policy options because the food production capacities of the donor countries in effect become a commons system. Access to ample food assistance, he believes, would encourage societies to continue increasing their populations for reasons that parallel the rationale that herdsmen have for adding cattle to the village commons. The "tragedy" occurs when world population significantly exceeds food production during years of poor harvests with the result being widespread famine and starvation.

If all requests for food assistance are denied, as under the third option, societies become "intrinsically responsible" for feeding themselves. The prospect of starvation is seen as a strong incentive for population limitation in the same way the prospect of personally bearing the costs of an overgrazed section of the pasture encourages the herdsmen to practice conservation. If countries fail to limit population growth, the resulting diebacks would bring population size into equilibrium with food production capacities, thereby preventing more serious population/food imbalances in the future (Hardin, 1974b: 563–565).

Let us now turn to an analysis of Hardin's analogies and the theories he has derived from them. The immediate urge is to attack what on the surface appears to be a repugnant and outrageous sense of values. If Hardin's analysis of the problem is valid, however, it is difficult to escape his conclusions, for the prospect of overshoot hardly seems any more palatable. The empirical and logical underpinnings are a more promising point of attack. In adopting this latter strategy, we shall examine Hardin's interpretation of ecological problems as well as the practicality of the "lifeboat" approach to environmental policy in the international context.

CARRYING CAPACITY AND THE NATURE OF ECOLOGICAL PROBLEMS

The concept of carrying capacity is a stock component of ecological theory which is used to refer to a threshold, the surpassing of which results in an overshoot evidenced by some type of eco-breakdown. In the commons analogy, carrying capacity is simply the number of cattle a pasture can sustain indefinitely without depleting its grasses. In the metaphor of the lifeboat, carrying capacity is the maximum number of people a raft will support without sinking or capsizing.

In applying the concept of carrying capacity to actual ecological problems, it is tempting to translate the numbers of cattle on the pasture or of occupants of a lifeboat in Hardin's metaphors into population sizes of countries. Defining carrying capacity solely in numbers of people logically leads to Hardin's conclusion that the greatest ecological perils lie in the high population growth rates of the less-developed regions, which already count for three-quarters of the world's population.

Overpopulation or Overconsumption?

Calculating carrying capacity becomes a more complex task when we recognize that all human beings do not necessarily count equally in an environmental sense. It is not only the existence of people that overburdens ecosystems, but also their levels of consumption and rates of waste discharge. When resources are finite and scarce, the exceeding of subsistence levels by any part of the world's population reduces the number of people that can be sustained by the natural endowments of the planet.

A few statistics should suffice to establish that levels of consumption are an important consideration in calculations of the planetary carrying capacity. Figures on the GNP/capita of countries provide an admittedly rough but nevertheless revealing approximation of overall consumption (Sivard 1982: 31). By 1979 the GNP/capita for several of the advanced industrial countries had surpassed $10,000, which is more than fifty times as great as the figures for the least developed countries that in many cases were less than $300. The latter group of countries accounts for nearly half of the world's population. In the same year, the average resident of the United States consumed an amount of energy equivalent to 11,382 kilograms of coal, whereas the comparable figure for the average citizen of India was only 190 kilograms (Sivard, 1981: 39). The per capita consumption of metals in the United States in 1975 was 200 pounds, compared to 4 and 8 pounds per capita in Africa and Asia, respectively (U.S. Council on Environmental Quality, 1980: 208). Daily food consumption in the developed world averages 3,440 calories per capita, compared to only 2,344 in the less developed countries (Sivard, 1982: 31). From these figures it is apparent that the ecological impact of the average citizen of the developed countries is at least several times greater than that of the inhabitants of the less-developed world.

The extent of these inequalities has two implications for our analysis of Hardin's theories. First, the roots of the major planetary ecological dangers of our times are, apparently, to be found not only in the demographic trends in less-developed regions, but to an even greater extent in the lavish life-styles of the western world. Limitations on consumption of resources and restraints on population growth are both important elements in global ecological policies. Second, reducing unnecessary and wasteful resource consumption in the industrial world would allow for a substantial increase in the number of people that the planet could accommodate. In terms of the lifeboat metaphor, the occupants of the American boat could potentially squeeze together, or better yet, diet to make considerably more than ten spaces available to the swimmers.

Overpopulation or Underdevelopment?

Whereas the capacity of the lifeboat is fixed, reseeding, fertilization, and irrigation can increase the grazing potential of a village pasture. The capacity of a country or region to sustain a population is more similar to the latter in that it can vary upward with the implementation of appropriate development strategies and the availability of technology and capital. For example, grain yields per acre in developed countries have been roughly fifty percent higher than in less-developed regions, a discrepancy that is less attributable to soil and weather conditions than to agricultural research and the availability of fertilizer, advanced seed varieties, pesticides, herbicides, machinery, and diesel fuel (Johnson, 1975: 62–64). By more fully developing their agricultural potential, less-developed countries may be able to reduce substantially their dependence on foreign sources of food. It should be borne in mind, however, that improper applications of agricultural technologies can have very adverse effects on the long-term productivity of a region, a lesson that man has been learning since ancient times (Hughes, 1975; Eckholm, 1976).

The potential for increasing the carrying capacity of the planet has also been demonstrated by a United Nations sponsored study which challenged some of the ominous findings of *The Limits to Growth*. It concluded that world resources are sufficient to support higher living standards for a growing population without inevitable environmental damage. The limits to accelerated development are seen as being political, social, and institutional in character with the key imperative being a reduction in the income gap between the rich and poor nations through significant changes in the world economic order (Leontieff, et al., 1977). Expressed in terms of the lifeboat metaphor, strengthening the structure of the rafts of the less-developed countries would enable them to support many of their occupants who otherwise would fall into the water and swim over to the American lifeboat.

Recognizing that carrying capacity is partly a function of capital and technology, it is difficult to distinguish overpopulation from poverty and low levels of economic development. Hunger and malnutrition, which Hardin sees as manifestations of overpopulation, may also be attributable to inequalities in the international distribution of wealth. That these inequalities are largely a consequence of centuries of colonialism as well as contemporary forms of international economic domination is a compelling reason to raise ethical challenges to Hardin's lifeboat policies, which would have the developed countries turn away from problems they played a considerable role in creating.

Population Growth and the Logic of the Commons

The strategies just cited for making fuller use of the natural resources of the planet may be rejected as merely being stopgap measures. Hardin argues that providing food assistance to the poor allows "excess" people to survive and to multiply relentlessly until eventually all mankind is struggling for survival. In making this point, Hardin (1975: 415) cites an axiom he refers to as "Gregg's Law" which states that "a cancer cannot be cured by feeding it." Does this "law" apply to population growth? Or should we accept Brown's (1974: 119) contention that "good nutrition is the best contraceptive."

Since there is no apparent motivation for the cast of characters in the lifeboat analogy to increase their numbers, let us focus on the commons metaphor. Hardin is concerned that couples will continue to add to their families and nations will increase their populations for reasons which parallel the calculation of gains and losses that motivated the herdsmen to continue adding cattle to an overgrazed pasture. Is this inference warranted?

Children can be an economic asset, particularly in rural regions of lesser-developed countries in which child labor is helpful and is not prohibited. Children also offer their parents security where governments are not able to provide social security for the elderly. Conversely, lower population growth rates in highly urbanized, industrial regions may be a consequence of the high cost of raising children who will contribute very little if anything to family income as they grow up and are not relied upon for financial support in old age.

Another basic factor in the decision of the herdsmen, however, is the extent to which the costs of grazing cattle are shared by the community. Thus, we would predict that countries having the greatest amount of publicly financed social services, such as education and health programs, which are in effect a commons arrangement, would also have the highest population growth rates. This expectation is not borne out empirically. For example, some of the most elaborate services are provided by European countries, which are also among the nations that most nearly approximate zero population growth. Similarly, among less-developed societies, those countries that have distributed income, employment, education, and health services most broadly, such as Sri Lanka, have experienced more substantial drops in population growth rates than those that have concentrated them within an elite (Holdgate et al., 1982: 312).

What accounts for these demographic trends? Perhaps in contrast to the grazing of cattle on the village commons, the financial costs of raising children in most societies falls more heavily on the individual family than on the community. Moreover, raising children is perceived as a greater sacrifice by prospective parents, particularly mothers, who could otherwise take advantage of a broad range of social opportunities. Thus, even with extensive social services, there is still a strong measure of intrinsic responsibility in providing for the needs of children.

Turning to national population policies, a few countries, including Brazil and Argentina, have adopted pro-natalist policies based on the premise that a larger population will facilitate economic growth. Even with generous food assistance from abroad, however, the expenses of providing the basic material needs and social services for a growing population still fall far more heavily upon national governments than upon the international community. This explains why 60 nations accounting for more than 95 percent of the population of less-developed regions have instituted programs designed to reduce birth rates (Holdgate et al., 1982: 310). A particularly noteworthy example is China which has adopted strong incentives and disincentives in an effort to reduce family size and achieve zero population growth by the year 2000 (Marden et al., 1982: 85–86).

To what can the population "explosion" in many lesser-developed regions be attributed, if not to a calculation of personal or national gains and losses? The theory of the demographic transition provides a more plausible explanation. In traditional societies, norms favoring large families became deeply ingrained as an adaptation to high infant and child mortality rates. With the widespread availability of health services and better nutrition during the post-war era, mortality rates have dropped sharply. Since compensating changes in social attitudes pertaining to fertility evolve more slowly, birth rates continue at high levels. In time, birth rates can be expected to follow the decline in death rates, thus stabilizing population sizes. The decline in world population growth rate to 1.7 percent a year from a peak of nearly 2.0 percent in the 1960s is an encouraging sign that the demographic transition has progressed to its latter stages on a worldwide basis. Also promising are rapid reductions in the fertility rates of a number of Third World countries, notable examples of which are Chile, Colombia, Venezuela,

China, South Korea, Malaysia, Singapore, and Sri Lanka (Marden et al., 1982: 124). A key factor in the development programs of these countries has been a more equitable distribution of income and social services, particularly in regard to education, health, nutrition, and employment.

The critique thus far has sought not to demonstrate that ecological concerns are unfounded, but rather to show that Hardin's analysis of the nature and immediacy of these problems is misleading. Not only are there possibilities for accommodating substantially more human beings with a measure of dignity, but there is evidence that the recent surge in population may be a temporary phenomenon triggered by unique historical circumstances. Optimism should be restrained, however, because the completion of a demographic transition is not inevitable, particularly in countries where little progress has been made toward economic development and social justice. Even where it does take place, the pace of change may not be fast enough to avert a disastrous overshoot.

SELF-RELIANCE AS ECOLOGICAL POLICY

Hardin (1972: 101–108) suggests that ecologically accountable behaviors can be encouraged most effectively by policies that incorporate intrinsic responsibility, an arrangement in which whoever commits an act, in this case one which overburdens the environment, is also the one who is most directly affected by its consequences. In critiquing this approach to ecological policy, let us adopt the technique of *reductio ad absurdum* by which the absurdity of a position is demonstrated by extending it to its logical conclusions. In particular, questions will be raised about the selectivity of Hardin's application of intrinsic responsibility as well as the practicality of applying the principle more broadly.

Intrinsic Responsibility in the Consumption of Food

To establish intrinsic responsibility in matters of population, Hardin would leave each society to fend for itself by denying it food assistance, even in the event of famines caused by fluctuations in climate, which he considers to be inevitable natural occurrences. Without access to a global food commons, either through bilateral assistance or a world food bank, he believes that greater efforts would be made to limit fertility in order to avoid the painful consequences of hunger and malnutrition.

Though it is clear that food assistance programs are inconsistent with the practice of intrinsic responsibility, is not the policy also violated by the sale of food to wealthier countries that are unable to meet their agricultural requirements from domestic production? Don't reliable opportunities to buy a commodity at readily affordable prices discourage restraint in consumption to as great a degree as uncertain prospects for timely foreign generosity? The primary distinction between food aid and trade is the financial capacity of the importer to pay the international market price. Thus, to suggest that a policy of intrinsic responsibility should rule out aid but not purchased imports confuses the environmental carrying capacity of a country with its purchasing power. The concept of carrying capacity is again inappropriately shifted from the environmental realm into the context of economics.

If food aid and trade are classified together, the list of countries that exceed their carrying capacity would be expanded considerably. A number of industrial countries are highly dependent on foreign supplies of food, Japan and the Soviet Union being notable examples. Much of the best agricultural land in less-developed countries where hunger is widespread is cash cropped, in some cases by large multinational agrobusinesses, for export to developed countries which can pay a higher price for what is produced on the land (Lappé and Collins, 1977: 270–288). Furthermore, developed nations, possessing technologically sophisticated factory ships, are the principal harvesters of fish taken in international waters. Ironically, even a sizeable proportion of the marine harvest of less-developed countries is exported to the developed world, partly for use as livestock feed and pet food. Thus, an extension of a policy of intrinsic responsibility to food trade would require major adjustments in the developed world, in some cases greater than the adaptations less-developed nations would have to make if the present meager flow of food assistance were discontinued.

Intrinsic Responsibility in the Consumption of Nonrenewable Resources

Throughout history man has learned to make use of an increasing variety of natural resources in pursuit of survival and an enhanced standard of living. In Hardin's application of "lifeboat ethics," the only type of resources mentioned is food. If for the sake of argument we temporarily accept the logic of intrinsic responsibility, aren't we faced with an equally compelling rationale for applying the practice to the consumption of other resources, such as fossil fuels and minerals? While nonfood resources are in most cases less basic to human survival, many are integral to a modern, industrial life-style, and, in some cases, even to the production of food. More importantly, unlike food supplies which can be replenished annually, assuming proper agricultural practices, reserves of fossil fuels and minerals are nonrenewable resources. A "tragedy" involving nonrenewable resource commons would be more serious because of its permanent consequences. Moreover, as with food, it could be argued that requiring national self-sufficiency in the consumption of nonrenewable resources would be a strong inducement for conservation.

The developed countries have become heavily dependent upon outside sources, especially in the Third World, for the nonrenewable natural resources essential to their industrial economies. Low prices for these resources on international markets during most of the post-World War II era encouraged high and wasteful levels of consumption. By the mid-1970s the United States had become a net importer of minerals and was almost completely dependent on foreign mines for 22 of 74 essential nonenergy minerals (Keyfitz, 1976). Japan depends on imports for virtually all of the petroleum that it consumes and 85 percent of its total energy needs (Murakami, 1982: 138). The European countries have looked to outside sources for more than half of their energy requirements.

Extending the logic of intrinsic responsibility to nonrenewable resources reinforces the conclusions drawn in preceding sections. First, population growth in the developing world should not be singled out as the only major ecological peril. High rates of resource consumption in the industrial world are a problem of comparable magnitude. Second, radical changes in consumption patterns by developed societies would be necessary to realize resource self-sufficiency. In view of Hardin's allegation that the leaders of the less-developed countries lack sufficient wisdom and power, it is interesting to note that more is being done to limit population growth in these regions than to conserve nonrenewable resources in the industrial world.

Intrinsic Responsibility and a Rational Use of Resources

Would it be practical to apply the doctrine of "lifeboat ethics" to imports as well as to aid and to extend the same practice to nonrenewable resources as well as to food? In essence, such an approach to ecological policy would require all societies to become fully resource self-sufficient. To explore the ramifications of this possibility let us further refine each of Hardin's analogies.

Recall that Hardin proposes dividing the village pasture into privately owned sections as a means of establishing intrinsic responsibility. Let us assume that the boundaries are drawn in such a manner that the only watering hole lies entirely within one section, leaving the owner little area for grazing cattle. In contrast, other sections have grass in bountiful quantities, but no access to water. If each section is to be a self-sufficient unit, of what value will any of the plots be for supporting cattle? In the case of the lifeboat analogy, let us assume that one lifeboat has the only containers of food, a second has the only containers of water, and a third has the only instrument that will open the containers. How favorable will their survival prospects be if the occupants of each lifeboat doggedly maintain their self-sufficiency by refusing to cooperate with the occupants of the other lifeboats?

In the original versions of the analogies, as presented by Hardin, no provision is made for interdependence as a factor relevant to the choice of environmental policies. In the modified analogies, self-sufficiency would clearly be impractical and would preclude an effective utilization of what resources are available. The modified analogies better reflect the irregular distribution of the natural endowments of the planet, for no country or even region is completely self-sufficient in resources.

Viewed from this perspective, the excess food growing capacity of the United States becomes an element in a global web of interdependencies, which parallels the concentrations of reserves of petroleum in the OPEC countries or chromite in the Republic of South Africa and the Soviet Union. If food is withheld from world trade by the United States, either vast amounts of surplus food would be wasted, or large areas of land would have to be taken out of production while substantial "diebacks" of people would be taking place in traditional food importing countries. At the same time the United States would be unable to import petroleum and minerals it lacks domestically, but which are nevertheless essential to its industrial and agricultural production. Likewise, if the OPEC countries were to withhold petroleum from international trade in the interests of energy conservation in the developed world, the economies of these importing countries would be severely jolted, touching off sharp economic reverberations throughout the international economic system. The OPEC members would have more petroleum reserves than their present or future populations could ever hope to consume, and would not be allowed to import the many resources that they lack domestically. Additionally, in the unlikely event that all nations become resource self-sufficient, some major mineral exporting countries in the developing world would lose much of their export revenue as well as foreign investments of capital and technology needed to produce these resources.

International trade is a necessary ingredient of a rational utilization of natural resources of the planet, given irregularities in their distribution. Without these exchanges, the effective carrying capacity of the planet would be substantially reduced. The residents of many nations are already living far beyond a level that could be sustained by relying solely on the natural resources found within their boundaries. Major reductions would be necessary both in the size of national populations and the quality of life for those who remain. At the same time, immense quantities of resources that could be consumed in an ecologically responsible manner would be underutilized. In effect, an enforced policy of self-reliance would avert an overshoot having global proportions at the expense of numerous national overshoots that collectively could be far more costly and disruptive.

THE VULNERABILITY OF DEVELOPED SOCIETIES

Let us consider the practicality of lifeboat ethics from one additional perspective. Hardin suggests that one of the greatest dangers to the developed world is, paradoxically, the sympathy and generosity of its residents. Implicit in the commons analogy, however, is an assumption that the individual herdsman can divorce himself from the destiny of his neighbors simply by fencing off his privately owned section of the pasture. Likewise, there is no recognition in Hardin's presentation of the lifeboat metaphor that the desperate swimmers pose any threat to the comfortable occupants of the American raft. Is it realistic to assume that a prosperous, overfed minority of the world's population can insulate itself from the problems of a poor, hungry majority that believes its plight is largely a result of a long history of exploitation?

The developed world is not impregnable. On the contrary, the process of industrialization increases the vulnerability of a nation. As societies become accustomed to an abundant variety of goods and services, their welfare becomes more and more dependent upon events beyond their boundaries (Sprout and Sprout, 1974: 18). In previous sections, mention has been made of a growing reliance of industrial countries on foreign sources of petroleum and minerals. The actions of the OPEC countries in 1973–1974 revealed the detrimental impact that embargoes, sharp price increases, or cutbacks in production can have on the highly integrated economic processes of the developed world.

Food shortages may exacerbate political and economic instabilities within less-developed societies that can have serious implications for the industrial world. Financially profitable investments by multinational corporations may, for example, be jeopardized by unsympathetic revolutionary movements that capitalize on the resentments that would inevitably be provoked by an imposition of lifeboat policies. Perhaps the lifeboat metaphor would be more realistic if it were rewritten with all of humanity being placed on one lifeboat, such that a hole in any part of the boat would doom both the rich and poor occupants alike. A Hardinist may notice that a leak has sprung, but because it is in the section of the less developed peoples, mistakenly conclude that it should be of little concern to Americans (Howe and Sewell, 1975: 62).

Militarily, Hardin (1976: 129) doubts that less-developed countries will ever pose a worrisome threat to the United States. While overwhelming military strength can provide security against an open armed attack by a weak nation, it does not eliminate the possibility that political extremists, incensed by the magnitude of international injustices, could cause discomfort for rich societies by a variety of forms of sabotage, terrorism, kidnapping, and blackmail. Nuclear explosives may become available to terrorists who could threaten to detonate them in heavily populated areas as a way of extorting concessions from the developed countries. Relatively inexpensive chemical or biological weapons could have considerable nuisance potential in industrial countries if introduced into the water systems of metropolitan areas. Because of the complexity and impersonality of social relations in modern industrial societies, disrupters have a tactical advantage over those attempting to maintain order (Giddings, 1974; Segre and Adler, 1973).

Saboteurs may even be citizens of the target country, who are knowledgeable of its vulnerabilities and are sympathetic to the plight of the disadvantaged peoples of the world. Past experience with skyjacking reveals that even marginally adequate efforts to prevent sabotage require sizeable commitments of resources as well as the cooperation of many other states in denying disrupters a sanctuary. Moreover, residents of industrial countries may be called upon to tolerate additional inconveniences and restrictions on their personal freedoms.

It is doubtful that wealthy societies can fully secure themselves, especially if a policy of indifference toward hunger and poverty in the less-developed regions sharpens and intensifies hostilities among those who are less fortunate. The response of the frustrated may take the form of a vengeful striking out against the bastions of wealth and privilege. It may be designed more purposively to call attention to injustices in the distribution of the world's wealth or even to coerce a transfer of food and resources from the rich to the poor countries. In terms of Hardin's metaphor, imagine the possibility of the American lifeboat being rocked or capsized by desperate, vindictive swimmers or that one of them possesses a knife that could be used to slash and sink the lifeboat.

A GLOBALIST ALTERNATIVE TO LIFEBOAT ETHICS

The preceding analysis has not questioned Hardin's concern with ecological problems, but only his interpretation of these problems and the suitability of lifeboat ethics as a response to them. A critical analysis of Hardin's preferred solutions to these problems would not be complete without at least a brief mention of alternative possibilities.

To broaden the scope of policy alternatives under consideration, let us focus on what can be described as a "globalist" response to environmental problems, which in several respects is a polar opposite of lifeboat ethics. In contrast to lifeboat ethics, which presumes that the destiny of Americans can be divorced from the plight of the poorer peoples of the world, globalism assumes that the future welfare of all societies is closely intertwined. Thus, rather than each nation turning inward in pursuit of narrowly defined interests, the imperative is for a coordinated response by all nations to ecological problems.

If a globalist approach is to be adopted, what institutional mechanisms for resource conservation could be applied? Interestingly enough, we need look no further than Hardin's "Tragedy of the Commons" essay for an applicable resource management strategy. Rather than opting for the "private enterprise" arrangement that incorporates intrinsic responsibility as advocated in lifeboat ethics, features of a commons system could be retained or even instituted where they do not exist. Since unrestricted access to natural resources might lead to a resource "tragedy," it would be necessary to adopt limitations on consumption, or what Hardin (1968, 1972: 130) refers to as "mutual coercion, mutually agreed upon." In the metaphor, a village council would be empowered to formulate and implement restrictions on the number of cattle each herdsman could graze on the pasture.

A shortcoming of the lifeboat analogy is the absence of a policy alternative that parallels the regulated commons arrangement. Moreover, it is difficult to imagine how the analogy could be modified to incorporate this alternative to self-sufficiency and intrinsic responsibility. In making his case for lifeboat ethics, Hardin (1974b: 561) briefly acknowledges the potential role of a regulatory authority, but dismisses it as being unrealistic in the international context, arguing that the United Nations is a "toothless tiger, because the signatories of the charter wanted it that way." To observe that the United Nations is inadequately equipped to effectively perform these environmental regulatory functions is hardly a sufficient rationale for ruling out the possibility that stronger international regulative authorities could be established in the future.

What changes in practices of national and international resource management would be needed to implement a regulated commons system? Basic to a commons in its purest form is a presumption that the resources of the planet are a common possession of humanity, including future generations as well as contemporary ones. In effect, this doctrine extends the "common heritage of mankind" principle, which has been applied to the seabed and outer space, to resources located on the territory of off-shore areas of nation-states. To avoid a resource "tragedy," restrictions would be placed on the quantities of natural resources that are produced and consumed by the countries entering into the arrangement. Nations would be guaranteed secure access to a fair share of food as well as energy and mineral resources at affordable prices. Such a guarantee would preclude the possibility of food or resources being withheld as a unilateral means of exercising political leverage.

Transforming private property into a regulated commons is likely to encounter stronger resistance than the placing of limitations on a previously unrestricted commons or the dividing of a commons into private sections, two possibilities taken into account by Hardin (1968, 1972). In the international context, instituting a regulated commons arrangement would violate the strongly held presumption that natural resources are the property of the state in which they are located, with the government of that state being allowed to exercise full sovereignty over their exploitation. Less-developed countries have made national sovereignty over resources a basic provision in their demands for a "new international economic order."

Regardless of how convincing the rationale for a regulated commons system may be, the prospects for its implementation in a pure, comprehensive form are remote. Such a transformation in natural resource control and management is unlikely in the absence of a widespread perception of impending crisis. A crisis atmosphere, however, would hardly be suitable for reaching agreements on a complex restructuring of international relationships. Past experiences indicate that severe scarcities in food and resources are more likely to elicit nationalistic policies in pursuit of narrowly defined self-interests.

A more practical approach to the management of food and natural resources may lie between the more extreme forms of lifeboat ethics and globalism. Aspects of a regulated commons system would be more feasible on a selective basis for those natural resources which are in shortest supply and would be irreversibly depleted in the near future unless consumption is limited. Resources for which world reserves may be inadequate within the next fifty years if current trends in consumption continue include petroleum and natural gas. The need for international management is far less immediate in the case of more plentiful resources, such as coal, chromium, nickel, iron, cobalt, potassium, and vanadium.

Instituting a regulated commons system would not necessarily constitute as fundamental a political and economic transformation as might first appear. Allowing nations to profit from exploiting resources on their territories is an inherent feature of a commons arrangement and is not necessarily inconsistent with a doctrine that resources are the common possession of mankind. National governments could continue to make decisions on the method and pace of resource extraction within guidelines set forth to conserve resources by an international authority. An inherent policy problem would be to reconcile the interests of the international community in resource conservation with the sometimes competing economic needs and aspirations of the states which have relied upon these resources for export income. Ideally, the rate of production and pricing policies could be designed to provide a relatively high, stable, long-term payoff to resource-rich states.

Restrictions on consumption may meet resistance from wealthy industrial societies that could afford to purchase larger quantities of resource than allocated by an international authority. As the reserves of certain resources begin to dwindle rapidly, it should be recognized that a diminished consumption of scarce resources is inevitable even without limitations imposed by an international administrative authority. Reductions in consumption by administrative regulation could be planned to take effect gradually without steep price rises. There would be less disruption for existing economic systems than if reductions were dictated by existing market mechanisms.

It may be noted that international regulations have been instituted successfully in the case of the Alaskan fur seal and, rather belatedly, in efforts to preserve endangered species of whales and a number of depleted fisheries (Caldwell, 1972: pp. 61–70). Whether these experiences can be applied to energy and mineral resources remains to be seen.

In comparison to Hardin's strategy of lifeboat ethics, even a partial implementation of a regulated commons arrangement within the context of a globalist orientation is a potentially more humane and equitable response to humanity's ecological predicament. Such an approach is consistent with the reality of international food and resource interdependence and provides a rational plan for the immediate utilization of scarce resources as well as their conservation for the benefit of future generations. In contrast to lifeboat ethics with its reliance on cycles of overshoot and diebacks as automatic ecological correctives, the regulated commons promises a more stable relationship between man and his environment and the avoidance of the permanent ecological damage that can result from an overshoot. Finally, a globalist response would tend to ameliorate rather than intensify the hostility that has become prevalent in the relations between the industrial and less-developed countries of the world.

REFERENCES

BROWN, L. R. (1974) In the Human Interest. New York: Norton

CALDWELL, L. K. (1972) In Defense of Earth: International Protection of the Biosphere. Bloomington: Indiana University Press.

ECKHOLM, E. P. (1976) Losing Ground: Environmental Stress and World Food Prospects. New York: Norton.

GIDDINGS, J. C. (1973) "World Population, Human Disaster, and Nuclear Holocaust," Bulletin of the Atomic Scientists 29 (September): 21–25, 45–50.

HARDIN, G. (1981) "An Ecolate View of the Human Predicament," Alternatives 7 (Fall): 242–262.

———— (1977) The Limits to Altruism: An Ecologist's View of Survival. Bloomington: Indiana University Press.

———— (1976) "Carrying Capacity as an Ethical Concept," pp. 120–137, in G.R. Lucas

Jr. and T.W. Ogletree (eds.) Lifeboat Ethics: The Moral Dilemmas of Hunger. New York: Harper & Row.

—————— (1975) "Gregg's Law," Bioscience 25 (July): 415.

—————— (1974a) "Lifeboat Ethics: The Case Against Helping the Poor." Psychology Today 8 (September): 38–43, 124–126.

—————— (1974b) "Living on a Lifeboat." Bioscience 24 (October): 561–568.

—————— (1972) Exploring New Ethics for Survival: The Voyage of the Spaceship Beagle. Baltimore: Penguin.

—————— (1968) "The Tragedy of the Commons." Science 162 (December 18): 1243–1248.

HOLDGATE, M. W., M. KASSAS, and G. F. WHITE (1982) The World Environment 1972–1982: A Report by the United Nations Environment Program. Dublin: Tycooly International Publishing Ltd.

HOWE, J. W. and J. W. SEWELL (1975) "Triage and Other Challenges to Helping the Poor Countries Develop," pp. 55–71, in J.W. Howe (ed.), The U.S. and World Development: Agenda for Action—1975. New York: Praeger.

HUGHES, J. D. (1975) Ecology in Ancient Civilizations. Albuquerque: University of New Mexico.

JOHNSON, D. G. (1975) World Food Problems and Prospects. Washington, D.C.: American Enterprise Institute.

KEYFITZ, N. (1976) "World Resources and the World Middle Class." Scientific American 235 (July): 28–35.

KOTHARI, R. (1981–1982) "On Eco-Imperialism," Alternatives 7 (Winter): 383–394.

LAPPÉ, F. M. and J. COLLINS (1977) Food First: Beyond the Myth of Scarcity. Boston: Houghton Mifflin.

LEONTIEFF, W. et al. (1977) The Future of the World Economy. New York: Oxford University Press.

LUCAS, G. R., Jr. and T. R. OGLETREE (eds.) (1976) Lifeboat Ethics: The Moral Dilemmas of Hunger. New York: Harper & Row.

MARDEN, P. G., D. G. HODGSON, and T. L. McCOY (1982) Population in the Global Arena. New York: Holt, Rinehart and Winston.

MEADOWS, D. H., D. L. MEADOWS, J. RANDERS, and W. W. BEHRENS, III (1972) The Limits to Growth: A Report for the Club of Rome's Project on the Predicament of Mankind. New York: Universe.

MURAKAMI, T. (1982) "The Remarkable Adaption of Japan's Economy," pp. 138–167, in D. Yergin and M. Hillenbrand (eds.), Global Insecurity. A Strategy for Energy and Economic Renewal. Boston: Houghton Mifflin.

SEGRE, D. V. and J. H. ADLER (1973) "The Ecology of Terrorism." Survival 15 (July/August): 178–183.

SIVARD, R. (1982) World Military and Social Expenditures 1982. Leesburg, Virginia: World Priorities.

—————— (1981) World Energy Survey (2nd ed.). Leesburg, Virginia: World Priorities.

SPROUT, H. and M. SPROUT (1974) Multiple Vulnerabilities: The Context of Environmental Repair and Protection. Princeton, N.J.: Center for International Studies.

U.S. Council on Environmental Quality and Department of State. (1980) The Global 2000 Report to the President. New York: Penguin Books.

34

The International State of Nature and the Politics of Scarcity

WILLIAM OPHULS

Is international conflict more or less probable in a world of scarcity? William Ophuls argues the former. Noting the absence of higher law or authority in the international system, implied in the principle of sovereignty to which all nation-states subscribe, he concludes that while ecological scarcity may cry out for international cooperation, "the clear danger is that, instead of promoting world cooperation, ecological scarcity will simply intensify the Hobbesian war of all against all." Ophuls has served as a commissioned officer in the United States Coast Guard and as a foreign service officer in the United States Department of State.

THE INTERNATIONAL MACROCOSM

If in the various national microcosms constituting the world political community the basic dynamics of ecological scarcity apply virtually across the board, in the macrocosm of international politics they operate even more strongly. Just as within each individual nation, the tragic logic of the commons brings about the overexploitation of common property resources like the oceans and the atmosphere. Also, the pressures toward inequality, oppression, and conflict are even more intense within the world political community, for it is a community in name only, and the already marked cleavage between rich and poor threatens to become even greater. Without even the semblance of a world government, such problems depend for their solution on the good will and purely voluntary cooperation of nearly 150 sovereign states—a prospect that does not inspire optimism. . . .

THE GLOBAL TRAGEDY OF THE COMMONS

The tragic logic of the commons operates universally, and its effects are readily visible internationally—in the growing pollution of international rivers, seas, and now even the oceans; in the overfishing that has caused a marked decline in the fish catch, as well as the near extinction of the great whales; and in the impending scramble for seabed resources by maritime miners or other exploiters. There is no way to confine environmental insults or the effects of ecological degradation within national borders; river basins, airsheds, and oceans are intrinsically international. Even seemingly local environmental disruption inevitably has some impact on the quality of regional and, eventually, global ecosystems. Just as within each nation, the aggregation of individual desires and actions overloads the international commons. But, like individuals, states tend to turn a blind eye to this, for they profit by the increased production while others bear most or all of the cost, or they lose by self-restraint while others receive most or all of the benefit. Thus, Britain gets the factory output, while Scandinavia suffers the ecological effects of "acid rain"; the French and Germans use the Rhine for waste disposal even though this leaves the river little more than a reeking sewer by the time it reaches fellow European Economic Community member Holland downstream.

However, if the problems are basically the same everywhere, the political implications of the tragedy of the commons are much more serious in the international arena. It has long been recognized that international politics is the epitome of the Hobbesian state of nature: despite all the progress over the centuries toward the rule of international law, sovereign states, unlike the citizens within each state, acknowledge no law or authority higher than their own self-interest; they are therefore free to do as they please, subject only to gross prudential restraints, no matter what the cost to the world community. Brazil, for example, has made it plain that it will brook no outside interference with its development of the Amazon, and well-meaning ecological advice is castigated as "scientific colonialism" (Castro 1972). Also, despite strong pressures from the international community, the U.S.S.R. and Japan have openly frustrated the effort to conserve whale stocks—both at the negotiating table and at sea. In international relations, therefore, the dynamic of the tragedy of the commons is even stronger than within any given nation state, which, being a real political community, has at least the theoretical capacity to make binding, authoritative decisions on resource conservation and ecological protection. By contrast, international agreements are reached and enforced by the purely voluntary cooperation of sovereign nation states existing in a state of nature. . . . [T]he likelihood of forestalling by such means the operation of the tragedy of the commons is extremely remote. Worse, just as any individual is nearly helpless to alter the outcome by his own actions (and even risks serious loss if he refuses to participate in the exploitation of the commons), so too, in the absence of international authority or enforceable agreement, nations have little choice but to contribute to the tragedy by their own actions. This would be true even if each individual state was striving to achieve a domestic steady-state economy, for unless one assumes agreement on a largely autarkic world, states would still compete with each other internationally to maximize the resources available to them. Ecological scarcity thus intensifies the fundamental problem of international politics—the achievement of world order—by adding further to the preexisting difficulties of a state of nature. Without some kind of international governmental machinery with authority and coercive power over sovereign states sufficient to oblige them to keep within the bounds of the ecological common interest of all on the planet, the world must suffer the ever greater environmental ills ordained by the global tragedy of the commons.

THE STRUGGLE BETWEEN RICH AND POOR

Ecological scarcity also aggravates very seriously the already intense struggle between rich and poor. As is well known, the world today . . . is sharply polarized between the developed, industrialized "haves," all affluent in a greater or lesser degree and all getting more affluent all the time, and the underdeveloped or developing "have nots," all relatively and absolutely impoverished and with few exceptions tending to fall relatively ever farther behind despite their often feverish efforts to grow. The degree of the inequality is also well known: the United States, with only 6 percent of the world's population, consumes about 30 percent of the total energy production of the world and comparable amounts of other resources, and the rest of the "haves," although only about half as prodigal as the United States, still consume resources far out of proportion to their population; conversely, per capita consumption of resources in the Third World ranges from one-tenth to one-hundredth that in the "have" countries. To make matters worse, the resources that the "haves" enjoy in inordinate amounts are largely and increasingly imported from the Third World; thus economic inequality and what might be called ecological colonialism have become intertwined. In view of this extreme and long-standing inequality (which moreover has its roots in an imperialist past), it is hardly surprising that the Third World thirsts avidly for development or that it has become increasingly intolerant of those features of the current world order it perceives as obstacles to becoming as rich and powerful as the developed world.

Alas, the emergence of ecological scarcity appears to have sounded the death knell for the aspirations of the LDC's. Even assuming, contrary to fact, that there were sufficient mineral and energy resources to make it possible, universal industrialization would impose intolerable stress on world ecosystems. In short, the current model of development, which assumes that all countries will eventually become heavily industrialized mass-consumption societies, is doomed to failure. Naturally, this conclusion is totally unacceptable to the modernizing elites of the Third World; their political power is generally founded on the promise of development. Even more important, simply halting growth would freeze the current pattern of inequality, leaving the "have nots" as the peasants of the world community in perpetuity. Thus an end to growth and development would be acceptable to the Third World only in combination with a radical redistribution of the world's wealth and a total restructuring of the world's economy to guarantee the maintenance of economic justice. Yet it seems absolutely clear that the rich have not the slightest intention of alleviating the plight of the poor if it entails the sacrifice of their own living standards. Ecological scarcity thus greatly increases the probability of naked confrontation between rich and poor.

WHO ARE NOW THE "HAVES" AND "HAVE NOTS"?

An important new element has been injected into this struggle. The great resource hunger of the developed and even some parts of the developing world has begun to transfer power and wealth to those who have resources to sell, especially critical resources like petroleum. As a result, the geopolitics of the world has already been decisively altered.

This process can be expected to continue. The power and wealth of the major oil producers is bound to increase over the next two decades, despite North Sea and Alaskan oil and regardless of whether the Organization of Petroleum Exporting Countries (OPEC) manages to maintain its current degree of unity.

Some believe that oil is a special case and that the prospect of OPEC-type cartels for other resources is dim (Banks 1974; Mikesell 1974). While these assessments may be correct, it seems inevitable that in the long run an era of "commodity power" must emerge. The hunger of the industrialized nations for resources is likely to increase, even if there is no substantial growth in output to generate increased demand for raw materials, because the domestic mineral and energy resources of the developed countries have begun to be exhausted. Even the United States, for example, already imports 100 percent of its platinum, mica, chromium, and strontium; over 90 percent of its manganese, aluminum, tantalum, and cobalt; and 50 percent or more of twelve additional key minerals (Wade 1974). However, the developed countries seem determined to keep growing, and assuming even modest further growth in industrial output, their dependence on Third World supplies is bound to increase markedly in the next few decades. Thus, whatever the short-term prospects for the success of budding cartels in copper, phosphates, and other minerals, the clear overall long-term trend is toward a seller's market in basic resources and therefore toward "commodity power," even if this power grows more slowly and is manifested in a less extreme form than that of OPEC.

Thus, the basic long-standing division of the world into rich and poor in terms of GNP per capita is about to be overlaid with another rich-poor polarization, in terms of resources, that will both moderate and intensify the basic split. Although there are many complex interdependencies in world trade—for example, U.S. food exports are just as critical to many countries as their mineral exports are to us—it is already clear that the resource-rich Third World nations stand to gain greater wealth and power at the expense of the "haves." . . .

Other problems abound. For example, international financial and monetary institutions, established for a simpler world of indefinite growth and a clear demarcation between "haves" and "have nots," are creaking under the unprecedented strain of the rapid shift in economic and geopolitical realities. In addition, poor countries without major resources of their own will suffer—indeed, already have suffered—major setbacks to their prospects for development. This is true not only of the hopelessly poor Fourth World, but also of countries whose development programs have already acquired some momentum. In India, for example, the quadrupled price of energy has dealt an all but mortal blow to the energy-intensive Green Revolution, on which so many of the country's hopes for development were pinned.

In sum, world geopolitics and economics are in for a radical reordering. Western economic development has involved a net transfer of resources, wealth, and power from the current "have nots" to the "haves," creating the cleavage between the two that now divides the world. In particular, the enormous postwar growth in output and consumption experienced by the industrialized nations was largely fueled by the bonanza of cheap oil that they were able to extract from relatively powerless client states in the Middle East. The success of the oil cartel is a signal that, from now on, wealth and power will begin to flow in the opposite direction. But only the relatively few "have nots" who possess significant amounts of resources will gain; the plight of the rest of the poor is more abject than before. Thus the old polarization between rich and poor seems likely to be replaced by a threefold division into the rich, the hopelessly poor, and the nouveaux riches—and such a major change in the international order is bound to create tension.

CONFLICT OR COOPERATION?

The overall effect of ecological scarcity in the international arena is to intensify the competitive dynamics of the preexisting international tragedy of the commons, so that increased commercial, diplomatic, and, ultimately, military confrontation over dwindling resources is more likely. At the same time the poor, having had their revolutionary hopes and rising aspirations crushed, will have little to lose but their chains. Also, to many of the declining "haves," ill-equipped to adapt to an era of "commodity power" and economic warfare, the grip of the nouveaux riches on essential resources will seem an intolerable stranglehold to be broken at all costs. Thus the disappearance of ecological abundance seems bound to make international politics even more tension ridden and potentially violent than it already is. Indeed, the pressures of ecological scarcity may embroil the world in hopeless strife, so that long before ecological collapse occurs by virtue of the physical limitations of the earth, the current world order will have been destroyed by turmoil and war—a truly horrible prospect, given the profoundly anti-ecological character of modern warfare. . . .

Some, on the other hand, hope or believe that ecological scarcity will have just the opposite effect—because the problems will become so overwhelming and so evidently insoluble without total international cooperation, nation states will discard their outmoded national sovereignty and place themselves under some form of planetary government that will regulate the global commons for the benefit of all humankind and begin the essential process of gradual economic redistribution. In effect, states will be driven by their own vital national interests—seen to include ecological as well as traditional economic, political, and military factors—to embrace the ultimate interdependence needed to solve ecological problems (Shields and Ott 1974). According to this hypothesis, the very direness of the outcome if cooperation does not prevail may ensure that it will.

Unfortunately, the accumulating evidence tends to support the conflictual rather than the cooperative hypothesis. Faced with the new power of the oil barons, the first impulse of the United States was to try to go it alone in "Project Independence," while Japan, France, and others maneuvered individually to ensure their own future supplies, torpedoing the solidarity of the consuming countries confronting OPEC. Canada has served notice on the United States that it intends to end America's ecological colonialism; henceforth, the resources of Canada will be saved for its own use. Thus, the rich seem readier to follow "beggar thy neighbor" policies than to cooperate among themselves. Sympathy for the plight of the poor is even less evident. Some talk about expanding still further the scale of ecological colonialism; a West German research group has even put forward a scheme for the diversion of West Africa's Niger River to supply Europe with heat for energy (Anon. 1974). For others, continued interdependence of any kind with the poor is seen as so problematic and so full of threats to the sovereign independence and high living standards of the rich that the only sensible course is autarkic self-sufficiency.

Naturally, there has been considerable talk about cooperative international action to deal with the problems of ecological scarcity, but little or no momentum toward greater cooperation has developed. In fact, all the talk may have served chiefly to heighten further the tensions within the world community.

AN UPSURGE OF CONFERENCE DIPLOMACY

By the late 1960's some of the alarming global implications of pollution and general ecological degradation had become widely apparent, and preparations began for a major international conference at Stockholm in 1972. Depending on one's point of view, the Stockholm Conference—to give it its proper title, the United Nations Conference on the Human Environment—was either a major diplomatic success or an abysmal failure. On the positive side, the elaborate preparations for the conference (each country had to make a detailed inventory of its environmental problems), the intense publicity given the over two years of preliminary negotiations, and the conference itself fostered a very high level of environmental awareness around the globe. Virtually ignored by diplomats in 1969, the environmental crisis had by 1972 rocketed right up alongside nuclear weapons and economic development as one of the big issues of international politics. The second major achievement of the Stockholm Conference was the establishment of the United Nations Environment Program (UNEP) to monitor the state of the world environment and to provide liaison and coordination between nation states and among the multitude of governmental and non-governmental organizations concerned with environmental matters. Finally, a few preliminary agreements covering certain less controversial and less critical ecological problems, like setting aside land for national parks and suppressing trade in endangered species, were reached either at the conference or immediately thereafter.

Despite these acknowledged achievements, environmentalists were by and large rather unhappy with the conduct and outcome of the conference. They were especially disillusioned, for example, by the way in which the original ecological purity of the conference's agenda was rapidly watered down by pressures from Third World countries, who made it plain that they would have nothing to do with the conference unless, in effect, underdevelopment was converted into a form of pollution. Moreover, a great part of the proceedings was devoted not to the problems on the agenda, but to the kind of "have" versus "have not" debate discussed above, and routine ideological posturing on political issues like "colonialism" consumed additional time. Also, cold-war politics refused to take a vacation; for example, the U.S.S.R. boycotted the conference because East Germany was not given full voting status. Thus the perhaps naively idealistic hope of many that the ecological issue would at last force quarrelsome and self-seeking sovereign nation states to put aside stale old grudges, recognize their common predicament, and act in concert to improve the human condition was completely dashed.

Worse, some of the features of the current world order most objectionable from an ecological point of view were actually reaffirmed at Stockholm—namely, the absolute right of sovereign countries to develop their own domestic resources without regard to the potential external ecological costs to the world community, and the unrestricted freedom to breed guaranteed by the Universal Declaration of Human Rights. In addition, established international institutions, like the World Health Organization and the Food and Agriculture Organization, extended distinctly lukewarm cooperation to the organizers of the conference, both because of bureaucratic jealousy and because of fear that environmental concerns would force them to alter or abandon programs, like all-out support for the Green Revolution and the eradication of malaria with DDT, that are a large part of their raison d'être. As a result, the Secretariat of UNEP was given little real power and only a minimum of resources to perform its coordinating and monitoring functions. Also, the headquarters of UNEP were eventually established in Nairobi, and although this has had the very positive effect of keeping the Third World interested in UNEP and its programs, it has definitely hampered the expansion and effectiveness of the global environmental monitoring and liaison that was to be UNEP's prime responsibility.

Since 1972, there have been more environmentally oriented conferences—principally the U.N. World Population Conference in 1974, the U.N. World Food Conference in 1974, and a series of U.N. Law of the Sea Conferences from 1974 to the present. However, there has been little progress since Stockholm. The World Population Conference somehow managed to end "without producing explicit agreement that there was a world population problem" (Walsh 1974). The World Food Conference produced few concrete achievements and left crucial problems on its agenda unsolved. The Law of the Sea Conferences have promoted progress toward a global consensus that seems likely to become the basis of an international treaty once future negotiating meetings dispose of some of the still unsettled issues. Unfortunately, the basis of this emerging consensus is an agreement to carve the oceans into national zones of exploitation, instead of making them into the common heritage of mankind; thus, as at Stockholm, the principle of national sovereignty has been even further entrenched.

The forces that prevented Stockholm from fulfilling its promise were even more strongly in evidence at these and other post-Stockholm international meetings directly or indirectly concerned with environmental issues. First, the spirit of militant nationalism that has animated so much of the history of the postwar world has not abated. Thus states insist on the absolute and sovereign right of self-determination in use of resources, population policy, and development in general, regardless of the wider consequences. Second, the demand by Third World countries for economic development has, if anything, increased in intensity, and whatever seems to stand in the way, like ecological considerations, gets rather short shift. Third, largely because their prospects for development are so dim, Third World countries have begun to press even harder for fundamental reform of the world system (a "new international economic order"); thus every discussion of environmental issues like food and population is inevitably converted by Third World spokesmen into a discussion of international economic justice as well, which enormously complicates the process of negotiation. In short, environmental issues have become pawns in the larger diplomatic and political struggle between the nations.

In addition, diplomats, like national leaders, have attempted to handle the issues of ecological scarcity not as part of a larger problematique, but piecemeal, so that their interaction with other problems is all but ignored. For example, the World Food Conference was solely concerned with the problem of feeding the hungry and gave virtually no attention to the eventual ecological consequences of growing more food or subsidizing further overpopulation with radically increased food aid. To some extent, therefore, the successes of international conferences that simply try to solve one small piece of the larger problem are as much to be feared as their failures.

If one wished to be optimistic, one could conclude that the world community has taken the first halting attitudinal and institutional steps toward meeting the challenges of ecological scarcity. A more realistic assessment would be that little has been accomplished so far and that major impediments to further progress loom large. One might even be forced to conclude, more pessimistically, that the world political community as presently constituted is simply incapable of coping with the challenges of ecological scarcity, at least within any reasonable time.

PLANETARY GOVERNMENT OR THE WAR OF ALL AGAINST ALL

. . . Even before the emergence of ecological scarcity, the world's difficulties and their starkly Hobbesian implications were grave enough. Some saw the "revolution of rising expectations" pushing the world toward a situation in which wants greatly exceeded the capacity to meet them, provoking Hobbesian turmoil and violence (Spengler 1969). Also, ever since Hiroshima the world has lived in a state of highly armed peace with a nuclear Sword of Damocles dangling over its head. We have all learned to live with the bomb, and the hair suspending the nuclear Sword has indeed held, although for how much longer no one can say.

Now the world must live under the blade of another Sword of Damocles, slower to fall but equally deadly. Unfortunately, the hair holding this environmental Sword has come loose; pollution and other environmental problems will not obligingly postpone their impact while diplomats haggle, so the Sword is already slicing down toward our unprotected heads. There is thus no way for the world community to put the environmental issue out of mind and go on about its business, as it has done with the bomb. The crisis of ecological scarcity is a Sword that must be parried, squarely and soon.

Thus the already strong rationale for a world government with enough coercive power over fractious nation states to achieve what reasonable men would regard as the planetary common interest has become overwhelming. Yet we must recognize that the very ecological scarcity that makes a world government ever more necessary has also made it much more difficult of achievement. The clear danger is that, instead of promoting world cooperation, ecological scarcity will simply intensify the Hobbesian war of all against all and cause armed peace to be replaced by overt international strife.

LIST OF SOURCES

Anon. 1974 "Take Water and Heat from Third World," *New Scientist* 62:549.

Banks, Fred. 1974 "Copper Is Not Oil," *New Scientist* 63:255–257.

Castro, Joao A. de A. (1972) "Environment and Development: The Case of the Developing Countries," *International Organization* (26): 401–416.

Mikesell, Raymond F. 1974 "More Third World Cartels Ahead?" *Challenge* 17(5):24–31.

Shields, Linda P., and Marvin C. Ott. 1974 "Environmental Decay and International Politics: The Uses of Sovereignty," *Environmental Affairs* 3:743–767.

Spengler, Joseph J. 1969 "Return to Thomas Hobbes?" *South Atlantic Quarterly* 68:443–453.

Wade, Nicholas. 1974 "Raw Materials: U.S. Grows More Vulnerable to Third World Cartels," *Science* 183:185–186.

Walsh, John. 1974 "UN Conferences: Topping Any Agenda Is the Question of Development," *Science* 185:1143–1144, 1192–1193.

35

Alternative Views of a World in Crisis

ANTONY J. DOLMAN

World order studies may usefully be described as systematic speculations about alternative world futures. Antony J. Dolman first discusses the background against which many such studies have been conducted during the past decade. He then offers a summary, based on an analysis of sixteen world order studies, of the world views implicit in them in a way that can usefully be applied to a broad range of analyses of international relations belonging to this genre of research. The excerpt is from among the reports of the RIO (Reshaping the International Order) Foundation. Dolman is senior fellow, Foundation Reshaping the International Order, Rotterdam.

CRISIS SYNDROME: THE PASSING OF THE POST-WAR PERIOD

Every generation is inclined to believe that it lives in a period which is historically unique. In a certain sense of course it does. There are very serious reasons for believing, however, that the period we have just passed through and are about to enter involves thresholds unknown in human history. Never before have so many problems converged in a world so small, so fragile and so vulnerable to the consequences of the failure to find answers to those problems. The competitive armaments race, growing inequalities, the struggle for resources, the disruption of global life-support systems, the structural crisis of capitalism are all problems which carry their own threats and dangers. As linked processes they conspire to form a problematique which, having already surpassed our capacity to manage it, threatens even to outrun our imagination.

Global problems are a new phenomenon. One hundred years ago there were no such problems. There could be none for there was no world system to give them global dimensions. Today we have a world system which, shaped by the forces of modern science-based technology, has given us world problems, problems which demand global responses. In some cases, the demands for global 'solutions' emanates, not from individual or groups of nations, but from the system as a whole. In such cases the world system will have to go beyond confrontation in order to prevent a catastrophe which could engulf all the world's nations. A century ago, British cavalry officers lowered their lances and headed for annihilation on the battlefield of Balaclava. Today, the whole world could become one giant battlefield and every man, woman and child a potential victim.

When history is written the 1970s will undoubtedly be recorded as a watershed decade. It was the decade that witnessed the passing of the post-war period. It saw the end of an order created in the aftermath of the Second World War and based upon the supremacy and hegemony of the United States. It brought to a close a period of relative stability and, for a handful of nations, of unparalleled prosperity.

Was there a single event which heralded the passing of the post-war period, the end of the Americo-centric world? Was it the decision of Richard Nixon in 1971 to devalue the dollar and to withdraw its gold convertibility, a decision which effectively pulled the rug from under the financial and monetary institutions created at Bretton Woods and from which the Western World has so much benefitted? Was it the 1973 'oil crisis' when, for the first time since the rise of Western capitalism, a decision affecting the world economy was taken outside the West? Was it the forced withdrawal of the U.S. from a country it had laid to waste? Or was it earlier? Was it the Cuban missile crisis when the superpowers learnt that their nuclear arsenals could not be used and that from that point on, in the words of Robert McNamara, "there is no longer any such thing as strategy, only crisis management"? Or was it perhaps the killing of John F. Kennedy in November 1963? Did the death of a President, a man who, in Alistair Buchan's judgement, was more mourned than any other leader since Pericles, also mark the demise of an order?[1] It was all of these things and much more.

The 1970s were a traumatic decade for the United States, the world's dominant power. It witnessed the end of the 'American Century', a century that lasted barely three decades.[2] In the space of just ten years supreme self-confidence and unshakable belief in the American dream gave way to doubt and uncertainty. As they entered the 1970s, Americans saw themselves as the chosen people, the sole inhabitants of a Noah's Ark, free from doubt, desolation and the afflictions which beset more ordinary people. It was an armor-plated Noah's Ark, full of richness, variety and vitality, symbolic of hope and progress. In the 1970s the Noah's Ark ran aground and Americans are still picking up the pieces of what was once their world.

Cherished beliefs were dashed on the jagged rocks of the decade: the belief that the U.S. was invincible; that it was inherently and intrinsically 'good'; that its leaders were men of wisdom and unimpeachable integrity; that it was feared and respected and revered as a 'model' of what others should seek to become. Vietnam was to demonstrate that the country could be defeated and that it was capable of monstrous crimes. Watergate showed that its faith in its leaders was sadly misplaced. Iran was to signal the sharpest rejection of the U.S. 'model' in a world that has grown to distrust and resent the U.S. rather than to respect and fear it. . . .

In the 1970s the world became immensely more complex both substantively and politically. Complexity is the enemy of power politics. Whether the United

States can adjust to these new complexities is . . . a very significant world order question. . . .

The world will become still more complex in the 1980s. Problems will become bigger, more intractable, more urgent. As the need for positive intervention becomes greater, so the scope for intervention threatens to become smaller. The signs are that deepening crises will further blur the visions of nations. Their concerns will become more parochial, their interests more narrowly defined, their time-frames more short-term. Some nations, the most privileged among them, may seek to escape the crises which are piling up rather than to meet them head on. But in turning away they will discover that there are no longer any sanctuaries, not even for the rich.

As we enter the 1980s there are many rational causes for serious concern. Many new ones will emerge. Where the deepening economic crisis will take us, for example, is a matter of grave concern. Already the most severe in half a century, the signs are that it will worsen rather than improve. Consider briefly the situation. In the West, the 1970s witnessed a dramatic fall in real output, a tripling of inflation rates, and the replacement of a trading surplus with a staggering deficit. The outlook for the 1980s, in the words of the OECD [Organization for Economic Cooperation and Development], an organization mandated to look on the bright side, does "not look particularly encouraging".[3] Unemployment, around 3 per cent at the end of the '60s, now tops 10 per cent in some Western nations and is expected to reach 15 per cent by the mid 1980s. Inflation, around 4 per cent a decade ago, is currently running at 10 per cent and steadfastly refusing to respond to treatment. Unemployment and inflation have effectively subverted the traditional apparatus of Western hope and self-improvement: hard work and saving. As prosperity gives way to doubt and uncertainty, the economic malaise may be the harbinger of political and social stresses and strains which will follow in its wake.

Doubt and uncertainty have entered the daily perceptions of millions of people in the Western world. There is a gnawing feeling that the good times are over. Polls are showing that, for perhaps the first time in history, Westerners are no longer sure that the future will be better than—or even as good as—the past. Politicians, businessmen and scientists of all kinds are telling them that their standards of living can be expected to decline, that their aspirations are unlikely to be fulfilled. In the space of little more than a decade they have been forced, in historian Geoffrey Barraclough's words, into a "growing awareness of the fragility and precariousness of civilization".[4]

The curtailment of the future is a traumatic experience and like all such experiences its consequences are incalculable. Will the new pessimism and cynicism, the rising tide of discontent and anxiety become a force which can be mobilized for change? Is disillusionment a first step in a process of learning? Will it give rise to questioning which is challenging as well as skeptical? Or will it give rise to apathy and defencism? To increased fragmentation, growing tensions, still further weakened institutions and, eventually, civil disorder? Must the 'new world' be built on the ruins of the old?[5]

Similar questions haunt the future of the centrally planned economies of Eastern Europe. Once believing themselves to be islands of socialist tranquility in a sea of economic turmoil, immune from the evils that bedevil capitalism, they have discovered that, in an integrating world economy, it is impossible to build protective walls.

Their growing trade with the West has inevitably brought debt to the West. The indebtedness of Eastern Europe was around $40 billion in 1976. It had increased to $60 billion by 1979 and, according to some estimates, could reach $200 billion by the end of the 1980s.[6] Poland and the Soviet Union have been responsible for two-thirds of the debt accumulated to date. Poland, an economic disaster by any standard, currently has to devote 60 per cent of its export earnings just to service its mushrooming debt.

Economic recession, rising prices combined with shortages of consumer goods, severe housing problems and, in some countries, energy deficiencies are much in evidence in Eastern Europe and are fuelling political and social unrest. Such problems, Edward Giereck once observed, "keep me awake at night".[7] They were also the cause of his downfall, just as they were the downfall of his predecessor. The same problems no doubt interfere with the sleep of Janos Kádár. He told the 12th Party Congress held in March 1980 that the fat years are over for good and that the future will be one of lean years. Hungarians, he said, must from now on expect slower rates of growth of income and standards of living. Similar messages have echoed around other Eastern European capitals.

If the economic and social situation is gloomy in the West and East, it is one of darkness in large parts of the Third World. The situation actually deteriorated in the 1970s and is now more critical than at any other time in the post-war period. . . .

According to the ILO [International Labor Organization], the standard of living of about one half of the population of the Third World actually declined in the period 1965–1975, a decline which is continuing. Even industrial workers, the privileged few in many developing countries, saw their real wages fall.[8] Nationally, economies strained under the growing pressure of rising import bills and oil prices. The combined deficits on current account of the developing countries increased from $31 billion in 1978 to around $75 billion in 1980, largely as a result of increases in oil prices. To keep afloat, the majority of Third World countries have been forced to borrow, some of them very heavily. Total Third World debt stood in 1980 at a staggering $325 billion and 60 per cent is supposedly due for repayment in 1982. Overall debt service, at present equivalent to 15 per cent of annual exports, is growing rapidly. Some countries have already reached the impossible stage where they must spend 90 per cent of their foreign exchange earnings just to satisfy their modest fuel needs and to pay their creditors.

The prospects for many non-oil exporting developing countries are grim. A further deterioration can only mean, in Jamal's words, "political chaos. It means violence, it means turbulence, upsetting of the order".[9]

Even the 'economic miracles' within the Third World—the so-called newly industrializing countries (NICs)—are finding it increasingly difficult to disguise acute economic and social problems. Their industrialization has been indebted industrialization and much of the debt is owed to Western banks. The figures are now so large that major defaults could throw the Western banking system into chaos.[10] The City Bank, for example, has lent Brazil an amount equivalent to its own capital. The consequence is that banks have to lend more money under the threat of default and the NICs are forced to borrow money just to service their ballooning debts. This is a process which has its inherent limits.

The style of their industrialization—offering Western transnationals a cheap and well-disciplined labor force and a high rate of return on investments of capital and technology—is also giving rise to growing internal inequalities and social unrest. Whether the NICs will first crack under the weight of their growing debts or under the pressure of internal social tensions is a question which remains to be answered. In an 'economic miracle' even optimism can seem grim. . . .

ESCAPING THE CRISES: WORLDVIEWS COMPARED

Is there an answer to the crises which increasingly threaten to engulf the world's nations? For more than a decade this question has been studied by distinguished groups of specialists around the world and it is to the various views presented on 'strategies for survival' that we will now turn. We do so with the intention of pulling together the variegated strands of world order thinking and the aim of weaving them into a richer understanding of the 'global problematique' and of the steps required to come to terms with it. . . .

. . . We will call the different approaches 'systems-maintaining', 'systems-reforming' and 'systems-transforming'. Before setting out to describe these approaches to world order thinking . . . , however, a few general observations . . . appear to be in order.

The world order studies keep alive the tradition of scholastic speculation on the future of international relations, a tradition which dates back certainly to Dante, perhaps even to the Greeks with their concern for the political, social and economic relations between autonomous communities.[11] Although the tradition is long and honorable it is only in the past decade that such studies have begun to be taken seriously and their acceptance has been fitful and controversial. In many respects they are themselves the product of an age of uncertainty and it is the need to search out new directions which has promoted their acceptance.

Acceptance does not necessarily imply utility. While it has no doubt contributed to a better understanding of the 'global problematique', world order thinking has yet to prove that it has a direct policy relevance.[12] Much of the thinking has certainly been characterized by naive rationalism. 'Relevance' in policy-making is, however, notoriously difficult to define and it would be absurd to believe that world order studies could ever contain the 'golden key' required to unlock the door to a brave new future.[13] The world, of course, does not work like that. Solutions to today's problems will not be found in the combination of intellectual analysis and 'goodwill'.[14]

There are many similarities in the studies reviewed. They all share a common concern about the state of the international order. There are concerns with respect to growing inequities (in income, in opportunity, in power, in access to resources, etc.), to the structures which define and govern the behavior of the system, and to the substantive problems which must be confronted (energy, food, science and technology, environment, and so on).[15] Many studies also express a deep dissatisfaction with present concepts of development in both the North and South and call, in the words of *What Now,* for "another development". Although the development models proposed vary in many important respects, there is a general consensus that new models of development should have a strong basic needs orientation. . . .

There is also considerable agreement that the solution of world problems, however defined, will require a major institutional build up at the global level. In some cases recognition of the need for stronger institutions is grudging, in others it verges on the ecstatic.

All studies express concern—some a very grave concern—about the consequences of failure to formulate appropriate national and international responses to global problems. Apocalyptic visions are painted in vivid colors and words like 'catastrophe', 'collapse', 'chaos', 'disaster' and 'despair' are *de rigeur.* Indeed the Four Horsemen of the Apocalypse seem permanently to ride over large areas of world order thinking. Some studies save their most declamatory language to describe the consequences of failing to come to terms with the 'widening gap' between the rich and poor worlds. A number of studies contend that the two worlds are locked into a collision course. . . .

40-yr. chapter

The studies document changes in thinking with respect to 'limits to change'. Whereas early world order studies, especially computer models in the Malthusian tradition, saw physical scarcities as the source of political conflicts and major obstacles to the formulation of required policy responses, more recent studies convey the clear message that the big problems are political, social and institutional and not physical. . . .

At face value, many of the studies reviewed are guided by common value premises. Few would disagree, for example, with WOMP's "world order values" or RIO's "guiding principles". These common value premises translate into general world order goals which could be expected to and indeed do command wide support. . . . This surface level consensus conceals fundamental disagreements on the problems which must be addressed in strategies, how they are to be tackled and why. Shared goals do not translate into common objectives for reshaping the international order nor into criteria required for evaluating its performance. And even if broad agreement could be reached, it is characteristic of strategies that they are unable to simultaneously achieve all the objectives which are set. There are always basic conflicts and tensions in a set of norms which govern prescription. In such cases, the 'right course of action' is never a matter of fact but always of choice. And choice, as we know, is always a matter of politics and ideology. Common goals and starting points can thus easily conceal fundamentally different interpretations of what is wrong and what needs to be done.

Let us now try to classify the studies reviewed according to the tripartite distinction 'systems-maintaining', 'systems-reforming' and 'systems-transforming' in an attempt to discover some of the basic disagreements concerning diagnosis and prescription.[16] The classification is not nor can it be watertight. It is at best an approximation predicated on the belief that each of the three approaches draws upon the theoretical, analytical and normative apparatus of different traditions. This leads the approaches to different interpretations of the 'problematique' and thus to different strategies for coming to grips with it.

THE SYSTEMS-MAINTAINING APPROACH

This approach to world order thinking is concerned with identifying the means for sustaining a system and maintaining its stability under changing conditions. It acquaints order with established patterns of privilege and power and the institutions which serve and service the status quo. The theoretical and analytical apparatus is derived from such sources as neoclassical economics, structural functionalism in sociology and functionalist approaches to the study of international relations. Its spiritual fathers include Adam Smith, Durkheim, Pareto, Milton Friedman, Talcott Parsons, R.A. Dahl and Daniel Bell. It is inherently conservative.

Characteristic of the systems-maintaining approach is an image of society based upon consensus, order and the forces that maintain the integrated functioning of its different components. The ideal order is traditionally portrayed as an equilibrium. The approach castigates attempts which might be made by the state or international bodies to regulate 'natural' processes and contends that such interference, despite the goodness of the underlying intentions, will upset the desired equilibrium and its balance of functions in unpredictable ways. Intervention can only result in a reduction of overall levels of welfare and serves to impede rather than enhance the adaptive evolution of the system. The market mechanism is deified. It is uncritically accepted as the only possible resource allocation mechanism.

In terms of international relations, different breeds of systems maintainers can be identified:

- *Isolationists:* Isolationists seek to restore the tradition of rich world detachment from geopolitical concerns. Although it was an Englishman, Lord Salisbury, who declared nearly 100 years ago that it was Britain's duty to pursue its policies in "splendid isolation", isolationists, as a breed, are mainly found today in the United States. The policy recommendations which emerge from world order thinking are, however, sometimes addressed to them: remember Forrester advises the rich countries to keep away from the Third World because it could pull them under when it goes down.
- *Imperialists:* Imperialists are those who, in the words of Richard Falk, "identify various categories of barbarians at the gates and seek to bar their entry".[17] They are attracted to such concepts as 'lifeboats' and 'triage'. They stress the importance of military power and tend to confuse 'might' with 'right'. Imperialists are critical of attempts to appease the developing countries, the leaders of which are seen to be abusing the rich countries in their desperate efforts to find an external scapegoat for their miserable failures on the home front. The imperialists' attitude to the Third World has been neatly summarized in an editorial in the *Wall Street Journal*, the voice of Western capitalism. Addressing itself to the Third World it warned: "Don't expect (us) to serve you up prosperity and don't think you can get it through extortion". And along

the same lines: "If the Third World countries want to be rich like us, they might try doing a few things our way".[18]

• *Managers:* Systems-maintaining managers are those who recognize that the world does not stand still and that the future of the rich countries is dependent upon them striking a series of bargains around those issues which challenge the system by disturbing the status quo or by threatening to throw it into chaos. The key expression is 'the management of interdependence' and it has been much in evidence in . . . world order thinking.

The managers believe that the post-war economic order has "served the world well" but recognize that it has in some respects become deficient and is in need of repair. The main cause of the disruption is viewed in terms of difficulties within the rich world–mainly between the Trilateral partners–and not, or very much less so, between the rich countries and the Third World. Since the solution to some of the problems is seen to reside in higher levels of cooperation, such cooperation is first sought among the dominant Western powers, especially the 'locomotives of growth', and then the rich world as a whole. . . .

The manager's ideal is a fully integrated world economy. This vision requires that the Third World, especially the few nations with a capacity for disruption, be 'fitted in'. The developing countries are seen to have no other future than one which organically links them to the capitalist world economy. Even the interests of the poorest of the poor, the managers argue, will be better served by such an association.[19] Managers go so far as to argue that it is the duty of the poor countries to seek more effective integration, to eschew disruptive action, to contribute to the growth and expansion of the world economic system for, in the words of Fishlow, "there can be no basis for repayment of accumulated debt, no assurance of efficient industrialization, no guarantee of greater production of foodstuffs and raw materials unless an expanding and competitive market in the industrialized nations is assured".[20]

Interdependence managers are keen to stress the diversity within the Third World. They advocate policies toward it based upon 'differentiation', policies geared to worlds within the Third World. The prime concern of this differentiated approach has been to find a basis for accommodation with the OPEC group. Most managers now seem to subscribe to the view that the group has come to learn which side its bread is buttered and no longer constitutes a threat. As *Interfutures* noted, the OPEC countries "have gradually come to realize that their own development depends upon the prosperity of the OECD countries". The main emphasis today is on integrating a handful of NICs into the world economy. These countries are seen, again to quote from *Interfutures*, as the "middle class of an evolving world society" and of being of "fundamental importance for future equilibrium".

In the manager's scheme of thinking, the NICs are allowed to develop into regional hegemonic powers and function as citadels of Western capitalism in their own universe of want and deprivation.

Transnational corporations are regarded as the embodiment of an interdependent world economy dominated by the rich capitalist nations. Not surprisingly, the attitude of systems-maintainers to international business ranges from congeniality to idolatry, the latter characterized by Moynihan's observation that transnational corporations are "arguably the most creative international institutions of the twentieth century".[21]

Systems-maintaining managers search for 'efficient' technical and functional solutions to world problems. They worship at the altar of economic growth and measure success in GNP increases. They disregard or downplay political issues. These only become relevant when and to the extent that they pose managerial challenges. And when they become too intractable, when they refuse to succumb to technical and functional logic, the manager readily discovers that his imperialist brethren are only too prepared to take up the matter further

The management of interdependence is seen to call for new arrangements around those problems in which the 'hidden hand' remains permanently invisible and which threaten the status quo. The challenge, in the words of Daniel Bell, is "to design effective international instruments–in the monetary, commodity, trade, and technology areas–to effect the necessary transition to a new international division of labor that can provide for economic and, perhaps, political stability".[22] Innate conservatism and the strong mercantilist tradition in the systems-maintaining approach which insists that greater emphasis be placed on national political and economic objectives than on considerations of global economic efficiency mean that this challenge cannot easily be met. The insistence of the NICs that comparative advantage should also be allowed to apply to them also does not help much.

The search for solutions is kept alive by the fear that the world economic system, a system which has been so bountiful, could unravel, producing grave domestic crises and international conflicts which could get so out of hand that they plunge the whole system into chaos. In a world which is armed to the teeth, a plunge into chaos could easily mean a plunge over the nuclear precipice. . . . [A] large number of world order studies have found it necessary to speculate on this eventuality.

THE SYSTEMS-REFORMING APPROACH

This approach reflects the realization that structural modifications over a broad number of issues will be required in response to new problems and changing geopolitical realities. These modifications, however, are not seen to be so fundamental as to require or to result in a basic reordering of established power configurations. Unlike systems-maintainers, reformers characteristically stress the problems rather than the advantages resulting from established patterns of privilege and power. Instead of beating the drum for free trade and *laissez-faire,* for example, they argue the need to 'correct' and 'augment' market mechanisms.

The approach is sustained by and can draw upon a long tradition of reformist thinking from religious and secular fields. Humanitarianism, christianity and socialism are all tributaries which have fed the flow of reformism. The sources are so diverse that attempts to list the spiritual fathers of the tradition can easily degenerate into a pointless exercise. The social sciences alone have contributed so many stars to the reformist firmament that it is difficult to list the names of those who have most illuminated the tradition. If restricted to the recent past, however, such a list would certainly include John Kenneth Galbraith, Gunnar Myrdal, Jan Tinbergen, Celso Furtado and Ralf Dahrendorf.

The ideal world of the systems reformer is a mixed economy with regulating agencies (the state or 'democratic' international institutions) playing the role of arbiter in social and economic conflicts. Whereas systems-maintainers tend to regard conflict as "deviant behavior" or an illness to be treated,[23] reformists recognize it as a basic consequence of pluralistic systems and divergent interests and seek to provide dispute settlement procedures in an effort to ensure that such conflicts are contained.

At the level of international relations, reformists are much more sensitive to the grievances of the Third World, grievances which are perceived to be just and which need to be taken seriously. The tone of the reformer is accommodating and propitiatory, his goal one of seeking to effect a reconciliation between the 'legitimate' interests of the rich and poor countries and the collective needs of the planet as a whole. The reformer is the guardian of the interests of the unborn. He has many constituencies and talks in terms of 'mutual interest', 'positive sum games' and the exercise of 'enlightened self-interest', the need to sacrifice today in order to safeguard tomorrow. The frame of reference is long enough to fall beyond current contexts of choice and expedient definitions of political feasibility but short enough to engage the normative receptivities of outward looking policymakers.

While firmly predicated on the primacy of the nation-state, reformist thinking has firm global aspirations. As in the case of some systems-maintaining thinking, the emphasis is managerial, only more so. More so leads to a greater stress on the potential role of international institutions . . . in the complex process of reform. Systems-reformers seek to use existing institutional mechanisms–although when in doubt they do not hesitate to suggest the creation of new ones–for directing change in deliberate ways with the intention of institutionalizing fundamental values and of maximizing welfare. The reformers' faith in the ability of mankind to make something of the United Nations borders on the demonic.

Systems reformers are critical yet basically friendly toward such phenomena as the transnational corporation. They acknowledge that some activities of big business in the developing world have been injurious and disruptive, guided by motives which are too narrowly defined, but nurture the belief that transnationals, with judicious encouragement and a little coercion, "can play a positive role in improving the living conditions of the poor masses in the Third World".[24]

For all their good intentions, reformers traditionally underestimate the influence of power on the probability of positive outcomes as well as the depths of antagonisms between the world's nations and the durability and robustness of the structures–cognitive and social–which maintain them. They are also prone to exaggerate the negotiability of the 'planetary agenda' and they presuppose the efficacy of moderation and the spirit of compromise. They are prevented from seeing the dark corners of world order by the stars in their eyes. They cling to hope that justice must prevail over injustice and have confidence in the exercise of reason and in the spirit of reasonableness. When their confidence is shaken, as indeed it often is, they resort to stressing the 'power of ideas' and the need to 'educate public opinion'.

THE SYSTEMS-TRANSFORMING APPROACH

This approach is predicated upon the belief that the cause of the world's predicament is deeply rooted in the structures which determine and legitimize the operation of the social and economic system and that the only hope for the future lies in the transformation of these structures.

There are two main types of systems-transformers. The most important are those of the 'radical left', the representatives of the Marxist and neo-Marxist traditions. These—for want of a better word we will call them the radicals—stress the dialectical interplay between ideology and social relations. They do not view change as an evolutionary or natural process but rather as being conditioned by the interests of dominant and powerful classes. Peoples' consciousness is conditioned by their milieu and position in society. The social system, however, is seen to be characterized by basic contradictions without which the system could not exist. These contradictions offer potential for the development of a revolutionary consciousness which is the motive force for the process of transformation. The radical tradition draws heavily upon the Marxist paradigm and is represented by such social scientists as Ernest Mandel, Samir Amin, Andre Gunder Frank, Herbert Marcuse and Perry Anderson.

The second school of systems-transformers can be termed the 'supranationalists' or 'superreformers'.[25] They see today's predicament as being rooted in an archaic system of antagonistic nation-states, the prerogatives of which are being increasingly eroded by powerful economic and technological forces. Mankind is viewed as a whole rather than as a collection of autonomous political units and although cultural and political differences are recognized, increasing social interdependence is seen to have virtually eliminated the ability of one government to live and act in isolation from others. More than any other tradition, they invoke the analogy of 'spaceship earth' and 'global village' to illustrate the dangers to which a shrinking and highly vulnerable planet is exposed.[26]

Supranationalists stress that the economic and technological forces are irresistible and are pressing for world integration. These forces, they believe, will eventually predominate over the political and make essential some form of world governments or, at least a world institution which, in the words of Marxist Silviu Brucan, is "vested with the authority to plan, to make decisions, and to enforce them".[27] Supranationalists argue that the main contours of a global community are already clearly discernable and that global governance cannot be far behind. Global governance is not a choice but rather an objective necessity which will be forced upon mankind by the pressure of events. It will come whether we like it or not. In the words of Saul Mendlovitz, director of the World Order Models Project: "It is my considered judgement that there is no longer a question of whether or not there will be world government by the year 2000. As I see it the questions we should be addressing at ourselves are: how it will come into being—by cataclysm, drift, more or less rational design—and whether it will be totalitarian, benignly elitist, or participatory (the probabilities being in that order)".[28]

In terms of rich-poor relations whereas the radicals emphasize the need for Third World autonomy-building, the supranationalists argue that the North-South distinction has become or is rapidly becoming obsolete and that the only framework—theoretical, analytical, normative—is 'one-worldism'.

Both radicals and supranationalists are highly sceptical about mankind's ability to shape the kinds of international institutions which can help steer the world out of crisis. The radicals contend that there is little or nothing which the poor can gain from negotiations with the rich and they view the United Nations as deeply conservative, Western dominated, and unresponsive to the needs of the poor. The supranationalists despair of a world committed to the nation-state and, at a time when super-strong international institutions are desperately required, see the United Nations as so ineffective and powerless that the only sensible thing to do is to 'start again' with a fresh sheet of paper. Gloom prevails in the worlds of both radicals and supranationalists. The radicals are sustained by a deep sense of outrage, the supranationalists by an optimism born out of the belief that when it has exhausted all other possibilities, mankind must surely resort to the rational.

The greatest weakness of the systems-transformers is their inability to mobilize widespread support partly because they are unable to depict a credible transition process–how do you go about overthrowing capitalism or building world government–and partly because those with vested interests in the status quo are able to shape, or at least confuse, public opinion on prospects for and the effects of a transition. Both groups are left to preach to the converted. Moreover, their insistence on structural change alienates them from public opinion and the policy-making mainstream, both of which are inherently conservative, overwhelmingly gradualist and intolerant and fearful of things which smack of 'extremism'. . . .

NOTES

1. See Alistair Buchan, *Change Without War*, Chatto and Windus, London, 1974, p. 21.
2. See Daniel Bell, 'The End of American Exceptionalism', *The Public Interest*, no. 41, Fall 1975, pp. 193–224.
3. See Sylvia Ostry, 'The World Economy in the 1970s and 1980s', *OECD Observer*, no. 103, March 1980, pp. 13–15, at p. 13.
4. Geoffrey Barraclough, *Turning Points in World History*, Thames and Hudson, London, 1979, p. 87.
5. For arguments to the effect that it must, see Robert L. Heilbroner, *An Inquiry into the Human Prospect*, W.W. Norton, New York, 1974; Harrison Brown, *The Human Future Revisited: The World Predicament and Possible Solutions*, W.W. Norton, New York, 1978; and Ronald Higgins, *The Seventh Enemy*, Hodder and Stoughton London, 1978. For works of fiction which share the same apocalyptic mood, see, for example, Doris Lessing, *Briefing for a Descent into Hell*, Knopf, New York, 1971; and Walker Percy, *Love in the Ruins*, Farrar, Straus, New York, 1971. For the view that the present 'age of chaos' is an age of transition to something else which, if not paradise,

promises to be much more acceptable than today's world, see William Irwin Thompson, *Darkness and Scattered Light*, Anchor Books, Garden City, New York, 1978.

6. Estimates of the Vienna based Institute for Comparative Economic Studies reported in 'A World Deep in Debt', *Newsweek*, December 3, 1979, p. 50.

7. Quoted in *The Observer*, January 6, 1980.

8. See ILO, *Yearbook of Labour Statistics, 1979*, Geneva, 1980.

9. Amir Jamal, interviewed in *D + C* (publication of the German Foundation for International Development), no. 1, 1981, pp. 28–29, at p. 29.

10. On this see, for example, Patrik Engellau and Birgitta Nygren, *Lending Without Limits–On International Lending and Developing Countries*, Secretariat for Futures Studies, Sweden, 1979.

11. For a review of world order thinking from the twelfth century onwards, see F.H. Hinsley's admirable *Power and the Pursuit of Peace*, Cambridge University Press, Cambridge, 1963.

12. For an assessment of the policy relevance of world order thinking see Sam Cole, 'The Global Futures Debate 1965–1976', in Christopher Freeman and Marie Jahoda, *World Futures: The Great Debate*, Martin Robertson, Oxford, 1978, pp. 9–49. See also John M. Richardson, 'Global Modelling: A Survey and Appraisal', paper prepared for the Seminar on Natural Resource Policies, University of Wisconsin, Madison, Wisconsin, December 1977 (mimeo); Don Munton, 'Global Models, Politics and the Future', paper presented to the Annual Meeting of the Canadian Political Science Association, London, Ontario, May 1978 (mimeo); Guy Poquet, 'The Limits to Global Modelling', *International Social Science Journal*, vol. 30, no. 2, 1978; Dick A. Leurdijk, *World Order Studies: World Order Studies, Policy-Making and the New International Order*, Foundation Reshaping the International Order, Rotterdam, February 1979; and Jorge Lozoya, Jaime Estevez and Rosario Green, *Alternative Views of the New International Economic Order: A Survey and Analysis of Major Academic Research Reports*, Pergamon Press, New York, 1979. A useful discussion can also be found in OECD, *A Comparative Evaluation of World Models*, chapter 11 of the 'Intermediate Results' of the Interfutures Project, Paris, 7 April 1977.

13. Richardson, op.cit., p. 41, argues that a world order model can be considered implemented "when the perspective of the model becomes part of the perspective of one or more decision-makers". It could also be argued that the main purpose of a model is simply to reveal the limitations of another model.

14. This is argued by William Irwin Thompson in *Evil and World Order*, Harper and Row, New York, 1976. The evil is systems analysis and its main cousins.

15. According to Leurdijk, op.cit., the questions of aid, industrialization and trade, food, and energy and raw materials have received the greatest attention in the world order studies published in the past decade. The questions of science and technology and human environment have received somewhat less attention and treatment of such matters as disarmament and ocean management has been conspicuous through its absence.

16. In defining the characteristics of the three approaches to world order thinking considerable use has been made of the following sources: Richard A. Falk, 'Contending Approaches to World Order', *Journal of International Affairs*, vol. 31, no. 2, Fall/Winter 1977, pp. 171–198; Richard A. Falk, 'Beyond Internationalism', *Foreign Affairs*, vol. 23, 1976, pp. 65–113; Ian Miles, 'Worldviews and Scenarios', in Freeman and Jahoda, op.cit., chapter 8.

17. 'Beyond Internationalism', p. 84.

18. 'A Word to the Third World', *Wall Street Journal*, July 17, 1975, p. 18.

19. For another lengthy study which reaches this conclusion, see William R. Cline, 'A

Qualitative Assessment of the Policy Alternatives in the NIEO Negotiations', in W.R. Cline (ed.), *Policy Alternatives for a New International Economic Order*, Praeger Publishers, New York, 1979.

20. Albert Fishlow, 'A New International Economic Order: What Kind?', in Roger D. Hansen (ed.), *Rich and Poor Nations in the World Economy*, McGraw-Hill, New York, 1978, p. 56.
21. Daniel P. Moynihan, 'The United States in Opposition', *Commentary*, March 1975, pp. 31–44, at p. 41.
22. Daniel Bell, 'The Future of World Disorder', *Foreign Policy*, vol. 27, Summer 1977, pp. 109–136, at p. 134.
23. This is the conclusion reached by Bart van Steenbergen in his review of Talcott Parsons' thinking on the subject of conflict. See *Orde of Conflict: Tegengestelde Maatschappijvisies Binnen de Futurologie*, Euroboekje, Wolters-Noordhoff, Groningen, 1969, p. 12.
24. The RIO Report [Jan Tinbergen (coordinator), *Reshaping the International Order: A Report to The Club of Rome*, E.P. Dutton, New York, 1976], p. 157.
25. For an extensive profile of the supranationalist, see Robert Gilpin, 'Three Models of the Future', in C. Fred Bergsten and Lawrence B. Krause (eds.), *World Politics and International Economics*, The Brookings Institution, Washington, D.C., 1975, pp. 37–60, viz. pp. 39–42.
26. For a description of the characteristic elements of the 'spaceship earth' world order paradigm, see Alan D. Buckley's 'Foreword' to the Fall/Winter 1977 edition of the *Journal of International Affairs*.
27. See Silviu Brucan, 'The World Authority: An Exercise in Political Forecasting', in Antony J. Dolman (ed.), *Global Planning and Resource Management: International Decision-Making in a Divided World*, Pergamon Press, New York, pp. 49–66, at p. 50.
28. Saul Mendlovitz in his introduction to Saul H. Mendlovitz (ed.), *On the Creation of a Just World Order: Preferred Worlds for the 1990s*, Free Press, New York, 1975, p. xvi.

36

New Non-Land Resources as Global Issues

JAMES N. ROSENAU

In this essay, James N. Rosenau asks whether traditional analytical devices are appropriate for examining issues relating to the global commons, which he describes as "non-land" resources, or whether the characteristics of these issues so set them apart that new modes of thinking are required. Arguing, among other things, that because such issues embrace scientifically oriented judgments, he concludes the latter—that new issues require new perspectives. Rosenau is professor and director of the Institute for Transnational Studies at the University of Southern California. He is a prolific writer on foreign policy and international politics; *The Study of Global Interdependence* (1980) is among his recent publications.

Do the conflicts over new non-land resources that have recently come onto the global agenda differ from those that have long been on the world scene? Do such issues seem new because the resources are new or because their structures and processes are atypical? In short, are non-land resource issues simply new wine in old bottles, or do they have characteristics that set them apart in terms of the dynamics that sustain them and the parameters within which attempts to resolve them must be undertaken?

I am far from certain of the answers to these questions. New resources have been coming onto the world scene for centuries. Each major technological innovation, from the railroad to the combustion engine to the microchip, has given rise to new resources over which conflicts subsequently ensue. Hence one could easily resort to historical analysis to demonstrate that humankind is once again faced with familiar conflicts that will be addressed in the usual, long-established ways. Perhaps, though, the new resources of the late twentieth century are different. Their availability, too, is the product of major technological innovations, but conceivably this time the resources, being located in non-land realms, are of such a different kind that they will be confronted through new forms of socio-political management.

While uncertainty marks my response to the foregoing questions, I do know that the answers to them are important. For the way in which the questions posed above are initially answered will determine how creative research into new re-

This paper was especially adapted for this book. An earlier version was presented at a Workshop on the Resolution of Disputes on the New Natural Resources, co-sponsored by the Hague Academy of Law and the United Nations University, Peace Palace, The Hague, The Netherlands, November 8–10, 1982.

source issues will be undertaken and, consequently, how the issues will come to be understood by observers and confronted by politicians. If such issues are seen as merely the latest additions to the global agenda, then they will and should be analyzed in terms of widely accepted models of international conflict, nation-state behavior, diplomatic bargaining, and individual motivation. If, on the other hand, they are conceived to have special dimensions that render them unique as issue-areas, then we need to push our conceptual imaginations to identify the new variables and interactive processes that constitute their structure.

It seems clear to me that the latter alternative is the only way to proceed with respect to this choice. If we proceed as if the new resources have given rise to differentiable issue-areas, we will at least compel ourselves to think afresh and theorize anew. To state the point differently, not to proceed in this way would be to run the risk of misreading or overlooking crucial dynamics of world politics. And, if it turns out that the new resources are really only new wine in old bottles, then the established models for examining them can be applied with greater confidence in their appropriateness.

Such, then, is the purpose of the inquiry that follows: to explore the new non-land resources associated with outer space, the seabed, environmental pollution, radio frequencies, and weather climate as issue-areas,[1] as foci of conflict that are different as well as recent additions to the global agenda.

ARE THE BOTTLES THE SAME?

An assessment of these seemingly new issues requires differentiating between the dynamics of the issues and the changing structures of the global system in which they have surfaced. For it is conceivable that the increasing interdependence in world affairs has altered the ways in which all issues on the global agenda are processed, with the result that what appears unique to new resource issues is no more than structural alterations at a more encompassing level. Conceivably, in other words, what appears to be new wine in old bottles is actually old wine in new bottles.

I believe there are a number of good reasons to conclude that the global system has undergone major structural alterations in the last two decades as a consequence of technological innovations that have lessened the geographical and social distances separating people and nations. Today, more than ever, the course of events and the routines of life in any part of the world are shaped by—and thus partly dependent on—decisions made and forces at work in other parts of the world. This greater interdependence, combined with declines in such basic resources as water, forests, and energy, has helped foster a surge of ethnic, racial, linguistic, and other forms of consciousness at sub-national levels (what I call "sub-groupism") that, in turn, has reduced the capacity of national governments to govern effectively. More accurately, heightened subgroupism and increased dependence on decisions and forces abroad have together limited the scope within which governmental authority can on its own bring about the realization of policy goals.[2]

For analytical purposes it is useful to distinguish between those "traditional" issue-areas that, relatively speaking, still remain primarily within the range of competence of national governments and those "interdependence" issue-areas that are only partly within their scope. In the former category are such policy questions as urban renewal, civil liberties, taxation, and a host of other domestic matters that fall fully within national jurisdictions. In addition, national governments can still frame foreign policies, pursue defense strategies, make alliance commitments, and in many other ways maintain control over how they participate in the traditional issues of diplomatic bargaining and military conflict. With the advent of greatly intensified global interdependence, however, a variety of new socio-economic issues have emerged—from terrorism to currency crises, from energy shortages to refugee flows, from inflation to agricultural imbalances—in which forces beyond the authority of national governments have greatly narrowed their control over when and how they become involved in the course of events.

It follows that the changing structures of the global system have significantly increased the complexity of the process through which the issues on its agenda are managed. In the traditional areas they continue to be processed through such long-standing mechanisms as diplomatic negotiation, government-to-government interaction, and balance-of-power politics. In the interdependence areas, on the other hand, the old structures have been supplemented by new mechanisms that allow for the participation of non-governmental, inter-governmental, and supranational actors through a diverse set of formal and ad hoc institutional arrangements—such as summit conferences, specialized UN conferences, and OPEC-like organizations—that were not part of the global scene only a few decades ago.

In short, and reverting for a final time to the spirits analogy, the global system's wine cellar now contains both old wine in old bottles and new wine in new bottles. Assuming this is the case, the task of the ensuing analysis can be restated in more precise form: to explore whether new non-land resources are likely to develop as traditional issues, whether they will evolve as merely a form of interdependence issue, or whether they have unique characteristics that will set them apart as still another type of global structure.

NEW NON-LAND RESOURCES AS ISSUES

It does not require much insight to discern that the new resource issues are unlikely to evolve into traditional structures. Virtually by definition, they are at least interdependence issues. Every one of the new resources is located in heretofore unexplored or unclaimed dimensions of the universe, dimensions that either span national boundaries or lie wholly outside national jurisdictions. Indeed, the fit between the global distribution of the resources and the state structure of the global system is not even close. Being located elsewhere than on or under land, the new resources are ubiquitous and encompass whole regions and continents through processes of nature over which nation-states have never exercised control. Moreover, not only do these processes unfold in non-land realms, but the resources are also fluid rather than fixed in geographical space, moving like (and sometimes with) the winds across and around national boundaries, as well as spanning them.[3]

To be sure, myriad are the proposals in which responsibility for the development and management of the new resources [is to] be placed under national jurisdictions—either on behalf of the global commons or to enhance national interests[4]—but even if such proposals were to be translated into political realities, the resulting structures would still be quite unlike the traditional type. For responsibility to the global commons would inevitably operate as a limitation upon national jurisdictions, just as such jurisdictions asserted on behalf of national interests would surely be constrained by the fact that the resources extend across state boundaries and thereby negate any legal claims or historical precedents that might be cited.

Thus it is hardly surprising that the seabed, outer space, climate, and other non-land regimes have evolved in such a way that national governments, supranational organizations, and sub-national actors have been thrown together in a variety of fora and through a variety of processes to cope with the problems posed by the growing competition for the new resources. The new resources cannot be utilized, in other words, without many actors' being affected. Conversely, no single state can fully determine the outcomes that follow from utilization. And thus it may even be that wholly unforeseen organizational structures lie ahead as means of managing new resource issues. The recently signed agreement between New York State and the government of Quebec to combat acid rain,[5] for example, may well be a harbinger of how new transnational structures that do not adhere to conventional diplomatic forms will evolve to cope with the ubiquity and fluidity of the new resources.

While the wide ramifications to which new non-land resources give rise are essential features of interdependence issues, there are several important ways in which the controversies they precipitate are quite different from any other type of issue on the global agenda. First and foremost, perhaps, the new resources give rise mainly to distributive rather than redistributive issues, a distinction that sets them apart from most interdependence issues. The latter foster conflict because they involve redistribution of a finite pie, with the result that the deprived want a larger share of it while the privileged wish to preserve or enhance their share. The disputes provoked by the New International Economic Order proposed by Third World countries exemplify this underlying characteristic of redistributive issues. On the other hand, because they have yet to be fully tapped, the new non-land resources can still be allocated without threat of deprivation to any actors (or, more accurately, any deprivation that may result from their allocation is likely to be widely, if not evenly, shouldered) and thus can be expected to exhibit the characteristic political structures and processes of distributive issues—including tendencies for log-rolling rather than ideology to serve as the basis of relations among the disputants, for decisions to be made through legislative rather than executive dynamics, and for the discussion of issues to be conducted at bureaucratic rather than top political levels.[6]

A second distinguishing feature of new resource issues is that they are much less infused with symbolic content than either traditional or interdependence issues. Their focus is on the allocation, utilization, and management of very concrete phenomena. Being tangible and observable products of nature, they are less subject to considerations of status, hierarchy, and the multitude of other intangible symbols that attach to the products of human relationships. Elsewhere I have elaborated on how the distinction between issue-areas encompassing tangible or intangible phenomena is likely to be relevant to the number of actors affected by the issue, the intensity of their motivations to act, the frequency with which they act, and the extent of their readiness to bargain with one another. More specifically, this formulation suggests that issue-areas encompassing tangible ends and means are more likely to involve fewer actors who are more highly motivated to act and more ready to bargain with one another than is the case when intangible ends or means are associated with a contested issue.[7] At first glance this description appears to fit new non-land resource issues rather well.

A third noteworthy characteristic of new non-land resource issues is that none of them embraces large constituencies. Unlike most interdependence issues—such as energy crunches, currency crises, food shortages, and population explosions, which involve masses of motorists, investors, farmers, and parents—the seabed, outer space, radio frequencies and other new non-land resources do not presently have any direct and immediate bearing on the daily lives of millions of people. Potentially, to be sure their relevance to humankind is considerable, but for the time being this relevance is largely circuitous and indirect. Consequently, those whose welfare might be threatened by proposed solutions to the issues are unlikely to be aware of the threats, because the causal chains that lead from the utilization of the resources to their doorsteps are so lengthy and complex; or, if they somehow become conscious of the chains and the threats lying behind them, they are likely to feel that there is not much they can do about breaking into and affecting such remote and intricate causal processes. In short, the politics of new resource issues is unlikely to be sustained by the hue and cry of mass publics or burdened or facilitated by their mobilization and intervention.

Fourth, partly because the interests of mass publics in the issues are not recognized, but mostly because of the slow pace at which nature's processes unfold, the issues associated with new non-land resources are not likely to be marked by dramatic climaxes. Where terrorism, territorial clashes, currency crises, and other types of issues erupt suddenly and compel attention as "hot" issues, those involving the non-land realm evolve in small increments and almost never command the headlines of the world's media. The specialist can discern droughts leading to famines or environmental pollution leading to disease, but forecasts of doomsday ahead if such patterns are allowed to continue carry little weight in the face of the current, more dramatic crises around which other types of issues revolve. To state the matter differently, the onset of problems derived from new non-land resources is likely to be detected only by specialists whose salience and clout in the political arena are quite limited.

Finally, and by no means least important, the issues associated with new non-land resources are highly technical and not readily assimilated by simple and overarching value systems. They involve levels of information and comprehension attained only by specialists, and thus they are issues that tend to be treated in the moderate discourse of science rather than the more inflammatory rhetoric of politics. Perhaps no issue-area on the global agenda relies more heavily on scientific proof as the means through which persuasion and influence are exercised than does the one embracing controversies over new non-land resources.[8]

Consider, for example, the growing issue of how much sewage the ocean can absorb without damage to its undersea life and to humans who consume its resources. This is not a question around which politicians can mobilize followers and debate on the basis of symbolic values or appeals to unqualified loyalties. Rather, to achieve agreement, compliance, or active support the facts must be offered, their derivation legitimated, and their application delineated. Changes in the amounts of silver, chromium, DDT, and other harmful compounds in ocean waters off metropolitan shores have to be clearly demonstrated and the ways in which the changes were measured have to be persuasive if those who contest such issues are to progress toward their goals. To be sure, facts never speak for themselves. They can only be developed in the context of some kind of value system, and obviously, different value systems can lead to different conclusions as to what the scientifically derived facts mean. It matters, for instance, whether one believes research on sewage systems should be oriented toward uncovering how humans can least disturb ocean habitats or toward discovering how much disruption the ocean can accommodate. Notwithstanding the centrality of such important value dimensions in any new resource issue, however, it is still the case that issues involving nature's structures and processes are bound to be differentiated from all other types of issues by the large degree to which the procedures of science underlie their argumentation and resolution.

CONCLUSIONS

A crucial dynamic of new resource issues is that all of their unique dimensions interact so as to reinforce each other and thus add further to the uniqueness of the issue-area. That such issues do not embrace mass constituencies, for example, seems both to contribute to and to stem from the fact that they also do not get framed in terms of grand symbols, and much the same can be said about the interaction among these characteristics and the non-dramatic, scientifically oriented bases on which the issues unfold. If this is so, it seems clear that there are a number of good reasons to anticipate that even as they mature and become more permanent fixtures on the global agenda, new resource issues will continue to be distinguishable from all the others that command attention on the world stage.

For those who have a vision of how the new non-land resources should be conserved, consumed, or otherwise managed in the future, such a conclusion might be disheartening. Strong advocates might readily regret that their concerns are handled at bureaucratic levels and do not preoccupy chiefs of state or otherwise command top spots on the global agenda. In turn, such a regret might well lead advocates to wish they could rely on periodic crises or resort to compelling symbols to mobilize mass support on behalf of their positions on the issues. Further reflection, however, can lead to quite the opposite conclusion. It can easily be asserted that issues cast in terms of concrete problems open to scientific proof and contested by specialists at lower political levels are more likely to be amenable to resolution, or at least to quiet but steady progress, than either the traditional or interdependence issues that dominate the world's headlines.

Admittedly the force of this argument may be weakened as awareness grows that the supply of new non-land resources is decreasing relative to the demand for them. In all likelihood, increasing scarcities and a growing awareness of them will foster an increasing politicization of such issues. With respect to radio frequencies, for example, there is already evidence of such politicization as the Third World, having begun to recognize that its interests are being compromised by the increasing congestion of the radio spectrum and the geosynchronous orbit, have drawn telecommunication issues into the larger North-South dialogue.[9]

Yet, to the extent that the new non-land resources undergo transformation from distributive to redistributive issues, their greater politicization may still be of a different order than obtains for other types of issues. Even if they come to occupy a more permanent and visible place on the world's agenda, the resources will continue to be located mainly in the global commons and their utilization will still pose questions that cannot be addressed without a commitment to establishing scientific proof. Thus, for better or worse, new resource issues seem destined to remain distinguishable in important respects and, accordingly, to require unique forms of conflict management.

NOTES

1. Since the word "resource" suggests a desirable asset, it is a bit awkward to classify environmental pollution as a new non-land resource. For present purposes, however, it is so classified in the sense that unpolluted environments need to be developed in the same way that the resources of outer space or the seabed await development.
2. For an elaboration of these dynamics of increasing global interdependence, see James N. Rosenau, *The Study of Global Interdependence* (N.Y.: Nichols Publishing Company, 1980).
3. Seyom Brown, Nina W. Cornell, Larry L. Fabian, and Edith Brown Weiss, *Regimes for the Ocean, Outer Space, and The Weather* (Washington, D.C.: Brookings Institution, 1977), pp. 3–8.
4. Ibid., pp. 8–18.
5. *The New York Times*, August 1, 1982, p. 21.
6. These distinctions between distributive and redistributive issues are cogently discussed in Theodore J. Lowi, "American Business, Public Policy, Case Studies, and Political Theory," *World Politics*, Vol. XVI (July 1964), pp. 677–715.
7. See James N. Rosenau, "Pre-Theories and Theories of Foreign Policy," in R. B. Farrell, ed., *Approaches to Comparative and International Politics* (Evanston, Ill.: Northwestern University Press, 1966); reproduced in J. N. Rosenau, *The Scientific Study of Foreign Policy* (N.Y.: Nichols Publishing Company, 1980, rev. ed.), pp. 160–168. For discussions of other theoretical approaches to the issue-area concept as an analytic tool in international relations, see Richard W. Mansbach and John A. Vasquez, *In Search of Theory: A New Paradigm for Global Politics* (N.Y.: Columbia University Press, 1981), Ch. 2; and William Zimmerman, "Issue Area and Foreign-Policy Pro-

cess: A Research Note in Search of a General Theory,'' *American Political Science Review*, Vol. 67 (December 1973), pp. 1204–1212.

8. For an extended discussion of the growing role of scientific proof in the global arena, see James N. Rosenau, ''Capabilities and Control in an Interdependent World,'' *International Security*, Vol. 1 (October 1976), pp. 32–49; reproduced in J. N. Rosenau, *The Study of Global Interdependence*, Ch. 3.

9. See Marvin S. Soroos, ''The Commons in the Sky: The Radio Spectrum and Geosynchronous Orbit as Issues in Global Policy,'' *International Organization*, Vol. 36 (Summer 1982), pp. 665–677.

About the Editors

CHARLES W. KEGLEY, JR., is Professor and Chair of the Department of Government and International Studies at the University of South Carolina. He is co-editor of the *Sage International Yearbook of Foreign Policy Studies* and has published, among other books, *Analyzing International Relations, International Events and the Comparative Analysis of Foreign Policy*, and *After Vietnam: The Future of American Foreign Policy*. His recent scholarship includes articles in the *International Journal, International Organization, International Studies Quarterly*, the *Journal of Politics*, and *Orbis*.

EUGENE R. WITTKOPF is Professor of Political Science at the University of Florida. He has contributed articles on international politics and foreign policy to a number of edited books and journals, including the *American Political Science Review, International Organization, International Studies Quarterly*, the *Journal of Politics, Orbis*, and the *Social Science Quarterly*.

Together Professors Kegley and Wittkopf have published *Perspectives on American Foreign Policy: Selected Readings* (1983), *American Foreign Policy: Pattern and Process* (2nd ed., 1982), and *World Politics: Trend and Transformation* (1981).